C000093141

Quality Control in Preliminary Examination: Volume 2

Morten Bergsmo and Carsten Stahn (editors)

2018
Torkel Opsahl Academic EPublisher
Brussels

Dedicated to Hartwig Stahn

EDITORS' FOREWORD TO VOLUME 2

Chapter 1 of Volume 1 is common to both Volumes 1 and 2 of *Quality Control in Preliminary Examination*, so we kindly refer readers of the present volume to that chapter.

Volume 2 contains 18 chapters in three of the five parts of the two volumes: Part 3, "The Normative Framework of Preliminary Examinations"; Part 4, "Transparency, Co-operation and Participation in Preliminary Examination"; and Part 5, "Thematicity in Preliminary Examination". The two volumes make up one coherent whole and have been bifurcated for convenience given the high overall number of pages.

We would like to thank CHAN Ho Shing Icarus, TOAEP Editor, for his professional copy-editing of the two volumes. We also thank Devasheesh Bais, LAU Carin, LEE Vincent, Sean O'Reilly, Surabhi Sharma, TSANG Selina and TUNG Ernie for their editorial assistance.

Morten Bergsmo and Carsten Stahn

TABLE OF CONTENTS

PART 4

TRANSPARENCY, CO-OPERATION AND PARTICIPATION
IN PRELIMINARY EXAMINATION

PART 5
THEMATICITY IN PRELIMINARY EXAMINATION

Part 3
The Normative Framework of Preliminary Examinations

18

Prosecutorial Ethics and Preliminary Examinations at the ICC

Alexander Heinze and Shannon Fyfe*

18.1. Introduction

The increased power and independence of the Office of the Prosecutor ('OTP', or the 'Office'), especially in the preliminary examination phase, has brought more attention to the ways in which prosecutors can exercise discretion in choosing which situations warrant investigation by the International Criminal Court ('ICC').[1] Under Article 15 of the ICC Statute, the Prosecutor has the authority to initiate investigations *proprio motu* on the basis of information on crimes within the jurisdiction of the Court. There

---

* **Alexander Heinze** is a lawyer and an assistant professor of law at the University of Göttingen, Germany. He holds a Ph.D. in International Criminal Law (with honours), received his master's in International and Comparative Law from Trinity College Dublin, Ireland, with distinction, and published various papers on topics such as International Criminal Law and Procedure, Media Law, Comparative Criminal Law, Human Rights Law and Jurisprudence. His book *International Criminal Procedure and Disclosure* (Duncker & Humblot, 2014) won three awards. He is a member of the ILA's Committee on Complementarity in ICL, editor of the *German Law Journal* and book review editor of the *Criminal Law Forum*, has been working for the Appeals Chamber of the ICC as a visiting professional and was recently appointed as an expert of the Committee for Legal Affairs and Consumer Protection of the German Parliament in the public hearing of the draft law on the abolishment of Section 103 of the German Criminal Code (defamation of organs and representatives of foreign States). **Shannon Fyfe** is a lawyer and a Ph.D. candidate in philosophy at Vanderbilt University, where she obtained her J.D. in 2010. Her prior experience includes an internship with the International Criminal Tribunal for Rwanda's Office of the Prosecutor, the American Society of International Law's Arthur C. Helton Fellowship for international human rights law in Tanzania, and a fellowship with the Syria Justice and Accountability Centre. She recently published *International Criminal Tribunals: A Normative Defense* (with Larry May) with Cambridge University Press, 2017. The authors thank Dov Jacobs, Morten Bergsmo, Carsten Stahn, Gregory S. Gordon, and Christopher B. Mahony for their valuable comments and CHAN Ho Shing Icarus for his assistance.

1   See Carsten Stahn, "Damned If You Do, Damned If You Don't: Challenges and Critiques of Preliminary Examinations at the ICC", in *Journal of International Criminal Justice*, 2017, vol. 15, no. 3, pp. 413–34.

---

are no specific requirements as to where the Prosecutor is to get this information or how she is to analyse the seriousness of the information received. Similar concerns are raised with regard to other trigger mechanisms. Although the requirement that the Pre-Trial Chamber ('PTC') must grant an authorization for a *proprio motu* investigation constrains the Prosecutor's discretion, there are generally no checks on her determination that there is (or is not) a reasonable basis to proceed with an investigation. The regulations of the OTP entered into force in 2009 and the OTP's Code of Conduct only entered into force in September 2013, largely as a reference to the staff rules of the ICC.

We argue that the influence of political considerations is most apparent in prosecutorial discretion exercised during the preliminary examination phase, and that the permissible invocation of these political considerations generates significant concerns about fairness. Evaluations of selection decisions are much more important for the ICC's legitimacy than for that of most national criminal law systems, where prosecutors' discretionary decisions not to prosecute very rarely spark a challenge to the legitimacy of the entire criminal justice system. In contrast, since the ICC can only prosecute a handful of cases, each decision can be seen as a statement about how the Court views its role in the world.

In this chapter, we begin with a discussion of the normative foundations of prosecutorial ethics. We acknowledge that in most stages of a criminal trial, deontological constraints on the prosecution should be primary, but that consequentialist considerations should play a larger role in the pre-trial phase of a criminal trial. In the third section, we turn to prosecutorial ethics in international law, analysing the normative considerations that should underpin the ethical rules and accountability mechanisms that currently govern the OTP. Then, we turn to the preliminary examination phase – a form of a pre-investigation that precedes the actual 'formal' investigation of a situation and subsequently a case before the ICC[2] – and

---

2. Kai Ambos, *Treatise on International Criminal Law: Volume III: International Criminal Procedure*, Oxford University Press, Oxford, 2016, pp. 335–36; Héctor Olásolo, *Corte Penal Internacional: ¿Dónde Investigar?: Especial Referencia a la Fscalía en el Proceso de Activación*, Tirant lo Blanch, Valencia, 2003, pp. 118–19; Ignaz Stegmiller, *The Pre-Investigation Stage of the ICC: Criteria for Situation Selection*, Duncker & Humblot, Berlin, 2011, p. 57; Ignaz Stegmiller, "The ICC and Mali: Towards more Transparency in International Criminal Law Investigations", in *Criminal Law Forum*, 2013, vol. 24, no. 4, pp. 485 ff.

analyse the OTP's use of prosecutorial discretion pursuant to Article 53(1). We argue that the Prosecutor's discretion to invoke political considerations when analysing whether a case is in the "interests of justice" should be limited by both deontological and consequentialist constraints, and that consequentialist political considerations should sometimes be prioritized to ensure the functioning of the ICC. Finally, we offer several broad suggestions regarding changes to the ethical rules governing the OTP, and argue that the OTP must be accountable to more specific ethical standards applicable at the preliminary examination phase to ensure the legitimacy and fairness of the Court, both in terms of perception and actual practice.

18.2. Prosecutorial Ethics

In this section, we consider the broad normative foundations of prosecutorial ethics, briefly exploring the relationship between law and morality, the concepts of justice and fairness[3] in criminal trials, and the normative ethical theories that inform different kinds of prosecutorial obligations.

18.2.1. The Relationship between Law and Morality

When we say we are 'obligated'[4] to do something, we generally mean this in one of two ways. First, we might mean that we are legally obligated to do something. We may have a positive duty to act in a certain way based on a contract we have signed, or we may have a negative duty not to act in a certain way based on the existence of a law that constrains our behaviour. The other way we might use the term 'obligation' is with respect to a moral duty.[5] Moral obligations can also be positive or negative, demanding or prohibiting certain actions, but a failure to abide by a purely moral obligation does not result in legal sanctions. Moral failures may result in community-based, social, or interpersonal sanctions.

Both moral and legal obligations usually correspond to rights: if one has a right to something, then there is a corresponding obligation on the part of someone, or some entity or institution. So to say that one has a right to the performance of a contract means that someone else has an

---

[3] About the role of fairness in legal ethics, see Paolo Moro, "Rhetoric and Fair Play: The Cultural Background of Legal Ethics", in *US-China Law Review*, 2017, vol. 14, no. 2, pp. 72 ff.

[4] We use the terms 'duty' and 'obligation' interchangeably.

[5] For the purposes of this article, we use the terms 'ethical' and 'moral' interchangeably.

obligation to perform under that contract, and to say that one has a right to medical care means that some institution has an obligation to provide such medical care.

There is no consensus as to how to distinguish the law as a system of norms from morality as a system of norms.[6] There are two main conceptual theories about how to understand legal norms: those who affirm that there is a necessary conceptual relationship between law and morality, and those who deny it. The former – natural law theorists going back to the Greek philosophers and Aquinas – argue that a concept of law cannot be fully articulated without some reference to morals (*"lex injusta non est lex"*).[7] William Blackstone gives the argument for natural law by claiming that it is "binding over all the globe, in all countries, and at all times: no human laws are of any validity, if contrary to this; and such of them as are valid derive all their force, and all their authority, mediately or immediately, from this original".[8] Two modern legal theorists, Lon Fuller and Ronald Dworkin, maintain that the concept of law is imbued with morality of a certain kind (Dworkin) or contains an inner morality (Fuller).

Positivists argue that because law and morality are conceptually distinct, a legal system with no moral constraints on legal validity could exist.

---

[6] This is given that these systems are relatively autonomous as promoted by Niklas Luhmann and Gunther Teubner. See Niklas Luhmann, *Soziologische Aufklärung 1: Aufsätze zur Theorie sozialer Systeme*, 8th edition, Springer, Cham, 2009, p. 226; Gunther Teubner, *Recht als autopoietisches System*, Suhrkamp, Frankfurt am Main, 1989; Niklas Luhmann, "Introduction to Autopoietic Law", in Niklas Luhmann (ed.), *Autopoietic Law: A New Approach to Law and Society*, De Gruyter, Berlin, 1988, pp. 1, 3; Niklas Luhmann, *Einführung in die Systemtheorie*, 4th edition, Carl-Auer, Heidelberg, 2008, pp. 50 ff. (6th edition, 2011, p. 111); Brian H. Bix, *Legal Theory*, Oxford University Press, Oxford, 2004, p. 18; Roger Cotterrell, "Law in Social Theory and Social Theory in the Study of Law", in Austin Sarat (ed.), *The Blackwell Companion to Law and Society*, Blackwell, Malden, 2007, pp. 16, 22; Clemens Mattheis, "The System Theory of Niklas Luhmann and the Constitutionalization of the World Society", in *Goettingen Journal of International Law*, 2012, vol. 4, no. 2, pp. 626 ff.

[7] See Plato, Thomas L. Pangle (trans.), *The Laws of Plato*, University of Chicago Press, Chicago, 1980, book IV; Marcus Tullius Cicero, Clinton Walker Keyes (trans.), *De Re Publica: De Legibus; with an English Translation by Clinton Walker Keyes*, Harvard University Press, Cambridge (MA), 1988; Augustine, Thomas Williams (trans.), *On Free Choice of the Will*, Hackett Publishing Company, Indianapolis, 1993; St. Thomas Aquinas, *The Summa Theologica of St. Thomas Aquinas*, Burns Oates & Washbourne, London, 1912.

[8] William Blackstone, *Commentaries on the Law of England*, The University of Chicago Press, Chicago, 1979, p. 41.

John L. Austin claims that there is a difference between what law is and what it ought to be, that "the existence of law is one thing; its merit or demerit is another".[9] H.L.A. Hart notes that law and morals are certainly related in some ways, but he disputes the idea that "a legal system *must* exhibit some specific conformity with morality or justice, or *must* rest on a widely diffused conviction that there is a moral obligation to obey it".[10] Instead, he argues that the criteria for what makes a law valid does not have to include a "reference to morality or justice".[11] Realists also argue that law and morality are conceptually distinct, but they challenge the idea that legal decision-making can be explained purely by reference to positive law. Instead, realists draw from social interests and public policy when determining what constitutes the law.[12]

Whether or not we can explain or justify the law without morality, there is definitely a relationship between the professional obligations[13] of lawyers and morality. Lawyers are expected to abide by laws, professional rules, and informal professional norms, and in many jurisdictions, they are also required to abide by a professional code of conduct.[14] Professional legal ethics involve a recognition that the lawyers are often confronted with ethical dilemmas. Criminal lawyers in particular face "conflicting

---

[9]   John Austin, *The Province of Jurisprudence Determined*, Library of Ideas edition, Weidenfeld and Nicolson, London, 1954, p. 184.

[10] H.L.A. Hart, *The Concept of Law*, 2nd edition, Clarendon Press, Oxford, 1994, p. 185.

[11] *Ibid.*

[12] See, for example, Myres S. McDougal, "Law and Power", in *American Journal of International Law*, 1952, vol. 46, no. 1, pp. 102–14; Harold D. Lasswell and Myres S. McDougal, "Criteria for a Theory About Law", in *Southern California Law Review*, 1970, vol. 44, no. 2, pp. 362–94; Brian Leiter, "Rethinking Legal Realism: Toward a Naturalized Jurisprudence", in *Texas Law Review*, 1997, vol. 76, no. 2, pp. 267–315; Anja Matwijkiw and Bronik Matwijkiw, "A Modern Perspective on International Criminal Law: Accountability as a Meta-Right", in Leila Nadya Sadat and Michael P. Scharf (eds.), *The Theory and Practice of International Criminal Law: Essays in Honor of M. Cherif Bassiouni*, Martinus Nijhoff, Leiden, 2008, pp. 19–79.

[13] See David Luban and W. Bradley Wendel, "Philosophical Legal Ethics: An Affectionate History", in *Georgetown Journal of Legal Ethics*, 2017, vol. 30, pp. 337-364; see also Hugh Breakey, "Building Ethics Regimes: Capabilities, Obstacles and Supports for Professional Ethical Decision-Making", in *University of New South Wales Law Journal*, 2017, vol. 40, no. 1, pp. 322–52.

[14] See Donald Nicolson, "Making Lawyers Moral? Ethical Codes and Moral Character", in *Legal Studies*, 2005, vol. 25, no. 4, pp. 601–26.

values, aims and interests".[15] They are expected, however, to separate the "morality in their representation" from the "morality of the client's cause".[16] A criminal lawyer is expected to vigorously argue for her side of the case, whether as a defence lawyer or a prosecution lawyer, and whether or not she thinks that she in fact has the most compelling argument. But this vigour remains limited by ethical constraints, such as the moral requirement to respect the dignity of all persons involved in a criminal trial, and the moral prohibition on lying to advance a client's interests. While a defence lawyer may have little control over criminal justice proceedings other than determining how best to advocate for his client, a prosecutor has additional ethical obligations due to her ability to select defendants for trial and determine the scope of the criminal justice process.[17]

There is one final point to make about the relationship between legal obligations and moral obligations, specifically in the realm of legal ethics. A lawyer's moral obligations may in fact be legally binding, if they are also legal obligations, and these obligations may correspond with legal accountability mechanisms. But even in cases where a moral obligation has been clearly violated by a prosecutor, the legal obligation may be too vague to ensure that the legal accountability mechanisms can prevent or punish the violation. So while we will identify legal accountability mechanisms at points throughout the chapter, our focus will remain on prosecutorial ethics as moral and legal obligations.

18.2.2. Justice and Fair Trials

The normative foundations of prosecutorial ethics consist of two main concepts: a prosecutor's general duty to seek justice,[18] and the moral theories that inform the corresponding, specific ethical obligations of the pros-

[15] Richard Young and Andrew Sanders, "The Ethics of Prosecution Lawyers", in *Legal Ethics*, 2004, vol. 7, no. 2, pp. 190–209.

[16] David Luban, *Legal Ethics and Human Dignity*, Cambridge University Press, New York, 2007, p. 20.

[17] This of course applies more to the criminal justice process in the legal tradition of the common law than to a civil-law criminal process, cf. Alexander Heinze, *International Criminal Procedure and Disclosure*, Duncker & Humblot, Berlin, 2014, pp. 107 ff.

[18] See Fred C. Zacharias, "Structuring the Ethics of Prosecutorial Trial Practice: Can Prosecutors Do Justice?", in *Vanderbilt Law Review*, 1991, vol. 44, no. 1, pp. 45 ff.

ecutor. In both adversarial and inquisitorial systems of law,[19] regardless of other specific duties, the prosecutor is expected to seek justice.[20] While the particular features of what constitutes justice vary between, and sometimes within, criminal legal systems, we adopt the view that it is always tied to the concept of fairness.[21]

There are three main types of fairness that we will consider in this chapter: substantive, procedural, and distributive. First, substantive fairness involves the protection of substantive rights, such as the right to bodily autonomy, liberty from confinement, or a trial that does not result in a mistaken conviction.[22] A trial that results in an absurd outcome or one that is intuitively immoral or arbitrary would be considered substantively un-

---

[19] About the meaning of terms 'inquisitorial' and 'adversarial' in more detail, see Heinze, 2014, pp. 117 ff., see *supra* note 17; Kai Ambos and Alexander Heinze, "Abbreviated Procedures in Comparative Criminal Procedure: A Structural Approach with a View to International Criminal Procedure", in Morten Bergsmo (ed.), *Abbreviated Criminal Procedures for Core International Crimes*, Torkel Opsahl Academic EPublisher, Brussels, 2017, pp. 27, 28 ff. (http://www.toaep.org/ps-pdf/9-bergsmo).

[20] Shawn Marie Boyne, *The German Prosecution Service*, Springer, Berlin, Heidelberg, 2014, p. 5 ("[P]rosecutors possess an ethical obligation to pursue justice"). The fact that the search for truth in inquisitorial systems is a constitutive feature (Heinze, 2014, p. 107, see *supra* note 17) does not render justice as an ethical obligation of the prosecutor less relevant. In inquisitorial systems too, truth is a means to the end of justice, as Karl Peters famously pointed out in his seminal work about the German criminal process (Karl Peters, *Strafprozeß*, C.F. Müller, Heidelberg, 1985, p. 82 ("Das Strafverfahren kann das Ziel der Gerechtigkeit nur erreichen, wenn es die Wahrheit findet")). In the same vein, see Theodore L. Kubicek, *Adversarial Justice: America's Court System on Trial*, Algora, New York, 2006, p. 37 with further references. See also Barton L. Ingraham, *The Structure of Criminal Procedure*, Greenwood Press, New York, 1987, p. 13.

[21] See, for example, ICC, Situation in the Democratic Republic of the Congo, *The Prosecutor v. Thomas Lubanga Dyilo*, Trial Chamber, Judgment on the Appeal of Mr. Thomas Lubanga Dyilo against the Decision on the Defence Challenge to the Jurisdiction of the Court pursuant to article 19 (2) (a) of the Statute of 3 October 2006, 14 December 2006, ICC-01/04-01/06-772, para. 37 (http://www.legal-tools.org/doc/1505f7/): "Where fair trial becomes impossible because of breaches of the fundamental rights of the suspect or the accused by his/her accusers, it would be a contradiction in terms to put the person on trial. Justice could not be done. A fair trial is the only means to do justice. If no fair trial can be held, the object of the judicial process is frustrated and the process must be stopped". See also Catherine S. Namakula, "The Human Rights Mandate of a Prosecutor of an International Criminal Trial", in *International Criminal Law Review*, 2017, vol. 17, no. 5, pp. 935, 936.

[22] See, for example, Larry Alexander, "Are Procedural Rights Derivative Substantive Rights?", in *Law and Philosophy*, 1998, vol. 17, no. 1, p. 19.

---

fair.[23] Second, procedural fairness can be assessed on the basis of a system's rules.[24] Rights that are guaranteed by procedures "allow for a system of law to emerge out of a set of substantive rules and [...] minimize arbitrariness".[25] If the same established rules and procedures are applied to all defendants and (potential) suspects without bias, then a system could be said to be procedurally fair, regardless of outcomes. Third, distributive fairness in a criminal justice system involves who is actually tried for crimes, out of the group of all those who could possibly be tried before the court system.[26] We might think that a criminal justice system is fair with respect to distribution if it is willing and able to try all parties who deserve to be tried. It seems that we should care at least somewhat about all three types of fairness, yet sometimes they will be at odds with one another. We return to our concerns with justice and fairness later in the chapter, when we consider the system of international criminal law and its particular aims. But for now, we will use a broad concept of fairness as the main goal of a criminal prosecutor.

18.2.3. Normative Foundations for Specific Prosecutorial Duties

The prosecutor's specific obligations for guaranteeing fair trials can be thought of in terms of deontological norms and consequentialist norms.[27]

---

[23] Larry May, "Habeas Corpus and the Normative Jurisprudence of International Law", in *Leiden Journal of International Law*, 2010, vol. 23, no. 2, pp. 297-299; Lon L. Fuller, *The Morality of Law (Revised Edition)*, Yale University Press, New Haven (CT), 1969, pp. 152 ff.

[24] See, for example, *ibid.*; Yvonne McDermott, *Fairness in International Trials*, Oxford University Press, New York, 2016, pp. 22 ff. Lon Fuller and others argue that procedural fairness contains substantive requirements as well, but for the moment we will consider each type of fairness in isolation. See Fuller, 1969, *supra* note 23.

[25] Larry May, *Global Justice and Due Process*, Cambridge University Press, Cambridge, 2011, p. 52.

[26] Frédéric Mégret, "The Anxieties of International Criminal Justice", in *Leiden Journal of International Law*, 2016, vol. 29, no. 1, p. 211.

[27] Some have argued that virtue theory can and should inform prosecutorial ethics. See, for example, R. Michael Cassidy, "Character and Context: What Virtue Theory Can Teach Us About a Prosecutor's Ethical Duty to Seek Justice", in *Notre Dame Law Review*, 2006, vol. 82, no. 2, p. 635. We would argue that virtue ethics and its focus on the *character* of a prosecutor, rather than her decisions, does not provide clear deontic verdicts for how to act. We also assume that the duty to act with integrity is incumbent upon all participants in a criminal justice system. Therefore, we will only consider the tension between consequentialist and deontological norms here.

Consequentialism "takes the good to be primary and identifies right action as action that promotes value".[28] Right actions are determined solely by the outcomes they produce, so with respect to consequentialist norms, they evaluate end-states independent of the path by which the end-states were achieved. For purposes of this chapter, we will adopt a broad version of consequentialism, a theory which holds that the right action is the action that maximizes the good. The promotion of 'the good', however, requires a conception of what is good and therefore worthy of promotion. In a criminal trial, we would probably conceive of goodness in terms of the substantive results of the trial. We might think a criminal trial was 'good', or fair, if the person who committed a crime is correctly convicted through the criminal trial process. So a prosecutor who attempts to reach the correct substantive outcome in every case, and considers this to be the standard of what constitutes a fair trial, adopts a purely consequentialist view of her ethical obligations.

Deontology, conversely, "takes right action to be the primary evaluative notion; it recognizes various actions as obligatory, prohibited, or permitted on the basis of their intrinsic natures and independently of the value they produce".[29] Unlike consequentialism, a deontological ethical theory may permit, and even require, that agents sometimes not maximize the good.[30] Rather, deontological constraints identify what actions are impermissible because they violate duties, in the form of prohibitions on what we may do, specifically prohibiting harming people in various ways.[31] For instance, Kant argues that one should: "[a]ct so that you use humanity, as much in your own person as in the person of every other, always at the same time as end and never merely as means".[32] We may incur particular responsibilities due to special relationships, which may require us to take actions that do not maximize the good.[33] Beyond the

---

[28] David O. Brink, "Some Forms and Limits of Consequentialism", in David Copp (ed.), *The Oxford Handbook of Ethical Theory*, Oxford University Press, New York, 2006, p. 381.

[29] *Ibid.*

[30] David McNaughton and Piers Rawling, "Deontology", in David Copp (ed.), *The Oxford Handbook of Ethical Theory*, Oxford University Press, New York, 2006, p. 424.

[31] *Ibid.*, p. 425.

[32] Immanuel Kant, Allen W. Wood (ed., trans.), *Groundwork for the Metaphysics of Morals*, Yale University Press, New Haven (CT), 2002, G4:429.

[33] *Ibid.*, G4:425.

actions that are specifically required by duty, deontology allows for freedom of choice in our actions.[34] For a strict deontologist, there is no general duty to 'do good' beyond the duties we have to abide by the constraints and duties of special relationships. A moderate deontologist, on the other hand, will be willing to forgo some duties, in service of good outcomes, when abiding by strict deontology will result in a disastrous outcome. In a criminal trial, deontological constraints on a prosecutor will align more with considerations of procedural fairness. A prosecutor who is focused on deontological norms will be concerned with the way choices are made, defendants' rights are respected, and trials are conducted, independent of the end-states the trials produce.

Deontological constraints are well suited to play the primary role in shaping prosecutorial ethics and promoting fair trials. Allison M. Danner has argued that prosecutorial decisions will be both actually legitimate and perceived as such if they are taken in a principled, reasoned, and impartial manner.[35] As we shall see, the OTP has adopted this approach in several policy papers. The duty to treat every individual as an end in herself and thus apply the same rules without bias or concern about outcomes lends itself to ensuring procedural fairness. The prosecutor is constrained by "rules which apply in an all-or-nothing, categorical manner without reference to the particular context or consequences of the prohibited or required behaviour".[36] The impartiality demanded by deontological constraints applies "separately to every relation between persons", which means that no one's rights may be violated, even if the violation could be "offset by benefits that arise elsewhere" in the justice system.[37] Deontological considerations support the view that: "as the prosecutor has abided by a number of sign posts, and even if the results may, with the benefit of hindsight, look less than ideal, then s/he is effectively considered to have acted ethically".[38] These signposts can be part of the criminal procedure

---

[34]   *Ibid.*, G4:426.

[35]   Allison M. Danner, "Enhancing the Legitimacy and Accountability of Prosecutorial Discretion at the International Criminal Court", in *American Journal of International Law*, 2003, vol. 97, no. 3, pp. 536–37.

[36]   Nicolson, 2005, p. 606, see *supra* note 14.

[37]   Daniel Markovits, *A Modern Legal Ethics: Adversary Advocacy in a Democratic Age*, Princeton University Press, New York, 2010, p. 7.

[38]   Frédéric Mégret, "International Prosecutors: Accountability and Ethics", in *Leuven Centre for Global Governance Studies*, Working Paper No. 18, 2008, p. 8.

of the justice system, but they can also involve internal constraints on prosecutors, such as formal or informal policies, strategies, standards, or regulations.[39] Deontological constraints can also support certain substantive rights, such as *habeas corpus*. We see these deontological constraints as crucial to the foundations of prosecutorial ethics and procedural fairness. While strict deontological lines cannot always be drawn, we agree that the rights of individual defendants should not be violated in service of achieving a particular outcome.

On the other hand, concerns about the substantive outcomes of criminal trials, the overall performance or record of a prosecutor, or the social and political impacts of criminal trials will likely involve more consequentialist considerations.[40] A prosecutor with an impeccable record of respect for defendants' rights, faced with the prospect of removal due to her failure to convict several of these defendants, must consider whether she should treat a few defendants as means to her end of staying employed. Another prosecutor, tasked with determining which members of a large criminal enterprise should be indicted and which should receive plea deals, will certainly take the results of his decisions into account – and will likely be unable to achieve a 'distributively' fair result.

Here we can see the tension between deontological and consequentialist considerations, as well as the varying types of justice, as it will not always be possible for a prosecutor to abide by strict deontological duties while also striving to convict every defendant who is guilty. Consequentialist considerations will be inappropriate at many points in a criminal trial, because they will constitute an impermissible failure of procedural fairness. A prosecutor who has been prevented by the applicable criminal procedure from presenting the most compelling evidence at a murder trial cannot go on to bribe a judge to rule in her favour, even if the murder conviction would serve an important social purpose in consoling the murder victim's family. We maintain that consequentialist considerations should be impermissible during a criminal trial phase when they are incompatible with deontological constraints.

Yet in most criminal justice systems, including the ICC, there are specific sites of prosecutorial discretion, and some of these are appropri-

---

[39] *Ibid.*, p. 7.
[40] *Ibid.*, p. 8.

ate sites for the influence of consequentialist ethical considerations. In an ideal system of criminal justice, each suspect is subject to a fourth kind of justice – retributive justice – in line with the wrongfulness of the respective conduct and the ensuing blame (*culpa*) to be accorded to her. Yet the uniform delivery of this classical, retributive justice is not possible in any criminal justice system. There are simply too many individuals who could be investigated and tried for prosecutors to take on every single situation or case. In practically all domestic criminal justice systems, justice is distributed selectively according to certain, often policy-based, criteria.[41] As we will see in the next section, this is also the case at the ICC.

Prosecutorial discretion may be appropriate in other parts of a trial as well. In the sentencing phase, for instance, it may be appropriate to consider a defendant's particular circumstances before determining the best method and duration of punishment. This offers an opportunity for the prosecutor to respond to concerns about general deterrence, as well as deterring the specific individual, and it can also allow for a prosecutor to mitigate or intensify the political impact of the criminal conviction within the community.

We argue, however, that the most appropriate site for an expanded use of consequentialist considerations is prior to the trial. A prosecutor's office might have a deontological aim of prosecuting all crimes that are of the same gravity, and attempt to seek distributive justice. Yet resources are always limited, in terms of time, money, personnel, and access to evidence. It is impossible for a prosecutor to treat every *potential* defendant equally, even if it is possible to treat every *actual* defendant equally.[42] While a prosecutor's conduct should always be limited by deontological constraints prohibiting bias and the use of individuals as means rather

---

[41] See Jörg-Martin Jehle and Marianne Wade, *Coping with Overloaded Criminal Justice Systems: the Rise of Prosecutorial Power across Europe*, Springer, Berlin, 2006, pp. 24, 60–61; see also Mirjan R. Damaška, "What is the Point of International Criminal Law?", in *Chicago Kent Law Review*, 2008, vol. 83, no. 1, pp. 362–63, referring to the discrimination from a historical perspective; from a comparative perspective, with a view to mandatory prosecution or prosecutorial discretion (principle of opportunity), see Hanna Kuczyńska, The *Accusation Model before the International Criminal Court*, Springer, Cham, 2015, pp. 94–106.

[42] See, in a similar vein, Andre Vartan Armenian, "Selectivity in International Criminal Law: An Assessment of the 'Progress Narrative'", in *International Criminal Law Review*, 2016, vol. 16, no. 4, p. 646.

than respecting them as ends, it is appropriate, and perhaps even obligatory in some instances, for a prosecutor to consider the potential consequences of the decisions she makes regarding which situations to investigate and which individuals to prosecute. In Sections 18.3. and 18.4., we expand this argument and apply it to the preliminary examination phase at the ICC.

18.3. Prosecutorial Ethics in International Criminal Law

In the previous section, we explored prosecutorial ethics generally, as it might play out for domestic prosecutors in a well-established criminal justice system. There are, however, at least two reasons why we might have more to consider when we turn to the specific ethical issues facing international prosecutors.

First, the institutions that purport to carry out international criminal law remain in their early stages. There are still concerns about both internal and external acceptance of the institutions, and so prosecutors will sometimes need to take into account how their decisions will influence the system of international criminal justice as a whole. This is also a concern for prosecutors in States with fledgling domestic criminal legal systems, in that the system must be seen as legitimate by a State's people for it to function effectively.[43]

Second, international criminal law exists as a complement to domestic criminal law, and therefore it cannot simply claim jurisdiction over any situation or case without considering the interests and positions of sovereign States. Domestic criminal law is often tiered as well, in States containing both federal and local laws and systems of accountability. Yet in most States, the federal jurisdiction takes priority over any local or regional jurisdictional claims. This is not necessarily so in the relationship between domestic and international criminal law, and thus international prosecutors have additional ethical factors to consider when exercising discretion.

Additionally, there are a variety of domestic criminal laws and principles that underlie international criminal law, so it is not always easy to identify what principles should prevail when international criminal prosecutors are asked to balance competing values or interests. In this section,

---

[43] *Ibid.*, pp. 644–45.

we will explore the particular features of ethics in international criminal law. We begin by exploring the system of international criminal law generally, in terms of the purpose of and power to punish. We then turn to foundational moral and political questions of international criminal law, namely how we should conceive of the shared jurisdiction between domestic and international criminal legal systems. Finally, we turn to the OTP at the ICC and analyse the specific ethical rules that govern this particular body's functioning.

18.3.1. *Ius Puniendi* and Purpose of Punishment in International Criminal Law

As we have seen, the prosecutor's work necessarily interferes with the rights of suspects and accused persons. The power of the prosecutor as a State agent/organ can only be justified by the State's power to punish (*ius puniendi*) and eventually by certain purposes of punishment. We lean towards translating *ius puniendi* as 'power' and not 'right' to punish, to avoid confusion with *ius poenale*. Reinhard Maurach and Heinz Zipf distinguish *ius poenale* and *ius puniendi* as the objective and subjective right to punish, respectively.[44] *Ius poenale* describes the sum of rules about offences, sentences and other forms of punishment; *ius puniendi* is the State power to punish, that is, the State's capacity – resulting from its sovereignty – to declare certain conduct as punishable and to determine a sentence.[45] Thus, *ius poenale* is the result of *ius puniendi*.[46]

Others also distinguish between the subjective and objective right to punish, but for them, the subjective right to punish is more of a right and less of an inherent power.[47] Their premise is different from ours: while we believe that *ius poenale* presupposes *ius puniendi*, for Franz von Holtzen-

---

[44] See Reinhard Maurach and Heinz Zipf, *Strafrecht – Allgemeiner Teil, Vol. 1: Grundlehren des Strafrechts und Aufbau der Straftat*, 8th edition, C.F. Müller, Heidelberg, 1992, p. 3.

[45] *Ibid.*

[46] See, in a similar vein, Hans-Heinrich Jescheck, *Lehrbuch des Strafrechts*, 3rd edition, Duncker & Humblot, Berlin, 1978, p. 8: "Das Strafrecht beruht auf der **Strafgewalt** ('ius puniendi') des Staates, und diese ist wiederum Teil der Staatsgewalt" (emphasis in the original, footnote omitted).

[47] See Hilde Kaufmann, *Strafanspruch und Strafklagerecht*, Otto Schwartz & Co, Göttingen, 1969, pp. 71–72 with further references.

dorff, for example, it is the other way around.[48] In other words, only when there exists a body of rules about offences, sentences, and other forms of punishment, does the State have the *right* to punish. This goes to Wesley Hohfeld's classical analysis of 'right' that includes – among other things – a power. More concretely, that is to say that the right to punish comprises both the normative power and the State's permissibility to punish.[49] Especially a State's jurisdiction – and eventually universal jurisdiction, as we elaborate in more detail below – stems from a State's power to punish and only indirectly from a right.[50]

For three reasons, however, the emanation of a power to punish (*ius puniendi*) from a right to punish (*ius poenale*) is not convincing. First, the Hobbesian 'right' to punish should not be confused with a Hohfeldian 'right' to punish.[51] According to Hobbes, State punishment stems from the right to self-preservation.[52] Even though, strictly speaking, this right be-

---

48 Franz von Holtzendorff, "Einleitung in das Strafrecht", in Franz von Holtzendorff (ed.), *Handbuch des deutschen Strafrechts in Einzelbeiträgen: Vol. 1: Die geschichtlichen und philosophischen Grundlagen des Strafrechts*, Lüderitz'sche Verlagsbuchhandlung, Berlin, 1871, p. 3: "Jedes staatliche Recht auf Bestrafung (jus puniendi) ist an das Vorhandensein eines positiven Rechtssatzes (jus poenale) geknüpft, durch welchen eine Handlung als verbrecherisch erklärt und die darauf anzuwendende Strafe bestimmt wird"; Kaufmann, 1969, p. 72, see *supra* note 47.

49 Alejandro Chehtman, "Jurisdiction", in Markus D. Dubber and Tatjana Hörnle (eds.), *The Oxford Handbook of Criminal Law*, Oxford University Press, Oxford, 2014, p. 402.

50 Permanent Court of International Justice, *The Case of the S.S. "Lotus" (France v Turkey)*, Judgment, 7 September 1927, para. 45: "Now the first and foremost restriction imposed by international law upon a State is that – failing the existence of a *permissive rule* to the contrary – it may not exercise its *power* in any form in the territory of another State. In this sense jurisdiction is certainly territorial; it cannot be exercised by a State outside its territory except by virtue of a permissive rule derived from international custom or from a convention". (emphasis added) (http://www.legal-tools.org/doc/a6fa72/). This was overlooked by Anthony R. Reeves, "Liability to International Prosecution: The Nature of Universal Jurisdiction", in *European Journal of International Law*, 2018, vol. 28, no. 4, pp. 1047–1067.

51 Alice Ristroph, "Respect and Resistance in Punishment Theory", in *California Law Review*, 2009, vol. 97, no. 2, p. 603, footnote 8.

52 Thomas Hobbes, *Leviathan*, Richard Tuck (ed.), Cambridge University Press, Cambridge, 2003, p. 214: "[E]very man had a right to every thing, and to do whatsoever be thought necessary to his own preservation; subduing, hurting, or killing any man in order thereunto. And this is the foundation of that right of Punishing, which is exercised in every Commonwealth. For the Subjects did not give the Soveraign that right; but onely in laying down theirs, strengthned him to use his own, as he should think fit, for the preservation of them all: so that it was not given, but left to him, and to him onely; and (excepting the limits set

---

longs to all natural, mortal humans, the sovereign possesses it through the State's existence in a specific state of nature *vis-à-vis* a natural person.[53] Second, especially at an extraterritorial and/or international level, beyond a right to punish, "we must also account for a specific body having the authority to exercise that right".[54] Third, should *ius puniendi* really pre-suppose *ius poenale*, the question of why a State has the right to punish is obsolete – a classical vicious cycle.[55]

Here, the development of the term '*ius puniendi*' deserves closer consideration. It originally only described the power to punish, also known as '*potestas criminalis*', and included the State's power to punish, resulting from superiority (*Selbstherrlichkeit, Imperium*), a superior right and duty to protect (*hoheitliches Schutzrecht mit Schutzpflicht*) or *ius eminens*, comparable with Hobbes' right to self-preservation.[56] The power to punish had a pre-positive origin[57] and became successively intertwined with the positive right to punish as result of the triumph of liberal criminal law,[58] constructing juridical relationships between the State as a (criminal law) legislator, and the State as possessing the right to punish.[59] This, however, ignores that *ius poenale* can hardly have the function of being both the criminal law (right), which is addressed to the citizens, and the basis of punishment (power), at the same time.

Nevertheless, both theoretical elements – *ius puniendi* and the purpose of punishment – are highly disputed on an international level. International criminal law lacks a consolidated punitive power in its own right, since it does not operate pursuant to a legislative body, but instead claims

---

him by naturall Law) as entire, as in the condition of meer Nature, and of warre of every one against this neighbour"; see also *ibid.*, pp. 613–14. ·

[53] Ristroph, 2009, p. 615, see *supra* note 51.

[54] Alejandro Chehtman, *The Philosophical Foundations of Extraterritorial Punishment*, Oxford University Press, Oxford, 2010, p. 6.

[55] In the same vein, see Peter Klose, "'Ius puniendi' und Grundgesetz", in *Zeitschrift für die gesamte Strafrechtswissenschaft*, 1974, vol. 86, p. 36.

[56] *Ibid.*

[57] Heinrich Luden, *Handbuch des teutschen gemeinen und particularen Strafrechts*, vol. 1, Friedrich Luden, Jena, 1847, p. 6.

[58] Klose, 1974, pp. 39–41, see *supra* note 55.

[59] Karl Binding, *Handbuch des Strafrechts*, Duncker & Humblot, Berlin, 1885, p. 191.

---

the ability to punish without the status of a sovereign nation.[60] This alone renders the OTP's broad discretionary power theoretically unfounded. In fact, what we have said earlier about the definition of law might well be used as arguments against prosecutorial discretion on an international level: (a) at the international level, a normative order is absent where norms are recognized by the society as a whole and determine social communication, which is required for the power to punish (Günther Jakobs);[61] (b) law cannot exist without the State (Thomas Hobbes);[62] and (c) law cannot exist without a public power to enforce it (Immanuel Kant) – for Kant, law implies the *Rechtsstaat* and "a republican form of governance",[63] which is not necessarily limited to the institutional form of a nation State but "allows for the creation, interpretation, and, where necessary, enforcement of law".[64]

However, a more fundamental question arises as to whether it makes sense at all to apply the theories of validity of norms, developed with classical sovereign nations in mind, to a supranational order that follows different rules of organization.[65] Here, the enforcement of fundamental human rights by international criminal law comes to the rescue of the international community's *ius puniendi*, eventually blurring the lines

---

[60] Kai Ambos, "Punishment without a Sovereign? The Ius Puniendi Issue of International Criminal Law: A First Contribution towards a Consistent Theory of International Criminal Law", in *Oxford Journal of Legal Studies*, 2013, vol. 33, no. 2, p. 298.

[61] Günther Jakobs, "Untaten des Staates – Unrecht im Staat", in *Goltdammer's Archiv für Strafrecht*, 1994, pp. 13–14. Jakobs *expressis verbis* refers to the state's 'power' and not 'right' to punish, since a power to punish is a necessary requirement for the right to punish. In Jakobs' own words: "Ohne staatliche Gewalt gibt es kein staatliches Recht" (p. 13). See also Kenneth Anderson, "The ICC Would Increase Its Prevention Ability If the Prosecutor's Discretion Were More Visibly Limited", in Richard H. Steinberg (ed.), *Contemporary Issues Facing the International Criminal Court*, Brill Nijhoff, Leiden, Boston, 2016, p. 188 ("Since I do not regard what passes for the international community as constituting a social order – a society, in Weber's sense – it seems to me mere metaphor and analogy to consider that the ICC can play a role globally that criminal courts play domestically"). See generally Ambos, 2013, pp. 299–300, see *supra* note 60 with further references.

[62] Thomas Hobbes, *Leviathan*, J.C.A. Gaskin (ed.), 1998 (1651) Oxford University Press, London, pp. 114 ff.

[63] Immanuel Kant, Mary J. Gregor (trans.), *The Metaphysics of Morals*, Cambridge University Press, Cambridge, 1991, p. 124 [313].

[64] Interpretation by Patrick Capps and Julian Rivers, "Kant's Concept of International Law", in *Legal Theory*, 2011, vol. 16, p. 229, 234.

[65] Ambos, 2013, p. 303, see *supra* note 60.

---

between the community's obligation to protect human rights abuses and its power to punish.

As previously mentioned, it was Immanuel Kant who had the idea of human dignity as a source of fundamental human (civil) rights[66] that, ultimately, must be enforced by a supra- or transnational (criminal) law.[67] Kant's conception of human dignity is complemented by his view of 'perpetual peace'.[68] Klaus Günther follows from Kant's Third Definitive Article ("Cosmopolitan Right shall be limited to Conditions of Universal Hospitality (principle of cosmopolitan right)"), that the application of public human rights is a necessary precondition for a permanent peace.[69]

---

[66] Immanuel Kant, Mary J. Gregor (ed., trans.), *Groundwork of the Metaphysics of Morals*, Cambridge University Press, Cambridge, 1997, p. 15 [402]. See also Marie E. Newhouse, "Two Types of Legal Wrongdoing", in *Legal Theory*, 2017, vol. 22, pp. 59 ff.; Ulfried Neumann, "Das Rechtsprinzip der Menschenwürde als Schutz elementarer menschlicher Bedürfnisse. Versuch einer Eingrenzung", in *Archiv für Rechts- und Sozialphilosphie*, 2017, vol. 103, p. 293; Thomas Gutmann and Michael Quante, "Menschenwürde, Selbstbestimmung und Pluralismus: Zwischen sittlicher Vorgabe und deontologischer Konstruktion", in *Archiv für Rechts- und Sozialphilospie*, 2017, vol. 103, no. 3, pp. 322 ff.; Laura Valentini, "Dignity and Human Rights: A Reconceptualisation", in *Oxford Journal of Legal Studies*, vol. 37, no. 4, p. 867.

[67] Ambos, 2013, p. 304, see *supra* note 60.

[68] The structure of his work *Toward Perpetual Peace* is as follows: six "Preliminary Articles" ban treacherous dealings among States, including preparation for war (Immanuel Kant, "Perpetual Peace", in Hans Reiss (ed.), H.B. Nisbet (trans.), *Immanuel Kant, Political Writings*, Cambridge University Press, Cambridge, 1991, pp. 93 ff.). They describe steps that can be taken to 'wind down' a war and avoid armed conflict. Kant's preliminary articles basically "seek to ground the federation on measures of good faith, self-determination and non-interference" (interpretation by Garrett Wallace Brown, "Kantian Cosmopolitan Law and the Idea of a Cosmopolitan Constitution", in *History of Political Thought*, 2006, vol. 27, pp. 661, 678). Three "Definitive Articles" establish actions and institutions deemed necessary for a cosmopolitan system to sustain itself over time and end a war: 1. The Civil Constitution of Every State shall be Republican (principle of civil right); 2. The Right of Nations shall be based on a Federation of Free States (principle of international right); 3. Cosmopolitan Right shall be limited to Conditions of Universal Hospitality (principle of cosmopolitan right) (Kant, *ibid.*, p. 98). Compared to the Preliminary Articles, the Definitive Articles present "stronger terms for membership [in the federation] and the normative conditions upon which the federation stands" (Brown, *ibid.*, p. 681). For a both historical and conceptual account of Kant's understanding of war and peace see Philipp Gisbertz, "The Concepts of 'War' and 'Peace' in the Context of Transnational Terrorism", in *Archiv für Rechts- und Sozialphilosophie*, 2018, vol. 104, no. 1, pp. 3, 9.

[69] Klaus Günther, "Falscher Friede durch repressives Völkerstrafrecht?", in Werner Beulke *et al.* (eds.), *Das Dilemma des rechtsstaatlichen Strafrechts*, Berliner Wissenschafts-Verlag, Berlin, 2009, p. 84.

Kant justifies this precondition through a two-step argument: First, "[The] universal law of Right [*Rechtsgesetz*], so act externally that the free use of your choice can coexist with the freedom of everyone in accordance with a universal law, *is indeed a law [Gesetz]*, which lays an obligation on me, but it does not at all expect, far less demand, that I myself should limit my freedom to those conditions just for the sake of this obligation; [...]".[70] Second, "if (as must be the case in such a constitution) the agreement of the citizens is required to decide whether or not one ought to wage war, then *nothing is more natural* than that they would consider very carefully whether to enter into such a terrible game, since they would have to resolve to bring the hardships of war upon themselves [...]".[71] In sum, with this conception, Kant laid the foundations for all current conceptions of human dignity and world peace, an "international rule of law".[72]

This not only gives the world community *ius puniendi* – it also affects the purposes of punishment and eventually the theoretical basis of the prosecutor's ethical obligations. The argument goes thus: prosecutorial ethics at the ICC are shaped by both the justification of the world community's *ius puniendi* and the mandate of the ICC, that is, its goals and purposes of punishment.[73] The justification of *ius puniendi* can have either a deontological (human dignity as a source of fundamental human (civil) rights) or consequentialist (confirmation and reinforcement of fundamental human rights norms) aspect. The same applies to the mandate of the ICC. While retribution as a purpose of punishment has a moral dimension, it is fair to say that most of the ICC's goals are consequentialist in nature.

---

[70] Immanuel Kant, Mary J. Gregor (trans.), *The Metaphysics of Morals*, Cambridge University Press, Cambridge, 1991, p. 56 [231], emphasis added.

[71] Immanuel Kant, *Toward Perpetual Peace and Other Writings on Politics, Peace, and History*, Yale University Press, London, 2006, [8:351], emphasis added.

[72] Wade L. Huntley, "Kant's Third Image", in *International Studies Quarterly*, 1996, vol. 40, pp. 45, 49; Alec Stone Sweet, "A Cosmopolitan Legal Order: Constitutional Pluralism and Rights Adjudication in Europe", in *Global Constitutionalism*, 2012, vol. 1, pp. 53, 58; Jorrik Fulda, "Eine legitime Globalverfassung? Die US-Hegemonie und die weltgesellschaftlich gerechte Vollendung des Kantischen Projektes", in *Archiv des Völkerrechts*, 2016, vol. 54, pp. 334, 345. About the role of human dignity in International Human Rights Law and International Criminal Law, see Stefanie Schmahl, "Human Dignity in International Human Rights, Humanitarian and International Criminal Law: A Comparative Approach", in Eric Hilgendorf and Mordechai Kremnitzer (eds.), *Human Dignity and Criminal Law*, Duncker & Humblot, Berlin, 2018, pp. 79 ff.

[73] See, in a similar vein, Reeves, 2018, p. 1047, *supra* note 50.

This is especially true for the expressivist purpose of punishment.[74] Moreover, the mere existence and work of the Court help to promote human rights by: creating a historical record for past wrongs;[75] offering a forum for victims to voice their opinions and receive satisfaction and compensation for past violations;[76] creating judicial precedent; and deterring potential violators of the gravest crimes[77] while punishing past offenders.[78] Thus, human rights norms in the ICC Statute "provide a blueprint for the common good of a community".[79]

18.3.2. Ethics and International Criminal Law

18.3.2.1. Normative Moral Foundations for International Criminal Law

Hugo Grotius and other early natural law theorists drew a distinction between voluntary law (*ius dispositivum*) and obligatory law (*ius scrip-*

---

[74] See, for example, David Luban, "Fairness to Rightness: Jurisdiction, Legality and the Legitimacy of International Criminal Law", in Samantha Besson and John Tasioulas (eds.), *The Philosophy of International Law*, Oxford University Press, Oxford, 2010, p. 576; Diane Marie Amann, "Group Mentality, Expressivism, and Genocide", in *International Criminal Law Review*, 2002, vol. 2, no. 2, p. 117.

[75] Statement of Judge Claude Jorda, U.N. SCOR, 55th session, 4161st meeting, UN Doc. S/PV.4161, 20 June, 2000, p. 3; Jens D. Ohlin, "A Meta-Theory of International Criminal Procedure, Vindicating the Rule of Law", in *UCLA Journal of International Law and Foreign Affairs*, 2009, vol. 14, no. 1, pp. 86 ff.; in more detail Heinze, 2014, pp. 218 ff., see *supra* note 17.

[76] Bert Swart, "Damaska and the Faces of International Criminal Justice", in *Journal of International Criminal Justice*, 2008, vol. 6, no. 1, p. 100; Minna Schrag, "Lessons Learned from ICTY Experience", in *Journal of International Criminal Justice*, 2004, vol. 2, no. 2, p. 428. For Ralph, this helps to constitute a world society, Jason Ralph, "International Society, the International Criminal Court and American Foreign Policy", in *Review of International Studies*, 2005, vol. 31, no. 1, pp. 28, 39.

[77] Kai Ambos, *Treatise on International Criminal Law: vol. 1: Foundations and General Part*, Oxford University Press, Oxford, 2013, p. 71.

[78] ICTR, *Prosecutor v. Omar Serushago*, Trial Chamber, Sentence, 5 February 1999, ICTR-98-39-S, para. 20 (http://www.legal-tools.org/doc/e2dddb/); ICTR, *Prosecutor v. Rutaganda*, Trial Chamber, Judgement, 6 December 1999, ICTR-96-3-T, para. 455 (http://www.legal-tools.org/doc/f0dbbb/); ICTR, *Prosecutor v. Ndindabahizi*, Trial Chamber, Judgement, 15 July 2004, ICTR-2001-71-I, para. 498 (http://www.legal-tools.org/doc/272b55/); ICTR, *Prosecutor v. Karera*, Trial Chamber, Judgement, 7 December 2007, ICTR-01-74-T, para. 571 (http://www.legal-tools.org/doc/7bc57f/).

[79] John M. Czarnetzky and Ronald J. Rychlak, "An Empire of Law: Legalism and the International Criminal Court", in *Notre Dame Law Review*, 2003, vol. 79, no. 1, p. 110.

---

tum).[80] Hugo Grotius claimed that the necessary principles of natural law were "the dictate of right reason involving moral necessity, independent of any institution – human or divine".[81] As John Finnis notes, Grotius and his counterparts believed that a determination of right or wrong "depends on the nature of things (and what is *conveniens* to such nature), and not on a decree of God; but the normative or motivating significance of moral rightness and wrongness".[82] Grotius saw that there was an international community of sovereign States for whom these necessary principles were non-voluntary laws.[83] He and his contemporaries "laid down unreservedly that Natural Law is the code of states, and thus put in operation a process which has continued almost down to our own day, the process of engrafting on the international system rules which are supposed to have been evolved from the unassisted contemplation of the conception of Nature".[84] One particularly important aspect of this natural law doctrine was the idea that since men are, by nature, all equal, so too are the "independent communities, however different in size and power", that make up the international order.[85]

An additional concept is the creation of a *civitas maxima* – which Christian Wolff described as an organic whole uniting all nations on the basis of the universal natural law[86] – that lies within the so-called revolu-

---

80 Evan J. Criddle and Evan Fox-Decent, "A Fiduciary Theory of Jus Cogens", in *Yale Journal of International Law*, 2009, vol. 34, no. 2, p. 334.

81 Lauri Hannikainen, *Peremptory Norms (Jus Cogens) in International Law: Historical Development, Criteria, Present Status*, Coronet Books Inc., Helsinki, 1988, p. 30.

82 John Finnis, *Natural Law and Natural Rights*, 2nd edition, Oxford University Press, Oxford, 2011, p. 44. Italics in original.

83 Hugo Grotius, *De Jure Belli Ac Pacis Libri Tres*, 1625, 1, chap. 1, sect. X, para. 5; see also Rafael Nieto-Navia, "International Peremptory Norms (Jus Cogens) and International Humanitarian Law", in Lal Chand Vohrah *et al.* (eds.), *Man's Inhumanity to Man: Essays on International Law in Honour of Antonio Cassese*, International Humanitarian Law Series, Kluwer Law International, The Hague, 2003, pp. 595–640.

84 Henry Sumner Maine, *Ancient Law*, CreateSpace Independent Publishing Platform, Lexington, 2013, p. 30.

85 *Ibid.*

86 Christian L.B. Wolff, *Institutiones Juris Naturae et Gentium in Quibus ex Ipsa Hominis Natura Continuo Nexu Omnes Obligationes et Jura Omnia Deducuntur*, Apud F. ex N. Pezzana, Venetiis, 1769, part IV, cap. I, sect. 1090: "Quemadmodum vero lex naturae praestat consensum in civitatem maximam; ita eadem quoque eumdem supplet in condendis legibus". This rather rough translation was provided by Armin von Bogdandi

tionist tradition, for which Kant is identified as a forerunner,[87] although both concepts – Grotius' and Kant's – overlap in certain regards.[88] The revolutionist view of a "world society" is "identified by those rights claims of individuals and non-State groups that are asserted by 'a third image of international [or cosmopolitan] law' and enforced by global institutions when states are unwilling and unable to do so".[89] The different notions of the international community are mirrored in the ICC Statute.

For legal positivists, the existence of a legal system depends on the procedures and structures that created the legal system, not on the content of the laws. In the realm of international law, this means that law could only exist as part of a system with accepted procedures and structures. Alberico Gentili, one of the earliest scholars of international law, argued that international law was based on the consent of States and attempted to show that "the [codified] Roman law was valid in the extra-European domain and between sovereign polities and empires".[90] He claimed that "it was possible to apply rules taken from the Roman law of the *Institutes* and the *Digest* to the relations between different European polities and to some relations beyond Europe".[91] Jeremy Bentham talked of "international jurisprudence" in reference to "mutual transactions between sovereigns",[92] and other positivists who followed pointed to State recognition of customs and treaty obligations.

---

and Sergio Dellavalle, "Universalism and Particularism", in Stefan Kadelbach *et al.* (eds.), *System, Order, and International Law*, Oxford University Press, Oxford, 2017, p. 489.

[87] Ralph, 2005, p. 34, see *supra* note 76; Barry Buzan, "The English School: An Underexploited Resource in IR", in *Review of International Studies*, 2001, vol. 27, no. 3, p. 475.

[88] Andrew Hurrell, "Kant and the Kantian Paradigm in International Relations", in *Review of International Studies*, 1999, vol. 16, no. 3, p. 200.

[89] Ralph, 2005, p. 34, see *supra* note 76, citing Andrew Hurrell, "Conclusion International Law and the Changing Constitution of International Society", in Michael Byers (ed.), *The Role of Law in International Politics: Essays in International Relations and International Law*, Oxford University Press, Oxford, 2000, p. 337.

[90] Benedict Kingsbury and Benjamin Straumann, "State of Nature Versus Commercial Sociability as the Basis of International Law: Reflections on the Roman Foundations and Current Interpretations of the International Political and Legal Thought of Grotius, Hobbes, and Pufendorf", in Samantha Besson and John Tasioulas (eds.), *The Philosophy of International Law*, Oxford University Press, Oxford, 2010, p. 38.

[91] *Ibid.* Italics in the original.

[92] Jeremy Bentham, *An Introduction to the Principles of Morals and Legislation*, Batoche Books, Kitchener, 1999, p. 236.

Although legal positivism has overshadowed natural law theory since the seventeenth and eighteenth centuries, it remains the case that we think, even without international positive law, that States cannot avoid certain obligations to the international community. Natural law theories remain the most straightforward way to justify an international legal system, especially one that has expanded to include claims of authority over a much wider range of issues, including criminal law and mass atrocity. The moral underpinnings of international criminal law reflect the continuing influence of natural law theory at least through the twentieth century. In the wake of World War II, as the international community sought to impose accountability for atrocities on individual actors, there was no positive international criminal law to assist with such an undertaking. Thus, one of the main justifications for the International Military Tribunal ('IMT') was a shared understanding within the international community that the atrocities of World War II were exceptionally serious. The individual trials were an expression of the universal moral judgment of the wrongness and seriousness of the crimes. While positive international criminal law has proliferated in the years since the IMT, the purported universal condemnation of genocide and crimes against humanity remains a source of respect for both the positive law and the norms against such crimes.

Moreover, contrary to the Nuremberg International Military Tribunal, the Tokyo International Military Tribunal for the Far East, and the Iraqi Special Tribunal (before it was turned into a national tribunal),[93] 'ordinary' international criminal tribunals[94] depend, as a general rule, on the co-operation of the relevant territorial State(s), with regard to both the investigation and prosecution of the crimes committed on the State territo-

---

93   Annalisa Ciampi, "Other Forms of Cooperation", in Antonio Cassese *et al.* (eds.), *The Rome Statute of the International Criminal Court: A Commentary*, vol. 2, Oxford University Press, Oxford, 2002, pp. 1711–12.

94   Generally on the ICC's approach to co-operation, see Rod Rastan, "The Responsibility to Enforce – Connecting Justice with Unity", in Carsten Stahn and Göran Sluiter (eds.), *The Emerging Practice of the International Criminal Court*, Nijhoff, Leiden, 2009, pp. 171 ff.; Karin N. Calvo-Goller, *La Procédure et la Jurisprudence de la Cour Pénale Internationale*, Gazette du Palais, Paris, 2012, p. 133.

ry, and the enforcement of the respective sentences.[95] States are and remain the key actors in co-operation with respect to criminal matters.[96] In this regard, the ICC Statute promotes the Grotian solidary international society.[97]

Some claim that legal positivist theories are unable to pass moral judgment on 'bad' State or individual actors, and that we should instead rely on these natural law theories. But as international criminal law has grown over the last half century, positive law theorists have gained force in passing legal judgments on such 'bad' actors. Many of the documents creating international criminal law are filled with moral language, reflecting expressions of the global community as to the wrongness of certain types of heinous crimes. This influence on the positive law seems to deny that positive law has to be free of moral judgment, but even if the moral language in the documents is ignored, States remain in a position to pass moral judgment as individual States while working within the international criminal justice systems to pass legal judgment.

18.3.2.2. Universal Jurisdiction

From the time of the IMT, holding individuals accountable under international criminal law has been related to the idea that those who commit international crimes do so not just against individuals, or ethnic groups, or States, but against humanity (the political community/global public) as a whole.[98] The concept of universal jurisdiction is premised on the moral argument that some crimes are "so calculated, so malignant, and so devastating, and civilization cannot tolerate their being ignored, because it can-

---

[95] See, generally, Claus Kreß and Kimberly Prost, "Part 9 – Preliminary Remarks", in Otto Triffterer and Kai Ambos (eds.), *Rome Statute of the International Criminal Court: A Commentary*, 3rd edition, C.H. Beck, Munich, 2016, marginal no. 1.

[96] Darryl Robinson, "Inescapable Dyads: Why the International Criminal Court Cannot Win", in *Leiden Journal of International Law*, 2015, vol. 28, no. 2, p. 339.

[97] Ralph, 2005, p. 37, see *supra* note 76.

[98] See Luigi D.A. Corrias and Geoffrey M. Gordon, "Judging in the Name of Humanity: International Criminal Tribunals and the Representation of a Global Public", in *Journal of International Criminal Justice*, 2015, vol. 13, no.1, pp. 98 ff.; Anthony Duff, "Authority and Responsibility in International Criminal Law", in Samantha Besson and John Tasioulas (eds.), *The Philosophy of International Law*, Oxford University Press, 2010, pp. 595 ff.; see also Hannah Arendt, *Eichmann in Jerusalem: A Report on the Banality of Evil*, Penguin Books, New York, 2006, p. 251.

---

not survive their being repeated".[99] When the whole of civilization or humanity is identified as the relevant entity who has been harmed by a crime, some argue that this should correspond with universal jurisdiction, which allows any State to prosecute individuals, no matter where the crime was committed.[100] Grotius, for instance, argued that every State should have jurisdiction over "gross violations of the law of nature and of nations, done to other States and subjects".[101] The concept of universal jurisdiction has foundations in natural law, but with the proliferation of positive international criminal law, it can be defended (and challenged) by theorists in both camps.[102]

18.3.2.3. Normative Moral Foundations for the ICC

The ICC was established with the concepts of universal jurisdiction in mind, although some of the parties who worked on the ICC Statute rejected the idea.[103] The Preamble of the Statute notes that the purpose of the ICC was to have jurisdiction over "the most serious crimes of concern to the international community as a whole", and that the aim of the ICC is to "guarantee lasting respect for and the enforcement of international jus-

---

[99] As noted in Justice Robert Jackson's opening statement before the Nuremberg Tribunal, speaking on behalf of the prosecution team. Justice Jackson's opening statement is published in *Trial of the Major War Criminals before the International Military Tribunal*, vol. 2, International Military Tribunal, Nuremberg, 1947, pp. 98–155. About the moral basis of universal jurisdiction in more detail, see Jochen Bung, "Naturrecht – Völkerrecht – Weltrecht: Der Code des Hugo Grotius", in *Archiv des Völkerrechts*, 2017, vol. 55, no. 2, pp. 126 ff.

[100] See Hans-Peter Kaul and Claus Kreß, "Jurisdiction and Cooperation in the Statute of the International Criminal Court", in *Yearbook of International Humanitarian Law*, 1999, vol. 2, pp. 143–75; see also Claus Kreß, "Universal Jurisdiction over International Crimes and the *Institut De Droit International*", in *Journal of International Criminal Justice*, vol. 4, no. 3, 2006, pp. 561–85.

[101] Hugo Grotius, Archibald C. Campbell (trans.), *The Rights of War and Peace, Including the Law of Nature and of Nations*, Elibron Classics reprint, M. Walter Dunne, Washington and London, 1901, book II, chap. XX, para. XL, p. 247.

[102] This diversity of the concept is overlooked by Reeves, 2018, pp. 1047-1067, see *supra* note 50, whose attempt to combine the *ius puniendi* question with the justification for universal jurisdiction is laudable but both lacks an examination of the literature on the *ius puniendi* of the international community (Reeves uses the rather anodyne term of "prerogative" [to prosecute] and superelevates it metaphysically) and demonstrates a rather selective analysis of the existing views on universal jurisdiction.

[103] See Kaul and Kreß, 1999, *supra* note 100.

---

tice".[104] The ICC Statute is not only the "culmination of international law-making".[105] Rather, it codifies the customary international humanitarian laws,[106] and the jurisprudence of previously established international or internationalised tribunals such as the ICTY and the ICTR.[107] Thus, the law with regard to grave international crimes, customary and treaty-based international law, the applicable general principles of law and internationally recognised human rights, "consolidated over a century's worth of jurisprudence and customary law", have been 'constitutionalized' by the ICC Statute.[108]

These declarations are significant, but they are vague in terms of how they should inform the specific ethical commitments of institutions like the ICC. If seeking justice is the aim of all adversarial, inquisitorial, and international criminal justice systems, then we need to know more about what the ICC is seeking when it seeks justice. We return to this question when we explore the parameters of the prosecutor's discretionary powers during the preliminary examination phase in Section 18.4. The most important thing to identify at this point is that it is necessary for the OTP to exercise these discretionary powers within a system of prosecutorial ethical obligations.

18.3.3. Ethical Obligations for the OTP

The OTP at the ICC is governed by several different sets of ethical rules relating to professional conduct and ethics. We focus on the ICC Statute and the OTP Code of Conduct, the latter of which was adopted in 2013, but the OTP is also bound by the Rules of Procedure and Evidence, the Regulations of the Court, and the Prosecution Regulations.[109] While we

---

[104] Rome Statute of the International Criminal Court, adopted 17 July 1998, entry into force 1 July 2002, Preamble ('ICC Statute') (http://www.legal-tools.org/doc/7b9af9/).

[105] Marc Weller, "Undoing the Global Constitution: UN Security Council Action on the International Criminal Court", in *International Affairs*, 2002, vol. 78, no. 4, p. 693.

[106] Errol P. Mendes, *Peace and Justice at the International Criminal Court*, Elgar, Cheltenham, 2010, p. 22.

[107] *Ibid.*, p. 24.

[108] *Ibid.*, pp. 15, 21–22.

[109] The applicable provisions in each of these documents were identified by the Trial Chamber V(B) in ICC, Situation in the Republic of Kenya, *Prosecutor v. Uhuru Muigai Kenyatta*, Trial Chamber, Decision on the Defence application concerning professional ethics applicable to prosecution lawyers, 31 May 2013, ICC-01/09-02/11-747, para. 10 (http://www.

briefly identify some of the corresponding external accountability mechanisms, such as disciplinary measures and judicial review, our focus is on specific obligations of the OTP. Therefore, the only accountability mechanisms that we discuss in any detail are those that create new obligations on the part of the OTP.

18.3.3.1. General Ethical Rules

18.3.3.1.1. The ICC Statute

The ICC Statute contains specific ethical requirements[110] of the OTP in several sections of the Statute. Article 42(2) gives the Prosecutor "full authority over the management and administration of the Office, including the staff, facilities and other resources thereof",[111] while Article 42(3) notes that the "Prosecutor and the Deputy Prosecutors shall be persons of high moral character".[112] This kind of institutional independence of the OTP, supported by a strong administrative autonomy, is a novelty.[113] Its purpose is to prevent a factual dependency of the OTP on the Registry, which occurred in the early stages of the ICTR.[114]

---

legal-tools.org/doc/d27ea0/). The case also referred to ICC Staff Rules and Regulations, which we have not considered here due to the high-level nature of the ethical obligations we are considering.

[110] On the ethical obligations of all legal professionals in international criminal courts and tribunals, see Chandra Lekha Sriram, in Vesselin Popovski (ed.), *International Rule of Law and Professional Ethics*, Ashgate Publishing, 2014, pp. 171-188.

[111] ICC Statute, Article 42(2), see *supra* note 104. See, in detail, Hector Olásolo, "Issues Regarding Article 42", in Morten Bergsmo, Klaus Rackwitz and SONG Tianying (eds.), *Historical Origins of International Criminal Law: Volume 5*, Torkel Opsahl Academic EPublisher, Brussels, 2017, pp. 423 ff. (http://www.toaep.org/ps-pdf/24-bergsmo-rackwitz-song).

[112] ICC Statute, Article 42(3), see *supra* note 104.

[113] See also John R.W.D. Jones, "The Office of the Prosecutor", in Antonio Cassese *et al.* (eds.), *The Rome Statute of the International Criminal Court: A Commentary*, vol. 1, Oxford University Press, Oxford, 2002, p. 273; Jan Wouters, Sten Verhoeven and Bruno Demeyere, "The International Criminal Court's Office of the Prosecutor: Navigating between Independence and Accountability", in *International Criminal Law Review*, 2008, vol. 8, no. 1, p. 277; William A. Schabas, *An Introduction to the International Criminal Court*, 5th edition, Cambridge University Press, Cambridge, 2017, p. 372; Namakula, 2017, pp. 937-938, see *supra* note 21.

[114] See Report of the Secretary-General on the Activities of the Office of Internal Oversight Services (Annex), UN Doc. A/51/789, 6 February 1997, para. 8 ("The Registrar has declined to meet administrative requests from the judges or the Office of the Prosecutor

The Court's internal dimension of independence is complemented by the rule according to which no OTP member[115] shall "seek or act on instructions from any *external* source".[116] Similar provisions can be found in the law of the *ad hoc* and mixed international criminal tribunals.[117] They reaffirm that the OTP shall exercise its authority on its own behalf and without external influence or pressure from governments, international organizations, NGOs or individuals.[118]

where in his judgement they were insufficiently justified. [...] Because of this perception, almost no decision can be taken by the other organs of the Tribunal that does not receive his review and agreement or rejection."); in more detail Luc Côté, "Independence and Impartiality", in Luc Reydams, Jan Wouters and Cedric Ryngaert (eds.), *International Prosecutors*, Oxford University Press, Oxford, 2012, pp. 335–36, see also Jones, 2002, p. 273, see *supra* note 113; Héctor Olásolo *et al.*, *Assessing the Role of the Independent Oversight Mechanism in Enhancing the Efficiency and Economy of the ICC*, Universiteit Utrecht, Utrecht, 2011, p. 54; Philipp Ambach and Klaus Rackwitz, "A Model Of International Judicial Administration? The Evolution of Managerial Practices at the International Criminal Court", in *Law and Contemporary Problems*, 2013, vol. 76, no. 3 and 4, p. 142.

[115] This provision applies to the Prosecutor, the Deputy Prosecutors, staff and gratis personal; see William A. Schabas, *The International Criminal Court: A Commentary on the Rome Statute*, 2nd edition, Oxford University Press, Oxford, 2016, p. 740.

[116] ICC Statute, Article 42(1) clause 3, see *supra* note 104 (emphasis added). cf. also Yvonne McDermott, "Article 42", in Mark Klamberg, *Commentary on the Law of the International Criminal Court*, Torkel Opsahl Academic EPublisher, Brussels, 2017, para. 1 (https://www. legal-tools.org/doc/aa0e2b/).

[117] Statute of the International Tribunal for the former Yugoslavia, adopted 25 May 1993 by Security Council resolution 827, Article 16(2) ('ICTY Statute') (https://www.legal-tools. org/doc/b4f63b/); Statute of the International Tribunal for Rwanda, adopted 8 November 1994 by Security Council resolution 955, Article 15(2) ('ICTR Statute') (http://www.legal-tools.org/doc/8732d6/); Statute of the United Nations Mechanism for International Criminal Tribunals, adopted 22 September 2010 by Security Council resolution 1966, Article 14(2) ('UNMICT Statute') (http://www.legal-tools.org/doc/30782d/); Statute of the Special Court for Sierra Leone, enacted 16 January 2002, in force 1 July 2002, Article 15(1) ('SCSL Statute') (http://www.legal-tools.org/doc/aa0e20/); Statute of the Residual Special Court for Sierra Leone, in force 12 August 2012, Article 14(2) ('RSCSL Statute'); Law on the Establishment of the Extraordinary Chambers in the Courts of Cambodia, 27 October 2004, Article 19 ('ECCC Law') (http://www.legal-tools.org/doc/9b12f0/); Statute of the Special Tribunal for Lebanon, adopted 30 May 2007 by Security Council resolution 1757, Article 11(2) ('STL Statute') (http://www.legal-tools.org/doc/da0bbb/).

[118] ICC, Situation in the Democratic Republic of the Congo, Pre-Trial Chamber, Prosecution's Reply on the Applications for Participation 01/04-1/dp to 01/04-6/dp, 15 August 2005, ICC-01/04-84, para. 32 (http://www.legal-tools.org/doc/4aa811/); in a similar vein Fabricio Guariglia, "The Selection of Cases by the Office of the Prosecutor of the International Criminal Court", in Carsten Stahn and Göran Sluiter (eds.), *The Emerging Practice of the International Criminal Court*, Nijhoff, Leiden, 2009, p. 212; Côté, 2012, p. 337, see *supra*

As to the OTP's external independence, the Prosecutor and the Deputy Prosecutors must refrain from engaging in any activity that is likely to interfere with their prosecutorial functions or to affect confidence in their independence.[119] Moreover, they must not engage "in any other occupation of a professional nature".[120] These requirements are deontological, in that they require that the OTP hold itself to a high standard of self-respect and refuse to permit others to bias their decisions. Yet they also reflect a consequentialist concern about the likely result, unfairness, of permitting such biases to influence the OTP.

Article 44 provides for the appointment of staff, including the requirement that the OTP "shall ensure the highest standards of efficiency, competency and integrity" in its employment of staff.[121]

Article 54(1) relates to the investigations phase and requires that the Prosecutor "investigate incriminating and exonerating circumstances equally",[122] take measures to "respect the interests and personal circumstances of victims and witnesses, including age, gender as defined in Article 7, paragraph 3, and health, and take into account the nature of the crime, in particular where it involves sexual violence, gender violence or violence against children" in the investigations,[123] and "[f]ully respect the

---

note 114. See also ICC, *Staff rules of the International Criminal Court*, adopted 21 April 2005, entry into force 3 December 2005, Rule 101.3(a) ("Staff members shall ensure their independence from any person, entity or authority outside the Court.") ('ICC Staff Rules') (http://www.legal-tools.org/doc/10f5c7/); Wu Wei, *Rolle des Anklägers eines internationalen Strafgerichtshofs*, Lang, Frankfurt am Main, 2007, p. 13; Hilde Farthofer, "The Prosecutor", in Christoph Safferling (ed.), *International Criminal Procedure*, Oxford University Press, Oxford, 2012, p. 151; Margaret M. deGuzman and William A. Schabas, "Initiation of Investigations and Selection of Cases", in Göran Sluiter *et al.* (eds.), *International Criminal Procedure: Principles and Rules*, Oxford University Press, Oxford, 2013, p. 167. Article 42(1)(3) of the ICC Statute does not, of course, forbid the Prosecution to seek assistance from external sources, in particular from member states, see SCSL, *Prosecutor v. Sesay et al.*, Trial Chamber, Judgment, 2 March 2009, SCSL-04-15-T, para. 44 (http://www.legal-tools.org/doc/7f05b7/).

119 ICC Statute, Article 42(5), see *supra* note 104.

120 See also Stefanie Bock, *Das Opfer vor dem Internationalen Strafgerichtshof*, Duncker & Humblot, Berlin, 2010, p. 215; Schabas, 2016, p. 741, see *supra* note 115; Isabelle Moulier, "Article 42", in Julian Fernandez and Xavier Pacreau (eds.), *Statut de Rome de la Cour Pénale Internationale*, vol. 1, Editions A. Pedone, Paris, 2012, p. 1024.

121 ICC Statute, Article 44(2), see *supra* note 104.

122 *Ibid.*, Article 54(1)(a).

123 *Ibid.*, Article 54(1)(b).

rights of persons arising under this Statute".[124] Article 54(1)(a) draws on the jurisprudence of the *ad hoc* Tribunals in making impartiality and objectivity statutory obligations.[125] In particular, the Prosecutor's duty to search actively for exonerating information may be regarded as a measure to achieve factual equality of arms between the prosecution and defence, since the latter may lack the necessary resources and powers to conduct extensive investigations on its own.[126] The obligations under Article 54(1) are deontological, where they correspond to specific procedural requirements or the rights of individuals. Yet they also involve some amount of discretion, which means that the OTP should consider the results of their decisions when balancing deontological obligations to defendants with deontological obligations to victims and witnesses.

---

[124] *Ibid.*, Article 54(1)(c).

[125] See, in more detail, Fabricio Guariglia, "Policy and Organisational Questions", in Bergsmo, Rackwitz and SONG (eds.), 2017, pp. 286 ff., *supra* note 111. See also Bock, 2010, p. 216, see *supra* note 120; Côté, 2012, pp. 359–60, see *supra* note 114; Heinze, 2014, pp. 257–58, see *supra* note 17.

[126] See also Caroline Buisman, "The Prosecutor's Obligation to Investigate Incriminating and Exonerating Circumstances Equally – Illusion or Reality?", in *Leiden Journal of International Law*, 2014, vol. 27, no. 1, p. 206; Vanessa Thalmann, "The Role of the Judge and the Parties in Proceedings", in Robert Kolb and Damien Scalia (eds.), *Droit International Pénal*, 2nd edition, Helbing Lichtenhahn, Bâle, 2012, p. 467; Hanna Kuczyńska, 2015, p. 52, see *supra* note 41. This appears to resemble more a civil law ('inquisitorial') than a common law ('adversarial') type of prosecutor. For, although the prosecution in the adversarial system is also obliged to follow the principles of truth and objectivity, the adversarial two-case approach entails that the submission of evidence by the prosecution is separated from the one by the defence, thereby forcing the prosecutor more in a partisan party position; cf. Mirjan R. Damaška, "Problematic Features of International Criminal Procedure", in Antonio Cassese (ed.), *The Oxford Companion of International Criminal Justice*, Oxford University Press, Oxford, 2009, p. 176, arguing that "it becomes difficult" for the Prosecutor "to refrain from using […] evidence selectively, focusing only on information favourable to their allegations"; see also Håkan Friman, "Investigation and Prosecution", in Roy S. Lee (ed.), *The International Criminal Court: Elements of Crimes and Rules of Procedure and Evidence*, Transnational Publishers, Ardsley (NY), 2001, p. 537; Vladimir Tochilovsky, "Legal Systems and Cultures in the ICC", in Horst Fischer *et al.* (eds.), *International and National Prosecution of Crimes under International Law: Current Developments*, Berlin-Verlag Spitz, Berlin, 2001, p. 637; Christoph Safferling, *Towards an International Criminal Procedure*, Oxford University Press, Oxford, 2003, pp. 79, 86; Kai Ambos and Stefanie Bock, "Procedural Regimes", in Luc Reydams, Jan Wouters and Cedric Ryngaert (eds.), *International Prosecutors*, Oxford University Press, Oxford, 2012, p. 489; Heinze, 2014, pp. 250, 253, see *supra* note 17.

Some critics argue that the Prosecution has so far "largely ignored its obligation under Article 54(1)(a)", "failed to investigate any of its cases with the thoroughness expected from a diligent prosecutor", and failed to acknowledge the weaknesses of certain cases.[127] In *Gbagbo*, the PTC, quite straightforwardly, expressed doubts whether the Prosecutor really had followed "all relevant incriminating and exonerating lines of investigation in order to establish the truth".[128] The *Mbarushimana* PTC characterised the OTP's interrogation technique, which involved manipulative feedback on witness testimony with frequent leading questions, as "utterly inappropriate when viewed in light of the objective, set out in Article 54(1)(a) of the Statute, to establish the truth by 'investigating incriminating and exonerating circumstances equally'".[129] Seeking the truth is a strict deontological obligation on the part of the OTP, and these cases demonstrate ethical failures on the part of the OTP.[130] Kant demanded that respect for the dignity of oneself and the dignity of others could never

---

[127] Buisman, 2014, pp. 223, 226, see *supra* note 126. See also ICC, Situation in the Democratic Republic of Congo, *Prosecutor v. Lubanga*, Trial Chamber, Closing Submission of the Defence, 15 July 2011, ICC-01/04-01/06-2773, para. 13 (http://www.legal-tools.org/doc/calfcd/), arguing that the OTP has seriously failed to fulfil its obligation to investigate exculpatory circumstances. Similar complaints were made in ICC, Situation in the Republic of Kenya, *Prosecutor v. Muthaura et al.*, Pre-Trial Chamber, Public Redacted Version of Final Written Observations of the Defence Team of Ambassador Francis K. Muthaura on the Confirmation of Charges Hearing, 2 December 2011, ICC-01/09-02/11-374, paras. 71–72 (http://www.legal-tools.org/doc/be93c9/); ICC, Situation in Darfur, Sudan, *Prosecutor v. Abu Garda*, Pre-Trial Chamber, Decision on the Confirmation of Charges, 8 February 2010, ICC-02/05-02/09-243-Red, paras. 46–47 (http://www.legal-tools.org/doc/cb3614/); ICC, Situation in the Republic of Kenya, *Prosecutor v. Ruto et al.*, William Samoei Ruto Defence Brief following the Confirmation of the Charges Hearing, 24 October 2011, ICC-01/09-01/11-355, paras. 19–23 (http://www.legal-tools.org/doc/3977e1/); Antonio Cassese *et al.*, *Cassese's International Criminal Law*, Oxford University Press, Oxford, 2013, p. 344 ("the prosecutor is every bit as partisan as his counterparts at the ICTY and ICTR").

[128] ICC, Situation in the Republic of Côte d'Ivoire, *Prosecutor v. Gbagbo*, Pre-Trial Chamber, Decision adjourning the hearing on the Confirmation of Charges Pursuant to Article 61(7)(c)(i) of the Rome Statute, 3 June 2013, ICC-02/11-01/11-432, para. 37 (http://www.legal-tools.org/doc/2682d8/).

[129] ICC, Situation in the Democratic Republic of Congo, *Prosecutor v. Mbarushimana*, Pre-Trial Chamber, Decision on the Confirmation of Charges, 16 December 2011, ICC-01/04-01/10-465, para. 51 (http://www.legal-tools.org/doc/63028f/).

[130] For a psychological, legal and sociological account of truth and international fact-finding, see Shiri Krebs, "The Legalization of Truth in International Fact-Finding", in *Chicago Journal of International Law*, 2017, vol. 18, no. 1, pp. 83 ff.

permit lying.[131] He does, however, limit this unconditional duty to explicit lies, or "intentionally untrue declaration[s] to another".[132] Failures to disclose to the truth may be permissible unless they are intentional deceptions. It is clear that under Article 54, there is a specific obligation to explore and disclose "all relevant incriminating and exonerating lines of investigation",[133] and any failure to do so would constitute a violation of a strict deontological duty.

There are other specific ethical obligations that the OTP incurs indirectly, such as those from sections of the ICC Statute that grant rights on other parties. Article 55, for instance, provides for specific rights on the part of persons during an investigation. These rights create corresponding deontological obligations on the part of the OTP, such as the obligation that the OTP not subject an individual "to arbitrary arrest or detention", nor deprive an individual "of his or her liberty except on such grounds and in accordance with such procedures as are established in this Statute".[134]

18.3.3.1.2. The OTP Code of Conduct

Like the ABA Model Rules for Professional Conduct in the United States,[135] the ICC also has Codes of Conduct that ensure the compliance of trial participants with ethical rules and values. The ICC has three Codes of Conduct: the Code of Judicial Ethics, the Code of Professional Conduct for counsel, and the Code of Conduct for the OTP ('OTP Code'). The Code of Judicial Ethics was adopted by the judges pursuant to Regulation 126 of the Regulations of the Court.[136] The Code of Professional Conduct

---

[131] Immanuel Kant, Mary Gregor (ed., trans.), *The Metaphysics of Morals*, Cambridge University Press, New York, 1996, 6:429; see also Immanuel Kant, "On a Supposed Right to Lie from Philanthropy", in Mary Gregor (ed., trans.), *Practical Philosophy*, Cambridge University Press, New York, 1996, 8:427.

[132] Kant, 1996, *supra* note 131.

[133] ICC Statute, Article 54(1)(a), see *supra* note 104.

[134] *Ibid.*, Article 55(1)(d).

[135] See Heinze, 2014, pp. 432 ff., see *supra* note 17.

[136] ICC Code of Judicial Ethics, 9 March 2005, Article 1 (http://www.legal-tools.org/doc/383f8f/). ICC, Regulations of the Court, 26 May 2004, Regulation 126 ('RegCourt') (http://www.legal-tools.org/doc/2988d1/) reads: "1. The Presidency shall draw up a Code of Judicial Ethics, after having consulted the judges. 2. The draft Code shall then be transmitted to the judges meeting in plenary session for the purpose of adoption by the majority of the judges".

for Counsel was adopted by the Assembly of States Parties ('ASP') and applies "to defence counsel, counsel acting for States, *amici curiae* and counsel or legal representatives for victims and witnesses practising at the International Criminal Court".[137] Since the Prosecutor was given the authority to set up his own office,[138] the Code of Professional Conduct for Counsel does not apply to the OTP.[139] Furthermore, Rule 9 of the ICC Rules of Procedure and Evidence ('RPE') provides that it is the Prosecutor's responsibility to "govern the operation of the office", including whether or not he would have a code of conduct and regulations.[140] Therefore, when the OTP started working, it had neither regulations nor a code of conduct (which was still the case when the first stay of the proceedings was imposed by the Trial Chamber in the *Lubanga* case in June 2008).[141] The OTP eventually published regulations on 23 April 2009, and one can only assume that it is linked to the disclosure failures in the *Lubanga* case.

On 5 September 2013, the OTP Code was adopted to regulate the ethical conduct of the individuals working at the OTP.[142] Prior to 2013, there was no set of ethical standards "specifically regulat[ing] the conduct of members of the OTP".[143] Many of the rules and regulations listed in the following sub-sections, which were in place prior to the adoption of the OTP Code, were "general in scope and not tailored to apply to the specific

---

[137] Cf. Code of Professional Conduct for Counsel, 2 December 2005, Article 1.

[138] Cf. ICC Statute, Article 42(2), see *supra* note 104.

[139] See also Theresa Roosevelt, "Ethics for the Ethical: A Code of Conduct for the International Criminal Court Office of the Prosecutor", in *Georgetown Journal of Legal Ethics*, 2011, vol. 24, no. 1, p. 840, who also provides an interesting reason for this: "The Prosecutor may have been given the responsibility to set up his own office as a carrot to take the job. Negotiations over how to set up the OTP took a great deal of time at the conference where the ICC Statute was drafted. It was difficult to recruit someone for the position of Prosecutor because there were many uncertainties about how much support he or she would have from states. This would mean the Prosecutor would be operating in a new, international arena, possibly without a government behind him or her." (footnote omitted).

[140] *Ibid.*

[141] See Heinze, 2014, pp. 454 ff., see *supra* note 17.

[142] *Ibid.*

[143] Lawrence Pacewicz, "Introductory Note to International Criminal Court Code of Conduct for the Office of the Prosecutor", in *International Legal Materials*, 2014, vol. 53, no. 2, p. 397.

---

role that the OTP plays at the ICC and the specific obligations and duties which that role entails".[144]

The OTP Code was drafted by the OTP and provides for internal enforcement of its provisions.[145] It involves many general deontological constraints on the conduct of the OTP that are also applied to other counsel acting before the ICC, such as those related to faithfulness, conscientiousness, impartiality, independence, confidentiality, and conflicts of interest.[146] The OTP Code includes ethical obligations related to the duty to establish the truth under Article 54(1)(a) of the ICC Statute, which are deontological as they relate to procedural requirements for a fair trial and the investigation of incriminating and exonerating circumstances equally.[147] But it also includes the requirement to consider all relevant circumstances, and the requirement that investigations be conducted "with the goal of establishing the truth, and in the interests of justice", each of which involves discretion and potentially consequentialist considerations.[148] The OTP Code contains other deontological constraints on the effective investigation and prosecution practices of the OTP, including the requirements to:

1. act with competence and diligence, make impartial judgments based on the evidence and consider foremost the interests of justice in determining whether or not to proceed;

2. fully respect the rights of persons under investigation and the accused and ensure that proceedings are conducted in a fair manner;

3. refrain from prosecuting any person whom they believe to be innocent of the charges;

4. refrain from proffering evidence reasonably believed to have been obtained by means of a violation of the Statute or internationally recognised human rights if the violation casts substantial doubt on the reliability of the evidence or the admission of evidence would

---

[144] *Ibid.*

[145] *Ibid.*

[146] ICC, *Code of Conduct for the Office of the Prosecutor*, 5 September 2013, chap. 2 ('OTP Code') (http://www.legal-tools.org/doc/3e11eb/).

[147] *Ibid.*, chap. 3, Section 1.

[148] *Ibid.*

be antithetical to and would seriously damage the integrity of the proceedings.[149]

The OTP Code also contains deontological provisions related to disclosure,[150] handling of information and evidence,[151] and security.[152] It has been argued that while the OTP Code contains a more comprehensive set of ethical guidelines for the OTP, it is still too vague to account for significant ethical concerns.[153] We will address this question in Section 18.5., when we present our recommendations for ensuring prosecutorial ethics in the preliminary examination phase.

18.3.3.1.3. Strategy and Policy Papers

Regulation 14 of the Regulations of the OTP obliges the OTP to make public its strategy and make use of policy papers that reflect the key principles and criteria of this strategy.[154] The OTP currently combines strategy papers, which clarify the Office's strategic objectives for a time period of three to four years, with policy papers addressing particular fundamental issues on which the Office wants to provide more clarity and transparency. We address these papers within the context of the OTP's application of Article 53, regarding the initiation of an investigation during the preliminary examination phase. The strategy papers are useful working agendas,

---

[149] *Ibid.*, chap. 3, Section 2.

[150] *Ibid.*, chap. 3, Section 3.

[151] *Ibid.*, chap. 3, Section 4.

[152] *Ibid.*, chap. 3, Section 5.

[153] See Pacewicz, 2014, p. 398, see *supra* note 143; see also Anna Oriolo, "The 'Inherent Power' of Judges: An Ethical Yardstick to Assess Prosecutorial Conduct at the ICC", in *International Criminal Law Review*, 2016, vol. 16, no. 2, p. 307. About vagueness and prosecutorial discretion from a domestic (US) perspective, see George D. Brown, "McDonnell and the Criminalization of Politics", in *Virginia Journal of Criminal Law*, 2017, vol. 5, no. 1, pp. 8–11.

[154] This corresponds to No. 17 of the UN Guidelines on the Role of Prosecutors ("In countries where prosecutors are vested with discretionary functions, the law or published rules or regulations shall provide guidelines to enhance fairness and consistency of approach in taking decisions in the prosecution process, including institution or waiver of prosecution."). A good example in this regard is ICC-OTP, *OTP Report on Preliminary Examination Activities 2013*, 25 November 2013 (http://www.legal-tools.org/doc/dbf75e/) setting out the principles and criteria of preliminary examinations (paras. 1 ff.) and aiming to promote transparency (para. 15). See recently ICC-OTP, *Strategic Plan 2016-2018* (2015), especially para. 36, referring to the policy paper on preliminary examinations and to case identification and prioritisation within a formal investigation.

which – due to their temporal limitation – also give the OTP the opportunity to critically evaluate and, if necessary, adjust its strategy on a regular basis. The policy papers clarify key issues such as the "interests of justice",[155] victim's participation,[156] preliminary examinations[157] and the prosecution of sexual and gender based crimes.[158] The OTP recently published policy papers on children[159] and 'case selection'.[160] This practice involves a broad ethical obligation on the part of the OTP, which could be considered deontological in that the duty might be seen as reflective of an obligation to be transparent with the international community, the general public, and all possible defendants that could come before the ICC. This commitment to transparency can also be seen as consequentialist, as one of its aims might be to support the appearance of the legitimacy of the ICC.[161]

18.3.3.2. Accountability Mechanisms

In this section, we analyse internal accountability mechanisms, including those previously identified in Section 18.3.2.1, and briefly identify some of the external accountability mechanisms that serve an important legal

---

[155] ICC-OTP, *Policy Paper on the Interests of Justice*, September 2007 (http://www.legal-tools. org/doc/bb02e5/).

[156] ICC-OTP, *Policy Paper on Victims' Participation*, 12 April 2010 (http://www.legal-tools. org/doc/3c204f/).

[157] ICC-OTP, 2013, see *supra* note 154; on the respective draft paper, see Kai Ambos and Ignaz Stegmiller, "Prosecuting International Crimes at the International Criminal Court: Is there a Coherent and Comprehensive Prosecution Strategy?", in *Crime, Law and Social Change*, 2012, vol. 58, no. 4, pp. 397–99; see also the OTP's annual reports on Preliminary Examination Activities 2011-2016.

[158] ICC-OTP, *Policy Paper on Sexual and Gender-Based Crimes*, 6 June 2014 (http://www. legal-tools.org/doc/7ede6c/).

[159] ICC-OTP, *Policy on Children*, 15 November 2016 (http://www.legal-tools.org/doc/ c2652b/).

[160] ICC-OTP, *Policy Paper on Case Selection and Prioritisation*, 15 September 2016 (http:// www.legal-tools.org/doc/182205/). For a detailed analysis see Nadia Bernaz, "An Analysis of the ICC Office of the Prosecutor's Policy Paper on Case Selection and Prioritization from the Perspective of Business and Human Rights", in *Journal of International Criminal Justice*, 2017, vol. 15, no. 3, pp. 527-542.

[161] Stahn, too, seems to view transparency (including publicity) as involving consequentialist considerations, when he points out: "Publicity is in line with the public nature of criminal proceedings. It may facilitate the alert effect and strengthen prevention", Stahn, 2017, p. 18, see *supra* note 1.

---

purpose in encouraging OTP compliance with ethical obligations. As noted previously, we do not go into any detail about external accountability mechanisms.

18.3.3.2.1. Internal Accountability Mechanisms

It is first and foremost the Prosecutor herself[162] who has to ensure that the OTP staff respect the legal rules and the principles of good professional practice.[163] The OTP Code provides for internal measures to ensure ethical behaviour within the OTP Rule 74 addresses the disciplinary measures that may be taken in light of prosecutorial misconduct within the OTP, noting that such instances shall be addressed "in accordance with Staff Rule 110.1, or listed as unsatisfactory in Section 5(3) of the *Code of Conduct for Staff Members*".[164] Disciplinary measures can also be directed against the OTP pursuant to the Staff Rules of the ICC. The Staff Rules are directed especially at alleged wrongdoing within the Prosecutor's office and situations when this wrongdoing falls within the Prosecutor's own disciplinary powers.[165] Since neither the ICC Statute nor the RPE specifically define a violation of the Staff Rules as "serious misconduct" or "a serious breach of duty", a violation of the Staff Rules alone cannot serve as a basis for the ASP to remove the Prosecutor or the Deputy Prosecutor.[166] However, the Prosecutor is responsible for determining whether

---

[162] On external, civil society control (by NGOs), see Carsten Stahn, "Judicial Review of Prosecutorial Discretion", in Carsten Stahn and Göran Sluiter (eds.), *The Emerging Practice of the International Criminal Court*, Nijhoff, Leiden, 2009, p. 261; on informal sanctions/control mechanisms, see Jenia I. Turner, "Accountability of International Prosecutors", in Carsten Stahn (ed.), *Law and Practice of the International Criminal Court*, Oxford University Press, Oxford, 2015, pp. 402–04.

[163] Frédéric Mégret, "Accountability and Ethics", in Luc Reydams, Jan Wouters and Cedric Ryngaert (eds.), *International Prosecutors*, Oxford University Press, Oxford, 2012, p. 457; see also Milan Markovic, "The ICC Prosecutor's Missing Code of Conduct", in *Texas International Law Journal*, 2011–12, vol. 47, no. 1, p. 206; Jenia I. Turner, "Policing International Prosecutors", in *New York University Journal International Law & Political Sciences*, 2012, vol. 45, no. 1, p. 256; Turner, 2015, pp. 386–87, see *supra* note 162; Olásolo *et al.*, 2011, p. 65, see *supra* note 114. The Prosecutor, however, must delegate his or her disciplinary powers if s/he has a personal interest in the case, see *Mr C.P. v ICC*, Judgement No. 2757 of the ILO Administrative Tribunal, 9 July 2008, para. 19 (http://www.legal-tools.org/doc/73bd48/).

[164] OTP Code, chap. 5, Section 2, Rule 74, see *supra* note 146 (italics added).

[165] Cf. Mégret, 2012, p. 477, see *supra* note 163 (italics added).

[166] Markovic, 2011–12, p. 207, see *supra* note 163.

OTP staff members have violated the Staff Rules and what disciplinary measures should be imposed.[167] Disciplinary proceedings can be instituted in case a staff member fails to act "in accordance with any official document of the Court governing rights and obligations of staff members" or fails "to observe the standards of conduct expected of an international civil servant", which amounts to "unsatisfactory conduct".[168]

These internal mechanisms for discipline are related to the Prosecutor's obligation to respect her staff in her dealings with them, but the obligations they create are not deontological in the sense that we generally associate deontology with retributive punishment. Disciplinary measures are not like criminal punishment, where a retributive view would tell us that each individual should get the punishment they are owed, in accordance with the wrongfulness of their conduct. They may involve some sorts of deontological fairness considerations, so that similar actors receive similar punishments. But disciplinary measures likely involve more consequentialist considerations, aimed at preventing future misconduct and ensuring a respectful and efficient work environment. These goals will support the larger OTP aims of seeking justice and fair trials.

18.3.3.2.2. External Accountability Mechanisms

The OTP is subject to external accountability mechanisms, in the form of disciplinary measures and judicial review, which do not generate new ethical obligations on the part of the OTP. Article 70 of the ICC Statute gives the ICC jurisdiction over intentional offences against the ICC's administration of justice,[169] while Article 71 provides for sanctions against persons who commit misconduct related to proceedings before the ICC.[170] Article 47 of the ICC Statute and Rule 25 of the RPE provide that Prosecutors and Deputy Prosecutors, among others, are subject to disciplinary measures for: "(i) Interfering in the exercise of the functions of a person referred to in Article 47; or (ii) Repeatedly failing to comply with or ignoring requests made by the Presiding Judge or by the Presidency in the

---

[167] *Ibid.*, p. 206.
[168] ICC Staff Rules, Rule 110.1, see *supra* note 107.
[169] ICC Statute, Article 70, see *supra* note 104.
[170] *Ibid.*, Article 71.

exercise of their lawful authority".[171] The aforementioned disclosure failures in *Gbagbo* and *Mbarushimana* certainly meet the threshold for failure in Rule 25(1)(a)(ii) of the RPE. Rule 26 of the RPE directs complaints about Article 47 misconduct to the Presidency, which has the discretion to either initiate proceedings against an individual or set aside complaints.[172]

Arguably, the only new ethical obligation that this complaint procedure places on the OTP is in the case of misconduct by a Deputy Prosecutor. If disciplinary measures against a Deputy Prosecutor are requested by the Presidency, "[a]ny decision to give a reprimand shall be taken by the Prosecutor"[173] and "[a]ny decision to impose a pecuniary sanction shall be taken by an absolute majority of the Bureau of the Assembly of States Parties upon the recommendation of the Prosecutor".[174] This obligation mirrors other mixed deontological and consequentialist general obligations on the part of the Prosecutor in her role as the leader of the OTP. She must treat all of her staff impartially, with respect and dignity, and use her best judgment about the expected consequences of using formal or informal mechanisms to discipline and redirect her staff.

Another external tool to investigate the alleged misconduct of staff and elected officials of the ICC is the Independent Oversight Mechanism ('IOM'), which was established by the ASP[175] in accordance with Article 112(4) of the ICC Statute.[176] The IOM "may receive and investigate reports of misconduct or serious misconduct" on the part of ICC staff and elected officials, including OTP staff.[177] The results of investigations con-

---

[171] ICC, *Rules of Procedure and Evidence*, 9 September 2002, Rule 25 ('ICC RPE') (http://www.legal-tools.org/doc/8bcf6f/).

[172] *Ibid.*, Rule 26(2).

[173] *Ibid.*, Rule 30(3)(a).

[174] *Ibid.*, Rule 30(3)(b).

[175] Official Records of the Assembly of States Parties to the ICC Statute of the International Criminal Court, Eighth session, The Hague, 18–26 November 2009 (ICC-ASP/8/20), vol. 1, part II, ICC ASP/8/Res.1.

[176] "The Assembly may establish such subsidiary bodies as may be necessary, including an independent oversight mechanism for inspection, evaluation and investigation of the Court, in order to enhance its efficiency and economy."

[177] Including "staff subject to the Staff and Financial Regulations and Rules of the Court [...] and all contractors and/or consultants retained by the Court and working on its behalf", see ASP, Resolution ICC-ASP/9/Res.5, adopted at the fifth plenary meeting (10 December 2010), Annex, para. 2. Interestingly, the term 'contractor' or 'consultant' does not include an 'intermediary', see ASP, Resolution ICC-ASP/9/Res.5, adopted at the fifth plenary

ducted by the IOM related to the OTP include "recommendations for consideration of possible disciplinary or jurisdictional action".[178] Interestingly, the IOM has the power to "recommend that the Court refer [a] matter for possible criminal prosecution to relevant national authorities, such as those of the State where the suspected criminal act was committed, the State of the suspect's nationality, the State of the victim's nationality and, where applicable, of the host State of the seat of the Court".[179] Thus, the IOM may have the ability to sanction prosecutorial misconduct through domestic criminal prosecution, although the ASP has taken steps to limit the independence of the IOM.[180] The IOM does not generate any specific ethical obligations on the part of the OTP.

Now that we have explored the general ethical rules and corresponding accountability mechanisms that apply to the OTP, we turn to the crux of the chapter, namely the ethical considerations for the OTP as they play out in the preliminary examination phase.

18.4. Prosecutorial Discretion and Preliminary Examinations at the ICC

18.4.1. Legal Principles of Prosecutorial Discretion

Given the high number of international crimes committed in crises, it is not possible to prosecute all potential perpetrators at the international level. After more than 10 years, it has become clear that not even those who are most responsible for mass atrocities will all face international criminal justice.

As we noted earlier, domestic criminal justice systems face similar challenges. There are different methods of dealing with the case overload, by balancing procedural principles like the search for the objective or

---

meeting (10 December 2010), Annex, para. 2 with fn. 3. About intermediaries and disclosure in more detail see Heinze, 2014, pp. 458 ff., see *supra* note 17.

[178] *Ibid.*, Annex, para. 4.

[179] *Ibid.*, Annex, para. 31. In that case, the IOM is also entitled to recommend that "privileges and immunities be waived", see *ibid.*, Annex, para. 32.

[180] Turner, 2012, pp. 181, 243–44, see *supra* note 163; see also ASP, Resolution ICC-ASP/9/Res.5, adopted at the fifth plenary meeting (10 December 2010), Annex, paras. 21–22.

material truth, the principle of full judicial clarification of the facts,[181] the principle of legality (*legalité de poursuites* – mandatory prosecution) and the principle of opportunity (*opportunité des poursuites* – prosecutorial discretion). Thus, some legal systems rest on the idea of 'legality' or 'compulsory/mandatory prosecution', whereby the relevant official agencies are expected to act upon a formal standard when dealing with all breaches of criminal law that come to their knowledge.[182]

In some countries, like Italy, the principle of legality (*principio di legalità*) is primarily related to the substantive (material) criminal law, thus prohibiting the punishment of a crime that was not explicitly punishable at the time it was committed.[183] The (procedural) principle of legality is either subject to important exceptions or qualified by prosecutorial discretion.[184] Thus, most countries operate in practice on both legality and opportunity principles, as they each have advantages and disadvantages. The opportunity principle "allows prosecutors to target resources for serious offences; it is effective against organised crime by facilitating charge-bargaining and opens up opportunities for diversionary[185] disposal of of-

---

181 See Strafprozessordnung (The German Code of Criminal Procedure), 12 September 1950, Section 244(2) ('StPO') (http://www.legal-tools.org/doc/741f12/; http://www.legal-tools. org/doc/19df38/): "In order to establish the truth, the court shall, *proprio motu*, extend the taking of evidence to all facts and means of proof relevant to the decision" (translated to English in Brian Duffett and Monika Ebinger (trans.), authorised by the German Federal Ministry of Justice).

182 See generally Kuczyńska, 2015, pp. 94–106, see *supra* note 126; Christopher Harding and Gavin Dingwall, *Diversion in the Criminal Process*, Sweet and Maxwell, London, 1998, p. 1. About the application of the principles of mandatory prosecution and discretion on the level of International Criminal Justice see Kai Ambos, "The International Criminal Justice System and Prosecutorial Selection Policy", in Bruce Ackerman, Kai Ambos and Hrvoje Sikirić (eds.), *Visions of Justice: Liber Amicorum Mirjan Damaška*, Duncker & Humblot, Berlin, 2016, p. 30; Kuczyńska, 2015, pp. 106–11, see *supra* note 41.

183 Ferrando Mantovani, *Diritto Penale, Parte Generale*, 6th edition, CEDAM, Padova, 2009, p. 3; however, there are procedural forms of the principle of legality in Italy, namely 'the principle of the legitimate judge' and the 'principle of legality'. On the distinction between legality in substantive and procedural law, see also Michele Caianiello, "Disclosure before the ICC: The Emergence of a New Form of Policies Implementation in International Criminal Justice?", in *International Criminal Law Review*, 2010, vol. 10, no. 1, p. 98.

184 Harding and Dingwall, 1998, p. 1, see *supra* note 182.

185 For a detailed analysis of 'diversion' see Kai Ambos and Alexander Heinze, "Abbreviated Procedures in Comparative Criminal Procedure: A Structural Approach with a View to International Criminal Procedure", in Morten Bergsmo (ed.), *Abbreviated Criminal Proce-*

fenders".[186] On the other hand, there is a danger of "inappropriate government interference" and the risk of "corrupt decision-making".[187] While the legality principle does not share these disadvantages, when considered with the principle of full clarification of the facts, the legality principle can be seen as a kind of luxury in an overloaded criminal justice system, generating "a backlog of cases, which can be destructive of the right to a fair and speedy trial"[188] and effectively impeding alternative procedures that may expedite trial proceedings.[189]

The rational and transparent selection and prioritization of cases at the ICC, accompanied by a coherent prosecution strategy, is of utmost importance for the success and legitimacy of any international criminal tribunal,[190] and the international criminal justice system as a whole.[191]

---

dures for Core International Crimes, Torkel Opsahl Academic EPublisher, Brussels, 2017, pp. 77 ff. (http://www.toaep.org/ps-pdf/9-bergsmo).

[186] Richard Vogler and Barbara Huber, *Criminal Procedure in Europe*, Duncker & Humblot, Berlin, 2008, p. 25; see also Kuczyńska, 2015, p. 94, see *supra* note 41.

[187] *Ibid.*

[188] *Ibid.*

[189] Gerhard Fezer, "Inquisitionsprozess ohne Ende? Zur Struktur des neuen Verständigungsgesetzes", in *Neue Zeitschrift für Strafrecht*, 2010, vol. 30, no. 4, p. 177.

[190] For an instructive comparative evaluation of the selection policies and practices of international criminal tribunals, see Guariglia, 2017, pp. 284 ff., see *supra* note 125; Christopher Keith Hall, "Prosecutorial Policy, Strategy and External Relations", in Bergsmo, Rackwitz and SONG (eds.), 2017, pp. 293 ff., see *supra* note 111. About various forms of selectivity Celestine Nchekwube Ezennia, "The of the International Criminal Court System: An Impartial or a Selective Justice Regime?", in *International Criminal Law Review*, 2016, vol. 16, no. 3, pp. 450 ff.; Frederick de Vlaming, "Selection of Defendants", in Luc Reydams, Jan Wouters and Cedric Ryngaert (eds.), *International Prosecutors*, Oxford University Press, Oxford, 2012, pp. 547–70; deGuzman and Schabas, 2013, pp. 133–54, see *supra* note 118; also Jeffrey Locke, "Indictments", in Luc Reydams, Jan Wouters and Cedric Ryngaert (eds.), *International Prosecutors*, Oxford University Press, Oxford, 2012, pp. 607–12; specifically on the ICTY, see Claudia Angermaier, "Case Selection and Prioritization Criteria in the Work of the International Criminal Tribunal for the Former Yugoslavia", in Morten Bergsmo (ed.), *Criteria for Prioritizing and Selecting Core International Crimes Cases*, 2nd edition, Torkel Opsahl Academic EPublisher, Oslo, 2010, pp. 27–43 (http://www.toaep.org/ps-pdf/4-bergsmo-second); on the ICTR, see Alex Obote-Odora, "Case Selection and Prioritization Criteria at the International Criminal Tribunal for Rwanda", in *ibid.*, pp. 45–67.

[191] See previously Ambos and Stegmiller, 2012, p. 392, see *supra* note 157. See also Human Rights Watch, *The Selection of Situations and Cases for Trial before the International Criminal Court*, 2006, p. 7 (http://www.legal-tools.org/doc/753e9b/); Human Rights Watch, *Unfinished Business: Closing Gaps in the Selection of ICC Cases*, 2011, pp. 4, 46 (http://

This holds particularly true for the ICC, given that its Prosecutor[192] has not only the power to select individual defendants, but also – for the first time in history – entire situations for investigation.[193] Accordingly, the complex process of selecting defendants and concrete charges[194] can be divided into two main steps: first, the primary selection of situations, and

---

www.legal-tools.org/doc/738f10/); Morten Bergsmo, "The Theme of Selection and Prioritization Criteria and Why it Is Relevant", in Bergsmo (ed.), 2010, pp. 8, 12, 14, *supra* note 190; Vlaming, 2012, pp. 542–43, see *supra* note 190; Locke, 2012, p. 614, see *supra* note 190; Côté, 2012, pp. 354–55, see *supra* note 114; deGuzman and Schabas, 2013, pp. 131–32, see *supra* note 118; from a victims' perspective, see Richard Dicker, "Making Justice Meaningful for Victims", in Bergsmo (ed.), 2010, pp. 267–68, *supra* note 190; Bock, 2010, p. 606, see *supra* note 120; Thompson, "The Role of the International Prosecutor as a Custodian of Global Morality", in Charles C. Jalloh and Alhagi B.M. Marong (eds.), *Promoting Accountability under International Law for Gross Human Rights Violations in Africa: Essays in Honour of Prosecutor Hassan Bubacar*, Brill Nijhoff, Leiden, 2015, p. 54.

[192] See also ICC, Situation in the Central African Republic, *Prosecutor v Bemba*, Pre-Trial Chamber, Decision on Request for Leave to Submit Amicus Curiae Observations Pursuant to Rule 103 of the Rules of Procedure and Evidence, 17 July 2009, ICC-01/05-01/08-453, para. 10, leaving the "issue of selection of cases" to the Prosecutor (http://www.legal-tools.org/doc/351d29/).

[193] Ambos and Stegmiller, 2012, p. 392, see *supra* note 157; see also Ambos and Bock, 2012, pp. 532, 541, see *supra* note 126; Alette Smeulers, Maartje Weerdesteijn and Barbora Hola, "The Selection of Situations by the ICC – An Empirically Based Evaluation of the OTP's Performance", in *International Criminal Law Review*, 2015, vol. 15, no. 1, p. 2.

[194] In the case against Lubanga, the Prosecutor decided to concentrate on the recruitment and use of child soldiers and suspended investigations concerning other alleged crimes, in particular sex crimes; ICC, Situation in the Democratic Republic of Congo, *Prosecutor v Lubanga*, Prosecutor's Information on Further Investigations, 28 June 2006, ICC-01/04-01/06-170, para. 7 (http://www.legal-tools.org/doc/e668a0/). As expected the OTP did not bring additional charges in the course of the appellate proceedings. Thus, the first case finished at the ICC has already shown that the selection of charges entails another discretionary decision that might enlarge the impunity gap; see Bock, 2010, pp. 322–23, see *supra* note 120; Ambos and Bock, 2012, p. 538, see *supra* note 126; also Paul Seils, "The Selection and Prioritization of Cases by the Office of the Prosecutor of the International Criminal Court", in Bergsmo (ed.), 2010, pp. 73–75, *supra* note 190; generally on the OTP's failure to charge Lubanga with sex crimes, see Kai Ambos, "The First Judgment of the International Criminal Court (Prosecutor v. Lubanga): Comprehensive Analysis of the Legal Issues", in *International Criminal Law Review*, 2012, vol. 12, no. 2, pp. 137–38 with fn. 156; on its impact on the reparation decision, see Stefanie Bock, "Wiedergutmachung im Völkerstrafverfahren vor dem Internationalen Strafgerichtshof nach Lubanga", in *Zeitschrift für Internationale Strafrechtsdogmatik*, 2013, vol. 8, no. 7–8, pp. 302–03.

second, the subsequent extraction of cases from these situations.[195] We focus on the latter, which is a core issue for prosecutorial coherence.

It follows from the principles of equality before the law and non-discrimination[196] that selection decisions must not be "based on impermissible motives such as, *inter alia*, race, colour, religion, opinion, national or ethnic origin".[197] Accordingly, the Prosecutor is required to investigate, as a rule,[198] all sides of a conflict without favour or bias toward any person or groups.[199] This is, in fact, necessary to overcome the stigma of victor's justice, which has been attached to international criminal justice since the Nuremberg and Tokyo tribunals.[200] Apart from these con-

---

[195] ICC, *Regulations of the Office of the Prosecutor*, entry into force 23 April 2009, Regulations 34–35 ('RegOTP') (http://www.legal-tools.org/doc/a97226/); see Smeulers, Weerdesteijn and Hola, 2015, p. 3, see *supra* note 193.

[196] ICC Statute, Articles 21(3), 67(1) see *supra* note 104.

[197] ICTY, *Prosecutor v Delalić et al.*, Appeals Chamber, Judgment, 20 February 2001, IT-96-21-A, para. 605 (http://www.legal-tools.org/doc/051554/); see also ICTR, *Prosecutor v Bizimungu et al.*, Decision on Defence Motions for Stay of Proceedings and for Adjournment of the Trial, including Reasons in Support of the Chamber's Oral Ruling delivered on Monday 20 September, 24 September 2004, ICTR-2000-56-T, para. 26 (http://www.legal-tools.org/doc/cf6400/); Côté, 2012, pp. 364, 366–70, see *supra* note 114; deGuzman and Schabas, 2013, pp. 146, 167, see *supra* note 118; also Thompson, 2015, p. 55, see *supra* note 191.

[198] An exception is that the investigation is limited to the alleged perpetrators if jurisdiction is based on active personality pursuant to Article 12(2)(b) ICC Statute; thereto Rod Rastan, "Jurisdiction", in Carsten Stahn (ed.), *Law and Practice of the International Criminal Court*, Oxford University Press, Oxford, 2015, p. 152 and generally Ambos, 2016, pp. 244 ff., see *supra* note 2.

[199] Côté, 2012, p. 370, see *supra* note 114; deGuzman and Schabas, 2013, p. 167, see *supra* note 118; see also Mégret, 2012, p. 439, see *supra* note 163; Hitomi Takemura, "Prosecutorial Discretion in International Criminal Justice: Between Fragmentation and Unification", in Larissa J. van den Herik and Carsten Stahn (eds.), *The Diversification and Fragmentation of International Criminal Law*, Nijhoff, Leiden, 2012, p. 643. Against this background, the decision of the ICTY Prosecution not to investigate alleged war crimes committed by NATO Forces during 'Operation Allied Forces' was heavily criticized; see Ambos and Bock, 2012, p. 502 with further references, see *supra* note 126. In general, on the difficulty and necessity of prosecuting peacekeepers on the international level, see Melanie O'Brien, "Prosecutorial Discretion as an Obstacle to Prosecution of United Nations Peacekeepers by the International Criminal Court", in *Journal of International Criminal Justice*, 2012, vol. 10, no. 3, p. 525.

[200] Côté, 2012, p. 370, see *supra* note 114. In more detail on the limited competencies of the IMT and the IMTFE which had no jurisdiction over alleged war crimes of the Allies, see Ambos and Bock, 2012, pp. 491–92, 497–98 with further references, see *supra* note 126.

---

straints, which are drawn from human rights norms, the Prosecutor is largely free to develop her own prosecutorial policy.

18.4.2. Preliminary Examinations and Article 53(1)

We briefly explain the legal framework of Article 53(1) and the OTP's approach to preliminary examinations in this sub-section. The two sub-sections that follow focus on the specific ethical obligations related to Article 53(1)(c) and the "interests of justice", and the judicial review that aims to hold the OTP accountable for following through on its ethical obligations, respectively.

The preliminary examination phase at the ICC is solely directed toward determining whether there are sufficient grounds (a "reasonable basis") to commence a formal investigation.[201] Thus, it acts as a kind of procedural filter for the OTP.[202] While the OTP has recently added a separate section on preliminary examinations to its website,[203] this phase still lacks transparency, and it is impossible for an 'outsider' to know about or evaluate the fate of the thousands of communications sent to the OTP. Although the term 'preliminary examination' is only explicitly referenced in Article 15(6) of the ICC Statute and Regulations 25-31 of the Regulations of the OTP,[204] all proceedings contain a preliminary examination, regardless of the trigger mechanism used to bring the situation before the ICC, that is, whether it comes through a referral by a State Party, referral by the UN Security Council, or by a *proprio motu* initiation of the Prosecutor.[205]

---

[201] Ambos, 2016, p. 336, see *supra* note 2; Stefan van Heeck, *Die Weiterentwicklung des formellen Völkerstrafrechts: Von den ad hoc Tribunalen der Vereinten Nationen zum ständigen Internationalen Strafgerichtshof unter besonderer Berücksichtigung des Ermittlungsverfahrens*, Duncker & Humblot, Berlin, 2006, pp. 181–82; deGuzman and Schabas, 2013, p. 144, see *supra* note 118, stressing the reasonable basis requirement; Kuczyńska, 2015, p. 74, see *supra* note 41.

[202] Stegmiller, 2013, p. 486 ("procedural filtering tool"), see *supra* note 2.

[203] ICC, "Office of the Prosecutor: Preliminary Examinations" (available on its web site).

[204] Cf. Stahn, 2017, p. 2, see *supra* note 1.

[205] Ambos, 2016, pp. 336–37, see *supra* note 2; ICC-OTP, *Annex to the "Paper on some policy issues before the Office of the Prosecutor": Referrals and Communications"*, p. 7 (http://www.legal-tools.org/doc/5df43d/); Wouters, Verhoeven, and Demeyere, 2008, p. 294, see *supra* note 113; Jan Wouters, Sten Verhoeven, and Bruno Demeyere, "The International Criminal Court's Office of the Prosecutor: Navigating between Independence and Accountability?", in José Doria, Hans-Peter Gasser and M. Cherif Bassiouni (eds.), *The*

The OTP's Policy Paper on Preliminary Examinations[206] explains the structure of a preliminary examination in four phases.[207] *Phase 1* is concerned with the evaluation of the 'communications', that is, the information submitted on alleged crimes received in accordance with Article 15(1) ("information on alleged crimes").[208] *Phase 2* represents the formal commencement of a preliminary examination[209] and consists of the thorough assessment of the preconditions of jurisdiction pursuant to Article 12 of the ICC Statute, and an inquiry as to whether the alleged crimes fall within the Court's subject-matter jurisdiction. *Phase 3* is concerned with the admissibility of 'potential' cases – since defined cases do not exist at this stage[210] – in terms of complementarity and gravity according to Arti-

---

Legal Regime of the International Criminal Court: Essays in Honour of Professor Igor Blishchenko, Nijhoff, Leiden, 2009, p. 365; Karel de Meester, Kelly Pitcher, Rod Rastan and Göran Sluiter, "Investigation, Coercive Measures, Arrest and Surrender", in Göran Sluiter *et al.* (eds.), *International Criminal Procedure: Principles and Rules*, Oxford University Press, Oxford, 2013, p. 182; David Bosco, "Discretion and State Influence at the International Criminal Court: The Prosecutor's Preliminary Examinations", in *American Journal of International Law*, 2017, vol. 111, no. 2, pp. 395-414; Ambos and Stegmiller, 2012, pp. 420 ff., see *supra* note 157; on the three trigger mechanisms, see Ambos, 2016, pp. 255 ff., see *supra* note 2.

[206] ICC-OTP, 2013, paras. 77–84, see *supra* note 154; summarising ICC-OTP, *Report on Preliminary Examination Activities*, 2013, para. 14, see *supra* note 142; see also RegOTP, Regulations 25–31, see *supra* note 195; for a detailed analysis see Ambos, 2016, pp. 337 ff., see *supra* note 2; see also Stegmiller, 2013, p. 487, see *supra* note 2. On the OTP's previous practical approach, see Kai Ambos, "Prosecuting International Crimes at the National and International Level: Between Justice and Realpolitik", in Wolfgang Kaleck *et al.* (eds.), *International Prosecution of Human Rights Crimes*, Springer, Berlin, 2006, pp. 56 ff.; Kai Ambos, "The Structure of International Criminal Procedure", in Michael Bohlander (ed.), *International Criminal Justice: a Critical Analysis of Institutions and Procedures*, Cameron May, London, 2007, pp. 435 ff.; Kai Ambos, "Die Rolle des Internationalen Strafgerichtshofs", in *Aus Politik und Zeitgeschichte*, 2006, vol. 42, pp. 14–15; Stegmiller, 2013, pp. 486–87, see *supra* note 2.

[207] See also the analysis by Stahn, 2017, p. 16 with further references, see *supra* note 1.

[208] ICC-ASP, *Report of the Court on the Basic Size of the Office of the Prosecutor*, 17 September 2015, ICC-ASP/14/21 (http://www.legal-tools.org/doc/b27d2a/).

[209] *Ibid.*

[210] ICC, Situation in the Republic of Kenya, Pre-Trial Chamber, Request for Authorisation of an Investigation pursuant to Article 15, 26 November 2009, ICC-01/09-3, paras. 51, 107 (http://www.legal-tools.org/doc/c63dcc/); and ICC, Situation in the Republic of Kenya, Pre-Trial Chamber, Decision Pursuant to Article 15 of the ICC Statute on the Authorization of an Investigation into the Situation in the Republic of Kenya, 31 March 2010, ICC-01/09-19, paras. 50, 182, 188 (assessment of admissibility "against certain criteria defining a 'potential case'") (http://www.legal-tools.org/doc/338a6f/).

---

cle 17 of the ICC Statute.[211] *Phase 4* analyses the "interests of justice" pursuant to Article 53 (1)(c),[212] and results in an 'Article 53(1) report'.[213] This report contains an "initial legal characterization of the alleged crimes" and a preliminary summary of the basic facts, indicating the temporal and geographical circumstances of the alleged commission, and the persons and/or groups involved.[214] It serves as a basis to determine whether to commence a formal investigation in accordance with Article 53(1), or to stop proceedings based on the "interests of justice".[215]

The OTP recently issued a Policy Paper on Case Selection and Prioritisation,[216] which states that the Prosecutor is only bound by the general principles of equality before the law and non-discrimination, that is, she must act independently, impartially[217] and objectively investigating all parties to a conflict without favouring or discriminating against any of them.[218] Otherwise, she has a broad discretion that may be guided by policy criteria regarding selection and prioritization.[219] "Broad discretion" is a phrase the OTP itself used in a previous draft of the Policy Paper: "Nonetheless, the Office has broad discretion in selecting individual cases for

---

[211] ICC-ASP, 2015, p. 39, see *supra* note 208; ICC-OTP, *Report on Preliminary Examination Activities 2016*, 14 November 2016, para. 15 (http://www.legal-tools.org/doc/f30a53/); about this report, see also Stahn, 2017, p. 3, see *supra* note 1. Sa. Andre V. Armenian, "Selectivity in International Criminal Law: An Assessment of the 'Progress Narrative'", in *International Criminal Law Review*, 2016, vol. 16, no 4, pp. 642 ff.; Celestine N. Ezennia, "The Modus Operandi of the International Criminal Court System: An Impartial or a Selective Justice Regime?", in *International Criminal Law Review*, 2016, vol. 16, no. 3, pp. 448 ff.

[212] ICC-ASP, 2015, p. 40, see *supra* note 208; ICC-OTP, 2016, para. 15, see *supra* note 211.

[213] Cf. RegOTP, Regulation 29(1), see *supra* note 195; also referring to ICC Statute, Article 15(3).

[214] Ambos, 2016, p. 339, see *supra* note 2.

[215] Cf. RegOTP, Regulations 29, 31, see *supra* note 195.

[216] ICC-OTP, 2016, see *supra* note 160.

[217] 'Impartiality' can be understood, however, in either procedural or political terms. See Sophie T. Rosenberg, "The International Criminal Court in Côte d'Ivoire: Impartiality at Stake?", in *Journal of International Criminal Justice*, 2017, vol. 15, no. 3, pp. 471-490.

[218] *Ibid.*, para. 16–23.

[219] On the governing principles of the selection process by the OTP, see also Fabricio Guariglia and Emeric Rogier, "Selection of Situations and Cases by the OTP of the ICC", in Carsten Stahn (ed.), *Law and Practice of the International Criminal Court*, Oxford University Press, Oxford, 2015, pp. 358–59; Kuczyńska, 2015, pp. 112–15, see *supra* note 41.

investigation and prosecution".[220] However, this sentence does not appear in the final version of the Policy Paper.[221] The relevant criteria, with respect to case selection and prioritization, include focusing on those who are "most responsible";[222] focusing on specific crimes with a special international/public interest/expressivist function (for example, sexual and gender-based crimes and crimes against children);[223] focusing on gravity of the crimes;[224] focusing on certain qualitative considerations; focusing

---

[220] ICC OTP, 2016, para. 4 *in fine*, see *supra* note 160.

[221] See *ibid.*

[222] Cf., for example, ICC, Situation in the Republic of Kenya, Pre-Trial Chamber, Decision Pursuant to Article 15 of the ICC Statute on the Authorization of an Investigation into the Situation in the Republic of Kenya, 31 March 2010, ICC-01/09-19, para. 188, see *supra* note 210; RegOTP, Regulations 34(1), see *supra* note 195. This may include "lower level-perpetrators where their conduct has been particularly grave or notorious", ICC-OTP, 2016, para. 42, see *supra* note 160. See also, regarding other tribunals, ICTY, Rules on Procedure and Evidence, adopted on 11 February 1994, Rule 28(A) ('ICTY-RPE') (http://www.legal-tools.org/doc/02712f/) (additional screening of indictment, introduced as part of completion strategy in 2004, to ensure that it "concentrates on one or more of the most senior leaders suspected of being most responsible [...]"; thereto Håkan Friman, Helen Brady, Matteo Costi, Francisco Guariglia and Carl-Friederich Stuckenberg, "Charges", in Göran Sluiter *et al.* (eds.), *International Criminal Procedure: Principles and Rules*, Oxford University Press, Oxford, 2013, p. 385) and SCSL Statute, Article 1(1), see *supra* note 117 (limiting the mandate to "persons who bear the greatest responsibility"); Guariglia and Rogier, 2015, pp. 351–52 (regarding ICTY), 360–61, see *supra* note 219.

[223] Cf. ICC-OTP, *Strategic Plan 2012-2015*, 11 October 2013, paras. 58–63; as well as OTP, *Strategic Plan 2016-2018*, 6 July 2015, paras. 40, 49 ff.; and Annex I, paras. 22 ff. regarding the results of the *Strategic Plan 2012-2015*. About the *Strategic Plan 2012-2015*, see also Fatou Bensouda, "The Sexual and Gender-Based Crimes Policy Paper of the Office of the Prosecutor of the International Criminal Court", in Charles C. Jalloh and Alhagi B.M. Marong (eds.), *Promoting Accountability under International Law for Gross Human Rights Violations in Africa: Essays in Honour of Prosecutor Hassan Bubacar*, Brill Nijhoff, Leiden, 2015, pp. 329 ff.; critics on "thematic prosecution of sex crimes", that is, the primary selection and prioritization of these crimes over others: Kai Ambos, "Thematic Investigations and Prosecution: Some Critical Comments from a Theoretical and Comparative Perspective", in Morten Bergsmo (ed.), *Thematic Prosecution of International Sex Crimes*, Torkel Opsahl Academic EPublisher, 2nd edition, Brussels, 2018, pp. 301 ff. (http://www.toaep.org/ps-pdf/13-bergsmo-second); critics of the ICC practice so far, but optimistic because of the new course under Prosecutor Bensouda as evidenced by the OTP policy paper: Niamh Hayes, "La Lutte Continue: Investigating and Prosecuting Sexual Violence at the ICC", in Carsten Stahn (ed.), *Law and Practice of the International Criminal Court*, Oxford University Press, Oxford, 2015, pp. 801 ff.

[224] Cf. RegOTP, Regulation 29(2), see *supra* note 195; ICC-OTP, 2013, paras. 9, 59 ff., see *supra* note 206; ICC-OTP, *Report on Preliminary Examinations Activities 2014*, 2 December 2014, para. 7 (http://www.legal-tools.org/doc/3594b3/); Guariglia and Rogier, 2015, pp.

---

on incidents that are "most representative of the scale and impact of the crimes" and on "crimes that have been traditionally under-prosecuted";[225] balancing the interests of justice within the meaning of Article 53; and identifying practical considerations.[226] The ultimate selection or prioritization decision remains in the hands of the Prosecutor and is subject to only limited judicial review.[227]

18.4.3. Prosecutorial Discretion and the "Interests of Justice"

18.4.3.1. The OTP and Article 53(1)(c)

Article 53(1)(c) contains the main site of discretion that invokes our previously outlined argument for including consequentialist considerations in the ethical obligations of the OTP during the preliminary examination

---

359–60, see *supra* note 219; ICC, Situation in the Republic of Kenya, Pre-Trial Chamber, Decision Pursuant to Article 15 of the ICC Statute on the Authorization of an Investigation into the Situation in the Republic of Kenya, 31 March 2010, ICC-01/09-19, para. 188, see *supra* note 210; ICC, Situation in the Republic of Kenya, *The Prosecutor v. Francis Kirimi Muthaura et al.*, Pre-Trial Chamber, Decision on the Confirmation of Charges Pursuant to Article 61(7)(a) and (b) of the Rome Statute, No. ICC-01/09-02/11-382-Red, para. 50, referring to sentencing RPE, Rule 145(1)(c) (http://www.legal-tools.org/doc/4972c0/). For a discussion, see Ambos, 2016, pp. 284 ff., see *supra* note 2. The OTP points out that it "may apply a stricter test when assessing gravity for the purposes of case selection than that which is legally required for the admissibility test under article 17", see ICC-OTP, 2016, para. 36 see *supra* note 160. With regard to the gravity test, in its recent policy paper on case selection, the OTP deviated from its November 2013 policy paper by adding a reference to crimes committed "by means of, or that result in [...] the destruction of the environment, the illegal exploitation of natural resources or the illegal dispossession of land" (*ibid.*, para. 41). See thereto Bernaz, 2017, p. 528, see *supra* note 160.

225 RegOTP, Regulation 34(2), see *supra* note 195; ICC-OTP, 2016, para. 45–46, see *supra* note 160.

226 Cf., for example, ICC-OTP, 2003, p. 1 ("feasibility of conducting an effective investigation in a particular territory"), see *supra* note 160; ICC-OTP, *Paper on Some Policy Issues Before the Office of the Prosecutor*, 5 September 2003, p. 2 (availability of the necessary cooperation) (http://www.legal-tools.org/doc/f53870/).

227 Only pursuant to legal regulation, especially Article 53(3) ICC Statute. It is however questionable to interpret Article 53(1)(a) and (b) as providing for "exacting legal requirements" (ICC, Situation on the Vessels of Comoros, Pre-Trial Chamber, Decision on the request of the Union of the Comoros to review the Prosecutor's decision not to initiate an investigation, 16 July 2015, ICC-01/13-34, para. 14 (http://www.legal-tools.org/doc/2f876c/)); on the criticism regarding the trigger and scope of the judicial review, see Guariglia and Rogier, 2015, pp. 362–63, see *supra* note 219.

---

phase.[228] There is no other clause in the ICC Statute allowing so explicitly for policy considerations.[229] The concept of the "interests of justice" within the meaning of Article 53(1)(c) and (2)(c) is nowhere defined in the ICC's legal framework. The OTP understands the concept as "a potential *countervailing* consideration that might produce a reason *not* to proceed" even where jurisdiction and admissibility are satisfied.[230] Thus, "interests of justice" is a negative requirement that may exclude an investigation (or prosecution), even if the positive requirements of Article 53(1) and (2) are

---

[228] Our argument is only for the expanded influence of consequentialist considerations. About the so-called "consequentialist approach" as a way to address preliminary examinations (*vis-à-vis* the "gateway approach") see Stahn, 2017, pp. 7 ff., see *supra* note 1. For the consequentialist approach, "there is a certain virtue in the conduct of a preliminary examination as such, irrespective of whether or not it leads to investigation at the ICC" (p. 7 with further references). According to the narrower "ICC-centric" gateway approach, "preliminary examinations are investigation-centred", which means that "they mainly serve as a means to deciding whether or not to open an ICC investigation and are essentially a filter that determines the pathway towards investigations" (p. 6).

[229] Cf. Ali Arsanjani, "The International Criminal Court and National Amnesty Laws", in ASIL, *Proceedings of the Ninety-Third Annual Meeting of the American Society of International Law*, ASIL, Washington, D.C., 1999, p. 67 ("broad range of possibilities"); Richard J. Goldstone and Nicole Fritz, "In the Interests of Justice and Independent Referral: The ICC Prosecutor's Unprecedented Powers", in *Leiden Journal of International Law*, 2000, vol. 13, no. 3, pp. 662–63; Matthew R. Brubacher, "Prosecutorial Discretion within the International Criminal Court", in *Journal of International Criminal Justice*, 2004, vol. 2, no. 1, pp. 80 ff. (p. 81: "broader interests of the international community"); Talita de Souza Dias, "'Interests of justice': Defining the scope of Prosecutorial discretion in Article 53(1)(c) and (2)(c) of the Rome Statute of the International Criminal Court", in *Leiden Journal of International Law*, vol. 30, no. 3, pp. 731-751; Maria Varaki, "Revisiting the 'Interests of Justice' Policy Paper", in *Journal of International Criminal Justice*, 2017, vol. 15, no. 3, pp. 455-470; Paul Seils and Marieke Wierda, *The International Criminal Court and Conflict Mediation*, Occasional Paper, International Center for Transitional Justice, New York, 2005, p. 12; Frank Meyer, "Complementing Complementarity", in *International Criminal Law Review*, 2006, vol. 6, no. 4, p. 580. Christ Gallavin, "Article 53 of the Rome Statute of the ICC: In the Interests of Justice?", in *King's College Law Journal*, 2003, vol. 14, no. 3, pp. 195, 197, draws a comparison to the 'public interest' criterion in English and Welsh law arguing that while the Prosecutor must be independent she must at the same time be aware of the political realities; on this parallel, see also Brubacher, 2004, p. 80, see *supra* note 217. On the public interest criterion in English and Welsh law in general see Antony Duff, "Discretion and Accountability in a Democratic Criminal Law", in Máximo Langer and David Alan Sklansky (eds.), *Prosecutors and Democracy*, Cambridge University Press, Cambridge, 2017, pp. 9, 24-32.

[230] ICC-OTP, 2007, pp. 2–3 (emphasis in the original), see *supra* note 155.

---

met. It will only be utilised "in exceptional circumstances" as a kind of last resort.[231]

18.4.3.2. Whose Justice?

The notion of *'justice'* involves a broader assessment that just a single situation or case[232] and is not limited to what we might think of as typical criminal justice considerations,[233] but rather it includes alternative forms of justice, and entails an overall assessment of the situation.[234] As we noted previously in Section 18.2.2., the particular features of what constitutes justice vary, and while we do not aim to construct a theory of justice in this chapter, we adopt the view that it always has something to do with fairness. Again, this can involve the protection of substantive rights, or the protection of procedural rights through strict adherence to rules, or ensuring that all potential defendants are treated the same before the law. Because they will sometimes be in conflict, we see justice as a balancing of various fairness considerations.

---

[231] *Ibid.*, p. 3. See also Rohrer, *Legalitäts- oder Opportunitätsprinzip beim Internationalen Strafgerichtshof*, Heymann, Köln, 2010, pp. 253–54, 313.

[232] Jessica Gavron, "Amnesties in the Light of Developments in International Law and the Establishment of the International Criminal Court", in *International and Comparative Law Quarterly*, 2002, vol. 51, no. 1, p. 110.

[233] Namely, considerations which concern the proper administration of justice, for example, the admission of additional evidence on the basis of "interests of justice", cf. ICTY, *Prosecutor v Kupreškić et al.*, IT-95-16-A, paras. 52–54, 61–69 (on former Rule 115(B) RPE ICTY); for more examples, see Stegmiller, 2011, p. 367, see *supra* note 2; also ICC-OTP, 2007, p. 8 (to be understood more broadly "than criminal justice in a narrow sense"), see *supra* note 155.

[234] Ambos, 2016, p. 387, see *supra* note 2. See also Goldstone and Fritz, 2000, p. 662, see *supra* note 229; Darryl Robinson, "Serving the Interests of Justice: Amnesties, Truth Commissions and the International Criminal Court", in *European Journal of International Law*, 2003, vol. 14, no. 3, p. 488; Meyer, 2006, p. 579, see *supra* note 229; Kenneth A. Rodman, "Is Peace in the Interest of Justice? The Case for Broad Prosecutorial Discretion at the International Criminal Court", in *Leiden Journal of International Law*, 2009, vol. 22, no. 1, pp. 101 ff., 108 ff.; Stegmiller, 2011, pp. 358, 367–68, 378–79, see *supra* note 2; Rohrer, 2010, pp. 314 ff., see *supra* note 231. On judicial intervention in ongoing atrocities and the assumption that justice can be pursued neutrally during conflicts, see Leslie Vinjamuri, "The ICC and the Politics of Peace and Justice", in Carsten Stahn (ed.), *Law and Practice of the International Criminal Court*, Oxford University Press, Oxford, 2015, pp. 20–25; on the interests of justice in conjunction with the principle of positive complementarity, see Justine Tillier, "The ICC Prosecutor and Positive Complementarity: Strengthening the Rule of Law?", in *International Criminal Law Review*, 2013, vol. 13, no. 3, pp. 542–45; Stahn, 2017, p. 9, see *supra* note 1.

To analyse whether or not an investigation (or a possible corresponding prosecution) serves the "interests of justice", we have two threshold questions to answer. The first is what counts as justice, and whether and which alternative justice mechanisms count as justice. Domestic criminal justice can be thought of as strictly procedural in nature, in that justice has been served if the domestic criminal procedures have been followed. Or we might think of domestic criminal justice as serving a more social purpose, albeit still local, in allowing a community to take ownership over crimes of mass atrocity and use transitional justice mechanisms to repair and reconcile. Some authors consider "interests of justice" as the most explicit gateway of the ICC Statute for the recognition of alternative processes of national reconciliation, including the granting of amnesties or other exemption measures for the sake of achieving peace.[235] Whether or not it should be primary, the domestic situation should be an important consideration in assessing the "interests of justice". Even with *ius puniendi* firmly established, it will be quite difficult to justify punishing defendants if the ICC acts completely counter to the interests of the domestic criminal justice systems.

Global criminal justice, on the other hand, might look more like an objective practice of holding individuals accountable for crimes of mass atrocity. This is one way of thinking about universal jurisdiction, where a crime is subject to prosecution in *any* jurisdiction in the world, because it

---

[235] John Dugard, "Dealing with Crimes of a Past Regime. Is Amnesty Still an Option?", in *Leiden Journal of International Law*, 1999, vol. 12, no. 4, p. 1014; John Dugard, "Possible Conflicts of Jurisdiction with Truth Commissions", in Antonio Cassese *et al.* (eds.), *The Rome Statute of the International Criminal Court: A Commentary*, vol. 1, Oxford University Press, Oxford, 2002, p. 702; Goldstone and Fritz, 2000, pp. 656, 662, see *supra* note 229; Robinson, 2003, p. 486, see *supra* note 234; Héctor Olásolo, "The Prosecutor of the ICC before the Initiation of Investigations: A Quasi-judicial or a Political body?", in *International Criminal Law Review*, 2003, vol. 3, no. 3, p. 111 (referring to a TRC); Brubacher, 2004, pp. 81–82, referring to post-conflict reconciliation processes, see *supra* note 229; Seils and Wierda, 2005, p. 12 ("most direct significance to mediators"), see *supra* note 229; Meyer, 2006, p. 579, see *supra* note 229; Rodman, 2009, pp. 101 ff., 108 ff., considering the goal of peace at the core of his broad, consequentialist approach, see *supra* note 234; Marta Valiñas, "Interpreting Complementarity and Interests of Justice in the Presence of Restorative: Based Alternative Forms of Justice", in Carsten Stahn and Larissa J. van den Herik (eds.), *Future Perspectives on International Criminal Justice*, TMC Asser Press, The Hague, 2010, pp. 277–78; Stegmiller, 2011, pp. 358, 367–68, 378–79, see *supra* note 2; less emphatic, Scharf, "The Amnesty Exception to the Jurisdiction of the International Criminal Court", in *Cornell International Law Journal*, 1999, vol. 32, no. 3, p. 524.

---

is a crime against the people in *every* jurisdiction in the world, and *ius puniendi* and *ius poenale* create the normative authorization for universal prosecutions. A commitment to universal jurisdiction reflects a cosmopolitan view of justice, which contains three important moral elements. First, "the ultimate units of concern are *human beings* or *persons* – rather than, say, family lines, tribes, ethnic, cultural, or religious communities, nations, or states. The latter may be units of concern only indirectly, in virtue of their individual members or citizens".[236] Second, "the status of ultimate unit of concern attaches to *every* living human being *equally* – not merely to some subset".[237] Finally, "persons are ultimate units of concern *for everyone* – not only for their compatriots, fellow religionists, or suchlike".[238] Some argue that the object and purpose of the ICC Statute (the fight against impunity) and the use of "interests of justice" in other provisions of the ICC and other Statutes [239] indicate that the non-investigation/prosecution cannot be based on transitional justice considerations.[240] While we would disagree with the idea that transitional justice

---

[236] Thomas W. Pogge, "Cosmopolitanism and Sovereignty", in *Ethics*, 1992, vol. 103, no. 1, p. 48. Italics in original. See also Thomas Pogge, *World Poverty and Human Rights: Cosmopolitan Responsibilities and Reforms*, Polity, Cambridge, 2002, p. 169; Immanuel Kant, "Metaphysics of Morals: Doctrine of Right, § 43–§ 62", in Pauline Kleingeld (ed.) and David L. Colclasure (trans.), *Toward Perpetual Peace and Other Writings on Politics, Peace, and History*, Yale University Press, New Haven, 2006, p. 139, 6:343–44; Derek Heater, *World Citizenship: Cosmopolitan Thinking and Its Opponents*, Continuum, London, 2002, pp. 13–14; Simon Caney, *Justice Beyond Borders: A Global Political Theory*, Oxford University Press, Oxford, 2005, p. 4; Andrea Sangiovanni, "Global Justice, Reciprocity, and the State", in *Philosophy & Public Affairs*, 2007, vol. 35, no. 1, p. 3; Gillian Brock, *Global Justice: A Cosmopolitan Account*, Oxford University Press, Oxford, 2009, p. 12; Roland Pierik and Wouter Werner (eds.), *Cosmopolitanism in Context: Perspectives from International Law and Political Theory*, Cambridge University Press, Cambridge, 2010, pp. 131–32; David Held, *Cosmopolitanism: Ideals and Realities*, Polity, 2010, p. 15.

[237] Pogge, 1992, p. 48, see *supra* note 236; see also Pogge, 2002, p. 169, see *supra* note 236; Sangiovanni, 2007, p. 3, *supra* note 236; Brock, 2009, p. 12, see *supra* note 236; Held, 2010, pp. 15–16, see *supra* note 236.

[238] Pogge, 1992, p. 48, see *supra* note 236; see also Pogge, 2002, p. 169, see *supra* note 236; Sangiovanni, 2007, p. 3, *supra* note 236; Brock, 2009, p. 12, see *supra* note 236; Held, 2010, pp. 15–16, see *supra* note 236.

[239] See Human Rights Watch, *Interests of Justice*, 2005, p. 6 referring to Articles 55(2)(c), 61, 65, 67, ICC Statute, and (in fn. 17) to Statutes of earlier international criminal tribunals where the notion was always understood in the sense of a fair administration of justice.

[240] See *ibid.*, pp. 4 ff. stating that "the prosecutor may not fail to initiate an investigation or decide not to proceed with the investigation because of national efforts, such as truth

---

considerations should never play a role, it also seems clear that the demands of cosmopolitan justice should be a factor in an assessment of justice. The concept of universality is central for the ICC.

The second, related question is who counts as a victim for purposes of the justice analysis. Immediate victims of mass atrocity are clearly included in this group. It may be that the OTP is only allowed to consider these immediate victims with respect to Article 53 and the interests of justice. But if we think of mass atrocity as a crime against humanity as a whole, the group of victims grows much larger. Universal (or nearly universal) jurisdiction could require us to factor all of humanity into an assessment of what would be in the interests of justice. Again, we might find that the interests of local and global 'victims' do not align.[241]

We argue that deontological obligations do not permit the OTP to pursue one form of justice to the serious detriment of the other form of justice. Since these different understandings of justice may conflict with one another, it may be impossible for the Prosecutor to make decisions that will maximize the justice interests of all the relevant constituencies. It remains within the purview of the Prosecutor to strike the right balance and decide, on a case-by-case basis, whether the formal initiation of an investigation or prosecution[242] would jeopardize justice interests.[243] In

---

commissions, national amnesties, or traditional reconciliation methods, or because of concerns regarding an ongoing peace process" (at pp. 4–5).

[241] For a recent account of the discussion of how the ICC has failed victims, see Gaelle Carayon and Jonathan O'Donohue, "The International Criminal Court's Strategies in Relation to Victims", in *Journal of International Criminal Justice*, 2017, vol. 15, no. 3, pp. 567-591.

[242] ICC Statute, Articles 53(1) and (2), see *supra* note 104.

[243] See, for example, Carsten Stahn, "Complementarity, Amnesties and Alternative Forms of Justice: Some Interpretative Guidelines for the International Criminal Court", in *Journal of International Criminal Justice*, 2005, vol. 3, no. 3, p. 698, arguing that abstinence from (immediate) prosecution may be allowed if otherwise reconciliation would be seriously put a risk; or Helmut Gropengießer and Jörg Meißner, "Amnesties and the Rome Statute of the International Criminal Court", in *International Criminal Law Review*, 2005, vol. 5, no. 2, p. 296, arguing that it is "possible to suspend the punishment even of serious offences in favour of higher-priority-interests" (similarly Karlijn van der Voort and Marten Zwanenburg, "From 'Raison d'État' to 'Ètat de Droit International': Amnesties and the French implementation of the Rome Statute", in *International Criminal Law Review*, 2001, vol. 1, no. 3, pp. 329–30) or, at p. 297 that the Prosecutor makes "his *own* decision on prognosis and balance" (emphasis in the original). For considerations governing the timing of indictments, see ICTJ, *UN Guidelines Meeting*, 2005, pp. 3 ff.

---

light of the fact that the ICC claims to have the goals of ending impunity for individual criminals and protecting the global community from the harms of mass atrocities, it seems that neither of these aims or constituencies can be ignored altogether.

18.4.3.3. Political Considerations and Article 53(1)(c)

The possibility of adverse State reactions to the investigation or prosecution of its officials must not subject the Prosecutor or the Court as a whole to intimidation by powerful States. Otherwise, the Court would rightly face criticism that it only prosecutes weak States, and thus undermine its legitimacy. International prosecutors have always been subject to pressure to achieve results, as was even admitted by the Trial Chamber in the *Lubanga* Judgment, which referred to the "degree of international and local pressure, once it was known that officials from the Court had arrived in the country".[244] The completion strategies at the *ad hoc* tribunals had a similar effect, as noted in Judge David Hunt's dissenting opinion to an admissibility decision of the ICTY in the *Milošević* case, in which he complained about a "consequential destruction of the rights of the accused", the "desire to assist the prosecution to bring the Completion Strategy to a speedy conclusion", and that it was "improper to take Completion Strategy into account [...] at the expense of those rights"; in sum: "Completion Strategy has been given priority over the rights of the accused".[245]

---

[244] ICC, Situation in the Democratic Republic of Congo, *Prosecutor v Lubanga*, Trial-Chamber, Judgment pursuant to Article 74 of the Statute, 14 March 2012, ICC-01/04-01/06-2842, para. 142 (http://www.legal-tools.org/doc/677866/); on the "natural tendency of the prosecutors to sympathize with victims of crimes at the expense of ICC defendants", see Markovic, 2011–12, p. 209, see *supra* note 163. See generally Ambos, 2012, p. 127, see *supra* note 194.

[245] ICTY, *Prosecutor v Milošević*, Dissenting Opinion of Judge David Hunt on Admissibility of Evidence-in-Chief in the Form of a Written Statement, 21 October 2003, IT-02-54-AR73.4, para. 20–22 (http://www.legal-tools.org/doc/41554b/). See also ICTR, *Prosecutor v Nyiramasuhuko*, Decision in the Matter of Proceedings Under Rule 15*bis*(D), Dissenting Opinion of Judge David Hunt, 24 September 2003, ICTR-97-21-T, para. 17 (http://www.legal-tools.org/doc/c56e1a/) (the completion strategy in Resolution 1503 should not be interpreted as an encouragement by the Security Council to the *ad hoc* Tribunals to "conduct its trials so that they would be other than fair trials"). About this dissent Fidelma Donlon, "The Judicial Role in the Definition and Implementation of the Completion Strategies of the International Criminal Tribunals", in Shane Darcy and Joseph Powderly (eds.), *Judicial Creativity at the International Criminal Tribunals*, Oxford University Press, Oxford, 2010, p. 360.

In a similar vein, Kevin J. Heller opined that completion strategies have often "(1) promoted impunity, (2) undermined OTP independence, (3) damaged the OTP's legitimacy, and (4) complicated post-closure projects".[246] In fact, the consequentialist tendencies go back to Nuremberg, where the prosecutor found himself in a structurally and procedurally superior position *vis-à-vis* the defence,[247] and some scholars and observers complained that inconsistent rulings favoured the prosecution.[248] Fair trial guarantees are considered to have been rather weak.[249] The separation of powers principle was diluted,[250] and a violation of the legality principle – the retroactivity element, to be concrete – has always been a matter of some dispute, not only with regard to the Nuremberg trials, but also the international criminal trials that followed.[251]

The ICC certainly depends on State co-operation, yet it must still ensure that it makes decisions about which situations and cases to pursue from a critical distance, especially with respect to the States in which the criminal situations take place. It would delegitimise the Court if the ICC had a practice of making political concession to States in terms of the

---

[246] Kevin J. Heller, "Completion", in Luc Reydams, Jan Wouters and Cedric Ryngaert (eds.), *International Prosecutors*, Oxford University Press, Oxford, 2012, p. 900. But see Lovisa Bådagård and Mark Klamberg, "The Gatekeeper of the ICC – Prosecutorial Strategies for Selecting Situations and Cases at the International Criminal Court", in *Georgetown Journal of International Law*, 2017, vol. 48, pp. 639-733 (arguing that the OTP should be more, not less focused on the goals of the Court in selection decisions).

[247] Hans Laternser, "Looking Back at the Nuremberg Trials with Special Consideration of the Processes Against Military Leaders", in Guénaël Mettraux (ed.), *Perspectives on the Nuremberg Trial*, Oxford University Press, Oxford, 2008, p. 480.

[248] See Bernard V.A. Röling, *The Tokyo Judgment*, APA-University Press, Amsterdam, 1977, pp. 633–34; Telford Taylor, *Anatomy of the Nuremberg Trials: A Personal Memoir*, Back Bay Books, Boston, 1992, p. 321.

[249] See, generally, Patricia M. Wald, "Running the Trial of the Century: The Nuremberg Legacy", in *Cardozo Law Review*, 2005–06, vol. 27, no. 4, pp. 1596–97; Ron Levi, John Hagan and Sara Dezalay, "International Courts in Atypical Political Environments: The Interplay of Prosecutorial Strategy, Evidence, and Court Authority in International Criminal Law", in *Law and Contemporary Problems*, 2016, vol. 79, no. 1, p. 297.

[250] Christoph Safferling and Philipp Graebke, "Strafverteidigung im Nürnberger Hauptkriegsverbrecherprozess: Strategien und Wirkung", in *Zeitschrift für die gesamte Strafrechtswissenschaft*, 2011, vol. 123, no. 1, p. 67.

[251] H.L.A. Hart, "Positivism and the Separation of Law and Morale", in *Harvard Law Review*, 1958, vol. 71, no. 4, p. 619; Andrew Ashworth and Lucia Zedner, "Defending the Criminal Law: Reflections on the Changing Character of Crime, Procedure, and Sanctions", in *Criminal Law and Philosophy*, 2008, vol. 2, no. 1, pp. 65 ff.

---

investigation and prosecution of the States' officials.[252] Rather, the "interests of justice" clause can only be invoked if the reason(s) that cause the Prosecutor to abstain from investigation and prosecution can really be traced back or are linked to justice interests, that is, if the abstention really serves the interests of justice.[253] It is here that we can see how deontological constraints on the OTP remain crucial for ensuring that the OTP seeks justice. The OTP must never treat potential defendants, or regions, or States, as mere means to serve a political end, whether it is personal or institutional. But these deontological constraints leave space for prosecutorial discretion and freedom of action, and it is here that we will see how consequentialist considerations may in fact be necessary to fill an ethical gap.

The "interests of justice" at the preliminary examination phase are not focused on whether or not a particular individual can receive a fair trial at the ICC. Justice at this phase is considering a constituency of victims, whether local or global, and not just a particular defendant. Because of the scope of this inquiry, we acknowledge that prosecutorial discretion with respect to analysing the "interests of justice" will involve political considerations. As noted above, political decisions based on bias or blackmail will never be appropriate. But as Frédéric Mégret has argued, while international criminal justice has tried to distance itself from any "blatantly political decision", the project of international criminal justice "cannot come about without some political power".[254] The factors in Article 53 make it clear that the Prosecutor has to take a legally substantiated decision on a case by case basis and cannot just invoke general policy considerations in their own right; otherwise, she could indeed "risk being mired in making political judgements that would ultimately undermine his [her] work" (or more exactly: her authority) and be subjected "to enormous political pressures and attempted manipulations by governments

---

[252] Ambos, 2016, p. 388, see *supra* note 2.

[253] Contrary to Human Rights Watch, *Interests of Justice*, 2005, pp. 19–20, the victims' justice interests cannot be limited to the interests of a criminal prosecution excluding *a limine* their possible interests in peace, traditional reconciliation etc. It is equally unconvincing to adduce as an additional factor in favour of criminal prosecution the victims' interest in the memory since this can normally be better preserved by a TRC.

[254] Frédéric Mégret, "The Anxieties of International Criminal Justice", in *Leiden Journal of International Law*, 2016, vol. 29, no. 1, p. 201.

and rebel groups".[255] The Prosecutor must always 'judicialize the politics' without being a political actor herself.[256] So we agree with Mégret that these political considerations are inevitable, and we further argue that these political considerations constitute consequentialist ethical obligations on the part of the OTP.

One important aspect of these political considerations that the OTP should be obligated to consider is the continued existence and functioning of the ICC as a legitimate international institution. This is especially so since the existence of a political community – here: the 'humanity' – to authorise international criminal adjudication has frequently been rejected.[257] If humanity fails to constitute a political community to legitimize an international criminal tribunal, "legitimacy must rest on the fairness [of this tribunal's] procedures".[258] Some have recently advanced a strategic view of the "interests of justice" concept, arguing that it should be used against the opening of an investigation – despite the existence of a reasonable basis within the meaning of Article 53(1)(a) – if such an investigation were detrimental to the Court's 'viability'.[259] This strategic approach goes too far, in our view, because we do not see the "interests of justice" as way for the Court to avoid its obligations to seek global and domestic justice. However, there may be instances in which Article 53(1)(c) is necessary to avoid the dissolution of the Court altogether. It may be reasonable, for instance, to take into account whether or not a region perceives the ICC as a fair institution before initiating another investigation into a situation from that region, especially if the region suggests that it may pull out of the ICC Statute altogether if it believes the ICC to be unfair and

---

[255] Human Rights Watch, *Interests of Justice*, 2005, p. 14.

[256] Stegmiller, 2011, p. 379, see *supra* note 2; see, in a similar vein, Brubacher, 2004, p. 95, arguing that prosecutorial "discretion must exclude partisan politics, but not the more statesmanlike politics of persuading state compliance", see *supra* note 229.

[257] David Luban, "A Theory of Crimes Against Humanity", in *Yale Journal of International Law*, 2004, vol. 29, no. 1, pp. 124–41.

[258] Antony Duff, "Authority and Responsibility in International Criminal Law", in Samantha Besson and John Tasioulas (eds.), *The Philosophy of International Law*, Oxford University Press, Oxford, 2010, p. 591.

[259] Cale Davis, "Political Considerations in Prosecutorial Discretion at the International Criminal Court", in *International Criminal Law Review*, 2015, vol. 15, no. 1, pp. 172, 174, 188–89.

biased.[260] In this situation, a strict deontological/retributive constraint on the OTP would require the investigation of the situation without considering the overall impact on the ICC or the region. Whether or not the ICC should continue with the investigation in this hypothetical situation is not immediately obvious without more information. What is obvious is that the OTP should have an ethical obligation to take its own continued existence into account when assessing the "interests of justice".

18.4.3.4. Deontological and Consequentialist Obligations under Article 53(1)(c)

Accordingly, we argue that there are some situations in which the OTP should be required to use consequentialist considerations to consider the moral weight of their discretionary decisions under Article 53(1)(c). We find that the continued existence of the ICC, or the maintenance of some particular global order, cannot be the only aims of the OTP unless the OTP ignores all of its deontological obligations related to treating all people as ends, never as mere means. Prosecutions cannot come about for purely consequentialist reasons, and we recognize that since we can't predict the future, the best we can hope for in our invocation of consequentialist considerations is that prosecutors will make decisions based on what is expected to be the best outcome.[261] Yet we would argue that the OTP is obligated to consider the continued existence of the ICC alongside these deontological constraints, because the deontological constraints are insufficient to account for the global politics that affect the ICC and its legitimacy, both perceived and actual. The ICC might never be popular, and we should not use the ICC's popularity as a metric for its successfulness, but the ICC's perception in the world is important because it relies

---

260 Jonathan Hafetz argues that the ICC should focus more on distributive considerations in order to ensure legitimacy. See Jonathan Hafetz, "Fairness, Legitimacy, and Selection Decisions in International Criminal Law", in *Vanderbilt Journal of Transnational Law*, 2017, vol. 50, pp. 1133-1172.

261 In less cautious language Anderson, 2016, p. 192, see *supra* note 61: "[T]he lack of predictability in a system in which the resources of the Prosecutor are so small in relation to the whole world that intervention looks like a lightning strike turns belief in the system into something no longer about legitimacy, or even about rational deterrence. It looks like just plain bad luck. A system for going after the world's worst crimes and worst international criminals that has a feeling of simple misfortune to the participants will not fulfil very adequately either legitimacy or rational deterrence".

on the co-operation of States in order to function.[262] If the OTP relies solely on deontological constraints to ensure that trials are fair, but the substantive focus of investigations remains largely focused on the African continent, the ICC may not be able to sustain the kind of support it has enjoyed from many African countries thus far,[263] if only due to the *perception* of unfairness rather than actual unfairness.

A flat-footed consequentialist or utilitarian theory might suggest that we should forgo procedural fairness considerations and corresponding deontological constraints in favour of purely substantive aims, seeking to prosecute only those individuals with overwhelming evidence against them, or attempting to ensure convictions even where the evidence is lacking. Such a simplistic consequentialist theory might even seek to justify the use of the OTP's prosecutorial discretion under Article 53(1)(c) in service of creating or sustaining a particular global order. This sort of theory could allow the OTP to refrain from investigating situations in any African countries, until the perception of the ICC has changed throughout the African continent. We do not endorse such a use of consequentialist

---

[262] Larry May and Shannon Fyfe, *International Criminal Tribunals: A Normative Defense*, Cambridge University Press, Cambridge, 2017, p. 188.

[263] See, for example, Charles Chernor Jalloh, "The African Union, the Security Council, and the International Criminal Court", in Charles Chernor Jalloh and Illias Bantekas (eds.), *The International Criminal Court and Africa*, Oxford University Press, Oxford, 2017, pp. 185-188. For a general discussion of the (now decreasing) support of (some) African states see Mandiaye Niang, "Africa and the Legitimacy of the in Question", in *International Criminal Law Review*, 2017, vol. 17, no. 4, pp. 615-624; Sanji Mmasenono Monageng, "Africa and the International Criminal Court: Then and Now", in Gerhard Werle, *et al.* (eds.), *Africa and the International Criminal Court*, Asser, Springer, The Hague, 2014, pp. 13 ff.; Sanji Mmasenono Monageng and Alexander Heinze, "The Rome Statute and Universal Human Rights", in Evelyn A. Ankumah (ed.), *The International Criminal Court and Africa*, Intersentia, Cambridge, Antwerp, Portland, 2016, pp. 63 ff.; Jean-Baptiste Jeangene Vilmer, "The African Union and the International Criminal Court: Counteracting the Crisis", in *International Affairs*, 2016, vol. 92, no. 6, pp. 1319-1342; Sarah Leyli Rödiger, Leonie Steinl and Valérie V. Suhr, "Das Völkerstrafrecht in Krisenzeiten", in *Kritische Justiz*, 2018, vol. 51, no. 1, 7 ff.; Jide Nzelibe, "The Breakdown of International Treaties", in *Notre Dame Law Review*, vol. 93, no. 3, pp. 1219 ff. About South Africa's and especially the African National Congress' (ANC) support and commitment international humanitarian and human rights law is well-documented, see Gerhard Kemp, "South Africa's (Possible) Withdrawal from the ICC and the Future of the Criminalization and Prosecution of Crimes Against Humanity, War Crimes and Genocide Under Domestic Law: A Submission Informed by Historical, Normative and Policy Considerations", in *Washington University Global Studies Law Review*, vol. 16, no. 3, p. 428.

---

considerations by the OTP. Rather, we argue that the OTP is obligated to consider the political implications of investigations during the preliminary examination phase as part of a more complex, institutional consequentialist theory. This sort of theory would not assess the consequences of each individual investigation or prosecution carried out by the OTP and the ICC. Maintaining the institution of the ICC becomes primary if we think of the world in which the ICC exists and functions as the scenario that is likely to create the best outcomes. Thus, this type of consequentialist analysis aims at ensuring the continued existence of the institution, rather than at attempting to predict the consequences of pursuing any one situation in particular. On this view, procedural justice remains the central type of fairness consideration, and deontological and consequentialist ethical considerations can (and must) co-exist in the OTP as they seek the same goals.

18.4.4. Accountability Mechanisms and Judicial Review

We focus in this sub-section on the internal accountability mechanisms and the ways they apply specifically to prosecutorial discretion during the preliminary examination phase, before outlining the external accountability mechanism of judicial review of the OTP.

Recall from Section 18.3.3.2.1. that the Prosecutor's ability to impose disciplinary measures on her staff applies at any phase. So the Prosecutor can use this power to prevent her staff from disrupting trial proceedings, or to chastise them for failing to act in an appropriately professional manner. Ethical failures at the level of prosecutorial discretion may be much more serious than conduct warranting a dismissal or a complaint or a mere slap on the wrist. Given the seriousness of these decisions, it seems unlikely that a lower-level staffer at the OTP would be in a position to influence the exercise of prosecutorial discretion under Article 53(1)(c). But it is certainly possible that a lower-level individual at the OTP could have failed to meet an ethical obligation in terms of information gathering or disclosure, and this could have played an important role in influencing the Prosecutor's assessment of the political considerations surrounding a situation. Thus, the Prosecutor and the OTP benefit from the Prosecutor's ability to threaten or utilize disciplinary procedures to establish a certain kind of respectful professional environment, but also to prevent large or small-scale misconduct.

The OTP's institutional independence, and the prosecutorial discretion that exists with respect to Article 53, is subject to limited judicial review,[264] drawing from the supervisory powers of the Chambers.[265] This judicial review serves as the corresponding legal accountability mechanism for the ethical obligations on the part of the OTP in exercising prosecutorial discretion. It does not create a new ethical obligation on the part of the OTP. In the case of a *proprio motu* investigation,[266] the Prosecutor must seek permission from the PTC if she wants to continue with the investigation.[267] The OTP may only commence the formal investigation if the PTC is satisfied that there is a reasonable basis to conduct such an investigation.[268] Otherwise, the OTP may submit a new request based on

---

[264] Morten Bergsmo, Frederik Harhoff and ZHU Dan, "Article 42", in Otto Triffterer and Kai Ambos (eds.), *Rome Statute of the International Criminal Court: A Commentary*, 3rd edition, C.H. Beck, Munich, 2016, mn. 8–9; Côté, 2012, p. 328, see *supra* note 114; Heinze, 2014, pp. 251–52, see *supra* note 17; see also ICC, Situation in the Democratic Republic of Congo, Pre-Trial Chamber, Prosecution's Reply on the Applications for Participation 01/04-1/dp to 01/04-6/dp, 15 August 2005, ICC-01/04-84, para. 32, see *supra* note 118; ICTR, *Prosecutor v Ndindiliyimana*, Pre-Trial Chamber, Decision on Urgent Oral Motion for a Stay of the Indictment, or in the Alternative a Reference to the Security Council, 26 March 2004, ICTR-2000-56-I, paras. 22–25 (http://www.legal-tools.org/doc/f8de3d/); SCSL, *Prosecutor v Sesay et al.*, Trial Chamber, Decision on Sesay Motion Seeking Disclosure of the Relationship between Governmental Agencies of the United States of America and the Office of the Prosecutor, 2 May 2005, SCSL-04-15-T, para. 22 (http://www.legal-tools.org/doc/fde087/); Daniel D. Ntanda Nsereko, "Prosecutorial Discretion before National Courts and International Tribunals", in *Journal of International Criminal Justice*, 2005, vol. 3, no. 1, pp. 136, 138; Peter C. Keen, "Tempered Adversariality: The Judicial Role and Trial Theory in the International Criminal", in *Leiden Journal of International Law*, 2004, vol. 17, no. 4, p. 797; Hakan Friman, "Procedures of International Criminal Investigations and Prosecutions", in Robert Cryer *et al.* (eds.), *Introduction into International Criminal Law and Procedure*, 3rd edition, Cambridge University Press, Cambridge, 2014, p. 430; Thalmann, 2012, p. 473, see *supra* note 126; Vladimir Tochilovsky, *The Law and Jurisprudence of the International Criminal Tribunals and Courts: Procedure and Human Rights Aspects*, 2nd edition, Intersentia, Cambridge, 2014, p. 470; Kuczyńska, 2015, pp. 40–42, see *supra* note 41; from a comparative perspective, Kai Ambos, "The Role of the Prosecutor", in Stephen Livingstone (ed.), *Towards a Procedural Regime for the International Criminal Court*, London, 2002, pp. 16–21, 63.

[265] From a comparative perspective, see Kai Ambos, "The Status, Role and Accountability of the Prosecutor of the International Criminal Court: A Comparative Overview on the Basis of 33 National Reports", in *European Journal of Crime, Criminal Law and Criminal Justice*, 2000, vol. 8, no. 2, p. 116.

[266] ICC Statute, Article 15(1), see *supra* note 104.

[267] Cf. *ibid.*, Article 15(3).

[268] *Ibid.*, Article 15(4). See also Ambos, 2016, p. 340, see *supra* note 2

---

new facts or evidence,[269] or it must drop the investigation. In the case of State or Security Council referrals,[270] the PTC can formally review the OTP decision "to initiate an investigation",[271] after the preliminary examination is concluded. The PTC is entitled to review OTP non-investigation or non-prosecution decisions under Article 53(1) and (2) pursuant to Article 53(3) of the ICC Statute. However, there generally is no possibility of judicial review in cases of prosecutorial inaction. Thus, a decision not to initiate an investigation under Article 15 cannot be reviewed.[272] After all, the decision to investigate or prosecute belongs to the realm of the Prosecutor, being the *dominis litis* over this part of the proceedings, and thus cannot be substituted by a judicial organ.[273]

Now that we have argued for our normative understanding of how prosecutorial discretion should be influenced by consequentialist ethical considerations during the preliminary examination phase, and identified the related OTP obligations and accountability mechanisms, Section 18.5. will outline policy recommendations that support our normative claims.

18.5. Specific Recommendations for OTP Ethics in the Preliminary Examination Phase

In this penultimate section, we argue that the OTP must be accountable to more specific ethical standards applicable to the preliminary examination phase in order to ensure the legitimacy and fairness of the Court, both in terms of perception and actual practice. We address both direct ethical duties and internal accountability mechanisms.

18.5.1. Suggested Ethical Obligations

18.5.1.1. Revisions to the OTP's Policy Guidelines

Our first recommendation is that the OTP should generate a more concrete set of policy guidelines to defend and explain the normative foundations of prosecutorial ethics, especially with respect to prosecutorial discre-

---

[269] ICC Statute, Article 15(5), see *supra* note 104.

[270] Cf. *ibid.*, Article 13(a) and (b).

[271] *Ibid.*, Article 53(1).

[272] Cf. Stahn, 2009, p. 255, see *supra* note 162.

[273] See, in a similar vein, Stahn, 2009, p. 255, *supra* note 162; Friman, Brady, Costi, Guariglia and Stuckenberg, 2013, p. 390 (Chamber "not empowered to substitute a negative decision with its own prosecution"), see *supra* note 222.

tion.[274] We do not think that relying on a common-sense understanding of morality is sufficient to ensure that individuals from a wide range of backgrounds pursue the same ethical aims. Rather, we suggest that the OTP should clearly identify when, which, and how deontological and consequentialist considerations should play a role in its selection and prioritization strategy, especially considering the mandate and purpose of the ICC. The OTP should be obligated to make selection decisions in accordance with the following theoretical underpinnings related to punishment.

18.5.1.1.1. Retribution

Retribution and deterrence[275] are of limited relevance at the international level.[276] It is therefore acceptable, that high selectivity undermines the

---

[274] In a similar vein, see Nicholas Cowdery, "The Exercise of the Powers of the Porsecutor", in Bergsmo, Rackwitz and SONG (eds.), 2017, pp. 421–22, see *supra* note 111. But see Bruce A. Green, "Prosecutorial Ethics in Retrospect", in *Georgetown Journal of Legal Ethics*, vol. 30, no. 1, pp. 461-484 (arguing that holding prosecutors more accountable may require developing alternatives to formal discipline or restructuring the process by which ethics rules for prosecutors are created and enforced).

[275] Roberto Bellelli, "The Establishment of the System of International Criminal Justice", in Roberto Bellelli (ed.), *International Criminal Justice: Law and Practice from the Rome Statute to Its Review*, Ashgate, Farnham, 2010, pp. 5, 13; Bradley E. Berg, "The 1994 I.L.C. Draft Statute for an International Criminal Court: A Principled Appraisal of Jurisdictional Structure", in *Case Western Reserve Journal of International Law*, 1996, vol. 28, no. 2, pp. 254 ff. For ICTR jurisprudence, see, for example, ICTR, *Prosecutor v. Serushago*, Trial Chamber, Sentence, 5 February 1999, ICTR-98-39-S, para. 20 (http://www.legal-tools.org/doc/e2dddb/); ICTR, *Prosecutor v. Rutaganda*, Trial Chamber, Judgment, 6 December 1999, ICTR-96-3-T, para. 455 (http://www.legal-tools.org/doc/f0dbbb/). For ICTY jurisprudence, see, for example, ICTY, *Prosecutor v. Erdemović*, Trial Chamber, Sentencing Judgment, 29 November 1996, IT-96-22-T, para. 65 (http://www.legal-tools.org/doc/eb5c9d/); ICTY, *Prosecutor v. Aleksovski*, Trial Chamber, Judgement, 24 March 2000, IT-95-14/1-A, para. 185 (http://www.legal-tools.org/doc/176f05/). Cautioning against the application of quantitative methods to determine the preventive effect of international criminal trials Anderson, 2016, p. 189, see *supra* note 61; Tomer Broude, "The Court Should Avoid all Considerations of Deterrence and Instead Focus on Creating a Credible and Legitimate Normative Environment in Which Serious Crimes are Not Tolerated", in Richard H. Steinberg (ed.), *Contemporary Issues Facing the International Criminal Court*, Brill Nijhoff, Leiden, Boston, 2016, p. 194 ("[S]pecific and general deterrence are empirically intangible – in the international criminal realm they can neither be proved nor disproved in a methodologically meaningful manner, beyond conjecture. Deterrence, therefore, cannot, and should not, serve as an appreciable objective to be achieved by the Court"). See, however, David Scheffer, "Maximizing Opportunities to Deter Further Atrocity Crimes", in *ibid.*, p. 220: "Recent empirical research demonstrates the deterrence value of international

---

Court's capacity to achieve retributive justice.[277] As Mark Drumbl remarks: "The retributive function is hobbled by the fact that only some extreme evil gets punished, whereas much escapes its grasp, often for political reasons anathema to Kantian deontology".[278] Thus, retribution cannot justify the selection of some suspects over others.[279] Ranking potential suspects in terms of their relative desert is impractical.[280] Deontological retributivists have provided theoretical tools to measure desert.[281] For instance, 'harm-ratings' which examine the consequences of a crime under consideration of certain assumed social situations and evaluate the "consequences in the light of certain assumed basic values";[282] or by the

---

and domestic prosecutions of human rights violators, including perpetrators of atrocity crimes").

[276] Ambos, 2013, p. 68, see *supra* note 77; Leslie P. Francis and John G. Francis, "International Criminal Courts, the Rule of Law, and the Prevention of Harm: Building Justice in Times of Injustice", in Larry May and Zachary Hoskins (eds.), *International Criminal Law*, Cambridge University Press, Cambridge, 2010; Deirdre Golash, "The Justification of Punishment in the International Context", in Larry May and Zachary Hoskins (eds.), *International Criminal Law and Philosophy*, Cambridge University Press, Cambridge, 2010, pp. 201 ff.; Berg, 1996, p. 254, see *supra* note 275.

[277] This criticism has been voiced in Mark A. Drumbl, *Atrocity, Punishment and International Law*, Cambridge University Press, Cambridge, 2007, pp. 151–54, 156–57 (citing Letter "Hannah Arendt to Karl Jaspers 17.8.1946", in Hannah Arendt and Karl Jaspers, *Briefwechsel 1926-1969*, R. Piper GmbH, Munich, 1985, p. 4 (translated to English in Lotte Köhler & Hans Saner (eds., trans.), *Correspondence 1926-1969*, Harcourt, 1992). See also Margaret M. deGuzman, "Choosing to Prosecute: Expressive Selection at the International Criminal Court", in *Michigan Journal of International Law*, 2012, vol. 33, no. 2, p. 302.

[278] Drumbl, 2007, p. 151, see *supra* note 277.

[279] deGuzman, 2012, p. 303, see *supra* note 277; Michael T. Cahill, "Retributive Justice in the Real World", in *Washington University Law Review*, 2007, vol. 85, no. 4, p. 870.

[280] deGuzman, 2012, p. 303, see *supra* note 277; Cahill, 2007, p. 852, see *supra* note 279.

[281] These theoretical tools may even comprise utilitarian approaches, as the so-called retributarianism does, see Hadar Dancig-Rosenberg and Netanel Dagan, "Retributarianism: A New Individualization of Punishment", in *Criminal Law and Philosophy*, 2018, Advance Article, p. 1 ("These retributarian approaches are characterized by the individualization of retributivism. On one hand, retributarianism shares with classic retributivism the rhetoric of justice, a focus on the moral evaluation of the severity of the offense, and the primary importance ascribed to maintaining proportionality. On the other hand, it shares with utilitarianism the possibility of taking into account, in addition to the severity of the offense, the offender's personal circumstances, with a future-oriented perspective that also considers developments subsequent to the commission of the offense").

[282] Andrew von Hirsch and Nils Jareborg, "Gauging Criminal Harm: A Living-Standard Analysis", in *Oxford Journal of Legal Studies*, 1991, vol. 11, no. 1, pp. 6–7.

impairment of personal interests such as 'welfare interests',[283] which comes close to the (rather consequentialist) German *Rechtsgutslehre*[284] and might – in our view – not be a deontological tool at all. Whether these tools can be applied in practice, however, especially in context of the ICC, seems doubtful.

Efficiency has been at the core of reform efforts within and outside of the ICC.[285] It is clear from these efforts that the necessary reforms can be more easily and quickly achieved by changes in practice (via practice manuals like the Chambers Practice Manual) than by – usually more cumbersome – normative reforms (via amendments of the RPE or even

---

[283] Joel Feinberg, *Harm to Others*, Oxford University Press, New York, 1987, pp. 41 ff.

[284] See in more detail Kai Ambos, "The Overall Function of International Criminal Law: Striking the Right Balance Between the *Rechtsgut* and the Harm Principles", in *Criminal Law and Philosophy*, 2015, vol. 9, no. 2, pp. 301–29; Kai Ambos, "Rechtsgutsprinzip und harm principle: theoretische Ausgangspunkte zur Bestimmung der Funktion des Völkerstrafrechts", in Mark A. Zöller (ed.), *Gesamte Strafrechtswissenschaft in internationaler Dimension: Festschrift für Jürgen Wolter zum 70 Geburtstag am 7 September 2013*, Duncker & Humblot, Berlin, 2013, pp. 1285–310.

[285] See, on the one hand, ICC, *Chambers Practice Manual*, May 2017 (http://www.legal-tools. org/doc/f0ee26/). About the creation of the Manual, see, for example, Hirad Abtahi and Shehzad Charania, "Expediting the ICC Criminal Process: Striking the Right Balance between the ICC and States Parties", in *International Criminal Law Review*, 2018, Advance Article, pp. 35 ff.; the various Reports of the Study Group on Governance (2011–15), especially the most recent Report of the Working Group on Lessons Learnt in ICC-ASP, *Report Study Group on Governance*, 2015, Annex II, 29 ff. and, last but not least, ICC, *Second Court's report on the development of performance indicators for the ICC*, 11 November 2016, p. 12–13 (formulating as an autonomous second goal '[T]he ICC's leadership and management are effective'); for a comprehensive overview of this Court-led initiative since its inception see Philipp Ambach, "A Look towards the Future: The ICC and 'Lessons Learnt'", in Carsten Stahn (ed.), *Law and Practice of the International Criminal Court*, Oxford University Press, Oxford, 2015, pp. 1284 ff.; Philipp Ambach, "The 'Lessons Learnt' Process at the ICC: a Suitable Vehicle for Procedural Agreements?", in *Zeitschrift für internationale Strafrechtsdogmatik*, 2016, vol. 11, no. 12, pp. 857 ff.; Birju Kotecha, "The ICC's Office of the Prosecutor and the Limits of Performance Indicators", in *Journal of International Criminal Justice*, 2017, vol. 15, no. 3, pp. 543-565. On the other hand, see Guénaël Mettraux, Shireen A. Fisher, Dermot Groome, Alex Whiting Gabrielle McIntyre, Jérome de Hemptinne, and Göran Sluiter, *Expert Initiative on Promoting Effectiveness at the International Criminal Court*, 2 December 2014 (http://www.legal-tools. org/doc/3dae90/) and the summary by Jürg Lindenmann, "Stärkung der Effizienz der Verfahren vor dem Internationalen Strafgerichtshof", in *Zeitschrift für Internationale Strafrechtsdogmatik*, 2015, vol. 10, no. 10, p. 529.

---

the ICC Statute).[286] The ensuing management needs to not only concern the judges but also the Prosecutor who bears the main responsibility for the conduct of the preliminary and investigation stage.[287] Given the Prosecutor's broad discretion at this procedural stage, with virtually no judicial supervision[288] and great freedom to select situations and cases,[289] a coherent and transparent prosecution strategy with the respective policies is required as a counterbalance.[290]

18.5.1.1.2. Deterrence

Deterrence is also unable to provide the theoretical basis for concrete selection criteria[291] – even though deterrence emanates from utilitarian moral philosophy. However, read together with other utilitarian goals of the ICC, such as strengthening the protections of international humanitarian law; creating a historical record of atrocities; providing satisfaction to the victims of crimes committed by an offender; and to promoting a process of reconciliation,[292] it might still be a better option for grounding punish-

---

[286] Cf. *ibid.* (calling for "changes of practice", and only subsidiary for normative changes); see also Ambach, 2016, p. 862 (referring to "practice adjustments short of the 'article 51 threshold'", that is, "internally" without an amendment of the RPE) and pp. 847–64 (on the amendments of the RPE via Article 51(2)(a) and (3), especially highlighting the smoother avenue for the judges pursuant to Article 51(3)), see *supra* note 285.

[287] For a critical discussion of the management structures of the OTP, see Mettraux, Fisher, Groome, Whiting McIntyre, de Hemptinne and Sluiter, 2014, p. 51 (paras. 4 ff.) (recommending, among other things, a streamlining of the prosecutorial investigations, pp. 65–66 para. 55), see *supra* note 285.

[288] Cf. Ambos, 2016, pp. 381 ff., see *supra* note 2. From a policy perspective against judicial oversight during investigation, see Mettraux, Fisher, Groome, Whiting McIntyre, de Hemptinne and Sluiter, 2014, p. 8, para. 8, p. 11, para. 36, see *supra* note 285.

[289] Cf. Ambos, 2016, pp. 376 ff., see *supra* note 2; Ambos, 2016, pp. 33 ff., see *supra* note 182. With a special focus on fairness see also May and Fyfe, 2017, pp. 177 ff., see *supra* note 262.

[290] See now – long expected – ICC-OTP, 2016 (establishing general principles, repeating the legal criteria and – most importantly – proposing case selection [gravity of the crime, degree of responsibility of the accused and representativity of charges, para. 34 ff.] and prioritisation criteria [cf. especially para. 50–51]), see *supra* note 160.

[291] In this vein also deGuzman, 2012, pp. 306 ff., see *supra* note 277; Anderson, 2016, pp. 189 ff, see *supra* note 61. For a nuanced account of deterrence see Broude, 2016, pp. 194 ff., see *supra* note 275.

[292] Heinze, 2014, pp. 216 ff., see *supra* note 17; John D. Jackson and Sarah J. Summers, *The Internationalisation of Criminal Evidence*, Cambridge University Press, Cambridge, 2012, pp. 111–12 (using the term 'purpose'); Jens D. Ohlin, "Goals of International Criminal Jus-

---

ment, since it includes the Court's mandate. After all, a prosecutorial strategy must always be measured against the legitimacy and effectiveness of the ICC; the effectiveness of an institution – in turn – depends on the execution of its mandate.[293] This mandate serves as the purpose or the goals of an institution. These goals cannot be assigned or determined *a placere*. They are established by the mandate provider or stakeholder,[294] especially in a rule-based international order.[295] In case of the *ad hoc* tribunals, the mandate provider is the UN Security Council.[296] Since the UN is bound by human rights norms based on its Charter, so are those tribunals and their prosecutors.[297] This, of course, also has an impact on the prosecutors' understanding of the tribunals' goals and purposes when selecting suspects. Thus, human rights law-related goals, such as satisfac-

---

tice and International Criminal Procedure", in Göran Sluiter *et al.* (eds.), *International Criminal Procedure: Principles and Rules*, Oxford University Press, Oxford, 2013, pp. 55, 58–60; Jenia I. Turner, "Plea Bargaining", in Linda Carter and Fausto Pocar (eds.), *International Criminal Procedure: The Interface of Civil Law and Common Law Legal Systems*, Edward Elgar, Cheltenham, 2013, pp. 34, 51; Douglas Guilfoyle, *International Criminal Law*, Oxford University Press, Oxford, 2016, p. 89; Nerida Chazal, *The International Criminal Court and Global Social Control: International Criminal Justice in Late Modernity*, Routledge, London, 2016, p. 2 (albeit claiming that providing satisfaction and reparation to victims is of secondary importance, which might not reflect the Statute's *telos*). See also – albeit with regard to the ICTY – Minna Schrag, "Substantive and Organisational Issues", in Bergsmo, Rackwitz and SONG (eds.), 2017, pp. 392 ff., *supra* note 111. For arguments for restorative justice or healing, See, for example, Mark J. Osiel, "Ever Again: Legal Remembrance of Administrative Massacre", in *University of Pennsylvania Law Review*, 1995, vol. 144, no. 2, pp. 471–78, 512.

[293] Yuval Shany, "Assessing the Effectiveness of International Courts: A Goal-Based Approach", in *American Journal of International Law*, 2012, vol. 106, no. 2, p. 237.

[294] *Ibid.*, p. 240.

[295] Ohlin, 2013, p. 61, see *supra* note 292.

[296] Security Council Resolution 827 (1993), UN Doc. S/RES/827(1993), 25 May 1993; Security Council Resolution 955 (1994), UN Doc. S/RES/955(1944), 8 November 1994; Iain Bonomy, "The Reality of Conducting a War Crimes Trial", in *Journal of International Criminal Justice*, 2007, vol. 5, no. 2, p. 353.

[297] Masha Fedorova and Göran Sluiter, "Human Rights as Minimum Standards in International Criminal Proceedings", in *Human Rights and International Legal Discourse*, 2009, vol. 3, no. 1, p. 21; Krit Zeegers, *International Criminal Tribunals and Human Rights Law*, Springer, The Hague, 2016, p. 57; Lorenzo Gradoni, "International Criminal Courts and Tribunals: Bound by Human Rights Norms … or Tied Down?", in *Leiden Journal of International Law*, 2006, vol. 19, no. 3, p. 849.

tion and restitution,[298] have arguably a more prominent position within the system of the *ad hoc* tribunals than at the ICC due to the different mandate providers.[299] In other words, 'core goals' of the ICTY/ICTR and the ICC do not necessarily have to coincide. At the ICC, the States Parties determine the mandate of the Court, and although international treaties or other instruments creating international courts will always be the result of a diplomatic compromise in which the framing of a text is a part of the bargaining process, this mandate is first and foremost consequentialist.

18.5.1.1.3. Expressivism and Communication

We are well aware that selection and prioritization criteria written in the ink of consequentialism risk widening the power of the Prosecutor to the detriment of fairness and justice. Both the expressivist and communicative purpose of punishment,[300] in particular and in its several variants, cannot

---

[298] Krešimir Kamber, *Prosecuting Human Rights Offences*, Brill, Leiden/Boston, 2017, pp. 186–87.

[299] Stahn, 2017, p. 9 with further references, see *supra* note 1, who views the "consequentialist approach" (in more detail *supra* note 228) of the OTP to preliminary examinations as carrying the potential of turning the ICC "into a human rights monitoring body or even cast[ing] irreversible shadows of incrimination on individuals prior to investigations".

[300] We understand expressivism as the expression of condemnation and outrage of the international community, where the international community in its entirety is considered one of the victims, see also Kai Ambos, "Review Essay: Liberal Criminal Theory", in *Criminal Law Forum*, 2017, vol. 28, pp. 589, 601 with further references. Even though expressivism can be traced back to Hegel's theory of punishment (for Hegel punishment is the "cancellation [*Aufheben*] of crime", which "is *retribution* in so far as the latter, by its concept, is an infringement of an infringement [of right] and in so far as crime, by its existence [*Dasein*], has a determinate qualitative and quantitative magnitude, so that its negation, as existent, also has a determinate magnitude", Georg Wilhelm Friedrich Hegel, *Elements of the Philosophy of Right*, Allen W. Wood (ed.), H.B. Nisbet (trans.), Cambridge University Press, Cambridge, 1821/1991, § 101, emphases in the original; see Antje Du Bois-Pedain, "Hegel and the Justification of Real-world Penal Sanctions", in *Canadian Journal of Law & Jurisprudence*, 2016, vol. 29, no. 1, pp. 37, 42; see also the analysis of Thom Brooks, *Hegel's Political Thought*, 2nd edn, Edinburgh University Press, Edinburgh, 2013, p. 172), Feinberg is usually named as its proponents, especially by authors from the common law system (for more references see May and Fyfe, 2017, pp. 61 ff., see *supra* note 262). What is commonly overlooked is that Feinberg speaks of "expression" rather than "communication" of punishment: "[P]unishment is a conventional device for the expression of attitudes of resentment and indignation. [...] Punishment, in short, has a *symbolic significance* largely missing from other kinds of penalties", Joel Feinberg, *Doing and Deserving*, Princeton University Press, Princeton, New Jersey, 1974, p. 98, emphasis in the original. There are several attempts to distinguish expressivist and communicative theories of punishment, evolving around the existence of a recipient (for our purposes, this admittedly

be transferred beyond the domestic realm, where the recognition of valid criminal laws can be empirically proven, to an area where these criminal laws do not exist. Here, international criminal law is not only "educating society about its past" through the truth-telling function of international criminal trials;[301] it also very bluntly aims to *create* an awareness of the existence of a norm, instead of strengthening this norm's perception. This, however, arguably bestows upon criminal law the function of *creating* morality, which is neo-colonialism par excellence.[302] Especially the OTP's policy of "positive complementarity"[303] – "a concept aimed at encourag-

---

rough and almost simplistic identification of a common criterion needs to suffice): Expressivist theories too are based on communication but that communication does not require a recipient and is audience-independent while communicative theories are based on an communicative act that is aimed at a certain recipient and is audience-dependent (see, for example, Andy Engen, "Communication, Expression, and the Justification of Punishment", in *Athens Journal of Humanities and Arts*, 2014, vol. 1, no. 4, pp. 299, 304 ff.; Bill Wringe, "Rethinking expressive theories of punishment: why denunciation is a better bet than communication or pure expression", in *Philosophical Studies*, 2017, vol. 174, no. 3, pp. 681-708). Communicative punishment theories therefore recognise the social communication between offender, victim and society through punishment (Ambos, *ibid.*, p. 601 with further references). This stems from the idea that a communication *with* (instead of about) the offender is both possible and necessary (*ibid.*, p. 602). Beyond that, through punishment society not only communicates with the offender, but also "with itself" (Klaus Günther, "Criminal Law, Crime and Punishment as Communication", in Andrew P. Simester *et al.* (eds.), *Liberal Criminal Theory*, Hart, Oxford, 2014, p. 131). In the words of Anthony Duff: "In claiming authority over the citizens, it [that is, criminal law] claims that there are good reasons, grounded in the community's values for them to eschew such wrong [...]. It speaks to the citizens as members of the normative community." (Antony Duff, *Punishment, Communication and Community*, Oxford University Press, Oxford, 2001, p. 80).

301 Mina Rauschenbach, "Individuals Accused of International Crimes as Delegitimized Agents of Truth", in *International Criminal Justice Review*, 2018, Advance Article, p. 3 with further references.

302 Cornelius Prittwitz, "Die Rolle des Strafrechts im Menschenrechtsregime", in Arno Pilgram *et al.* (eds.), *Einheitliches Recht für die Vielfalt der Kulturen? Strafrecht und Kriminologie in Zeiten transkultureller Gesellschaften und transnationalen Rechts*, LIT, Wien, 2012, pp. 23, 31.

303 Ambos, 2016, p. 327 with further references, see *supra* note 2; Cedric Ryngaert, "Complementarity in Universality Cases: Legal-Systemic and Legal Policy Considerations", in Morten Bergsmo (ed.), *Complementarity and the Exercise of Universal Jurisdiction for Core International Crimes*, Torkel Opsahl Academic EPublisher, Oslo, 2010, pp. 165, 172 ff. (http://www.toaep.org/ps-pdf/7-bergsmo); Olympia Bekou, "The ICC and Capacity Building at the National Level", in Carsten Stahn (ed.), *Law and Practice of the International Criminal Court*, Oxford University Press, Oxford, 2015, pp. 1245, 1252 ff.; William W. Burke-White, "Maximizing the ICC's Crime Prevention Impact Through Positive Complementarity and Hard-Nosed Diplomacy", in Richard H. Steinberg (ed.), *Contempo-*

---

ing domestic criminal justice systems to conduct their own criminal proceedings" – has been subjected to such a criticism.[304] Yet we see this consequentialist dimension of prosecutorial discretion as Larry May understands it, invoking an 'international harm principle', or a moral argument
for thinking that group-based rather than individualized harms are the
proper subject of international prosecutions.[305] May focuses on humanity's interest rather than individual interests, claiming: "One interest of
humanity is that its members, as members, not be harmed. This is similar
to the claim that a club has an interest that its members, as members, not
be harmed. For when the club's members are harmed in this way, the
harms adversely affect the reputation of the club, and even the ability of
the club to remain in existence".[306] This mirrors an objective understanding of legal goods, as promoted by Feinberg with his understanding of
harm (see above). Thus, according to May, "justified international prosecutions require either that the harm must be widespread in that there is a
violation of individuality of a certain sort epitomized by group-based
harmful treatment that ignores the unique features of the individual victim,
or the harm must be systematic in that it is perpetrated in pursuance of a
plan by an agent of a State or with active involvement from a State or
State-like entity".[307] These purposes of punishment (and their respective
limitations) should be more clearly reflected in the OTP policies.

18.5.1.2. Concretization of the OTP's General Ethic Rules (Especially its Code of Conduct)

Second, we follow Morten Bergsmo in our argument for more precise
obligations on the part of the OTP with respect to their conduct, pursuant

---

rary Issues Facing the International Criminal Court, Brill Nijhoff, Leiden, Boston, 2016, pp. 203 ff.

[304] Stahn, 2017, p. 9 with further references, see *supra* note 1.

[305] Larry May, *Crimes Against Humanity: A Normative Account*, Cambridge University Press, Cambridge, 2005, p. 81. In support of and applying May's harm principle (especially with-in the context of the IMT), see Andrew Altman and Christopher Heath, "A Defense of In-ternational Criminal Law", in *Ethics*, 2004, vol. 115, no. 1, pp. 40 ff. But see Reeves, 2018, p. 1060, see *supra* note 50, who denies that we should treat the harm of crimes against humanity as a "precondition of legitimate prosecution" and instead claims that universal jurisdiction should not require special standing. Again, we disagree with his conflation of questions about universal jurisdiction with those of *ius puniendi*.

[306] May, 2005, p. 82, see *supra* note 305.

[307] *Ibid.*, p. 90.

---

to the OTP Code. In 2003, Morten Bergsmo, Senior Legal Advisor at the ICC-OTP Legal Advisory Section at the time, led a team which drafted a Prosecutorial Code of Conduct ('Draft Code'), which appeared on the ICC's website.[308] In comparison to the then-existing Professional Conduct for Prosecution Counsel at the *ad hoc* tribunals, Bergsmo's draft was much more specific.[309] The draft is not available at the ICC's website anymore, but was kindly provided to the authors by Bergsmo himself and has recently been reprinted.[310] The Draft Code begins by identifying a moral obligation that is not legally enforceable, yet it is one that may go a long way toward cultivating an impressive sort of professional environment at the OTP. Regulation 5.1 of Chapter 2 of the Draft Code explains that the Prosecutor "promulgates this Code of conduct to inculcate and uphold the standard of excellence expected from all members of the Office".[311] Similarly, Regulation 6.2 of Chapter 2 proposes that members of the OTP "shall establish and promote a unified international legal culture within the Office, rooted in the principles and purposes of the Statute, without bias for the rules and methods of any one national system or legal tradition".[312] A written expectation of excellence and a certain professional culture could serve to generate pride and determination on the part of the OTP staff in their approach to other ethical obligations. A more explicit demand for the deontological obligations of self- and other-respect could only improve the culture of the OTP. Regulations 7 through 12 also provide for more precise parameters of the sort of character and conduct that should be expected of someone at the OTP, with respect to standards of independence,[313] honourable and professional conduct,[314] faithful con-

---

[308] Theresa Roosevelt, "Ethics for the Ethical: A Code of Conduct for the International Criminal Court Office of the Prosecutor", in *Georgetown Journal of Legal Ethics*, 2011, vol. 24, no. 3, p. 844.

[309] *Ibid.*, p. 846.

[310] Salim A. Nakhjavani, "The Origins and Development of the Code of Conduct", in Bergsmo, Rackwitz and SONG (eds.), 2017, Annex 1, pp. 964 ff., see *supra* note 111.

[311] Draft Code, Chapter 2, Regulation 5.1.

[312] *Ibid.*, Regulation 6.2. About this "legal culture" in more detail, see Christopher Staker, "Observations on Legal Culture, Legal Policy and the Management of Information", in Bergsmo, Rackwitz and SONG (eds.), 2017, pp. 637–38.

[313] Draft Code, Chapter 2, Regulation 7.

[314] *Ibid.*, Regulation 8.

duct,[315] impartial conduct,[316] contentious conduct,[317] and confidentiality.[318] Again, there should be more than a reliance on commonsense morality in establishing constructive ethical obligations for the OTP.

In terms of more specific issues relating to prosecutorial discretion, Regulation 6.3 of Chapter 2 of the Draft Code obligates all members of the OTP to: "in all their dealings with and relations to the Court and in all matters arising in the performance of their duties or the exercise of their powers, (a) maintain the independence of the Office and refrain from seeking or acting on instructions from any external source; (b) conduct themselves honourably, professionally, faithfully, impartially and conscientiously; [...] (d) endeavour to establish the truth in preliminary examinations, investigations and prosecutions, in accordance with Article 54 of the Statute and Regulation 13; (e) promote the effective [and expeditious] investigation and prosecution of crimes within the jurisdiction of the Court". Regulation 6.3(e) in particular obligates the OTP to work fairly, but also effectively, which is important for maintaining the ICC as an international criminal justice institution. If the OTP cannot function effectively, the wheels of the ICC will grind to a halt.

A possible objection by the OTP to the focus on substantive truth-finding is that it is overly utopian. The OTP Code in fact counters the draft in its footnote to the corresponding provision: "This standard of *truth-seeking* is excerpted from the statement of purpose supporting the duty of the Prosecutor to investigate all relevant facts and evidence, that is, 'In order to establish the truth...' (Article 54(1)(a)). As the search for truth cannot be an obligation of result, the term 'strive' is used to convey an obligation of means of central importance for individual choices of conduct".[319] Yet we would argue that the language should not be modified to reflect a less stringent obligation.

Regulation 13 provides for useful, specific standards of 'truth-seeking', among other things: first, "to provide the factual and evidentiary basis for an accurate assessment of whether there may be criminal respon-

---

[315] *Ibid.*, Regulation 9.
[316] *Ibid.*, Regulation 10.
[317] *Ibid.*, Regulation 11.
[318] *Ibid.*, Regulation 12.
[319] Reprinted in Nakhjavani, 2017, Annex 1, p. 840, see *supra* note 310.

sibility under the Statute"; second, the "investigation of both incriminating and exonerating circumstances as a matter of equal priority and with equal diligence"; and third, "prompt reporting of concerns which, if substantiated, would tend to render a previous conviction made by the Court unsafe, bring the administration of justice into disrepute or constitute a miscarriage of justice; and full conformity to the applicable rules on disclosure of new evidence".[320] The second and third standards are especially compelling. The second standard does not only highlight the (policy-implementing) feature of investigating both incriminating *and* exonerating evidence, but also stresses the importance of the word "equally" in a footnote: "The Statute requires that incriminating and exonerating circumstances be investigated 'equally'. This standard interprets 'equally' as equality in priority, diligence and resource-allocation, and thus relevant to several professions and levels of seniority within the Office".[321]

The investigation of exonerating evidence, as an element of truth finding that a prosecution team may find particularly challenging to demand of itself, is further specified in Regulation 46 of the Draft Code: "During evidence collection, all care shall be taken to identify exonerating evidence [...] If any material points to further potentially exonerating material, this potential shall be recorded. If the lead is not pursued further, the reasons for this decision shall be recorded on the Evidence Registration Form".[322] It is useful that there is no discretion available here, where the obligation is strict and straightforward.

Our final recommendation for adoption from the Draft Code is Regulation 14, which establishes the "standard of effective investigation and prosecution".[323] This regulation uses the modifier "reasoned" to limit what counts as an acceptable "evaluation of facts, evidence, and law, particularly in preparing and conducting the tests of reasonable basis, *prima facie* admissibility, interests of justice and reconsideration, considering applicable factors and criteria and taking into account the interests protected in the Statute in each case".[324] It is necessary that the OTP not be in

---

[320] Draft Code, Chapter 2, Regulation 13.
[321] Reprinted in Nakhjavani, 2017, Annex 1, p. 840, see *supra* note 310.
[322] Draft Code, Chapter 2, Regulation 46.
[323] *Ibid.*, Regulation 14.
[324] *Ibid.*, Regulation 14(b).

a position to shy away from clear expectations for upstanding conduct in associated with the preliminary examination phase, and one way to do that is to be more precise about the standard of evaluation that is acceptable. This standard means reasons must be available for any exercise of prosecutorial discretion, and this seems more than reasonable given the stakes of ICC investigations.

18.5.2. Suggested Internal Accountability Mechanisms

In line with our argument throughout this chapter that the Prosecutor should act in accordance with deontological constraints and also in light of consequentialist considerations, we find that the existing internal accountability mechanisms give her suitable discretion in determining how to hold her staff accountable for failed ethical obligations. There is little that can be done internally to ensure that the Prosecutor herself is held legally accountable for her purely ethical obligations, other than the passage and revision of the OTP, which constitutes the basis for several internal accountability mechanisms. We thus rely on the suggestions revisions to the OTP Code listed in Section 18.5.1. above, and would insist that external bodies who play a role in selecting the Prosecutor are obligated to ensure that the Prosecutor is of the highest moral calibre.

18.6. Conclusion

We have argued that the foundations of prosecutorial discretion, particularly in the OTP at the ICC, cannot be mere platitudes about doing one's job with honour and avoiding serious misconduct in carrying out one's duty. We have analysed the normative foundations of prosecutorial ethics in international criminal law and argued for the necessity of relying on consequentialist considerations during the preliminary examination phase at the ICC, as carefully constrained by deontological obligations. In particular, we have argued that in Article 53, the concept of the "interests of justice" should include both global and local concerns and victims, which will sometimes require the OTP to balance conflicting interests and make decisions that promote the 'expectably best' outcome for all interested parties.

19

Politics, Power Dynamics, and the Limits of Existing Self-Regulation and Oversight in ICC Preliminary Examinations

Asaf Lubin[*]

Should the normative framework that governs the International Criminal Court's ('ICC') oversight concerning preliminary examinations undergo a reform? The following chapter answers this question in the affirmative, making the claim that both self-regulation by the Office of the Prosecutor ('OTP') and quality control by the Pre-Trial Chamber ('PTC') currently suffer from significant deficiencies, thus failing to reach the optimum point on the scale between absolute prosecutorial discretion and absolute control. The chapter demonstrates some of these inadequacies using the example of the preliminary examination concerning the situation in Palestine. The chapter first maps out the legal structures and mechanisms that regulate the preliminary examination stage. The chapter then explores a number of key areas in which the OTP has considerable independence, and concerning which sufficient quality control is critical to ensuring the legitimacy of the preliminary examination process, and of the Court itself. This review includes an analysis of the Court's potential for politicization, the problems faced by the OTP when attempting to articulate generalized prioritization policies and exit strategies, the regulation of evidentiary standards at the preliminary examination stage, and the role of transparency in the preliminary examination process. The chapter concludes with four suggestions for potential reform of the existing control mechanisms over prosecutorial discretion in preliminary examinations: (1) re-phasing

---

[*] **Asaf Lubin** is J.S.D. candidate at Yale Law School (2018 expected); Resident Fellow at Yale's Information Society Project; Visiting Scholar at Hebrew University Cyber Security Research Center; and Robert L. Bernstein International Human Rights Fellow at Privacy International. He would like to thank Morten Bergsmo, Carsten Stahn, as well as the team at the Centre for International Law Research and Policy and Torkel Opsahl Academic EPublisher, for all of their invaluable support in the drafting and publication of this piece. He wishes to also thank Shannon Kisch for her continued guidance and assistance.

of the preliminary examination phase and the introduction of a Gantt-based review process and a sliding scale of transparency requirements; (2) redefinition of the relationship between the OTP and PTC at the preliminary examination stage; (3) redrafting the existing OTP policy papers on Preliminary Examinations and Interests of Justice, as well as adopting a new policy paper on Evidence, Evidentiary Standards, and Source Analysis; and (4) introducing a 'Committee of Prosecutors' as a new external control mechanism.

19.1. Introduction

In her famous speech at Sanders Theater, before the gathered masses attending the 1993 Harvard Law School Class Day Program, then recently confirmed Attorney General Janet Reno presented a stirring account of the role and mandate of criminal prosecutors. "We cannot forget the need to use the law as a shield, but we must remember other forces of the law", she told the cheering crowd of young law students, stressing the point that "the prosecutor who thinks that they have done their job when they get a conviction and see somebody sentenced [...] have another think coming". In her speech, Reno was underlying the need, indeed the ultimate duty of prosecutors, "to look beyond the narrow aspects of the courtroom".[1] This obligation is perhaps magnified in the international sphere, where political pressures[2] and economic costs,[3] as well as mandate constraints and juris-

---

[1] Text of speech given by Janet Reno, United States Attorney General, Harvard Law School Class Day Program, 9 June 1993.

[2] See, for example, M. Cherif Bassiouni, "The Philosophy and Policy of International Criminal Justice", in Lal Chand Vonrah *et al.* (eds.), *Man's Inhumanity to Man: Essays on International Law in Honour of Antonio Cassese*, Kluwer Law International, The Hague, 2003, p. 107 ("political manipulation will derive from *realpolitik*, which will use international criminal justice as a tool to achieve its goals"); see also Felix Olick, "Ocampo remarks spark fury over 'politics' around Kenyan ICC cases", in *Standard Digital*, 9 February 2014 (citing criticism by lawyers over what they perceived to be an infiltration of "international politics" into the Court, following a statement made by former prosecutor Ocampo that diplomats had attempted to exert pressure on him as he launched his investigation into Kenya: "There were some diplomats asking me to do something more to prevent Mr. Kenyatta or Mr. Ruto to run in the elections. I said, it's not my job. Judges in Kenya should do that. And if they authorise them to run, people will vote. And if people vote for them, we have nothing to say"); David Bosco analysed the Court's dependence and interdependence, noting that:

> on paper at least, the International Criminal Court is a striking advance for the legalist worldview against the traditional concept of sovereignty [...] the ICC is designed to be

dictional limitations,[4] prove a constant hindrance to formal criminal prosecution.

The preliminary examination stage, briefly introduced in the Rome Statute, has the potential to be a procedural vessel by which the Prosecutor may indeed look "beyond the narrow aspects of the courtroom".[5] The

---

largely free from political control. The court's prosecutor and its judges are asked to work on the basis of the court's governing statute, a set of carefully defined crimes, and the court's rules of evidence and procedure […] Yet the Rome Statute also made clear that the court would be entirely dependent on state resources to succeed. Negotiators gave the court no enforcement tools of its own. Investigations on national soil require official permission and access. To apprehend suspects, the court leans on state police and military forces. Financially, the court relies on annual dues from members […] If the court needs support of states in general, those major powers that enjoy global reach and influence are particularly important. These states have the economic, diplomatic, intelligence, and military resources needed to help turn the court's writ into reality either directly or via pressure on those whose cooperation is essential in particular cases.

See David Bosco, *Rough Justice: The International Criminal Court in a World of Power Politics*, Oxford University Press, Oxford, 2014, pp. 3–4.

[3] See, for example, William W. Burke-White, "Regionalization of International Criminal Law Enforcement: A Preliminary Exploration", in *Texas International Law Journal*, 2003, vol. 38, p. 738 ("The monetary costs of international criminal law enforcement have been and will continue to be a significant hindrance to the effective operation of international tribunals"); Pierre-Richard Prosper, former U.S. Ambassador-at-Large for War Crimes, Statement before the House International Relations Committee on the U.N. Tribunals for Rwanda and the Former Yugoslavia and the ICC, 28 February 2002 ("the process [of international criminal justice as seen through the work of the Tribunals], at times, has been costly, has lacked efficiency, has been too slow"); Patricia M. Wald, "To Establish Incredible Events by Credible Evidence: The Use of Affidavit Testimony in Yugoslavia War Crimes Tribunal Proceedings", in *Harvard International Law Journal*, 2001, vol. 42, p. 536 (Wald, a former US judge at the ICTY, noted that the "United Nations is understandably anxious to bring to closure the ICTY and the tribunal for Rwanda (ICTR), which together consume almost ten percent of the total UN budget").

[4] See, generally, Awa Njoworia Valerie Adamu, *The Jurisdictional Limitations of the Statute of the ICC: The International Criminal Court, Jurisdiction and the Crimes Under the Jurisdiction of the Court*, LAP LAMBERT Academic Publishing, Saarbrücken, 2012.

[5] This echoes what Professor Mirjan Damaška coined as the 'didactic function' of the ICC, and the role of international criminal law actors as 'moral teachers'. As Damaška explains, international criminal courts should "look beyond the effect of their decisions on potential criminals. Instead, they should aim their denunciatory judgments at strengthening a sense of accountability for international crime by exposure and stigmatization of these extreme forms of inhumanity. This exposure is apt to contribute to the recognition of basic humanity. To the extent that international criminal courts are successful in this endeavor, humanitarian norms would increasingly be respected – the low probability of their violations be-

---

preliminary examination stage, as Carsten Stahn writes, could thus be understood not purely in a technical sense, as a 'filter' for determining when to launch an investigation, but rather taking into account its broader virtues underpinned "in its alert function and its communicative power towards the creation of a broader 'international system of justice'".[6] This approach is further reflected in the declared goals of the preliminary examination stage. As the OTP clarified in its 2013 Policy Paper on Preliminary Examinations, "in the course of its preliminary examination activities, the Office will seek to contribute to the two overarching goals of the Rome Statute: the ending of impunity, by encouraging genuine national proceedings, and the prevention of crimes".[7] These goals are clearly more far-reaching than the expeditious indictment of a carefully drawn up list of alleged perpetrators.[8]

---

ing visited with criminal punishment notwithstanding". Mirjan R. Damaška, "What is the Point of International Criminal Justice?", in *Chicago-Kent Law Review*, 2008, vol. 83, no. 1, p. 329, p. 345.

[6] Carsten Stahn, "Damned if you do, damned if you don't: Challenges and Critiques of ICC Preliminary Examinations" (on file with the author). See also Grotius Centre for International Legal Studies, "Preliminary Examination and Legacy/Sustainable Exit: Reviewing Policies and Practices" (hereinafter 'Grotius Centre Report'), para. 5:

> [T]he OTP may have more leverage over States during preliminary examinations than during investigation, due [to] the scope of choice/discretion involved and the unpredictability of the outcome. OTP action might have most effects on actors on the ground at this stage, since unlike in the context of arrest warrants, the Office was not yet 'locked in'. It was argued that in situations where the context is right, preliminary examinations could be used to facilitate choices in relation to peace and justice. Preliminary examinations could be used to facilitate a number of goals: prevention of atrocity crimes, shape the agenda of peace negotiations, or serve as catalyst for complementarity and/or transitional justice. Preliminary examinations could also have a certain deterrent effect due to their element of surprise, their 'watchdog function' (that is, the fact of 'being watched'), and the structural relationship between the OTP and the state concerned (that is, monitoring, putting pressure, providing reward for behaviour). These factors make preliminary examinations a powerful instrument [...].

[7] ICC Office of the Prosecutor, *Policy Paper on Preliminary Examinations*, para. 93 (http://www.legal-tools.org/doc/acb906/).

[8] At the same time, however, it is important to clarify that the ICC will not open a preliminary examination "merely with the purpose of prevention or 'positive complementarity'", and in that regard the need for the information relating to the situation must substantiate some form of initial basis for a potential investigation. See Grotius Centre Report, see *supra* note 6, para. 8.

It should thus come as no surprise that for the ICC Prosecutor, Fatou Bensouda, preliminary examinations have proved to be "one of the most remarkable efficiency tools" the OTP has at its disposal.[9] But the efficiency of the preliminary examination stage hinges on balanced, impartial utilization by the Prosecutor that is conducive to both political stability and the legitimacy of the Court.[10] This is a matter of concern to some since, during a preliminary examination, significant latitude is in the hands of the Prosecutor, who already enjoys "extremely wide" discretion "when compared to national courts and even *ad hoc* tribunals".[11] This

---

[9] Fatou Bensouda, "Reflections from the International Criminal Prosecutor", in *Case Western Reserve Journal of International Law*, 2012, vol. 45, no. 1, p. 509. Phakiso Mochochoko, the Director of the Jurisdiction, Complementarity and Cooperation division had hinted the same: "The Office of the Prosecutor can make a substantial contribution, in proactively collecting information and monitoring situations under preliminary examination". See Phakiso Mochochoko, "Open Debate of the United Nations Security Council on Peace and Justice, with a special focus on the role of the International Criminal Court: Address on behalf of the Prosecutor", 17 October 2012 (http://www.legal-tools.org/doc/a7d99b/).

[10] As noted by Damaška, "as the interdisciplinary literature on norm acceptance through persuasion suggests, there exists a necessary condition for [international criminal courts] success in performing [the] socio-pedagogical role [that is their 'didactic function']: they should be perceived by their constituencies as a legitimate authority. Lacking coercive power, their legitimacy hangs almost entirely on the quality of their decisions and their procedures". See Damaška, see *supra* note 5, p. 345.

[11] Antonio Coco, "Article 13(c)", in Mark Klamberg (ed.), *Commentary on the Law of the International Criminal Court*, Torkel Opsahl Academic EPublisher, Brussels, 2017, fn. 183 (http://www.legal-tools.org/doc/aa0e2b/). One reflection of this concern can be found in the January 2017 resolution by the African Union, which welcomed notifications by Burundi, South Africa, and The Gambia of withdrawal from the ICC and further adopted a withdrawal strategy for the Union. The Resolution also included calls for reforming the ICC, given the dissatisfaction of the AU with the Court and what they perceive as an inequitable international criminal justice system. For further reading see Emmanuel Igunza, "African Union backs mass withdrawal from ICC", in *BBC News*, 1 February 2017. See also Russian Federation, "Decree on the Intention not to become a Party to the Rome Statute of the International Criminal Court", 16 November 2016 (http://www.legal-tools.org/doc/02c22f-1/):

> Unfortunately the Court failed to meet the expectations to become a truly independent, authoritative international tribunal. The work of the Court is characterized in a principled way as ineffective and one-sided in different fora, including the United Nations General Assembly and the Security Council. It is worth noting that during the 14 years of the Court's work it passed only four sentences having spent over a billion dollars. In this regard the demarche of the African Union which has decided to develop measures on a coordinated withdrawal of African States from the Rome Statute is understandable. Some of these States are already conducting such procedures.

project on "Quality Control in Preliminary Examination" thus asks contributors the following research question: in light of the above considerations, how can we ensure greater awareness and improvement of quality in the work of the OTP at the preliminary examination stage?

To answer this question, I begin by adopting a definition of 'quality control' that is similar to that introduced by Morten Bergsmo in the 2013 CILRAP-project on 'Quality Control in Fact-Finding', tweaked to accommodate the unique features of preliminary examinations. For the purposes of this chapter, a quality control approach "invites consideration of how the quality of every functional aspect" of a preliminary examination can be improved including "work processes to identify, locate, obtain, verify, analyse, corroborate, summarise, synthesise, structure, organise, present, and disseminate" law and facts as they relate to each specific situation under prosecutorial review, and to the decision as to whether or not to open an investigation.[12] In line with this definition, the chapter looks at only one institutional component that may serve to ensure greater quality awareness and ultimate improvement: effective control mechanisms over prosecutorial discretion in the review of situations in the pre-investigation phase.

The topic of controlling prosecutorial discretion, both in the domestic and the international planes, has been the subject of significant scholarship.[13] Judge Gerard E. Lynch summarized this literature by suggesting

---

[12] Morten Bergsmo, "Foreword by the Editor", in Morten Bergsmo (ed.), *Quality Control in Fact-Finding*, Torkel Opsahl Academic EPublisher, Florence, 2013, p. viii (http://www.toaep.org/ps-pdf/19-bergsmo).

[13] For domestic analysis see, for example, Stephanos Bibas, "Prosecutorial Regulation Versus Prosecutorial Accountability", in *University of Pennsylvania Law Review*, 2007, vol. 157, no. 4, p. 1002 (noting that "[m]uch management literature bemoans excessive corporate hierarchies and praises the recent trend toward flattening and slimming layers of bureaucracy [...] General Electric, for example, became leaner and more flexible by slimming down from twenty-nine to six levels [...] In contrast, prosecutors' offices have nowhere near six levels of review. Many prosecutors' offices are at the other extreme of the spectrum, with virtually no effective oversight in most cases. Rather than being regulated to death, even line prosecutors express frustration with the lack of coordination. Because the problem is the opposite one, the solution is as well"); John H. Langbein, "Controlling Prosecutorial Discretion in Germany", in *University of Chicago Law Review*, 1974, vol. 41, no. 3, p. 439; Sara Sun Beale, "Prosecutorial Discretion in Three Systems: Balancing Conflicting Goals and Providing Mechanisms for Control", in Michele Caianiello and Jacqueline S. Hodgson (eds.), *Discretionary Criminal Justice in a Comparative Context*, Carolina Academic Press, Durham, 2015, p. 52 (looking at prosecutorial discretion in the U.S.,

---

that while critics of broad discretion wish to see clear self-executing rules that would "prevent officials from applying subjective and potentially biased standards", defenders of discretion claim that such a view would be "intolerable if pressed to extremes". Discretion, they argue, is "part of the function of the criminal law, that must in turn be moderated by sensible officials who understand that not every case that falls within the literal terms of the law is meant to be punished". Yet, even were we to accept some measure of prosecutorial discretion as inevitable, it would not follow that "the discretion should be exercised without public accountability, or that some form of review of the resulting decisions should not be permitted".[14]

This chapter seeks to examine what model of prosecutorial control was adopted by the drafters of the Rome Statute in the context of preliminary examinations, and where this model has proved ineffective in the work of the ICC to date. The chapter proceeds in the following order. Section 19.2. briefly summarizes the normative framework that governs the preliminary examination stage, with a particular focus on prosecutorial independence.

Section 19.3. maps out the existing control mechanisms over OTP activities at the preliminary examination stage, looking at both internal oversight in the form of self-regulation, or 'office common law', and external oversight in the form of mandatory review by the PTC. Particular emphasis will be given to development of oversight mechanisms as part of the Court's evolution and on particular cases during which this oversight was put to the test.

Germany, and France the author concludes "all three national systems have structural mechanisms designed to provide a degree of democratic accountability. The issue in both is how to balance the need for accountability with the commitment to prosecutorial neutrality and independence, especially in cases involving the investigation of politically prominent suspects who are members – or opponents – of the current government"); CHEN Siyuan, "The Limits of Prosecutorial Discretion in Singapore: Past, Present, and Future", in *International Review of Law*, 2013, vol. 5, p. 1. For analysis of prosecutorial discretion in the ICC, see DONG Jingho, "Prosecutorial Discretion at the International Criminal Court: A Comparative Study", in *Journal of Politics and Law*, 2009, vol. 2, no. 2, p. 109; Allison Marston Danner, "Enhancing the Legitimacy and Accountability of Prosecutorial Discretion at the International Criminal Court", in *American Journal of International Law*, 2003, vol. 97, p. 510.

[14] Gerard E. Lynch, "Prosecution: Prosecutorial Discretion", in *Encyclopedia of Crime and Justice*, 2002.

Section 19.4. will discuss the difficulties with which the currently existing oversight framework is faced, using the Palestinian preliminary examination as a case study. The section will focus on three key issues related to preliminary examinations that are exemplified in the Palestinian case: (1) the potential for the politicization of the Court; (2) the problems faced by the OTP when attempting to articulate generalized prioritization policies and exit strategies; and (3) the regulation of evidentiary standards at the preliminary examination stage.

Finally, as mentioned at first, Section 19.5. will suggest four areas for potential reform, including (1) re-phasing of preliminary examinations and the introduction of a Gantt-based review process and a sliding scale of transparency requirements; (2) redefinition of the relationship between the OTP and PTC at the preliminary examination stage; (3) redrafting existing OTP policy papers on Preliminary Examinations and Interests of Justice and the adoption of a new Policy Paper on Evidence, Evidentiary Standards, and Source Analysis; and (4) introducing a 'Committee of Prosecutors' as a new external control mechanism.

19.2. Normative Framework

19.2.1. Legislative Structures

It is obvious that the drafters of the Rome Statute "did not anticipate the significance that is now attached to Preliminary Examinations".[15] If anything, the drafters assumed that preliminary examinations would be a far weaker process with a much shorter leash, since the general obligation to co-operate under Part 9 of the Statute only applies to investigations and cases.[16] As a result, the Rome Statute stipulates only general and largely

---

[15] William A. Schabas, *The International Criminal Court: A Commentary on the Rome Statute*, Oxford University Press, Oxford, Second Edition, 2016, p. 46. See also, Stahn, see *supra* note 6, p. 3 ("When the Rome Statute was drafted, hardly anyone contemplated how important preliminary examinations would become in the operation of the ICC").

[16] See Rome Statute of the International Criminal Court (last amended 2010), Article 86 (http://www.legal-tools.org/doc/7b9af9/). Surprisingly, the preliminary examination stage is now considered by some to have provided the OTP more power than any other stage. See Grotius Center Report, see *supra* note 6, para. 5:

> Several participants argued that PEs have a certain intrinsic value that goes beyond investigations. The point was made that the OTP may have more leverage over States during PEs than during investigation, due the scope of choice/discretion involved and the unpredictability of the outcome. OTP action might have most effects on actors on

---

vague factors that must be considered during the preliminary examination phase as detailed in Article 53(1):

> The Prosecutor shall, having evaluated the information made available to him or her, initiate an investigation unless he or she determines that there is no reasonable basis to proceed under this Statute. In deciding whether to initiate an investigation, the Prosecutor shall consider whether:
>
> (a) The information available to the Prosecutor provides a reasonable basis to believe that a crime within the jurisdiction of the Court has been or is being committed.
>
> (b) The case is or would be admissible under Article 17; and
>
> (c) Taking into account the gravity of the crime and the interests of victims, there are nonetheless substantial reasons to believe that an investigation would not serve the interests of justice.
>
> If the Prosecutor determines that there is no reasonable basis to proceed and his or her determination is based solely on subparagraph (c) above, he or she shall inform the Pre-Trial Chamber.[17]

The term 'preliminary examination' itself is introduced in the Rome Statute only indirectly. Article 15(6) refers to the procedural obligations of the Prosecutor when exercising her *proprio motu* powers to review a potential situation.[18] The Prosecutor is called to "analyse the seriousness of the information received" and "seek additional information from States,

---

the ground at this stage, since unlike in the context of arrest warrants, the Office was not yet 'locked in'. It was argued that in situations where the context is right, PEs could be used to facilitate choices in relation to peace and justice.

[17]   Rome Statute, *ibid.*, Article 53(1).

[18]   *Ibid.*, Article 15(6) ("If, after the preliminary examination referred to in paragraphs 1 and 2, the Prosecutor concludes that the information provided does not constitute a reasonable basis for an investigation, he or she shall information those who provided the information. This shall not preclude the Prosecutor from considering further information submitted to him or her regarding the same situation in the light of new facts or evidence"). Article 42(1) of the Statute, in laying out the mandate of the OTP, also makes an implied mention of preliminary examinations, noting that: "The Office of the Prosecutor shall act independently as a separate organ of the Court. It shall be responsible for receiving referrals and any substantiated information on crimes within the jurisdiction of the Court, for examining them and for conducting investigations and prosecutions before the Court".

---

organs of the United Nations, intergovernmental or non-governmental organizations, or other reliable sources that he or she deems appropriate".[19] On the basis of this information, gathered over the course of this stage, coined by the Statute as a preliminary examination, the Prosecutor is instructed to decide whether there is "reasonable basis for an investigation".[20] Although this is not expressly stated, it is inferred from Article 53 that the preliminary examination stage is required not only in *proprio motu* decisions, but in fact in all scenarios, including those where the review is triggered by the United Nations Security Council or by a referral from a State Party.[21] Furthermore, the practice of the OTP has been to open a preliminary examination, "as a matter of policy", in all situations where a declaration pursuant to Article 12(3) is made by a non-State Party.[22]

---

[19]   *Ibid.*, Article 15(2). Note that the creation of this pre-investigation stage is unique to the ICC, compared with the *ad hoc* tribunals which had specific jurisdiction over a single situation. As further explained by Ambos and Stegmiller, the

> preliminary examination stage is an important and necessary innovation compared to the pre-trial procedure of former International Criminal Tribunals (the International Military Tribunals in Nuremberg and Tokyo, the ICTY and ICTR, the Special Court for Sierra Leone, the Extraordinary Chambers in the Courts of Cambodia and the Special Tribunal for Lebanon). Contrary to these *Ad Hoc* International Criminal Tribunals that all possessed jurisdiction over a specific situation, limited in temporal and territorial terms, the ICC does not have such jurisdictional limitations. Instead, the ICC must pre-investigate and select its own situations. Even in the case of *prima facie* pre-defined situations, by way of a SC or State referral.

Kai Ambos and Ignaz Stegmiller, "Prosecuting international crimes at the International Criminal Court: is there a coherent and comprehensive prosecution strategy?", in *Crime, Law and Social Change*, 2012, vol. 58, no. 4, p. 421.

[20]   *Ibid.*, Article 15(1), (2), (6).

[21]   Schabas, see *supra* note 15, p. 829 ("This is implied by Article 53 because it is necessarily the basis for the decision of the Prosecutor about whether or not to proceed with an investigation. The consequences of this scheme is that an investigation under Article 53 cannot begin until the Prosecutor has carried out a preliminary examination."). ICC OTP, *Report on Preliminary Examination Activities*, 14 November 2016, para. 10 (http://www.legal-tools.org/doc/f30a53/) ("As required by the Statute, the Office's preliminary examination activities are conducted in the same manner irrespective of whether the Office receives a referral from a State Party or the Security Council or acts on the basis of information on crimes obtained pursuant to article 15").

[22]   *Ibid.*, pp. 358–359 ("as a matter of policy the Prosecutor responds to Article 12(3) declaration by conducting a 'preliminary examination' in accordance with Article 15, treating the declaration in the same way as it treats a referral by a State Party or by the Security Coun-

---

Rule 48 of the Rules of Procedure and Evidence establishes that in determining whether there is "reasonable basis to proceed with an investigation" the Prosecutor shall consider the three factors set out in Article 53(1)(a) to (c).[23] Based on this rule, the OTP has adopted a four-phased 'filtering process' which is flexible enough, according to the Office, to allow for engagement in a "holistic approach" throughout the preliminary examination stage.[24]

Phase 1 consists of a 'pre-preliminary examination', which encompasses the analysis of communications to conclude whether the information available is serious enough to warrant the launching of a preliminary examination, and whether such examination would not be frivolous. Of all phases, there is the least amount of public information available about the general procedures and structures adopted by the OTP at this phase, as well as statistics regarding the number and nature of Phase 1 processes launched or closed.[25]

---

cil. However, unlike a referral the Article 12(3) declaration does not entitle a non-party State that has made the declaration to contest a decision by the Prosecutor not to proceed").

[23] Rules of Procedure and Evidence of the International Criminal Court, as amended on 22 May 2013, ICC-ASP/1/3, U.N. Doc. PCNICC/2000/1/Add.1, Rule 48 (2000).

[24] *2016 Preliminary Examination Report*, see *supra* note 21, para. 15 (by "holistic approach" the OTP intends that while each phase focuses on a distinct statutory factor, the analysis itself is not formalistically rigid). See also Schabas, see *supra* note 15, p. 400 ("The first phase consists of a general analysis of the seriousness of information provided to the Court. Situations that are outside the jurisdiction can be quickly weeded out. No doubt there are many frivolous submissions, filed by cranks or by well-meaning but ill-informed activists, perhaps searching for a bit of publicity rather than out of any serious hope that prosecutions could result. Phase two, which is really the formal beginning of the examination, deals with the precondition for the exercise of jurisdiction set out in Article 12 of the *Statute* and whether a reasonable basis exists to think that the alleged crimes are within the Court's subject-matter jurisdiction. Already attention is given to whether or not potential cases may exist. The third phase concerns the admissibility of potential cases, applying the two main criteria of complementarity and gravity. Finally, phase four examines whether the 'interest of justice' may nevertheless tip the balance against prosecution. An internal report that analyses the relevant factor s and concludes with a recommendation is then submitted to the Prosecutor, who decides whether there is a reasonable basis for an investigation").

[25] It is in this context that Amitis Khojsteh, "The Pre-Preliminary Examination Stage: Theory and Practice of the OTP's Phase 1 Activities", in Morten Bergsmo and Carsten Stahn (eds), *Quality Control in Preliminary Examination: Volume 1*, Torkel Opsahl Academic EPublisher, Brussels, 2018, chap. 8 offers some unique insight into this under-researched and under-discussed phase.

Phase 2, the formal initiation of a preliminary examination, correlates with Article 53(1)(a) and involves an examination of the preconditions to the exercise of jurisdiction by the Court, including territorial or personal, temporal and subject-matter jurisdiction.

Phase 3 correlates with Article 53(1)(b) and focuses on the admissibility of potential cases in terms of complementarity and gravity.

Finally, Phase 4 correlates with Article 53(1)(c) and involves the consideration of the interests of justice prior to the formulation of a final recommendation to the Prosecutor on whether a reasonable basis to initiate an investigation exists.[26]

As of the date of writing, the OTP is reviewing 8 ongoing preliminary examinations. Three (Gabon, Palestine, and Ukraine) are at Phase 2, four (Colombia, Guinea, Iraq/UK, and Nigeria) are at Phase 3, and one, concerning Afghanistan, is pending authorization from the Pre-Trial Chamber III to initiate an investigation.[27] This growing list of situations includes some of the most politically fraught and highly publicized con-

---

[26] Originally the OTP delineated only three phases of the Preliminary Examination process. See OTP, "Annex to the "Paper on some policy issues before the Office of the Prosecutor": Referrals and Communications (September 2003)" (http://www.legal-tools.org/doc/f53870/):

> The first phase of analysis is an initial review to identify those communications that manifestly do not provide any basis for further action. Following this determination, acknowledgements will be sent, either providing reasons for the decision not to proceed or else advising that further analysis will be undertaken. Once the initial backlog of communications is cleared, the Office will endeavour to ensure that this first phase is completed and acknowledgements are sent within one month of receipt of any communication sent in a working language of the Court. The second phase of analysis is a more detailed legal and factual analysis of significant communications, carried out by JCCD, with support from the Investigation Division, under supervision of the Executive Committee and the Prosecutor. The most serious situations will proceed to the third phase, advanced analysis and planning. During this phase, the Office may develop an investigation plan, in which case a joint team will be created, led by the Investigation Division and including members of the Investigation Division, Prosecution Division and JCCD. In this third phase, a decision may be taken to initiate an investigation under Article 53 or to seek Pre-Trial Chamber authorization under Article 15(3).

[27] ICC OTP, *Report on Preliminary Examination Activities*, 4 December 2017 (http://www.legal-tools.org/doc/e50459/). The number of situations under phase 1 review is not disclosed by the OTP. On 29 November 2017, the Prosecutor notified the PTC of her "final decision" regarding the preliminary examination pertaining to registered vessels of Comoros, Greece and Cambodia, ending an examination which began with a referral dating 14 May 2013 from the Government of the Union of Comoros.

---

flicts and hotspots around the world, and thus stands in stark contradiction to the limited number of predominantly African cases currently on the ICC docket. While some of these situations relate to alleged crimes that are relatively recent (for example, those committed in Gabon since May 2016), others concern crimes allegedly committed years ago (for example, the preliminary examination into the situation in Afghanistan which has been ongoing since 2007, and which concerns alleged crimes committed since 2003).

Some critics have raised the concern that "[t]he OTP's lengthy open-ended analysis of several situations", coupled with "the absence of reporting over long periods", have "strained the credibility of its preliminary examinations" and have made its few public statements appear "more like posturing".[28] For example, concerning the aforementioned preliminary examination in Afghanistan, in its November 2016 update on preliminary examinations, the OTP made the much-anticipated statement that "a final determination" with respect to the situation, which has been ongoing for a decade, will be made "in the very near future".[29] It took an additional year for the Office to conclude the examination and request authorization from the Court to initiate an investigation into alleged war crimes and crimes against humanity committed as part of or with a nexus to the armed conflict in Afghanistan since 1 May 2003.[30]

---

[28] Human Rights Watch, *ICC: Course Correction: Recommendations to the Prosecutor for a More Effective Approach to "Situations under Analysis"*, 16 June 2011 (http://www.legal-tools.org/doc/43aefb/).

[29] OTP, "Annex to the "The Prosecutor of the International Criminal Court, Fatou Bensouda, issues her annual Report on Preliminary Examination Activities (2016)" (http://www.legal-tools.org/doc/834809/).

[30] OTP, "Public redacted version of "Request for authorisation of an investigation pursuant to article 15", 20 November 2017" (http://www.legal-tools.org/doc/db23eb/). For an analysis of the potential reasons for the delay see David Bosco, "Will the ICC Launch a Full Investigation in Afghanistan?", in *Lawfare*, 8 May 2017. Same criticisms can be raised with regard to the Preliminary Examination on Colombia, which has been open for more than ten years, and some NGOs are criticizing as "unacceptable". See Stéphanie Maupas, "ICC Prosecutor at a Turning Point", in *JusticeInfo*, 7 March 2017; see also Luis Moreno-Ocampo, "The ICC's Afghanistan Investigation: The Missing Option", in *Lawfare*, 24 April 2017.

19.2.2. Prosecutorial Independence and External Review

Interestingly enough, the drafters of the Rome Statute were never concerned with prosecutorial thumb-twiddling of the kind described above; they were far more worried about prosecutorial foot-stomping. This concern may be noted in the debates that led to the introduction of prosecutorial powers *proprio motu* under Article 15 of the Statute. The image of an all-mighty global prosecutor with *proprio motu* powers, a "lone ranger running wild",[31] concerned the US delegation (and many other delegations), as expressed in an official statement circulated towards the end of the Rome Statute negotiations in 1998:

> The United States strongly supports an effective ICC Prosecutor who will be able to exercise independent judgment and who will be perceived as impartial and fair. [...] The United States is strongly of the view that the principles of prosecutorial independence and effectiveness are not only fully consistent with, but ultimately will be best served by, the structure proposed by the ICC under which the Prosecutor's authority to embark on an investigation is triggered by a referral by a State or the Security Council. It is our firm view that the proposal for a *proprio motu* prosecutor – one tasked with responding to any and all indications that a crime within the potential jurisdiction of the Court may have been committed – not only offers little by way of advancing the mandate of the Court and the principles of prosecutorial independence and effectiveness, but also will make much more difficult the Prosecutor's central task of thoroughly and fairly investigating the most egregious crimes.[32]

---

31 Danner, see *supra* note 13, p. 513 ("Opponents argued that the Prosecutor could become either a "lone ranger running wild" around the world targeting highly sensitive political situations or a weak figure who would be subject to manipulation by states, NGOs, and other groups who would seek to use the power of the ICC as a bargaining chip in political negotiations").

32 Statement of the United States Delegation Expressing Concern Regarding the Proposal for a *Proprio Motu* Proecutor (22 June 1998), reprinted in Rod Grams (ed.), *Is a U.N. International Criminal Court in the U.S. National Interest?*, Hearing before the Subcommittee on International Operations of the Committee of Foreign Relations of the U.S. Senate (23 July 1998), pp. 147–150. The International Law Commission further promoted this position. The ILC was of the view that, absent support from a State Party or the UNSC, prosecution of crimes under the Statute should not be undertaken. The ILC assumed the Prosecutor would be vulnerable to political pressure, and that therefore the support of State parties or

---

Supporters of *proprio motu* powers, on the other hand, were equally concerned with the independence and effectiveness of the OTP, arguing that by limiting the Prosecutor's investigatory capabilities "to situations identified by overtly political institutions like States and the Security Council", the drafters would "decrease the independence and credibility of the Court as a whole".[33] The final wording of Article 15 was therefore a compromise, "one of the most delicate provisions of the Statute" and the product of "extensive debates and divisions of views throughout the drafting process and until the end of the Rome Conference".[34] The proposal was put forward by German and Argentina. While it granted the Prosecutor *proprio motu* powers, it simultaneously put checks on those powers. As was further explained by Judge Fernandez in his separate opinion on the Côte d'Ivoire situation: "there was growing recognition that there were some real risks of abuse of power and that some checks and balances were needed, both in order to prevent arbitrary decisions taken in a solitary fashion by the Prosecutor, and to help insulate the Prosecutor from external pressure".[35]

---

the UNSC would prevent "frivolous, groundless, or politically motivated campaigns". Draft Statute of the International Criminal Court in Report of the International Law Commission on the Work of its Forty-Sixth Session A/CN.4/SER.A/1994/Add.1 (Part 2), reprinted in *Yearbook of the International Law Commission 1994: Report of the Commission to the General Assembly on the work of its forty-sixth session*, 1997, p. 46.

[33]   Danner, see *supra* note 13, p. 514.

[34]   Situation in the Republic of Kenya, Pre-Trial Chamber II, Decision Pursuant to Article 15 of the Rome Statute on the Authorization of an Investigation into the Situation in the republic of Kenya, 31 March 2010, ICC-01/09, paras. 17–18. See also Dissenting Opinion of Judge Hans-Peter Kaul to the same judgment, para. 12 (Article 15 was "one of the most fervently negotiated provisions of the Rome Statute"). In favour of the *proprio motu* powers were Thailand, Lesotho, Jordan, Mexico, Costa Rica, Venezuela, Morocco, Australia, New Zealand, the Czech Republic, Romania, Trinidad and Tobago, the Netherlands, Norway, Italy, South Africa, Tanzania, Brazil, Denmark, Madagascar, Germany, Sweden, Slovenia, Canada, Chile, Bahrain, Andorra, Greece, Senegal, Azerbaijan, Republic of Korea, Switzerland, Togo, Sierra Leon, Portugal, Burkina Paso, Peru, Uruguay, Namibia and Poland. Opposing the powers were the US, Nigeria, Iran, Kenya, Yemen, Iraq, Indonesia, India, Israel, Libya, Cuba, Egypt, Saudi Arabia, China, Russian Federation, Tunisia, Algeria, Turkey, United Arab Emirates, Pakistan, and Bangladesh. For further reading, see Schabas, see *supra* note 15, p. 396.

[35]   Situation in the Republic of Côte d'Ivoire, Judge Fernandez de Gurmendi's Separate and Partially Dissenting Opinion to the Decision Pursuant to Article 15 of the Rome Statute on the Authorization of an Investigation into the Situation in the Republic of Côte d'Ivoire, 3 October 2011, ICC-02/11, para. 8. See also, Situation in the Republic of Kenya, see *supra*

Stepping outside Article 15 and looking at the power to launch preliminary examinations more broadly, two primary checks and balances are included in the Statute. The first check concerns the obligation to provide reasoning in cases of dismissal as a matter of general fairness. If the Prosecutor seeks not to initiate an investigation, under Rule 105 of the Rules of Procedure and Evidence she is required to "promptly inform in writing" the State(s) that referred the situation to the Prosecutor under Article 14 or the Security Council in respect of situations covered by Article 13(b). This obligation to notify applies, under Article 15(6), in respect of "those who provided information" for a *proprio motu* preliminary examination. Such notifications must include the reasons for the dismissal/decision not to investigate, while taking into account any potential danger to the safety, well-being, or privacy of victims or witnesses.[36]

A second check on the preliminary examination activities of the OTP was introduced in Articles 15 and 53, in the form of judicial review by the PTC. This judicial review is limited to certain specific scenarios: (a) when the Prosecutor decides to proceed *proprio motu* with an investigation it must seek the authorization of the PTC;[37] (b) in situations of Security Council or State Party referrals, the referring parties are entitled to request judicial review by the PTC of the Prosecutor's decision (in relation to determinations not to open an investigation on the basis of jurisdiction or admissibility);[38] and (c) in the case of a decision by the Prosecutor not to open an investigation, based solely on the conclusion that an investigation would not serve the interests of justice, the PTC may review the decision on its own initiative, and the decision shall be effective only if confirmed by it.[39]

---

note 34, para. 18 (where it noted that the drafters sought a "balanced approach that rendered the *proprio motu* power of the Prosecutor to initiate an investigation acceptable to those who feared it" by introducing the PTC as a check so to alleviate the "risk of politicizing the Court and thereby undermining its credibility").

[36] See Rules of Procedure and Evidence, see *supra* note 23, at Rule 105; Rome Statute, see *supra* note 16, Article 15(6). Note, that no obligation to provide such notification is required in the case of Article 12(3) declarations.

[37] Rome Statute, *ibid.*, Article 15(3)-(4).

[38] *Ibid.*, Article 53(3)(a).

[39] *Ibid.*, Article 53(3)(b).

It is in this context that Articles 15 and 53 are "closely associated" and lay out the full scope of prosecutorial discretion by mapping the Prosecutor's independent role in the selection of situations for prosecution.[40] The PTC, however, may not become engaged following a decision to close an examination launched *proprio motu* (including those launched on the basis of Article 12(3) declarations), or in cases where the UNSC or referring States do not seek to challenge the decision of the OTP to close an investigation (or where such investigations are eventually launched).[41] This significantly reduces the potential scope of judicial review over preliminary examination decisions.[42]

Some have contemplated whether the Assembly of State Parties ('ASP') offers some additional form of control over the Prosecutor. The ASP does elect the Prosecutor and Deputy Prosecutor, and in theory has the power of removing them by a majority vote.[43] Such removal can only occur if serious misconduct or a serious breach of duties has occurred.[44] Additionally, a few scholars have pondered whether the ASP may use its

---

[40] Schabas, see *supra* note 15, p. 394 (noting further that the Prosecutor is "beyond any doubt the most important individual at the Court. She may also be one of the most powerful, perhaps indeed the most powerful, official in any international organization, including the United Nations").

[41] The Prosecutor is also subject to judicial review in a case where it seeks to take the testimony or a statement, examine, collect or test evidence of a witness which may not be available subsequently for the purposes of a trial (cases of "unique investigative opportunities"). See Rome Statute, see *supra* note 16, article 56.

[42] The PTC may theoretically examine a decision by the Prosecutor not to open a Preliminary Examination under Regulation 46(3) of the Regulations of the Court; however, the PTC has interpreted that power narrowly. See Request under Regulation 46(3) of the Regulations of the Court (ICC-RoC46(3)-01/14), Decision on the 'Request for review of the Prosecutor's decision of 23 April 2014 not to open a Preliminary Examination concerning alleged crimes committed in the Arab Republic of Egypt, and the Registrar's Decision of 25 April 2014', Pre-Trial Chamber II, 12 September 2014 (the Pre-Trial Chamber rejected the request by President Mohamed Morsi and the Freedom and Justice Party of Egypt to review of the Prosecutor's decision not to open a Preliminary Examination, limiting the scope of their review).

[43] Judges may only be removed by a two-thirds vote, making the Prosecutor slightly more accountable to the ASP than the judges.

[44] Rome Statute, see *supra* note 16, Article 46. This control is made possible through the work of the independent oversight mechanism established in 2009 under the Office of Internal Audit. For further reading see Assembly of State Parties to the Rome Statute, "Establishment of an Independent Oversight Mechanism", ICC-ASP/8/Res.1, adopted by consensus at the 7th Plenary Meeting, 26 November 2009.

significant control over budgetary decisions to micromanage prosecutorial decision-making at the pre-trial stage.[45]

Overall, the regulatory framework under the Statute at the preliminary examination stage grants significant discretion to the Prosecutor, establishes minimal guidelines on specific aspects of preliminary examination proceedings, and offers, at least on paper, only limited institutional checks on the work of the OTP throughout this crucial phase. On a glorified altar of prosecutorial independence and impartiality, the drafters thus willingly sacrificed significant portions of institutional and mandatory control. This observation recalls a sentiment expressed in the seminal work of Kenneth Culp Davis on "Discretionary Justice":

> If all decisions involving justice to individual parties were lined up on a scale with those governed by precise rules at the extreme left, those involving unfettered discretion at the extreme right, and those based on various mixtures of rules, principles, standards, and discretion in the middle, where on the scale might be the most serious and most frequent injustice? [...] I think the greatest and most frequent injustice occurs at the discretion end of the scale, where rules and principles provide little or no guidance, where emotions of deciding officers may affect what they do, where political or other favoritism may influence decisions, and where the imperfections of human nature are often reflected in the choices made. I think that in our system of government, where law ends tyranny need not begin. Where law ends discretion begins, and the exercise of discretion may mean either beneficence or tyranny, either justice or injustice, either reasonableness or arbitrariness.[46]

In his book, Davis makes two important assertions. First, for every agency decision there is "an optimum point on the scale between rule-of-law at one end and total discretion at the other end", and second, that once this optimum level is achieved discretionary power is "confined, structured, and checked" so as to ensure "the greatest amount of discretionary

---

[45] Danner, see *supra* note 13, p. 524.

[46] Kenneth Culp Davis, *Discretionary Justice: A Preliminary Inquiry*, Louisiana State University Press, Baton Rouge, 1969, p. V.

---

justice and the least amount of discretionary injustice".[47] In the following section, we will examine what actions both the Prosecutor and the PTC have taken since the ICC opened its doors in order to reach this optimum level. We will examine both internal and external control mechanisms and how they have evolved over time.

19.3. Existing Oversight Mechanisms

In the years since the Court's establishment, a number of mechanisms have been put in place in an attempt to improve the transparency and pre-dictability of the preliminary examination stage and thereby optimize quality controls over the assessment process of the OTP. These mecha-nisms have evolved, in great part, due to the institutional evolution of the OTP,[48] the surge in Article 15 communications coming before the Court for examination,[49] and the natural transformations resulting from changes in the identity of the prosecutors and prosecutorial staff. Of these mecha-nisms, the most fundamental is self-regulation by the OTP. This practice involves the self-imposition of a series of internal guidelines and policies, mandatory checkpoints, reporting obligations, and transparency standards to be applied equally across situations.

---

[47] Frank J. Remington, "Review: Discretionary Justice: A Preliminary Inquiry", The Univer-sity of Chicago Law Review, vol. 36, 1969, p. 884, p. 889.

[48] Jens Meierhenrich, "The Evolution of the Office of the Prosecutor at the International Criminal Court: Insights from Institutional Theory", in Martha Minow *et al.* (eds.), *The First Global Prosecutor: Promise and Constraints*, University of Michigan Press, Ann Ar-bor, 2015, pp. 100–102 (noting that "between 2002 and 2012, the OTP underwent a num-ber of far-reaching institutional transformations, all of which had profound effect on the everyday life of international prosecution at the ICC", mapping four developments as "crit-ical junctures" in the institutional development of the OTP during that period: (1) the in-vention of the JCCD, (2) the introduction of joint teams, (3) the creation of ExCom, and (4) the drafting of an Operational Manual).

[49] As of the 2016 reporting period, and since it opened its doors in July 2012, the OTP has received a total of 12,022 Article 15 communications. That said, on average the OTP re-ceives 520 communications a year, more than 70% of which are deemed manifestly ill-founded, and only a handful warrant further analysis (44 in 2014; 42 in 2015; and 28 in 2016). For further reading see 2016 preliminary examination report, see *supra* note 21, pa-ra. 18; OTP, *Report on Preliminary Examination Activities*, 12 November 2015, para. 18 (http://www.legal-tools.org/doc/ac0ed2/); *idem*, *Report on Preliminary Examination Ac-tivities*, 2 December 2014, para. 18, (http://www.legal-tools.org/doc/3594b3/). See Ambos and Stegmiller, *supra* note 19, p. 422 (noting that "only when the number of communica-tions on potential situations increased, a policy with regard to preliminary examinations became a matter of urgency").

In addition to self-regulation, as we have already discussed, the PTC affords a complementary layer of external oversight over the work of the Prosecutor at a number of limited, but nonetheless crucial, junctures throughout specific preliminary examination review processes. The jurisprudence of the Chamber, in a few key decisions, offers further clarity as to the regulatory framework that governs the Prosecutor's assessment of situations. Further, such rulings play a role in conveying to the OTP the Court's level of comfort regarding certain prosecutorial decisions actions, and policies. Self-regulation and judicial review, which together are currently the only substantive control mechanisms at the preliminary examination stage, will be analysed in this section to determine their effectiveness in ensuring quality control over prosecutorial discretion.

19.3.1. Self-Regulation ('Office Common Law')

Under Rule 9 of the Rules of Procedure and Evidence, the Prosecutor is required to put in place "regulations to govern the operation of the Office".[50] In line with this requirement, at a very early stage (June 2003), the OTP issued a comprehensive draft of regulations that included an in-depth discussion on the values, principles, and structures that should govern the preliminary examination stage.[51] On 5 September 2003, the Prosecutor adopted *ad interim* an abridged version of the draft regulations.[52] Howev-

---

[50] See Rules of Procedure and Evidence, *supra note* 23, Rule 9.

[51] OTP, Draft Regulations of the Office of the Prosecutor (annotated) (3 June 2003), Part 2: The Management of Preliminary Examination, Article 53(1) Evaluation, and Start of Investigation, pp. 14–20 (amongst other things the draft sets three values and principles that must be met at the Preliminary Examination stage: "(a) ensure the efficient and timely implementation of preliminary examinations and evaluations; (b) establish a transparent and rational decision making process during preliminary examinations and evaluations that guarantees accurate, reasonable and consistent results; (c) enable the Chief Prosecutor to base his decision of whether to start an investigation on a reliable basis, both factually and legally". The draft additionally establishes a log of Article 15 preliminary examinations and Article 53 evaluations, and the designation of Article 15 communications and preliminary examinations by the Deputy Prosecutor (Investigations) to teams within the OTP. The Draft also included a process whereby reports are to be handed to the Deputy Prosecutors, and the way in which decisions on whether a reasonable basis to proceed with an investigation are to be made. Finally, the Draft introduced the concept of a "draft investigative plan" which, together with a recommendation, should form the basis of an application by the OTP to the PTC for opening an investigation *proprio motu*).

[52] For a complete history of the development of the draft regulations, see Carlos Vasconcelos, "Draft Regulations of the Office of the Prosecutor", in Morten Bergsmo *et al.* (eds.), *Historical Origins of International Criminal Law: Volume 5*, Torkel Opsahl Academic EPub-

er, it took more than six years for a limited version of those guidelines –
excluding most, if not all, of the substantive policies relating to preliminary examinations – to be formally adopted.[53]

The importance of prosecutors developing internal policies has been
reflected, for example, in the 1990 UN "Guidelines on the Role of Prosecutors". While this document is aimed at domestic public prosecutors, it
nonetheless offers "standards and principles which are generally recognized internationally as necessary for the proper and independent prosecution of offenses".[54] Article 17 of the UN Guidelines, titled "Discretionary
Powers", confirms that:

> In countries where prosecutors are vested with discretionary
> functions, the law or published rules or regulations shall pro-
> vide guidelines to enhance fairness and consistency of ap-
> proach in taking decisions in the prosecution process, includ-
> ing institution or waiver of prosecution.[55]

---

lisher, Brussels, 2017, pp. 801-824 (http://www.toaep.org/ps-pdf/24-bergsmo-rackwitz-
song).

[53] Regulations of the Office of the Prosecutor, ICC-BD/05-01-09, 23 April 2009, Section 3:
Preliminary Examination and Evaluation of Information (http://www.legal-tools.org/doc/
a97226/) (these regulations adopt most of the language of Articles 15 and 53 as they are,
offering little additional information as to OTP policies at the Preliminary Examination
stage. That said, Regulation 29 clarifies that the OTP should "produce an internal report
analyzing the seriousness of the information, considering the factors set out in Article
53(1), and offering a recommendation on whether there is reasonable basis in opening an
investigation").

[54] UN Office of the High Commissioner for Human Rights, "Guidelines on the Role of Prosecutors", adopted by the Eighth United Nations Congress on the Prevention of Crime and
the Treatment of Offenders, Havana, Cuba (September 1990), Article 1.3(d)
(http://www.legal-tools.org/doc/15b063/).

[55] *Ibid.*, at Article 17. See further, United Nations Office of Drugs and Crime and International Association of Prosecutors, "The Status and role of Prosecutors: A Guide (2014)", p.
17 (noting that "there are tangible benefits in having established policies and guidelines in
prosecution services for all to follow in the performance of their duties. Many prosecution
services worldwide have established guidelines for many aspects of a prosecutor's practice,
some of them being annotated with recent case law, thus providing a legal backdrop for the
policy and allowing prosecutors to take direction from the law. The guidelines (often also
known as "policy manuals", "desk books" or "codes") provide both prosecutors and man-
agers with a quick reference to common questions that arise during the daily practice of
their profession and allow for quick reference and consistent responses to those queries
within the prosecution service and outside it. Making reference to a manual can provide
not only direction to the individual prosecutor but also protection from accusations of arbitrary conduct if a decision to pursue or not pursue a certain course of action is challenged

It is indeed a common feature across legal jurisdictions that most prosecutorial discretionary decisions "follow a sort of office common law, that is, habits and patterns of disposition that treat like cases alike".[56] Establishing mandatory structures, procedural hoops, and internal frameworks is a necessary step, since it serves as a compass in the organic evolution of prosecutorial habits, and ensures greater predictability and objectivity in the overall work of the OTP. Looking at both the June 2003 Draft Regulations and the September 2003 paper on "Some Policy Issues before the Office of the Prosecutor" with its accompanying annex on referrals and communications,[57] it is clear that the Court's first prosecutor, Louis Moreno-Ocampo, was receptive to the calls for the Prosecutor to adopt a "public articulation of prosecutorial guidelines that will shape and constrain his discretionary decisions".[58]

However, and intriguingly, despite the fact that Ocampo welcomed the development of internal regulations and policies on preliminary examinations, he insisted that the work products of those processes remain confidential. For example, the Draft Regulations established both logging procedures of preliminary examinations by the Deputy Prosecutor for Investigations, and reporting procedures by OTP-designated preliminary examination teams. Under Ocampo's guidelines, both the logs and the progress reports – including the final 'draft investigative plan' incorporating the recommendation as to whether to open an investigation – were to be treated as confidential internal materials not subject to disclosure.[59] At

---

at a future date. Reference to how the guidelines guided their decisions can provide an articulable, legally sound response to any challenges that may arise and further promotes transparency in the decision-making process") (http://www.legal-tools.org/doc/f782ce/).

[56] Bibas, see *supra* note 13, p. 373.

[57] See *supra* note 26.

[58] Danner, see *supra* note 13, p. 511.

[59] Draft Regulations, see *supra* note 51, Part 2, Regulation 3 ("the Deputy Prosecutor (Investigations) shall keep a Log of all Article 15 preliminary examinations conducted (Preliminary Examinations Log). The Log shall be considered an internal document prepared by the Office of the Prosecutor in connection with the investigation or presentation of a case as specified by rule 81(1) of the Rules of Procedure and Evidence, and not be subject to disclosure"); Regulation 8 ("The Deputy Prosecutor (Investigations) shall keep a Log of all Article 53(1) evaluations conducted. The Log shall be considered an internal document prepared by the Office of the Prosecutor in connection with the investigation or presentation of a case as specified by rule 81(1) of the Rules of Procedure and Evidence, and not be subject to disclosure."); and Regulation 6 ("The report prepared by the Preliminary Exam-

---

most, the Guidelines established that teams engaged in preliminary examination analysis could provide the Prosecutor with "a recommendation" as
to how to "explain and communicate" a decision not to open an investigation "to the general public".[60] So in essence, early-term Ocampo laid the
foundations for prosecutorial decision-making at the ICC, by introducing
the 'black box', as Stephanos Bibas defined it,[61] and providing the general
public with a glimpse of the box's contours. It was left for Ocampo at the
end of his tenure, and more pressingly for his successor Bensouda, to
open this black box, inviting the public to look inside.[62] This is of course a
welcome development, as Bibas explains:

> Opening the black box can help to make prosecutors' deci-
> sions more legitimate in the eyes of the public as well as fer-
> ret out suspicious patterns that might reflect bias or sloth.
> Opening the black box would also invite more public input,
> helping to refine patterns of discretion to better track the
> public's shared sense of justice. The shared sense of justice is
> contextual, so this process of refining discretion can make
> justice more reasoned and reasonable than any set of rules
> alone could.[63]

The 'opening of the black box' and the increase in transparency regarding the preliminary examination process did not happen spontaneous-
ly – it was a slow, gradual process whereby the policies of the OTP ma-

---

ination Team and the draft investigation plan shall be considered internal documents prepared by the Office of the Prosecutor in connection with the investigation or presentation
of a case as specified by rule 81(1) of the Rules of Procedure and Evidence, and not be
subject to disclosure").

60 *Ibid.* at Part 2, Rule 11.2.

61 Bibas, see *supra* note 13, at 373 ("even though outsiders see only a black box with no
evident law, insiders recognise norms and customs that yield predictable results").

62 One example of this could be the publicity of preliminary examinations. As Seils write:
"during the first two years of operations, the OTP indicated that it would not make public
which situations were under preliminary examination. This practice was reversed in 2007".
Paul F. Seils, "Making Complementarity Work: Maximizing the Limited Role of the Prosecutor", in Stahn *et al.* (eds.), *The International Criminal Court and Complementarity:
From Theory to Practice*, Cambridge University Press, Cambridge, 2011.

63 *Ibid.* See also Staphanos Bibas, "Transparency and Participation in Criminal Procedure",
New York University Law Review, vol. 81, no. 3, 2006, p. 911, pp. 947–948 ("for criminal
punishment to communicate consistently and effectively, criminal procedure must be
transparent. Other-wise, current and prospective criminals, victims, and the public do not
see justice done or hear the law's message").

tured, its statements to the public increased, and its inclination towards greater elaboration of the reasoning behind its decisions became more profound and inherent. This is what has led William Schabas to conclude that the OTP has exemplified "an impressive and unprecedented degree of transparency, at least by comparison with the equivalent bodies in the *ad hoc* tribunals".[64] Current examples of transparency at the preliminary examination stage abound and include the OTP Policy Paper on Preliminary Examinations, annual reports on the status of ongoing preliminary examinations, detailed analysis of decisions to terminate preliminary examinations, reporting to the UNSC and the ASP, and additional statements and engagements (both in official and non-official capacities) by high-level OTP personnel.[65] Each of these examples deserves individual consideration.

19.3.1.1. Policy Paper on Preliminary Examinations

As we have already seen, since its inception, the OTP has been engaged in a process with the goal of developing and advancing its internal policies and guidelines on how to conduct preliminary examinations. Some of these policies, like the June 2006 "Criteria for Selection of Situations and Cases" draft policy paper, were even circulated for comments among external experts and NGOs.[66] Nonetheless, until November 2013, the OTP operated without a public, official and finalized document detailing the

---

[64] William A. Schabas, *An Introduction to the International Criminal Court*, Cambridge University Press, Cambridge, 5th edition, 2017, p. 372.

[65] It is important to note that other policy papers by the OTP may reference preliminary examinations. For example, the November 2016 Policy on Children devoted a section to preliminary examinations. Nonetheless, the Prosecutor seems to merely re-echo positions raised in the Policy Paper on Preliminary Examination, rather than establishing new policies or changing course on existing guidelines. See OTP, *Policy on Children*, November 2016 (http://www.legal-tools.org/doc/c2652b/).

[66] See Human Rights Watch, "The Selection of Situations and Cases for Trial before the International Criminal Court: HRW Policy Paper", 26 October 2006 (http://www.legal-tools.org/doc/753e9b/); Ambos and Stegmiller, see *supra* note 19, p. 422 ("In October 2010 the OTP published a Draft Policy Paper on preliminary examinations which was widely circulated and invited critical commentary. This Preliminary Examinations Paper is largely based on an earlier (internal) draft paper on situation and case selection of 2006, which was also circulated, albeit not that widely, for comments among (external) experts.").

legal interpretations employed by the OTP over the course of its preliminary examination determinations.[67]

The release of the final policy paper in 2013 reflected a strong interest by Prosecutor Bensouda in the enhancement of the legitimacy of the
Court by formulating "standardized, clear, transparent, and predictable
working methods".[68] This helped distinguish between Bensouda and her
predecessor, under the direction of whom the OTP faced extensive criticism "for failing to be sufficiently transparent in its decision-making processes".[69] The preliminary examination Policy Paper set forth further
transparency-increasing policies, including: OTP yearly reports on preliminary examinations, early interaction with stakeholders, information on
high-level visits, and the publication of situation-specific reports (both in
cases where a decision to open an investigation or close a situation is
made, and for ongoing preliminary examinations, providing the public
with an interim analysis of specific topics, such as jurisdiction or admissibility).[70]

On the other hand, the Policy Paper raises certain concerns. One element of the Policy Paper worth noting is its distinction between 'general
principles' and 'policy objectives'. The former includes independence,
impartiality, and objectivity, which serve as three 'overarching principles'
that guide the preliminary examination stage. Missing from that list is the
principle of transparency, which is only introduced at the end of the Paper
as a 'policy objective'. The OTP thus connects transparency with the other
stated 'policy objectives' of positive complementarity and prevention of

---

[67] This document saw an early draft edition being circulated in October 2010, with the continuous delays being explained by the need for a robust consultative process with 'partners'. See Thomas Obel Hansen, "The Policy Paper on Preliminary Examinations: Ending
Impunity through 'Positive Complementarity'?", p. 3 (on file with the author). As Hansen
details there, criticism has been raised about the slow pace at which these policy briefs
have been produced.

[68] Fatou Bensouda, "Reflections from the International Criminal Court Prosecutor", in *Case
Western Reserve Journal of International Law*, vol. 45, 2012, p. 506.

[69] *Ibid.*, p. 1.

[70] See also OTP, *Strategic Plan 2016-2018*, 6 July 2015, para. 54 ("to promote a better understanding of the process, correct possible misperceptions and increase predictability, the
Office will continue to provide information on its preliminary examination activities
through, amongst others, the publication of a yearly overview report and related press release, the issuance of situation-specific reports or statements, and where appropriate, undertaking field activities") (http://www.legal-tools.org/doc/7ae957/).

crimes. In essence, what the OTP is acknowledging is that it is not being transparent for the sake of transparency, but rather that it will utilize disclosures when it deems necessary, as a tool to advance other policy objectives.[71] Transparency, in the eyes of the OTP, is a means, not an end.

Moreover, the OTP uses the following terminology when describing its policy objectives. On positive complementarity, the OTP writes:

> The nature of the Office's efforts towards encouraging genuine national proceedings will be dependent on the prevailing circumstances. The Office will engage with national jurisdictions provided that it does not risk tainting any possible future admissibility proceedings. Nonetheless, the Office can report on its monitoring activities, send in-country missions, request information on proceedings, hold consultations with national authorities as well as with intergovernmental and non-governmental organisations, participate in awareness-raising activities on the ICC, exchange lessons learned and best practices to support domestic investigative and prosecutorial strategies, and assist relevant stakeholders to identify pending impunity gaps and the scope for possible remedial measures.[72]

On the topic of crime prevention, the OTP notes:

> The Office will seek to perform an early warning function. For this purpose, it will systematically and proactively collect open source information on alleged crimes that appear to fall within the jurisdiction of the Court.
>
> This will allow the Office to react promptly to upsurges of violence by reinforcing early interaction with States, international organisations and non-governmental organisations in order to verify information on alleged crimes, to encourage genuine national proceedings and to prevent reoccurrence of crimes.
>
> The Office may also issue public, preventive statements in order to deter the escalation of violence and the further

---

[71] Thus, for example, the OTP "generally makes all preliminary examinations public, except for those that are in Phase I. A situation in Phase 1 may be made public when there is considerable interest, or if the Office receives many inquiries", see Stahn, see *supra* note 6, p. 13.

[72] OTP, *Policy Paper on Preliminary Examinations*, see *supra* note 7, para. 102.

commission of crimes, to put perpetrators on notice, and to
promote national proceedings [...].[73]

In essence, the Policy Paper reaffirms the view that the preliminary
examination stage, from the perspective of the OTP, is not centred on the
prompt conclusion of the examination as to whether a full investigation
should be opened. The OTP has grown to realize that it is in fact most
effective when it positions situations in the preliminary examination's
figurative parking lot.[74] Once placed there, the OTP is free to actively
monitor ongoing political developments, relying on the "shadow of the
Court",[75] and the threat of an investigation. The fact that it is not yet
committed to specific cases against individual perpetrators further allows
the OTP to exert its influence equally on all parties to a situation. Coupled
with the fact that "there are no timelines provided in the Statute for bringing a preliminary examination to a close",[76] the OTP is empowered to
engage in this leverage strategy, which Stahn coins the 'consequentialist
approach', for extensive periods.[77] At the preliminary examination stage,

---

[73] *Ibid.*, paras. 104–06.

[74] Kersten used a culinary analogy to describe the phenomenon, noting that of the Court's
"long-lasting examinations like Afghanistan and Colombia, it has often been said that they
are left on the 'low-heat' of preliminary examination status as a means for the Court to be
able to say it is interested and active in those situations and not because it actually is". See
Mark Kersten, "How Long Can the ICC Keep Palestine and Israel in Purgatory?", in *Justice in Conflict*, 29 February 2016.

[75] See, for example, "We Should at All Costs Prevent the ICC from Being Politicised",
Vereinte Nationen, German Review of the United Nations, vol. 62, no. 1, 2014 (where
Prosecutor Bensouda explains: "over time, as the ICC encourages national systems to develop their national jurisdiction and their capacity to try these crimes, people will recognise that the fewer cases we have, the more successful the Court is. "Success" for the ICC
should not be gauged by the number of cases we have. Success will be gauged by the deterrent effect of the shadow of the Court in preventing crimes; and by the increase in capacity and ability of national jurisdictions to investigate and prosecute their own crimes.
Then the ICC's role will have been fulfilled"); see also, James Verini, "The Prosecutor and
the President", 22 June 2016, in *The New York Times* (Ocampo takes a similar position to
that of Bensouda, as the author describes – Ocampo believed in the pre-emptive power of
prosecution – "the shadow of the court", as he liked to call it. In his inaugural address at
The Hague, Moreno-Ocampo said the Court's success would be measured not by how
many cases it tried but by how few).

[76] *Ibid.*, para. 14.

[77] Stahn, see *supra* note 6, pp. 5–6

---

the OTP becomes in essence a hybrid human rights monitoring body and a fact-finding mission with a forceful whip.[78]

However, as Human Rights Watch has criticized: "using preliminary examinations to influence national authorities or potential violators is no easy task and requires a careful balancing act. While the fact that a situation may come before the ICC initially provides an incentive for authorities to stop crimes or to start their own investigations, that leverage is likely to wane with the passage of time".[79] Some scholars go even further, claiming that there is no empirical evidence to support the proposition that the consequentialist approach is at all effective in achieving the Court's agenda.[80] Stahn summarizes:

> One of the most forceful critiques of the consequentialist approach is the uncertainty regarding the desired effects. The use of preliminary examination as leverage for 'positive complementarity' may trigger unintended political effects: a risk of derailing peace negotiations, rising victim expectations, or 'mimicking' of ICC processes at the national level. Existing experiences show that ICC engagement has promoted complementarity in countries with a strong rule of law culture. It has been less effective in fragile environments. One lesson is that the side effects must be analysed better. The ICC should not open a preliminary examination merely for the purpose of promoting rationales, such as complemen-

---

[78] *Ibid.*, p. 13 ("The OTP has developed the practice of developing annual reports. They are in some respects comparable to country monitoring under human rights mechanisms"), but cf. p. 2 ("ICC preliminary examinations differ partly from human rights documentation by NGOs and fact-finding bodies. They are part of the justice process and address violations specifically through the lens of individual criminal responsibility").

[79] Human Rights Watch, "ICC: Course Correction", see *supra* note 28.

[80] Seils, see *supra* note 55, p. 998 (as he writes, there is no evidence that publicizing preliminary examinations has "made a difference" in the context of increasing positive complementarity); Geoff Dancy and Florencia Montal, "Unintended Positive Complementarity: Why International Criminal Court Investigations May Increase Domestic Human Rights Prosecutions", *American Journal of International Law*, forthcoming, 2017, pp. 13, 17 ("We contend that the launch of a formal ICC investigation of a particular country is associated with a spike in domestic prosecutions for all human rights violations, and further, that this effect is larger than the impact of the target state's ratification of the Rome Statute or the Prosecutor's decision to begin a preliminary examination. [...] Preliminary examinations do not carry costs as high for states, since the Court in this phase is mainly limited to an information collection and assessment role").

tarity or deterrence. In certain contexts, the rationales of pre-vention may require respect for peace processes. Using pre-liminary examination as a catalyst for other rationales re-quires a deeper commitment to in-depth situational analysis over time.[81]

19.3.1.2. Public Reporting on Preliminary Examinations

Beginning 13 December 2011,[82] the OTP has annually released reports to the public, summarizing the activities conducted during the reported year for each of the preliminary examinations under review.[83] Interestingly, the length of the reports has been increasing (25 pages in 2011, 63 in 2014, 73 in 2017). The increase in length is not anecdotal, nor is it a mere reflection of the rise in the number of preliminary examinations over the course of those years. It is evidence of the current Prosecutor's motivation to effec-tively disseminate information concerning its monitoring operations and assessments to the general public. It is also a reflection of the significant investment of OTP resources into this reporting. Despite the addition of content and information, in the six years since the first report the format has remained largely the same. These reports consist of an introduction to preliminary examination activities, and a review of each of the situations before the OTP, including examinations that were concluded during the relevant year, organized by phase.

The reports of the OTP serve as a pressure relief valve, providing critics with proof that the OTP remains active. This is done by voluntarily providing information regarding both the factual and legal narratives as they emerge from the assessment, while keeping the situations parked at the preliminary examination stage. Reviewing the reports shows that the OTP adopts an expansive definition of 'situation' at this stage, allowing it to expand its monitoring to cover all alleged crimes potentially surround-

---

[81] Stahn, see *supra* note 6, p. 13.

[82] Incidentally, this was the day after the election of Fatou Bensouda as Prosecutor.

[83] Throughout almost all of Ocampo's tenure as Prosecutor there was no significant reporting on ongoing preliminary examinations, *let alone* an annual report. In 2006, a single report was published on the activities which were performed during the first three years in opera-tion of the OTP. Preliminary examinations were discussed only briefly in this report, chief-ly concerning the importance of gravity when making decisions on case selection (see OTP, *Report on the activities performed during the first three years (June 2003 - June 2006)* (http://www.legal-tools.org/doc/c7a850/)).

ing a particular conflict or tension hotspot.[84] Moreover, knowing that all concerned parties carefully read these reports, statements made in their framework allow the Prosecutor to signal to States its views on certain political developments, in the hopes of guiding their behaviour.[85] The affected States, let alone potential defendants, have very little recourse at this stage to challenge factual or legal characterizations made by the Prosecutor as part of her monitoring. These examples thus indicate that, at the preliminary examination phase, "the balance between prosecutorial discretion and the rights of the defense leans the most toward discretion".[86]

19.3.1.3. Termination of Preliminary Examinations Reports

Another means by which the OTP has increased transparency relates to notification and publication of the reasoning surrounding the termination of preliminary examinations. The first decision to terminate an ongoing preliminary examination came in 2006 and concerned alleged crimes against humanity by the Government of Venezuela, targeting political opponents. The decision issued by the OTP, headed by then Prosecutor Ocampo, consisted of a short five-page letter, signed by Ocampo and mailed to those who submitted the communication to the Court under Ar-

---

[84] Consider, for example, the expansion of the preliminary examination regarding the Situation in Afghanistan to cover CIA operations in Poland, Romania and Lithuania. See 2016 Preliminary Examination Report, see *supra* note 21, para. 199 ("In addition, a limited number of alleged crimes associated with the Afghan armed conflict are alleged to have been committed on the territories of Poland, Lithuania and Romania, which are parties to the Statute. This is because individuals captured in the context of the armed conflict in Afghanistan, such as presumed members of the Taliban or Al Qaeda, were allegedly transferred to detention centres located in those countries.").

[85] Consider, for example, the comments of the OTP regarding the recent political appointments and election results in Guinea as part of the 2016 Preliminary Examination Report, *ibid.*, paras. 272, 276 ("in this context, the reappointment of Me Cheick Sako in the position of Minister of Justice signals the continued support of the authorities for the investigation carried out by the Guinean panel of judges [...] the Office notes that the appointment in March 2016 of General Mathurin Bangoura, former member of the CNDD indicted in 2015, as Governor of Conakry was perceived by victims and civil society organisations as a troubling signal in the context of Guinean authorities' stated intention to bring to justice the persons allegedly involved in the 28 September case").

[86] Carsten Stahn and Dov Jacobs, "The Interaction between Human Rights Fact-Finding and International Criminal Proceedings", in Phillip Alston *et al.* (eds.), *The Transformation of Human Rights Fact-Finding*, Oxford University Press, Oxford, 2016.

---

ticle 15.[87] The letter notes that the OTP conducted a "crime analysis", which included "preparation of tables of allegations and pattern analysis" as well as "legal research and analysis of the main doctrinal issues".[88] The letter was eventually published online, but no public statement or press release was ever produced to accompany it.

This decision is a stark contrast to the one published by the OTP, led by the present Prosecutor, when the preliminary examination into Honduras was terminated. In that case, the Prosecutor made a general public statement on 28 October 2015,[89] which was immediately followed by a three-day country visit "to announce and explain in detail the conclusions reached by the OTP to Honduran authorities and civil society organisations".[90] The OTP produced a 49-page analysis of the legal issues surrounding its decision, focusing on subject-matter jurisdiction.[91] Additionally, a two-page Questions and Answers document was published in both English and Spanish to facilitate broader dissemination.[92] Finally, the decision was included in the November 2015 preliminary examination report of the OTP.[93] A similar approach was taken by the Prosecutor in the termination decision regarding the situation in the Republic of Korea.[94] In

---

[87]   OTP, "Response to Communications Received Concerning Venezuela", 9 February 2006 (http://www.legal-tools.org/doc/c90d25/). The Court took the same approach in its response in Iraq which was issued the same day and consisted of a ten-page letter. OTP, "Response to Communications Received Concerning Iraq", 9 February 2006 (http://www.legal-tools.org/doc/5b8996/).

[88]   *Ibid.*, p. 2.

[89]   Office of the Prosecutor, "Statement of the Prosecutor of the International Criminal Court, Fatou Bensouda, on the conclusion of the preliminary examination into the situation in Honduras", 28 October 2015 (http://www.legal-tools.org/doc/1d09c8/).

[90]   See *2015 Preliminary Examination Report*, see *supra* note 49, para. 287.

[91]   OTP, *Situation in Honduras: Article 5 Report*, October 2015 (http://www.legal-tools.org/doc/54755a/).

[92]   OTP, "On the decision of the ICC Prosecutor to close the preliminary examination in Honduras" (http://www.legal-tools.org/doc/f0035a/).

[93]   See *2015 Preliminary Examination Report*, see *supra* note 49, paras. 268–289.

[94]   On 23 June 2014 the Prosecutor made a public statement that the two maritime incidents in the Yellow Sea of 2010 did not satisfy the requirements for an initiation of an investigation (OTP, "Statement of the Prosecutor of the International Criminal Court, Fatou Bensouda, on the conclusion of the preliminary examination of the situation in the Republic of Korea", 23 June 2014 (http://www.legal-tools.org/doc/8d0a96/)). That statement was immediately followed by a 24-page report summarizing the complete legal analysis of the subject-matter jurisdiction, on the basis of which its termination decision was made (OTP, *Situa-*

other words, the OTP has reinterpreted its obligations under Article 15(6) and Rule 105 and committed itself to far broader obligations of notification, transparency, and reasoning.

The very act of giving a public reason for the conclusions of a preliminary examination creates a powerful mechanism of control.[95] Providing a robust legal analysis and argumentation forces the Prosecutor not only to justify its interpretation and logic through the Statute's terminology, but more importantly it sets a principle and a precedent to be relied on in the future (both internally within the OTP, and externally by critics). These are all positive developments. However, there is a fly in the ointment. Recognizing the power of the Prosecutor to produce this detailed legal analysis, which is not subject to adversarial scrutiny or judicial review, risks the development of 'prosecutorial adjudication' at the ICC. The term, first coined by Lynch, involves a situation whereby the Prosecutor becomes a "central adjudicator of facts (as well as replacing the judge as arbiter of most legal issues [...])".[96] In the context of international crimes, the Prosecutor additionally becomes the final authority in establishing the pseudo-legal, pseudo-political narrative surrounding the situation under review. This is especially important in cases where the preliminary examination was not launched on the basis of a State referral, and even more so in situations involving non-members of the Rome Statute. In those instances, the relevant countries might be relieved to learn that an investigation will not ensue, but at the same time they are offered no means to challenge any characterizations made by the Prosecutor,[97] which

---

tion in Republic of Korea: Article 5 Report, June 2014 (http://www.legal-tools.org/doc/ef1f7f/)). The decision was also reported in *2014 Preliminary Examination Report*, see *supra* note 49, paras. 218–245.

[95] David Moshaman, "Reasoning as Self-Constrained Thinking", *Human Development*, vol. 38, no. 1, 1995, p. 53 ("reasoning is best construed as a form of thinking in which the thinker purposely constrains processing of information in an effort to realise the epistemic advantages of making justifiable inferences").

[96] Gerard E. Lynch, "Screening Versus Plea Bargaining: Exactly What Are We Trading Off?", in *Stanford Law Review*, vol. 55, no. 4, 2003, pp. 1403–04.

[97] Note further that in accordance with the policies of the OTP "before making a determination on whether to initiate an investigation, the Office will also seek to ensure that the States and other parties concerned have had the opportunity to provide the information they consider appropriate" (2016 Preliminary Examination Report, see *supra* note 21, para. 12). However, a similar policy is not stated for decisions to close preliminary examinations,

they might not accept, and which, considering the Court's standing, will ultimately be instrumental in framing the political memory and legal reality concerning these situations in future discussion.

19.3.1.4. Press Releases and Reporting to the UNSC and the ASP

The Prosecutor and other high-ranking officials at the OTP and the Court additionally brief the UNSC (regarding situations referred to it under UNSC resolutions)[98] and the ASP.[99] These public statements may place additional constraints upon the work of the OTP by forcing it to answer to other institutions. At the same time, however, it gives an opportunity for the Prosecutor to continue the game of political signalling by openly speaking about ongoing preliminary examinations. One recent example is the May 2017 statement by the Prosecutor made during a routine briefing to the UNSC on the situation in Libya: "I take this opportunity before the council to declare that my office is carefully examining the feasibility of opening an investigation into migrant-related crimes in Libya should the court's jurisdictional requirements be met".[100] This statement further demonstrates how the OTP uses its innate discretion during the preliminary examination stage to expand the reach of situations it reviews to cover as much international activity as possible (including the most hotly contested contemporary human rights abuses, regardless of their immediate connection to the situation under review), thus enabling it to monitor and influence them from within, and thereby win political capital.

---

and even if it did, there is surely no requirement to reflect the States' and other parties' positions in the final termination report.

[98] See, for example, OTP, *Twelfth Report of the Prosecutor of the International Criminal Court to the United Nations Security Council pursuant to UNSCR 1970 (2011)* (http://www.legal-tools.org/doc/461c14/); OTP, "Statement of ICC Prosecutor to the UNSC on the Situation in Libya, pursuant to UNSCR 1970 (2011)", 9 November 2016 (http://www.legal-tools.org/doc/f093e8/).

[99] See, for example, OTP, "Mrs. Fatou Bensouda, Prosecutor of the International Criminal Court, Address at the First Plenary, Fifteenth Session of the Assembly of States Parties", 16 November 2016 (noting that "beyond increasing the quality of our preliminary examinations, investigations and prosecutions, one of the main goals of my tenure as Prosecutor is to strengthen trust and respect for the Office by ensuring further transparency and predictability in our operations") (http://www.legal-tools.org/doc/4f0ecf/).

[100] OTP, "Statement of ICC Prosecutor to the UNSC on the Situation in Libya, pursuant to UNSCR 1970 (2011)", 8 May 2017, para. 29 (http://www.legal-tools.org/doc/a943f7/).

It is further a common feature in the Office's work for the Prosecutor to issue press releases at times of deteriorating security situations, reminding all parties to the conflict that the OTP is watching.[101] Some of these press releases are issued as part of a field mission, an area of activity not originally provided for under Article 15, but one nonetheless undertaken by both Prosecutors.[102] The OTP additionally engages in other forms of outward communication including academic writing, interviews, and lectures.[103]

19.3.2. Judicial Review by the PTC

The drafters' conceptualization of the relationship between the OTP and the PTC did not materialize. As we have seen, the system of checks and balances which they created follows the notion of an over-zealous Prosecutor eager to launch investigations, constrained by an active PTC pro-

---

[101] See, for example, OTP, "Statement of the Prosecutor of the International Criminal Court, Mrs. Fatou Bensouda, following growing tensions reported in Guinea", 14 October 2015 ("As part of its ongoing preliminary examination, my Office has been closely following developments in the situation in Guinea, including as they relate to the risk of possible violence leading to crimes falling under the jurisdiction of the International Criminal Court. [...] I would like to reiterate my call for calm and restraint to all political actors, and their supporters. I wish to reiterate that anyone who commits, orders, incites, encourages or contributes in any other way to the commission of atrocity crimes falling within the jurisdiction of the ICC is liable to prosecution either in Guinea or at the Court in The Hague") (http://www.legal-tools.org/doc/10190c/); OTP, "Statement of the Prosecutor of the International Criminal Court, Fatou Bensouda, regarding the worsening security situation in Burundi", 6 November 2015 ("I recall that any person in Burundi who incites or engages in acts of mass violence including by ordering, requesting, encouraging or contributing in any other manner to the commission of crimes falling within the jurisdiction of the International Criminal Court ("ICC" or "Court") is liable to prosecution before this Court. Should any conduct in Burundi – whether by the Security Forces, militias or any armed group – amount to war crimes, crimes against humanity, or genocide, no-one should doubt my resolve to fulfill my mandate so that the perpetrators do not go unpunished") (http://www.legal-tools.org/doc/65d51f/).

[102] See, for example, OTP, "Statement by the Prosecutor of the International Criminal Court, Fatou Bensouda, on her Office's mission to the Democratic Republic of the Congo from 16 to 20 October 2016" (http://www.legal-tools.org/doc/c374e0/).

[103] See, for example, Bensouda, see *supra* note 9; Fatou Bensouda, "The Office of the Prosecutor of the International Criminal Court: Successes, Challenges and the Promise of International Criminal Justice", UN Audiovisual Library of International Law (available on its web site); Mark Kersten, "A Test of Our Resilience – An Interview with the ICC Deputy Prosecutor", in *Justice in Conflict*, 10 August 2016.

---

tecting the Court's legitimacy through fighting against politicization.[104] The reality is reversed. The Prosecutor is in no rush to conclude preliminary examinations and proceed to investigations, and the PTC is criticized by its own judges as being in danger of becoming "a mere rubber-stamping instance",[105] likely to "automatically [agree] with what the Prosecutor presents".[106] The PTC has adopted, for example, an approach

---

[104] See *supra* note 32. See also Situation in the Republic of Kenya, Decision Pursuant to Article 15 of the Rome Statute, see *supra* note 34, para. 32 (noting that the goal of PTC review is "to prevent the Court from proceeding with unwarranted, frivolous, or politically motivated investigations that could have a negative effect on its credibility"). Situation in Georgia, Pre-Trial Chamber I, Decision on the Prosecutor's Request for Authorization of an Investigation, 27 January 2016, ICC-01/05, Separate Opinion of Judge Péter Kovács, para. 9 (noting that "[a]ccording to my recollection, when the idea of providing the Prosecutor with such power in the absence of a State's complaint was first tabled by one member of the International Law Commission ("ILC") in the course of preparing the 1994 Draft Statute for an International Criminal Court (the "1994 ILC Draft"), there was a clear resistance by the ILC working group members, as they thought that the international community was not ready to provide a free hand to a world Prosecutor").

[105] Situation in the Republic of Kenya, Decision Pursuant to Article 15, see *supra* note 34, Dissenting Opinion of Judge Hans-Peter Kaul, para. 19.

[106] Situation in Georgia Decision on the Prosecutor's Request for Authorization of an Investigation, Separate Opinion of Judge Kovács, see *supra* note 104, paras. 6, 11:

I consider that "judicial control", be it at the article 15 stage or a subsequent stage of the proceedings, is not an empty term. Judicial control entails more than automatically agreeing with what the Prosecutor presents. It calls for "an independent judicial inquiry" of the material presented as well as the findings of the Prosecutor that there is a reasonable basis to proceed with the opening of an investigation. This process requires a full and proper examination of the supporting material relied upon by the Prosecutor for the purpose of satisfying the elements of article 15(4) in conjunction with article 53(1)(a)-(c) of the Statute, as well as the victims' representations, which are referred to in article 15(3) of the Statute. To say otherwise means that the Pre-Trial Chamber will not be exercising what the Majority describes as "judicial control". Nor will the Pre-Trial Chamber be acting in a manner which can prevent the abuse of power on the part of the Prosecutor. [...] The degree of seriousness of the Pre-Trial Chamber's examination should not depend on the stage of the proceedings as the Majority Decision suggests. Being at the early stages of the proceedings does not justify a marginal assessment. It just means that the assessment should be carried out against a low procedural standard ("reasonable basis to proceed") and a low evidentiary standard ("reasonable basis to believe") on the basis of the request, the available material and the victims' representations. Still such an assessment should be carried out thoroughly and the decision should demonstrate the thoroughness of the assessment conducted by the Chamber.

whereby its examination of Article 15 requests is "strictly limited".[107] As a result, all three of the Prosecutor's applications to launch investigations under Article 15 to date have been authorized by the PTC.[108] Similarly, the scope of judicial review has been the subject of contestation, even between the Pre-Trial Chambers.[109] Schabas has attempted to explain, in part, the Chamber's difficulty when attempting to conduct a robust judicial review at the preliminary examination stage (looking at the inherent disadvantage of the PTC at the preliminary examination stage, as it lacks adversarial debate):

> [T]he judicial approval of the Prosecutor's application has been relatively perfunctory [...] Nothing of [the Court's] inquiry suggests a genuine effort to come to terms with issues of 'politicization' or concerns about prosecutorial abuse. It would be difficult for them to do so given that the hearings take place *ex parte*, that is, without an opposing party. The Prosecutor can hardly be expected to provide the Court with evidence of abusive or improper intent.[110]

Moreover, the OTP adopted the policy of informing relevant State(s) prior to seeking authorization from the PTC to launch an investigation in *proprio motu* situations (with the hope that the relevant State(s) would take steps to simply refer the situation directly).[111] Essentially, despite the

---

[107] Situation in Georgia, Decision on the Prosecutor's Request for Authorization of an Investigation, *ibid.*, para. 3.

[108] Schabas, see *supra* note 64, p. 161 ("All three of the applications made by the Prosecutor have been granted by the Pre-Trial Chambers although in each decision judges have penned individual opinions indicating that there is no consensus within the Court about the function of the judicial review provided for in paragraphs 3 and 4 of Article 15").

[109] See the positions of a group of international experts convened on 29 September 2015 by the Grotius Centre for International Legal Studies and the Centre for International Law Research and Policy. Their concluding report notes: "It remains contested to what extent Article 53 review powers apply to *proprio motu* action under Article 15, what qualifies as a 'decision' of the Prosecutor 'not to proceed', triggering powers of judicial review under Article 53 (1) and (2), and to what extent such a decision must be formalised. Differences also exist between how Pre-Trial Chambers have interpreted the scope of judicial review in relation to Article 15 at the end of the preliminary examination, that is, regarding authorization to investigate ongoing and continuing crimes, or only crimes committed until the date of the filing of the request for authorization". Grotius Center Report, see *supra* note 6, para. 21.

[110] Schabas, see *supra* note 64, pp. 162–63.

[111] OTP, *Policy Paper on Preliminary Examinations*, see *supra* note 7, paras. 94–99.

Chamber's leniency in authorizing investigations, the OTP prefers to operate with as little judicial scrutiny as possible and will not shy away from utilizing loopholes in the Statute to do so.

Peculiarly, the PTC has been an active check to the powers of the OTP concerning one type of decision, when responding to attempts by the Prosecutor to delay or close ongoing preliminary examinations. When given a chance to criticize the Prosecutor for either stalling or terminating a preliminary examination, the PTC has been quick to do so.[112] In this regard, it is useful to analyse both the 2006 Central African Republic ('CAR') decision, and the 2014 decision concerning the situation on certain registered vessels of Comoros, Greece, and Cambodia.

19.3.2.1. Central African Republic

The Chamber's involvement in the situation in the CAR offers good insight into both the dynamics between the PTC and the OTP at the preliminary examination stage, and their divergent interpretations of the temporal scope of prosecutorial discretion. On 27 September 2006, almost two years after making its initial referral to the OTP under Article 14, the Government of the CAR requested the Chamber's intervention. This Re-

---

[112] In fact, this strand of activism by the PTC has been reflected at the investigation stage as well. The first decision ever made by the PTC was a February 2005 decision to convene a "Status Conference" relating to the ongoing investigation into the situation in the Democratic Republic of the Congo. The Chamber, which was frustrated by the slow nature of the investigation of the OTP, relied on a broad interpretation of a general provision contained in Article 57(3)(c) of the Statute to increase its control over the Prosecutor. This in turn led to a minor controversy in which the Prosecutor publicly rejected the purported authority of the Chamber to convene a status conference, claiming that "the system enshrined in the Statute is one where the investigation is not performed or shared with a judicial body, but rather entrusted to the prosecution [...] at the same time, the system also includes a closed number of provisions empowering the Pre-Trial Chamber to engage in specific instances of judicial supervision over the Prosecution's investigative activities. The prosecution submits that this delicate balance between both organs must be preserved at all times in order to honour the Statute, and to enable the Court to function in a fair and efficient manner" (Situation in the Democratic Republic of the Congo (ICC-01/04), Prosecutor's Position on Pre-Trial Chamber I's 17 February 2005 Decision to Convene a Status Conference, 8 March 2005, para. 3). The Pre-Trial Chamber by a ruling dismissed the Prosecutor's objections and the Statute Conference took place. For further reading see Michela Miraglia, "The First Decision of the ICC Pre-Trial Chamber: International Criminal Procedure Under Construction", *Journal of International Criminal Justice*, vol. 4, no. 1, 2006, pp. 188–95.

quest was based on the Prosecutor's alleged "failure to decide, within a reasonable time" whether or not to initiate an investigation.[113]

The PTC, in its decision, reaffirmed the right of a referring State to be informed by the Prosecutor of developments concerning a preliminary examination, and the right of the PTC to request that the Prosecutor make such information available.[114] The PTC further made reference to a series of terms used by both the Statute and the Rules constraining the temporal scope of prosecutorial discretion ("reasonable time", "without delay", "promptly", and "in an expeditious manner"). While the PTC did not interpret any of these terms directly, it did recall that "the preliminary examinations of the situations in the Democratic Republic of the Congo and Northern Uganda were completed within two to six months".[115] On the basis of this, the PTC requested that the Prosecutor issue a report no later than 15 December 2006, containing information as to the current status of the preliminary examination, including "an estimate of when the preliminary examination of the CAR situation will be concluded".[116]

The Prosecutor's response was decisive. Although it did provide the PTC and the CAR with a report detailing its activities, it clarified that it was doing so without accepting "the existence of a legal obligation to submit this type of information [...] nor adopting any precedent that it may follow in future cases".[117] As we have already discussed, that report did in fact lay the groundwork for the eventual voluntary adoption of this method of reporting in all preliminary examination situations beginning in 2011.[118]

From the Prosecutor's perspective, it was crucial to ensure that the equilibrium in the PTC-OTP relationship not be skewed. Therefore, the

---

[113] Situation in the Central African Republic, Pre-Trial Chamber I, Decision Requesting Information on the Status of the Preliminary Examination of the Situation in the Central African Republic, 30 November 2006, ICC-01/05, p. 3.

[114] *Ibid.*, pp. 4–5.

[115] *Ibid.*, p. 4.

[116] *Ibid.*, p. 5.

[117] Situation in the Central African Republic, Pre-Trial Chamber I, Prosecution's Report Pursuant to Pre-Trial Chamber III's 30 November 2006 Decision Requesting Information on the Status of the Preliminary Examination of the Situation in the Central African Republic, 15 December 2006, ICC-01/05, para. 11.

[118] See *supra* Section 19.3.1.2.

Prosecutor stated that the Chamber's supervisory role was limited to "a review of a decision under Article 53(1) and (2) by the Prosecutor not to proceed with an investigation".[119] If the OTP delays this decision, the Prosecutor stressed, "there is no exercise of prosecutorial discretion susceptible to judicial review by the Chamber".[120] Similarly, the Prosecutor refused to commit to any specific deadlines, noting that:

> [T]he OTP, while committed to reaching decisions under Article 53 (1) as expeditiously as possible, submits that no provision in the Statute or the Rules establishes a definitive time period for the purposes of the completion of the preliminary examination. The OTP submits that this was a deliberate legislative decision that provides the required flexibility to adjust the parameters of the assessment or analysis phase to the specific features of each particular situation. That choice, and the discretion that it provides, should remain undisturbed.[121]

The matter was left there, with no resolution of the objection's core issue: whether 'inaction' in the form of a delay in OTP decision-making during the preliminary examination phase (be it intentional or unintentional) constitutes an exercise of prosecutorial discretion subject to judicial review.[122]

19.3.2.2. Registered Vessels of Comoros, Greece, and Cambodia

On 6 November 2014, the OTP announced that, based on the information available to it, there was no reasonable basis to proceed with an investigation of the situation on certain registered vessels of Comoros, Greece, and Cambodia.[123] The situation, which concerned the May 2010 interception of a flotilla that left Turkey with the goal of breaking the maritime block-

---

[119] Situation in the Central African Republic, Prosecution's Report Pursuant to Pre-Trial Chamber III's 30 November 2006 Decision, see *supra* note 117, para. 1.

[120] *Ibid.*

[121] *Ibid.*, para. 10.

[122] It is worth nothing that since the voluntary adoption of greater reporting and transparency during preliminary examinations, we have not seen any further criticism by the PTC of the OTP for delaying, even in the context of prolonged preliminary examinations such the one related to the situation in Afghanistan.

[123] OTP, *Situation on Registered Vessels of Comoros, Greece and Cambodia: Article 53(1) Report*, 6 November 2014 (http://www.legal-tools.org/doc/43e636/).

ade on the Gaza strip, was referred to the OTP by the Government of the Union of Comoros on 14 May 2013.[124] Based on a detailed report issued by the Prosecutor, dealing with jurisdictional and admissibility issues, the OTP concluded that any potential cases likely to arise from an investigation into the situation would not be of sufficient gravity to justify further action by the Court, and therefore would be inadmissible pursuant to Articles 17(1)(d) and 53(1)(b).[125]

On 29 January 2015, the Representatives of the Union of Comoros filed an application for review of the Prosecutor's decision not to proceed, pursuant to Article 53(3)(a) of the Statute. The application raised two complaints. The first concerned an alleged failure by the Prosecutor to take into account other facts (a complaint the PTC later dismissed). The second concerned alleged analytical errors in the Prosecutor's assessment of gravity under Article 17(1). The PTC issued its decision on 16 July 2015, calling on the Prosecutor to reconsider her decision not to open an investigation.[126] It was the first review of its kind. The PTC identified

---

[124] This is a unique preliminary examination in the sense that in concerns a single incident, and not a full situation. After the Hamas terrorist organization seized control of the Gaza Strip in June 2007, the Government adopted various measures, including a 3 January 2009 naval blockade on the Gaza Strip. In the days preceding May 31, 2010, a flotilla of six vessels advanced towards the coastline of Israel, with approximately 700 persons on board. The largest of the ships in the flotilla, the *Mavi Marmara*, was the location of the incident that is the sole subject of the preliminary examination. On May 31, 2010, in the early hours of the morning, IDF forces boarded the Mavi Marmara and took control of the vessel. During the boarding and taking control of the ship, the IDF forces encountered violent resistance. When the conflict ended, it was found that nine of the ship's passengers had been shot dead, and fifty-five passengers and nine IDF soldiers had been wounded. The Preliminary Examination was the subject of extensive investigation concluding in two national reports (produced by both Turkey and Israel) and two international reports (produced by a fact-finding mission of the United Nations Human Rights Council and a panel of inquiry appointed by the UN Secretary-General). For further reading, see Report of the Secretary-General's Panel of Inquiry on the 31 May 2010 Flotilla Incident (http://www.legal-tools.org/doc/f2de32/).

[125] *Ibid.*, para. 150. The OTP focuses its conclusion on the limited nature of these potential cases ("considering the scale, impact and manner of the alleged crimes, the Office is of the view that the flotilla incident does not fall within the intended and envisioned scope of the Court's mandate… in the context of the current referral, it is clear that the potential case(s) that could be pursued as a result of an investigation into this situation is limited to an event encompassing a limited number of victims of the alleged ICC crimes, with limited countervailing qualitative considerations" (*ibid.*, paras. 142–44).

[126] Situation on the Registered Vessels of the Union of the Comoros, The Hellenic Republic, and the Kingdom of Cambodia, Pre-Trial Chamber I, Decision on the Request of the Union

---

errors in every aspect of the gravity analysis of the OTP, including in its consideration of potential perpetrators, the scale of the crimes, the nature of the crimes, the manner of their commission, and their impact.[127] This decision by the PTC is a troubling one, in terms of both its legal merits and its policy implications.

Within the limits of this chapter, I will not touch on the substantive legal arguments, which have been the subject of extensive criticism. It has been argued that the Judges applied a "bizarre" test for "potential perpetrators" (one which ignores the relative importance of the potential perpetrators), and moreover conflated situational gravity with case gravity in their analysis of the scale of the crimes.[128] Moreover, the majority decision called on the Prosecutor to take into consideration "the attention" that the *Mavi Marmara* incident had attracted (including "fact-finding efforts"

---

of the Comoros to Review the Prosecutor's Decision not to Initiate an Investigation, 16 July 2015, ICC-01/13, p. 26 (http://www.legal-tools.org/doc/2f876c/).

[127] *Ibid.* paras. 20–48.

[128] For a complete review see Kevin Jon Heller, "The Pre-Trial Chamber's Dangerous Comoros Review Decision", in *Opinio Juris* 17 July 2015 (noting in particular that "The PTC's approach to "potential perpetrator" gravity would thus seems to be based on a basic misunderstanding of the difference between situational and case gravity". Focusing on the argument raised by the Court that the scale of the crimes is similar to that in the case against Bahar Idriss Abu Garda and Abdallah Banda, Heller writes "here the PTC explicitly compares the gravity of the Comoros situation to the gravity of one case within a situation. The number of victims in the Comoros situation is indeed comparable to the number of victims in the JEM attack on the UN peacekeepers in Darfur. But the Abu Garda and Abdallah Banda case was one of many cases within the Darfur situation; when we compare the number of victims in the Comoros situation to the Darfur situation as a whole, it is clear that the PTC has no basis whatsoever to insist that the "scale" factor counsels in favour of finding the Comoros situation grave enough to formally investigate. The comparison is then between 10 civilian deaths and hundreds of thousands); see also Dov Jacobs, "ICC Judges ask the Prosecutor to reconsider decision not to investigate Israeli Gaza Flotilla conduct", in *Spreading the Jam*, 20 July 2015 (noting that Chamber's interpretation of the "potential perpetrators" test is at odds with the case law of Pre-Trial Chamber II in the Kenya situation); Geert-Jan Alexander Knoops and Tom Zwart, "The Flotilla Case before the ICC: The Need to Do Justice While Keeping Heaven Intact", in *International Criminal Law Review*, vol. 5, no. 6, 2015. But cf. Marco Longobardo, "Everything Is Relative, Even Gravity: Remarks on the Assessment of Gravity in ICC Preliminary Examinations, and the Mavi Marmara Affair", in *Journal of International Criminal Justice*, vol. 14, no. 4, 2016 (suggesting that the "OTP should have properly considered that the admissibility threshold at the stage of preliminary examinations is less stringent than the one embodied in Article 53(2)").

---

launched by the United Nations).[129] The Chamber's request has the potential of greatly politicizing the Court, and in any event involves the reintroduction of 'social alarm' as a gravity test (a test which was already rejected by the Appeals Chamber in 2006).[130]

Far more troubling than the debates on the merits is the Chamber's overall conceptualization of its standard for review of OTP decisions and the scope of the Prosecutor's discretion under Article 53, to which most of the following analysis is devoted. The majority decision put forward the presumption that Article 53(1)(a)–(b) involve no discretionary power, merely requiring the "application of exacting legal requirements".[131] By doing so, they sought to shift power back to them by allowing the PTC to micromanage precisely this legal application, without being branded as interfering with or infringing on prosecutorial independence. The PTC in essence sought to place itself as a second-tier prosecutor. However, the Chamber's approach may only encourage the OTP to offer less reasoning, as such detailed reporting is not required under the Statute or the Rules. If the OTP provides no robust legal analysis of its decisions, there is nothing to micromanage, and that will be a detrimental blow to transparency and predictability.

Moreover, the majority decision attempted to further narrow the scope of prosecutorial discretion by establishing an extremely low bar for launching investigations. As they wrote in their decision:

> If the information available to the Prosecutor at the pre-investigative stage allows for reasonable inferences that at least one crime within the jurisdiction of the Court has been committed and that the case would be admissible, the Prose-

---

[129] Situation on the Registered Vessels of the Union of the Comoros, The Hellenic Republic, and the Kingdom of Cambodia, Decision on the Request of the Union of the Comoros, see *supra* note 126, para. 51.

[130] Situation in the Democratic Republic of the Congo, Appeals Chamber Judgment on the Prosecutor's appeal against the decision of Pre-Trial Chamber I entitled "Decision on the Prosecutor's Application for Warrants of Arrest, Article 58", 13 July 2006, ICC-01/04 (http://www.legal-tools.org/doc/083c1a/). See also Dov Jacobs, *supra* note 128.

[131] Situation on the Registered Vessels of the Union of the Comoros, The Hellenic Republic, and the Kingdom of Cambodia, Decision on the Request of the Union of the Comoros, see *supra* note 126, para. 14.

---

cutor shall open an investigation, as only by investigating
could doubts be overcome.[132]

Adopting this model of interpretation of the preliminary examination stage completely overturns the role of the OTP as it has evolved over
the years since the Court's establishment. This approach forces the Prosecutor to adopt the position of a legal technician, not a consequentialist,
and it urges the OTP to launch more investigations in less time, as (in the
Chamber's view) those could assist in 'overcoming any doubts' about the
circumstances.[133] Judge Péter Kovács' partly dissenting opinion is telling,
as it reflects exactly the dangers of adopting the majority's approach in the
dynamic relationship between the OTP and the PTC. He writes:

> I do not believe that the Pre-Trial Chamber is called upon to
> sit as a court of appeals with respect to the Prosecutor's deci-
> sions. Rather the Pre-Trial Chamber's role is merely to make
> sure that the Prosecutor has not abused her discretion in ar-
> riving at her decision not to initiate an investigation on the
> basis of the criteria set out in article 53(1) of the Statute. This
> view calls for a more deferential approach when reviewing
> the Prosecutor's decision on the basis of the criteria set out in
> article 53(1), and is implied in the text of article 53. It pro-
> vides the Prosecutor with some margin of discretion in de-
> ciding not to initiate an investigation into a particular situa-
> tion. This interpretation is more in line with the main idea
> underlying article 53 namely, to draw a balance between the
> Prosecutor's discretion/independence and the Pre-Trial
> Chamber's supervisory role in the sense of being limited to
> only requesting the Prosecutor to reconsider her decision if
> necessary. To argue that the power of the Pre-Trial Chamber
> exceeds this point is daring. The Majority does not go in this
> direction. Instead, it preferred to conduct a stringent review,

---

[132] *Ibid.*, para. 13.

[133] A similar concern was raised by a group of international experts: "Some concerns were
expressed in relation to the consequences of the Comoros decision. It was argued that the
decision might have negative side effects on preliminary examinations, since it curtails
prosecutorial discretion and might indirectly force the OTP to open investigations in many
situations. This might deprive the space for analysis under preliminary examinations, and
might ultimately make the OTP more reluctant to open preliminary examinations, since it
would inevitably be expected to follow up by an investigation" (see Grotius Center Report,
see *supra* note 6, para. 22).

which clearly interferes with the Prosecutor's margin of discretion.[134]

In an attempt to reassert her prosecutorial discretion, Prosecutor Bensouda applied for an appeal under Article 82(1)(a), claiming the Chamber's decision was a decision on admissibility. By a 3 to 2 vote, the majority dismissed the Prosecutor's appeal, determining that the decision did not in fact concern admissibility (correctly, as it was a review of a pre-trial decision not to open an investigation). The Appeals Court did note that whereas "the Prosecutor is obliged to reconsider her decision not to investigate", she nonetheless "retains ultimate discretion over how to proceed".[135] The Prosecutor, thus, reaffirmed her prosecutorial power *vis-à-vis* the PTC regarding the decision of whether to open an investigation.[136] On 29 November 2017 the Prosecutor notified PTC I of her "final decision", under Rule 108(3), and after carrying out a "thorough review of all submissions made and all the information available, including information newly made available in 2015-2017".[137] The Prosecutor concluded that there was no reasonable basis to proceed with an investigation, and made sure to clarify that, as far as her Office is concerned, this "closes the preliminary examination", subject only to the "Prosecutor's ongoing and residual discretion under article 53(4) of the Statute".[138]

---

[134] Situation on the Registered Vessels of the Union of the Comoros, The Hellenic Republic, and the Kingdom of Cambodia, Decision on the Request of the Union of the Comoros, Partly Dissenting Opinion of Judge Péter Kovács, ICC-01/13-34-Anx-Corr, paras. 7–8, see *supra* note 126.

[135] Schabas had argued similarly, noting that "[i]n the *Gaza Flotilla* situation, the Pre-Trial Chamber 'requested' the Prosecutor 'to reconsider' the decision, according to the terms of Article 53(3)(a). The language seems mild and less than mandatory. Can anything further be done if the Prosecutor 'reconsiders' and decides to maintain her decision? It seems that as long as the Prosecutor bases her decision on the grounds of jurisdiction or admissibility, this is where the matter ends". See Schabas, see *supra* note 64, p. 241.

[136] Situation on Registered Vessels of the Union of the Comoros, the Hellenic Republic and the Kingdom of Cambodia, Decision on the admissibility of the Prosecutor's appeal against the "Decision on the request of the Union of the Comoros to review the Prosecutor's decision not to initiate an investigation", Appeals Chamber, 6 November 2016, ICC-01/13, para. 59. For further reading see Giulia Pecorella, "The Comoros situation, the Pre-Trial Chamber and the Prosecutor: the Rome Statute's system of checks and balances is in good health", in *International Law Blog*, 30 November 2015.

[137] *2017 Preliminary Examination Report*, see *supra* note 27, para. 320.

[138] *Ibid.*, at para. 344.

19.4. The Palestinian Preliminary Examination and the Limits of Existing Oversight Mechanisms

What is evident from the analysis up this point is that both self-regulation by the OTP and judicial review by the PTC are underperforming in their role of maximization of quality control over prosecutorial discretion at the preliminary examination stage. The PTC has adopted a narrow interpretation of prosecutorial discretion, in accordance with which it is pushing the OTP to avoid consequentialism at all costs. The PTC is thus encouraging or attempting to strong-arm the Prosecutor into focusing its limited prosecutorial resources on launching investigations. The OTP, on the other hand, has adopted a set of regulations that, while introducing a certain degree of transparency and adherence to procedure, nonetheless enhances prosecutorial discretion at the preliminary examination stage. These guidelines further incentivize 'parking' more situations for more extensive periods of time. The OTP is thus at a risk of becoming too involved in the political monitoring game and overcautious in proceeding with investigations or, when appropriate, concluding preliminary examinations.

Davis' 'optimum point' has not been reached, and this lack of balance results in the occasional power struggle between the OTP and the PTC, in addition to insufficient checks on the Prosecutor's evolving consequentialist role at the preliminary examination stage. These limitations of the existing control mechanisms are the subject of this section, and will be exemplified relying on the case study of the preliminary examination in Palestine. In particular, the section will focus on three primary concerns resulting from this lack of adequate oversight: (1) the potential politicization of the Court; (2) issues relating to prioritization policies and exit strategies; and (3) insufficient regulation of evidentiary standards at the preliminary examination stage.

19.4.1. The Preliminary Examination on Palestine: Background

On 1 January 2015, the Palestinians lodged an Article 12(3) declaration with the Registrar of the ICC,[139] stating their wish to accept the Court's jurisdiction over alleged crimes committed "in the occupied Palestinian

---

[139] Mahmoud Abbas, "Declaration Accepting the Jurisdiction of the International Criminal Court", 31 December 2014 (http://www.legal-tools.org/doc/60aff8/).

territory, including East Jerusalem, since June 13, 2014".[140] The next day, the Palestinians deposited their instrument of accession to the Court with the United Nations Secretary-General (which entered into force for Palestine on 1 April 2015).[141] On 7 January 2015, the Registrar of the ICC informed President Abbas of his acceptance of the Article 12(3) declaration, which was then transmitted to the Prosecutor.

This was not the Palestinians' first attempt to grant jurisdiction to the Court, the first declaration being lodged in 2009. Back then, Prosecutor Ocampo ultimately rejected the declaration in April 2012, based on the inability of the OTP to determine Palestinian statehood for the purposes of the Statute. The Prosecutor stated that it was "for the relevant bodies at the United Nations or the Assembly of States Parties to make the legal determination whether Palestine qualifies as a State for the purpose of acceding to the Rome Statute and thereby enabling the exercise of jurisdiction by the Court under article 12(1)".[142] This statement was problematic in and of itself, ultimately broadening the interpretation of 'statehood' beyond its usual parameters, by essentially empowering the United Nations General Assembly ('UNGA') and the ASP to make determinations that would be binding on an international judicial body.

In 22 November 2012, the UNGA adopted resolution 67/19, upgrading Palestine's status from 'observer entity' to 'non-member observer State'. In 2014, Prosecutor Bensouda published an article in *The Guardi-*

---

[140] *2016 Preliminary Examination Report*, see *supra* note 21, para. 111.

[141] United Nations Secretary General, "State of Palestine Accession to the Rome Statute of the International Criminal Court", 6 January 2015 (http://www.legal-tools.org/doc/f7411b/) (note that the UNSG accepted the accession of the Palestinians in his technical and administrative capacity as depository of the Rome Statute. As a later note by the UNSG clarifies "[i]n conformity with the relevant international rules and his practice as a depositary, the Secretary-General has ascertained that the instruments received were in due and proper form before accepting them for deposit, and has informed all States concerned accordingly through the circulation of depositary notifications This is an administrative function performed by the Secretariat as part of the Secretary-General's responsibilities as depositary for these treaties. It is important to emphasize that it is for States to make their own determination with respect to any legal issues raised by instruments circulated by the Secretary-General". United Nations Secretary-General, "Note to Correspondents – Accession of Palestine to Multilateral Treaties", 7 January 2015 (http://www.legal-tools.org/doc/864b39/).

[142] ICC Office of the Prosecutor, *Report on Preliminary Examination Activities 2012*, November 2012, para. 201 (http://www.legal-tools.org/doc/0b1cfc/).

---

an, titled "The truth about the ICC and Gaza".[143] While the situation in Palestine was no longer the subject of a preliminary examination, the Prosecutor still thought it useful to note that her Office had "examined the legal implications of this development and concluded that while this change did not retroactively validate the previously invalid 2009 declaration, Palestine could now join the Rome statute". She further suggested that "is a matter of public record that Palestinian leaders are in the process of consulting internally on whether to [lodge a new Article 12(3) declaration]; the decision is theirs alone and as ICC prosecutor, I cannot make it for them".[144] There is a question of whether or not this type of political signalling and public winking is appropriate for an ICC Prosecutor.

Following the above-mentioned lodging of the declaration and accession to the Statute at the beginning of 2015, the OTP issued a statement on 16 January 2015, confirming that it found the adoption of UNGA resolution 67/19 "determinative of Palestine's ability to accede to the Statute pursuant to article 125, and equally, its ability to lodge an article 12(3) declaration".[145]

A preliminary examination was immediately launched. Based on its policy, the OTP is examining alleged crimes committed by both the IDF and members of Palestinian armed groups as part of the conflict that erupted over the course of the summer of 2014 (Operation Protective Edge), along with specific alleged crimes in the West Bank and East Jerusalem (namely alleged settlement activities, ill-treatment and escalation of violence).[146] The preliminary examination is currently at the jurisdiction phase (Phase 2), and the OTP is reviewing open source materials and reports from individuals, groups, States, IGOs and NGOs. The Office specifically mentions "monthly reports" from the Government of Palestine regarding alleged ongoing crimes and other developments. The OTP is

---

[143] Fatou Bensouda, "[T]he truth about the ICC and Gaza", in *Guardian*, 29 August 2014.

[144] *Ibid.*

[145] ICC Office of the Prosecutor, "The Prosecutor of the International Criminal Court, Fatou Bensouda, opens a preliminary examination of the situation in Palestine", 16 January 2015 (http://www.legal-tools.org/doc/1dcbe5/).

[146] *2017 Preliminary Examination Report*, see *supra* note 27, paras. 58–66.

also developing and running a number of databases, and conducting field missions.[147]

The Palestinian case study is intriguing because, as the Prosecutor herself notes, "[t]he alleged crimes that have been the subject of analysis to date involve complicated factual and legal assessments, such as in relation to conduct of hostilities issues, thereby necessitating careful analysis in reference to the relevant law applicable and information available".[148] But it is not only that the legal questions lead to significant complications;[149] the facts surrounding the dispute are also unique. As noted by the former Legal Advisor of Israel's Ministry of Foreign Affairs, Alan Baker:

> This unique and *sui generis* situation, including the history and circumstances of the Israeli-Palestinian conflict regarding the territories, as well as the series of agreements and memoranda that have been signed between the Palestinian leadership and the Government of Israel, have produced a special independent regime – a *lex specialis* – that governs all aspects of the relationship between them, including the respective status of each party vis-à-vis the territory.[150]

The combination of legal issues, which lack sufficient clarity in international criminal law jurisprudence especially insofar as they relate to a prolonged situation of belligerent occupation, and the one-of-a-kind nature of the Israeli-Palestinian conflict, poses a series of concerns regarding quality control of this preliminary examination. It goes to heart of the question of how the Court will square issues relating to territorial or personal jurisdiction without making political determinations that should be decided in bilateral negotiations between the parties. Note, in this regard, that in both the 2015 and 2016 annual preliminary examination reports, the Prosecutor maps out a series of alleged crimes "without prejudice to any future determinations by the Office regarding the exercise of territori-

---

[147] *Ibid.*, paras. 72–77; see also *2016 Preliminary Examination Report, supra* note 21, paras. 135–44.

[148] *2016 Preliminary Examination Report, ibid.*, para. 139.

[149] Note in this regard, as an example, the fact that the *2016 Preliminary Examination Report* (see *supra* note 21, paras. 130–132) does not explain how the settlements come within the jurisdiction of the Court. See also Stahn, *supra* note 6, p. 14.

[150] Alan Baker, "International humanitarian law, ICRC and Israel's status in the Territories", in *International Review of the Red Cross*, vol. 94, no. 888, Winter 2012, p. 1515.

---

al or personal jurisdiction by the Court".[151] In other words, the Prosecutor is entering this political minefield without a methodology for determining thorny jurisdictional questions as well as interpretive matters as they relate to the novel legal issues at hand. The Palestinian preliminary examination thus offers a useful case study to examine the limitations of extant oversight, insofar as it may become an instance of 'prosecutorial adjudication' where the OTP would apply subjective values in its analysis.

19.4.2. Politicization of the Court

The decision of the Prosecutor to launch a preliminary examination concerning the situation in Palestine encompassed a number of adjudicative decisions. First, as noted by Schabas, "that the Prosecutor considers a declaration by a non-party State pursuant to Article 12(3) as an automatic trigger for a preliminary examination is an innovation, something not provided for in the Rome Statute or anywhere else in the legal instruments applicable to the Court".[152] Moreover, the decision to recognize Palestine as a State for the purposes of an Article 12(3) referral was in itself a highly contentious decision criticized by a number of scholars.[153] Indeed,

---

[151] See, for example, *2016 Preliminary Examination Report, supra* note 21, para. 119.

[152] Schabas, see *supra* note 21, p. 400.

[153] CHAN James, "Judicial Oversight over Article 12(3) of the ICC Statute", FICHL Policy Brief Series No. 11 (2013), Torkel Opsahl Academic EPublisher, Oslo, 2013 (http://www.toaep.org/pbs-pdf/11-chan), pp. 3–4 ("The Palestinian Declaration also sends a message to quasi-States that a declaration can be used to their advantage […] the OTP has allowed the ICC to be used as a forum for questions of statehood. Submissions to the OTP have argued that accepting the Palestine Declaration would create precedent for other non-State entities such as Kosovo or Taiwan to assert political independence"); Zachary Saltzman, "Much Ado About Nothing: Non-Member State Status, Palestine and the International Criminal Court", *St. John's Journal of International & Comparative Law*, vol. 3, no. 2, 2013, p. 207 ("The General Assembly resolution upgrading Palestine to a non-member state status thus has little effect on ICC jurisdiction pursuant to 12(3). The criteria for statehood were either met or not met prior to the General Assembly's vote. The vote did little to change the existing calculus prior to the vote"); XIAO Jingren and ZHANG Xin, "A Realist Perspective on China and the International Criminal Court", FICHL Policy Brief Series No. 13 (2013), Torkel Opsahl Academic EPublisher, Beijing, 2013 (http://www.toaep.org/pbs-pdf/13-xiao-zhang) ("Practice regrettably shows that the ICC Office of the Prosecutor has allowed the Court to be used as a forum for the consideration of political questions of statehood through its discretionary preliminary examination powers. This is a most serious matter from the perspective of China which impacts on the legitimacy of the Court. The protracted and monarchical manner in which the former ICC Prosecutor indulged in his preliminary examination of the Palestinian Article 12(3) declaration for more than three years sets

States do not declare their independence in The Hague, nor are they formed by the Court. The traditional criteria for the recognition of state-hood under international law, codified in the Montevideo Convention and rooted in effective control, offer the most widely accepted prescription to be applied at the outset of making any determination regarding state-hood.[154] These rules should not, of course, be applied rigidly – they re-quire a case-by-case analysis, as noted by James Crawford:

> It has been argued that international law does contain worka-ble rules for determining whether a given entity is or is not a State. Of course, these rules are not, so to speak, self-executing: as with rules in other areas of international law, their application by international lawyers, or by States and other international persons, requires the exercise of judgment in each case.[155]

What is of concern is, therefore, the *procedure* whereby the deter-mination of Palestinian statehood was made in January 2015. Leaving open the question of whether Palestine is a State in the traditional sense, one should ask: who applied the rules and who exercised judgment in recognizing Palestinian statehood at the ICC? The Prosecutor merely ac-cepted as determinative a UNGA resolution which was nothing more than a symbolic vote upgrading Palestine's representation at the *United Na-tions* to "somewhere in between the other observers, on the one hand, and member states on the other".[156] Did the delegates voting at the General Assembly realize that they were voting on Palestinian accession to the

---

a landmark precedent for how the Office might disregard legitimate state interests during the examination of such declarations as well as complaints. There is little, if anything, af-fected governments can do during such preliminary examination, except to wait for what may be a very long time, even when the complaint is politically motivated. The present au-thors fail to comprehend how the ICC Prosecutor could spend more than three years exam-ining the Palestinian declaration.").

[154] See, for example, J.D. van der Vyver, "Statehood in International Law", in *Emory Interna-tional Law Review*, vol. 9, 1991, p. 12 (explaining that the declaratory theory, consisting of the Montevideo Convention requirements, is widely accepted).

[155] James Crawford, "The Criteria for Statehood in International Law", in *British Yearbook of International Law*, vol. 48, no. 1, 1977, p. 181.

[156] Permanent Observer Mission of The State of Palestine to the United Nations, "Status of Palestine" (http://www.legal-tools.org/doc/15678f/).

Rome Statute, and if they were told would they have voted differently?[157] In any event, is it prudent to abrogate this pertinent decision to a single political action by one political arm of the United Nations?

This is of critical importance, because this kind of recognition by the Prosecutor has a norm-setting function. Decisions by the ICC, as an international Court, carry a different status from those of the International Olive Council, for example.[158] As noted by Yaël Ronnen:

---

[157] Reviewing the explanation of votes made by those States who either voted in favour of or abstained from UN General Assembly resolution 67/19 is quite telling and contradicts that conclusion. See, for example, UK Secretary of State for Foreign and Commonwealth Affairs, William Hague (abstained), who remarked: "We continue to believe that the prospects for a swift return to negotiations on a two state solution – the only way to create a Palestinian state on the ground – would be greater today if President Abbas had been able to give the assurances we suggested, and without which we were unable to vote in favor of the resolution. In particular, we called on President Abbas to set out a willingness to return to negotiations without preconditions, *and to signal that the Palestinians would not immediately seek action in the International Criminal Court, which would be likely to make a return to negotiations impossible*" (emphasis added) (Jill Reilly, "U.N agrees to recognise Palestine but UK abstains from vote after Hague issues peace deal demands", in *Daily Mail*, 30 November 2012); Japan's Ambassador to the United Nations General Assembly, Jun Yamazaki (voted in favour): "It is not acceptable to use this resolution to act in a way that might negatively affect or hinder direct negotiations with Israel. *We ask for prudence with respect to conduct such as accession to international organizations, action which might negatively affect the prospect for the resumption of negotiations*" (emphasis added) (Permanent Mission of Japan to the United Nations, "Statement by H.E. Jun Yamazaki, At the Debate of the United Nations General Assembly on Agenda Item 36: "The Situation in the middle East" and Agenda Item 37: "The Question of Palestine", 30 November 2012 (http://www.legal-tools.org/doc/1e116d/)); Romania's Ambassador to the United Nations General Assembly Simona Mirela Miculescu (abstained): "Romania does not favor unilateral initiatives, regardless of which side they come from, as they may have adverse effects for the resumption of the peace process negotiations. *The adopted resolution is not facilitating the recognition of Palestine as a state nor its accession to international organisations and treaties*" (emphasis added) (Permanent Mission of Romania to the United Nations, "Romania's participation at the General Assembly Session on the resolution "The Status of Palestine in the United Nations", 29 November 2012 (http://www.legal-tools.org/doc/89c434/)); Deputy Prime Minister and Minister of Foreign Affairs of the Kingdom of Belgium, Didier Reynders (voted in favour): "For Belgium, the resolution adopted today by the General Assembly *does not yet constitute recognition of Palestine as a state in the full sense of the word*" (emphasis added) (Kingdom of Belgium Foreign Affairs, Foreign Trade and Development Cooperation, "Declaration by Minister Reynders following the awarding to Palestine of the status of observer/non-member state", 30 November 2012 (http://www.legal-tools.org/doc/f911f1/)).

[158] Isabel Putinja, "Palestine Becomes Olive Council's Newest Member", in *Olive Oil Times*, 20 April 2017.

---

a determination by a legal body such as the ICC (the prosecutor and, at a later stage, the Court) that a state of Palestine
exists (either generally or for the purpose of Article 12(3))
would carry significant weight. [...] Thus, if the Prosecutor,
or later the Pre-Trial Chamber, determines that the Palestinian declaration fulfills the requirements of Article 12(3), they
would be assuming an almost unprecedented competence,
which incurs onto the political sphere which is the traditional
prerogative of states.[159]

This argument will be further borne out to the extent that the Prosecutor proceeds with the preliminary examination, basing its decision on a
determination of territorial and personal jurisdiction which will go beyond
recognizing a Palestinian State, and which will *de facto* delineate its borders.[160] Although Bensouda emphasizes that any determination will be
strictly limited for the purposes of the preliminary examination, the Prosecutor in essence has placed her Office at the centre of any future negotiation between the parties. The determinations of the OTP are likely to be
raised in the future by the Palestinians, by Israel, and by other interested
parties, for the purposes of making territorial claims or objections. A recent statement by former Prosecutor Ocampo confirms this point. At a
visit to Al-Quds University in May 2017, Ocampo acknowledged that the
status of Palestine as a State has been indisputably solidified legally and
politically as a result of the launching of the Palestinian preliminary examination. He further noted that the Palestinian preliminary examination
"was not the goal but only one of the many political and diplomatic means
the Palestinian side is wisely utilizing to achieve its legitimate aim of ending the occupation".[161]

As Allison Danner wrote, the ICC Prosecutor sits "at a critical juncture in the structure of the Court, where the pressures of law and politics

---

[159] Yaël Ronen, "ICC Jurisdiction over Acts Committed in the Gaza Strip: Article 12(3) of the
ICC Statute and Non-state Entities", in *Journal of International Criminal Justice*, vol. 8,
no. 1, 2010, p. 22.

[160] William A. Schabas, *The International Criminal Court: A Commentary on the Rome Statute*, Oxford University Press, Oxford, 2010, p. 290 (noting that the "actual limits of the territory of Palestine are also a matter of dispute").

[161] Palestine News Network, "اوكامبو: اسرائيل ادانة إلى ستؤدي حرب جريمة الاستيطان" ("Ocampo:
Settlement of War Crimes will lead to Condemnation of Israel", in *Palestine News Network*, 30 May 2017 (translated from the original Arabic).

---

converge. The cases adjudicated by the ICC are infused with political implications and require sensitive decision making".[162] To avoid as much politicization of the Court as possible, Alex Whiting, former Prosecution Coordinator and Investigation Coordinator at the OTP, recommended that Prosecutors adopt a chess-master's mentality.[163] Given that the positions of the international community, the situation States, and the primary actors (including the victims and the accused) are all frequently in a state of flux, OTP investigations are inherently dynamic. As a result, at "any given time, the prosecutor has to consider and weigh all of the different variables when deciding where to investigate, what resources to dedicate, how fast to go, when there is enough evidence, and when to move to the next phase".[164]

The creation of facts on the ground by the OTP, and categorical determinations by the Prosecutor which will be very difficult to reverse, stand directly opposed to this necessary dynamism.[165] Further complications arise from the preliminary examination on Palestine, since it requires

---

[162] Danner, see *supra* note 13, p. 510.

[163] Alex Whiting, "Dynamic Investigative Practice at the International Criminal Court", in *Law and Contemporary Problems*, vol. 76, nos. 3–4, 2013, p. 185 ("To employ a cliché, planning and conducting an investigation at the ICC is like playing three-dimensional, or even four- or five-dimensional, chess").

[164] *Ibid.* A similar approach is suggested by Jacob Foster. See *generally*, Jacob N. Foster, "A Situational Approach to Prosecutorial Strategy at the ICC", in *Georgetown Journal of International Law*, vol. 47, 2016.

[165] Valérie Arnould, "The Limits of International Criminal Justice: Lessons from the Ongwen Case", 27 January 2015 (http://www.legal-tools.org/doc/b4fc01/) ("intervention in ongoing conflict exposes the Court to excessive politicisation, as it inexorably gets sucked into political wrangling and opens itself up to political manipulation by states. In the Ugandan case, President Museveni mobilised international justice to legitimise his government's military response to the conflict, divert attention away from the army's own human rights practices, and to depoliticise the northern conflict. Experiences in Sudan, Kenya and Palestine in turn show how the Court may be used as a bargaining chip in political power plays, either between states or domestic elites. This becomes particularly problematic if international justice is used as a substitute to the pursuit of a political or military solution. While it is impossible for the Court to completely act outside of politics, there is a need to reflect more on circumstances where too much politics may end up immobilising the Court and serving the interest of neither justice nor peace. The hard truth which thus needs to be confronted is that rather than ending conflict, international justice is at growing risk of becoming an additional terrain on which wars are fought out. While it would be unrealistic to simply state that the Court should therefore never intervene in ongoing conflicts, at the minimum a more critical reflection of the conditions under which this happens is needed.").

the Prosecutor to apply what was in essence created to be a *jus post bellum* criminal justice mechanism to a lingering, protracted, and drawn out *jus in bello* situation. No other conflict currently under preliminary examination, even other ongoing, volatile situations (for example, Ukraine), has this kind of historically magnified nature, reflected in a state of occupation now entering its fiftieth year. By opening the preliminary examination, the OTP bull has placed itself within the china shop that is the West Bank and Gaza Strip. Every legal interpretation, statement, or declaration must be vetted and thoroughly scrutinized, as each one is likely to make an immediate and lasting political impact.

19.4.3. Prioritization Policies and Exit Strategies

Setting aside the issue of semantics,[166] one key dilemma concerning the inner workings of the OTP involves how to prioritize between situations, and later cases, and also if, when and how to disengage from ongoing preliminary examinations.[167] Many of these questions are left to the dis-

---

[166] Grotius Centre Report, see *supra* note 6, para. 30 ("It was pointed that some of the existing semantics are open to question. Experience across institutions suggests that disengagement/'exit' is not simply a moment in time, but a complex process in itself. In line of this, it might be more appropriate to speak of 'completion', rather than 'exit'").

[167] At present the OTP "has no exit strategy in place for any of the situations in which it operates" (see Rebecca J. Hamilton, "The ICC's Exit Problem", in *New York University Journal of International Law and Policy*, 2014, vol. 47, p. 5). The Office of the Prosecutor had promised that as part of a Policy Paper on Case Selection and Prioritisation it will include a clearer working definition and structure for "exit strategies", see Strategic Plan 2016-2018, see *supra* note 70, para. 36 ("the Office will define its policy on how it proposes to end its involvement in a situation under investigation, the so-called: "exit strategy" for situations"). The Policy Paper adopted in 15 September 2016 does not even mention the term, *let alone* provide any meaningful analysis (see Office of the Prosecutor, *Policy Paper on Case Selection and Prioritisation*, 15 September 2016 (http://www.legal-tools.org/doc/182205/)). For the purposes of this chapter, I adopt a definition of 'exit strategy' similar to that of Richard Caplan, it is "a plan for disengaging and ultimately withdrawing" from a situation, "ideally having attained the goals that inspired international involvement originally. If the goals have been attained, an exit strategy may envision follow-on measures to consolidate the gains [...] However, if the goals have not been attained and, it is concluded, cannot be attained, then a different set of considerations will govern the formulation of an exit strategy. For instance, if there have been partial gains, are these worth preserving and, if so, how can that be achieved? If there are reputational costs associated with exit, such as perceived loss of credibility, how can these best be contained? If exit will leave others to pick up the pieces, how is the process to be managed without leaving the others high and dry? As these considerations suggest, exit is not merely a technical matter, to be accomplished (ideally) when requirements for sustainability have been achieved. It is also a polit-

---

cretion of the Prosecutor, given that there are no temporal limitations on preliminary examinations[168] (aside from a general obligation to complete them within a 'reasonable time' regardless of complexity),[169] and that the OTP Policy Paper only instructs in vague terms that preliminary examinations may be terminated depending on "the availability of information, the nature, scale and frequency of the crimes, and the existence of national responses in respect of alleged crimes".[170]

It is important to recall that the ICC has capacity limitations. The ICC is unlikely to act as a first, second, or even third responder to the commission of widespread atrocities, and the most important thing the OTP can do to enhance its positive image is to educate the public on the subject of its inevitable constraints. As clarified by Bibas and Burke-White:

> A system that idealistically promises justice to everyone will disappoint most of them. It must focus on the most intentional and flagrant crimes that caused the gravest harm to the most victims and sowed the most widespread grief and bitterness. Coherent screening policies can pick a handful of strong cases involving the worst crimes, to maximize public satisfaction and historic resolution. They can screen out all but the most serious international crimes and all but the highest-level persons responsible, such as political or military leaders.[171]

---

ical matter, whose pace may be determined by a host of domestic and international factors that may have little to do with the achievement of sustainable outcomes" (see Richard Caplan, "Exit Strategies and State Building", in Richard Caplan (ed.), *Exit Strategies and State Building*, 2012, Oxford University Press, Oxford, pp. 5–6). Devising an exit strategy at the beginning of the Preliminary Examination stage will entail reviewing all of the above factors to develop both the goals and the risks involved in the particular situation under review.

[168] OTP, *Policy Paper on Preliminary Examinations*, see *supra* note 7, para. 89.

[169] See *supra* Section 19.3.2.1. in this chapter.

[170] It is intriguing to note that the original regulations of the OTP envisioned a one-month maximum deadline for the first Phase, see *supra* note 26.

[171] Stephanos Bibas and William W. Burke-White, "International Idealism Meets Domestic-Criminal-Procedure Realism", *Duke Law Journal*, vol. 59, no. 4., 2010, pp. 681–682. Cf. Grotius Centre Report, see *supra* note 6, para. 33 ("Doubts were expressed whether international criminal courts and tribunals should focus strictly on 'big fish', while leaving 'small fish' to domestic courts").

This approach echoes the consequentialist model and has implications for gravity and complementarity considerations by the OTP. At the same time, the OTP must recognize that there are limits to the duration of even prolonged preliminary examinations as well as to their number,[172] not the least of which is its own budgetary constraints.[173] While proposals to set rigid time limits[174] may be counterproductive to the goals of positive complementarity and tailored prosecutorial strategies,[175] there could

---

[172] Vincent Dalpé, "The ICC-OTP's Approach to Preliminary Examinations: Complementarity in Action or Complete Inaction" (on file with the author) ("one must keep in mind that the ICC barely has the necessary resources to prosecute a handful of individuals every year. The ICC is not a development agency and by no means has the necessary resources to orchestrate the monumental rule of law project that positive complementarity would require. A clear line needs to be drawn between the court's mission to promote rule of law and that of adjudicating crimes of international concern").

[173] Assembly of States Parties, Proposed Programme Budget for 2016 of the International Criminal Court, ICC-ASP/14/10 2 September 2015, para. 135 ("This budget increase does not allow the Office to immediately respond to all the demands placed upon it [...] Situations that are under preliminary examination, and for which investigations could be opened, are being postponed as a result of insufficient resources").

[174] Grotius Centre Report, *ibid.*, para. 16 ("Some support was expressed in favour of fixed timelines and greater judicial review of prosecutorial action [...] preliminary examinations should be concluded within one year, with the possibility for the Prosecutor to request the Pre-Trial Chamber to extend the time limit, if necessary"). Kersten, see *supra* note 74 ("This issue of how long preliminary examinations should last was raised last year at a conference organized by the inestimable Carsten Stahn and his team at Leiden University. There, a number of participants raised the possibility of adopting reasonable timelines. The most convincing version of this argument, at least in my view, essentially prescribed a general time limitation on how long prosecutors would have to conduct a preliminary examination. Here, somewhere between three to five years would be considered fair, although some suggested a one-year time period (I think this is far too little). After the initial period of time passed, the Office of the Prosecutor would have three options: 1) close the preliminary examination; 2) proceed to an official investigation; or 3) apply to judges for an extension of the preliminary examination for an additional period of time, perhaps somewhere between 2–3 years. During such applications – which, if the record of preliminary examinations to date is any indication, would regularly be filed – those states under scrutiny as well as victims' representatives would be permitted to file their own declarations as to whether to proceed to an official investigation").

[175] Grotius Centre Report, *ibid.*, para. 18 ("other participants remained skeptical towards the idea of specifying time limits for prosecutorial action. Questions were raised about the feasibility of time limits in 'hard' cases. Would the Prosecutor have to proceed with an investigation even if she does not have enough information or should the Preliminary Examination be closed? How should the OTP and Chambers address situations where it is not clear whether an investigation should be initiated? Concerns were expressed that the complexity and fluidity of the situations make it difficult to impose timelines. Difficulties would arise

---

be other means to regulate generalized temporal considerations at the pre-liminary examination stage.[176] The Court must devote more resources to developing tailored engagement strategies with affected States at an early stage of preliminary examinations, and to continuously updating those strategies. Moreover, the Court needs to ensure that extending preliminary examination periods does not serve to politically misuse preliminary examinations in domestic PR campaigns.[177] This directly ties into the issue of prioritization, and in light of the increase in referrals to the Court, and the Chamber's pushback in the case of the Registered Vessels of Comoros, Greece, and Cambodia, it has become critical for the Court to have clear, public and defensible prioritization policies.

One area of particular importance, in this context, concerns peace negotiations and their impact on "interests of justice" interpretations and broader exit strategies.[178] For these purposes, 'victims' are defined under the Rules of Procedure and Evidence as "natural persons who have suffered harm as a result of the commission of any crime within the jurisdic-

---

in particular in situations of continuing or recurring violence (for example, Nigeria and Honduras), or when peace negotiations are ongoing or agreements have been reached and the OTP has to give the state time to proceed with its own investigations and prosecutions").

[176] *Ibid.*, paras. 16–17 (the group of experts considered other ways including granting the territorial or personal jurisdiction state (or even the victims) the possibility of asking the PTC to request that the OTP make a decision (similar to the CAR situation). Alternatively, it might be possible to allow the OTP to request PTC rulings on jurisdiction or admissibility at the Preliminary Examination stage, or to establish reasonable timeframes for each phase of a Preliminary Examination assessment).

[177] James, see *supra* note 153, pp. 2–3 (noting that the "publicity generated" through activities done at the Preliminary Examination stage "could be politically advantageous" for one of the parties).

[178] As explained above, as part of the preliminary examination process, the Prosecutor considers whether, taking into account the gravity of the crimes and the interests of victims, there are nonetheless substantial reasons to believe that an investigation would not serve the interests of justice. Rome Statute, see *supra* note 18, Article 53(1)(c).

tion of the Court".[179] Any decision not to open an investigation on the basis of "interests of justice" is subject to mandatory judicial review.[180]

In its 2007 Policy Paper on the Interests of Justice, the OTP adopted a narrow understanding of "interests of justice" incorporating a "presumption in favour of investigations or prosecution" and a standard of "exceptionality" (a course of last resort).[181] Concerning peace processes specifically, the OTP refers to the recognized role of the UNSC in maintaining peace and security and its power to delay investigations and prosecutions by means of a resolution under Chapter VII of the UN Charter (thus stressing that the "broader matter of international peace and security is not the responsibility of the Prosecutor").[182] Concerning the conflict in Uganda, the Juba peace talks were launched two years after the OTP concluded its preliminary examination and opened an investigation. As a result, the negotiations were not considered as part of the Ugandan preliminary examination. On the other hand, both in the context of Colombia and in the context of the Palestine, negotiations may play a role in the Prosecutor's analysis.

The position that interests of peace are distinguishable from interests of justice and fall outside the mandate of the OTP is discouraging. In a world where the UNSC is paralysed due to conflicting agendas among permanent members with veto power, to abrogate all responsibilities to that institution seems unreasonable. The Court must engage in determining whether pursuing criminal justice during a preliminary examination would serve stability. The fact that the PTC is required to review such determinations further justifies the OTP in considering interests of justice rather than ignoring them. The Policy Paper is so limiting that it seems very unlikely that the Prosecutor will ever find an investigation should not be launched under Article 53(1)(c). As Schabas has noted:

---

[179] Rules of Procedure and Evidence, see *supra* note 23, Rule 85. This definition of victimhood is slightly vague, as the means whereby interests of different groups of victims could be discerned and compared are unclear. Consider the following: will an Israeli settler in the West Bank be considered a victim? Would her interests be ranked differently or the same as the interests of a Palestinian?

[180] Rome Statute, see *supra* note 18, Article 53(3)(b).

[181] OTP, *Policy Paper on Interests of Justice*, September 2007, pp. 3–4.

[182] *Ibid.*, pp. 8–9.

It is often said that without justice there can be no peace, but the opposite is also a valid proposition: without peace there can be no justice. It is probably unwise to reduce the debate to absolute propositions, whereby one objective, be it justice or peace, trumps the other. Advocates of uncompromising justice build their argument on the rights of victims, whose claim is secured by contemporary human rights norms. But while individual victims are perfectly entitled to see their perpetrators brought to book, like many rights, this must sometimes acknowledge competing interests, including the right to peace. The real issue is whether the Prosecutor, in making determinations under article 53, engages with the peace and justice dialectic or instead positions himself as an advocate for justice, leaving others to defend the interests of peace. The Prosecutor's policy paper takes the latter approach, although a good case can be made for a more holistic perspective. Perhaps future Prosecutors of the Court will attempt to balance the interests of justice and peace in the selection of cases, invoking the 'interests of justice' where deferral of prosecution may be useful in promoting an end to conflict.[183]

The public statements of the OTP in the wake of the signing of a peace accord between Colombia and the FARC-EP were also disconcerting. On 1 September 2016, the Prosecutor welcomed the "historic achievement", noting specifically the Special Jurisdiction for Peace which was supposed to be established and take into consideration the victims "legitimate aspirations for justice".[184] Following the narrow victory of 'no' voters in the October 2016 referendum, all direct references to the Rome Statute were removed from the revised deal. As some have contended, "reaching a peace accord and ending 52 years of armed conflict between the State and the FARC-EP would not have been possible at all without a transitional justice system that prioritizes the needs of Colombians for peace and reconciliation higher than the Rome Statute and the

---

[183] Schabas, see *supra* note 21, p. 839.

[184] OTP, "Statement of ICC Prosecutor, Fatou Bensouda, on the conclusion of the peace negotiations between the Government of Colombia and the Revolutionary Armed Forces of Colombia – People's Army", 1 September 2016 (http://www.legal-tools.org/doc/c64dd0/).

increasingly controversial ICC".[185] The Prosecutor ignored these considerations and published a column in the weekly *Semana*, in which she clarified that the OTP would intervene and prosecute cases if Colombia's transitional justice system "fails to effectively prosecute military and guerrilla commanders over war crimes or crimes against humanity".[186]

This precedent is worrisome in the context of the preliminary examination on Palestine. The Israeli-Palestinian conflict has known high and low tides of bilateral negotiations, often supported by the United States as an intermediary. Unlike a final and comprehensive status agreement achieved through bilateral compromise, bringing the Chairman of the Yesha Council or a high-ranking Hamas official to The Hague is unlikely to end the occupation, dismantle a single settlement, or reduce violence in the region; in fact, the reverse is true, it will likely only raise antagonism. The Prosecutor's unwillingness to acknowledge the role her Office might play in derailing such negotiations, and her refusal to recognize that her mandate actually requires her to take these considerations under review,[187] is troubling, as this refusal could, in and of itself, lead to significant political implications.

19.4.4. Evidentiary Standards at the Preliminary Examination Stage

The information available at the preliminary examination stage is neither expected to be "comprehensive" nor "conclusive", compared to evidence gathered during an investigation.[188] According to Regulation 24 of the

---

[185] Christof Lehmann, "ICC Chief Prosecutor Bensouda Threatens With Intervention in Colombia", in *MSNBC*, 27 January 2017.

[186] *Ibid.*

[187] In this context it might be useful to note that the expression "interests of justice" was proposed by the United Kingdom in an amendment to what was then Article 26 of the draft statute. In an accompanying discussion paper, the UK delegation clarified that "the reference to the "interests of justice" is intended to reflect a wide discretion on the part of the prosecutor to decide not to investigate comparable to that in (some) domestic systems, eg [...] there were good reasons to concluded that a prosecution would be counter-productive": see UK Discussion Paper, "International Criminal Court: Complementarity", 29 March 1996, para. 30 (https://www.legal-tools.org/doc/45b7f5/). Based on this Schabas concludes that "had there been an amendment to article 53(1)(c) to the effect that 'the interests of justice shall not be confused with the interests of peace', it would surely not have met with consensus", Schabas, see *supra* note 21, p. 836.

[188] Situation in the Republic of Kenya, Decision Pursuant to Article 15, see *supra* note 34, para. 27; 2016 *Preliminary Examination Report*, see *supra* note 21, para. 11.

Regulations of the OTP, the Office is required to develop and apply "a consistent and objective method for the evaluation of sources, information and evidence", taking into consideration their credibility and reliability while ensuring bias control by inspecting multiple sources.[189] The Prosecutor has full discretion in conducting preliminary examinations and is provided with a broad range of investigatory powers, short of the formal mechanisms utilized by the Office at the investigation stage (including in particular Part 9 co-operation),[190] to conduct her examination:

> According to Article 15(2), the tools available to the Prosecutor at this stage include: received information; additional information from States, organs of the UN, intergovernmental or non-governmental organizations or other reliable sources and 'written or oral testimony' received at the seat of the Court (whereby the ordinary procedures for questioning shall apply and the procedure for preservation of evidence for trial may apply pursuant to Rule 47). Although apparently limited in scope, the sources described under this rule are potentially rich in terms of the information they may in practice be able to provide. Moreover, there is arguably no reason to restrictively interpret the type of non-governmental or governmental organization that may and should be approached by the ICC Prosecutor under this provision. Flexibility and creativity should be employed in this regard, depending on the type of information sought.[191]

Thomas Hansen, relying on OTP Reports, mapped out the "wide range" of activities conducted within this phase. Amongst those he

---

[189] Regulations of the Office of the Prosecutor, see *supra* note 42, Regulation 24.

[190] For an analysis of different interpretations as to whether Part 9 Cooperation should apply to preliminary examinations, see OTP, *Informal Expert Paper: Fact-finding and investigative functions of the office of the Prosecutor, including international co-operation*, 2003, paras. 22–29 (https://www.legal-tools.org/doc/ba368d/).

[191] *Ibid.*, para. 21. Although the above description refers specifically to the conditions concerning the receipt of information by the Prosecutor acting *proprio motu*, in reality these conditions are not really any different from those when she acts pursuant to a State Party or Security Council referral. "The Prosecutor must always 'analyse the seriousness' of information provided, even when it comes from a State Party or the Security Council, as the Rules of Procedure and Evidence make quite clear. Moreover, she may always seek additional information from various 'reliable sources' and receive written or oral testimony at the seat of the Court" (Schabas, see *supra* note 21, p. 402).

notes:[192] (1) creating databases relating to incidents and crimes under examination; (2) conducting various forms of legal analysis, including in the context of determining the existence of an armed conflict; (3) analysing decisions by national courts, as well as non-criminal domestic processes; (4) verifying information provided in communications, including from other States, and assessing the senders' reliability, using open source information such as international organizations and NGO human rights reports and statements; (5) reviewing legislative developments that may have an impact on the conduct of national proceedings; (6) analysing provisions in peace agreements; (7) shedding further light and filling informational gaps relying on the jurisprudence of regional courts; (8) conducting meetings at both the seat of the Court and in examination countries with various stakeholders (governmental, civil society, victims); and (9) conducting missions to situation countries to undertake outreach and education activities.[193]

The OTP 2016-2018 Strategic Plan on Prosecutorial Strategy notes further that "[t]he high pace of technological evolution changes the sources of information, and the way evidence is obtained and presented in court".[194] As a result, the Strategic Goal 4 of the OTP involves adapting the Office's investigative capabilities and network to "the technological environment" and has included hiring cyber investigators and digital forensic analysts as well as training and capacity building.[195]

The preliminary examination process is opaque inasmuch as the OTP does not have a clearly defined, publicly available policy on eviden-

---

[192] Hansen, see *supra* note 67, pp. 11–12.

[193] More generally regarding the OTPs methods at the Preliminary Examination phase, see OTP, *Policy Paper on Preliminary Examinations*, see *supra* note 7, paras. 31–32 ("As information evaluated at the preliminary examination stage is largely obtained from external sources, rather than through the Office's own evidence-gathering powers (which are only available at the investigation stage), the Office pays particular attention to the assessment of the reliability of the source and the credibility of the information. The Office uses standard formats for analytical reports, standard methods of source evaluation, and consistent rules of measurement and attribution in its crime analysis. It checks internal and external coherence, and considers information from diverse and independent sources as a means of bias control").

[194] Strategic Plan 2016-2018, see *supra* note 70, para. 3.

[195] *Ibid.*, paras. 23, 59.

tiary standards and the analysis of sources at that stage.[196] It is submitted that the Prosecutor should provide additional information (and actual past examples) of how it corroborates and verifies information, as well as how much weight is given to different source types. This is predominantly because of the extensive weight given to open-source materials – including materials by UN fact-finding missions and monitoring bodies, as well as human rights NGOs. It is also taking into consideration situations whereby the affected States might not co-operate with the Prosecutor during the preliminary examination analysis. This problem was exemplified in the 2014 Report concerning the Situation on Registered Vessels of Comoros, Greece, and Cambodia. The OTP relied on four different reports[197] and seemingly gave all four identical weight. However, Israel has reason to be concerned about legal and factual determinations based on insufficient evidence. As Judge Thomas Buergenthal wrote in his dissenting opinion in the 2004 *Wall Advisory Opinion*, the ICJ supported its findings:

> with evidence that relates to the suffering the wall has caused along some parts of its route. But in reaching this conclusion the Court fails to address any facts or evidence specifically rebutting Israel's claim of military exigencies or require-

---

196 For example, in the context of activities conducted in 2017 as part of the Preliminary Examination into Palestine the Office clarifies that it has:

> reviewed and assessed a large body of information from various types of sources, including publicly available information as well as information and materials provided to the Office by relevant individuals, local and international NGOs, international organizations and States. Consistent with standard practice, the Office has subjected such information to rigorous source evaluation, including in terms of the reliability of the sources and credibility of the information received. In this regard the Office has continued to take steps to verify and corroborate a number of relevant factual issues, including, for example, by requesting additional information from relevant actors (2017 Preliminary Examination Report, *supra* note 27, at para. 74).

The Office does not provide any information about the "various types of sources" it collected, the nature of its "standard practice" of "rigorous source evaluation", or the ways by which it verifies sources to determine reliability and credibility.

197 Namely, (1) the report from the fact-finding mission established by the UN Human Rights Council, (2) the report of the four-member panel of inquiry established by the UN Secretary-General and chaired by Geoffrey Palmer, (3) the report by the national commission of inquiry established by the Turkish Government, and (4) the report of the investigate commission established by the Israeli Government and headed by former Israeli Supreme Court Justice Jacob Turkel.

ments of national security. It is true that in dealing with this subject the Court asserts that it draws on the factual summaries provided by the United Nations Secretary-General as well as some other United Nations reports. It is equally true, however, that the Court barely addresses the summaries of Israel's position on this subject that are attached to the Secretary-General's report and which contradict or cast doubt on the material the Court claims to rely on. Instead, all we have from the Court is a description of the harm the wall is causing and a discussion of various provisions of international humanitarian law and human rights instruments followed by the conclusion that the law has been violated. Lacking is an examination of the facts that might show why the alleged defences of military exigencies, national security or public order are not applicable to the wall as a whole or to the individual segments of its route. The Court says that it "is not convinced" but it fails to demonstrate why it is not convinced, and that is why these conclusions are not convincing.[198]

Greater contemplation as to the means by which the Prosecutor analyses, verifies, and disseminates information is absolutely critical, especially considering that the OTP acts as a quasi fact-finding mission and human rights monitoring body, at the preliminary examination stage, one that is occasionally known for taking the strategy of "naming and shaming".[199]

---

[198] *Legal Consequences of the Construction of a Wall in the Occupied Palestinian Territory (Advisory Opinion)*, International Court of Justice, 9 July 2004, Separate Declaration by Judge Buergenthal, pp. 243–244.

[199] James Verini, see *supra* note 75 ("Moreno-Ocampo seemed to see the ICC not as a forensic body so much as a "naming and shaming" organization, like Human Rights Watch or Amnesty International. And while it was true that the court's small budget limited the size of his investigations, he was, some say, already more interested in prominence than evidence. A former court attorney told me: "He would see the leader of a state and say: 'There must be evidence out there. Go get it for me.'"). More generally regarding criticism of the OTP as a monitoring body, see Grotius Centre Report, see *supra* note 5, para. 27 ("questions were raised regarding the role of the ICC in terms of monitoring: whether it should monitor domestic trial proceedings until a final judgment is rendered or simply make sure that proceedings are genuine at a given time, with the possibility of reopening the situation if circumstances change. Several participants shared reservations about the idea of long-term monitoring. They highlighted that the scope of Pes is quite different than trial monitoring and raised concerns with regard to resource limitations and the potential prolongation of

Moreover, to the extent that the Court intends to increase its usage of digital evidence, including through the reliance on the collection, storage, (algorithmic) analysis, verification, and promulgation of intercepted communications, bulk data sets, or computerized digital depositories, to name but a few examples, clearer policies must be put in place to ensure both the accuracy of the conclusions and the privacy of individuals.[200] The United Nations Global Pulse, an initiative by the United Nations Secretary-General, focuses on the means by which UN agencies and authorities harness big data safely and responsibly in pursuit of a public good. The Global Pulse's Data Privacy Advisory Group adopted a set of "Privacy and Data Protection Principles" in July 2016, which themselves were an evolution of UNGA resolution 45/95 of 15 December 1989 establishing "Guidelines for the Regulation of Computerized Personal Data Files".[201] The United Nations High Commissioner for Refugees has recently adopted a robust policy on the protection of personal data of persons of concern to the agency. Among the standards to be adhered to are basic principles of personal data processing.[202] The policy also includes guidelines covering data processing by implementing partners and the transfer of data to

---

Pes. It was suggested that closure, with potential re-opening, might be a more suitable methodology. This power, however, has thus far not been exercised or tested").

[200] Note in this regard that the Rome Statute only addresses the protection of the "dignity and privacy of victims and witnesses" (see Rome Statute, see *supra* note 18, at Articles 68(1) and 57(3)(c)). However, such investigative techniques could interfere with the rights to privacy of the accused as well as the rights to privacy of uninvolved third parties (what is commonly known as 'collateral data'), and their right to privacy does not seem to receive statutory protection under the Statute.

[201] For further reading, see United Nations Global Pulse, "Privacy and Data Protection Principles" (available on its web site) (the guidelines cover individual privacy protections, data security, lawful collection, right and purpose of use, risk and harm assessment and mitigation, data sensitivity, data minimization, data quality and accountability, data retention, and collaboration with others on data-related matters). UNGA Resolution 45/95 (the precursor to the Privacy and Data Protection Principles) not only adopted the guidelines for the regulation of computerized personal data files across the United Nations, but also called on "all governmental, intergovernmental, and non-governmental organizations to respect those guidelines in carrying out the activities within their field of competence". This would seem to include the ICC.

[202] Namely legitimate and fair processing, purpose specification, necessity and proportionality, accuracy, respect for data subjects' rights (including rights to access, correct and delete data, and to object to processing), confidentiality, security, the practice of conducting data protection impact assessments, and rules on retention, accountability and supervision.

---

third parties.[203] At the very least, the OTP needs to have a similar policy developed which will provide more comprehensive information and assurances as to how its investigative policies, as they relate to new technologies and greater volumes of electronic data, are in compliance with those basic standards.[204]

Further, the question of the evidentiary standard to be met is equally as open-ended and discretionary as the decision on investigative tools and methods. The Prosecutor must show that there is "a reasonable basis to proceed with an investigation".[205] That will of course depend on whether the OTP finds in Phase 2 that there is "reasonable basis to believe" that the criteria under Article 53(1)(a)–(c) are met. The two threshold criteria ("to believe" and "to proceed") "mutually relate" and the "underlying purpose of this check is to control for frivolous or politically motivated charges".[206] This requirement applies equally to all three trigger mechanisms moving a situation from a preliminary examination to an investigation. While the bar is essentially low, "the question how low the threshold

---

[203] For further reading, see United Nations High Commissioner for Refugees, *Policy on the Protection of Personal Data of Persons of Concern to UNHCR*, May 2015 (http://www. legal-tools.org/doc/6b6aef/).

[204] Certain limited aspects of this novel legal problem were raised in the Special Tribunal for Lebanon, in the context of a challenge by the Defense Counsel of call sequence tablets (CSTs) that the Prosecution sought to bring into evidence. The Prosecution created the CSTs using the call data records ('CDRs') pertaining to the metadata of every mobile phone call and text message in Lebanon between 2003 and 2010. The CDRs were transferred from Lebanese telecommunications providers to the United Nations International Independent Investigation Commission ('UNIIIC') and the Tribunal's Prosecution. Both the Trial Chamber and the Appeals Chamber agreed that the Prosecutor could legally request and obtain the CDRs without judicial authorization because such authorization was not required under their respective governing legal instruments. The Appeals Chamber further held that while there is a compelling case as to the CDRs protection by international standards on the right to privacy, the transfer of the CDRs in the absence of judicial control in this particular case did not violate the right to privacy because the transfer was provided for by (domestic) law, was necessary and proportionate. For further reading see *The Prosecutor v. Salim Jamil Ayyash et al.* (STL-11-01/T/AC/AR126.9, Special Tribunal for Lebanon, The Appeals Chamber, Decision on Appeal by Counsel for Mr. Oneissi Against the Trial Chamber's Decision on the Legality of the Transfers of Call Data Records).

[205] See Rome Statute, see *supra* note 18, at Articles 15(3)-(4) and 53(1).

[206] Mark Klamberg (ed.), *Commentary on the Law of the International Criminal Court*, Torkel Opsahl Academic Epublisher, Brussels, 2017, p. 188 (http://www.legal-tools.org/doc/aa0e2b/).

---

actually is remains unsettled in present ICC jurisprudence".[207] Once again, some greater elucidation regarding the interpretations of the necessary evidentiary standard by the Prosecutor could significantly improve quality control of the Office's work.

19.5. Areas for Potential Reform

In this section, I aim to propose a number of potential reforms relating to the internal operations of the OTP, the relationship between the OTP and the PTC, and external oversight over the Office's work during the preliminary examination stage, each of which, I believe, could have a positive impact in helping to ensure greater quality control throughout all phases of the preliminary examination process. While some of the proposed reforms would require, by their nature, the unlikely accord of a wide range of actors in and around the Court (the Prosecutor, the Judges, and the States Parties), others are subtler or more moderate and would therefore be easier to implement. Together, or individually, these proposals should serve as the beginning of a conversation, and are by no means its conclusion.

19.5.1. Re-phasing of the Preliminary Examination Phase

One possible reform that the OTP should consider is restructuring its phasing of the preliminary examination stage. As Stahn wrote, "the phased-based approach involves a certain tension between a sequenced and a parallel consideration of selection criteria. The idea to break preliminary examination down into phases seems to suggest that the analysis is sequenced. It implies that one phase comes after the next. According to this logic, analysis may get stuck at one phase, like jurisdiction, for years, without considering information related to other phases. Given these con-

---

[207] *Ibid.*, pp. 188–89. For further analysis of the application of the "reasonable basis to believe" standard, questioning whether the ICC Prosecutor may have adopted a "too high a threshold for making this determination and hence proceeding to the next phase of the preliminary examination", see Thomas Obel Hansen, "Policy Choices, Dilemmas and Risks in the ICC's Iraq-UK Preliminary Examination", FICHL Policy Brief Series No. 83 (2017), Torkel Opsahl Academic EPublisher, Oslo, 2017, pp. 2-3 (http://www.toaep.org/pbs-pdf/83-obel-hansen/).

cerns, it might make sense to adopt a more holistic methodology towards the respective situation".[208]

Potential re-phasing could be based on various stages at the preliminary examination that are already sequenced (that is, collection of materials, extraction of information and arrangements in databases, mandated consultation processes, routine internal and external progress reports and reviews, meetings with stakeholders and missions to situation countries). This re-phasing would involve breaking the preliminary examination into each of its sub-components and replicating the natural sequencing. Stepping outside of strictly delimited conception of preliminary examination phases that merely mimic the statutory provisions of Article 53 will allow the Prosecutor to open the 'black box' of the preliminary examination review process once more, this time inviting the public to look even deeper inside.

The more the preliminary examination stage could be broken down to its vital or basic elements, the easier it would be to produce a visual 'Gantt chart' of prosecutorial work to be used internally to enhance results-driven action and quantifiable achievements by the OTP, and provide greater transparency to the ASP in budgeting decisions. Gantt charts are a common practice in business, providing a graphical depiction of a project schedule, from start to finish, that maps flexible beginning and end dates of all elements of a particular project (including resources, milestones, tasks, and dependencies). This could allow for the further formalization of "internal benchmarks and channels of communication"[209] as well as for holding individuals accountable within the OTP. As part of this reform, it is worth considering the introduction of a formal 'exit strategy development' phase, preferably early on in the preliminary examination, which could even be subject to a mandatory dialogue with ASP delegates.[210] In

---

[208] Stahn, see *supra* note 6, p. 12. As discussed above, the Prosecutor already purports to adopt a "holistic approach" regarding the preliminary examination stage, see *supra* note 24. The Prosecutor claims that the analysis during the preliminary examination stage is not rigid and does not follow the statutory stages inflexibly. That said, very little is known about what the OTP actually means by this. Restructuring the preliminary examination stage would make it possible to put meat on the skeleton of the Office's self-proclaimed holistic methodology.

[209] *Ibid.*

[210] It is important to stress that the comments received from ASP members, under such a potential mandatory consultation, must not be binding on the Prosecutor. In developing an

any event, as previously mentioned, Gantt charts are not to be adhered to religiously. Start and end dates may move or change to ensure flexibility. The original Gantt chart will merely provide a model for preliminary examinations (that could further elucidate what the Prosecutor considers as 'reasonable time' for each of the examination's phases), but will be routinely updated in accordance with the dynamics of any given examination. As such, this proposal does not purport to set strict time frames for preliminary examinations, nor does it find such an endeavour useful.

19.5.2. Redefining the Relationship between the OTP and the PTC

As demonstrated, the PTC needs to more substantively acknowledge the significant margin of discretion of the OTP at the preliminary examination stage, especially in connection with its consequentialist policies. At the same time, it would be useful to consider whether greater judicial review of OTP decisions might be a welcome step. The addition of more procedural structure to the preliminary examination stage, through re-phasing as discussed above, could allow for a PTC review that is far more technical and tailored to analysis of actual abuse of powers or improper intent (addressing Schabas' valid concerns about the effectiveness of judicial review).[211] In fact, insofar as the review is limited to those procedural elements (as opposed to micromanagement of subject-matter determinations, as happened in the *Comoros* decision), it might even be possible to mandate a PTC review of every decision to launch an investigation (and not only those launched *proprio motu* – ending what is an arbitrary distinction between Article 14 and Article 15 judicial review). There is also justification for allowing the Prosecutor, when she deems necessary, to apply to the Court for an advisory opinion on matters related to the preliminary examination stage – a mechanism currently unavailable to her.[212]

---

early conceptualization of 'exit strategies' (see discussion on the definition of the term at *supra* note 167) at the preliminary examination stage, the OTP should be advised by as many actors as possible in order to map out the key goals and the broader objectives to be achieved in 'consequentially' engaging a particular situation; but the final decision rests with the Prosecutor.

[211] See *supra* note 110.

[212] Stahn, see *supra* note 6, pp. 14–15 (noting that judicial review in the process of deliberating the question of Palestinian statehood could have been useful, but that "Regulation 46 was not meant to provide a judicial forum for such disputes" – further concluding that this situation is "unsatisfactory". According to Stahn there is need to provide a channel through

Any proposed increase in the role of the PTC at the preliminary examination stage must be considered with great caution. The intention here is not to turn the preliminary examination stage into a quasi-trial and certainly not to establish legal judgments (which might ultimately be perceived as binding on the Court) at an early stage. This is because, at the pre-investigation stage, any engagement with the Court is by default conducted on an *ex parte* basis, with no one representing the affected States or presenting broader counter-arguments to the position of the OTP.[213]

19.5.3. Redrafting Existing OTP Policy Papers and the Adoption of New Policies

Another significant area of reform could be the amendment by the OTP of some of its policies and the adoption of new policy papers, correcting some of the existing flaws in the Court's prosecutorial system, discussed and analysed throughout this chapter. In this regard, the Prosecutor should clarify that transparency is not merely a 'policy objective' but indeed a 'general principle' that guides every preliminary examination. It is true that not everything must be disclosed, and that the question of transparency itself should be subject to discretion. Certain elements in the preliminary examination process might indeed be better served if carried out with some degree of secrecy (consider, for example, sensitive consultations with victims' groups or with the affected States). The question, therefore, is not whether transparency should be uniformly and rigidly applied, but

---

which judicial guidance can be sought prior to, or during, preliminary examinations. I would further suggest that such guidance not be binding on the Prosecutor, but should nonetheless hold significant weight). At the moment, the only external legal advice available to the Prosecutor comes in the form of thematic experts the OTP may consult with on a routine or *ad hoc* basis (for example, roundtable consultations, academic engagements, and workshops).

[213] Some might say that any attempt to involve the PTC will inevitably lead to conclusions that will have far-reaching legal and political consequences not unlike those of the OTP today, and in that case even greater caution is required. One can potentially conceive of means that could introduce structured adversarial PTC proceedings at the preliminary examination stage (beyond what exists today, which is the ability of States to request to submit amicus briefs). For example, the establishment of a "red team" within the OTP (that would be required to submit an alternative account to that of the Prosecutor to the PTC) or a special advocate in the Court that might engage with interested States and could raise their concerns during PTC proceedings. For now, the proposal does not go that far; it merely suggests greater PTC involvement, limited however solely to a technical, rather than substantive, review of procedure.

---

rather whether transparency should be treated as a general principle to be followed, to the extent possible, with some degree of consistency. Transparency should thus be aspired to, and not seen solely through utilitarian lenses as a means to achieve ever-changing objectives.

If my Gantt chart-based approach is adopted, the question then arises as to whether these charts are shared with the public, a question that goes to the heart of the tension between transparency and efficacy. I would recommend that a generic Gantt chart be disclosed, in order to educate the public about the various sub-stages of the preliminary examination process and to elucidate the time frames envisioned by the Office for each sub-stage as a matter of best practice in an ideal scenario. The disclosure of elements of specific Gantt charts from specific preliminary examinations, on the other hand, should be part of a sliding scale approach to transparency. So, while initially the balance would be tilted against such disclosures, the longer the preliminary examination was ongoing without a determination, the more reasons there would be to increase transparency by providing greater information about specific challenges and time frames.

Further, the OTP should reconsider its Policy Paper on the Interests of Justice, due in part to the political deadlock at the UNSC, which prevents it from offering an effective check on the work of the OTP as it relates to decisions that could hinder stability and the broader maintenance of peace and security. This is of specific importance in the context of decisions relating to peace negotiations and agreements. The drafters of the Rome Statute included this parameter within the Prosecutor's discretionary powers (which reflected the notion that the Court does not operate in vacuum), and it is wrong of a Prosecutor to abrogate this responsibility. Similarly, the OTP should elaborate on its policies regarding the formulation of disengagement plans from situations ('exit strategies').[214]

Finally, the Prosecutor should adopt a new Policy Paper on evidentiary standards and policies related to sources of information, including at the preliminary examination stage. The Prosecutor should use that paper to set out in detail the process whereby it examines open-source materials and what legal weight her Office gives them, including by reference to actual examples from past preliminary examinations which have already

---

[214] See *supra* note 167.

been closed. The Prosecutor should further introduce standards concerning the collection, access to, analysis, and dissemination of digital communications and digital forensic evidence, predominantly as they relate to data protection and privacy regulation.

19.5.4. External Review Processes

Finally, there is some basis to the contention that the OTP could be checked by other external oversight mechanisms beyond the PTC.[215] In this context, Senior Legal Advisor to the Pre-Trial Division of the ICC, Gilbert Bitti, has suggested the radical idea of "a structural reform of the office of the prosecutor", replacing the Prosecutor with a three-member 'Committee of Prosecutors' ('College de Procureurs'). Bitti claimed that this would "ensure greater credibility of the institution's choices" by enhancing the stability of penal policies within the Office.[216] While such a

---

[215] Some commentators have suggested that external review processes should even extend beyond the OTP and cover the entire Court. See Morten Bergsmo *et. al.*, "A Prosecutor Falls, Time for the Court to Rise", FICHL Policy Brief Series No. 86 (2017), Torkel Opsahl Academic EPublisher, Oslo, 2017 p. 4 (http://www.toaep.org/pbs-pdf/86-four-directors/) ("Ov-ersight of the ICC cannot be left to States Parties alone […] Immunizing the Court through the good intentions of officials and civil society actors may inadvertently numb the normal sense of vigilance within the organization, on which its self-preservation depends. An unarticulated sense within the Court that it will not be held accountable, that Governments will conceal problematic information from the public, should not be allowed to take hold").

[216] Gilbert Bitti, "Article 53. Ouverture d'une enquête", in Javier Fernandez and Xavier Pacreau (eds.), *Commentaire du Statut de Rome de la Cour pénale internationale*, Pedone, Paris, 2012, vol. II, p. 1173, at p. 1227 ("On peut également envisager, pour assurer une meilleure transperance, et done une plus grande crédibilité des choix de l'institution, une réforme structurelle du Bureau du Procureur. La première chose à afaire serait de remplacer le Procureur par un collège de procureurs, à savoir trois procureurs elus pour 9 ans, non rééligible, et dont le renouvellement se ferait par tiers tous les trois ans. On aboutirait ainsi sans doute aune plus grande stabilité de la politique pénale et donc à une meilleure coherence des choix de politique pénale"). Bitti then proceeds by suggesting that the OTP would be split into two, with the Committee of Prosecutors working alongside a "Commission of Inquiry and Analysis" (Commission D'enquête et D'analyse). The latter will be composed of qualified investigators and analysts under the direction of a senior investigator and a senior analyst that would be of the same rank as the Prosecutors in the Committee. Within six months from a referral or Article 15 communication, the Commission would be required to submit its final report to the Committee of Prosecutors. The Committee would then have six months to make a determination regarding the launch of an investigation, subject to review by the PTC.

---

dramatic reform may be unnecessary, Bitti's creative idea is certainly one that is worth more than a passing thought.

One could envision a less drastic version of Bitti's proposal through the establishment of an external 'Committee of Prosecutors' that would serve the purpose of guiding the OTP in its exercise of prosecutorial discretion. Such a Committee might include former Prosecutors from the ICC and other international courts and tribunals, along with a regional representation by high-ranking State prosecutors. This Committee could issue reports, guidance, and support at the request of the Prosecutor or, in cases of prolonged preliminary examinations, at their own volition. Such decisions would not replace the Prosecutor's overall discretion or final say, but could further support it by offering more detailed reasoning and greater objectivity to the determinations – thus enhancing the overall legitimacy of the Court.[217]

19.6. Conclusion

Celebrating its fifteenth anniversary, the ICC is at a crossroads. The political reality that embraced the Court with the signing of the Rome Statute in 1998 is not the same political reality in which the Court must manoeuvre today. The Prosecutor faces opposition from African States, increased nationalism in the United States under the current administration, and populist rhetoric across Europe, financial crises that force the Court's primary donors to cut their budget, and grotesque war crimes and crimes against humanity in war zones like Syria with no available means to seek ICC redress.

It is in this context that the Prosecutor's power to engage in preliminary examinations is both a promise and a curse. The OTP should continue to push for crime prevention and positive complementarity, looking "beyond the narrow aspects of the court room", while using the means available to it through Article 53(1) examinations. At the same time, however, the Prosecutor should be fully cognizant of the limits of its own power to effect change, and should ensure that good faith is not confused

---

[217] The controversy that arose in 2010 following the establishment of the Independent Oversight Mechanism and the debates over its monitoring functions over the OTP, makes me believe this recommendation is likely to endure similar resistance. See, generally, Bertham Kloss, *The Exercise of Prosecutorial discretion at the International Criminal Court: Towards a more Principled Approach*, Herbert Utz Verlag, Munich, 2016, pp. 74–77.

with impotent idealism. A number of politically contentious preliminary examinations are threatening to further degrade public perception of the Court. In trying to achieve Davis' 'optimum point', mechanisms at the preliminary examination stage should be re-conceptualized, first and foremost by the OTP. This chapter has attempted to analyse the limitations of existing mechanisms, and to offer potential reforms which may aid the advancement of quality awareness and improvement throughout the preliminary examination process.

20

Disarming the Trap:
Evaluating Prosecutorial Discretion in
Preliminary Examinations beyond
the False Dichotomy of Politics and Law

Jens Iverson[*]

This chapter interrogates the assumption that the choices faced by the Office of the Prosecutor in preliminary examinations can be adequately summarized as a conflict between law and politics. It argues in favour of a more open discussion of the trade-offs inherent in pursuing international criminal justice, particularly on a limited budget. International criminal law practitioners and scholars are too often stuck in a rhetorical trap that ill-serves the goals of making and explaining collective value choices and critiques. Time and resources are wasted in a discursive framework pairing unsubstantiated allegations of politicization with unsatisfying invocations of professionally simply following where the law and the evidence lead. Not only does this sterile back-and-forth fail to explain the actual actions and motivations of decision makers, but it neuters the didactic potential of international criminal law mechanisms, even (or perhaps especially) in the preliminary examination stage.

20.1. Introduction

The spectre of politicization is never far from the exercise of prosecutorial discretion, and the scope of prosecutorial discretion in preliminary examinations is wide. At the preliminary examination stage, there is ordinarily no check to the Prosecutor's discretion from any judge, defence counsel, or victims' representative. The Office of the Prosecutor must be, in large

---

[*] **Jens Iverson** is Assistant Professor of Law, Leiden University. This chapter builds on previous online writings of the author, particularly "Spreading the jam". Many thanks to Professors Carsten Stahn, Ascanio Piomelli, and Naomi Roht-Arriaza for inspiration, and Dr. Joe Powderly, Dr. Dov Jacobs, and Cale Davis for their thoughtful comments. Errors are the author's own.

---

part, guided by its own principles at this early stage. The Office of the Prosecutor's Policy Paper on Preliminary Examinations declares that "[t]he preliminary examination process is conducted on the basis of the facts and information available, and in the context of the overarching principles of independence, impartiality and objectivity".[1] Similarly, in the Policy Paper on Case Selection it proclaimed that "[t]he Office shall conduct its case selection and prioritisation on the basis of the overarching principles of independence, impartiality and objectivity".[2] All of these principles are efforts in part to prevent politicization, real or perceived.

Independent, objective, impartial analysis is as an essential foundation for criminal justice. Rawls' theory of 'justice as fairness' underscores that the principles of justice should be best chosen through a 'veil of ignorance' in which people do not know of their own partial interests, but instead approach choices pertaining to justice as objectively as possible.[3] Partiality is thus viewed, from a Rawlsian perspective, as an impediment to achieving justice, and politics conceived as a form of partiality an unalloyed negative. This sets up the dichotomy of partial politics on the one hand and objective application of the law to a given set of facts on the other hand. This dichotomy is usually assumed without examination, and guides the debate over the choices of actors within international criminal law. Anything not framed as law is assumed to be politics, and politics are to be avoided.

This chapter disputes the assumption that the choices faced by the Office of the Prosecutor in preliminary examinations can be adequately summarized as a conflict between law and politics. This conflict may exist, but reducing the spectrum of choices of the Office of the Prosecutor to this conflict is a thin and inadequate framework to understand those choices. This chapter argues in favour of a more open discussion of the trade-offs inherent in pursuing international criminal justice, particularly with a limited budget. International criminal law practitioners and scholars are too often stuck in a rhetorical trap that ill-serves the goals of making and explaining collective value choices and critiques. Time and re-

---

[1]   Office of the Prosecutor, *Policy Paper on Preliminary Examinations*, November 2013, p. 7, para. 25 (http://www.legal-tools.org/doc/acb906/).

[2]   Office of the Prosecutor, *Policy Paper on Case Selection and Prioritisation*, 15 September 2016, p. 7, para. 16 (http://www.legal-tools.org/doc/182205/).

[3]   John Rawls, *A Theory of Justice*, Harvard University Press, Cambridge (MA), 1971.

sources are wasted in a discursive framework pairing unsubstantiated allegations of politicization with unsatisfying invocations of professionally "simply following where the law and the evidence lead".[4] Not only does this sterile back-and-forth fail to explain the actions and motivations of decision makers, but it neuters the didactic potential of international criminal law mechanisms, even in the preliminary examination stage.

The chapter does not follow the pattern employed by some critical theorists in which apparently apolitical, objective analyses are deconstructed and revealed as mere subjective expressions of power. If that technique is 'critical' the argument made by this chapter is for a Pragmatic 'anti-critical' approach. This Pragmatic[5] approach is more than simple apology. It maintains that the Office of the Prosecutor's choices are *not* determined entirely by law or politics, but at least in part is an expression of value prioritization best understood on its own terms.

This argument finds particular purchase in the context of preliminary examination stage. The didactic function of preliminary examination is underappreciated, except to the degree it is included in the overall discussion of 'positive complementarity'.[6] If freed from the trap of avoiding public discussion of prioritization made for fear of being slandered as 'politicized' comparatively transparent explanations of the Office of the Prosecutor's choices can play an important role in driving public discussion of what values undergird international criminal law.

Isaiah Berlin asserted "collisions of values are of the essence of what they are and what we are".[7] The Office of the Prosecutor, its supporters, and critics, should directly confront the collisions of values inher-

---

4   For an example of discourse on politics and international law, see, for example, Martti Koskenniemi, "The Politics of International Law", in *European Journal of International Law*, 1990, vol. 1, no. 1, p. 4.

5   On the value of Pragmatism and human rights, see, for example, Richard Rorty, "Human rights, rationality, and sentimentality", in Rathore, Aakash Singh, and Alex Cistelecan (eds.), *Wronging Rights?: Philosophical Challenges for Human Rights*, Routledge, 1993, pp. 1–34. For a skeptical approach to Pragmatism and jurisprudence see, for example, Richard A. Posner, *The Problems of Jurisprudence*, Harvard University Press, 1993.

6   On the neglected importance of the didactic function, see, for example, Mirjan Damaška, "What is the point of international criminal justice", in *Chicago-Kent Law Review*, 2008, vol. 83, no. 1, p. 329.

7   Isaiah Berlin, "The pursuit of the ideal", in *The Crooked Timber of Humanity: Chapters in the history of ideas*, Princeton University Press, 2013.

ent in the use of prosecutorial discretion. Openly discussing the possibility that, with a limited budget, addressing crimes in Palestine may mean that crimes in Afghanistan may go largely un-investigated by the Office of the Prosecutor, or that crimes of sexual violence may have to be prioritized above other crimes, and doing so with minimal unfounded allegations of politicization, will not only promote the values behind each of these options. It will also enrich our understanding of each option, help the Office of the Prosecutor to come to better decisions, and may ultimately result in greater support and financial backing for the project of international criminal law in general.

The chapter begins in Section 20.2. with a brief discussion of the context of preliminary examinations at the International Criminal Court, and proceeds in Section 20.3. to interrogate what 'quality' means in terms of 'quality control' in preliminary examinations. Section 20.4. emphasizes Mirjan Damaška's prioritization of the didactic effect of international criminal courts and ties it to the idea of quality in preliminary examination. The chapter continues in Section 20.5. with a discussion of Amartya Sen's distinction between optimal and maximal choices, where a maximal alternative need not be 'best'.[8] The idea of didactics from an experimentalist or Pragmatic point of view is explored in Section 20.6. Section 20.7. brings together the idea of a choice by the Office of the Prosecutor being maximal from a Pragmatic perspective. The limits to approaching choices in preliminary examination through a purely didactic lens are discussed in Section 20.8, followed by concluding reflections.

This work relies in part on the contributions of scholars (Mirjan Damaška, Amartya Sen, and John Dewey) who are widely familiar as intellectuals. Applying their work to the challenges of International Criminal Law, particularly the practical demands of quality control in preliminary examinations, may require a bit more explanation than building on the work of scholars whose contributions are focused exclusively or primarily on international criminal law. Hopefully, any patience required in following their potential contribution to understanding the demands of quality control will be rewarded by the utility of bringing fresh approaches to the problems faced by practitioners. Damaška, Sen, and Dewey all

---

[8] Amartya Sen, "Reason and Justice: The Optimal and the Maximal", in *Philosophy*, 2017, vol. 92, no. 1, pp. 5–19.

hail from different disciplines, but share a common emphasis on the importance of paying attention to local generation of law and meaning. Damaška is a consummate comparativist, bringing a unique perspective to his scholarship on international criminal law. Sen's work is replete with a discussion of social choice and justice. Dewey is a foundational Pragmatist whose work revolutionized early twentieth century philosophy with respect to re-founding liberal democratic values on the basis of experimentation and locally-constructed meaning. In addition, there is a rich scholarship emphasizing international criminal law's expressive function.[9] Before exploring selected contributions of these scholars, the basic argument of the chapter will be amplified. In the following sections, the trap of falling into a discourse that eliminates any useful public discussion of the choices that may be available will be examined, and an argument will be made for particular emphasis on the didactic function of international criminal justice.

20.2. Defining the Trap:
The Context of Quality Control in Preliminary Examinations

The Office of the Prosecutor is of course not wrong to insist on "independence, impartiality and objectivity" as guiding principles for preliminary examinations,[10] case selection,[11] and its practice generally. Its main

---

[9]   See, for example, Mark A. Drumbl, "The expressive value of prosecuting and punishing terrorists: Hamdan, the Geneva Conventions, and international criminal law", in *George Washington Law Review*, 2006, vol. 75, nos. 5–6, p. 1165; Alexander K.A. Greenawalt, "Justice without Politics-Prosecutorial Discretion and the International Criminal Court", in *New York University Journal of International Law and Politics*, 2006, vol. 39, no. 3, p. 583 (arguing that the choices of the Office of the Prosecutor are inherently political); Robert D. Sloane, "The Expressive Capacity of International Punishment: The Limits of the National Law Analogy and the Potential of International Criminal Law", in *Stanford Journal of International Law*, 2007, vol. 43, no. 1, p. 39; William Schabas, "Victor's Justice: Selecting "situations" at the International Criminal Court", in *John Marshall Law Review*, 2009, vol. 43, no. 3, p. 535; Rod Rastan, "Comment on Victor's Justice & the Viability of Ex Ante Standards", in *John Marshall Law Review*, 2009, vol. 43, no. 3, p. 569; Margaret M. deGuzman, "Choosing to prosecute: Expressive selection at the International Criminal Court", in *Michigan Journal of International Law*, 2012, vol. 33, no. 2, p. 265; Darryl Robinson, "Inescapable Dyads: Why the International Criminal Court Cannot Win", in *Leiden Journal of International Law*, 2015, vol. 28, no. 2, p. 323.

[10] Office of the Prosecutor, *Policy Paper on Preliminary Examinations*, 2013, p. 7, para. 25, see *supra* note 1.

[11] Office of the Prosecutor, *Policy Paper on Case Selection and Prioritisation*, 2016, p. 7, para. 16, see *supra* note 2.

---

approach to engaging with local actors at the preliminary examination stage appears to be through the concept of "positive complementarity".[12] The hope is that: "A Court based on the principle of complementarity ensures the international rule of law by creating an interdependent, mutually reinforcing system of justice".[13] Positive complementarity in practice appears to be "encouraging genuine national proceedings",[14] noting that:

> [T]he Office can report on its monitoring activities, send in-country missions, request information on proceedings, hold consultations with national authorities as well as with inter-governmental and non-governmental organisations, partici-pate in awareness-raising activities on the ICC, exchange lessons learned and best practices to support domestic inves-tigative and prosecutorial strategies, and assist relevant stakeholders to identify pending impunity gaps and the scope for possible remedial measures.[15]

There is little guidance from the Office of the Prosecutor as to whether its engagement with local actors helps determine a ranked priori-ty of the gravity of potentially criminal conduct. Gravity is primarily treated as a threshold determination for admissibility pursuant to Article 17(1)(d) of the Rome Statute.[16] Regulation 29(2) provides a non-exhaustive list of factors for the Office of the Prosecutor to consider when assessing the gravity of alleged crimes: "In order to assess the gravity of the crimes allegedly committed in the situation the Office shall consider various factors including their scale, nature, manner of commission, and impact". The Policy Paper on Preliminary Examinations amplifies the meaning of these factors:

> 62. The scale of the crimes may be assessed in light of, *inter alia*, the number of direct and indirect victims, the extent of the damage caused by the crimes, in particular the bodily or psychological harm caused to the victims and their families, or their geographical or temporal spread (high intensity of

---

12 Office of the Prosecutor, *Policy Paper on Preliminary Examinations*, 2013, p. 23, paras. 100 ff., see *supra* note 1.

13 *Ibid.*, p. 23, para. 100.

14 *Ibid.*, p. 24, para. 102.

15 *Ibid.*

16 Rome Statute of the International Criminal Court, adopted 17 July 1998, entry into force 1 July 2002 ('ICC Statute') (http://www.legal-tools.org/doc/7b9af9/).

---

the crimes over a brief period or low intensity of crimes over an extended period).

63. The nature of the crimes refers to the specific elements of each offence such as killings, rapes and other crimes involving sexual or gender violence and crimes committed against children, persecution, or the imposition of conditions of life on a group calculated to bring about its destruction.

64. The manner of commission of the crimes may be assessed in light of, inter alia, the means employed to execute the crime, the degree of participation and intent of the perpetrator (if discernible at this stage), the extent to which the crimes were systematic or result from a plan or organised policy or otherwise resulted from the abuse of power or official capacity, and elements of particular cruelty, including the vulnerability of the victims, any motives involving discrimination, or the use of rape and sexual violence as a means of destroying groups.

65. The impact of crimes may be assessed in light of, *inter alia*, the sufferings endured by the victims and their increased vulnerability; the terror subsequently instilled, or the social, economic and environmental damage inflicted on the affected communities.[17]

This is an admirable start. The jurisprudence cited in the Policy Paper on Preliminary Examinations warning against excessively formulistic grounds for the assessment of gravity is indeed persuasive.[18] Nonetheless, these general principles provide little check on the Office's determination of the gravity of possible crimes (at least at this early stage), nor much guidance as to how or whether a determination of relative gravity will inform the allocation of resources. Criticisms such as Human Rights

---

[17] Office of the Prosecutor, *Policy Paper on Preliminary Examinations*, 2013, pp. 15–16, paras. 62–65, see *supra* note 1.

[18] ICC, Situation in the Democratic Republic of the Congo, Appeals Chamber, Judgment on the Prosecutor's appeal against the decision of Pre-Trial Chamber I entitled "Decision on the Prosecutor's Application for Warrants of Arrest, Article 58", under seal 13 July 2006; reclassified as public 23 September 2008, ICC-01/04-169, paras. 69–79 (http://www.legal-tools.org/doc/8c20eb/).

Watch's report *ICC: Course Correction*[19] alleging inconsistency in approach across various situations will likely persist. Such criticism will also be largely unanswerable because the introduction of so many subcriteria in an overall balancing test provides little transparency or ground for any kind of objective metric.

Beyond the policy papers cited above, observers of international criminal law may detect a more general cautious pattern in statements and responses from the Office of the Prosecutor. For example, when the particular charges chosen by the Office in the first trial are questioned, they will emphasize that they follow evidence's lead. When members of only one side of a conflict are charged, the Office of the Prosecutor will argue that to charge leaders from both sides, when that is not where the evidence leads, would be a political choice – and they must avoid politics. When the question arises of whether there is a tension between prosecution and peace, the Office of the Prosecutor representatives will typically point to the United Nations Security Council's power to pause investigation and prosecution, indicating that political choices should be made by the Security Council. When it is pointed out that every situation country is in Africa, the response is much the same as to the question about refusing to "balance" prosecutions on both sides of a conflict – the Prosecution will not "balance" their work by opening an investigation elsewhere if that is not where the evidence leads. The Office of the Prosecutor will not be politicized. It will follow the law.

This approach is understandable, but it is part of what is being described here as a trap that needs to be disarmed. What is needed is a conversation where those interested in the Office of the Prosecutor's decisions can discuss them without falling into an artificial dichotomy where everything is either political or legal, with no room for additional criteria to be considered.

The unique horrors of forcing children to kill, the particular structural threat of election violence, the specific values threatened by forced marriage – choosing to prioritize addressing one of these at the expense of another must unfortunately be done by the decision makers at the Office

---

[19] Human Rights Watch, *ICC: Course Correction: Recommendations to the Prosecutor for a More Effective Approach to "Situations under Analysis"*, 16 June 2011 (http://www.legal-tools.org/doc/43aefb/).

of the Prosecutor, and yet cannot be fully evaluated either through a legal or political framework. Even combined, the legal and political frameworks merely provide a needlessly binary worldview. This dichotomy places the Office of the Prosecutor in a position of unnecessary opacity with respect to explaining their choices. They cannot discuss non-legal values easily without being subject to the critique of politicization. So, functionally, they are quiet.

The Office of the Prosecutor and its critics are caught in a rhetorical trap. No one realistically expects that the Office behaves as a creature of pure logic, able to rationalize all choices into the single logical choice made evident by the evidence. Thus, when a choice is made, it is easy to paint that choice not based on the application of the law to the facts, what might be described as a professional choice or a legal choice, but rather a political choice. If it cannot be wholly made clear by law, then the political explanation is the only remaining option.

It should be evident to any observer that the Office of the Prosecutor has to make choices. It is neither omniscient nor omnipotent. Any choice it makes is liable to be attacked as a political choice, by academics, activists, and defence counsel (Chambers largely limits itself to pointing out errors of law and professionalism). The Office of the Prosecutor does its best to make clear that they have not been politicized, but it cannot convincingly explain its actions merely with a wave at the law, or the evidence, and an invocation of gravity, without anything further.

It is perhaps helpful to think more about what we mean by such terms as 'political', 'legal' and 'prosecutorial discretion'. One can, of course define political and legal in the negative, where political is the non-legal and the legal is the non-political. This is implied by the pattern of responses from the Office of the Prosecutor, and often from the statements of their detractors.

What positive definitions can be offered? Positively defining 'law' is perhaps easier in the context of evaluating the actions of the Office of the Prosecutor with reference to the legal texts that created and govern it, including: the Rome Statute,[20] the Rules of Procedure and Evidence, and Regulations of the Court. Positively defining 'politics' is of course difficult, with many wanting to define it broadly, but it might be helpful in this

---

[20] ICC Statute, see *supra* note 16.

context to tie it to the term 'politicization', with a focus on power relations between humans and groups of humans, particularly with respect to governmental power. The issue of politics as power relations is particularly heated in the context of armed conflict, and indeed haunts international criminal law. When Justice Robert Jackson famously described the International Military Tribunal as "one of the most significant tributes that Power has ever paid to Reason", it spoke not only to pride in the law, but the concern over victor's justice as a particular politicization of law that lies at the nexus of international criminal law and international humanitarian law.

The tension between the two frameworks of law and politics is a real one, and virtually any choice by the Office of the Prosecutor can usefully be analysed both in terms of its relation to specific legal texts and its effects in power relations. But the analysis need not, and should not, stop there. All this chapter suggests is a richer discussion. A discussion that acknowledges the legal limitations of the Office of the Prosecutor, the effects of power relations, but that also recognizes that the Prosecutor's decisions may express human values that are neither wholly legal nor political.

Charging an accused for recruitment of child soldiers but not for gender or sexual based violence despite evidence of both, can be thought of not only as a legal or political choice, but also as a performance choice. The Office of the Prosecutor can be praised for delivering a message with special emphasis (given the simple charge and as it happens, conviction) that recruitment of child soldiers is wrong and may have repercussions for the perpetrator. The Office of the Prosecutor can be criticized by implicitly sending a message that gender and sexual based violence is not important enough to charge even when it would not necessarily involve additional accused or evidence. Either of these statements has legal and political ramifications, but they need not be, at their core, legal or political. Regardless of one's opinion on the choice, the conversation is enriched by consciously avoiding unnecessary simplification into a political-legal dichotomy.

Similarly, should the Prosecutor decide she will not proceed on an investigation based on the authority granted by UN Security Council referral specifically because the UN Security Council failed to provide the necessary funding for such an investigation, that decision would be an example of prosecutorial discretion not wholly determined or explainable by law or politics. Such a decision would have political and legal effects, but is not fundamentally political or legal in nature. More fundamentally, such an exercise of discretion goes to a clash of values that can exist between, for example, pursuing accountability for specific alleged crimes and building a sustainable and responsible relationship between institutions.

20.3. What is Quality in Quality Control?

There are a range of best practices that pertain to quality control in preliminary examinations that are beyond the scope of this chapter: avoiding unforced errors in terms of, for example, acquiring, preserving, and analysing inculpatory and exculpatory evidence while respecting the rights of the accused and the interests of the victims. This section will instead focus on the goals of international criminal justice as a useful guide to the meaning of quality in quality control. Even without evidentiary errors, for example, if the choices made do not ultimately serve to achieve the goals of international criminal justice, the 'quality' of the choices made must be questionable.

Mirjan Damaška's provocatively titled *What is the point of international criminal justice* discusses the overabundance of goals international criminal courts have set for themselves as a curable weakness of those courts.[21] He notes that such goals include retribution for wrongdoing, general deterrence, incapacitation, rehabilitation, producing a historical record, giving voice to the victims of international crime, propagate human rights values, achieve peace and security objectives, and protecting the rights of the accused.[22] These goals are not only too ambitious, but also too diverse. Adopting a myriad of different Herculean goals threatens to pull these courts in too many directions at once, making completion of even just one of their goals difficult.[23] Damaška goes beyond the peace versus justice chestnut to include the tension between individualization of proven criminal responsibility and creating an accurate history, or the rights of the accused and the desire to satisfy crime victims (framed as a tension between procedural and substantive justice).[24] He particularly

---

[21] Damaška, 2008, p. 330, see *supra* note 6.

[22] *Ibid.*, p. 331.

[23] *Ibid.*, pp. 331–32.

[24] *Ibid.*, pp. 332–34.

notes the case of *Barayagwiza*, in which an initial decision to release an accused due to a violation of his rights to a speedy trial was reversed apparently due to the Rwandan government's decision to suspect co-operation with the Tribunal.[25] Most interesting is Damaška's analysis of the tension between the didactic[26] goals of international criminal justice and the (asserted) desire of victims to see the direct perpetrators of crimes committed against them convicted.[27] Damaška suggests that the greatest didactic impact can be achieved primarily from dramatic prosecutions of high-level superiors.[28]

Damaška suggests that the goals of international criminal courts should have direct impacts on their work. For example, Damaška provides rationales as to why an emphasis on didactic effect (in contrast with general deterrence) should lead the Office of the Prosecutor (in any international criminal tribunal) to hesitate before relying heavily on joint criminal enterprise or anything that resembles it, or to depend upon superior responsibility unless necessary. Damaška seems to indicate that 'quality' is not avoiding error, or applying the law as mechanistically as possible to facts, but rather, active analysis as to the goals of the institution and allowing those goals to influence policy and practice.

20.4. Quality in Preliminary Examination as Potential Didactic Effect

After noting the superabundance of goals of international criminal courts and the tensions between them, Damaška turns to a theme that can be connected to Sen's analysis described below, the absence of a ranking order among the goals.[29] He makes a compelling case for the primary importance of the didactic function.[30] He specifically ranks didactic effects above deterrence, noting the very limited capacity of international criminal courts to provide a credible threat for most perpetrators, whereas

---

[25] ICTR, *Barayagwiza v. Prosecutor*, Appeals Chamber, Decision (Prosecutor's Request for Review or Reconsideration), 31 March 2000, ICTR-97-19-AR72, paras. 34, 74 (https://www.legal-tools.org/en/doc/1c0fe7/).

[26] Damaška uses the term "pedagogical".

[27] Damaška, 2008, pp. 334–35, see *supra* note 6.

[28] *Ibid.*

[29] *Ibid.*, pp. 339–40.

[30] *Ibid.*, pp. 343 ff.

the didactic effect does not rely on such a threat.[31] Such a didactic effect, lacking coercive power, rests almost entirely on the quality of the decisions and procedures – legitimacy and integrity are critical for such an effect.[32]

Damaška also notes that the didactic effect of a choice within international criminal justice can vary depending on local experience, customs, sensibilities and loyalties. The same conviction may produce one effect in one community and another in a different community, or in the international community as a whole.[33] Ideally, international criminal justice would command 'thick acceptance' by being tailored to local sensibilities, but this would necessarily entail fragmentation of international criminal law, leading to incoherence and a lack of integrity.[34] How can this tension be resolved? Damaška suggests the following:

> International prosecutors-who have great leeway in choosing whom to prosecute, when, and on what charges-should carefully weigh local factors in discharging their responsibilities. Dismissive or condescending attitudes toward local culture or laws and insensitivity to state identity (especially if fragile) should be anathema. And international judges, while following the uniform legal regime, should make it their habit always to explain, in their decisions, the reasons or special needs that induce international criminal law to deviate from whatever local norms or practices are deemed fair and appropriate.[35]

This has particular application within the context of preliminary examinations. When comparing the various aspects of gravity of multiple possible crimes,[36] and with an eye towards thick acceptance and didactic effect of the choices made, the Office of the Prosecutor would be well advised to take into account not only gravity, but also the comparative gravity of the crimes as felt by the affected communities. Ideally this would occur with all relevant organs of the Court supplementing this

---

[31] *Ibid.*, p. 345.

[32] *Ibid.*

[33] *Ibid.*, p. 335.

[34] *Ibid.*, p. 349.

[35] *Ibid.*

[36] See *supra* Section 20.2.

evaluation with respectful explanations of any differences between its practice and the legal norms of said communities. This may be useful when the mode of liability has no local equivalent, and where the appearance of selective prosecution of local leaders may be seen as an expression of power and partiality.[37]

A focus on didactic effect suggests a particular approach the Office of the Prosecutor should take with respect to investigations: to concentrate on establishing whether particular individuals committed specific wrongs, and shy away from attempting to providing a broad narrative history of peoples and groups leading up to the alleged crimes.[38] That said, focusing on selected semi-representative episodes of atrocity may have a more profound impact than relying on a strict evaluation of gravity if that implies the same didactic notes will be struck repeatedly.[39] The didactic effect of the prosecutions pursuant to Control Council Law No. 10, for example, was likely enhanced by the thematic nature of those prosecutions.[40]

20.5. Contrasting 'Optimal' and 'Maximal' Choices

Early in *Reason and Justice: The Optimal and the Maximal*, Sen provides an example of optimal decision-making that can be usefully repurposed for the question of choices facing the Office of the Prosecutor during preliminary examination.[41] The example is worth quoting in full, as it cannot be much reduced without a loss of explanatory power.

> Let me begin with an example. Consider a person, Ashraf, with a strong anti-terrorism commitment in contemporary West Asia who is considering the possibility of two terrible events, both of which a terrorist group has threatened to carry out. One threatened event – let us call it x – is the total destruction of the historic city of Nineveh (with, however, no one being killed), and the other – called y – involves the killing of a thousand people at a different spot (without any

---

[37] See Damaška, 2008, pp. 350 ff., see *supra* note 6.

[38] See *ibid.*, p. 360.

[39] See *ibid.*

[40] Trials of War Criminals Before the Nuernberg Military Tribunals Under Control Council Law No. 10, vol. XV, Procedure, Practice and Administration, October 1946–April 1949, pp. 23–28 (http://www.legal-tools.org/doc/ffda62/).

[41] Sen, 2017, see *supra* note 8.

destruction of Nineveh). Both are hugely bad things to happen, and Ashraf is considering what can be done to stop them. If it turns out that he and his fellow anti-terrorists can prevent one of the two ghastly events, but not both, then his decision would have to be about choosing between x and y.

The point is not only that it is a difficult choice, nor that the considerations involved in the two alternatives are quite different: one is the prevention of the murder of a large number of people (a thousand in this example) and the other the preservation of a great historical sight which can be thought to be valuable in itself, but would also be hugely valued by a great many generations to come. The point rather is that we may have good reasons to give decisional priority in one direction, or alternatively in the other – a plurality of answers that need not be eliminated by what Rawls calls a 'reflective equilibrium'. It may be quite acceptable, and yet not obligatory, that by the force of reasoning Ashraf will decide in favour of one of the alternatives, rejecting the other (for example, choosing to sacrifice a thousand human lives, for preventing the destruction of Nineveh).[42]

Here, relying on Nikolas Bourbaki,[43] an 'optimal' choice or result is one that is the 'best', whereas a 'maximal' choice or result is one that is "no less satisfactory than any other conclusion (an alternative that cannot be bettered)".[44] Using this formal definition, all optimal choices are maximal, but not all maximal choices have the unique quality of being optimal. While this may seem like an esoteric distinction useful in mathematics but not for legal professionals, Sen asserts this distinction is "absolutely central to the nature of substantive ethical arguments, including the assessment of the respective claims of alternative theories of justice".[45] To the degree Sen's argument is correct, and to the degree the Office of the Prosecutor must address competing claims to justice, consideration of this distinction may prove useful.

---

[42] *Ibid.*, pp. 8–9.

[43] Nicolas Bourbaki, *Elements de Mathématique*, Hermann, 1939; translated to English in Springer-Verlag, 1939.

[44] Sen, 2017, p. 7, see *supra* note 8.

[45] *Ibid.*, p. 7.

The Office of the Prosecutor often faces an array of choices not unlike Ashraf. In the preliminary examination of any given situation, multiple events like x (the destruction of cultural property) and y (the murder of many people) may have already occurred, and with a limited set of resources, not every event can be fully investigated. Indeed, as the Office of the Prosecutor may in some cases provide early warning, the Office of the Prosecutor may be placed in an even more similar situation to Ashraf than the investigation of past crimes.[46] Further, difficult choices such as these occur on every scale, from which situations should be prioritized, to which events or course of potentially criminal conduct should merit particular investigation, to which particular crimes should be emphasized, to aspects of an individual charge. How can the Office of the Prosecutor make the best choice at every level?

Sen's contribution is to indicate that there may not be a best ('optimal') choice, but rather a set of 'maximal' choices (as well as objectively non-maximal and (necessarily) non-optimal choices). Ashraf, in Sen's example, can come to the end of his impartial and reasoned assessment without ranking x above y or vice versa. If he could rank one above the other, he could respond with an optimal choice. If he prevents x but not y, even if he cannot objectively and impartially rank x and y, his choice may be considered maximal, because preventing x is "no less satisfactory than any other conclusion", including preventing y. Put another way, preventing y (the alternative maximal choice) does not represent a better choice *because* x and y are an unranked pair with respect to each other.

For some readers, graphic representations of these quantitative concepts may be of assistance. Before jumping to 'x' and 'y' from Sen's example, an easier example will be provided.

---

[46] "18. The Office will also seek to react promptly to upsurges of violence by reinforcing early interaction with States, international organisations and non-governmental organisations in order to verify information on alleged crimes, to encourage genuine national proceedings, and to prevent the recurrence of crimes". Office of the Prosecutor, *Policy Paper on Preliminary Examinations*, 2013, p. 4, para. 18, see *supra* note 1.

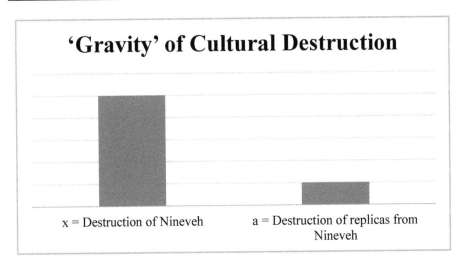

Figure 1

Here, 'x', the destruction of Nineveh, clearly has a greater 'gravity' than the destruction of replicas from Nineveh. Even if the replicas are artfully crafted, and even without a clear, rigorous, objective definition and means of evaluation of the definition of 'gravity' with respect to the destruction of cultural heritage, an unambiguous ranking is possible, placing preventing x above preventing a. Preventing x is thus both the maximal and optimal choice between the two. Gravity is put in quotes not to denigrate the concept of gravity as used in international criminal law, but as a gentle reminder that it operates in part as an analogy with real, measurable, physical gravity (in the sense of an attractive force between mass), and that like all analogies, it has limits (in this case, precise quantification). Not only may 'a' not necessarily pass the gravity threshold for admissibility pursuant to Article 17(1)(d) of the Rome Statute,[47] even if it did (perhaps as part of an additional course of conduct) it might not merit the same level of analysis and attention.

---

[47] ICC Statute, see *supra* note 16.

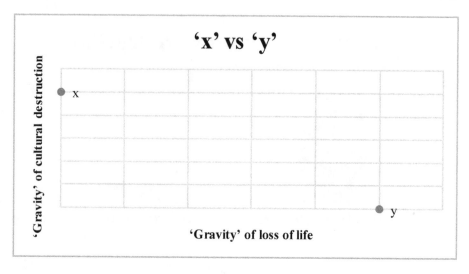

Figure 2

Here, choosing to prevent either x or y may be maximal, but neither is optimal without some sort of 'total gravity index' that can somehow equate the gravity of a (measurable) unit of to something arguably incomparable, such as the loss of life. This is similar to the situation in a standard economics textbook, where a range of goods can be produced along a simple production – possibility frontier – any choice along that frontier will be maximal (usually goods like bread and butter are used), while none will be optimal without some clear index between the two maximands – in this example the goods being produced. In terms of the choices faced by the Office of the Prosecutor, it will rarely be two simple choices, but rather a range of possible crimes to investigate.

The following figure is an extremely simplified example of an array of six events with various levels of destruction of cultural property or loss of life.

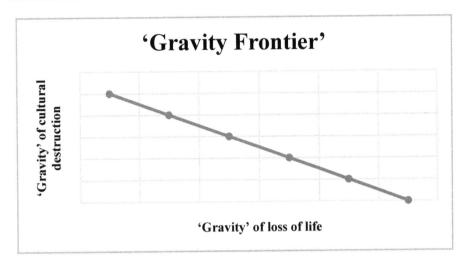

Figure 3

Here, again, investigating any particular event, if only one could be picked, could be said to be maximal. Without some agreed upon way to compare units of one type of gravity with another, choosing the optimal event to prioritize above all others on the basis of 'gravity' alone is impossible. Any event along the 'frontier' could be considered a maximal choice. Prioritizing any event below the frontier would be considered non-maximal (and non-optimal). Any quality control rubric measuring the choices of the Office of the Prosecutor has to consider the real constraints of the Office, in which not every investigatory lead can be pursued. The complications of real investigations may make such comparisons appear foolish, but at the risk of trying the patience of the reader, one last figure will be ventured to illustrate the basic concept.

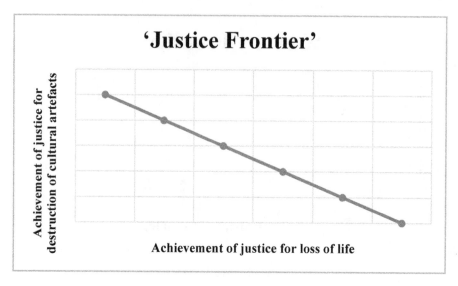

Figure 4

Ultimately, the choices of the Office of the Prosecutor must respond to more than the gravity of the crimes within their jurisdiction, including such factors as the availability and reliability of evidence, co-operation of States, the interests of the victims, and the rights of the accused. Nonetheless, the basic point holds; there may be multiple choices that are maximal, without any one of them being clearly optimal. Were this visualization to be carried out further, even with respect to the gravity alone, many additional variables representing the various values involved would have to be represented. Given the inherent difficulty with assessment of evidence at the stage of preliminary examination, as well as the arbitrary nature of comparing arguably incomparable qualities, some indication of uncertainty akin to error bars would need to be introduced.[48] But that would be taking the exercise too far; the point here is not to introduce or encourage some sort of 'total gravity index' that would allow an optimal choice to be determined, but rather to illustrate the problem that in any actual preliminary examination the best that can be hoped for is that the choices made are not clearly inferior to alternative options, given the knowledge available at the time.

---

[48] Sen discusses this in terms of "unbridgeable gaps in in information" and "tentative incompleteness". Sen, 2017, p. 12, see *supra* note 8.

At this point the reader may contrast the Office of the Prosecutor's list of sub-criteria with respect to gravity and Sen's simple thought experiment, and feel that neither provides a great deal of guidance as to quality or limits to the Office's discretion. Combining Damaška's insights as to the local specificity of the didactic function and Sen's framework allowing a range of acceptable approaches to the same facts is of some help. Sen's framework should allow the Office of the Prosecutor and its critics to relax and admit a variety of acceptable (approaching maximal) choices, while Damaška's insights can provide some guidance as to how the Office of the Prosecutor can approach the question of how and whether to proceed with a degree of local nuance and a clearer prioritization of goals (emphasizing the didactic function). Damaška's warnings regarding patronizing tone or approach are particularly valuable here – while the primary long-range goal of international criminal courts may be didactic (to consolidate and reinforce fundamental values underpinning international criminal law so as to enhance voluntary compliance and enforcement), the individuals receiving the most education at the preliminary examination stage are the staff of the Office of the Prosecutor, not the individuals in affected communities.

The staff of Office of the Prosecutor has the opportunity during preliminary examination not only to receive and analyse communications and learn about evidence and allegations to which they may apply the law and plan further investigations, but also to learn in a more nuanced way what the impact of crime is, which is inextricably bound up in how it is defined and experienced on an individual and community basis. The Office of the Prosecutor notes "The impact of crimes may be assessed in light of, *inter alia*, the sufferings endured by the victims and their increased vulnerability; the terror subsequently instilled, or the social, economic and environmental damage inflicted on the affected communities".[49] The role of affected communities in evaluating the gravity of various crimes for themselves is not made clear by this list of sub-criteria. Prioritizing the didactic function provides a particular opening to interact with affected communities and individuals in a manner that allows them to contribute to the discussion as to priorities of the Office of the Prosecutor without necessarily feeling that any variance from the public line of proceeding mechanisti-

---

[49] Office of the Prosecutor, *Policy Paper on Preliminary Examinations*, 2013, p. 16, para. 65, see *supra* note 1.

cally "on the basis of the facts and information available, and in the context of the overarching principles of independence, impartiality and objectivity" will subject the Office to unfounded allegations of politicization.

20.6. Pragmatism and Didactics

The Office of the Prosecutor is, of course, not the only actor with respect to the didactic effect of a preliminary investigation and any subsequent proceedings at the International Criminal Court. Local civil society, local government, and other local actors may all play a role, and other organs of the Court play a role at any later stage. To examine their role, particularly with respect to didactics, it may be helpful to look towards foundational theorists of education.

One rediscovered theorist who may be helpful with respect to the philosophy of education is John Dewey, a leading (some would say *the* leading)[50] US public intellectual of the 1920s through the early 1940s.[51] Dewey is generally considered a Pragmatist, although he preferred the term 'Experimentalism' to 'Pragmatism' because his emphasis was on the evaluation of practices by their consequences.[52] Dewey's contributions were rich and varied, providing important insight to the theory of participatory democracy and legitimacy of government amongst other matters.[53]

From the outset, Dewey emphasized the importance of local legitimacy. He asserted that "Humanity cannot be content with a good which is procured from without, however high and otherwise complete that good".[54] Dewey's Experimentalist/Pragmatist approach to legitimacy and to education emphasizes the necessity of widespread participation in political life. He suggested that values are not formed from on high and pushed

---

[50] Ascanio Piomelli, "The Democratic Roots of Collaborative Lawyering", in *Clinical Law Review*, 2005, vol. 12, p. 541, at p. 565. Note that the author served as research assistant for Ascanio Piomelli. My thanks to him for his support.

[51] Sheldon S. Wolin, *Politics and vision: Continuity and innovation in Western political thought*, Princeton University Press, 2009, p. 503 (comparing Dewey favorably with John Rawls and John Stewart Mill).

[52] Piomelli, 2005, p. 566, see *supra* note 50.

[53] *Ibid.*, p. 549.

[54] John Dewey, "The Ethics of Democracy" (1888), in *The Early Works of John Dewey*, Southern Illinois University Press, 2008, vol. 1, p. 228, reprinted in John Dewey, in Debra Morris and Ian Shapiro (eds.), *The Political Writings*, Hackett Publishing, 1993, p. 49, at p. 61; also as cited in Piomelli, 2005, p. 541, see *supra* note 50.

down, but rather that there existed a "necessity for the participation of every mature human being in formation of the values that regulate the living of men together",[55] and further:

> The very fact of exclusion from participation is a subtle form of suppression. It gives individuals no opportunity to reflect and decide upon what is good for them. Others who are supposed to be wiser and who in any case have more power decide the question for them and also decide the methods and means by which subjects may arrive at the enjoyment of what is good for them. This form of coercion and suppression is more subtle and more effective than is overt intimidation and restraint.[56]

Imagining Sen's Ashraf deciding between addressing event x or event y, one might suggest that Ashraf would be best served not by following some *a priori* abstract determination of how these types of issues should be balanced, but rather guided by the values of affected communities. While cultural property may be in part a universal heritage, it is also part of specific heritage. Ashraf facing a similar choice on the surface level could and *should* come to a different determination depending on what he could ascertain about the affected communities. One does not need to adopt a particular philosophical outlook such as Pragmatism to emphasize the importance of allowing local individuals (particularly victims), civil society and representative government a role in defining 'quality'. 'Quality control' is in a sense always in the hands of the Prosecutor and in the testing of her decisions in subsequent proceedings, but the Office of the Prosecutor would be well-served by listening to and learning from affected communities, and by incorporating local perspectives into decision-making. This cannot be done adequately through the passive receipt of communications or communicating only to government officials at the apex of local authority and influence. To the degree possible, perspectives from those most directly affected by criminal conduct, often made available only through civil society, should be sought out and responded to.

---

55 John Dewey, *The Later Works of John Dewey: 1925-1953: 1932: Ethics*, Southern Illinois University Press, 2008, vol. 7, p. 217.

56 *Ibid.*, p. 218.

Civil society and the Office of the Prosecutor must inevitably remain separate and independent actors, including during preliminary examination. The question is how, not whether, they will relate to each other. The main mode may be one in which the Office of the Prosecutor receives communications, which may include both potential evidence and legal characterization of that evidence, from civil society. What Ascanio Piomelli and others have called "collaborative lawyering"[57] may be looked upon nervously by those who fear anything that may be characterized as 'political' (indeed this type of lawyering is also known as "political lawyering"[58]), but by any name, local lawyers working in collaboration with individuals and communities affected by crimes within the jurisdiction of the Court should be encouraged by all involved to make their case publicly as a welcome part of the discussion as to what 'quality' means in a particular context.

20.7. A Pragmatic Approach to the Didactic Effect of Choices Made in Preliminary Examinations

Dewey and his more famous colleague and intellectual predecessor William James emphasized truth-testing[59] and idealized a scientific approach to contested social questions.[60] The decision in *Lubanga* not to prioritize sexual violence and to prioritize the conscripting and using child soldiers has been widely criticized.[61] One critical question that might be posed is how attitudes and concepts towards sexual violence and child soldiers has changed in communities that have paid particular attention to the *Lubanga* trial. Empirically determining the effect of choices on goals such as deter-

---

[57] Piomelli, 2005, p. 541, see *supra* note 50.

[58] *Ibid.*, p. 545.

[59] See, for example, James T. Kloppenberg, "James's Pragmatism and American Culture: 1907-2007", in John J. Stuhr (ed.), 100 Years of Pragmatism: William James's Revolutionary Philosophy, Indiana University Press, 2009, p. 7.

[60] Piomelli, 2005, p. 569, see *supra* note 50.

[61] See, for example, Susana SáCouto and Katherine Cleary, "The Importance of Effective Investigation of Sexual Violence and Gender-Based Crimes at the International Criminal Court", in *American University Journal of Gender, Social Policy & the Law*, 2009, vol. 17, no. 2, p. 337; Dustin A Lewis, "Unrecognized Victims: Sexual Violence Against Men in Conflict Settings under International Law", in *Wisconsin International Law Journal*, 2009, vol. 27, no. 1, p. 1; Anne-Marie de Brouwer, "Reparation to Victims of Sexual Violence: Possibilities at the International Criminal Court and at the Trust Fund for Victims and Their Families", in *Leiden Journal of International Law*, 2007, vol. 20, no. 1, pp. 207–37.

---

rence is notoriously difficult, as imagining the counterfactual scenario without investigation and prosecution tends towards speculation as to what might be in the mind of individual potential perpetrators. Empirically determining the didactic effect of choices made by the Office of the Prosecutor may be comparatively easier, as one could use qualitative interview research or quantitative survey research to determine baseline and post-trial attitudes and concepts regarding relevant criminal conduct.

Disappointment and other reactions from investigation and trial outcomes should matter. Just to take one example, one set of hypotheses that might be put forward is that the *Lubanga* investigation and charging decisions created local disappointment from affected individuals and possibly even local minimization of the importance of the issue of sexual violence – an unwanted didactic effect. But for these reactions to matter institutionally, they must be measured, considered, and incorporated into the Office of the Prosecutor's understanding of how it will make choices and evaluate those choices going forward.

Incorporating social science tools to measure affected communities and individuals as part of quality control may not be a comfortable or familiar process for the Office of the Prosecution. It may, in fact be a responsibility that may be a better fit for the Registry (as such or in the operation of Trust Fund for Victims), an outside party, or a collaborative effort. The institutional fact of making such measurements will likely change the way decision makers evaluate their decisions. Making such measurements may also serve to provide a signal that may itself be helpful. A commitment to making the results of such social science research may available would also further the degree of transparency and accountability for the Office of the Prosecutor and the Court in general.

20.8. Limitations to Using Criminal Proceedings as a Means to a Didactic End

This chapter has suggested that the Office of the Prosecutor embrace Damaška's recommendation that the didactic goal of international criminal justice be prioritized over, for example, deterrence, or incapacitation, due in part to the inherent limitations of scalability of the International Criminal Court's capacity and the inherent ends-based evaluation of the importance of the didactic function. That said, there are limitations to the pursuit of this goal, both ethically and inherently.

Ethically, the retributive justification for criminal punishment is limited by the imperative not to use individuals as merely a means to an end, but rather to act in accordance with the inherent dignity and rights of each affected individual. There is no need to engage in a lengthy discourse on Kantian ethics at this point, but rather just to emphasize a few aspects of the Rome Statute.[62] Not only must the "application and interpretation of law pursuant to this article [...] be consistent with internationally recognized human rights" (pursuant to Article 21(3)), protect the rights of the accused throughout (particularly: Articles 20, 22, 23, 63, 66, 67, and 85), as well as the rights and interests of the victims and witnesses (particularly Articles 57(3), 64(2), 64(6), 65(4), 68, 70, 75, and 79), but the Office of the Prosecutor must, pursuant to Article 54(1)(a): "investigate incriminating and exonerating circumstances equally".

Investigating exonerating circumstances is potentially one of the more difficult areas of quality control for the Office of the Prosecutor. The Article 54(1)(a) obligation, combined with the Article 67(2) disclosure obligation,[63] create an area of potential conflict between the goals described by Damaška. Exonerating circumstances not only make it difficult to get a conviction (or lengthy sentence), but may arguably make certain, simplistic didactic efforts more difficult. If the evidence may create reasonable doubt with regards to any element of any count, the Office of the Prosecutor may have difficulty switching between its largely adversarial role during the pre-trial, trial, and appeals stages and the more inquisitorial, investigative judge-like role apparently envisaged by the command to investigate exonerating circumstances equally with incriminating circumstances.

This can be resolved in part by emphasizing that the didactic function envisaged by Damaška and others is broader and more fundamental than the desire that no crime remain unpunished (*ne crimina remaneant impunita*).[64] The primary didactic function from Damaška's perspective is

---

[62] ICC Statute, see *supra* note 16.

[63] "In addition to any other disclosure provided for in this Statute, the Prosecutor shall, as soon as practicable, disclose to the defence evidence in the Prosecutor's possession or control which he or she believes shows or tends to show the innocence of the accused, or to mitigate the guilt of the accused, or which may affect the credibility of prosecution evidence."

[64] Damaška, 2008, p. 356, see *supra* note 6.

to "propagate human rights values".[65] It is precisely by doing what is difficult, to scrupulously respect the rights of the accused *especially* when it makes the conviction of an accused more challenging, that this lesson is at its most potent. It is inherently self-defeating for the Office of the Prosecutor to abuse human rights in order to propagate human rights values. To put it more positively, placing the didactic function more squarely at the heart of the Office of the Prosecutor's goals when the 'lessons' include modelling the rule of law and the rights of the accused is likely to improve quality control in the difficult area of the production and disclosure of potentially exculpatory evidence. The more that the Office of the Prosecutor can internalize the idea that gathering, producing and providing such evidence can also be framed as a 'win' in the way a conviction is often seen as a victory, the more the Office of the Prosecutor is likely to check itself when its discretion is very broad. In the context of preliminary examination, the Office of the Prosecutor does not have the same investigative and disclosure obligations as in later stages, but the basic approach is likely to inform the workings of Prosecution staff – the full and rigorous evaluation of alternative theories and interpretation of communications that do not support proceeding to trial.

More fundamentally, Damaška's warning about the limited capacity of international criminal courts applies even when the prioritized goal is comparatively scalable. Mark Drumbl has written particularly well about the potential and the limits of the expressive value of international criminal justice.[66] Because the Office of the Prosecutor must make choices, that selectivity inherently undercuts certain values that one might wish it could express, in terms of the equality before the law, universal application of the law, the equal dignity of all people, the universal nature of human rights of all people including victims of crimes not fully investigated by the Office of the Prosecutor. But these limitations should serve more as a call to arms, to address and expand the capacity of international criminal

---

65 *Ibid.*, p. 331.

66 See, for example, Mark A. Drumbl, "Collective Violence and Individual Punishment", in *Northwestern University Law Review*, 2005, vol. 99, no. 2, p. 593; Mark A. Drumbl, "The Expressive Value of Prosecuting and Punishing Terrorists: Hamdan, the Geneva Conventions, and International Criminal Law", in *George Washington Law Review*, 2006, vol. 75, no. 5–6, p. 1165; Mark A. Drumbl, *Atrocity, Punishment, and International Law*, Cambridge University Press, 2007, pp. 173–76.

justice, than a signal to stop the discussion about the choices being made by limiting the discussion to a sterile circular discourse as to whether the Prosecutor's choices are optimal or 'political'.

20.9. Conclusions

In order for the discussion to be more productive, for the Office of the Prosecutor to use its discretion in the best possible manner, and for international criminal law to best address the terrible issues necessarily in its portfolio, we must have a richer, franker discussion over what to do with limited resources. Discussing directly the implication that addressing crimes in Kenya, Côte d'Ivoire, and Libya may mean that crimes in the Democratic Republic of the Congo may go un-investigated by the Office of the Prosecutor, and doing so without unfounded allegations of politicization, may not only promote the values behind each of the options, enrich our understanding of them, and help us come to better decisions, they may ultimately result in greater support and financial backing for the project of international criminal law in general.

Then again, it may not. Discussing these trade-offs may not, for example, motivate States to properly fund the International Criminal Court – maybe nothing will. There will certainly be disagreement and lack of consensus. There is no single value to maximize, no single criterion to satisfy in every case. But that is where the conversation should begin, not end.

As mentioned at the outset, Isaiah Berlin stated in his 1988 address *The Pursuit of the Ideal*, "collisions of values are of the essence of what they are and what we are".[67] He was addressing such grand issues as the different choices made by cultures over history. This chapter is discussing the choices of the Office of the Prosecutor, particularly in the context of preliminary examinations. But the principle holds true. We should directly confront the collisions of values inherent in the use of prosecutorial discretion. We may not discover anything as grand as who we are, but it is still a better option than reflexively falling back into further fruitless rounds of allegations of politicization on one side and defensive invocations of the law and the evidence on the other. By addressing the collision of values beyond law and politics, we will get closer to the heart of what we, as international criminal lawyers, think we are doing.

---

[67] Berlin, 2013, see *supra* note 7.

This chapter is, at heart, a plea for a more open discussion of the trade-offs inherent in pursuing international criminal justice, particularly with a limited budget. Too much time is wasted in unsubstantiated allegations of politicization and unsatisfying invocations of simply following the evidence. The Office of the Prosecutor and its critics are stuck in a rhetorical trap that ill serves the goals of making and explaining their value choices and critiques. To disarm this trap, international criminal law scholars are well served to review general, friendly criticism from scholars such as Damaška, and broaden such criticism to include the insights of leading ethical philosophers of the twentieth and twenty-first centuries on the interconnected issues of education, legitimacy, and social choice. The goal should not be to eradicate or minimize politics where it exists, but not to let complaints about politics occupy and silence the entire field of discussion about the value-laden choices the Office of the Prosecutor must inevitably make.

21

Make the ICC Relevant:
Aiding, Abetting, and Accessorizing as
Aggravating Factors in Preliminary Examination

Christopher B. Mahony[*]

21.1. Introduction

To date, preliminary examinations by the International Criminal Court ('ICC') have focused on the culpability of local actors. There is scarce evidence on any deterrent effect of international criminal justice. This chapter considers the absence of empirical basis for the ICC's objective of deterring atrocity by considering whom the Court targets for prosecution, and whom it implicates in its preliminary examinations. It places this consideration in the context of the increased prevalence of intra-State conflict with external actors supporting various parties. The chapter argues that conduct enabling conflict and *jus in bello* crimes should constitute a key aggravating criterion for opening a formal investigation, particularly after the activation of the crime of aggression. It further argues that in making reports on preliminary examination, the ICC Office of the Prosecutor

---

[*] **Christopher B. Mahony** is Political Economy Adviser in the Disaster Risk Financing and Insurance Program at the World Bank (where he was formerly Political Economy Adviser at the Independent Evaluation Group), Consultant Strategic Policy Adviser at the United Nations Development Program (where he was formerly Rule of Law, Justice, Security and Human Rights Adviser), Visiting Research Fellow at Georgetown University Law Center. He was admitted to the bar of the High Court of New Zealand in 2006 where he appeared for the Crown in criminal and refugee matters. In 2003, he drafted the recommendations on governance and corruption for the Sierra Leone Truth and Reconciliation Commission, and co-authored the "Historical antecedents to the conflict" chapter. In 2008, he directed the design of Sierra Leone's witness protection programme. From 2012 to 2013, he was Deputy Director of the New Zealand Centre for Human Rights Law, Policy and Practice, Faculty of Law, Auckland University. He holds Bachelor of Commerce (B.Com.) and of Laws (LL.B.) degrees from the University of Otago, and a Master's in African Studies (M.Sc.) and a D.Phil. in Politics from the University of Oxford. The author thanks Benjamin Mugisho and Joshua McCowen for their invaluable research assistance in preparing this chapter.

('OTP') is also duty-bound to report on credible evidence of conduct that constitutes aiding, abetting or otherwise acting as an accessory ('accessorizing') to international criminal conduct.

The chapter will consider if the OTP adequately considers the role of external aiders, abettors and accessories in key situations under preliminary examination. Is this conduct, which is criminalized by the Rome Statute, attracting sufficient attention from the OTP and domestic criminal justice actors?

The chapter will start by considering literature on the effect of international criminal justice on the inclination of actors to use force and commit core international crimes. It will then consider the nature of violent conflict and the role of external actors, highlighting the emblematic case of Syria.

Then, it will turn to the process and criteria for making a determination regarding a preliminary examination. In describing the process, it will discuss where aiding, abetting and accessorizing fit, and should fit, in this process. After that, it will consider the jurisprudence on the technical elements on the modes of liability of aiding, abetting and accessorizing. It will then consider the ICC's preliminary examination of Afghanistan. Finally, it will assess the ICC-OTP's conduct in this respect, how it has evolved, its efficacy, and where it could go for the greatest impact to those at risk of core international crimes.

It is argued that an effective prosecutorial strategy that advances the interests of justice, peace, and security must not abstain from pursuing the external actors that fuel conflict. Focusing on aiding, abetting and accessorizing is a strategy that marries *jus in bello* with *jus ad bellum*. This chapter will identify how the prevalence of international humanitarian law violations in conflict means that prosecuting the conduct of aiding, abetting and accessorizing allows a prosecutor to effectively prosecute the crime of aggression. This is so where the aggressive behaviour is apparent in external actors' support of "armed bands, groups, irregulars or mercenaries, which carry out acts of armed force against another State".[1] In relation to the crime of aggression, this applies only to external State support for non-State actors on another territory. However, this chapter will

---

[1]   Rome Statute of the International Criminal Court, 17 July 1998, Article 8*bis*(2)(g) ('ICC Statute') (http://www.legal-tools.org/doc/7b9af9/).

also consider the peace and security implications of targeting all external actors aiding, abetting and accessorizing to government actors as well as other domestic actors.

Lastly, the chapter will survey some of the situations under investigation and those under preliminary examination before the OTP. The situations, it is argued, indicate that those engaged in aiding, abetting and accessorizing are not attracting the attention they deserve. Given the public policy positioning of some aiding, abetting and accessorizing conduct, it is further argued that the omission brings into question the authenticity of preliminary examination objectives stated by the OTP, including enhanced efficiency and independence.

21.1.1. Considering the ICC's Deterrent Effect

At the heart of this chapter is the idea that violent conflict is often accompanied by international humanitarian law violations. The first judgement at Nuremburg stated:

> To initiate a war of aggression is not only an international crime; it is the supreme international crime, differing only from other war crimes in that it contains within itself the accumulated evil of the whole.[2]

Today, battle deaths remain high. However, as the United Nations and World Bank have noted in their flagship study on conflict prevention,

---

[2] International Military Tribunal (Nuremberg), The United States of America, The French Republic, The United Kingdom of Great Britain and Northern Ireland, and the Union of Soviet Socialist Republics, v. Hermann Wilhelm Göring, Rudolf Hess, Joachim von Ribbentrop, Robert Ley, Wilhelm Keitel, Ernst Kaltenbrunner, Alfred Rosenberg, Hans Frank, Wilhelm Frick, Julius Streicher, Walter Funk, Hjalmar Schacht, Gustav Krupp von Bohlen und Halbach, Karl Dönitz, Erich Raeder, Baldur von Schirach, Fritz Sauckel, Alfred Jodl, Martin Bormann, Franz von Papen, Artur Seyss-Inquart, Albert Speer, Constantin von Neurath, and Hans Fritzsche, individually and as members of any of the following groups namely: Die Reichsregierung (Reich Cabinet); Das Korps der Politischen Leiter der Nationalsozialistischen Deutschen Arbeiterpartei (Leadership Corps of the Nazi Party); Die Schutzstaffeln der Nationalsozialistischen Deutschen Arbeiterpartei (commonly known as the 'SS ') and including Der Sicherheitsdienst (commonly known as the 'SD '); Die Geheime Staatspolizei (Secret State Police, commonly known as the 'GESTAPO '); Die Sturmabteilungen der N.S.D.A.P. (commonly known as the 'SA ') and the General Staff and High Command of the German Armed Forces, Judgment, 1 October 1946, in The Trial of German Major War Criminals: Proceedings of the International Military Tribunal sitting at Nuremberg, Germany, Part 22 (22 August 1946 to 1 October 1946), 25 (421), para. 426 (http://www.legal-tools.org/doc/45f18e/).

violence increasingly targets urban areas and public spaces. Civilians, therefore, are becoming more and more vulnerable, despite (if not because of) technological advancement.[3] Between 2010 and 2016, the number of civilian deaths in violent conflicts had doubled just as the ICC expanded its situations and indictments.[4]

Reviews of the ICC's impact have at times sought cause for incremental optimism. Jo and Simmons find that neither ICC ratification nor domestication of the Rome Statute appears to reduce rebel killing of civilians.[5] They also find, at a low level of significance, that rebel groups appear to respond to ICC actions.[6] They find that ratification of the ICC may be associated with increased violence among rebel groups.[7] They find that relative strength and government behaviour are the most consistent predictors of rebel intentional killing.[8] They note a stronger effect attributable to the ICC on governments than rebels, including "weak yet notable improvements" on domestic reforms in Uganda, Kenya and Côte d'Ivoire.[9] They also observe that the Court has had little effect in situations such as Sudan and Libya,[10] which also appears to be the case in the Democratic Republic of Congo and the Central African Republic. A simplistic observation identifies that in four of the seven countries where suspects have been indicted, violent conflict has recurred.

Jo and Simmons' language suggests a level of confirmation bias in their research. They state that:

> prosecutorial deterrence theory implies that investigations, indictments and especially successful prosecutions *should* trigger a reassessment of the likelihood of punishment and a boost to deterrence – a result consistent with Kim and Sik-

---

[3] United Nations and World Bank, *Pathways for Peace: Inclusive Approaches to Preventing Violent Conflict*, Washington, D.C., 2018, p. xix (http://www.legal-tools.org/doc/7bb4c2-1/).

[4] Uppsala University, Department of Peace and Conflict Research, "UCDP Data for download" (available on the University's web site).

[5] Jo Hyeran and Beth A. Simmons, "Can the International Criminal Court Deter Atrocity?— CORRIGENDUM", in *International Organization*, 2017, vol. 71, no. 2, pp. 419–21.

[6] *Ibid.*

[7] *Ibid.*

[8] *Ibid.*

[9] *Ibid.*

[10] *Ibid.*

kink's study of national human rights trials in transition countries.[11]

Jo and Simmons cite the work of Kim and Sikkink, which tests for the association of prosecutions with repression instead of conflict recurrence.[12] Further, the theory has long been debunked by what Simon calls the counter-intuitive behaviour of social systems.[13] After correcting a mistake in the data, Jo and Simmons observed that:

> ratification of the ICC [Statute] may be associated with *increased* violence among rebel groups, which differs from our initial conclusion of "no effect" and is contrary to theoretical expectations of prosecutorial deterrence.[14]

Sikkink suggests that domestic prosecutions are associated with human rights improvements.[15] Olsen, Payne and Reiter find that a combination of amnesties and prosecutions are associated with improvements in human rights and democracy.[16] However, they do not consider recurrence or non-recurrence of conflict. The link of domestic processes to the ICC occurs via the principle of complementarity, where the ICC cedes primacy of jurisdiction to States unless those States are unable or unwilling genuinely to prosecute crimes themselves. Jo and Simmons claim that ICC complementarity increases the quality of domestic criminal processes, and that better criminal trial processes are likely to have a more positive effect on conflict non-recurrence.[17] They identify the situations in Uganda, Kenya and Côte d'Ivoire, where domestic processes were established to prosecute crimes. They concede the weakness of those processes, but the critical element is that, in each case, the process is deferential to power. Ra-

---

[11] *Ibid.*

[12] Hunjoon Kim and Kathryn Sikkink, "Explaining the Deterrence Effect of Human Rights Prosecutions for Transitional Countries", in *International Studies Quarterly*, vol. 54, no. 4, pp. 939–63.

[13] Herbert Alexander Simon, *Models of Bounded Rationality: Empirically Grounded Economic Reason*, MIT press, 1997, vol. 3.

[14] Jo and Simmons, 2017, see *supra* note 5.

[15] Kathryn Sikkink, *The Justice Cascade: How Human Rights Prosecutions Are Changing World Politics (The Norton Series in World Politics)*, W.W. Norton & Company, 2011.

[16] Tricia D. Olsen, Leigh A. Payne and Andrew G. Reiter, *Transitional Justice in Balance: Comparting Processes, Weighing Efficacy*, United States Institute of Peace Press, Washington, D.C., 2010.

[17] Jo and Simmons, 2017, see *supra* note 5.

ther than enhance the rule of law and the confrontation of impunity, the cited cases embed it by building into the international system expedient domestic processes that reflect power. Those cited processes pursue only government adversaries or low-hanging fruits. At the same time, the processes provide legitimacy to the governments of States subject to ICC investigation based upon the States' ostensible co-operation with the ICC.[18]

The joint United Nations–World Bank *Pathways for Peace* study took the first step towards identifying the relationship between domestic prosecutions of international crimes and conflict (non-)recurrence. The UN-commissioned background study found that the rate of conflict recurrence decreases by approximately 70% when trials are pursued in respect of mid- and low-level actors while prosecution of high-ranking individuals is associated with a 65% increase in the rate of conflict recurrence.[19]

Like common international criminal justice approaches, the high-ranking individuals that are prosecuted in domestic courts are all persons within situations. However, the countries experiencing violent conflict are rarely themselves the manufacturers of weapons. International criminal justice tends to attribute responsibility very narrowly and without regard to the evidence about the true nature of violent conflict. The following section highlights the nature of conflict and queries whether international criminal justice targets the right people.

21.2. Globalization, Liberalism and Proxy-War's Enablement

Grievances relating to exclusion of social groups from political power, access to land and resources, access to justice and security, and access to services, are not novel.

---

[18] Christopher B. Mahony, "If You're Not at the Table, You're on the Menu: Complementarity and Self-Interest in Domestic Processes for Core International Crimes", in Morten Bergsmo and SONG Tianying (eds.), *Military Self-Interest in Accountability for Core International Crimes*, 2nd edition, Torkel Opsahl Academic EPublisher, Brussels, 2018, pp. 229–60 (http://www.toaep.org/ps-pdf/25-bergsmo-song-second).

[19] Leigh Payne, Andrew G. Reiter, Christopher B. Mahony and Laura Bernal-Bermudez, "Conflict Prevention and Guarantees of Non-Recurrence", Background paper for United Nations-World Bank Flagship Study, *Pathways for Peace: Inclusive Approaches to Preventing Violent Conflict*, World Bank, Washington, D.C., 2017.

Two historical 'functions' affecting the increased phenomena of local conflict's 'transnationalization' can be observed. The first is the breaking down of State sovereignty via the economic liberalism that accompanies globalization. The second is that the United Nations Security Council, the critical infrastructure for managing armed conflict, is focused upon managing conflict between States – particularly conflict between its five permanent members.[20] It is not designed to prevent domestic violent conflict. The decline in inter-State conflict indicates the emergence of adherence to certain norms and law. Since the post-World War II establishment of the United Nations, the United Nations Security Council's five veto-wielding permanent members have also constituted the world's largest military powers and arms manufacturers.[21] They have peacefully managed and mitigated the risk of direct violent conflict between themselves. Yet, particularly since the end of the Cold War, they have (albeit to variant degrees) unanimously come to embrace economic liberalism as a foundation for inter-State commerce.

21.2.1. Conflict's Multi-dimensional Causes

After the last great inter-State armed conflict – World War II – anti-colonial and post-colonial violent conflicts and Cold War proxy-wars came to affect a number of African and Asian States.[22] At the end of the Cold War, new proxy-contestations emerged in the Third World, particularly in Africa, where the United Kingdom, the United States and France contested spheres of influence via proxies.[23] A comparative surge in

---

[20] Simon Chesterman, "The UN Security Council and the Rule of Law", 7 May 2008, NYU School of Law, Public Law Research Paper No. 08-57; Annex to the letter dated 18 April 2008 from the Permanent Representative of Austria to the United Nations addressed to the Secretary-General, Doc. A/63/69-S/2008/270, 7 May 2008.

[21] Adam Roberts, "The United Nations and International Security", in *Survival*, vol. 35, no. 2, pp. 3–30; Adam Roberts and Benedict Kingsbury (eds.), *United Nations, Divided World: The UN's Roles in International Relations*, 2nd edition, Clarendon Press, 1994.

[22] See, for example, Frederick Cooper, *Africa since 1940: The Past of the Present*, Cambridge University Press, Cambridge, 2002; Cemil Aydin, *The Politics of Anti-Westernism in Asia: Visions of World Order in Pan-Islamic and Pan-Asian Thought*, Columbia University Press, 2007; Shashi Tharoor, *An Era of Darkness: The British Empire in India*, Aleph Book Company, 2016.

[23] See John Dumbrell, *A Special Relationship: Anglo-American Relations from the Cold War to Iraq*, Palgrave Macmillan, 2006; Bruce Russett, "The Democratic Peace", in *Conflicts and New Departures in World Society*, Routledge, 2017, pp. 21–43; Adda Bruemmer Bozeman, *Conflict in Africa: Concepts and Realities*, Princeton University Press, 2015.

---

peacekeeping and prevention, among other factors, helped reduce conflict in a post-Cold War global order until the mid-2000s.[24] Intra-State conflicts proliferated, commonly driven by resource scarcity, demographic pressures, and group-specific grievances surrounding exclusion from access to political power, land and resources, justice and security, and services.[25] At the same time, a window of opportunity opened to focus the international system on its capacity to manage and mitigate intra-State conflicts in the same way the system has managed the risk of direct conflict between P5 actors. However, in 2005, the number of persons killed in violent conflict reached a low point, signalling a different turn as the scope and fatalities of conflict began to increase – a trajectory that accelerated in 2010 (see Figure 3 below).

The level of global contextual risk is currently increasing because of the emergence of 'stressors', which are cumulative for two reasons: (1) increasing complexity due to greater interconnectedness of people, and (2) faster rates of economic, social and technological change. With regard to violent conflicts, multi-dimensional risks could simultaneously affect geographic, infrastructural, societal, political and economic dimensions. Some of the most prominent areas of risk that interface with risks and effects of violent conflicts include climate change, natural disaster, epidemics, economic shocks, demographic expansion, and so on.

Financial liberalization and transnationalization of capital embed inequality of access to capital and consequently, to economic, educational and other sources of economic mobility. It also enables transnational support for armed groups engaged in violent conflict. For example, in the second half of 2010, before the Arab Spring, key staple food prices had risen by over 25%, acting as a shock multiplier to the drought that Syria encountered.[26] Economic historians cite increasing deregulation of capital markets as increasing the frequency and severity of boom and bust eco-

---

24 World Bank, 2018, p. 11, see *supra* note 3.
25 *Ibid.*
26 Elena I. Ianchovichina, Josef L. Loening and Christina A. Wood, "How Vulnerable are Arab Countries to Global Food Price Shocks?", in *The Journal of Development Studies*, vol. 50, no. 9, pp. 1302–19; George Joffé, "The Arab Spring in North Africa: Origins and Prospects", in *The Journal of North African Studies*, vol. 16, no. 4, pp. 507–32.

---

nomic cycles.[27] Increasingly regular and severe global economic adjustments themselves drive up commodity prices, fuelling speculation, disproportionately affecting marginalized communities, and elevating grievances relating to social groups about their exclusion from power, resources, justice, security and services.[28]

21.2.2. Syria: A Permissive Global System's Emblematic Proxy-War

The conflict in Syria has by far the highest number of conflict-related deaths (see Figure 1). It is worth considering, therefore, the impact of the transnational phenomena described in the previous section on the situation in Syria.

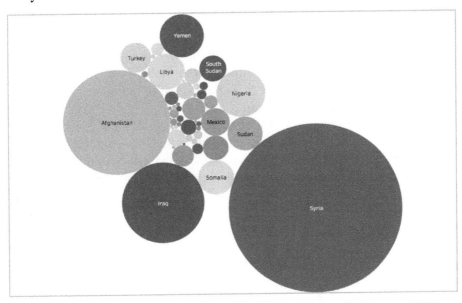

Figure 1: Number of Conflict-Related Deaths Worldwide, by Country, 2016

---

27 Hyman P. Minsky and Henry Kaufman, *Stabilizing an Unstable Economy*, McGraw-Hill, New York, 2008, vol. 1.

28 For example, fiscal space in Saudi Arabia allowed the government to rapidly deploy USD 130bn in social spending at the outset of protests in that country. See F. Gregory Gause III, "Why Middle East Studies Missed the Arab Spring: The Myth of Authoritarian Stability", in *Foreign Affairs*, 2011, vol. 90, no. 4, pp. 81–90; Neil MacFarguhar, "In Saudi Arabia, Royal Funds Buy Peace for Now", in *New York Times*, 8 June 2011.

Between 2005 and 2010, the Fertile Crescent[29] witnessed the worst drought in recorded history, which intensified during the winter of 2006-2007.

Syria's drought and its economic and social implications are uncommon themes among influential explanations of Syria's conflict. The conflict's onset occurred in the context of the Arab Spring protests, influenced by the demonstration effect of organized protests and local conditions, including "microfoundations and emotions".[30]

It has been indicated that the drought cannot be explained by natural causes, instead, it is consistent with models of anthropogenic climate change. The drought affected, with particular intensity, Syria's territory. Agriculture collapsed in the north-eastern region of Syria – the breadbasket of the country that produces two-thirds of the country's cereal output. Food prices went through the roof, more than doubling between 2007 and 2008. However, violent conflict did not occur in 2006 or 2007. The population in the northeast provinces of Syria witnessed a dramatic increase in nutrition-related diseases in children due to their inability to afford food as a result of a combination of high prices and deprivation of income and livelihood. School enrolment also dropped by 80%. An aggravating factor accompanying these socio-economic conditions was migration of displaced persons. As many as 1.5 million people were internally displaced in Syria, moving, along with many Iraqi refugees, to the periphery of urban areas.

---

[29] Civilization emerged for the first time in the 'Fertile Crescent' more than 10 millennia ago. Crops and animals were domesticated, institutions were created, agriculture and technology flourished. The interactions between humans and ecosystems that enabled civilization to emerge have sustained populations in the region since then.

[30] Wendy Pearlman, "Emotions and the Microfoundations of the Arab Uprisings", in *Perspectives on Politics*, 2013, vol.11, no. 2, pp. 387–409.

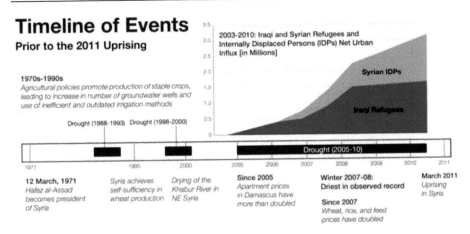

Timeline of Events
Prior to the 2011 Uprising

2003-2010: Iraqi and Syrian Refugees and Internally Displaced Persons (IDPs) Net Urban Influx [in Millions]

Syrian IDPs

Iraqi Refugees

1970s-1990s
Agricultural policies promote production of staple crops, leading to increase in number of groundwater wells and use of inefficient and outdated irrigation methods

Drought (1988-1993)   Drought (1998-2000)

Drought (2005-10)

1971   1995   2000   2005   2006   2007   2008   2009   2010   2011

12 March, 1971
Hafez al-Assad becomes president of Syria

Syria achieves self-sufficiency in wheat production

Drying of the Khabur River in NE Syria

Since 2005
Apartment prices in Damascus have more than doubled

Winter 2007-08:
Driest in observed record

Since 2007
Wheat, rice, and feed prices have doubled

March 2011
Uprising in Syria

Figure 2: Syrian Conflict Timeline

By 2010, 20% of Syria's urban population was composed of internally displaced persons and Iraqi refugees, mostly on the urban periphery. The displaced population had no legal settlement options, and was faced with overcrowding, lack of basic services, rampant unemployment, and rising crime.[31] These peripheral urban areas became the cradle of the civil unrest that began to intensify in March 2011, which was inspired by the examples of Tunisia and Egypt but also supported by an influx of arms and foreign nationals supported by regional and global governments.[32] As the conflict unfolded, it became clear that Saudi Arabia, co-ordinating with the United States, began importing arms and people into Syria to fight the Syrian government. Similarly, the Russian and Iranian governments provided significant support to the Syrian government to repel the rebels. The direct engagement of one superpower in a conflict appeared, in the eyes of another, to be a decision between either inevitably engaging with that superpower or accepting that non-direct engagement would constitute concession of the military imperative to that superpower. Goldberg,

---

[31] Colin P. Kelleya, Shahrzad Mohtadib, Mark A. Canec, Richard Seagerc and Yochanan Kushnirc, "Climate change in the Fertile Crescent and implications of the recent Syrian drought", in *Proceedings of the National Academies of Sciences*, 2015, vol. 112, no. 11, pp. 3241–46.

[32] Ambrose Evans-Pritchard, "Saudis offer Russia secret oil deal if it drops Syria", in *The Telegraph*, 27 August 2013; Mark Mazzetti, Anne Barnard and Eric Schmitt, "Military Success in Syria Gives Putin Upper Hand in U.S. Proxy War", in *New York Times*, 6 August 2016.

who had an interview with the then US President, Barak Obama, described it as follows:

> "When you have a professional army," he once told me, "that is well armed and sponsored by two large states" – Iran and Russia – "who have huge stakes in this, and they are fighting against a farmer, a carpenter, an engineer who started out as protesters and suddenly now see themselves in the midst of a civil conflict ..." He paused. "The notion that we could have – in a clean way that didn't commit U.S. military forces – changed the equation on the ground there was never true."[33]

He further described Obama's view on the regional contestation between Iran and Saudi Arabia that feeds many violent conflicts in the Middle East:

> At one point I observed to him that he is less likely than previous presidents to axiomatically side with Saudi Arabia in its dispute with its arch-rival, Iran. He didn't disagree.
>
> Iran, since 1979, has been an enemy of the United States, and has engaged in state-sponsored terrorism, is a genuine threat to Israel and many of our allies, and engages in all kinds of destructive behavior," the president said. "And my view has never been that we should throw our traditional allies" – the Saudis – "overboard in favor of Iran.
>
> But he went on to say that the Saudis need to "share" the Middle East with their Iranian foes. "The competition between the Saudis and the Iranians – which has helped to feed proxy wars and chaos in Syria and Iraq and Yemen – requires us to say to our friends as well as to the Iranians that they need to find an effective way to share the neighborhood and institute some sort of cold peace," he said. "An approach that said to our friends 'You are right, Iran is the source of all problems, and we will support you in dealing with Iran' would essentially mean that as these sectarian conflicts continue to rage and our Gulf partners, our traditional friends, do not have the ability to put out the flames on their own or decisively win on their own, and would mean that we have to start coming in and using our military power to settle scores.

---

[33] Jeffrey Goldberg, "The Obama Doctrine", in *The Atlantic*, April 2016.

And that would be in the interest neither of the United States
nor of the Middle East.

The United Nations Security Council encourages permanent members to settle disputes between themselves without coming into direct
military conflict. However, there is no such mechanism to deter proxy-war.

21.2.3. How the Global System and Its Leadership Ignore Contemporary Conflicts

The joint United Nations and World Bank flagship study on conflict prevention does not consider prevention issues that appear at the forefront of
the mind of the former US President. Obama failed to consider how the
risk of violent conflict may be lowered by development of norms and
rules that stigmatize, dissuade, deter or even prevent external actors from
inserting weapons, armed actors, and other material support of armed
groups into situations of instability.

Conflicts with increasing non-State armed groups also reduces formal State involvement, rendering traditional dispute resolution less appropriate. The plurality of armed groups and their diverse nature (from
rebels, militias and violent extremist groups to traffickers and other organized criminal groups) adjust the political economy of conflict. The function of international criminal justice has failed to respond appropriately.

As the international criminal justice system is preoccupied with
more expedient indictees located within domestic military and political
structures, both internationalized conflicts where external actors are engaged and the number of non-State groups have increased dramatically
(see Figures 3–4).

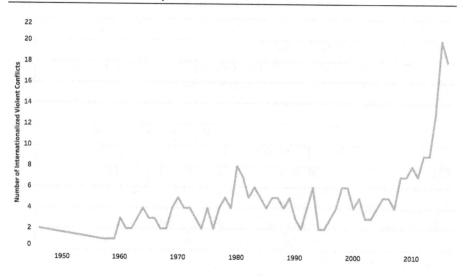

Figure 3: Number of Internationalized Violent Conflicts, 1946-2016[34]

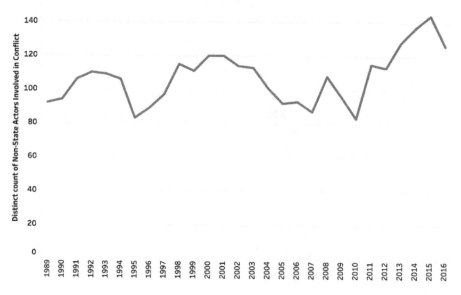

Figure 4: Number of Non-State Groups Active in Violent Conflict Worldwide, 1989-2016[35]

---

[34] World Bank, 2018, p. 18, see *supra* note 3.

The UN–World Bank *Pathways for Peace* report acknowledges the existence of the increased incidence of internationalized conflict and the role of the United Nations Security Council in resolving disputes between States. Obama acknowledged the engagement of external actors, including himself in his capacity as US President. However, he failed to consider the efficacy of global peace and security for this type of behaviour, or the efficacy of potential collective responses by nations.

The following section considers the role of the modes of liability of aiding, abetting and accessorizing, where they might sit in the preliminary examination process, and where the legal threshold lies for aiding, abetting and accessorizing international crimes.

21.3. Prosecuting Aiding, Abetting and Accessorizing as a Response to Proxy-War

The OTP enjoys an opportunity to play a role in dissuading actors, or at least momentarily disrupting, delaying, or adjusting the incentives and disincentives of actors from waging war. It can do so by adopting an approach that focuses on the conduct of external enabling actors.

Confronting the self-interest of States that seek to permit war by proxy, something which is prohibited under international law, could constitute a much more substantive contribution to the prevention of violent conflict than dealing with the crimes that occur only after conflict has started. This approach considers the interaction of the crime of aggression of supporting a party to a conflict in another State (where an external actor is supporting a non-State actor) along with the conduct of the party being supported (given the commonality of international crimes committed by non-State actors).

External actors play a prominent role in causing the onset, escalation and persistence of violent conflict with which core international crimes are associated. For the prevention of violent conflicts, employing available means to prosecute those actors is equally important as prosecuting local direct perpetrators and persons with command responsibility.

---

[35] *Ibid.*, p. 16.

21.3.1. Gravity in Preliminary Examination and the Aiding, Abetting and Accessorizing of Crimes

As noted elsewhere in these volumes, the OTP receives and analyses referrals and communications to determine whether there is a reasonable basis to investigate and prosecute persons responsible for crimes under the Statute before the Court. The factors and procedures applied by the Office to carry out a preliminary examination are outlined in its 2010 Draft Policy Paper on Preliminary Examinations.[36]

In determining whether a reasonable basis to proceed with an investigation exists or not, the Prosecutor considers jurisdiction, admissibility and interests of justice.[37] Presuming a situation moves to Phase 3, admissibility under Article 17[38] requires consideration of the role of aiding, abetting and accessorizing. Firstly, in considering complementarity,[39] it should determine whether a domestic process has jurisdiction over the modes of liability of aiding, abetting and accessorizing, and whether investigations are credibly pursuing such persons. Secondly, it should consider aiding, abetting and accessorizing to third parties as a significant aggravating factor in determining gravity[40] regarding the most serious crimes and those bearing greatest responsibility for them.[41]

Finally, the OTP should, where there are positive determinations on both jurisdiction and admissibility,[42] consider the role of aiding, abetting

---

[36] ICC OTP, *Draft Policy Paper on Preliminary Examinations*, 4 October 2010, p. 1 (http://www.legal-tools.org/doc/bd172c/).

[37] *Ibid.*

[38] ICC Statute, Article 53(1)(b), see *supra* note 1.

[39] *Ibid.*, Article 17(1)(a)–(c). The Court is intended to complement national criminal justice systems, hence in general a case will be inadmissible if it has been or is being investigated or prosecuted by a State with jurisdiction. However, a case may be admissible if the investigating or prosecuting state is unwilling or unable to genuinely carry out the investigation or prosecution.

[40] *Ibid.*, Article 17(1)(d).

[41] ICC OTP, *Draft Policy Paper on Preliminary Examinations*, 2010, para. 51, see *supra* note 36.

[42] ICC OTP, *Report on activities performed during the first three years (June 2003 – June 2006)*, 12 September 2006, p. 2 (http://www.legal-tools.org/doc/c7a850/).

---

and accessorizing in identifying the "countervailing consideration"[43] of the interests of justice.

In relation to gravity, there is a specific guiding consideration for determining if the gravity threshold is met in respect of war crimes.[44] Article 8(1) states that these crimes exist when they are "committed as part of a plan or policy or as part of a large-scale commission of such crimes".[45] This means that the role of external actors would suggest a degree of planning. Therefore, a perpetrating group or actor would be more likely to have a plan or a policy.

The prosecutor enjoys a great deal of discretion in interpreting "gravity", which is not defined in the Rome Statute. This opens the door to employing the modes of liability of aiding, abetting and accessorizing as an interpretive mechanism of aggravation.[46] In determining whether to open an investigation, the OTP's intention is to establish a basic standard that is not overly restrictive.[47] At the stage of initiating an investigation, there is not yet a 'case'. Preliminary examination, therefore, should consider situations generally, with awareness of likely cases. Given the role of external actors in materially (and often lethally) supporting perpetrators, a part of this general consideration includes consideration of aiding, abetting and accessorizing. It may also better inform the Prosecutor as to the perpetrator's extent of responsibility during case selection.[48]

---

43   ICC OTP, *Draft Policy Paper on Preliminary Examinations*, 2010, para. 10, see *supra* note 36.

44   ICC OTP, "OTP Response to Communications received concerning Iraq", 9 February 2006, p. 8 (http://www.legal-tools.org/doc/5b8996/).

45   ICC Statute, Article 8(1), see *supra* note 1.

46   See William A. Schabas, "Prosecutorial Discretion *v.* Judicial Activism at the International Criminal Court", in *Journal of International Criminal Justice*, 2008, vol. 6, no. 4, p. 731, at pp.736–41. For a wider discussion of gravity, including information on the origins of the gravity threshold and an analysis of Pre-Trial Chamber I's approach to Article 17, see War Crimes Research Office, *The Gravity Threshold of the International Criminal Court*, American University Washington College of Law, 2008.

47   ICC OTP, *Draft Policy Paper on Preliminary Examinations*, 2010, at para. 68, see *supra* note 36.

48   Fabricio Guariglia, "The Selection of Cases by the Office of the Prosecutor of the International Criminal Court", in Carsten Stahn and Goran Sluiter (eds.), *The Emerging Practice of the International Criminal Court*, Martinus Nijhoff Publishers, Leiden/Boston, 2009, pp. 209–17, at p. 213.

The OTP provides a number of criteria for determining gravity that are relevant to the role of persons that aid and abet or act as accessories to international crimes.[49] The role of external actors goes in particular to the 'nature' of crimes, particularly high-level killings, the manner of commission of crimes (in terms of participation), and abuse of power (where external actors experience comparatively little consequence). Similarly, external aiding, abetting and accessorizing has a long-term 'impact' because conflicts involving external actors last longer, thus increasing the possibility of cross-border conflicts.

If the OTP makes a positive determination on admissibility, the OTP will weigh the gravity and victims' interests to determine the "interests of justice".[50] This includes consideration of the interests of the victims, the conflict parties' views, victims' interest in seeing justice done, and witnesses' physical and psychological well-being, as well as the dignity and privacy of victims and witnesses.[51] In making such a determination, in particular of the victims' interest, the role of external actors is significant.

In weighing the above considerations, the OTP should provide, in its reports on preliminary examinations, an outline of credibly alleged external actors with potential criminal liability. It should also lay out how the credibly alleged conduct relates to the aforementioned preliminary examination considerations.

---

[49] ICC OTP, *Draft Policy Paper on Preliminary Examinations*, 2010, at para. 70, see *supra* note 36. For more information regarding the origins of these criteria, see Paul Seils, "The Selection and Prioritization of Cases by the Office of the Prosecutor of the International Criminal Court", in Morten Bergsmo (ed.), *Criteria for Prioritizing and Selecting Core International Crimes Cases*, 2nd edition, Torkel Opsahl Academic EPublisher, Oslo, 2010 (http://www.toaep.org/ps-pdf/4-bergsmo-second).

[50] ICC Statute, Articles 53(1)(c) and 53(2)(c), see *supra* note 1. Article 53(1)(c) provides: "Taking into account the gravity of the crime and the interests of victims, there are nonetheless substantial reasons to believe that an investigation would not serve the interests of justice". Article 53(2)(c) additionally requires consideration of the particular circumstances of the accused.

[51] ICC OTP, *Policy Paper on the Interests of Justice*, September 2007, at p. 5 (http://www.legal-tools.org/doc/bb02e5/).

21.4. The Legal Threshold of Aiding, Abetting and Accessorizing

The mode of liability of aiding and abetting in international criminal law was first established at the International Criminal Tribunal for the former Yugoslavia ('ICTY'). Article 7(1) of the ICTY Statute ascribes criminal responsibility where an actor "aided and abetted in the planning, preparation or execution of a crime".[52] The mode of liability was not present in the Charters of the Nuremburg or Tokyo tribunals.[53] It has taken on normative acceptance in international criminal law and has been included in the Statutes of all the post-Cold War international criminal courts and tribunals. The existence of this mode of liability has facilitated successful prosecution of political leaders and external commercial or State actors because it is not necessary to show command responsibility over perpetrators.[54] In effect, the mode of aiding, abetting and accessorizing also criminalized the conduct of waging war by proxy (where proxy forces commit crimes).[55]

The ICTY in *Perišić* preferred a *mens rea* element that demands that the aider or abettor specifically intend for support to be used for the specific acts that occurred (known as 'specific direction').[56] However, it was rejected by later jurisprudence at the ICTY and at the Special Court for Sierra Leone.[57]

---

[52] Statute of the International Criminal Tribunal for the Former Yugoslavia, adopted 25 May 1993, amended 17 May 2002, Article 7(1) ('ICTY Statute') (http://www.legal-tools.org/doc/b4f63b/).

[53] Charter of the International Military Tribunal, 8 August 1945 (http://www.legal-tools.org/doc/64ffdd/); Charter of the International Military Tribunal for the Far East, adopted 19 January 1946, amended 26 April 1946 (http://www.legal-tools.org/doc/a3c41c/).

[54] Andrew Clapham, "Extending international criminal law beyond the individual to corporations and armed opposition groups", in *Journal of International Criminal Justice*, 2008, vol. 6, no. 5, pp. 899–926.

[55] *Ibid.*

[56] ICTY, *Prosecutor v. Perišić*, Appeals Chamber, Judgment, 28 February 2013, IT-04-81-A, para. 44 (http://www.legal-tools.org/doc/f006ba/).

[57] ICTY, *Prosecutor v. Šainović et al.*, Appeals Chamber, Judgment, 23 January 2014, IT-05-87-A, paras. 1648–49 (http://www.legal-tools.org/doc/81ac8c/); ICTY, *Prosecutor v. Popović et al.*, Appeals Chamber, Judgment, 30 January 2015, IT-05-88-A, para. 1758 (http://www.legal-tools.org/doc/4c28fb/); ICTY, *Prosecutor v. Stanišić and Simatović*, ICTY Appeals Chamber, Judgment, 9 December 2015, IT-03-69-A, paras. 104–07 (http://www.legal-tools.org/doc/198c16/).

21.4.1. Aiding and Abetting under the Rome Statute

Article 25(3)(c) of the Statute[58] provides for criminal liability if a person:

> For the *purpose of facilitating the commission of such a crime*, aids, abets or otherwise assists in its commission or its attempted commission, including providing the means for its commission [...]

The Pre-Trial Chamber has noted that a "substantial" contribution to the crime may be contemplated.[59] The Rome Statute, unlike the jurisprudence of the *ad hoc* tribunals, does not require the aider and abettor to share the perpetrator's intent to commit the crime.

However, the threshold remains unclear, as the language "or otherwise assists" is novel to the ICC. It suggests that the provision of means for the commission of a crime may simply constitute an example of assistance, and perhaps a lower threshold than the "substantial" contribution threshold.

Future ICC defendants may argue that Article 25(3)(c) expressly adopts a 'specific direction' standard because assistance must be given "for *the purpose* of facilitating the commission of such crime".[60] They may argue that the Article 25(3)(c) language of "otherwise provides" adds a mental element that must be proved in addition to intention and knowledge under Article 30.[61] This view is held by multiple observers,

---

[58] ICC Statute, Article 25(3)(c), see *supra* note 1; Special Court for Sierra Leone ('SCSL'), *Prosecutor v. Charles Taylor*, Appeals Chamber, Judgment, 26 September 2013, SCSL-03-01-A, para. 207 (http://www.legal-tools.org/doc/3e7be5/).

[59] ICC, Situation in the Democratic Republic of the Congo, *Prosecutor v. Mbarushimana*, Pre-Trial Chamber I, Decision on the Confirmation of Charges, 16 December 2011, ICC-01/04-01/10-465-Red, para. 279 (http://www.legal-tools.org/doc/63028f/); ICC, Situation in the Democratic Republic of the Congo, *Prosecutor v. Thomas Lubanga Dyilo*, Trial Chamber I, Judgment Pursuant to Article 74 of the Statute, 14 March 2012, ICC-01/04-01/06-2842, para. 997 (http://www.legal-tools.org/doc/677866/).

[60] Defendants may argue that "the Court was established to try the most serious crimes of international concern", which demand high thresholds: Sarah Finnin, *Elements of Accessorial Modes of Liability: Article 25(3)(b) and (c) of the Rome Statute of the International Criminal Court*, Martinus Nijhoff Publishers, 2012, p. 203. See also ICC Statute, Preamble, Articles 1 and 5(1), see *supra* note 1.

[61] Albin Eser, "Individual Criminal Responsibility", in Antonio Cassese (ed.), *The Rome Statute of the International Criminal Court: A Commentary*, Oxford University Press, New York, 2002, p. 767, at pp. 798–801; Finnin, 2012, p. 180, see *supra* note 60; K.J.M. Smith,

---

who argue that the inclusion of the "for the purpose" language would be otherwise meaningless.

However, David Scheffer and Caroline Kaeb argue that the word "purpose" indicates only the *de minimis* and neutral *mens rea* element of acting in a manner that has the consequence of facilitating the commission of crimes.[62] Their view is that the language "for the purpose of" reflects a lack of drafting consensus regarding *mens rea*. It is worth noting, in this relation, that Scheffer was present at the drafting. They conclude that the *mens rea* element of aiding and abetting is informed by Article 25(3)(d)(ii) requiring "knowledge" of the "near certainty" of a crime "in the ordinary course of events" because drafting consensus existed in that provision.[63] They argue that if the drafters intended that an accessory must share a perpetrator's intent, aiding and abetting would have been a co-perpetrator mode of liability under Article 25(3)(a).[64] Their argument may be supported by tracing the drafting of Article 25(3)(c) to the US Model Penal Code, which does not require specific direction.[65] Further, their argument is normatively supported by the Rome Statute's own intent to "put an end to impunity" via interpretations that "close accountability gaps".[66] When read alongside the existence of the crime of aggression, a specific direction interpretation of aiding and abetting becomes incompatible with the

---

A Modern Treatise on the Law of Criminal Complicity, Oxford University Press, Oxford, 1991, p. 142.

[62] David Scheffer and Caroline Kaeb, "The Five Levels of CSR Compliance: The Resiliency of Corporate Liability under the Alien Tort Statute and the Case for a Counterattack Strategy in Compliance Theory", in *Berkeley Journal of International Law*, 2011, vol. 29, no. 1, pp. 349–57.

[63] *Ibid.*

[64] *Ibid.*

[65] Finnin, 2012, p. 187, at p. 200, see *supra* note 60. It is beyond the scope of this chapter to fully engage with how "purpose" should be interpreted. For a helpful introduction, see SCSL, *Prosecutor v. Charles Taylor*, Appeals Chamber, Judgment, 26 September 2013, p. 5, at paras. 446–51, see *supra* note 58.

[66] ICC, Situation in the Democratic Republic of the Congo, *The Prosecutor v. Thomas Lubanga Dyilo*, Appeals Chamber, Judgment on the appeals of Mr Lubanga Dyilo and the Prosecutor against the Decision of Trial Chamber I of 14 July 2009 entitled "Decision giving notice to the parties and participants that the legal characterisation of the facts may be subject to change in accordance with Regulation 55(2) of the Regulations of the Court", 8 December 2009, ICC-01/04-01/06-2205, at para. 77 (http://www.legal-tools.org/doc/40d015/).

Rome Statute due to the impossibly high standard. The ICC is also likely to find that *Perišić* draws a false distinction between different 'types' of degree of contribution and awareness for remote actors. To argue that 'substantial contribution' before the ICC is, as per the ICTY, inadequate at the ICC is to presume a *mens rea* threshold of perceived inadequacy of knowledge, [67] despite the Rome Statute's adoption of purpose and knowledge together. Given that volition and cognition are demanded together, a specific direction element can reasonably be perceived as a further unstated, and therefore non-existent, component of Article 25(3)(c).

Defendants may cite Appeals Chamber Judge Silvia Fernández de Gurmendi's dissenting opinion in *Mbarushimana* as a recognition of *Perišić* that rejects the degree of contribution for interpreting Article 25(3)(d):

> I am not persuaded that such contributions would be adequately addressed by adding the requirement that a contribution be significant. Depending on the circumstances of a case, providing food or utilities to an armed group might be a significant, a substantial or even an essential contribution to the commission of crimes by this group. In my view the real issue is that of the so-called "neutral" contributions. This problem is better addressed by analysing the normative and causal links between the contribution and the crime rather than requiring a minimum level of contribution.[68]

Defendants, invoking Fernández de Gurmendi, will argue that the "normative and causal links" between the contributions of the accused, on the one hand, and the crimes' commission, on the other, must reflect the requirements of 'specific direction', or at least demand the crimes are the reason for assisting the accused. To reinforce that claim, defendants will

---

[67] James G Stewart, "The ICTY Loses Its Way on Complicity", *Opinio Juris*, 3 April 2013. But see Kevin Jon Heller, "Two Thoughts on Manuel Ventura's Critique of Specific Direction", *Opinio Juris*, 10 January 2014.

[68] ICC, Situation in the Democratic Republic of the Congo, *The Prosecutor v. Callixte Mbarushimana*, Appeals Chamber, Separate Opinion of Judge Silvia Fernandez de Gurmendi, Judgment on the appeal of the Prosecutor against the decision of Pre-Trial Chamber I of 16 December 2011 entitled "Decision on the confirmation of charges", 30 May 2012, ICC-01/04-01/10-514, at para. 12 (http://www.legal-tools.org/doc/6ead30/). Importantly, the rest of the bench in the Appeals Chamber decided the appeal without engaging the question of contribution. As such, Judge de Gurmendi's statement of principle should be considered persuasive.

likely emphasise that both Fernández de Gurmendi and the 'specific direction' jurisprudence at the ICTY were concerned with establishing an approach that appropriately responded to 'neutral contributions' or, as *Perišić* put it, "general assistance" that can be used for lawful or unlawful purposes.[69]

Given that the language of Article 25(3)(d) makes clear the level of contribution and knowledge, an interpretation in line with specific direction that contradicts the Article's intent (when read within the intent of the Rome Statute)[70] is unlikely to be adopted. The Court is also more likely to read the above paragraph in de Gurmendi's dissent as a guide for considering if a defendant's contribution was significant, rather than being specifically directed.[71] The jurisprudence advancing the *mens rea* element of specific direction has also been rejected by subsequent jurisprudence. The *Taylor* appeal judgement found that "aiding and abetting liability under customary international law is not limited to direct intent or [...] purpose".[72] At the ICTY, the *Šainović* appeal judgment, *Popović* appeal judgment, and *Stanišić and Simatović* appeal judgment all rejected specific direction.[73]

---

[69] ICTY, *Prosecutor v. Perišić*, Appeals Chamber, Judgment, 28 February 2013, at para. 44, see *supra* note 56.

[70] ICC, Situation in the Democratic Republic of the Congo, *The Prosecutor v. Thomas Lubanga Dyilo*, Appeals Chamber, Judgment on the appeals of Mr Lubanga Dyilo and the Prosecutor against the Decision of Trial Chamber I of 14 July 2009 entitled "Decision giving notice to the parties and participants that the legal characterisation of the facts may be subject to change in accordance with Regulation 55(2) of the Regulations of the Court", 8 December 2009, at para. 77, see *supra* note 66.

[71] ICC, Situation in the Republic of Kenya, *The Prosecutor v. William Samoei Ruto and Joshua Arap Sang*, Trial Chamber V, Defence Response to Prosecution's Submissions on the law of indirect co-perpetration under Article 25(3)(a) of the Statute and application for notice to be given under Regulation 55(2) with respect to William Samoei Ruto's individual criminal responsibility, 25 July 2012, ICC-01/09-01/11, at p. 3 (http://www.legal-tools.org/doc/be4424/); Randle C. DeFalco, "Contextualizing *Actus Reus* under Article 25(3)(d) of the ICC Statute", in *Journal of International Criminal Justice*, 2013, vol. 11, no. 4, at pp. 730–32.

[72] SCSL, *Prosecutor v. Charles Taylor*, Appeals Chamber, Judgment, 26 September 2013, para. 207, see *supra* note 58.

[73] ICTY, *Prosecutor v. Šainović et al.*, Appeals Chamber, Judgment, 23 January 2014, paras. 1648–49, see *supra* note 57; ICTY, *Prosecutor v. Popović et al.*, Appeals Chamber, Judgment, 30 January 2015, para. 1758, see *supra* note 57; ICTY, *Prosecutor v. Stanišić and*

In the ICC Trial Chamber's decision in *Bemba et al.*, the Chamber noted the word 'purpose' introduced a "higher subjective mental element" demanding "assistance with the aim of facilitating the offence".[74] The accessory's facilitation (not the principal offence) must be made with the knowledge of the assistance to the principal perpetrator in the commission of the offence.[75] With regard to the principal offence, knowledge of the offence in the ordinary course of events and its essential elements is required.[76] However, knowledge of the precise offence intended and committed in the specific circumstance is not required.[77] The *Bemba* decision at the Trial Chamber may not necessarily be adopted at the Appeals Chamber.

21.4.2. Accessorizing under the Rome Statute

A similar mode of liability, but with a different *mens rea* element, is that of acting as an accessory to crimes committed by a group under Article 25(3)(d) (herein referred to as 'accessorizing').[78] This is where a person makes an 'intentional' contribution to a crime.[79] Unlike aiding and abetting, Article 25(3)(d) does not refer to a 'purpose', but rather requires either a shared intent for the group's crimes, or *knowledge* of the group's crimes, including knowledge that they are likely to occur in "the ordinary course of events".[80] "Knowledge of the intention of the group to commit a

---

Simatović, Appeals Chamber, Judgment, 9 December 2015, paras. 104–07, see *supra* note 57.

74 ICC, Situation in the Central African Republic, *The Prosecutor v. Jean-Pierre Bemba Gombo, Aimé Kilolo Musamba, Jean-Jacques Mangenda Kabongo, Fidèle Babala Wandu and Narcisse Arido*, Trial Chamber VII, Public Redacted Version of Judgment pursuant to Article 74 of the Statute, 19 October 2016, ICC-01/05-01/13-1989-Red, paras. 97–98 (http://www.legal-tools.org/doc/fe0ce4/).

75 *Ibid.*

76 *Ibid.*, para. 98.

77 *Ibid.*

78 ICC Statute, Article 25(3)(d), see *supra* note 1.

79 *Ibid.*; Roger S. Clark, "*The Mental Element in International Criminal Law*", in *Criminal Law Forum*, 2001, vol. 12, no. 3, pp. 291, 320–21; Kai Ambos, in Otto Triffterer (ed.), *Commentary on the Rome Statute of the International Criminal Court: Observers' Notes, Article by Article*, 2nd edition, C.H. Beck/Hart/Nomos, München/Oxford/Baden-Baden, 2008, pp. 743–70.

80 ICC Statute, Article 30(3), see *supra* note 1.

---

crime"[81] is therefore a low bar to meet. The Appeals Chamber ruled that for 'mere' knowledge of a consequence "in the ordinary course of events", "*virtual* certainty" of the consequence is necessary.[82]

The ICC Pre-Trial Chamber has also found that criminal liability exists when a crime is attempted or committed, the crime was carried out by a group with common purpose, and the accused intentionally made a "significant"[83] contribution to the crime with the knowledge of the group's intention to commit the crime.[84]

Where a group is party to a conflict, which has carried out crimes over a number of years, as alleged by credible observers, the requirement of near certainty that the group will continue to carry out those crimes is met. Where credible organisations like United Nations human rights monitoring bodies, Human Rights Watch and Amnesty International publicly report a groups' previous conduct, the requisite threshold is met. It indicates an awareness of a high probability of existence of a fact.[85] The existing fact in such circumstances is that the intentionally supported group is nearly certain to continue to commit crimes in the ordinary course of events.

21.5. Aiders, Abettors and Accessories in Afghanistan

Afghanistan's conflict has significantly contributed to loss of life and global instability over the past three decades. There are also violent conflicts with a significant number of external actors supporting parties to conflict.

---

[81] *Ibid.*, Article 25(3)(d)(ii).

[82] ICC, Situation in the Democratic Republic of the Congo, *Prosecutor v. Thomas Lubanga Dyilo*, Appeals Chamber, Judgment on the appeal of Mr Thomas Lubanga Dyilo against his conviction, 1 December 2014, ICC-01/04-01/06-3121-Red, para. 447 (http://www.legal-tools.org/doc/585c75/) (emphasis in the original).

[83] ICC, Situation in the Democratic Republic of the Congo, *Prosecutor v. Mbarushimana*, Pre-Trial Chamber I, Decision on the Confirmation of Charges, 16 December 2011, para. 283, see *supra* note 59.

[84] ICC, Situation in the Democratic Republic of the Congo, *Prosecutor v. Mbarushimana*, Pre-Trial Chamber I, Decision on the Prosecutor's Application for a Warrant of Arrest against Callixte Mbarushimana, 28 September 2010, ICC-01/04-01/10-1, para. 39 (http://www.legal-tools.org/doc/04d4fa/).

[85] Ambos, 2008, p. 870, see *supra* note 79.

Record numbers of battle-related deaths were observed in 2016, increasing ten-fold from 2005, the low point since the end of the Cold War.[86] The three countries with the most casualties in 2016 are also conflicts with a high number of external actors: Afghanistan, Iraq, and Syria.[87] This section of the chapter considers some of the conduct that might be considered by an OTP that incorporates the accused in its preliminary examinations and related reports.

The United States has been involved in Afghanistan for the past 17 years. Much of that time has been spent fighting insurgent groups such as the Taliban and the Haqqani Network. Despite a successful ground campaign, the United States has been unable to defeat the Taliban. This is in large part due to the large international backing that the Taliban has from both foreign governments and private individuals who serve as donors. The governments of Iran and Pakistan have served as the Taliban's primary backers. In October 2017, the Taliban attacked the cities of Farah and Lashkar Gah in Western Afghanistan.[88] Afghan National Security Forces were barely able to contain the offensive. The Taliban withdrew only after the Afghan forces requested a series of US airstrikes. Afghan intelligence found four dead Iranian commandos after the attack.[89] March 2018 saw yet another Taliban offensive to capture Farah. Evidence suggests that Iran's Islamic Revolutionary Guard Corps provided support to the Taliban during the lead-up to the attack.[90] Iran has an interest in keeping the western province of Farah unstable because it is a focal point for the Saudi financed TAPI (Turkmenistan, Afghanistan, Pakistan and India) pipeline. Additionally, Iran holds an interest in preventing the construction of the

---

[86] Marie Allansson, Erik Melander and Lotta Themnér, "Organized Violence, 1989–2016", in *Journal of Peace Research*, 2017, vol. 54, no. 4, pp. 574–87; Ralph Sundberg, Kristine Eck and Joakim Kreutz, "Introducing the UCDP Non-State Conflict Dataset", in *Journal of Peace Research*, 2012, vol. 49, no. 2, pp. 351–62.

[87] Mihai Croicu and Ralph Sundberg, *UCDP GED Codebook version 17.1*, Department of Peace and Conflict Research, Uppsala University, Uppsala, 2017; Ralph Sundberg and Erik Melander, "Introducing the UCDP Georeferenced Event Dataset", in *Journal of Peace Research*, 2013, vol. 50, no. 4, pp. 523–32.

[88] Mujib Mashal and Fahim Abed, "On Their Own, Afghan Forces Strain to Combat Taliban Offensives", in *The New York Times*, 9 October 2016.

[89] Carlotta Gall, "In Afghanistan, The US Exits, Iran Comes In", in *The New York Times*, 5 August 2017.

[90] Ahmad Majidyar, "Afghans see Iran's hand in Taliban's latest gains in western Afghanistan", Middle East Institute, 14 March 2018.

Bakhshabad dam in Farah province because it would serve to limit Iranian access to Afghanistan's rivers.[91] Iran has allowed the Taliban to cross into Iran so that they may train and replenish their forces before an offensive. The Islamic Revolutionary Guard Corps has additionally become vocal in its support for the Taliban mainly because the Taliban manages to simultaneously fight Daesh/ISIS and US and NATO forces.[92]

Russian support for the Taliban in Afghanistan may seem very surprising given their history with Afghanistan. However, the current US commander in Afghanistan, General John Nicholson, has gone on the record in an interview with the BBC and has publicly accused the Russian Federation of supplying arms to the Taliban. In an interview, General Nicholson states:

> We've had stories written by the Taliban that have appeared in the media about financial support provided by the enemy. We've had weapons brought to this headquarters and given to us by Afghan leaders and said, this was given by the Russians to the Taliban. We know that the Russians are involved.[93]

Russia has conducted numerous counter terrorism exercises with the Tajik Army in southern Tajikistan along the border of Afghanistan. General Nicholson believes that when the Russian military moves weapons and equipment for an exercise they intentionally leave surplus materials behind so that they can be smuggled into Afghanistan for use by the Taliban.[94] While it is currently difficult to determine the quantity of weapons being smuggled in to Afghanistan, the Afghan Police and Afghan National Army believe that Russia is supplying medium and heavy machine guns, night vision goggles and small arms to the Taliban.[95]

Pakistan has long served as a refuge for the Taliban. In 2012, evidence emerged that showed direct ties between Pakistan's Inter-Services Intelligence ('ISI') branch and the Taliban. The report states that the "ISI is thoroughly aware of Taliban activities and the whereabouts of all senior

---

[91] *Ibid.*

[92] *Ibid.*

[93] Justin Rowlatt, "Russia 'arming the Afghan Taliban', says US", in *BBC*, 23 March 2018.

[94] *Ibid.*

[95] *Ibid.*

Taliban personnel".[96] The report also claims that ISI agents were able to sit in on the "Quetta Shura" (the Taliban's top leadership council). Observers claim that support of the Taliban is part of the ISI's official policy.[97] The United States government has requested that UN-proscribed NGOs al Rashid Trust, al Akhtur Trust and all successor organizations stop funnelling money and providing other forms of support to the Taliban and LeT (Lashkar-e-Taiba) from Pakistan.[98] The US has also identified the Pakistan-based Haqqani network as a conduit for funnelling weapons and fighters across the Afghan and Pakistan border.[99]

Saudi Arabia has long praised Pakistan's support to the Taliban while simultaneously supporting the United States in their efforts to defeat the Taliban in Afghanistan. Agha Jan Motasim, the former finance minister of the Taliban explained that he travelled to Saudi Arabia two to three times a year to raise funds and gauge support for the Taliban among donors.[100] Motasim accomplished all of this while on pilgrimage to Saudi Arabia's holy sites. Motasim would appeal to wealthy Saudi Sheikhs and other wealthy Muslims and urge them to donate to the Taliban as private individuals. Once Motasim raised money he would move it to Pakistan through a series of regional banks or through the 'Hawala' (an Islamic custom of informal money transfers). The amount of money raised by the Taliban in Saudi Arabia was so significant that Secretary of State Hillary Clinton said that Saudi Arabia was the "most significant source of funding to Sunni terrorist groups worldwide".[101] US diplomatic cables further disclosed fears and suspicions that that the Taliban were able to raise millions of dollars from private individuals during annual pilgrimages in Saudi Arabia.

The United States has been funding the fledging government of Afghanistan since its establishment after the Bonn Agreement in 2001. The

---

[96] Azmat Khan, "Leaked NATO Report Alleges Pakistani Support for Taliban", in *Frontline*, 1 February 2012.

[97] "Pakistani agents 'funding and training Afghan Taliban'", in *BBC*, 13 June 2010.

[98] United States Secretary of State, *Terrorist Finance: Action for request for senior level engagement on terrorism finance*, 30 December 2009, STATE 131801.

[99] *Ibid.*

[100] Carlotta Gall, "Saudis Bankroll Taliban, Even as King Officially Supports Afghan Government", in *The New York Times*, 6 December 2016.

[101] *Ibid.*

United States has taken a special interest in shaping and training the Afghan National Security Forces so that they may become a self-sustaining force capable of fighting against insurgents. From 2002-2015 the US Department of Defense has spent a total of USD 778.1 billion on the war in Afghanistan.[102] In 2016, the US State Department approved a USD 60 million arms sale to Afghanistan through the Defense Security Cooperation Agency, which specializes in foreign military sales. This arms package includes 4,891 M16A4 assault rifles, 485 M240B machine guns and 800 M2 machine guns listed under the Major Defense Equipment ('MDE') category. Non-MDE procurements include M249 light machine guns, M110 sniper rifles, MK-19 grenade launchers, machine gun mounts, spare parts, and repair kits.[103] A press release from the Defense Security Cooperation Agency on the sale further elaborates:

> The proposed sale will enhance the foreign policy and national security objectives of the United States by helping to improve the security of a strategic partner by providing weapons needed to maintain security and stability, as well as to conduct offensive operations against an ongoing insurgency. A stable and secure Afghanistan is vital to regional stability. This proposed sale will also demonstrate the U.S. commitment to Afghanistan's security.

However, the OTP has included Afghanistan as a part of its preliminary examination activities in 2017. In the report, the Afghan National Security Forces were accused of "[w]ar crimes of torture, outrages upon personal dignity and sexual violence".[104] The other major parties to the conflict are also accused of crimes.

21.6. Conclusion

As ICC observers begin to confront the institution's movement towards a status of irrelevance, an urgency surrounding the need for real and per-

---

[102] Ian S. Livingston and Michael O'Hanlon, *Afghanistan Index: Also including selected data on Pakistan*, Brookings Institute, 2017.

[103] Defense Security Cooperation Agency, "Afghanistan - Individual and Crew Served Weapons", 18 August 2016.

[104] ICC OTP, *Report on Preliminary Examination Activities 2017*, 4 December 2017 (http://www.legal-tools.org/doc/e50459/).

ceived integrity and impact emerges.[105] The post-Cold War re-emergence of international crimes prosecutions at the international level is at risk of capture by realist State self-interest.[106] A part of that capture is the exclusion from substantive international criminal justice jurisdiction of the crime of aggression – the focus on *jus in bello* crimes. Such a change demands change from a situation where those that fight wars be accountable to certain conduct but that those that start wars may do so with impunity. As identified, this status quo focuses international criminal justice on the symptoms of the problem – how war is fought – and not the problem – the waging of war. Further, the current practice of international criminal justice focuses accountability on local actors for the conduct of war while avoiding the conduct of those enabling it via material support.

The deterrence effect of international criminal justice and in particular of the ICC, has not been demonstrated. New approaches, aligned with the nature of the escalation in violent conflict, are required. Civil society, which has refrained from focusing on external actors' international criminal law liability, must also play its role in providing credible evidence to substantiate reports on preliminary examination.

As the situation in Afghanistan is considered, there is an opportunity to take a bold and meaningful step towards accountability for the conduct of local Afghan actors as well as those that enable it. Similarly, in Colombia, the US government provides military support to the Colombian government for its operations. Secret US assistance, such as eavesdropping, is funded via a multi-billion black budget. Since 2000, this secret support has been supplemented by a public USD 9 billion package of mostly military aid called 'Plan Colombia'.[107]

---

[105] See, for example the identification of the ICC as increasingly irrelevant in; Morten Bergsmo, Wolfgang Kaleck, Sam Muller and William H. Wiley, "A Prosecutor Falls, Time for the Court to Rise", in FICHL Policy Brief Series No. 86 (2017), Torkel Opsahl Academic EPublisher, Brussels, 2017 (http://www.toaep.org/pbs-pdf/86-four-directors/).

[106] Christopher B. Mahony, "The Justice Pivot: US International Criminal Law Influence from Outside the Rome Statute", in *Georgetown Journal of International Law*, 2015, vol. 46, no. 4, p. 1071.

[107] *Idem*, "If You're Not at the Table, You're on the Menu: Complementarity and Self-Interest in Domestic Processes for Core International Crimes", in Morten Bergsmo and SONG Tianying (eds.), *Military Self-Interest in Accountability for Core International Crimes*, Torkel Opsahl Academic EPublisher, Brussels, 2015, pp. 229–59 (http://www.toaep.org/ps-

It is likely that the US will have a hostile response to formal OTP investigations in Colombia and Afghanistan, particularly examination of external actors. However, the OTP's continued apprehensive approach, which avoids conflict with major powers, can be mitigated by pointing the finger at *all* external actors equally. Boxing oneself in by rendering the consideration of external actors a standardized practice, via a policy announcement, would render such an approach a *fait accompli*. Such a status would increase, via standardization, the consideration of external actors. It would establish a stigma around the conduct of providing such support. This is needed not only to provide justice to victims, but most importantly to reintroduce ICC credibility and efficacy for preventing future war and crimes we know accompany it.

---

pdf/25-bergsmo-song); Dana Priest, "Covert action in Colombia", in *The Washington Post*, 21 December 2013.

22

The Standard of Proof in
Preliminary Examinations

Matthew E. Cross[*]

The ICC is, at times, a controversial institution. Perhaps the most common allegation is that the Court, and especially the Office of the Prosecutor, has in some way exercised an inappropriate degree of selectivity in the situations where investigations are opened, or the time at which investigations are opened. The Prosecutor's answer has been to stress that situation selection is an essentially legal question:[1] an investigation *shall* be opened if and when it is determined that the conditions specified in Article 53(1) of the Statute are met. Such an answer is based on the intention of the international community in drafting the Rome Statute, as it is understood. Yet another question necessarily follows from this premise: *when* are the conditions of Article 53(1) met? In other words, what standard of proof is applied, and what are the implications of this standard? That is the focus of this chapter. Only with clarity about this concept can there be a meaningful assessment of the 'quality' of any preliminary examination.

Discussion of the standard of proof may seem prosaic, perhaps even trite, to most lawyers. After all, the standard of proof is usually the foundation for legal discussion, its meaning commonly accepted and the underlying assumptions well known and undisputed. But this may not be so

---

[*] **Matthew Cross** (LL.B. (Hons.), M.Jur. (Dunelm)) is an Appeals Counsel in the Office of the Prosecutor at the ICC. The views expressed in this chapter are those of the author, and do not necessarily represent the views of the Office of the Prosecutor or the International Criminal Court. With thanks to Helen Brady, Amitis Khojasteh, Rod Rastan, and Emeric Rogier, for the various fruitful discussions of these issues over the past years; and to Grace Goh, Anna Ivanovitch, Hesham Mourad, and Elena Martin Salgado, for their assistance in consulting other linguistic versions of the Rome Statute of the International Criminal Court (see *infra* note 61). Any errors remain, of course, my own. Case law references finalised on 26 April 2018.

[1] See also Matilde Gawronski, "The Legalistic Function of Preliminary Examinations", in Morten Bergsmo and Carsten Stahn (eds.), *Quality Control in Preliminary Examination: Volume 1*, Torkel Opsahl Academic EPublisher, Brussels, 2018, chap. 7.

in the context of preliminary examinations, given the unusual – perhaps even unique – object and purpose of this procedure. To the extent this object and purpose is contested, this may imply favouring different approaches. For example, many (but by no means all) domestic legal systems would accept the principle that all reported crimes should result in an investigation. Such a principle would suggest that any preliminary examination, as the gateway to investigation, should necessarily apply a *very* low standard of proof (in essence, merely looking to whether a criminal complaint exists). Yet it might equally be argued that the ICC cannot properly be compared with national authorities, and that the Statute reflects an inherent principle of selectivity. The Court is not mandated to investigate and prosecute *every* crime within its jurisdiction but, for example, only those which are *admissible* before it. Such a view favours a standard of proof which is somewhat higher, sufficient at least to provide a rational distinction between those situations which meet the conditions in the Statute and those which do not.

It is notable that the Court's (relatively few) judicial decisions addressing Article 53(1) are rarely unanimous.[2] Suspicions that there may not (yet) be universal agreement about the applicable standard of proof should also be raised by the recent *Comoros* litigation, in which for the first time a Pre-Trial Chamber (by majority) requested the Prosecutor to reconsider her decision not to open an investigation.[3] In seeking to appeal the decision, the Prosecutor asserted that the majority had erred not only in its conclusions and the standard of review applied but also in its interpretation of the 'legal standard' in Article 53(1)[4] – a matter which she

---

[2] Notably, and as further discussed below, Judges Kaul, Fernández de Gurmendi, and Kovács (twice) have all reasoned separately in relevant decisions in the Kenya, Côte d'Ivoire, Comoros, and Georgia situations, respectively. Although these separate opinions may not all directly have been occasioned by a difference of opinion concerning Article 53(1), nonetheless they do reveal varying insights into the meaning and application of this provision. The recent *Burundi* decision under article 15(4) is the only one, to date, which has not featured a separate opinion of some kind.

[3] International Criminal Court, Situation on the Registered Vessels of the Union of the Comoros, the Hellenic Republic and the Kingdom of Cambodia, Pre-Trial Chamber, Decision on the request of the Union of the Comoros to review the Prosecutor's decision not to initiate an investigation, 16 July 2015, ICC-01/13-34 ('*Comoros* Reconsideration Request') (http://www.legal-tools.org/doc/2f876c/).

---

described as being of "near-constitutional importance", with "the potential to affect all situations currently undergoing preliminary examination".[5] She concluded: "To any extent that the standard to be applied by the Prosecution is lower than that suggested by the plain words of the Statute, this may radically affect the scope of the Court's operations, now and for the years to come".[6]

Greater clarity about the standard of proof applicable to preliminary examinations will yield some particular benefits, beyond dispelling the myth that the Prosecutor's analysis is purely oriented to delivering some kind of 'preferred' consequence. To the extent that the Prosecutor must

---

[4]   International Criminal Court, Situation on the Registered Vessels of the Union of the Comoros, the Hellenic Republic and the Kingdom of Cambodia, Appeals Chamber, Notice of Appeal of "Decision on the request of the Union of the Comoros to review the Prosecutor's decision not to initiate an investigation" (ICC-01/13-34), 27 July 2015, ICC-01/13-35, para. 20 ('*Comoros* Notice of Appeal') (http://www.legal-tools.org/doc/50ca53/).

[5]   *Ibid.*, paras. 5, 23.

[6]   *Ibid.*, para. 23. By majority, the appeal was dismissed as inadmissible, since the *Comoros* Reconsideration Request was not considered a decision with respect to admissibility in the meaning of Article 82(1)(a) of the Statute. However, the Appeals Chamber emphasised that, consequently, the Pre-Trial Chamber's views do not bind the Prosecutor in conducting her reconsideration: International Criminal Court, Situation on the Registered Vessels of the Union of the Comoros, the Hellenic Republic and the Kingdom of Cambodia, Appeals Chamber, Decision on the admissibility of the Prosecutor's appeal against the "Decision on the request of the Union of the Comoros to review the Prosecutor's decision not to initiate an investigation", 6 November 2015, ICC-01/13-51, paras. 59–60, 64, 66 (http://www.legal-tools.org/doc/a43856/). The Prosecutor subsequently published her "final decision", in which she confirmed her disagreement with the standard of proof adopted by the majority of the Pre-Trial Chamber: International Criminal Court, Situation on the Registered Vessels of the Union of the Comoros, the Hellenic Republic and the Kingdom of Cambodia, Office of the Prosecutor, Notice of Prosecutor's Final Decision under Rule 108(3), 29 November 2017, ICC-01/13-57, Annex I, paras. 3-4, 8-9, 12-35 (http://www.legal-tools.org/doc/298503/). At the time of finalising this chapter, the Government of the Comoros and the Prosecution continue to dispute any binding quality of the legal reasoning in the *Comoros* Reconsideration Request, and the Pre-Trial Chamber is likely to rule further on the matter: International Criminal Court, Situation on the Registered Vessels of the Union of the Comoros, the Hellenic Republic and the Kingdom of Cambodia, Government of the Union of the Comoros, Public Redacted Version of "Application for Judicial Review by the Government of the Union of the Comoros", 26 February 2018, ICC-01/13-58-Red (https://www.legal-tools.org/doc/24c550/); International Criminal Court, Situation on the Registered Vessels of the Union of the Comoros, the Hellenic Republic and the Kingdom of Cambodia, Office of the Prosecutor, Prosecution's Response to the Government of the Union of the Comoros' "Application for Judicial Review" (ICC-01/13-58) (Lack of Jurisdiction), 13 March 2018, ICC-01/13-61 (https://www.legal-tools.org/doc/a17312/).

---

undertake a concrete legal assessment which surpasses a clear threshold, this has obvious implications for her approach – particularly in evaluating the available information; her possible actions when confronted with an apparent insufficiency of information; and in the nature and extent of the findings she may make in seeking to open an investigation, or terminating a preliminary examination. Furthermore, although there is no hierarchy of crimes within the Statute – in the sense that no Article 5 crime is *a priori* worthier of investigation than any other[7] – practical considerations may make some crimes more amenable to identification at the preliminary examination stage than others. An appreciation of the standard of proof also sheds further light on the nature and limits of the discretion afforded to the Prosecutor in situation selection, the applicable standard of judicial review, and the nature and scope of the Pre-Trial Chamber's oversight functions in this area.

From these considerations, it is concluded that the standard of proof in Article 53(1) may imply a relatively narrow, and essentially procedural, function for preliminary examinations. There is a clear need for comprehensive and reliable reporting of alleged human rights abuses and international crimes, in the fashion successfully implemented by many international bodies and NGOs, but this is not the primary role of preliminary examinations – even though, on occasion and as a matter of her discretion, the Prosecutor may choose to provide a more fulsome analysis than is legally required.

It follows from the application of a standard of proof that a preliminary examination – insofar as its external, public results are concerned – will not simply be an account of suspicions or allegations of crime, but a *selective* assessment of those allegations which meet the standard of proof. Accordingly, the public conclusion of a preliminary examination will not necessarily be a reliable guide to the contours of the subsequent investigation. Frequently, there may be alleged (or even unknown) crimes which cannot be substantiated to the Article 53(1) standard in the preliminary

---

[7] See Rome Statute of the International Criminal Court, 17 July 1998, Preamble, Articles 5, 53 ('ICC Statute') (http://www.legal-tools.org/doc/7b9af9/); International Criminal Court, Situation in the Central African Republic, *Prosecutor v. Jean-Pierre Bemba Gombo*, Office of the Prosecutor, Prosecution's Final Submissions following the Appeal Hearing, 19 January 2018, ICC-01/05-01/08-3597 A A2 A3, para. 25 (http://www.legal-tools.org/doc/70e8cd/).

examination stage, but which can be established by investigative measures thereafter. Conversely, it is only when a preliminary examination is closed *without* proceeding to open an investigation that the Prosecutor may be obliged – at least for situations referred to the Court – to give a reasoned analysis explaining the basis for her view that the available information does not support *any* alleged crime, to the requisite standard of proof. This is necessary in order to allow the Pre-Trial Chamber to undertake any review which might be triggered, applying an appropriate standard of scrutiny.

22.1. Interpreting Article 53(1) of the Statute: Defining the Standard of Proof

In its *chapeau*, Article 53(1) states generally that:

> The Prosecutor shall, having evaluated the information made available to him or her, initiate an investigation unless he or she determines that there is no reasonable basis to proceed under this Statute.

In making this determination, Article 53(1) further requires that:

a) the information available provides "a reasonable basis to believe" that a crime within the jurisdiction of the Court has been committed;[8]

b) there is at least one potential case which would be admissible, in the meaning of Article 17 (that is, complementarity and gravity);[9] and

---

[8] *Ibid.*, Article 53(1)(a).

[9] *Ibid.*, Article 53(1)(b). Although this provision refers to "the case", this means a "potential case": International Criminal Court, Situation in the Republic of Kenya, Pre-Trial Chamber, Decision Pursuant to Article 15 of the Rome Statute on the Authorization of an Investigation into the Situation in the Republic of Kenya, 31 March 2010, ICC-01/09-19, para. 50 ('*Kenya* Article 15 Decision') (http://www.legal-tools.org/doc/338a6f/); International Criminal Court, Situation in the Republic of Côte d'Ivoire, Pre-Trial Chamber, Decision pursuant to Article 15 of the Rome Statute on the Authorisation of an Investigation into the Situation in the Republic of Côte d'Ivoire, 3 October 2011, ICC-02/11-14, paras. 190–91 ('*Côte d'Ivoire* Article 15 Decision') (http://www.legal-tools.org/doc/7a6c19/). It suffices, moreover, if the admissibility of at least one "potential case" is established to the requisite standard: International Criminal Court, Situation in Georgia, Pre-Trial Chamber, Decision on the Prosecutor's request for authorization of an investigation, 27 January 2016, ICC-01/15-12, paras. 39, 46, 50 ('*Georgia* Article 15 Decision') (http://www.legal-tools.org/doc/a3d07e/).

---

c) there are not "substantial reasons to believe" that opening an investigation would be contrary to the interests of justice.[10]

From the plain text of these provisions, the last analysis – the "interests of justice"' assessment – is clearly different in nature from the other two. The first two address the Prosecutor's appreciation of the *facts* as they presently exist; the last is directed to the Prosecutor's anticipation of the *consequences* of any investigation and an evaluation of whether those consequences are consistent with the notion of 'justice'.

The text of the Statute further illustrates the distinction of the "interests of justice" assessment from the other criteria, not only by setting a different test ("substantial reasons" rather than "reasonable basis"), but also by providing a different oversight structure.[11] Likewise, both the Pre-Trial Chamber and the Prosecution have recognised Article 53(1)(c) as a more overt exercise of prosecutorial discretion.[12]

For these reasons, Article 53(1)(c) should be treated differently from Article 53(1)(a) and (b), and does not represent the straightforward application of a standard of proof to given information. In this chapter, therefore, it is recognised as a distinct and separate exercise of discretion, as a final restraint on the first two criteria (which are largely law- and fact-driven), but it is not considered within the discussion of the 'standard of proof' as such.

By contrast, Article 53(1)(a) and (b) – the jurisdiction and admissibility analyses – should be understood to be based on the *same* legal standard: whether or not there is a "reasonable basis" to believe the relevant facts exist, based on the information available. Unlike Article 53(1)(a), Article 53(1)(b) does not itself make any direct reference to the standard upon which the Prosecutor shall determine the facts relevant to whether a potential case is or would be admissible at the preliminary examination stage. Yet four cogent reasons support the view that these pro-

---

[10] ICC Statute, Article 53(1)(c), see *supra* note 7.
[11] *Ibid.*, Article 53(1), 53(3).
[12] See *Comoros* Reconsideration Request, para. 14, see *supra* note 3 (contrasting the "discretion" in Article 53(1)(c) with the "exacting legal requirements" of Article 53(1)(a) and (b)); Office of the Prosecutor, *Policy Paper on the Interests of Justice*, September 2007, p. 1 (referring to the "exercise of the Prosecutor's discretion" in Article 53(1)(c)) (http://www.legal-tools.org/doc/bb02e5/).

visions apply the same approach to different criteria.[13] First, both provisions are equally subject to the *chapeau* of Article 53(1), which refers to the requirement of a "reasonable basis to proceed".[14] Second, notwithstanding their different wording, both Article 53(1)(a) and (b) have a similar purpose: requiring an assessment of certain facts based on the available information – which is different from Article 53(1)(c). Third, the text of Article 53(1)(b), by referring to a conditional assessment of admissibility ("would be") manifestly does not require an absolute assessment. Fourth, if Article 53(1)(b) does not apply a "reasonable basis" standard, it is very hard to discern what alternative standard would be applied for the factual assessments which are no less inherent in determininations of complementarity and gravity than of jurisdiction.[15]

---

13   See also *Kenya* Article 15 Decision, "Dissenting Opinion of Judge Hans-Peter Kaul", para. 17, see *supra* note 9.

14   Notably, in concluding the negotiations for the ICC Statute, the diplomatic conference declined to adjust the reference to "reasonable basis" in the *chapeau* of Article 53(1), even though the question had been raised whether a broader term might be needed to capture the three criteria in what would become Article 53(1)(a) to (c). Consequently, it can be inferred that the drafters saw the concept of a "reasonable basis" as the threshold underlying all relevant determinations in Article 51(1). See M. Cherif Bassiouni, *The Legislative History of the International Criminal Court: an Article-by-Article Evolution of the Statute*, vol. 2, Transnational Publishers, 2005, pp. 337 (reproducing the Drafting Committee's 1998 draft, Article 54, which was the result of the diplomatic negotiations at Rome, stating that "[t]he Prosecutor shall, having evaluated the information made available to him or her, initiate an investigation unless he or she determines that there is no reasonable basis to proceed"), 338 (reproducing the Preparatory Committee's 1998 draft, Article 54, which was the basis for the diplomatic negotiations, stating that "the Prosecutor shall [...] initiate an investigation unless the Prosecutor concludes that there is no reasonable basis for a prosecution", accompanied by a note: "The term 'reasonable basis' in the opening clause is also used in the criteria listed in paragraph 2(i). If the latter is retained, a broader term in the opening clause might be necessary in order to cover all the criteria listed under paragraph 2") (hereinafter 'Bassiouni'). Cf. Manuel Ventura, "The 'Reasonable Basis to Proceed' threshold in the Kenya and Côte d'Ivoire *propio motu* investigation decisions: The International Criminal Court's lowest evidentiary standard?", in *The Law and Practice of International Courts and Tribunals*, 2013, vol. 12, no. 1, p. 49, at p. 61 (hereinafter 'Ventura').

15   See also, for example, International Criminal Court, Office of the Prosecutor, *Policy Paper on Preliminary Examinations*, 1 November 2013, paras. 46–58 (complementarity assessments are based on ascertaining the relevant facts, and applying the law to them) ('*Policy Paper on Preliminary Examinations*') (http://www.legal-tools.org/doc/acb906/); Giuliano Turone, "Powers and duties of the Prosecutor", in Antonio Cassese *et al.* (eds.), *The Rome Statute of the International Criminal Court: a Commentary*, Oxford University Press, Oxford, 2002, p. 1152 (describing the "fluctuating" nature of the admissibility assessment) (hereinafter 'Turone').

Consistent with the case law of the Court, and the general approach in public international law, provisions of the Statute should be interpreted according to the principles set out in the Vienna Convention.[16] Accordingly, this analytical framework should be adopted to consider the meaning of the "reasonable basis to believe" standard in Article 53(1).

22.1.1. Ordinary Meaning of the Term "Reasonable Basis to Believe" in Article 53(1)

Article 53(1) states that, based on the available information, the Prosecutor must be satisfied of a "reasonable basis" to proceed. More concretely, as specified in Article 53(1)(a), this means a "reasonable basis to believe" certain relevant facts.

There is wide consensus about the meaning of the word "reasonable", including in the specific context of Article 53(1). To begin with, the dictionary definition of a "reasonable belief" is one which is "in accordance with reason; not irrational, absurd or ridiculous" or which is "based on specific and objective grounds".[17] Pre-Trial Chambers of the Court –

---

[16] See, for example, International Criminal Court, Situation in the Democratic Republic of the Congo, Appeals Chamber, Judgment on the Prosecutor's Application for Extraordinary Review of Pre-Trial Chamber I's 31 March 2006 Decision Denying Leave to Appeal, 13 July 2006, ICC-01/04-168, paras. 6, 33, 40 (http://www.legal-tools.org/doc/a60023/); International Criminal Court, Situation in the Republic of Kenya, *Prosecutor v. Ruto and Sang*, Appeals Chamber, Judgment on the appeals of [Mr] William Samoei Ruto and Mr Joshua Arap Sang against the decision of Trial Chamber V (A) of 17 April 2014 entitled "Decision on Prosecutor's Application for Witness Summonses and resulting Request for State Party Cooperation", 9 October 2014, ICC-01/09-01/11-1598, para. 105 (http://www.legal-tools.org/doc/e5eb09/); International Criminal Court, Situation in [REDACTED], *Prosecutor v. [REDACTED]*, Appeals Chamber, Judgment on the appeal of the Prosecutor against the decision of [REDACTED], 15 February 2016, ICC-ACRed-01/16, paras. 53, 55–57, 61–62 (http://www.legal-tools.org/doc/c01204/); International Criminal Court, Situation in the Republic of Côte d'Ivoire, Pre-Trial Chamber, Judge Fernández de Gurmendi's separate and partially dissenting opinion to the Decision pursuant to Article 15 of the Rome Statute on the Authorisation of an Investigation into the Situation in the Republic of Côte d'Ivoire, 3 October 2011, ICC-02/11-15, para. 10 ('*Côte d'Ivoire* Article 15 Decision, Separate Opinion of Judge Fernández de Gurmendi') (http://www.legal-tools.org/doc/ea2793/).

[17] "Reasonable", in *Oxford English Dictionary Online*, meaning A.4.a, example sentence 2 (available on its web site). See also Georghios M. Pikis, *The Rome Statute for the International Criminal Court: Analysis of the Statute, the Rules of Procedure and Evidence, the Regulations of the Court and Supplementary Instruments*, Martinus Nijhoff, 2010, pp. 104 (mn. 256: "good reason"), 264 (mn. 624: "fair[] infer[ence]"), 268 (mn. 636) (hereinafter 'Pikis'); Morten Bergsmo *et al.*, "Article 53: initiation of an investigation", in Otto

---

which are also called upon to apply the Article 53(1) standard when making decisions under Article 15(4), pursuant to Rule 48[18] – have consistently characterised it as a rational or sensible conclusion based on the available information.[19] The late Judge Kaul, for example, stated that it requires "a serious, thorough and well-considered approach", which would not be

---

Triffterer and Kai Ambos (eds.), *The Rome Statute of the International Criminal Court: A Commentary*, 3rd edition, C.H. Beck/Hart/Nomos, 2016, p. 1370, mn. 12 ("due consideration") (hereinafter 'Bergsmo *et al.*').

[18] See also *Kenya* Article 15 Decision, para. 21, see *supra* note 9; *Côte d'Ivoire* Article 15 Decision, Separate Opinion of Judge Fernández de Gurmendi, para. 13, see *supra* note 16; International Criminal Court, Situation in the Republic of Burundi, Pre-Trial Chamber, Public Redacted Version of 'Decision Pursuant to Article 15 of the Rome Statute on the Authorization of an Investigation into the Situation in the Republic of Burundi', ICC-01/17-X-9-US-Exp, 25 October 2017, 9 November 2017, ICC-01/17-9-Red, para. 28 ('*Burundi* Article 15 Decision') (https://www.legal-tools.org/doc/8f2373/).

[19] *Kenya* Article 15 Decision, paras. 30 ("reasonable means 'fair and sensible', or 'within the limits of reason'"), 33 ("it is sufficient" that a conclusion "can be supported on the basis of the [...] information available"), 35 (Article 53(1), in the context of Article 15(4), requires "a sensible [...] justification for a belief"), see *supra* note 9; *Côte d'Ivoire* Article 15 Decision, para. 24, see *supra* note 9; *Georgia* Article 15 Decision, para. 25, see *supra* note 9; *Burundi* Article 15 Decision, para. 30, see *supra* note 18. In the context of the 'beyond reasonable doubt' standard, see further International Criminal Tribunal for Rwanda, *Rutaganda v. the Prosecutor*, Appeals Chamber, Judgment, 26 May 2003, ICTR-96-3-A, para. 488 (a reasonable possibility is "based on logic and common sense" and has "a rational link to the evidence, lack of evidence, or inconsistencies in the evidence"; it is not "imaginary or frivolous [...] based on empathy or prejudice") (http://www.legal-tools.org/doc/40bf4a/); International Criminal Tribunal for the former Yugoslavia, *Prosecutor v. Mrkšić and Šljivančanin*, Appeals Chamber, Judgment, 5 May 2009, IT-95-13/1-A, para. 220 ("a fair or rational hypothesis which may be derived from the evidence" and not any "hypothesis or possibility") (http://www.legal-tools.org/doc/40bc41/); International Criminal Tribunal for the former Yugoslavia, *Prosecutor v. Galić*, Appeals Chamber, Judgment, 30 November 2006, IT-98-29-A, para. 259 ("just because there is some possibility, however slight, that an incident could have happened in another way does not in itself raise reasonable doubt") ('*Galić* Appeal Judgment') (http://www.legal-tools.org/doc/c81a32/). The ICC Appeals Chamber has cited *Rutaganda* with approval: International Criminal Court, Situation in the Democratic Republic of the Congo, *Prosecutor v. Ngudjolo*, Appeals Chamber, Judgment on the Prosecutor's appeal against the decision of Trial Chamber II entitled "Judgment pursuant to article 74 of the Statute", 27 February 2015, ICC-01/04-02/12-271, para. 109 (http://www.legal-tools.org/doc/1dce8f/); International Criminal Court, Situation in the Democratic Republic of the Congo, *Prosecutor v. Ngudjolo*, Appeals Chamber, Joint Dissenting Opinion of Judge Ekaterina Trendafilova and Judge Cuno Tarfusser, 27 February 2015, ICC-01/04-02/12-271-AnxA, paras. 54–57 ('*Ngudjolo* AJ, Dissenting Opinion of Judges Trendafilova and Tarfusser') (http://www.legal-tools.org/doc/45f67c/).

satisfied by "a somewhat generous or only summary evaluation whereby *any* information, of even [a] fragmentary nature", suffices.[20]

Likewise, the drafting history of the Statute suggests that the 'reasonableness' standard ultimately employed in Article 53(1) requires something more than a mere "possibility" – a term rejected early in the drafting process[21] – and at least the existence of "objective criteria".[22] Article 42(1) also contemplates the Prosecutor receiving "*substantiated* information on crimes within the jurisdiction of the Court".[23]

It would seem to follow that while information meeting the Article 53(1) standard need not be comprehensive or conclusive,[24] it must amount to something more than an entirely unsupported allegation. In other words, it would not suffice for the Prosecutor to initiate an investigation based merely on her determination that the *allegations* in a referral or Article 15 communication, if true, could satisfy the elements of at least one crime under the Statute. She would, instead, need to be assured that there was at least some factual foundation for those allegations, consistent with the

---

[20] *Kenya* Article 15 Decision, Dissenting Opinion of Judge Kaul, para. 15, see *supra* note 9. See also *Côte d'Ivoire* Article 15 Decision, Separate Opinion of Judge Fernández de Gurmendi, para. 43, see *supra* note 16.

[21] For example, the Preparatory Committee in 1997 opted to replace the term "possible basis" with "reasonable basis": Bassiouni, pp. 348 (reproducing the Preparatory Committee's 1997 draft, Article 26, requiring an investigation "unless the Prosecutor concludes that there is no reasonable basis"), 354 ("reproducing the Preparatory Committee's 1996 draft, Article 27, requiring determination "whether the complaint provides or is likely to provide a [possible] [reasonable] basis"), 363 (reproducing Article 26 of the ILC's *Draft Code of Crimes against the Peace and Security of Mankind*), see *supra* note 14. See also Bergsmo *et al.*, pp. 1369–1370, mn. 10, see *supra* note 14.

[22] By analogy, in the context of then Article 59, concerning the arrest of a suspect: see *Report of the Preparatory Committee on the Establishment of an International Criminal Court*, UN Doc. A/Conf.183/2/Add.1, 14 April 1998, p. 86, fn. 10 ("reasonable grounds [...] embody objective criteria") (http://www.legal-tools.org/doc/816405/).

[23] ICC Statute, Article 42(1) (emphasis added), see *supra* note 7. If read in isolation, the relevant sentence of Article 42(1) could be read disjunctively to suggest that State and UN Security Council referrals need not be "substantiated", but only communications under Article 15(1) need to be. However, this interpretation is inconsistent with the context of Article 53(1) – also reflected in the constant practice of the OTP – which requires *all* preliminary examinations to be based on a substantive evaluation of the information made available. See Article 53(1); further *infra* note 26.

[24] *Kenya* Article 15 Decision, para. 27, see *supra* note 9; *Côte d'Ivoire* Article 15 Decision, Separate Opinion of Judge Fernández de Gurmendi, para. 31, see *supra* note 16; *Georgia* Article 15 Decision, para. 25, see *supra* note 9.

---

general practice of the Pre-Trial Chamber under Article 15(4).[25] Nothing in the Statute or the Rules supports any distinction in the application of Article 53(1) between referred and *proprio motu* preliminary examinations, once formally commenced.[26]

By contrast, in *Comoros*, the majority of the Pre-Trial Chamber suggested that the Prosecutor must, in her preliminary examination, accept as true allegations which are not "manifestly false".[27] This view, expressed in the context also of the majority's assertion that the Article 53(1) assessment "does not necessitate any complex or detailed process of analysis",[28] would seem to support a more formalistic approach, focusing on the characteristics of an individual referral, communication, or piece of information, and not on an overall assessment of whether the inference to be drawn – for example, an element of a crime – is reasonable.[29]

The majority did not address relevant previous jurisprudence on these issues, and it is unclear whether it viewed its analysis as following or departing from this prior case law. In *Georgia*, however, the same majority cited all this jurisprudence together, implying that these opinions are consistent.[30] Yet, on their face, it is difficult to see how this is so. It is thus appropriate to consider these interpretations of the standard of proof in Article 53(1) in the context of the Statute more broadly, and the object and purpose of these provisions. In particular, however, it is hard to see how

---

[25] *Kenya* Article 15 Decision, Dissenting Opinion of Judge Kaul, para. 18 ("the Prosecutor must demonstrate his determination under Article 53(1)(a) of the Statute and substantiate it with adequate material"), see *supra* note 9.

[26] *Policy Paper on Preliminary Examinations*, paras. 12, 27, 35, see *supra* note 15.

[27] *Comoros* Reconsideration Request, para. 35, see *supra* note 3.

[28] *Ibid.*, para. 13.

[29] In other contexts, this approach is not correct. The applicable standard of proof should be applied to the legal elements which must be satisfied, and should not be applied in isolation to specific pieces of evidence. See, for example, *Ngudjolo* AJ, Dissenting Opinion of Judges Trendafilova and Tarfusser, paras. 34, 40–41, see *supra* note 19; *Galić* Appeal Judgment, para. 218, see *supra* note 19.

[30] *Georgia* Article 15 Decision, para. 25, see *supra* note 9. Judge Kovács again wrote separately, disagreeing with the majority on the extent to which the Pre-Trial Chamber should, under Article 15(4), undertake an independent review of the available information.

this approach can be reconciled with the duty to *evaluate* the information available, which implies some kind of substantive analysis.[31]

The *Georgia* decision is also notable for its reference, in the context of admissibility under Article 53(1)(b), to "reasonable doubts" as to whether the Russian authorities were "unable" to investigate in the meaning of Article 17.[32] This may simply have been a recognition of a factual ambiguity. But if the term is afforded legal significance, it suggests that the majority considered the standard of proof under Article 53(1)(b) to be *higher* than that under Article 53(1)(a) – on the "reasonable basis to believe" standard, the existence of a "reasonable doubt" is irrelevant:[33] what matters is whether there is a reasonable basis to believe a given fact; the possibility that there is also a reasonable basis to doubt that fact is immaterial. Such an approach by the *Georgia* majority would also seem to be inconsistent with the approach of the same majority in *Comoros*, where they emphasised (still in the context of admissibility, albeit sufficient gravity rather than complementarity) that "reasonable alternative explanations" did not matter, provided that *one* reasonable explanation supported the requirements of Article 53(1).[34] The incidence of such linguistic ambiguities only underlines the need for clarity in the interpretation of Article 53(1).

22.1.2. Context of the Standard of Proof in Article 53(1)

The "reasonable basis to believe" standard is undoubtedly a "low" standard,[35] and the lowest "evidentiary threshold" in the Statute.[36] An obvious

---

[31] See *infra* text accompanying note 123. In this context, the *Burundi* Pre-Trial Chamber notably referred to a concept of "manifest[] unreasonable[ness]", which may be an attempt to reframe the *Comoros* concept of 'manifest falsity' more clearly within the terms of article 53(1): *Burundi* Article 15 Decision, para. 138, see *supra* note 18. Yet, if so, it is still unconvincing – while appropriately shifting the focus somewhat to what is a *reasonable* conclusion, this is still qualified by the concept of what is 'manifest' – which itself depends on the nature of the evaluation which has been undertaken and the amount of information made available.

[32] *Georgia* Article 15 Decision, para. 46, see *supra* note 9.

[33] See, for example, *infra* note 37, and accompanying text.

[34] See, for example, *Comoros* Reconsideration Request, para. 41 ("the Prosecutor erred in not recognising one of the reasonable alternative explanations of the available information, on the absence of which she then relied in concluding that the gravity requirement was not met"), see *supra* note 3.

[35] *Kenya* Article 15 Decision, Dissenting Opinion of Judge Kaul, para. 15, see *supra* note 9.

contextual analysis would thus suggest that it must be interpreted to ensure it is meaningfully distinct from the other standards of proof which the Statute contains. It is uncontroversial that it is less than proof beyond reasonable doubt (that is, the standard of proof for criminal conviction, requiring that the relevant conclusions constitute the *only* reasonable inference from the available information),[37] and less than "sufficient evidence to establish substantial grounds to believe" the relevant facts (that is, the standard for confirmation of charges).[38] But there may be insights to be drawn from consideration of the relationship between the standards of proof in Article 53(1), on the one hand, and Articles 53(2) and 58, on the other. In particular, it is quite a different thing to suggest that the Article 53(1) standard is the lowest of *three* alternative standards of proof than to suggest it is the lowest of *five* alternative standards of proof (which would, presumably, make it very low indeed). Answering this question depends on an analysis of Articles 53(2) and 58.

Article 53(2) provides that the Prosecutor must "inform the Pre-Trial Chamber and the State making a referral", or the UN Security Council if it made a referral, if she decides that "there is not a sufficient basis for a prosecution" in a situation under investigation. Given the independence of the Prosecutor in "conducting investigations" under Article 42(1), Article 53(2) is understood to apply *only* if the Prosecutor determines she cannot initiate "*a*" prosecution – in the sense of "any" or "at least one"[39] –

---

[36] *Côte d'Ivoire* Article 15 Decision, Separate Opinion of Judge Fernández de Gurmendi, para. 43, see *supra* note 16; *Burundi* Article 15 Decision, para. 30; see *supra* note 18.

[37] *Kenya* Article 15 Decision, paras. 33-34, see *supra* note 9; *Georgia* Article 15 Decision, para. 25, see *supra* note 9. See also International Criminal Court, Situation in Darfur, Sudan, *Prosecutor v. Al Bashir*, Appeals Chamber, Judgment on the appeal of the Prosecutor against the "Decision on the Prosecution's Application for a Warrant of Arrest against Omar Hassan Ahmad Al Bashir", 3 February 2010, ICC-02/05-01/09-73, paras. 32–33 ('*Al Bashir* Article 58 Appeal Decision') (http://www.legal-tools.org/doc/9ada8e/). See further, for example, ICC Statute, Article 66(3), see *supra* note 7; International Criminal Tribunal for the former Yugoslavia, *Prosecutor v. Vasiljević*, Appeals Chamber, Judgment, 25 February 2004, IT-98-32-A, para. 120 (http://www.legal-tools.org/doc/e35d81/).

[38] See ICC Statute, Article 61(7), see *supra* note 7.

[39] As such, it cannot properly be seen as a "step" in the process from preliminary examination to investigation to prosecution. Rather, it is an *alternative* to prosecution, leading to the termination of an investigation. It applies only if the Prosecutor decides that she cannot make *any* applications under Article 58. By contrast, provided the Prosecutor retains the intention to bring at least one prosecution within any open investigation, she retains full discretion as to whether to make an application under Article 58 or not in any particular

in a situation.[40] Article 53(2) further defines that an "insufficient basis" to prosecute means the absence of "a sufficient legal or factual basis to seek a warrant or summons under Article 58",[41] the inadmissibility of the case,[42] or a determination that a "prosecution is not in the interests of justice".[43] For all these reasons, it follows, therefore, that Article 53(2) does not contain an independent standard of proof,[44] but rather is contingent

---

case. Notably, and in contrast to the apparently limited scope of Article 53(2)(a), this ensures that she can determine whether to initiate a prosecution not only on the basis of her view that she will meet the Article 58 standard, but more broadly on the prospects of obtaining a successful conviction. See also International Criminal Court, Office of the Prosecutor, *Policy Paper on Case Selection and Prioritisation*, 15 September 2016, paras. 25–55 (http://www.legal-tools.org/doc/182205/). Cf. Bergsmo *et al.*, p. 1370 (margin no. 11), see *supra* note 17; De Meester, "Article 53: Initiation of an investigation", in Mark Klamberg (ed.), *Commentary on the Law of the International Criminal Court*, Torkel Opsahl Academic EPublisher, Brussels, 2017, pp. 389 (fn. 419), 395 (fns. 426–427) (http://www.legal-tools.org/doc/aa0e2b/); Matthew Brubacher, "Prosecutorial discretion within the International Criminal Court", in *Journal of International Criminal Justice*, 2004, vol. 2, no. 1, p. 71, at pp. 79–80 (hereinafter 'Brubacher').

40 Self-evidently, if the Prosecutor was required to inform the Pre-Trial Chamber and the referring party every time she determined that a particular person could not be prosecuted – a population which could run into the thousands – she would no longer be acting independently but under an intrusive form of supervision. See also Morten Bergsmo, Frederik Harhoff, and ZHU Dan, "Article 42: the Office of the Prosecutor", in Otto Triffterer and Kai Ambos (eds.), *The Rome Statute of the International Criminal Court: a Commentary*, 3rd edition, C.H. Beck/Hart/Nomos, 2016, p. 1267, at p. 1270, mn. 9 ("The Pre-Trial Chamber may not impose conditions as to how, when or where the investigations are to be carried out, for which alleged offences and against whom. These decisions fall within the purview of the Prosecutor's prerogative") (hereinafter 'Bergsmo *et al.*: Article 42'); Daniel D. Ntanda Nsereko, "Prosecutorial discretion before national courts and international tribunals", in *Journal of International Criminal Justice*, 2005, vol. 3, no. 1, p. 124, at p. 138 (hereinafter 'Nsereko'). See further Hassan B. Jallow, "Prosecutorial discretion and international criminal justice", in *Journal of International Criminal Justice*, 2005, vol. 3, no. 1, p. 145, at p. 155.

41 ICC Statute, Article 53(2)(a), see *supra* note 7.

42 *Ibid.*, Article 53(2)(b).

43 *Ibid.*, Article 53(2)(c).

44 Cf. Marco Longobardo, "Everything is relative, even gravity: Remarks on the assessment of gravity in ICC preliminary examinations, and the *Mavi Marmara* affair", in *Journal of International Criminal Justice*, 2016, vol. 14, no. 4, p. 1011, at p. 1022 (hereinafter 'Longobardo'); Bergsmo *et al.*, p. 1370 (mn. 11), see *supra* note 17; Kai Ambos, *Treatise on International Criminal Law: Volume III: International Criminal Procedure*, Oxford University Press, 2016, p. 380 (hereinafter 'Ambos'); Brubacher, pp. 79–80, see *supra* note 39.

upon the Prosecutor's assessment of the prospects for meeting (at least) the standard of proof contained in Article 58.[45]

Article 58 provides that the Pre-Trial Chamber shall issue a warrant of arrest or summons to appear, at the Prosecutor's application, if it is satisfied that: "[t]here are reasonable grounds to believe that the person has committed a crime within the jurisdiction of the Court".[46] Whether the Pre-Trial Chamber issues a warrant or summons depends on its further assessment whether: "[t]he arrest of the person appears necessary" to ensure their appearance for trial, to preserve the integrity of the investigation or Court proceedings, or to prevent the commission of relevant crimes;[47] or whether: "a summons is sufficient to ensure the person's appearance".[48]

The Appeals Chamber has emphasised that the Article 58 standard must be something less than the two aforementioned standards under Articles 61 and 66(3),[49] and stressed that, "at this preliminary stage, it does not have to be certain that th[e] person committed the alleged offence".[50] Although opinions may vary as to whether or not the Article 58 standard should properly be equated to the concept of 'reasonable suspicion' as articulated and understood by the European Court of Human Rights,[51] the

---

[45] It is in this sense that it is likely that the distinct terminology in Article 53(2) was advertent: cf. Longobardo, p. 1022 (citing United Nations Diplomatic Conference of Plenipotentiaries on the Establishment of an International Criminal Court: Official Records: Volume III: Reports and other documents, UN Doc. A/Conf.183/13 (Vol. III), August 2002, p. 292 (notes contained in the transmittal letters from the Chairman of the Committee of the Whole to the Chairman of the Drafting Committee) (http://www.legal-tools.org/doc/e03967/)), see *supra* note 44. The note of 26 June 1998 simply states that: "[i]n article 54", as it was, "the words 'reasonable basis' and 'sufficient basis' are used intentionally in different paragraphs". See also Bergsmo *et al.*, p. 1375, mn. 29, see *supra* note 17.

[46] ICC Statute, Article 58(1)(a), see *supra* note 7. See also Article 58(6), (7) (a summons may be issued if "there are reasonable grounds to believe that the person committed the crime alleged").

[47] *Ibid.*, Article 58(1)(b).

[48] *Ibid.*, Article 58(7).

[49] *Al Bashir* Article 58 Appeal Decision, para. 30 ("a Pre-Trial Chamber should not require a level of proof that would be required for the confirmation of charges or for conviction"), see *supra* note 37. See also paras. 32–33.

[50] *Ibid.*, para. 31.

[51] Cf. *Ibid.* See Michael Ramsden and CHUNG Cecilia, "'Reasonable grounds to believe': An unreasonably unclear evidentiary threshold in the ICC Statute", in *Journal of International Criminal Justice*, 2015, vol. 13, no. 3, p. 555 (hereinafter 'Ramsden and CHUNG'); Amrutanshu Dash and Dhruv Sharma, "Arrest warrants at the International Criminal Court:

practice of the ICC nonetheless shows that Article 58 is not concerned with mere abstract suspicions but rather "'grounds' *founded on evidential material* giving rise to a reasonable belief that a crime has been committed".[52] This necessarily follows from Article 58(2)(d), which requires the Prosecutor at least to summarise "the evidence and any other information" which "establish" that the standard of proof is met.[53]

Some authorities have gone further and suggested that the requirement of "reasonable *grounds* to believe" in Article 58 must therefore be a distinct (higher) standard of proof than Article 53(1) ("reasonable *basis* to believe"). Thus, the *Kenya* Pre-Trial Chamber stated without further reasoning that:

> bearing in mind that the 'reasonable basis' standard under article 15 of the Statute is *even lower than that provided under article 58 of the Statute* [...], the Chamber considers that in the context of the present request, all the information provided by the Prosecutor *certainly* need not point towards only one conclusion.[54]

This reasoning seems to have been accepted uncritically by the Office of the Prosecutor to date,[55] and by some academic commentators.

---

reasonable suspicion or reasonable grounds to believe?", in *International Criminal Law Review*, 2016, vol. 16, no. 1, p. 158; Ventura, pp. 63–65, see *supra* note 14.

[52] International Criminal Court, Situation in the Democratic Republic of the Congo, *Prosecutor v. Lubanga*, Appeals Chamber, Judgment on the appeal of Mr Thomas Lubanga Dyilo against the decision of the Pre-Trial Chamber I entitled "*Décision sur la demande de mise en liberté provisoire de Thomas Lubanga Dyilo*", 13 February 2007, ICC-01/04-01/06-824, "Separate Opinion of Judge Georghios M. Pikis", para. 5 (emphasis added) (http://www.legal-tools.org/doc/ff3bd8/).

[53] See, for example, Ambos, p. 401, see *supra* note 44. Cf. Ramsden and CHUNG, p. 572, see *supra* note 51.

[54] *Kenya* Article 15 Decision, para. 34 (emphasis added), see *supra* note 9. See also paras. 27, 29.

[55] See, for example, International Criminal Court, Office of the Prosecutor, *Situation in Honduras: Article 5 Report*, October 2015, para. 37 (fn. 3: referring to "the higher 'reasonable grounds' standard for arrest warrant applications under article 58", citing Kenya Article 15 Decision, para. 34, see *supra* note 9) (http://www.legal-tools.org/doc/54755a/); International Criminal Court, Office of the Prosecutor, Situation on Registered Vessels of the Union of the Comoros, the Hellenic Republic and the Kingdom of Cambodia, *Situation on Registered Vessels of Comoros, Greece and Cambodia: Article 53(1) Report*, 6 November 2014, ICC-01/13-6-AnxA, para. 4 (fn. 4) (http://www.legal-tools.org/doc/6b833a/). Indeed, it appears that this reasoning by the *Kenya* Pre-Trial Chamber was initially *proposed* by the Office: International Criminal Court, Situation in the Republic of Kenya, Pre-Trial Cham-

---

Conceiving Article 53(1) as a 'lower threshold' has been justified on the basis that "[t]he level of information available to the prosecutor at the time of the preliminary examination is deemed to be less comprehensive and conclusive as opposed to the evidence gathered at the end of such an examination [sic]" (understood to mean 'investigation').[56] It has also been suggested that the standard for commencing a prosecution (of an individual) should "logically" be higher than the standard for commencing an investigation of a situation "since the actual prosecution affects the rights of the accused, who should be presumed innocent".[57]

Yet on closer examination, this reasoning appears doubtful.[58] First, the wording of the standards in Articles 53(1) and 58 is "almost the same" and "strikingly similar".[59] The only difference – between "grounds" and "basis" – is, at most, very fine.[60] The other, equally authentic, linguistic versions of the Statute likewise reflect minor distinctions in terminology (not amounting to a substantive difference in connotation), and thus shed

---

ber, Request for authorisation of an investigation pursuant to Article 15, 26 November 2009, ICC-01/09-3, para. 103 ("The expression 'reasonable basis' in Article 15 indicates that a decision to authorize the commencement of an investigation shall be made pursuant to a lower standard than the one required for the issuance of a warrant of arrest or summons to appear.") (http://www.legal-tools.org/doc/c63dcc/).

56 Geert-Jan Alexander Knoops and Tom Zwart, "The Flotilla Case before the ICC: the need to do justice while keeping heaven intact", in *International Criminal Law Review*, 2015, vol. 15, no. 6, p. 1069, at p. 1082 (citing Bergsmo and Kruger in the first edition of Triffterer's commentary; for the analogous passage of the third edition, see Bergsmo *et al.*, p. 1370, mn. 12, see *supra* note 17) (hereinafter 'Knoops and Zwart').

57 Longobardo, p. 1022, see *supra* note 44. See also pp. 1023–24, 1030; Ramsden and Chung, pp. 570 ("The fact that the object and purpose of Article 58 – to ascertain criminal responsibility of an individual – differs from that of Article 15(4) suggests that a uniform test is inappropriate for the two distinct stages"), 577, see *supra* note 51.

58 *Ibid.*, p. 569 (acknowledging "the lack of definitive consensus" on this issue).

59 *Kenya* Article 15 Decision, para. 29, see *supra* note 9; Ramsden and CHUNG, p. 569, see *supra* note 51.

60 Compare, for example, "basis", in *Oxford English Dictionary Online*, meanings II.8. ("That by or on which anything immaterial is supported or sustained; a foundation, support"), 9.b. ("That on which anything is reared, constructed, or established, and by which its constitution or operation is determined; groundwork, footing: a thing immaterial; a principle, a fact"), with "ground" (noun), meanings II.5.a. ("That on which a system, work, institution, art, or condition of things, is founded; the basis, foundation"), 5.c ("A circumstance on which an opinion, inference, argument, statement, or claim is founded, or which has given rise to an action, procedure, or mental feeling; a reason, motive […]") (available on its web site).

little additional light; indeed, in Russian, the *same terms* are used for both Articles 53(1) and 58.[61] Accordingly, bearing in mind the principle that like terms should be interpreted alike,[62] the standards of proof in Articles 53 and 58 should be read to be the same.[63]

Second, although Articles 53 and 58 do indeed differ in their object and purpose (discussed further below),[64] this is more than adequately addressed by the different scope of their application. It is not necessary to interpret Article 58 as imposing a higher *standard of proof* than Article 53 because it requires proof of facts which are defined with much greater specificity, and hence necessarily more burdensome to establish.[65] Unlike Article 53(1), Article 58 requires proof (at the relevant standard) that a *particular identified person* "committed a crime" – thus, it not only requires evidence of the existence of a crime under Articles 5 or 70 but also that the identified person satisfied at least one mode of liability under Articles 25 or 28.[66] In practical terms, such evidence – often known as 'linkage' evidence (who did what, and how?), as differentiated from 'crime-based' evidence (what happened to the victims?) – is often the most difficult evidence to obtain in international criminal proceedings. It is thus appropriate to condition the beginning of a prosecution on the Prosecutor showing that the suspect is sufficiently implicated in the alleged crime – a

---

[61] Compare, for example, ICC Statute, Article 53(1) (Arabic: "معقول أساس"; Chinese: "合理根据"; French: "*base raisonnable*"; Russian: "разумные основания"; Spanish: "*fundamento razonable*"), with Article 58(1)(a) (Arabic: "أسباب معقولة"; Chinese: "合理理由"; French: "*motifs raisonnables*"; Russian: "разумные основания"; Spanish: "*motivo razonable*"), see *supra* note 7.

[62] See Richard Gardiner, *Treaty Interpretation*, 2nd edition, Oxford University Press, 2015, p. 209; see also p. 181.

[63] See also Pikis, p. 264, mn. 626, see *supra* note 17: "A question arises as to whether there is any material difference between the above term ['reasonable basis to proceed'] and the corresponding term used in article 15.3 [sic], notably 'reasonable grounds to believe'. To my mind, the answer is in the negative. 'Grounds' are what provide the basis for a proposition. 'Grounds' and 'basis' in the context under consideration are synonymous terms." Since the term "reasonable grounds" appears in the ICC Statute only in Article 58, Pikis' reference to "article 15.3" in this context must be a typographic error.

[64] *Kenya* Article 15 Decision, para. 29, see *supra* note 9.

[65] See also Ambos, pp. 380–81, see *supra* note 44.

[66] *Kenya* Article 15 Decision, para. 29 ("the criminal responsibility of an individual" is "not at stake for the authorization of an investigation"), see *supra* note 9. See Ventura, pp. 76–77, 80, see *supra* note 14.

---

showing which is not necessary to justify the opening of an investigation (when the perpetrator(s) may be unknown). But it does not necessarily follow from this that the standard of proof must be higher. Nor is such a view compelled simply by the fact that the Prosecutor has had the opportunity for investigation by this point.[67] The point is simply that Articles 53(1) and 58 are concerned with different questions.

Moreover, considering the suspect's right to liberty may be something of a red herring when defining the *standard of proof* under Article 58,[68] and consequently its relation with the standard of proof under Article 53(1). This is not because human rights are irrelevant to the work of the Court – far from it[69] – but because the determination whether to deprive the suspect of their liberty is not predicated on the standard of proof *per se* (that is, the standard by which the Prosecutor has supported her allegations of the suspect's criminal conduct), provided it is met, but on a further and separate assessment of the *necessity* of detention.[70] This is demonstrated, first and most obviously, by the fact that Article 58 applies the *same* standard of proof ("reasonable grounds to believe") irrespective whether the Prosecutor seeks an arrest warrant (triggering provisional detention) or a summons to appear (not triggering provisional detention).[71] What differs in these circumstances is merely the 'necessity' analysis.[72] Likewise, once a suspect has been detained, they are entitled to

---

[67] Cf. *Kenya* Article 15 Decision, para. 27, see *supra* note 9; Bergsmo *et al.*, p. 1370, mns. 11–12, see *supra* note 17.

[68] Cf. Ramsden and CHUNG, pp. 570-571, 573–575, see *supra* note 51; Longobardo, p. 1022, see *supra* note 44; Ventura, p. 76, see *supra* note 14.

[69] See, for example, ICC Statute, Article 21(3), see *supra* note 7; International Criminal Court, Situation in the Democratic Republic of the Congo, *Prosecutor v. Lubanga*, Appeals Chamber, Judgment on the Appeal of Mr Thomas Lubanga Dyilo against the Decision on the Defence Challenge to the Jurisdiction of the Court pursuant to Article 19(2)(a) of the Statute of 3 October 2006, 14 December 2006, ICC-01/04-01/06-772, para. 36 (http://www.legal-tools.org/doc/1505f7/).

[70] Christopher K. Hall and Cedric Ryngaert, "Article 58: issuance by the Pre-Trial Chamber of a warrant of arrest or a summons to appear", in Otto Triffterer and Kai Ambos (eds.), *The Rome Statute of the International Criminal Court: A Commentary*, 3rd edition, C.H. Beck/Hart/Nomos, 2016, p. 1447, mn. 15.

[71] Compare ICC Statute, Article 58(1), with Article 58(7), see *supra* note 7.

[72] See also International Criminal Court, Situation in Darfur, Sudan, *Prosecutor v. Banda*, Appeals Chamber, Judgment on the appeal of Mr Abdallah Banda Abakaer Nourain against Trial Chamber IV's issuance of a warrant of arrest, 3 March 2015, ICC-02/05-03/09-632-Red, para. 25 (http://www.legal-tools.org/doc/bb2b11/).

periodic reviews of the continuing *necessity* of their detention – but, in those reviews, a re-examination of the merits of the case against them will ordinarily be inappropriate and unnecessary.[73]

To the extent that issuing a summons or arrest warrant (if public) may have some adverse reputational implications for the suspect, this limited harm is justified even by the "reasonable basis" to believe that the suspect committed one or more crimes within the jurisdiction of the Court. The remedy also lies within their hands – appearing promptly before the Court (as a person still presumed to be innocent) triggers the confirmation of charges procedure, which will eliminate weak cases.[74]

Therefore, it is not the function of Article 58 to test the strength of the Prosecutor's case against the individual, and thus to control whether or not the case should be committed for trial.[75] That is the distinct function of the confirmation of charges procedure – which must be accomplished within a "reasonable time" after the suspect's arrival at the Court[76] – and which does indeed imposes a higher standard of proof ("substantial grounds to believe") than Articles 53(1) or 58. Precisely because Article 58 proceedings occur *ex parte*, they are not well suited to serve as a 'gateway' to trial. It is also plain that Article 58 is not concerned with examining the entirety of the Prosecutor's case against the suspect, but only in verifying that there is *a* case against the suspect. Thus, the Prosecutor may not only seek amendment of an arrest warrant by "modifying or

---

[73] See ICC Statute, Articles 60(2), 60(3), see *supra* note 7; International Criminal Court, Situation in Uganda, *Prosecutor v. Ongwen*, Pre-Trial Chamber, Decision on the "Defence Request for the Interim Release of Dominic Ongwen", 27 November 2015, ICC-02/04-01/15-349-Red, paras. 6–13 (http://www.legal-tools.org/doc/f20956/).

[74] Cf. Ramsden and CHUNG, pp. 574–75, see *supra* note 51.

[75] Cf. *Ibid.*, pp. 572–573 (arguing for a "high threshold" under article 58, but apparently justifying this on the basis that "a higher standard [...] applied at the *confirmation of charges* stage" might better filter out weak cases).

[76] ICC Statute, Article 61(1), see *supra* note 7; International Criminal Court, *Regulations of the Court*, 6 December 2016, ICC-BD/01-05-16, regulation 53 (the confirmation decision shall be delivered within 60 days of the close of the confirmation hearing) (http://www.legal-tools.org/doc/8a1f87/); International Criminal Court, *Chambers Practice Manual*, 3rd edition, May 2017, pp. 7–8, 16 (advocating "[e]fforts [...] to reduce the average time that passes between the first appearance and the commencement of the confirmation of charges hearing", takining into account "the circumstances of each particular case") ('Chambers Practice Manual') (http://www.legal-tools.org/doc/f0ee26/).

---

adding to the crimes specified therein",[77] but may also add charges prior to the confirmation hearing.[78]

For all these reasons, recognising the suspect's liberty interest does not require a distinction in principle between the standard of proof applicable when an *investigation* is initiated and when a *prosecution* is initiated. Rather, the suspect's right to liberty is adequately guaranteed in the period between initiating the prosecution and confirming the charges by the ongoing assessment of the necessity of their detention, if indeed they are taken into custody at all.

Third, even if we attempt, *arguendo*, to distinguish the standards of proof in Articles 53(1) and 58, there is the immediate practical difficulty of meaningfully doing so.[79] Already, even if there are only three relevant standards of proof in the Statute, there is a tendency to define them purely on a relative basis – the confirmation standard ("substantial grounds to believe") is 'lower' than the conviction standard ("beyond reasonable doubt") and 'greater' than the "reasonable basis"/"reasonable grounds" standard(s).[80] But in concrete terms, what is the difference between a "substantial ground" and a "reasonable ground"? And how much harder does this become to determine if it is further necessary to distinguish between a "substantial ground", a "reasonable ground", and a "reasonable basis"? In short, proliferating standards of proof are likely to lead to conceptual confusion, and gradations based on mere semantics. This serves only to obscure the nature of the analysis, and favours neither the suspect nor the economy of judicial proceedings.

---

[77] ICC Statute, Article 58(7), see *supra* note 7.

[78] See, for example, Chambers Practice Manual, pp. 11–12, see *supra* note 76; International Criminal Court, Situation in Uganda, *Prosecutor v. Ongwen*, Pre-Trial Chamber, Status Conference of 19 May 2015, ICC-02/04-01/15-T-6-ENG, pp. 6–18 (http://www.legal-tools.org/doc/18d506/). For example, in the *Ongwen* case, although Mr. Ongwen was originally arrested on seven counts, charges were subsequently confirmed against him on 70 counts: compare International Criminal Court, Situation in Uganda, *The Prosecutor v. Joseph Kony, Vincent Otti, Okot Odhiambo and Dominic Ongwen*, Pre-Trial Chamber, Warrant of arrest for Dominic Ongwen, 8 July 2005, ICC-02/04-01/05-57, para. 30 (http://www.legal-tools.org/doc/7a2f0f/); with ICC, Situation in Uganda, *Prosecutor v. Onwen*, Pre-Trial Chamber, Decision on the confirmation of charges against Dominic Ongwen, 23 March 2016, ICC-02/04-01/15-422-Red, pp. 71–104 (http://www.legal-tools.org/doc/74fc6e/).

[79] See Ventura, pp. 78–80, see *supra* note 14.

[80] See *supra* note 49, and accompanying text.

A contextual analysis of Article 53(1) thus favours interpreting the standard of proof to be the same as the standard in Article 58,[81] even though they are applied to different issues. Accordingly, the Article 53(1) standard of proof, while indeed being the lowest standard, is the lowest of *three* principal standards in the Statute.[82] Recognising the link in this way between the standards of proof in Articles 53 and 58 does not necessarily *lower* the Article 58 standard but, rather, may simply illustrate that Article 53(1) is *also* a meaningful legal requirement. It clarifies, in particular, that Article 53(1), like Article 58, requires at least some evidentiary basis.

22.1.3. Object and Purpose of the Statute and Article 53(1): A Selective Approach to Investigations

Finally, in interpreting the standard of proof in Article 53(1), it is helpful to consider its object and purpose, and indeed the object and purpose of the Statute as a whole.

In *Côte d'Ivoire*, the Pre-Trial Chamber described the "underlying purpose" of Article 15(4) – which may be considered analogous to the Prosecutor's function under Article 53(1) – as preventing "unwarranted, frivolous or politically motivated investigations".[83] But it may be that this statement still does not go quite far enough, or at least gives little clue as to what an 'unwarranted' investigation might mean, in the context of the Statute.

The Preamble to the Statute recalls: "that it is the duty of every State to exercise its criminal jurisdiction over those responsible for international crimes" and emphasises that: "the International Criminal Court

---

[81] See also Mark Klamberg, "Article 58: issuance by the Pre-Trial Chamber of a warrant of arrest of a summons to appear", in Mark Klamberg (ed.), *Commentary on the Law of the International Criminal Court*, Torkel Opsahl Academic EPublisher, Brussels, 2017, p. 426 (fn. 464: "The threshold 'reasonable grounds' is the least demanding evidentiary requirement used in the ICC Statute") (http://www.legal-tools.org/doc/aa0e2b/).

[82] At least, three principal standards relevant to significant milestones of the criminal process, such as investigation, prosecution, committal for trial, conviction, and so on. Other standards may apply as conditions for lesser procedural matters. See, for example, Ambos, p. 400 (noting that Article 55(2), relating to investigative safeguards for suspects, applies when there are mere "grounds to believe that a person has committed a crime"), see *supra* note 44. This standard, if based merely on the subjective opinion of the investigator, is indeed lower than the standard in Articles 53(1) and 58.

[83] *Côte d'Ivoire* Article 15 Decision, para. 21, see *supra* note 9. See also *Kenya* Article 15 Decision, Dissenting Opinion of Judge Kaul, para. 15, see *supra* note 9.

---

established under this Statute shall be complementary to national criminal jurisdictions". Moreover, although the crimes within the Court's jurisdiction are, as such, "the most serious crimes of concern to the international community as a whole",[84] the Statute nonetheless recognises that not all cases of such crimes are "of sufficient gravity to justify further action by the Court".[85] These principles thus imply that some element of selectivity, both of situations and cases, is inherent to the Court's operation, and thus favour an interpretation of the standard of proof in Article 53(1) which may properly give effect to that interest. In particular, it suggests that the Court is not mandated to investigate every allegation of an Article 5 crime, but must at least establish that the allegation is sufficiently well-founded on its facts (even without the Court itself conducting an investigation) as well as being sufficiently grave and not subject to relevant domestic proceedings.

There are also significant practical justifications confirming the necessity of a meaningful form of situation selectivity.

Although the Court and the Office of the Prosecutor are of a finite size, the Statute does not expressly allow for the resource implications of a new investigation to be taken into account in the Prosecutor's Article 53 determination. Although laudable in principle, this silence might seem anomalous from a practical point of view. In the first years of the Court's operation already, 11 situations are under investigation and/or prosecution, with another 10 under preliminary examination.[86] And this is still at a time when the Statute remains far from universal ratification, and when some notable situations of apparent international crimes have not even been referred to the Court. By contrast, even the 'basic size' of the Office of the Prosecutor – which is, itself, aspirational and not yet fully funded by the ICC Assembly of States Parties – imposes significant limits on the number of active investigations and prosecutions that can be pursued at any

---

[84]   ICC Statute, Article 5, see *supra* note 7; see also Preamble.

[85]   *Ibid.*, Article 17(1)(d); see also Article 8(1) ("The Court shall have in respect of war crimes *in particular when* committed as part of a plan or policy", emphasis added).

[86]   At the time of writing, the situations presently under investigation are: Burundi, Central African Republic (I and II), Côte d'Ivoire, Democratic Republic of Congo, Georgia, Kenya, Libya, Mali, Sudan (Darfur), and Uganda. The situations under preliminary examination are: Afghanistan, Colombia, Gabon, Guinea, Nigeria, Palestine, the Philippines, Ukraine, the United Kingdom (Iraq), and Venezuela. A request to the Pre-Trial Chamber, under article 15(3) of the Statute, is pending with regard to the Afghanistan situation.

one time.[87] This apparent lacuna in the Statute is, however, at least partially resolved if Article 53(1) is understood to apply a meaningful standard of proof, requiring allegations of crimes to be substantiated to a threshold level.[88] This means, at the very least, that investigations are not opened on a purely speculative basis, to resolve doubt even about the reasonable possibility that at least one international crime might have been committed. Rather, scarce resources are reserved for those situations where the threshold has been reached.[89]

Similar reasoning could also be applied to the apparent silence of the Statute, in the context of Article 53, concerning the Prosecutor's anticipation of any difficulties in collecting evidence or obtaining the co-operation of relevant States (which may be a crucial consideration for many of her activities). It is possible that such issues might be reflected in the assessment of the interests of justice under Article 53(1)(c) (on the theory, perhaps, that an ineffective investigation is less beneficial to the victims than the prospect of a more effective investigation later on). But by requiring the facts of at least one crime to be established to a meaningful threshold as a condition for opening investigations, again Article 53(1)(a) and (b) ensure that there is an adequate basis for the expenditure of the efforts of the Prosecutor and the Court (even if such difficulties may potentially impede initiating any prosecution).

These views may be supported by Judge Kaul's separate opinion in *Kenya*. Recalling that "[n]ational prosecutors are called upon to commence investigations if they become aware of *any* information that a crime may have occurred", he observes that this principle is "not entirely transferable" to Article 15 (and, accordingly, Article 53) of the Statute.[90]

---

[87] See, for example, ICC Assembly of States Parties, *Report of the Court on the Basic Size of the Office of the Prosecutor*, 17 September 2015, ICC-ASP/14/21, paras. 7–8, 21 (http://www.legal-tools.org/doc/b27d2a/).

[88] By analogy, see also *Kenya* Article 15 Decision, Dissenting Opinion of Judge Kaul, para. 10 (justifying the necessity of, in his view, a strict definition of crimes against humanity on the basis *inter alia* of "the limited financial and material means" of the ICC, and his concern that a relaxed definition could lead to the Court being "unable to tackle all the situations which could fall under its jurisdiction with the consequence that the selection of the situations under actual investigation might be quite arbitrary to the dismay of the numerous victims in the situations disregarded"), see *supra* note 9.

[89] See also Bergsmo *et al.*, p. 1368, mn. 5, see *supra* note 17.

[90] *Kenya* Article 15 Decision, Dissenting Opinion of Judge Kaul, para. 16, see *supra* note 9.

Rather, the Prosecutor has a "differ[ent] mandate".[91] Judge Kaul does not elaborate on exactly what this means, except by referring to Article 53(1). Nor indeed is it correct even to say that *all* domestic systems favour a system of obligatory prosecution; to the contrary, although some States favour such an approach, it is by no means universal.[92]

Finally, as reflected by the Statute's emphasis on complementarity, it is also important to recall that Article 53(1) balances the Court's effective operation in fulfilling its mandate against recognition of the sovereign powers and prerogatives of States, and their primary role in enforcing the criminal law. It is clear from the drafting history of the Statute that this balance was struck with great care, and after extensive negotiation and deliberation.[93] As such, it cannot be correct to imply that opening an ICC investigation, when it is ambiguous whether the Article 53(1) standard is met, does "no harm to anyone's rights".[94] The rights at issue may be the rights of States, rather than individuals, but this does not mean that the Court may disregard them lightly.[95] Indeed, transparent respect for these rights – while maintaining full independence, both of opinion and action – is highly important for the effective operation of the Prosecutor, and the success of international criminal justice more broadly.[96]

---

[91] *Ibid.*

[92] Philippa Webb, "The ICC Prosecutor's discretion not to proceed in the 'interests of justice'", in *Criminal Law Quarterly*, 2005, vol. 50, p. 305, at pp. 310–12 (hereinafter 'Webb').

[93] Bergsmo *et al.*, p. 1367, mn. 3, see *supra* note 17; Morten Bergsmo, Jelena Pejić, and ZHU Dan, "Article 15: Prosecutor", in Otto Triffterer and Kai Ambos (eds.), *The Rome Statute of the International Criminal Court: A Commentary*, 3rd edition, C.H. Beck/Hart/Nomos, 2016, p. 725, at pp. 726–29, mns. 1-7. See also Alison M. Danner, "Enhancing the legitimacy and accountability of prosecutorial discretion at the International Criminal Court", in *American Journal of International Law*, 2003, vol. 97, p. 510, at pp. 513–515 (hereinafter 'Danner'); generally Silvia A. Fernández de Gurmendi, "The role of the international prosecutor", in Roy S. Lee (ed.), *The International Criminal Court: The Making of the Rome Statute: Issues, Negotiations, Results*, Kluwer Law International, 1999, p. 175.

[94] Cf. Longobardo, p. 1026, see *supra* note 44. See also *Comoros* Reconsideration Request, para. 13, see *supra* note 3.

[95] See Ventura, p. 78, see *supra* note 14.

[96] See Brubacher, pp. 94–95, see *supra* note 39. See also Danner, pp. 551–52 (noting that "[p]rosecutorial guidelines will help the Prosecutor negotiate the tension between accountability and independence", enhancing the Prosecutor's legitimacy and fostering effective

---

22.1.4. The Article 53(1) Standard of Proof: A Summary

For all these reasons, Article 53(1) can only be correctly interpreted to impose a standard of proof which must be genuinely applied to all factual matters which require determination under Article 53(1)(a) and (b). It requires the Prosecution to be satisfied that the available information shows a rational or sensible factual basis to reach the necessary conclusions. In particular, the Prosecutor must be satisfied of a "reasonable basis to believe" that:

- at least one Article 5 crime has been committed (including all the requisite legal elements);[97] and

- all other facts which are material to her admissibility assessment exist (for example, if her 'sufficient gravity' analysis turns on the existence of a plan or policy under Article 8(1), the existence of those facts showing that plan or policy, which may not themselves be legal elements of the crime).[98]

This is no more and no less than the Pre-Trial Chamber's analogous duty under Article 15(4) and, albeit applied to more specific (and hence demanding) types of facts, under Article 58 of the Statute.

22.2. The Scope of Prosecutorial Discretion in Article 53(1)

If Article 53(1) applies an essentially legal test, requiring that an investigation be opened if the conditions in Articles 53(1)(a) to (c) are satisfied, it follows that the Prosecutor's discretion in opening an investigation is circumscribed. To be clear, the application of the standard of proof in Articles 53(1)(a) and (b) allows *no* discretion in the legal sense at all.[99] Rather, the only discretion lies in Article 53(1)(c).[100] And, so far in the history of this Court, this discretion has *never* been exercised. A clearer and wider understanding of this fact, as the present Prosecutor has repeatedly urged, would assist in answering many of the allegations of some kind of bias in the Court's approach to preliminary examinations.

---

cooperation from States), see *supra* note 93. Article 53(1) of the Statute is a prosecutorial 'guideline' *par excellence*.

[97] ICC Statute, Article 53(1)(a), see *supra* note 7.

[98] *Ibid.*, Article 53(1)(b).

[99] See also Webb, p. 319, see *supra* note 92; Turone, p. 1152, see *supra* note 15.

[100] See *supra* note 12, and accompanying text.

However, the non-discretionary nature of the standard of proof in Article 53(1) does not mean that there is no room for prosecutorial discretion at all,[101] but the specific nature and limits of the concept in this particular context must be understood. As Knoops and Zwart have recently recalled, "prosecutorial discretion" is an "integral part" of prosecutorial independence, which is guaranteed by Article 42(1) of the Statute.[102] But in the context of Article 53(1)(a) and (b),[103] this discretion does not manifest itself in discretionary *decision-making* (because the Prosecutor could be objectively wrong in her determination that there is not a reasonable basis to believe a given fact is true, whereas a discretionary decision is not amenable to such criticism),[104] but in discretion as to *methodology*. To

---

[101] Luc Côté, "Reflections on the exercise of prosecutorial discretion in international criminal law", in *Journal of International Criminal Justice*, 2005, vol. 3, no. 1, p. 162, at p. 163 ("discretion, like the hole in a doughnut, does not exist except as an area left open by a surrounding belt of restriction", quoting Ronald Dworkin, *Taking Rights Seriously*, Harvard University Press, 1977, p. 31). See also Webb, pp. 310–311 (noting that, even in States abiding by the "principle of legality" – which "theoretically compels the prosecutor (or investigating authority) to investigate when there are facts that give enough grounds for suspicion" – "in practice there are no 'pure' versions of the principle of legality", citing for example the "incidental areas of discretion" which remain and are "used to prioritize cases" in the Italian system, and greater latitude still in systems such as that in Germany), see *supra* note 92; Nsereko, pp. 127–129, see *supra* note 40.

[102] Knoops and Zwart, p. 1073, see *supra* note 56. See also Brubacher, p. 76, see *supra* note 39; Jallow, p. 146, see *supra* note 40.

[103] Specifically, this means there is no discretion concerning relevant factual matters in Phases 2–3 of the preliminary examination process, as conceived by the Office of the Prosecutor: see *Policy Paper on Preliminary Examinations*, paras. 77–83 (Phase 2 "represents the formal commencement of a preliminary examination of a given situation"), see *supra* note 15. By contrast, Phase 1 decision-making – determining which individual communications to the Prosecutor under Article 15 should lead to opening a preliminary examinations – *is* in part discretionary, and is not directly governed by Article 53(1): for more information, see Amitis Khojasteh, "The Pre-Preliminary Examination Stage: Theory and Practice of the OTP's Phase 1 Activities", in Morten Bergsmo and Carsten Stahn (eds.), *Quality Control in Preliminary Examination: Volume 1*, Torkel Opsahl Academic EPublisher, 2018, chap. 8. This is consistent with Article 15(1) of the Statute, given its ordinary meaning, context, and object and purpose, which states that "[t]he Prosecutor may initiate investigations *proprio motu* on the basis of information on crimes within the jurisdiction of the Court".

[104] Cf. Knoops and Zwart, p. 1079. "A discretionary power involves the right to choose between more than one possible course of action upon which there is room for reasonable people to hold differing opinions as to which is to be preferred. Therefore, discretion may be defined as the power to make a decision that cannot be determined to be right or wrong in an objective way", citing UK House of Lords, *Secretary of State for Education and Sci-*

---

borrow an analogy from trial proceedings, whereas it is well-established that final determinations about the guilt or innocence of the accused are *not* discretionary, the Trial Chamber's management of the trial itself (how long to allow the Parties to question witnesses, order of questioning, and so on) *is* a discretionary matter.[105]

The fact that Article 53(1)(a) and (b) determinations are not discretionary does not, however, mean that they may be judicially reviewed simply on a 'correctness' standard. To the contrary, as further explained below, such determinations remain entitled to a certain deference in the course of any judicial review.

So how does the residual *methodological* discretion of the Prosecutor manifest itself in Article 53(1)? As the very term implies, the Prosecutor has control of the process of conducting preliminary examinations, consistent with her statutory independence.[106] This control, and hence her discretion, extends to all aspects of the process. But three notable examples can quickly be identified, which may impact the preliminary examination function itself and allow for the Prosecution's particular approach to be suitably adapted to the circumstances.[107]

---

ence v. Tameside Metropolitan Borough Council [1977] AC 1014, 1064, *per* Lord Diplock; Grey, "Discretion in administrative law", in *Osgoode Law Journal*, 1979, vol. 17, no. 1, pp. 1070, 1090 (apparently referring to a "broad prosecutorial discretion whether to bring situations […] before the ICC"), see *supra* note 56. See also Nsereko, pp. 124–25, see *supra* note 40.

[105] See, for example, ICC Statute, Article 64; International Criminal Court, Situation in the Republic of Kenya, *Prosecutor v. Ruto and Sang*, Appeals Chamber, Judgment on the appeal of the Prosecutor against the decision of Trial Chamber V(a) of 18 June 2013 entitled "Decision on Mr Ruto's Request for Excusal from Continuous Presence at Trial", 25 October 2013, ICC-01/09-01/11-1066, para. 50 (http://www.legal-tools.org/doc/575657/); International Criminal Court, Situation in the Republic of Kenya, *Prosecutor v. Ruto and Sang*, Trial Chamber, Decision on Witness Preparation, 2 January 2013, ICC-01/09-01/11-524, para. 27 (http://www.legal-tools.org/doc/82c717/).

[106] ICC Statute, Article 42(1) ("The Office of the Prosecutor shall act independently as a separate organ of the Court. It shall be responsible for receiving referrals and any substantiated information on crimes within the jurisdiction of the Court, for examining them […] A member of the Office shall not seek or act on instructions from any external source"), see *supra* note 7.

[107] See also Carsten Stahn, "Damned if you do, damned if you don't: challenges and critiques of preliminary examinations at the ICC", in *Journal of International Criminal Justice*, 2017, vol. 15, no. 3, p. 413, at pp. 417–22 (hereinafter 'Stahn').

First, the Prosecutor allocates and assigns her (limited) resources to the various activities of her Office, including to the conduct of particular preliminary examinations.[108] It follows from this that she controls the timing and relative priority of different preliminary examinations. She may choose, consistent with her developing practice,[109] to explain some of the principles which guide her discretion in this respect (through means of a policy document), but she cannot be obliged to exercise her discretion in a particular fashion.

Second, the Prosecutor has discretion in the extent to which she seeks out open-source information concerning the subject-matter of a preliminary examination. Although she does not enjoy investigative powers under Article 54 at this stage of proceedings, as further discussed below, she "*may* seek additional information from [...] reliable sources that *he or she deems appropriate*, and *may* receive written or oral testimony".[110] This means that the Prosecutor is not limited to the content of a referral or Article 15 communication, but may seek additional information from States, the United Nations, NGOs, or other reliable sources. By these means, she may be able to fill 'gaps' which appear to exist in the information in her possession, if she thinks this is appropriate. But by the same token, if a referral or Article 15 communication contains such gaps, she cannot be perpetually compelled to seek additional information to resolve those deficiencies.[111] She is entitled, if she thinks appropriate,[112] simply to close the preliminary examination.[113]

---

[108] *Ibid.*, Article 42(2) ("The Prosecutor shall have full authority over the management and administration of the Office, including the staff, facilities and other resources thereof").

[109] The Prosecutor has, so far, published policies on procedural matters including the conduct of preliminary examinations, the meaning of the "interests of justice" in Article 53, and the process of case selection and prioritisation, as well as on substantive matters such as sexual and gender based crimes, and the relationship between international criminal law and children. See generally "Policies and Strategies", available on the Office's web site; Matthew E. Cross and Antonio Coco, "Foreword", *Journal of International Criminal Justice*, 2017, vol. 15, no. 3, p. 407, at p. 409.

[110] ICC, *Rules of Procedure and Evidence*, 9 September 2002, Rule 104(2) (emphasis added) (http://www.legal-tools.org/doc/8bcf6f/).

[111] See, for example, International Criminal Court, Situation in the Democratic Republic of the Congo, Appeals Chamber, Judgment on victim participation in the investigation stage of the proceedings in the appeal of the OPCD against the decision of Pre-Trial Chamber I of 7 December 2007 and in the appeals of the OPCD and the Prosecutor against the decision of Pre-Trial Chamber I of 24 December 2007, 19 December 2008, ICC-01/04-556, pa-

---

Third, and in part consequent on the first two discretions, the Prosecutor controls the *duration* of a preliminary examination, and when it is terminated (by seeking to open an investigation, or by closing), with reference to relevant circumstances.[114] She may be satisfied that the Article 53(1) standard is met within a matter of months (or, perhaps exceptionally, even weeks), or she may require years. Likewise, where she considers that the available information does not suffice, or her admissibility assessment relates to a manifestly changing or developing situation, she may properly decide to maintain a 'watching brief' and to defer reaching a determination until the facts become clearer.[115]

The Prosecutor's methodological discretion may be illustrated by one incident in the early case law of the Court, in which Pre-Trial Chamber III queried the progress of the CAR I preliminary examination.[116] Although providing this information, the Prosecutor stressed that "[t]he Pre-Trial Chamber's supervisory role, under Article 53(3), only applies to the review of a *decision* under Article 53(1) and (2) by the Prosecutor not to proceed with an investigation of a prosecution".[117] He continued to point out that, since Article 53(1) requires "an informed and well-reasoned de-

---

ra. 51 (http://www.legal-tools.org/doc/dca981/); *Côte d'Ivoire* Article 15 Decision, Separate Opinion of Judge Fernández de Gurmendi, paras. 20–22, see *supra* note 16.

[112] See also ICC Statute, Article 42(3) ("The Prosecutor and the Deputy Prosecutors shall be persons of high moral character, be highly competent in and have extensive practical experience in the prosecution or trial of criminal cases"), see *supra* note 7.

[113] This is without prejudice to the preliminary examination being reopened on the basis of new facts or information: see *infra* note 114.

[114] This is supported, furthermore, by the Prosecutor's discretion to reopen a closed preliminary examination: ICC Statute, Article 53(4) ("The Prosecutor *may*, at any time, reconsider a decision whether to initiate an investigation or prosecution based on new facts or information", emphasis added), see *supra* note 7.

[115] See further *Policy Paper on Preliminary Examinations*, paras. 90, 101–102, see *supra* note 15.

[116] International Criminal Court, Situation in the Central African Republic, Pre-Trial Chamber, Decision Requesting Information on the Status of the Preliminary Examination of the Situation in the Central African Republic, 30 November 2006, ICC-01/05-6, pp. 4–5 (http://www.legal-tools.org/doc/76e607/).

[117] International Criminal Court, Situation in the Central African Republic, Pre-Trial Chamber, Prosecution's Report Pursuant to Pre-Trial Chamber III's 30 November 2006 Decision Requesting Information on the Status of the Preliminary Examination of the Situation in the Central African Republic, 15 December 2006, ICC-01/05-7, para. 1 ('Prosecutor's CAR Report') (http://www.legal-tools.org/doc/1dd66a/). See also para. 10.

cision", preliminary examinations must be carried out "in a comprehensive and thorough manner" and that "it must be for him to determine the breadth and scope of this preliminary assessment".[118] Moreover, notwithstanding the uniform legal framework, the practical requirements of any particular preliminary examination are "situation-specific", and the "time taken" may depend "on the particular circumstances in each situation".[119] What Pre-Trial Chamber III thought of this response is lost to history, presumably because the Prosecutor nonetheless provided the information requested. Subsequently, moreover, the Prosecutor has herself adopted the practice of providing annual reports on preliminary examination activities,[120] which may go some way to increasing the transparency of her activities in this area.[121] But the Policy Paper on Preliminary Examinations, published in 2013, has nonetheless maintained this view of the Prosecutor's discretion in managing the 'process' of the preliminary examination.[122]

22.3. Consequences of the Standard of Proof in Article 53(1)

The nature of the standard of proof under Article 53(1)(a) and (b), and the confined role of prosecutorial discretion, has some important consequences for the conduct of preliminary examinations, and hence for any assessment of their 'quality'. These include: (1) the Prosecutor's duty to evaluate the information available to her; (2) her response to a lack of information on relevant issues; (3) the extent to which she may select and/or prioritise the Article 5 crimes on which to make findings under Article 53(1); and (4) the nature of the Pre-Trial Chamber's judicial review under Article 53(3).

---

[118] *Ibid.*, para. 7.

[119] *Ibid.*, para. 8. See also para. 9.

[120] This practice began in 2011, and has been maintained annually since that time. For the most recent annual report (at the time of writing), see, for example, International Criminal Court, Office of the Prosecutor, *Report on Preliminary Examination Activities 2016*, 14 November 2016 (http://www.legal-tools.org/doc/f30a53/).

[121] Cf. Anni Pues, "Towards the 'Golden Hour'? A critical exploration of the length of preliminary examinations", in *Journal of International Criminal Justice*, 2017, vol. 15, no. 3, p. 435.

[122] *Policy Paper on Preliminary Examinations*, para. 89, see *supra* note 15.

22.3.1. A Duty to Evaluate the Available Information

Article 53(1) conditions the Prosecutor's determination of whether the criteria in Article 53(1)(a) to (c) are met on "evaluat[ing] the information made available to him or her". Rule 104(1) further specifies that, "[i]n acting pursuant to Article 53, paragraph 1, the Prosecutor shall, in evaluating the information made available to him or her, analyse the seriousness of the information received".

Considering these prescriptions in the context of the standard of proof in Article 53(1), it is apparent that the Prosecutor is not obliged to accept the information presented to her at face value.[123] Admittedly, the meaning of the reference in Rule 104(1) to analysing the "seriousness" of the information is somewhat obscure, since this would seem to duplicate the requirements of Article 53(1)(a) or (b). But no matter the particular construction placed on it, the conclusion appears inescapable that the Prosecutor should reach her own assessment of the meaning, relevance and significance of the information available. It will likely be insufficient for the Prosecutor simply to accept the contents of a referral or Article 15 communication as true.[124] Consistent with her discretion to seek additional information (without 'investigating'), previously described, she may also attempt to contextualise the information she receives where she considers it appropriate.

It is implicit in these observations that the Prosecutor may weigh the available information as a whole. She may decide, on occasion, that some of the available information is less reliable than other information. In some instances, she may positively decide that she cannot rely on certain information, uncorroborated, even to establish a "reasonable basis to

---

[123] Cf. *Comoros* Reconsideration Request, para. 35, see *supra* note 3.

[124] Compare International Criminal Court, Situation in Georgia, Pre-Trial Chamber, Separate Opinion of Judge Kovács, 27 January 2016, ICC-01/15-12-Anx-Corr, paras. 6 ("Judicial control entails more than automatically agreeing with what the Prosecutor presents"), 20 ('*Georgia* Article 15 Decision, Separate Opinion of Judge Kovács') (http://www.legal-tools.org/doc/28b159/); *Kenya* Article 15 Decision, Dissenting Opinion of Judge Kaul, para. 19 (the Pre-Trial Chamber's article 15(4) analysis is not "a mere rubber-stamping" exercise), see *supra* note 9. *But* see *Côte d'Ivoire* Article 15 Decision, Separate Opinion of Judge Fernández de Gurmendi, paras. 15 ("while the Chamber and the Prosecutor need to examine the same factors and apply the same 'reasonable basis to proceed' standard, the examination by the Chamber should not become a duplication of the preliminary examination conducted by the Prosecutor"), 16, 18–19, 27–28, see *supra* note 16.

believe". This may include, for example, assertions which appear highly implausible in the context of all the relevant circumstances. Although the Prosecutor should take great care in such situations – and should not reject relevant available information merely because it challenges her preconceptions – she is not, for example, required to accept there is a reasonable basis to believe that aliens exist, merely because someone tells her so.

Consistent with the approach adopted in trial proceedings, however, the Prosecutor should not enter into the question whether particular pieces of information are themselves 'reasonable' or not.[125] Rather, she should apply the standard of proof to the factual findings which are indispensable to her determination (for example, the elements of the relevant Article 5 crime(s) and any factual matters material to her Article 53(1)(b) analysis). Only if such an indispensable finding depends on a single piece of information should she consider whether that information itself provides a reasonable basis to believe the finding in question.

22.3.2. Prohibitive Effect of Insufficient or Ambiguous Information

In *Comoros*, the majority of the Pre-Trial Chamber observed that: "[f]acts which are difficult to establish, or which are unclear, [...] are not valid reasons not to start an investigation but rather call for the opening of such an investigation".[126] The same majority hinted at similar reasoning in *Georgia*,[127] and an entirely different bench of the Pre-Trial Chamber repeated this statement, without further elaboration, in *Burundi*.[128] Yet, on the other hand, Judge Kaul, writing separately in the context of the Article 15(4) decision in *Kenya*, had previously stated that a "somewhat selective

---

[125] See *supra* note 29.

[126] *Comoros* Reconsideration Request, para. 13, see *supra* note 3. But see also *infra* note 130.

[127] *Georgia* Article 15 Decision, paras. 34–35 (noting concerns by the Prosecutor that, for certain allegations, the standard of proof was not met based, in her view, on concerns about its reliability, and opining that the Prosecutor had "acted too restrictively and [...] imposed requirements on the material that cannot reasonably be met in the absence of an investigation, the initiation of which is precisely at stake"), see *supra* note 9. Notwithstanding his dissent from the reasoning of the majority in *Comoros*, Judge Kovács appears to agree with the majority in this respect: *Georgia* Article 15 Decision, Separate Opinion of Judge Kovács, paras. 21–23 ("[t]he complexity of the crimes makes it even more compelling to commence an investigation to establish whether or not the elements of the offence are fulfilled"), see *supra* note 124.

[128] *Burundi* Article 15 Decision, para. 30, see *supra* note 18.

or summary examination in the hope […] that the investigation may bring about the missing pieces of his determination under Article 53(1)(a) of the Statute is not enough".[129]

To any extent that the *Comoros* majority was suggesting that investigations should nonetheless be opened even when the Article 53(1) standard of proof is *not* met,[130] Judge Kaul's opinion is to be preferred. To do otherwise – opening an investigation when one or more indispensable facts is not established to the Article 53(1) threshold – would defeat the entire exercise, and create a wholly circular logic: "an investigation cannot be opened until these conditions are met; if the information does not show that these conditions are met, then an investigation is still necessary in order to find such information". Such logic undermines the object and purpose of Article 53(1).

The correctness of Judge Kaul's view is moreover supported by the consistent statements – even by the *Comoros* majority – that, until the Prosecutor has made a positive Article 53(1) determination, and at least one other relevant authority has concurred that an investigation should be opened,[131] she may not take *any* 'investigative' measure which depends upon Article 54.[132] Although the exact definition of an investigative measure in this context is not yet established, it may be taken to involve active measures to obtain primary source information in order to assess

---

[129] *Kenya* Article 15 Decision, Dissenting Opinion of Judge Kaul, para. 18, see *supra* note 9.

[130] The significance of the majority's comment is not entirely clear, however, since it also (in the same paragraph) refers to the need for investigation to overcome doubts "*[i]f*" there are "reasonable inferences" that at least one crime has been committed: *Comoros* Reconsideration Request, para. 13, see *supra* note 3. An alternative interpretation of the majority's remarks might be to suggest that the Article 53(1) requires little or no evaluation of the available information, and that the standard of proof is satisfied by the mere allegation of Article 5 crimes.

[131] Article 13 of the Statute lists three such authorities: a referring State Party, the UN Security Council acting under Chapter VII of the UN Charter, and the Pre-Trial Chamber approving a request from the Prosecutor under Article 15(4). States and the UN Security Council provide the necessary authorisation through their referrals, prior to the Prosecutor's preliminary examination. By contrast, since it provides a check on the *proprio motu* powers of the Prosecutor, applying in the absence of a referral, the Pre-Trial Chamber provides (or withholds) the necessary authorisation *after* the Prosecutor's preliminary examination.

[132] See, for example, *Kenya* Article 15 Decision, para. 27, see *supra* note 9. See also *Comoros* Reconsideration Request, para. 13 ("only during the investigation may the Prosecutor use her powers under article 54 of the Statute; conversely, her powers are more limited under article 53(1)"), see *supra* note 3.

whether there is criminal responsibility under the Statute, beyond those measures which inhere in the preliminary examination process.[133] Notwithstanding the vagueness of the definition, the prohibition of the use of investigative measures of this kind seems incontrovertible – if the Prosecutor may not open an investigation until the conditions of Articles 13, 15, and/or 53 of the Statute are met (as applicable), then necessarily those measures which can only be used in the context of an 'investigation' cannot be used in order to bring about this state of affairs.

22.3.3. Selectivity in Publicly Reported Criminal Allegations in 'Positively-resolved' Preliminary Examinations

Judge Kovács, in his separate opinion in *Georgia*, emphasised the importance of "ensur[ing] that the threshold provided for in Articles 15 and 53 of the Statute is *equally* applied to all crimes under the jurisdiction of the Court, irrespective of the nature of the alleged crimes at stake".[134] Yet applying the standard of proof in Article 53(1) "equally" to all the Article 5 crimes does *not* mean that a preliminary examination which supports the opening of an investigation is likely to provide a 'full' account of all the types of crimes which might have been committed. Indeed, the opposite is true. Certain Article 5 crimes are, by their nature, more difficult to establish because they require a greater number of elements to be satisfied. Moreover, in the context of preliminary examinations, this logic applies even more strongly because some required elements, by their nature, may be difficult to establish to the standard of proof on the basis of the "infor-

---

[133] See generally ICC Statute, Article 54, see *supra* note 7. All intrusive measures are likely to be investigative measures. Preliminary examinations depend on open-source information, or information which is consensually provided to the Prosecutor. Certain measures are thus clearly not 'investigative' for these purposes, and are expressly contemplated by Article 53(1) and Rule 104(2). The Prosecutor may *receive* information (that is, "information made available"), and may seek information from any "reliable" source she deems appropriate; she may also receive "testimony". Accordingly, it is certain that the Prosecutor may consult any open-source or public domain material. It also may be the case that the Prosecutor may receive the accounts of individuals – for example, victims, or 'whistleblowers' – provided those accounts are made *voluntarily* and thus do not require the use of any measure under Article 54. Nor does anything in the Statute prevent other actors taking independent steps at least to preserve potential evidence pending the opening of an investigation.

[134] *Georgia* Article 15 Decision, Separate Opinion of Judge Kovács, para. 23, see *supra* note 124.

---

mation made available". For example, certain 'conduct of hostilities' offences may be especially prone to this phenomenon.[135] The extent to which inferences of these elements can reasonably be made from the general circumstances is an open, and difficult, question.

Notwithstanding this limitation, it will generally not impede most kinds of preliminary examinations which see allegations of multiple kinds of criminality.[136] After all, an investigation can be opened if "the information available [...] allows for reasonable inferences that *at least one* crime within the jurisdiction of the Court has been committed and that the case would be admissible".[137] Likewise, Judge Fernández has recalled that "the facts and incidents identified" in an Article 15 application "are not and could not be expected to be exhaustive [...], but are intended solely to give concrete examples to the Chamber of the gravest types of criminality that have occurred in the situation".[138] This same reasoning applies to the Prosecutor's reasoning not only when she seeks to open an investigation *proprio motu,* by applying to the Pre-Trial Chamber, but also when opening the investigation of referred situations.

Yet, although Judge Fernández's conclusion is correct, it cannot necessarily be assumed that the 'examples' demonstrating that the Article 53(1) requirements are met will necessarily prove to be the 'gravest' types of criminality in the situation. Rather, although the Prosecutor can be expected to enumerate the gravest types which she finds to be established according to the Article 53(1) standard of proof, practical considerations will necessarily inform which crimes actually meet the test.

The story is, of course, different if the Prosecutor resolves to *close* a preliminary examination without proceeding to open an investigation. In

---

[135] See, for example, ICC Statute, Article 8(2)(b)(iv), see *supra* note 7.

[136] It may, however, bite on situations which feature very narrowly framed allegations. Whether this is a negative or positive result of the Article 53(1) test may depend on the point of view. On the one hand, it could serve to prevent certain situations in which (for example) one or more types of 'conduct of hostilities' war crimes may have been committed from coming readily before the ICC. On the other hand, for a court of limited resources, it may help to ensure that attention is naturally focused on situations of more widespread 'atrocity', and to limit situations based on 'technical' (although nonetheless serious) breaches of IHL.

[137] *Comoros* Reconsideration Request, para. 13 (emphasis added), see *supra* note 3.

[138] *Côte d'Ivoire* Article 15 Decision, Separate Opinion of Judge Fernández de Gurmendi, para. 32, see *supra* note 16.

---

that situation alone must she address *all* the crimes alleged in a situation, or which might arguably be considered to have arisen, because Article 53(1) requires her to have concluded that there is *no* reasonable basis to proceed for *any* Article 5 crime. This is only possible if she has measured the available information against all the crimes in the Statute.

For these reasons, the Article 53(1) standard of proof, combined with the prohibition on investigative measures during preliminary examinations, means that the situation described when *opening* an investigation will be the 'truth', as it appears, but not necessarily the '*whole* truth'. Expecting a preliminary examination to correspond "as much as possible to the 'reality' on the ground" is reasonable in and of itself – but the caveat "as much as possible" is critical.[139] Inevitably, certain features, possibly key features, of the situation may well be suspected at the preliminary examination stage, but are only susceptible to proof by means of the investigation itself. This presents no legal problem as such, since the scope of the investigation once opened is not limited to the incidents discussed in any public outcomes of the preliminary examination.[140] But it is important to understand, consequently, that such public outcomes are not necessarily akin to a 'monitoring report' by a human rights organization, and may not even aspire to paint a complete picture of the situation. Perhaps paradoxically, it is only when the Prosecutor does *not* find a reasonable basis to proceed with an investigation that she may endeavour to

---

[139] Cf. *Georgia* Article 15 Decision, Separate Opinion of Judge Kovács, para. 20, see *supra* note 124.

[140] See, for example, *Georgia* Article 15 Decision, para. 63 ("for the procedure of article 15 to be effective it is not necessary to limit the Prosecution's investigation to the crimes which are mentioned by the Chamber in its decision authorizing investigation. To impose such limitation would also be illogical, as an examination under article 15(3) and (4) of the Statute is inherently based on limited information. [...] Binding the Prosecutor to the crimes mentioned in the decision authorizing investigation would also conflict with her duty to investigate objectively, in order to establish the truth"), see *supra* note 9; *Côte d'Ivoire* Article 15 Decision, Separate Opinion of Judge Fernández de Gurmendi, para. 34 ("this early and necessarily non-comprehensive identification of incidents serves only as the basis for determining whether the requirements of Article 53 of the Statute are met and [is] not determinative of the case selection that will take place later upon further investigation"), see *supra* note 16. In this context, the *Burundi* Pre-Trial Chamber's apparent criticism of the Prosecutor for basing her application under Article 15(3) on alleged crimes against humanity, and not finding it necessary or appropriate to enter into the question of any armed conflict, seems curious. See *Burundi* Article 15 Decision, paras. 137-141, see *supra* note 18.

---

provide a reasonably comprehensive account of the facts on the ground, in order to explain the basis of her conclusion.[141]

In this context, it is important to note, of course, that the public outcomes of preliminary examinations are not the *only* outcomes. Preliminary examination activities may also yield *internal* work product, which may be relevant to and relied upon by any subsequent investigation, even if it does not meet the Article 53(1) standard of proof and therefore may not form part of the Prosecutor's Article 53(1) determination (and thus publicly reported).[142]

22.3.4. No *De Novo* Judicial Review

Article 53(3)(a) provides that, for situations referred to the Court and at the request of the referring body, the Pre-Trial Chamber may review the Prosecutor's decision *not* to open an investigation when based on her view that one or more of the criteria in Article 53(1)(a) or (b) is not met. In essence, therefore, this provision allows the Pre-Trial Chamber to review the Prosecutor's evaluation of the facts through the lens of the standard of proof set out in Article 53(1), as well as the correctness of the law to which she directs herself.

Just like any other proceedings before the Court, however, the existence of a mechanism for judicial review does not necessarily mean that the reviewing body can automatically substitute its own opinion of the facts for that of the body under review. Even in criminal trials, where the standard of proof applied is especially rigorous, it is still settled that "two judges, both acting reasonably, can come to different conclusions on the basis of the same evidence, both of which are reasonable".[143] This reasoning may apply *a fortiori* at the lower standard of proof of a preliminary examination.

---

[141] See also Stahn, pp. 433-434, see *supra* note 107.

[142] See also International Criminal Court, Office of the Prosecutor, *Policy Paper on Sexual and Gender Based Crimes*, June 2014, paras. 6, 21, 38–40, 54–55, 71 (http://www.legal-tools.org/doc/7ede6c/); International Criminal Court, Office of the Prosecutor, *Policy on Children*, November 2016, paras. 53–54, 65, 117, 123 (http://www.legal-tools.org/doc/c2652b/).

[143] International Criminal Tribunal for Rwanda, *Ntawukulilyayo v. the Prosecutor*, Appeals Chamber, Judgment, 14 December 2011, ICTR-05-82-A, para. 15 (http://www.legal-tools.org/doc/42d81d/).

Accordingly, recognising that Article 53(1) imposes a standard of proof, with which the Prosecutor must comply, does not mean recognising that the Pre-Trial Chamber may overturn the Prosecutor's determination based merely on its own subjective disagreement.[144] This is most especially the case when the Pre-Trial Chamber does not necessarily have before it all the primary information which was available to the Prosecutor in making her determination.[145] Applying a standard of review with an appropriate measure of deference on factual matters is not directly a matter of prosecutorial independence as such, but one of judicial economy and judicial procedure. This much should be clear from the example of the Appeals Chamber, even if reasonable minds may disagree whether the precise standard of review to be applied is better analogised to the standard for judicial review of administrative or executive action, or the appellate standard for factual errors, or the appellate standard for an abuse of discretion.[146]

22.4. Conclusion

This chapter has sought to examine the standard of proof under Article 53(1) – which should be a bedrock principle for the conduct of preliminary examinations, and for the evaluation of preliminary examination activity by the Court's wider constituency in the international community. It seems a simple proposition that, subject to her residual discretion in Article 53(1)(c) – as yet, unused – the Prosecutor will open an investiga-

---

144 Cf. *Comoros* Reconsideration Request, paras. 14–15 ("paragraphs (a) and (b) require the application of exacting legal requirements [...] the Chamber considers it necessary to add that there is also no valid argument for the proposition that in order not to encroach on the independence of the Prosecutor, the Chamber should knowingly tolerate and not request reconsideration of decisions under Article 53(1) [...] which are erroneous, but within some field of deference"), see *supra* note 3. Compare International Criminal Court, Situation on the Registered Vessels of the Union of the Comoros, the Hellenic Republic and the Kingdom of Cambodia, Pre-Trial Chamber, Partly Dissenting Opinion of Judge Kovács, 16 July 2015, ICC-01/13-34-Anx, paras. 6–8 (doubting the standard of review applied by the majority, and calling for "a more deferential approach") (http://www.legal-tools.org/doc/c854cf/).

145 See, for example, Rules of Procedure and Evidence, Rule 107(2), see *supra* note 110.

146 See further, for example, International Criminal Court, Situation on the Registered Vessels of the Union of the Comoros, the Hellenic Republic and the Kingdom of Cambodia, Pre-Trial Chamber, Public Redacted Version of the Prosecution's Consolidated Response to the Observations of the Victims (ICC-01/13-27 and ICC-01/13-28), 14 July 2015, ICC-01/13-29-Red, paras. 15–18 (http://www.legal-tools.org/doc/248fd1/).

tion if she determines that the information available shows a reasonable basis to believe that the criteria in Article 53(1)(a) and (b) are met. Yet, despite her recent repeated emphasis on this fact, it remains on occasion misunderstood.

The Article 53(1) standard of proof is indeed relatively low, but it is not meaningless. Like any other fact-finding exercise, it requires that the standard be satisfied by information and not conjecture or assertion. It requires that the standard be genuinely and consistently applied to all the factual elements required by Article 53(1)(a) and (b). It requires resources, time, and professional analysis, and a due measure of co-operation from the international community. Moreover, the link between the standards of proof in Articles 53(1) and 58 underlines the view of the drafters of the Statute that opening an investigation is just as serious and significant a decision as requesting an arrest warrant, with the former impacting largely on States and the latter impacting largely on individuals.

The implications of this analysis are enlightening. First, it underscores that preliminary examinations are not a reflection of the Prosecutor's opinion, or preconceptions, but merely a statement of what the information made available to her reasonably suggests, *without* conducting an investigation. As such, preliminary examinations neither express a political opinion, nor represent a statement of what the Prosecutor (or anyone else) might *suspect* about a situation.

Second, consequently, preliminary examinations serve a fundamentally *procedural* purpose: they are a step to opening an investigation, when this is called for, rather than an end in themselves. Accordingly, although there may sometimes be benefits in publicising the Prosecutor's finding(s) of a reasonable basis to believe that certain crimes are being committed, this is not their core function. Even if an overtly pragmatic approach to preliminary examinations were to be taken, where the Prosecutor only ascertains the bare minimum necessary to open an investigation, this would not mean that the Prosecutor will not carry out the resulting investigation fully, comprehensively and impartially, nor that she has overlooked (or will overlook) any type of Article 5 crime. In this regard, the public outcomes of preliminary examinations may not always reflect (some of) the short-term interests of civil society – to the extent this means drawing public attention to certain allegations of crime – even if such allegations remain material to an ensuing criminal investigation.

Third, preliminary examinations reflect a sophisticated balance struck by the drafters of the Statute. While ensuring that pragmatic considerations are not a primary consideration in deciding whether to open or not to open an investigation, unless they rise to the level of a consideration relevant to Article 53(1)(c), the standard of proof in Article 53(1) also ensures that there is a meaningful and objective filter on those situations which come before the Court. Care should be taken in ensuring that this standard of proof remains fit for purpose. In this context, by giving the Prosecutor the primary and independent responsibility for the *process* by which the standard of proof is applied (within her limited resources), and giving the Pre-Trial Chamber an oversight role in ensuring that the standard of proof is applied *properly*, the Court employs a system which makes a fair and reasonable effort to meet the unique constraints under which it operates.

23

Reconceptualizing the Birth of the International Criminal Case: Creating an Office of the Examining Magistrate

Gregory S. Gordon[*]

23.1. Introduction

One of the features of the International Criminal Court ('ICC') that has been the subject of critical commentary is the preliminary examination, which seeks to determine if there is a reasonable basis to proceed with a criminal investigation.[1] Given its amorphous status as the 'pre-investigation stage' of a case, it permits the Office of the Prosecutor ('OTP') a wide berth in terms of investigatory subjects and topics, length of inquiry, and platform for airing views of the incipient case to the public. In addition, there is a lack of transparency with no oversight or assurance that this initial sifting of the evidence is being conducted in a sufficiently neutral or efficient manner. That said, preliminary examinations offer an array of possible advantages, including the potential for deterring fresh violence, fostering peace negotiations and sparking transitional justice efforts (and thus complementarity) on the ground.

---

[*] **Gregory Steven Gordon** is Associate Professor and formerly served as Associate Dean (Development/External Affairs) and Director of the Ph.D.–M.Phil. Programme at the Faculty of Law, Chinese University of Hong Kong (CUHK Law). He is also a Research Fellow at the Centre for International Law Research and Policy (CILRAP). In 2017, his book *Atrocity Speech Law: Foundation, Fragmentation, Fruition* (Oxford University Press), which coined a new term for the law related to hate speech in international criminal law, proposed a paradigm shift in the field with introduction of the "Unified Liability Theory for Atrocity Speech Law".

[1] See, for example, Carsten Stahn, "Damned if You Do, Damned if You Don't: Challenges and Critiques of ICC Preliminary Examinations", in *Journal of International Criminal Justice*, 2017, vol. 15, no. 3, p. 7, noting that the current approach to preliminary examinations "has been subject to a number of critiques".

So, is it possible to keep the preliminary examination, with all its advantages, while eliminating or reducing its problems? This chapter argues that it is possible through a reconceptualization of the preliminary examination phase by creating an Office of the Examining Magistrate ('OEM') within ICC Chambers. Thus reconceptualized, the preliminary examination would be handled by both the OTP and the OEM. Initial information on crimes would go through the OTP, which, upon analysis, could refer it to the OEM for further action. If the referral were found to be sufficiently credible by the OEM, it would analyse the evidence, interview witnesses and undertake other related activities. When necessary, the OEM could consult with the OTP during the process, at the end of which the OEM would submit a completed dossier to the OTP. If the OTP determined that a reasonable basis to investigate had been established, then it would apply to the Pre-Trial Chamber to open a formal investigation. The OTP would not be able to comment on the case in public during the OEM's processing. And a time limit of 24 months would be placed on the preliminary examination. If additional time were needed at the end of this period, then both offices could apply to the Pre-Trial Chamber for a 12-month extension (and would then need to apply for additional 12-month extensions, if necessary, thereafter). In this way, the OEM would serve both an investigative and a judicial function.

While certain discretion would still be vested in the OTP (initial referral, applications for time extensions and opening of formal investigations), the OEM would provide an independent set of eyes and a degree of oversight. For all stakeholders, the preliminary examination would have a greater veneer of neutrality and, given that it would be more detached from the OTP, the OEM would be more likely to collect evidence potentially favourable to future defendants and implicated victims. In this way, not only would the process be inherently more fair and efficient, but it would also promote equality of arms, as well as concern for restorative justice, at an early stage. At the same time, the preliminary examination would still be able to promote deterrence, transition and complementarity on the ground. To the extent preliminary examinations in municipal jurisdictions are premised on a comparable lack of initial prosecutorial oversight, this proposal could be adopted in them as well for purposes of integrating quality control into the process.

This chapter will proceed in five sections. Section 23.2. will outline the preliminary examination process and describe its various phases, standards and objectives. In light of those objectives, Section 23.3. will consider the shortcomings of the current preliminary examination regime. In particular, it will focus on the OTP's inconsistent practices across different preliminary examinations, including length of process, methods of information collection and determinations regarding requests to investigate via communication versus referrals. Section 23.4. will set forth a solution – creation of the OEM and its integration into the existing framework. The nature of the OEM's mandate, as well as the protocols and procedures governing its operation will be explored. This section will also consider the OEM's relationship with the OTP, which would be designed to promote not only oversight and gap-filling but synergistic collaboration and reinforcement. Finally, Section 23.5. will summarize the advantages as well as anticipate potential objections to the proposed creation of the OEM, such as the impingement of the prosecutor's discretion and strategic manoeuvring as well as complementarity-promotion-hampering, the imposition of time limits and possible inefficiency and cost of an expanded bureaucracy.

In the end, the chapter will demonstrate that, notwithstanding these possible downsides, integration of the OEM within the preliminary examination structure will have a net positive effect. In particular, it will better achieve the goals of the Rome Statute – promoting complementarity, deterrence, efficiency and equality of arms.

23.2. The Preliminary Examination Process and Objectives

As will be discussed in greater detail below, the purpose of the OTP's preliminary examination is to ascertain whether a full investigation is justified. This amounts to marshalling sufficient information on crimes of the required gravity, as well as an absence of municipal investigative/prosecutorial efforts, such that a reasonable basis to open an investigation appears. This analysis is conducted within the framework of four 'phases'. Before examining these 'phases', it is helpful to consider how the Prosecutor receives information that triggers a preliminary examination.

23.2.1. Preliminary Examination Triggers

23.2.1.1. Communications and Referrals

The OTP is alerted to the existence of possible relevant crimes, known as *notitia criminis*,[2] via communications or referrals. These channels are pegged to the two mechanisms that can activate the Court's jurisdiction: (1) State Party (Article 13(a)) and Security Council (Article 13(b)) referrals; and (2) *proprio motu* investigations (Articles 13(c) and 15).[3] 'Communications' (the OTP's nomenclature for 'information', the precise word used in the Statute)[4] are tied to the latter. Article 15 of the Rome Statute declares:

> 1. The Prosecutor may initiate investigations *proprio motu* on the basis of *information* on crimes within the jurisdiction of the Court.
>
> 2. The Prosecutor shall analyse the seriousness of the information received. For this purpose, he or she may seek additional information from States, organs of the United Nations, intergovernmental or non-governmental organizations, or other reliable sources that he or she deems appropriate, and may receive written or oral testimony at the seat of the Court.
>
> 3. If the Prosecutor concludes that there is a reasonable basis to proceed with an investigation, he or she shall submit to the Pre-Trial Chamber a request for authorization of an investigation, together with any supporting material collected. Vic-

---

[2]   See Carsten Stahn, Mohamed M. El Zeidy and Héctor Olásolo, "The International Criminal Court's *Ad Hoc* Jurisdiction Revisited", in *American Journal of International Law*, 2005, vol. 99, no. 2, pp. 421, 426, pointing out that "after receiving a *notitia criminis*, and before actually securing the Court's formal jurisdiction by way of an Article 12(3) declaration, the prosecutor might carry out a preliminary analysis under Article 15(2) to determine whether the situation falls within the Court's jurisdiction *ratione personae, loci*, and *temporis*".

[3]   Rome Statute of the International Criminal Court, adopted 17 July 1998, entered into force 1 July 2002, Articles 13, 15 ('ICC Statute').

[4]   See Human Rights Watch, *ICC Course Correction: Recommendations to the Prosecutor for a More Effective Approach to "Situations under Analysis"*, 16 June 2011 (http://www.legal-tools.org/doc/43aefb/): "'Communications' are information received by the OTP under article 15 of the Rome Statute, which permits the prosecutor to open an investigation proprio motu ('on his own initiative') with the authorization of a pre-trial chamber of judges".

---

tims may make representations to the Pre-Trial Chamber, in accordance with the Rules of Procedure and Evidence.

4. If the Pre-Trial Chamber, upon examination of the request and the supporting material, considers that there is a reasonable basis to proceed with an investigation, and that the case appears to fall within the jurisdiction of the Court, it shall authorize the commencement of the investigation, without prejudice to subsequent determinations by the Court with regard to the jurisdiction and admissibility of a case.

5. The refusal of the Pre-Trial Chamber to authorize the investigation shall not preclude the presentation of a subsequent request by the Prosecutor based on new facts or evidence regarding the same situation.

6. If, after the preliminary examination referred to in paragraphs 1 and 2, the Prosecutor concludes that the information provided does not constitute a reasonable basis for an investigation, he or she shall inform those who provided the information. This shall not preclude the Prosecutor from considering further information submitted to him or her regarding the same situation in the light of new facts or evidence.[5]

23.2.1.2. The Providers and Nature of Information Received

There are no restrictions on the identity of persons or entities permitted to furnish the Prosecutor with *notitia criminis* for purposes of triggering an ICC investigation. Thus, "the personal scope of the right of access to the ICC to report crimes contained in the [Rome Statute] is universal".[6]

'Information' on crimes within the jurisdiction of the Court can consist of a variety of materials, including non-governmental organization ('NGO') or intergovernmental organization ('IGO') reports, witness affidavits, news items or other documentary evidence provided to the OTP by members of civil society, IGOs, groups, individual concerned citizens, or any other reliable sources.[7] Nothing in the Rome Statute regulates the

---

[5] ICC Statute, Article 15 (emphasis added).

[6] Hector Olasolo, *The Triggering Procedure of the International Criminal Court*, Martinus Nijhoff Publishers, Leiden, 2005, p. 54.

[7] International Criminal Court, *Understanding the International Criminal Court*, p. 17 (http://www.legal-tools.org/doc/9ea9fa/).

form or substance of the communications.[8] That said, unlike State and Security Council referrals, it would be unreasonable to "impose upon the senders of communications the burden of investigating for themselves or conducting extensive inquiry for the purpose of sending detailed information to the Prosecutor".[9] By the same token, if the communication is too extensive or vague, it "might be impossible for [the Prosecutor] to assess its value without launching a full investigation, something the Prosecutor is not allowed to do without authorisation from the Pre-Trial Chamber".[10]

23.2.1.3. Procedural Presumptions

Assuming the communication fits within these parameters, it also triggers a procedural response different from that of a referral. Per Article 53, when the Prosecutor receives a referral, she *shall* initiate an investigation *unless* she determines that there is no reasonable basis to proceed (see 'Phase 2' below).[11] This default position is reinforced by the fact that the Pre-Trial Chamber may only review the Prosecutor's decision not to proceed, but does not review an affirmative determination to proceed.[12] The default position is reversed when the Prosecutor receives a communication – in other words, she shall not seek to initiate an investigation unless she first concludes it is warranted.[13] This will be referred to as 'Phase 1'.

23.2.2. The Four Phases

23.2.2.1. Phase 1: Initial Assessment

So now it is appropriate to outline and unpack the four 'phases'. As just suggested, for 'Phase 1', in analysing "the seriousness of information received" per Article 15(2), the Prosecutor may filter out data concerning

---

[8]   Jo Stigen, *The Relationship between the International Criminal Court and the National Jurisdictions: The Principle of Complementarity*, Martinus Nijhoff Publishers, Leiden, 2008, p. 99.

[9]   International Criminal Court, *Annex to the "Paper on Some Policy Issues Before the Office of the Prosecutor": Referrals and Communications*, September 2003, sect. I.B. ('Referrals and Communications') (http://www.legal-tools.org/doc/5df43d/).

[10] *Ibid.*

[11] ICC Statute, Article 53(1). Referrals and Communications, sect. I.A., see *supra* note 9.

[12] *Ibid.*

[13] *Ibid.*

---

offences patently outside the ICC's jurisdiction. Also excluded are situations already under preliminary examination or investigation, or forming the basis of a prosecution.[14] Situations that survive this initial sifting then move to 'Phase 2' and formally become 'situations under analysis'.[15]

23.2.2.2.   Phase 2: Jurisdiction Assessment

So Phase 2 marks the formal start of the preliminary examination proper. As part of this, the Prosecutor analyses the factors set out in Article 53(1) of the Rome Statute, which govern the Prosecutor's decision as to whether a formal investigation should begin. Article 53(1) declares:

> The Prosecutor shall, having evaluated the information made available to him or her, initiate an investigation unless he or she determines that there is no reasonable basis to proceed under this Statute. In deciding whether to initiate an investigation, the Prosecutor shall consider whether:
>
> (a)   The information available to the Prosecutor provides a reasonable basis to believe that a crime within the jurisdiction of the Court has been or is being committed;
>
> (b)   The case is or would be admissible under Article 17; and
>
> (c)   Taking into account the gravity of the crime and the interests of victims, there are nonetheless substantial reasons to believe that an investigation would not serve the interests of justice.
>
> If the Prosecutor determines that there is no reasonable basis to proceed and his or her determination is based solely on subparagraph (c) above, he or she shall inform the Pre-Trial Chamber.[16]

Thus, Phase 2 boils down to an Article 53(1)(a) inquiry as to whether there is "a reasonable basis to believe that a crime *within the jurisdiction of the Court* has been or is being committed".[17] This further bifur-

---

[14]   OTP, *Policy Paper on Preliminary Examinations*, 1 November 2013, para. 78 (http://www.legal-tools.org/doc/acb906). Communications considered clearly beyond the Court's jurisdiction may be reconsidered based on new information or circumstances, such as a change in the jurisdictional situation.

[15]   See Human Rights Watch, 2011, see *supra* note 4.

[16]   ICC Statute, Article 53(1).

[17]   *Ibid.*, emphasis added.

cates into 'Phase 2(a)', which looks at temporal and geographical or personal jurisdiction, and 'Phase 2(b)', which considers whether the alleged conduct constitutes crimes under the Rome Statute (that is, if there exists subject-matter jurisdiction).[18] The date of entry into force of the Rome Statute delineates the starting point for the Court's temporal jurisdiction, namely from 1 July 2002 onwards.[19] The Court's subject-matter jurisdiction is laid out in Article 5 of the Statute and extends to genocide (as defined in Article 6), crimes against humanity (Article 7), war crimes (Article 8) and, recently, aggression (Article 8*bis*).[20]

The Court's territorial or personal jurisdiction is established if an Article 5 offence is committed on the territory or by a national of a State Party (Article 12(2)) or when a non-State Party has lodged a declaration accepting the Court's jurisdiction (Article 12(3)).[21] Moreover, jurisdiction lies beyond these parameters where the Security Council refers a situation to the Court, acting pursuant to its Chapter VII powers under the UN Charter (Article 13(b)).

Phase 2 involves an extensive jurisdiction-focused evaluation of the facts and law in connection with the crimes that are the object of the communication. The Prosecutor "will pay particular consideration to crimes committed on a large scale, as part of a plan or pursuant to a policy".[22] And she may collect any available materials related to any relevant national proceedings. Phase 2 culminates in the submission to the Prose-

---

[18] Human Rights Watch, 2011, see *supra* note 4.

[19] Christoph Safferling, *International Criminal Procedure*, Oxford University Press, Oxford, 2012, p. 98.

[20] The Court may also exercise jurisdiction over the crime of aggression, once the necessary provision adopted by the Assembly of States Parties enters into force. More specifically, this can occur one year after the 30th ratification of the relevant amendment to the Rome Statute adopted at the Kampala Review Conference (2010), and no earlier than 2017. See Review Conference of the Rome Statute, Amendments on the Crime of Aggression to the Rome Statute of the International Criminal Court, 11 June 2010, UN doc. RC/Res.6 (http://www.legal-tools.org/doc/0d027b/); ICC Statute, Articles 15 *bis* and 15 *ter*. As this chapter goes to print, the aggression jurisdiction has been activated. On 15 December 2017, the International Criminal Court Assembly of States Parties adopted the 2010 Kampala aggression amendments – as of 17 July 2018, the Court will be able to prosecute State leaders responsible for the illegal use of force against other States.

[21] ICC Statute, Articles 12(2) and 12(3).

[22] OTP, 2013, para. 81, see *supra* note 14.

---

cutor of an 'Article 5 report' focusing on the Court's subject-matter jurisdiction as defined in Article 5 of the Statute.[23]

23.2.2.3. Phase 3: Admissibility Assessment

Consistent with Article 53(1)(b), admissibility is assessed in 'Phase 3'. This is tantamount to determining whether the 'complementarity' and 'gravity' factors have been satisfied. Pursuant to the principle of complementarity, primacy of jurisdiction lies with a State's domestic courts unless the ICC determines the State is "unwilling or unable genuinely to carry out the [...] prosecution".[24] The other admissibility criterion, gravity, requires that the crimes at issue be sufficiently serious to "the international community as a whole".[25] The Statute describes these crimes as "unimaginable atrocities" and "grave crimes" that "deeply shock the conscience of humanity".[26]

At this preliminary phase, where there is not yet a 'case' proper, the Prosecutor analyses only "potential" cases that "could be identified in the course of the preliminary examination based on the information available and that would likely arise from an investigation into the situation".[27] Thus, per the Pre-Trial Chamber in the Situation in the Republic of Kenya, "admissibility at the situation phase should be assessed against certain criteria defining a 'potential case' such as: (i) the groups of persons involved that are likely to be the focus of an investigation for the purpose of shaping the future case(s); and (ii) the crimes within the jurisdiction of the Court allegedly committed during the incidents that are likely to be the focus of an investigation for the purpose of shaping the future case(s)".[28]

Completion of Phase 3 entails submission to the Prosecutor of an 'Article 17 Report' related to the admissibility issues identified in Article 17 of the Statute.

---

[23] *Ibid.*

[24] ICC Statute, Article 17(1)(a).

[25] Margaret M. deGuzman, "Gravity and the Legitimacy of the International Criminal Court", in *Fordham International Law Journal*, 2008, vol. 32, no. 5, p. 1400.

[26] ICC Statute, Preamble.

[27] OTP, 2013, para. 43, see *supra* note 14.

[28] ICC, Situation in the Republic of Kenya, Pre-Trial Chamber, Decision Pursuant to Article 15 of the Rome Statute on the Authorization of an Investigation into the Situation in the Republic of Kenya, 31 March 2010, ICC-01/09-19, para. 50.

23.2.2.4. Phase 4: Interests of Justice Assessment

Assuming the requirements of jurisdiction and admissibility are met, the "interests of justice" prong is considered in Phase 4. Whereas the Phase 2 and 3 considerations (jurisdiction and admissibility) are positive requirements in the sense that they must be met to proceed with the inquiry, Phase 4 (interests of justice) is rather a "potentially countervailing consideration" that may give a reason not to proceed.[29] Thus, the OTP will go forward absent specific circumstances providing a substantial reason to conclude that the interests of justice would not be served by an investigation at that time.[30]

In doing its analysis during this phase, the OTP will take into account the best interests of victims (and, where relevant, victim representatives), and "other relevant actors, such as community, religious, political or tribal leaders, States, and "intergovernmental and non-governmental organisations".[31] That said, the OTP is conscious of not infringing on the Security Council's Article 16 'peace and security maintenance' role. Per that provision, "no investigation or prosecution may be commenced or proceeded with [...] for a period of 12 months after the Security Council, in a resolution adopted under [UN Charter] Chapter VII, has requested the Court to that effect [with allowance of renewal]".[32] Thus, Phase 4 does not "embrace all issues related to peace and security", given that it should not operate as "a conflict management tool requiring the Prosecutor to assume the role of a mediator in political negotiations".[33]

Phase 4 results in the issuance of an 'Article 53(1) Report', which provides a non-binding preliminary statement of facts, with relevant suspects, places and times, as well as an initial legal characterization of the alleged crimes within the Court's jurisdiction.[34]

---

[29] OTP, 2013, para. 67, see *supra* note 14.

[30] *Ibid.*

[31] *Ibid.*

[32] ICC Statute, Article 16.

[33] OTP, 2013, para. 69, see *supra* note 14.

[34] *Ibid*, paras. 83–84.

23.2.3. Preliminary Examination Activities

Article 15(2) of the Rome Statute identifies two principal categories of activity that the Prosecutor can engage in during preliminary examination: (1) seek additional information from States, organs of the United Nations, intergovernmental or non-governmental organizations, or other reliable sources that she deems appropriate; and (2) receive written or oral testimony at the seat of the Court.[35] Although, on its surface, this language may seem limiting, the actual scope of prosecutorial activity at this stage can be rather broad. Given that the OTP is not technically conducting an 'investigation', it cannot officially rely on the modes of co-operation set forth in Part 9 of the Statute. [36] However, the OTP can send information requests to States, UN organs, intergovernmental and non-governmental organisations and other reliable sources for the purpose of analysing the seriousness of the information received. [37]

In connection with this, the OTP may also carry out field missions to the relevant jurisdictions "to consult with the competent national authorities, the affected communities and other relevant stakeholders, such as civil society organisations".[38] In this context, the OTP acknowledges that, as part of the preliminary examination, the "Office also examines the general context within which the alleged crimes, in particular, sexual and gender based crimes, have occurred and assesses the existence of local institutions, international organisations, non-governmental organisations and other entities available as potential sources of information and/or of support for victims".[39]

In light of these and other considerations, Héctor Olásolo interprets the Article 86 'investigation and prosecution' restriction in Part 9 of the Statute as not forbidding access to certain parts of the Part 9 international

---

[35] ICC Statute, Article 15(2).

[36] See ICC Statute, Article 86, which declares that "States Parties shall, in accordance with the provisions of this Statute, cooperate fully with the Court in its *investigation and prosecution* of crimes within the jurisdiction of the Court" (emphasis added). By implication, activities outside of 'investigation' and 'prosecution' would furnish grounds for requesting State co-operation.

[37] OTP, *Regulations of the Office of the Prosecutor*, 23 April 2009, ICC-BD/05-01-09, Regulations 33–35 (http://www.legal-tools.org/doc/a97226/).

[38] OTP, 2013, para. 85, see *supra* note 14.

[39] *Ibid.*, para. 86.

co-operation regime, in particular those that are of a 'non-coercive' nature. As explained by Olásolo:

> In this regard, it is submitted that the States Parties duty to cooperate with the Court under art. 86 RS [Rome Statute] extends to all activities of the Court, including the preliminary examination and the subsequent triggering procedure. There are a number of reasons for this interpretation. First, the ultimate purpose of the cooperation scheme provided for in the RS is to facilitate the Court's exercise of any of its jurisdictional powers (not just its power to investigate and prosecute). Secondly, Part IX of the RS provides for several forms of cooperation that are closely connected with the Court's exercise of powers other than the investigative and prosecutorial ones, such as those to enforce sentences and to award and enforce reparations rewards. Thirdly, a number of provisions on the adoption and implementation of preventive measures in connection with the reparation proceedings are based on the general obligation to cooperate pursuant to art. 86 and on those other provisions that elaborate on such general obligation. Thus, as some have pointed out, [the "investigation/prosecution" language of art. 86] should be understood as a reference to all ways in which the ICC exercises its jurisdictional powers. That would include the preliminary examination, which is essential for the proper exercise by the ICC of the activation dimension of its jurisdictional power.[40]

Based on this, Olásolo arrives at the following conclusion:

> It is submitted that art. 15(2) RS leaves room for the OTP to resort to many of the forms of State Parties cooperation [of a non-coercive nature] provided for in art. 93 RS, including: (i) identification and location of persons or items; (ii) voluntary questioning of victims and witnesses in the territory of the States Parties; (iii) service of documents, including judicial documents; (iv) provision of records and documents, including official records and documents; (v) examination of places or sites; and (vi) any other type of assistance not of a co-

---

[40] Olásolo, 2005, p. 61, see *supra* note 6.

ercive nature which is not prohibited by the law of the requested state.[41]

We will revisit these preliminary examination activities later in this
chapter when considering them in the context of the proposed OEM.

23.2.4. Preliminary Examination Termination

The preliminary examination process is open-ended with the Prosecutor
taking the position that "imposing rigid timetables on this process of analysis would not be workable under the framework of the Rome Statute".[42]
This is so, per the OTP, because: (1) the nature of Article 5 crimes, along
with a broad jurisdictional scope and a mandate to analyse the interests of
justice, often dictates long monitoring periods before preliminary examination inquiries can be concluded; (2) given the principle of complementarity, sufficient time is needed to determine the genuine nature and status
of national investigation/prosecution efforts; and (3) the OTP's limited
resources means that not every situation can be immediately or expeditiously investigated.[43]

Relevant persons or entities will be informed of an ultimate decision by the Prosecutor not to investigate. Per Article 53(3), the Pre-Trial
Chamber may review such a decision in relation to a referral by a State or
the Security Council but not pursuant to a communication by other parties.[44]

23.2.5. Preliminary Examination Objectives

Clearly, as we have seen, the chief aim of the preliminary examination is
to consider if there is a reasonable basis to launch an official investigation
regarding a situation. However, important subsidiary goals also include
spurring domestic investigation/prosecution efforts (known as 'positive
complementarity'), deterring commission of future crimes, and contributing toward the end of a culture of impunity.

But, for these objectives to be realized, the OTP "must adopt a consistent method of analysis", "increasing transparency", and "clear time-

---

[41] *Ibid.*, p. 60.

[42] Referrals and Communications, sect. I.C., see *supra* note 9.

[43] *Ibid.*

[44] ICC Statute, Article 53(3); OTP, 2013, para. 92, see *supra* note 14.

lines".[45] Unfortunately, in its decade and a half of work, it has failed to live up to these standards. Examining how that has played out in individual cases will be the object of the next section.

23.3. A Preliminary Examination Record of Timeline Inconsistency, Politicization and Uneven Results

Despite theoretically furthering important interests beyond verification of a reasonable basis to proceed, including deterrence and positive complementarity, the preliminary examination has often worked at cross-purposes to the ICC's larger policy objectives. This is especially the case in reference to *proprio motu* investigations. In its relatively short life, the OTP has received over 10,000 Article 15 communications. And yet, only three have resulted in *proprio motu* investigations. Many communications have entailed years of OTP effort not yielding an eventual investigation, with many still in limbo at the time of writing. By the same token, the preliminary examinations themselves have raised political firestorms that have not been quelled by OTP strategy. Related to this, they have often been ineffective, yielding inconsistent results. These problems will now be explored in greater depth.

23.3.1. Timeline Inconsistencies

23.3.1.1. Preliminary Examinations Triggered by Communications

The disparity in timelines with regard to preliminary examinations triggered by communications is marked. Focusing on some case studies helps put this in perspective.

23.3.1.1.1. Expeditious OTP Decisions

23.3.1.1.1.1. Kenya

23.3.1.1.1.1.1. Background

In late December 2007, in a hotly contested presidential election, Kenya's sitting chief executive, Mwai Kibaki, a Kikuyu of the Party of National Unity ('PNU') was announced the victor by a razor-thin margin against opponent Raila Odinga, a Luo of the Orange Democratic Movement ('ODM'). The results enraged dissatisfied Luo voters and the country

---

[45] Claire Grandison, "Maximizing the Impact of ICC Preliminary Examinations", in *Human Rights Brief*, 10 February 2012.

exploded in violence that lasted through January 2008 and left over 1,000 dead, over 300,000 displaced, over 3,500 seriously injured, with nearly one thousand sexual assault victims, and extensive destruction of property.[46] These atrocities, along with the absence of a meaningful local law enforcement response, led to the OTP receiving communications and opening a preliminary examination in February 2008.[47] At the same time, an international commission of inquiry – the so-called Waki Commission – was established and ultimately recommended creation of a tribunal to investigate and prosecute post-election violence perpetrators.[48] The Waki Commission eventually sent evidence it collected to the OTP.[49]

23.3.1.1.1.1.2. Efforts to Create a National Tribunal and the OTP Request for Investigation

Through 2009, Kenyan authorities held serious discussions about creating a national tribunal to try perpetrators of post-election violence.[50] Toward the end of the year, those discussions had not yet yielded fruit. But as of 9 November, the Kenyan parliament had begun debate on enacting a constitutional amendment to form a local tribunal.[51] In spite of this, on 26 November 2009, the ICC Prosecutor filed a request seeking authorization from Pre-Trial Chamber II to open an investigation in relation to Kenya's post-election crimes.[52] That request was granted.[53]

---

46 ICC, Situation in the Republic of Kenya, Pre-Trial Chamber, Decision Pursuant to Article 15 of the Rome Statute on the Authorization of an Investigation into the Situation in the Republic of Kenya, 31 March 2010, ICC-01/09-19, para. 131, see *supra* note 28.

47 ICC Office of the Prosecutor, "OTP Statement in relation to events in Kenya", 5 February 2008 (http://www.legal-tools.org/doc/765584/).

48 Philip Waki, "Report of the Commission of Inquiry into Post-Election Violence", 15 October 2008, pp. 472 ff. (http://www.legal-tools.org/doc/a1063a/).

49 ICC Office of the Prosecutor, "ICC Prosecutor receives materials on post-election violence in Kenya", 16 July 2009.

50 Such discussions surrounded, in particular, the Special Tribunal for Kenya Bill 2009 and The Constitution of Kenya (Amendment) Bill 2009, 28 January 2009, Constitution of Kenya (Amendment) (No. 3) Bill 2009, 24 August 2009.

51 International Crisis Group, "Kenya: Impact of the ICC Proceedings", in *Crisis Group Africa Briefing no. 84*, 9 January 2012, p. 17.

52 ICC, Situation in the Republic of Kenya, Pre-Trial Chamber, Request for authorisation of an investigation pursuant to Article 15, 26 November 2009, ICC-01/09-3 (http://www. legal-tools.org/doc/c63dcc/).

In December 2010, the Prosecutor requested the issuance of 'summonses to appear' for six suspects in the Kenya investigation – William Samoei Ruto, Henry Kiprono Kosgey, Joshua arap Sang (Case One) and Francis Kirimi Muthaura, Uhuru Muigai Kenyatta, and Mohamed Hussein Ali (Case Two) – for their alleged responsibility in the commission of crimes against humanity.[54] Those summonses were issued with the Pre-Trial Chamber finding reasonable grounds to believe the suspects committed the alleged crimes.[55] The charges were eventually confirmed, but those against Ali and Kosgey were rejected.[56]

23.3.1.1.1.1.3. The Case Crumbles

In March 2013, the Prosecutor withdrew all charges against Muthaura, noting problems with recanting witnesses.[57] In December 2014, prior to trial, the Prosecutor withdrew charges against Kenyatta, again alluding to

---

[53] ICC, Situation in the Republic of Kenya, Pre-Trial Chamber, Decision Pursuant to Article 15 of the Rome Statute on the Authorization of an Investigation into the Situation in the Republic of Kenya, 31 March 2010, ICC-01/09-19 (http://www.legal-tools.org/doc/338a6f/).

[54] ICC, Situation in the Republic of Kenya, Pre-Trial Chamber, Prosecutor's Application Pursuant to Article 58 as to Francis Kirimi Muthaura, Uhuru Muigai Kenyatta and Mohammed Hussein Ali, 15 December 2010, ICC-01/09-31-Red2 (http://www.legal-tools.org/doc/72b726/).

[55] ICC, Situation in the Republic of Kenya, *The Prosecutor v. William Samoei Ruto, Henry Kiprono Kosgey and Joshua Arap Sang*, Pre-Trial Chamber, Decision on the Prosecutor's Application for Summons to Appear for William Samoei Ruto, Henry Kiprono Kosgey and Joshua Arap Sang, 8 March 2011, ICC-01/09-01/11-1 (http://www.legal-tools.org/doc/6c9fb0/); and ICC, Situation in the Republic of Kenya, *The Prosecutor v. Francis Kirimi Muthaura, Uhuru Muigai Kenyatta and Mohammed Hussein Ali*, Pre-Trial Chamber, Decision on the Prosecutor's Application for Summonses to Appear for Francis Kirimi Muthaura, Uhuru Muigai Kenyatta and Mohammed Hussein Ali, 8 March 2011, ICC-01/09-02/11-01 (http://www.legal-tools.org/doc/df8391/).

[56] ICC, Situation in the Republic of Kenya, *The Prosecutor v. Francis Kirimi Muthaura, Uhuru Muigai Kenyatta and Mohammed Hussein Ali*, Pre-Trial Chamber, Decision on the Confirmation of Charges Pursuant to Article 61(7)(a) and (b) of the Rome Statute, 29 January 2012, ICC-01/09-02/11-382-Red (http://www.legal-tools.org/doc/4972c0/).

[57] ICC, Situation in the Republic of Kenya, *The Prosecutor v. Francis Kirimi Muthaura and Uhuru Muigai Kenyatta*, Trial Chamber, Prosecution notification of withdrawal of the charges against Francis Kirimi Muthaura, 11 March 2013, ICC-01/09-02/11-687 (http://www.legal-tools.org/doc/9d2c58/).

---

witness availability issues.[58] In April 2016, a majority of judges in Trial Chamber V(A) concluded there was insufficient evidence to continue the Ruto/Sang trial, which had been running for a year.[59]

23.3.1.1.1.2. Côte d'Ivoire

Echoing the problems in Kenya, Côte d'Ivoire was wracked by sectarian violence following disputed presidential elections in November 2010. From then through April 2011, supporters of the two election opponents – Christian incumbent, Laurent Gbagbo, hailing from the south, and Muslim challenger Alassane Ouattara, from the north – attacked one another in various cities around the country. The violence left approximately 3,000 people dead and half a million displaced.[60] Many viewed this as a resuscitation of the Ivorian 2002-2007 civil war, wherein Muslim rebels from the north attacked the government-held south, including the then-capital Abidjan. International military forces, spearheaded by the French, ended the crisis and installed Ouattara as president.

Although, via Gbagbo's referral, the OTP had technically opened a preliminary examination in 2003 related to civil war violence, it had lain moribund for several years.[61] Thus, the 2010-2011 post-election violence triggered what was essentially a new preliminary examination. Alleged crimes connected to that violence had been committed as recently as April 2011. But already by 23 June, the Prosecutor requested authorization for an investigation.[62] That authorization was granted and Gbagbo, along with his key lieutenant Charles Blé Goudé, are currently on trial before ICC Trial Chamber I.[63] A warrant for arrest against Gbagbo's wife, former

---

58 ICC, Situation in the Republic of Kenya, *The Prosecutor v. Uhuru Muigai Kenyatta*, Trial Chamber, Notice of withdrawal of the charges against Uhuru Muigai Kenyatta, 5 December 2014, ICC-01/09-02/11-983 (http://www.legal-tools.org/doc/b57a97/).

59 ICC, Situation in the Republic of Kenya, *The Prosecutor v. William Samoei Ruto and Joshua Arap Sang*, Trial Chamber, Decision on Defence Applications for Judgments of Acquittal, 5 April 2016, ICC-01/09-01/11-2027-Red-Corr (http://www.legal-tools.org/doc/6baecd/).

60 See, for example, ICC, Situation in the Republic of Côte d'Ivoire, Pre-Trial Chamber, Request for authorisation of an investigation pursuant to article 15, 23 June 2011, ICC-02/11-3, paras. 2 and 113 (http://www.legal-tools.org/doc/1b1939/).

61 OTP, *Report on Preliminary Examination Activities*, 13 December 2011, para 120 (http://www.legal-tools.org/doc/4aad1d/).

62 *Ibid.*, para. 122.

63 ICC, *The Prosecutor v. Laurent Gbagbo and Charles Blé Goudé*, TC I, ICC-02/11-01/15.

First Lady Simone Gbagbo, has been issued but she is not in ICC custody. Thus, that case remains in the pre-trial phase.[64]

23.3.1.1.1.3. Other Situations

Although not as expeditious as the Kenya and Côte d'Ivoire decisions, the OTP has taken relatively quick decisions in other communications-triggered preliminary examinations. After a 2009 *coup d'état* in Honduras, the government of strong-man coup leader Roberto Micheletti allegedly engaged in crimes against humanity stemming from police violence against civilians and the murder of *campesinos* (peasants or farmers).[65] At the end of 2010, after receiving related communications, the OTP opened a preliminary examination.[66] The examination was closed in 2013 for want of a reasonable basis to proceed. The preliminary examination was then reopened in 2014 and summarily closed again in 2015.[67]

Two other communications-based preliminary examinations appear to have been conducted summarily. The OTP received communications in reference to alleged British troop offences during the invasion of Iraq in 2003.[68] The United Kingdom, a junior partner to the United States, re-mained an occupying authority, until 30 June 2004, when an Iraqi interim government assumed full authority. At some unknown point during this period, the OTP opened a preliminary examination based on the commu-nications related to British troop offences (the UK having ratified the Rome Statute in 2001). Given that the OTP did not begin operations until 2003 and was not up and running at full strength for some time after that, a February 2006 close date suggests a relatively truncated preliminary

---

[64] ICC, *The Prosecutor v. Simone Gbagbo*, PTC I, ICC-02/11-01/12.

[65] See, for example, OTP, 2011, paras. 33–41, see *supra* note 61.

[66] OTP, "Statement of the Prosecutor of the International Criminal Court, Fatou Bensouda, on the conclusion of the preliminary examination into the situation in Honduras", 28 October 2015 (http://www.legal-tools.org/doc/1d09c8/).

[67] OTP, *Situation in Honduras: Article 5 Report*, 28 October 2015 (http://www.legal-tools. org/doc/54755a/).

[68] OTP, "Communications Received by the Prosecutor of the ICC", 16 July 2003, p. 2 (http:// www.legal-tools.org/doc/df602e/).

examination.[69] That conclusion is bolstered by the fact that the OTP reopened the preliminary examination a few years later (in May 2014).[70]

Stemming from crimes allegedly perpetrated by the Hugo Chavez regime, Venezuela (another State Party to the Rome Statute) was also the object of a communications-triggered OTP preliminary examination opened on an unknown date. Like the Iraq preliminary examination, the one for Venezuela was also terminated in February 2006.[71] Again, allowing for the OTP's start-up period, the early 2006 end date also indicates a compressed timeframe.

23.3.1.1.2. Delayed OTP Decisions

In contrast, many communications-based preliminary examinations have been dragged out for years. The following cases illustrate this other side of OTP practice.

23.3.1.1.2.1. Colombia

From 1958 until 2012, when peace talks began, a civil war in Colombia claimed at least 220,000 lives and created one of the largest displaced persons populations in the world. The long conflict saw the rise and decline of various powerful drug cartels, guerrilla groups, and paramilitaries but the government's chief military antagonist was the guerrilla group known as the Revolutionary Armed Forces of Colombia ('FARC').[72]

The OTP opened a preliminary examination in Colombia in June 2004.[73] It has examined materials related to alleged killings, enforced disappearances, imprisonment, torture, and other grave crimes committed by both government and rebel groups from November 2002 onward.[74] In 2012, the OTP concluded the Phase 2 portion of the preliminary examina-

---

[69] OTP, "OTP response to communications received concerning Iraq" [untitled letter from Luis Moreno-Ocampo], 9 February 2006 (http://www.legal-tools.org/doc/c90d25/).

[70] OTP, "Prosecutor of the International Criminal Court, Fatou Bensouda, re-opens the preliminary examination of the situation in Iraq", 13 May 2014 (https://www.legal-tools.org/doc/d9d9c5).

[71] OTP, "OTP response to communications received concerning Venezuela" [untitled letter from Luis Moreno-Ocampo], 9 February 2006 (http://www.legal-tools.org/doc/c90d25/).

[72] See, for example, OTP, 2011, paras. 63–64, see *supra* note 61.

[73] OTP, *Report on Preliminary Examination Activities 2012*, 22 November 2012, para. 97 (http://www.legal-tools.org/doc/0b1cfc/).

[74] OTP, 2011, paras. 65–73, see *supra* note 61.

tion, finding there was a reasonable basis to believe crimes against humanity and war crimes had been committed by the Colombian army, guerrilla actors such as FARC and the National Liberation Army, and paramilitary groups.[75]

Five years later, and thirteen years after the preliminary examination first began, it lingers on – ostensibly due to efforts by Colombian officials to institute domestic proceedings. In 2005, the government had enacted the Justice and Peace Law ('JPL'), which established several Justice and Peace Tribunals ('JPTs') to prosecute members of illegal armed groups that demobilized between 2004 and 2006.[76] This law has been criticized for meting out token punishment and lacking coordination between judicial and administrative authorities while having inadequate technical capacity. In the words of Jennifer Easterday, as early as 2009:

> However, the JPL in effect does little to promote justice, truth, reparations, or reconciliation for victims in Colombia; instead, it serves as a quasi-amnesty for the worst perpetrators of crimes against humanity and human rights abuses. Indeed, many aspects of the JPL directly controvert President Uribe's proclamations of "justice," "truth" and "peace" [...] Worse still, the JPL is not a comprehensive plan involving all of the armed factions. [The focus has been] mainly on demobilizing the paramilitary groups. [Colombia has been taking advantage] of any ambiguities in its obligations under the Rome Statute[...] Other state parties to the Rome Statute, unsure of how the future of international criminal law will evolve and how the principle of complementarity will be applied in real world situations, are very likely to mimic the actions of Colombia by instituting their own sham prosecutions in the name of peace or transitional justice.[77]

---

[75] OTP, *Situation in Colombia: Interim Report*, 14 November 2012, para. 5 (http://www.legal-tools.org/doc/7029e5/).

[76] See, for example, OTP, *Report on Preliminary Examination Activities (2015)*, 12 November 2015, paras. 148 ff. (http://www.legal-tools.org/doc/ac0ed2/); OTP, *Report on Preliminary Examination Activities 2016*, 14 November 2016, para. 245 (http://www.legal-tools.org/doc/f30a53/).

[77] Jennifer Easterday, "Deciding the Fate of Complementarity: A Colombian Case Study", in *Arizona Journal of International and Comparative Law*, 2009, vol. 26, no. 1, pp. 82–83.

The 2016 peace deal, whose transitional justice approach seemingly flowed from the JPL, was rejected by Colombian voters, in large part because it was seen as promoting impunity for fighters who had committed grave offences.[78] And so, as of July 2017, after nearly a decade and a half of being open, the OTP's Colombian preliminary examination continued to be mired in Phase 3.

23.3.1.1.2.2. Afghanistan

After the attacks of 11 September 2011 against the United States, directed by Al-Qaeda from Afghanistan within the territorial jurisdiction of the Taliban government, a US-led military coalition invaded the country and attacked the Taliban and the Al-Qaeda terrorists it harboured. Coalition forces soon defeated the Taliban and a new Afghan government was installed. The Taliban regrouped and has continued fighting against the government, which has been supported by international forces, including NATO.[79] In connection with the conflict, the Taliban and other armed anti-government forces, as well as Afghan government soldiers in tandem with international forces, have allegedly committed crimes against humanity and war crimes.[80] The OTP has received communications alleging criminal conduct in reference to three separate groups of alleged perpetrators: members of the Taliban and their affiliates (anti-government groups); members of Afghan government forces; and members of international forces.

Afghanistan deposited its instrument of ratification to the Rome Statute on 10 February 2003. In 2007, the OTP publicly acknowledged the existence of the preliminary examination of the situation in Afghanistan, meaning the preliminary examination has been open since at least that time.[81] As of 2013, the preliminary examination entered into Phase 3,[82]

---

[78] Julia Symmes Cobb and Nicholas Casey, "Colombia Peace Deal Is Defeated, Leaving a Nation in Shock", in *New York Times*, 2 October 2016 (noting that "[t]o many Colombians who had endured years of kidnappings and killings by the rebels, the agreement was too lenient. It would have allowed most rank-and-file fighters to start lives as normal citizens, and rebel leaders to receive reduced sentences for war crimes").

[79] OTP, 2011, paras. 22–23, see *supra* note 61.

[80] *Ibid.*, paras. 24–29.

[81] *Ibid.*, para. 20.

[82] See Office of the Prosecutor, *Report on Preliminary Examination Activities 2013*, 25 November 2013, p. 14, para. 56 ("[The] Prosecutor has decided that the preliminary examina-

and as of 2016, the OTP has acknowledged that the case is admissible. Its 2016 "Report of Preliminary Examination Activities" recognized that the "Government has instituted only a limited number of proceedings against alleged perpetrators" and "has not provided any information on national proceedings to the Office, despite multiple requests for such information from the Office since 2008".[83] Moreover, the OTP has essentially declared that its Phase 4 assessment has concluded, that is, there are no interest of justice issues:

> In light of the mandate of the Office, as well as the object and purpose of the Statute, and taking into account the gravity of the crimes and the interests of victims, based on the information available the Office would have no substantial reasons to believe that the opening of an investigation would not be in the interests of justice.[84]

Thus, as of November 2016, at least nine years after the preliminary examination was opened, the OTP acknowledged that it was "concluding its assessment of factors set out in Article 53(1)(a)-(c), and will make a final decision on whether to request the Pre-Trial Chamber authorisation to commence an investigation into the situation [...] imminently".[85] As of July 2017, a full decade after the preliminary examination was initiated, no decision has been taken.[86]

23.3.1.1.2.3. Guinea

On 28 September 2009, 50,000 protesters gathered in a national stadium in Guinea to express discontent during Independence Day celebrations with then-leader Moussa Dadis Camara, who had taken power in a *coup*

---

tion of this situation should be expanded to include admissibility issues") (http://www.legal-tools.org/doc/dbf75e/).

[83] *Ibid.*

[84] *Ibid.*, p. 50, para. 225.

[85] *Ibid.*

[86] By memorandum of 30 October 2017, the Prosecutor notified the President of the Court, in accordance with regulation 45 of the Regulations of the Court, of her intention to submit a request for authorisation of an investigation into the situation in the Islamic Republic of Afghanistan pursuant to article 15(3) of the Statute. On 3 November 2017, the Presidency of the Court assigned the Situation in the Islamic Republic of Afghanistan to PTC III. As of April 2018, PTC III has not issued a decision regarding the Prosecutor's request for authorization of an investigation.

d'état the previous year. Protesters were shot, stabbed, beaten and raped by government forces. In all, 157 civilians were killed (although Guinean military personnel quickly removed bodies from the stadium, making it difficult to ascertain the true number of those killed) and dozens of women were raped.

In October 2009, after receiving related communications, the OTP opened a preliminary examination for this matter. In a December 2011 report, the OTP concluded that there is a reasonable basis to believe that Guinean government forces committed crimes against humanity in connection with the 28 September 2009 massacre. Five years later, the Guinean government had engaged in only limited justice efforts related to the massacre:

> Since legal proceedings began in 2010 [...] only eight people have been charged, though offenses were committed by scores of members of the armed forces [...] Administering justice for the victims is all the more urgent because scores of victims have died in the past five years from their injuries or disease without being vindicated [...] Despite the government's stated commitments, a lack of financial and political support has been a major obstacle to the progress of the investigation. The government needs to guarantee that all of the people summoned for questioning, including members of the security forces, regardless of their rank, answer the summonses issued by the judges. On several occasions, despite repeated summonses, the judges have not been able to interview people summoned for questioning about the events of September 28, 2009.[87]

Nearly three years later, despite some progress in the proceedings, there has still been no trial. In its latest Report of Preliminary Examination Activities (2016), the OTP concluded its analysis of the Guinea situation on a pessimistic note:

> Notwithstanding the concrete and progressive investigative steps adopted by the panel of judges during the reporting period, the Office notes that the appointment in March 2016 of General Mathurin Bangoura, former member of the CNDD indicted in 2015, as Governor of Conakry was perceived by

---

[87] "Guinea: 5 Years On, No Justice for Massacre", in *Human Rights Watch*, 27 September 2014 (http://www.legal-tools.org/doc/e1f24e/).

victims and civil society organisations as a troubling signal in the context of Guinean authorities' stated intention to bring to justice the persons allegedly involved in the 28 September case.[88]

And yet, as of July 2017, after nearly eight years of a preliminary examination for a relatively simple case (by the ICC's usual standards), the matter remains in Phase III.

23.3.1.1.2.4. Nigeria

Since at least 2009, the Nigerian Islamist group Boko Haram has been engaged in a violent campaign to control large swaths of territory in Northern Nigeria and create an 'Islamic State'.[89] Nigerian Security Forces have resorted to scorched-earth tactics to combat this violent uprising.[90] The OTP has received communications regarding alleged crimes committed by both sides of the conflict. Nigeria ratified the Rome Statute in 2001. And the existence of a preliminary examination in respect of it was announced to the public in 2010 (and thus the preliminary examination has been opened since at least that time). As of 2012, the OTP had found that there was a reasonable basis to conclude that Boko Haram had committed crimes against humanity and thus the preliminary examination could enter Phase 3.[91]

In the meantime, there is compelling evidence that Nigeria is turning a blind eye to human rights abuses and grave law of war violations committed by its own security forces. According to the 2016 Report on Nigeria by Human Rights Watch:

> Authorities have rarely prosecuted members of the police and military implicated in abuses. While some soldiers have been prosecuted in military tribunals for offences such as cowardice and mutiny, the pervasive culture of impunity

---

[88] Office of the Prosecutor, 2016, p. 62, para. 276, see *supra* note 76.

[89] "Explaining Boko Haram, Nigeria's Islamist Insurgency", in *New York Times*, 10 November 2014.

[90] Adam Nossiter, "Massacre in Nigeria Ignites Outcry Over Military", in *New York Times*, 29 April 2013, A1.

[91] Office of the Prosecutor, 2012, p. 22, para. 96, see *supra* note 73.

---

means almost no one has been held to account for human rights crimes.[92]

The OTP has implicitly acknowledged this in its 2016 Report of Preliminary Examination Activities by alluding to Nigeria's domestic justice efforts in hypothetical and vague terms:

> Crimes allegedly committed by the Nigerian security forces that could fall under the Court's jurisdiction *would be* exclusively investigated and prosecuted by the military and would not fall under the jurisdiction of the Attorney-General of the Federation.
>
> [Both] the DPPF and the military authorities provided supporting material including investigative reports and case files regarding *potentially relevant* individual cases, which are subject to further examination by the Office.[93]

And yet, as of July 2017, the preliminary examination is still locked in Phase 3 admissibility stature.

23.3.1.1.2.5. Georgia

On gaining independence from the Soviet Union in 1991, Georgia was soon engaged in its own two-year civil war with separatists from the would-be breakaway region of South Ossetia. Upon cessation of hostilities in 1992, although mostly unrecognized by the rest of the world, South Ossetia announced it was seceding from Georgia. This extremely fraught situation erupted in renewed armed conflict during the first week of August 2008, with Russia involved on behalf of the South Ossetians this time. By 12 August 2008, a ceasefire had been negotiated, although crimes are alleged to have continued after that date. The five-day conflict claimed the lives of hundreds of civilians, left approximately 2,000 wounded and resulted in a reported 138,000 individuals being displaced, with many ethnic Georgian villages in South Ossetia destroyed. War crimes and crimes against humanity were allegedly committed by all three of the warring parties.

After receiving numerous communications, the OTP opened a preliminary examination of the situation in Georgia in August of 2008. After

---

[92] Human Rights Watch, "Nigeria", in *World Report 2016* (http://www.legal-tools.org/doc/24ed21/).

[93] Office of the Prosecutor, 2016, pp. 66–67, paras. 300–301, see supra note 76.

a late 2015 request, opening of a *proprio motu* investigation was authorized on 27 January 2016, nearly eight years after commencement of the preliminary examination. And this delay occurred in spite of the fact that, early on, there was ample evidence of crimes committed (thanks to NGO reports and a European Union fact-finding mission)[94] and that South Ossetia could not conduct legitimate proceedings as an unrecognized State.[95]

23.3.1.2. Preliminary Examinations Triggered by Referrals

23.3.1.2.1. Expeditious OTP Decisions

Preliminary examinations triggered by referrals have also seen significant timeline discrepancies. Many referral cases have been subjected to lightning-quick preliminary examinations. For example, on an April 2004 referral from the government of the Democratic Republic of the Congo, where large-scale war crimes and crimes against humanity have been committed as part of an internal armed conflict since the mid-1990s (including sectarian murder and rape in the bloody Ituri region), a mere two months of preliminary examination spawned an authorized investigation in June 2004. A slew of other State party referrals have also involved preliminary examinations of mere months, including Uganda (January 2004 referral and July 2004 investigation authorization – seven months), Mali (July 2012 referral with a January 2013 green light for the investigation – a six-month preliminary examination), Central African Republic II (May 2014 referral and a September 2014 investigation opening – a preliminary examination of only four months).

Preliminary examinations pursuant to Security Council referrals have been similarly brief. Based on Sudan's genocidal actions in Darfur, a March 2005 Security Council referral triggered only a three-month preliminary examination that ended with the start of an investigation in June 2005. Gross human rights violations committed against protesters in the

---

94 See, for example, Human Rights Watch, "Up in Flames: Humanitarian Law Violations and Civilian Victims in the Conflict over South Ossetia", 23 January 2009 (http://www.legal-tools.org/doc/0ccc21/; http://www.legal-tools.org/doc/ab3fc5/); Council of the European Union, *Independent International Fact-Finding Mission on the Conflict in Georgia: Report*, September 2009, vols. 1-3 (http://www.legal-tools.org/doc/b6be61/; http://www.legal-tools.org/doc/d0e020/; http://www.legal-tools.org/doc/c273c2/).

95 Coalition for the International Criminal Court, "Georgia", available at http://www.coalition fortheicc.org/country/georgia, last accessed on 11 January 2018.

---

waning days of the Muammar Gaddafi regime spurred a Security Council referral in February 2011. And an investigation was authorized in March. Thus, the preliminary examination lasted approximately one month.

This shortened version of the preliminary examination in referral situations even applies to cases not selected for investigation. In connection with Israel blockading the Gaza territory (controlled by the Hamas terrorist organization), in May 2010 a flotilla of boats sailed to the territory to break the blockade and purportedly provide humanitarian aid to Gaza residents. The boats were registered to Comoros, Greece, and Cambodia, among other countries. The Israeli government declared that the flotilla was organized to provoke Israel and manufacture a confrontation that would generate negative publicity against it. On 28 May, Israeli military forces boarded the ships to inspect them and were violently confronted by some of the pro-Palestinian flotilla activists. In response, Israeli military personnel used force. Ten activists were killed and many others were wounded. Flotilla activists claimed Israeli force was excessive.

On 14 May 2014, ICC State Party Comoros, to which one of the ships was registered, referred the matter to the OTP alleging commission of crimes within the Court's jurisdiction.[96] Less than six months later, on 6 November 2014, the Prosecutor terminated the preliminary examination, finding that the requirements for opening an investigation into the situation had not been met.

Following a request for review filed by the Comoros government, on 16 July 2015, Pre-Trial Chamber I requested the Prosecutor to reconsider her decision. On 6 November 2015, this decision was upheld by the Appeals Chamber.[97]

23.3.1.2.2. Delayed OTP Decisions

In large part, referrals tend to yield quick decisions. But one case in particular may be different. In January 2009, the Palestinian Authority submitted a declaration recognizing the Court's jurisdiction over alleged ICC subject-matter crimes committed on its territory. Upon receipt, the OTP opened a preliminary examination. Nearly four years later, in November

---

[96] International Criminal Court, *Registered Vessels of the Union of the Comoros, the Hellenic Republic and the Kingdom of Cambodia* (available on the Court's web site).

[97] *Ibid.*

2012, the OTP decided that, given Palestine's UN 'observer entity' status, the declaration could not be accepted and closed the preliminary examination. Then, in January 2015, after a change to 'non-member observer State' status for Palestine and the filing of a new declaration, a new preliminary examination was opened. Two and a half years later, the preliminary examination is still in Phase 2. In effect, the case has been in the 'preliminary examination twilight zone' for almost nine years.

23.3.2. Politicization of Cases

23.3.2.1. Personality-Driven Politics

It is important not to evaluate the inconsistent timelines in a vacuum. Rather, a significant part of the problem, apart from more structural obstacles such as resource constraints and barriers to evidence collection, is arguably attributable to political considerations exogenous to the merits of the case. Some of these political issues are circumstance-driven while others are personality-driven. With respect to the latter, the ICC's first Prosecutor, Luis Moreno-Ocampo, exerted a tremendous impact on case selection and processing, allegedly in reference to consideration of his legacy as well as a desire to be in the spotlight. In considering what lies behind the 'charges of politicization' directed toward Moreno-Ocampo, Kai Ambos noted that:

> The sad truth is that he is a prosecutor who prefers holding press conferences to reading files. He enjoys making grand statements about being "the world's most powerful prosecutor", but does not spend much time diligently assessing intricate legal matters. One particularly embarrassing scene in the documentary "Prosecutor", which tries to paint a flattering portrait of Moreno-Ocampo, shows him stepping out of a helicopter on to a muddy village square in the northeast of the Democratic Republic of the Congo, dressed in a spotless white suit. It gives the impression that he had come to this godforsaken place to lecture the people about the importance of international criminal justice.[98]

David Bosco of *The Atlantic* acknowledged Moreno-Ocampo's reputation as "a poor manager who enjoys the limelight a bit too much and

---

[98] Kai Ambos, "Slow Wheels of Justice: The ICC's Disappointing Track Record", in *Der Spiegel*, 14 December 2011.

speaks a bit too freely".[99] Given this situation, Bosco added, "the court has been beset by delays". Mark Kersten has observed that "Moreno-Ocampo's willingness to bluntly 'stick his fingers in it' has been a constant source of exasperation".[100] The African Union Commission's former Chairman, Jean Ping attributed the AU's ICC antipathy to Ocampo himself: "Frankly speaking, we are not against the International Criminal Court. What we are against is Ocampo's justice – the justice of a man".[101]

How does this relate to specific cases? The quick decisions to pursue investigations in DR Congo and Sudan, for example, arguably signified the Prosecutor's "rush to pursue high-profile indictments, contemporaneous with his pursuit of the 'low-hanging fruit' (supposedly easy cases such as that of Thomas Lubanga Dyilo [the first defendant brought to trial at the ICC in connection with the DR Congo investigation] suggest a prosecutor with sharp political instincts and a recognition of the need for a new institution to have a few 'quick wins'".[102] In contrast, in the non-African situations, where there was less immediate political gain and possible high political costs, such as in Iraq or Venezuela, Ocampo was quick to dispense with preliminary examinations.[103]

By the same token, delaying processing of cases with little political value but the potential for political trouble affected the preliminary examinations in non-African cases like Georgia, Palestine, Colombia and Afghanistan. And again, this is in contrast to headline-grabbing African cases like the Kenya post-election crisis that garnered high initial international interest in prosecution. As explained by Chandra Lekha Sriram:

> [In these cases] the relatively muted approach of the prosecutor is noteworthy. In a rare official public statement on a non-African situation, the office of the prosecutor issued a two-sentence statement on Georgia in 2008, simply stating that it was a state party to the statute of the Court and that the

---

[99] David Bosco, "Luis Moreno-Ocampo", in *The Atlantic*, November 2011.

[100] Mark Kersten, "The ICC's Next Top Prosecutor", in *Justice in Conflict*, 23 May 2011.

[101] Nicole Fritz, "Congo Provides Justice without Theatrics", in *War and Law*, 22 February 2011.

[102] Chandra Lekha Sriram, "The Prosecutor of the ICC: Too Political, Not Political Enough, or Both?", in *Human Rights and Human Welfare*, May 2009.

[103] *Ibid.*, noting the Prosecutor failed "to take up cases regarding abuses in places such as Iraq and Venezuela given the surrounding "political controversies".

Court considers all information pertaining to crimes within its jurisdiction. This is notable in comparison to the public statements indicating the willingness of the prosecutor to pursue investigations into post-election violence in Kenya if local or hybrid investigations do not go forward, which have been far more forceful. Two other situations which public statements by the office of the prosecutor indicate are "under examination" – Palestine and Afghanistan – have not been the subject of comparable public scrutiny, and indeed reference to examination of them can only be found in public documents from the office of the prosecutor at the end of a press release on Kenya investigations. [This] prosecutorial strategy – in terms of situations and individual cases, and in terms of timing of crucial steps and engagement with peace negotiations – illustrate an approach that is [...] highly political [...].[104]

Even if the current Prosecutor, Fatou Bensouda, has adopted a much less overtly political strategy, it is noteworthy that the preliminary examinations in non-African situations such as Colombia still drag on.[105] Bensouda took over as Prosecutor in 2012 when the Colombia case, as well as that of Afghanistan, had been mired in preliminary examination purgatory for several years. Six years later, with Bensouda at the helm, Colombia is still in the same place and the Afghanistan preliminary examination has only recently wrapped up.

23.3.2.2. Situation-Driven Politics

23.3.2.2.1. Palestine and Afghanistan

Apart from any personal agenda that the Prosecutor may have, certain situations may be hamstrung by the political controversy that they generate in their own right. As summarized by Carsten Stahn:

[The OTP's current roster of preliminary examinations includes] assessments of the some of the most politically sensitive contexts: submissions related to ill-treatment of detainees and unlawful killings by British troops in Iraq from 2003 to 2008, analysis of alleged crimes committed in the Israel-Palestine conflict, including the 2014 Gaza conflict and set-

---

[104] *Ibid.*

[105] The Afghanistan preliminary examination was finally wrapped up toward the end of 2017.

tlement activities in the West Bank and Jerusalem, review of violations committed in the Ukraine conflict (Maidan events, Eastern Ukraine and Crimea), and analysis of alleged crimes in Afghanistan by the Taliban, Afghan forces and members of US armed forces and the CIA, including abuse of detainees and use of prohibited interrogation techniques.[106]

Apart from the preliminary examination in Iraq, which has already closed, each of the current ongoing preliminary examinations just mentioned bears separate consideration here. The Palestine preliminary examination is a prime example. It is a politically-charged situation since, as has been noted:

> [The] Palestinians' dualistic bid [declaring and acceding] to join the International Criminal Court (ICC) amounts to lawfare, in that they are not motivated by ideals of international justice. Instead, they are trying to get the best possible political deal for themselves in joining the court with hopes of enjoying the maximum benefits to be gained from membership.[107]

And this engulfs the Court in the cross-currents of strong geopolitical dynamics that can affect its freedom of movement. Thomas Obel Hansen explains:

> Palestine joining the ICC may be more a question of playing politics and strengthening its position towards Israel – and the international community more broadly – than obtaining justice for the crimes committed during the conflict. At the same time, key players, including the US, have so far been opposing active ICC intervention in Palestine, raising questions as to whether the Court is capable of advancing its agenda in the face of great power resistance. The ICC depends on the support of powerful countries, in particular the permanent members of the United Nations Security Council.[108]

---

[106] Stahn, 2017, p. 2, see *supra* note 1.

[107] Nimrod Karin, "The Establishment of the International Criminal Tribunal for Palestine (Part II)", in *Just Security*, 22 January 2015.

[108] Thomas Obel Hansen, "What Are the Consequences of Palestine Joining the International Criminal Court?", in *E-International Relations*, 6 April 2015.

The Afghanistan preliminary examination, which dragged on for over a decade, was beset by comparable political pressures. According to David Bosco:

> Any investigation there would be politically fraught, however, because Chief Prosecutor Fatou Bensouda has received information about alleged U.S. torture in the country. And a serious investigation of those crimes might lead to scrutiny of former U.S. leaders. In late October, the prosecutor declared that a decision on Afghanistan was "imminent." Six months later, and without an explanation, no decision has been made.[109]

23.3.2.2.2. Ukraine

Finally, the preliminary examination in Ukraine is also a potential political minefield. That case stems from mass violence inflicted against citizens gathered in Kiev's Maidan Square to protest the refusal of the perceived Russian-controlled government to enact reforms and accede to the European Union. In the resulting turmoil, then-President Viktor Yanukovych was removed from power. Pro-Russian separatist rallies in the Crimea/Donbas regions following Yanukovych's ouster resulted in a military takeover in those territories and then a disputed annexation of Crimea by Russia. This, in turn, sparked an international armed conflict among Ukrainian, separatist, and Russian forces. In April 2014, the Ukrainian government submitted an Article 12(3) declaration accepting ICC jurisdiction over alleged Article 5 crimes connected to the Maidan Square violence. Upon receipt, the Prosecutor opened a preliminary examination. A second declaration submitted by Ukraine caused the OTP to later expand the probe to cover atrocities allegedly committed in connection with the armed conflict.

On November 14, in its Report on Preliminary Examinations, the OTP announced its preliminary conclusion that "there exists a sensible or reasonable justification for a belief that a crime falling within the jurisdiction of the Court 'has been or is being committed'" within the Crimean and Donbas territories of Ukraine. On issuance of the report, Russia declared that it would withdraw from the ICC because it "failed to meet the

---

[109] David Bosco, "15 Years on, the International Criminal Court Is Still Trying to Deliver on Its Promise", in *Washington Post*, 5 May 2017.

expectations to become a truly independent, authoritative international tribunal".[110] Despite the OTP's initial finding, the preliminary examination is still currently in the Phase 2 subject-matter jurisdiction stage.

But having drawn Russia's ire, the process is perceived as vulnerable to political pressure. This is especially true in the case of Ukraine, where there is the added Russian animus in reference to the investigation in Georgia. Russia has declaimed that the Georgia preliminary examination resulted in accusations against South-Ossetian militia and Russian soldiers, while investigations against Georgian government officials were left to the discretion of the national authorities. Considering these developments, Russia has indicated that it "can hardly trust the ICC".[111] And, thus, David Bosco notes that, in reference to Ukraine, the Court "has dipped in a toe but not yet committed to a full investigation".[112]

As a result, in relation to the ostensibly politically explosive preliminary examinations in relation to Afghanistan, Palestine and Ukraine, Bosco concludes:

> Taken together, [these preliminary examinations] will mark an important crossroads for the court. If [Prosecutor Fatou] Bensouda moves forward on those fronts, she may eventually seek to prosecute the citizens of powerful states that have spurned the court. And that will almost certainly provoke new political turbulence. If she avoids those battles, the accusations that the court is politically hobbled will intensify.[113]

23.3.2.3. Uneven Results

From our survey of preliminary examinations to date, the record is littered with poor choices, snap decisions, inconsistent positions and on-again-off-again probes. In Kenya, the Prosecutor's blitzkrieg preliminary examination led to an eventual unravelling of the case when crucial evidence ended up being unavailable. In DR Congo, an abbreviated two-month preliminary examination in 2004 yielded the Court's first trial on the relatively

---

[110] Sheena McKenzie, "Russia Quits International Criminal Court, Philippines May Follow", in *CNN*, 17 November 2016.

[111] *Ibid.*

[112] Bosco, 2017, see *supra* note 107.

[113] *Ibid.*

insignificant charges of recruitment and use of child soldiers. As critics have noted:

> Given the widespread allegations of systematic rape, sexual enslavement and other forms of sexualised violence by the UPC military group [of which Lubanga was the leader] in the Ituri region of the DRC, the charges against Lubanga were too narrow, with special criticism that gender-based crimes were not prosecuted. This became even more apparent as evidence of gender-based crimes came out repeatedly through documentary and viva voce evidence during the trial.[114]

This was followed by less than satisfying results in the Ituri-focused trials of two other Congolese warlords. In particular, Mathieu Ngudjolo Chui was acquitted and Germain Katanga was convicted strictly of being an accessory in respect of one February 2003 incident in an Ituri village and sentenced to only 12 years' imprisonment. Once again, experts accused the OTP of taking shortcuts. Per Phil Clark:

> The more important charges around whether Katanga orchestrated these massacres in Ituri province in northeastern Congo; whether he was responsible for rape, sexual slavery, and the use of child soldiers. They'll be disappointed that those charges didn't stick[...] The prosecution has cut corners [and] these cases haven't been systematically built.[115]

Other cases have suffered from a herky-jerky decision-making approach. Honduras is a prime example. Triggered by communications received at the end of 2010, the OTP opened a preliminary examination in reference to that troubled country. The examination was closed in 2013 for want of a reasonable basis to proceed. It was then opened again in 2014 and summarily closed again in 2015. In Côte d'Ivoire, a 2003 preliminary examination connected to alleged crimes committed as part of

---

[114] Danya Chaikel, "The Prosecutor v. Thomas Lubanga Dyilo: A Turbulent but Promising Retrospective", in *Hague Justice Portal*, 17 November 2011. Other DRC cases at the ICC appear to be constructed on similarly shaky foundations. Although the trial of Bosco Ntaganda is ongoing, the charges against Callixte Mbarushimana were not confirmed and Mathieu Ngudjolo Chui was acquitted. See ICC, "Situation in the Democratic Republic of the Congo" (available on the Court's web site).

[115] Henry Ridgwell, "International Criminal Court Convicts Congolese Warlord", in *Voice of America*, 7 March 2014.

---

the north-south civil war lay fallow for years until 2010 violence flowing from the same conflict brought it back to life in 2011.

The Palestinian matters are further evidence of a schizophrenic approach. As we saw in *Registered Vessels of the Union of the Comoros, the Hellenic Republic and the Kingdom of Cambodia*, a 14 May 2014 referral led to a termination of preliminary examination only months later on the grounds the investigation-opening requirements had not been met. However, upon Comoros's motion, Pre-Trial Chamber I requested the Prosecutor to reconsider her decision. And that yielded, in fairly quick order, an Appeals Chamber decision sustaining the PTC. Similarly, when the Palestinian Authority itself tendered a 2009 declaration accepting the Court's jurisdiction over alleged Israeli offences perpetrated on its territory, the OTP was quick to initiate a preliminary examination only to shut it down in 2012, given Palestine's UN 'observer entity' status. Then, in January 2015, after Palestinian deposit of instruments of ICC accession, yet a new preliminary examination was launched.

Questionable outcomes also extend to preliminary examinations wherein Phase 1-4 criteria seem satisfied but the matters languish nonetheless. After a decade of documenting Colombia's failures to render meaningful justice to victims of that country's civil war, the OTP's continuing reluctance to request authorization for an investigation flies in the face of its own triggering criteria. The Guinea preliminary examination is arguably even more egregious given a one-day single-crime-scene matter and dithering government justice efforts for nearly ten years. The OTP has become a passive observer, transitioning through Phases 1 through 3 and then glacially shambling through an incomplete Phase 4. The Nigeria preliminary examination is frozen in the same procedural posture, despite ample evidence of the government's criminality disincentivizing it to take meaningful justice measures.

23.4. A Proposed Solution: Creation of the Office of the Examining Magistrate

23.4.1. Background

So how can the beneficial aspects of the ICC preliminary examination – new atrocity deterrence, peace negotiations fillip, and transitional justice facilitator – be preserved while curbing the temporal disparities, personal agendas, political pressures and compromised justice just documented? In answering this question, it is worth remembering that judicial oversight is a hallmark in ICC procedure. In an effort to convince the world's super-powers – especially the United States – that a politically-minded maverick prosecutor would not go on a figurative witch-hunt, tight control of the Prosecutor's investigatory prerogatives was built into the Rome Statute. It is exercised at various junctures throughout the investigative and prosecutorial phases with one glaring exception – the preliminary examination. In effect, from a judicial supervision perspective, the preliminary examination represents an evidence-collection blind spot. In other words, the Rome Statute's framers gave free rein for the Prosecutor to go on a pre-situation fishing expedition without time limit.

So it is posited that removing the blind spot will solve the problem. But what is the optimal way to achieve this? Rather than simply extending the Pre-Trial Chamber's writ to include preliminary examination oversight, this chapter proposes a solution that can be more proactive in terms of promoting prosecutor-defence equality of arms and sensitivity to victims' rights, while preserving the benefits of deterrence and positive complementarity. At the same time, it can offer a judicial authority with oversight capability but also with specialized expertise in preliminary examination techniques and issues. This is possible through creation of an 'Office of the Examining Magistrate'. As this proposal is based in part on the traditional civil law inquisitorial model, which Jacqueline Hodgson describes as a possible means of better controlling "discretion in the exercise of [investigatory powers]",[116] as well as that of the Office of the Co-Investigating Judges at the Extraordinary Chambers in the Courts of Cambodia, those institutions will be examined first. From that foundation, the details of the proposed ICC OEM will be considered.

---

[116] Jacqueline Hodgson, "The Police, The Prosecutor and the Juge d'Instruction: Judicial Supervision in France, Theory and Practice", in *British Journal of Criminology*, 2001, vol. 41, no. 2, p. 342.

23.4.2. Foundations: The Civil Law Examining Magistrate and the ECCC's Office of Co-Investigating Judges

23.4.2.1. The Traditional Civil Law Examining Magistrate

23.4.2.1.1. Background

The Examining Magistrate is a traditional feature of civil law jurisdictions such as France, Spain, Belgium and the Netherlands.[117] The criminal procedure of these jurisdictions is characterized by an 'inquisitorial' system, which denotes "an official inquiry, in contrast to the contest or dispute that characterizes the adversarial process [as found in England and the United States, for example]".[118] The centrepiece of that 'inquiry' is conducted by the Examining Magistrate (*juge d'instruction* in France, *juez de instrucción* in Spain, and *onderzoeksrechter* in the Netherlands).

23.4.2.1.2. A Tripartite System with Victim Participation

A helpful model for this chapter's proposal is provided in the French system, where the examining magistrate's traditional role in cases of serious crimes fits within a tripartite pre-appeal criminal justice process. It begins with a case initiation phase via the police/prosecutor (or by a complaint filed by a private citizen), 'instruction' under the aegis of the examining magistrate, and pre-trial/trial phase presided over by an adjudicating judge/jury (that is first filtered by a *Chambre des Mises en Accusation* – somewhat akin to a grand jury in American criminal procedure).[119]

It should be noted that the French system, consistent with its sister civil law jurisdictions, also allows a citizen to institute a separate civil case (*action civile*) arising from the crime at issue by filing a formal declaration demanding reparation.[120] This is significant since, as we shall see,

---

[117] It should be noted that the traditional role of the examining magistrate has been reduced or eliminated in many civil law jurisdictions. Illustrative, in this regard, is France, which Jacqueline Hodgson explains, has seen "a shift of power away [...] from the juge d'instruction in favour of the procureur giving her significant dispositive powers". Jacqueline Hodgson, "The French Prosecutor in Question", in *Washington and Lee Law Review*, 2010, vol. 67, no. 4, p. 1362.

[118] Harry R. Dammer and Jay S. Albanese, *Comparative Criminal Justice Systems*, 5th edition, Wadsworth Publishing, Boston, 2012, p. 128.

[119] Doris Jonas Freed, "Aspects of French Criminal Procedure", in *Louisiana Law Review*, 1957, vol. 17, no. 4, pp. 734–735, 741–744.

[120] *Ibid.*, pp. 734–735.

---

the ICC's victim-centred schema is largely modelled on this feature. It therefore provides greater conceptual support for the notion of instituting the OEM, which is clearly of a piece with the ICC's inspirational template.

Within the tripartite system outlined above, there is a rather symbiotic relationship between the prosecutor and the examining magistrate. The prosecutor's office initiates the case via citizen's complaint or *sua sponte* filing. But then it is turned over to the examining magistrate for further investigation. Doris Jonas Freed explains the range of the examining magistrate's activities at this juncture in the French system:

> To carry out his duties effectively, the *juge d'instruction* is given extensive authority. He may issue warrants of detention [...] make searches and seizures, order a visit to the scene of the crime, and require expert testimony. If proceedings must be held outside the jurisdiction of the *juge*, he can issue letters rogatory to a *juge* in the proper jurisdiction empowering him to hold the necessary hearings. The formal investigation is a secret proceeding before the *juge* and his clerk in which the *juge* examines and cross-questions witnesses and confronts them with the accused.[121]

23.4.2.1.3. The End-Phase for the Examining Magistrate

The results of the investigation, including the depositions of any testimony, are rendered in an expository document with supporting exhibits. This constitutes the '*dossier*' of the case. Based on this record, the examining magistrate makes recommendations for further action to the prosecutor, to whom he refers the entire record.[122] After that referral, the prosecutor has a period of time in which to plead (that is, to frame the case for trial-level proceedings). It should be noted that, in cases of insufficient basis for proceeding, the examining magistrate has the option of entering an *ordonnance de non-lieu*, similar to a *nolle prosequi* in American law (a dismissal of the case).[123]

---

[121] *Ibid.*, p. 732.

[122] *Ibid.*, p. 733.

[123] *Ibid.*

23.4.2.1.4. The System's Advantages

Although the prosecutor in the French system is technically regarded as part of the judiciary and an 'officer of the court', Jacqueline Hodgson has commented on the fundamentally adversarial nature of her writ. Thus, the examining magistrate is crucial in terms of furnishing a kind of "independence of the criminal justice system".[124] She refers to this as a crucial "due process protection" in the form of "judicial oversight provided by the officer in control of the investigation – an investigation that does not focus simply on the suspect, but which is oriented towards the discovery of both incriminating and exculpating evidence".

The French themselves see greater efficiency and procedural fairness in this arrangement *vis-à-vis* the more strictly adversarial process with the prosecutor assuming sole investigative duties. In the words of former French Justice Minister Élisabeth Guigou, in addressing the *Sénat* on 15 June 1999:

> The adversarial system of justice is by nature unfair and unjust. It favours the strong over the weak [...] Our own system is better, both in terms of efficiency and the rights of the individual. I prefer, and I want to make this quite plain, an independent judge who investigates evidence both for and against the suspect, to police officers who carry out large parts of the criminal investigation without any judicial supervision.[125]

23.4.2.2. The Internationalization of the Examining Magistrate: The Office of the Co-Investigating Judges at the ECCC

23.4.2.2.1. Background

The examining magistrate model has been implemented at the international level by the Extraordinary Chambers in the Courts of Cambodia ('ECCC'), which was established pursuant to an agreement between the Cambodian government and the United Nations to render justice in relation to the crimes of the Khmer Rouge regime. In contrast to previous *ad hoc* or hybrid internationalized tribunals whose criminal procedure was

---

[124] Hodgson, 2010, pp. 1362–1363, see *supra* note 115.

[125] Jacqueline Hodgson, *French Criminal Justice: A Comparative Account of the Investigation and Prosecution of Crime in France*, Hart Publishing, Portland, 2005, p. 28.

---

modelled on the adversarial schema, the ECCC follows the French inquisitorial template (including the *juge d'instruction*) incorporated into Cambodian law during its colonial time.

23.4.2.2.2. Role of the Co-Investigating Judges

Thus, pre-trial investigations at the ECCC are carried out not by the Prosecution and the Defence but by the two Co-Investigating Judges (one international and one domestic – in line with the 'hybrid' nature of the institution). After initial referral of the matter by the Co-Prosecutors via an 'Introductory Submission' (setting out the basic case parameters – the prosecution may also file so-called 'Supplementary Submissions', if any new information comes into its possession), the Co-Investigating Judges ('CIJs') begin an investigation.[126]

The CIJs are tasked with gathering evidence in order to determine: (1) whether the information in the Introductory Submission constitute crimes within the subject-matter jurisdiction of the ECCC; (2) whether the suspects identified were senior leaders or most responsible for the crimes at issue); and (3) whether the person under investigation should be bound over for trial or released for want of sufficient evidence.[127]

In performing these tasks, the CIJs are under a duty to: (1) investigate impartially with a view to finding evidence regardless of whether it is incriminating or exculpatory; (2) act independently and not accept or seek any instructions from any government or any other source; (3) strike a balance among the interests and rights of the different parties, that is, defence, victims and prosecution; and (4) conduct the investigation under confidentiality in order to protect the rights and interests of the Parties, especially the presumption of innocence, to allow for potential protective measures for the identity of witnesses and victims, and to conduct an efficient and effective investigation.[128]

---

[126] Extraordinary Chambers in the Courts of Cambodia, "Office of the Co-Investigating Judges" (available on their web site).

[127] *Ibid.*

[128] *Ibid.*

23.4.2.2.3. Concluding Duties

At the conclusion of an investigation, the CIJs notify the parties who then have fifteen days to request further investigative action. At the expiration of this period, the CIJs forward the case file to the Co-Prosecutors, who issue a written final submission, wherein they may request that the CIJs indict the suspect at issue or dismiss the case. Not bound by the Co-Prosecutors' submissions, the CIJs will issue a 'Closing Order' consisting of either an indictment or dismissal – both of which are subject to appeal by the Co-Prosecutors (and by the defendant and/or civil parties pursuant to certain conditions/limitations).[129]

If no appeal is filed against a Closing Order, in the case of indictment, the CIJs forward the case file to the Trial Chamber so that a trial date can be set (or to the archives in case of dismissal). From this point forward, the CIJs play no further role in the case. If new evidence becomes available subsequent to a dismissal, though, the judicial investigation may be re-opened by the CIJs upon request of the Co-Prosecutors.

23.4.2.2.4. Benefits of the ECCC's Co-Investigating Judges Framework

In the context of an internationalized mass crimes tribunal, the CIJ model is beneficial both in terms of procedural fairness and restorative justice responsiveness.[130] With regard to the former, the mechanism may be viewed as superior in terms of its truth-seeking function. As explained by Lise Reuss Muff:

> The introduction of investigating judges, whose sole purpose is to conduct an impartial investigation, examining all kinds of evidence regardless of its nature, is a better guarantee of the factual correctness of the findings than leaving the investigative responsibility with the respective parties. No facts will be hidden even though neither the defense nor the pros-

---

[129] *Ibid.*

[130] That said, it does have a dysfunctional quality linked to its dual domestic-international identity. This embeds a kind of schizophrenic quality to the office as disagreements between the Cambodian and the expatriate CIJs can irretrievably gridlock proceedings. See Lise Reuss Muff, "The Investigating Judges within the ECCC: Beneficial or a Bureaucratic Burden?", in *Documentation Centre of Cambodia*, Summer 2011, p. 42 ("Having two Co-Investigating judges has caused numerous suspicions and distrust in the system.") (http://www.legal-tools.org/doc/d8e9a5/).

ecutor might find a particular interest in them, and the final result and thereby the events found to have occurred should only to a very limited extent depend on the skills and capabilities of the lawyers in question but instead reflect the reality. Rather than being viewed as a dispute between parties, the inquisitorial process is thought of as an official and thorough inquiry, and the vital role of the trial judge combined with the impartial investigation of the investigating judge ensures the best possible investigation of the virtual reality.[131]

At the same time, as the ECCC takes into account the interests of victims and makes them juridical parties, the CIJ schema also serves the interests of restorative justice. The CIJs, as neutral probers focused on gathering all relevant evidence pursuant to no litigation agenda, can organically take victims' interests into account throughout the investigatory process.[132]

23.4.3. Integrating the Office of the Examining Magistrate into the ICC Preliminary Examination Framework

In considering introduction of the OEM to the ICC preliminary examination process, it is necessary to examine four main aspects of the proposal: (1) the stages of the process; (2) the timeline of the process; (3) other logistical considerations; and (4) potential benefits of the process. Each of these shall be considered in turn.

23.4.3.1. The Stages of the Process

In general, tracking the chronology of initial case management, six main stages can be discerned: (1) OTP initial intake; (2) OTP referral to the OEM; (3) OEM initial intake credibility assessment; (4) conduct of the Phases 2 through 4 probe; (5) OEM submission of a dossier to the OTP; and (6) OTP request for additional examination period or application to the Pre-Trial Chamber to open an investigation. It is helpful to unpack each of these stages.

---

[131] *Ibid.*, p. 25.
[132] *Ibid.*

23.4.3.1.1. Stage 1: OTP Initial Intake

According to this proposal, initial receipt of communications and referrals would still go through the OTP. In this way, the OTP could take initial decisions regarding patently frivolous communications and filter them out. At the same time, for communications that appear facially plausible, as well as for State or Security Council referrals, this preliminary intake function permits the OTP to register case-initiation activity and put in place any case-tracking mechanisms. More generally, especially in light of the initial filtering, it signifies that the OTP remains an important actor in the preliminary examination process. In other words, while the OEM will assume the central probing function during the preliminary examination, as confirmed by the OTP role in subsequent stages of the process, it will not monopolize it.

23.4.3.1.2. Stage 2: The OTP's Referral to the OEM

Assuming the communication or referral is facially plausible, the OTP will transfer the matter to the OEM to conduct the balance of preliminary examination activities. It should be noted that, either way, the OTP will be required to respond to the author of the communication within a reasonable amount of time (six months are recommended here). That response must indicate that no further action will be taken at that time or that the matter will be referred to the OEM. In cases of non-referral, the author of the communication shall have the right to appeal the non-referral to the OEM. The relevant regulations shall specify that the OTP's initial decision must be granted great deference and the OEM may only open a file in such cases if the OTP has engaged in abuse of discretion.

23.4.3.1.3. Stage 3: The OEM's Own Initial Intake Credibility Assessment

Of course, assuming the matter is transferred to the OEM, it must then make an independent initial credibility determination. Thus, assuming OTP transfer of what it perceives as a facially credible communication, a second set of eyes at the OEM may find a fault not at first transparent. In this sense, it can be said that the OTP and the OEM would share Phase 1 responsibilities. Of course, if the OEM has questions for the OTP concerning its initial assessment, it can communicate with the OTP to request any relevant information.

23.4.3.1.4. Stage 4: Conduct of the Phases 2 through 4 Probe

Conduct of the Phases 2 through 4 probe is the heart of the process. As we have seen, Article 15(2) of the Rome Statute clarifies the scope of would-be OEM activities: (1) seeking additional information from States, organs of the United Nations, intergovernmental or non-governmental organizations, or other reliable sources that the office considers germane; and (2) receiving written or oral testimony at the seat of the Court.[133]

This could entail, as noted earlier, field visits to implicated countries "to consult with the competent national authorities, the affected communities and other relevant stakeholders, such as civil society organisations".[134] Thus, consistent with OTP policy, the OEM would likely scrutinize "the general context within which the alleged crimes, in particular, sexual and gender based crimes, have occurred and [assess] the existence of local institutions, international organisations, non-governmental organisations and other entities available as potential sources of information and/or of support for victims".[135]

Moreover, per the interpretation of preliminary examination scope put forth by Hector Olásolo, Article 15(2) of the Rome Statute may permit the OEM to avail itself of certain limited forms of non-coercive State Party co-operation provided for in Article 93, including: (1) identifying and locating persons or items; (2) questioning victims and witnesses on a voluntary basis on the territory of States Parties; (3) serving documents, including those of a judicial nature; (4) seeking records and documents, including those of an official nature; (5) inspecting places or sites; and (6)

---

[133] ICC Statute, Article 15(2) ((1) seeking additional information from States, organs of the United Nations, intergovernmental or non-governmental organizations, or other reliable sources that the office considers germane; and (2) receiving written or oral testimony at the seat of the Court).

[134] OTP, *Policy Paper on Preliminary Examinations*, 2013, para. 85, see *supra* note 14 ("to consult with the competent national authorities, the affected communities and other relevant stakeholders, such as civil society organisations").

[135] *Ibid.*, para. 86 ("[examine] the general context within which the alleged crimes, in particular, sexual and gender- based crimes, have occurred and [assess] the existence of local institutions, international organisations, non-governmental organisations and other entities available as potential sources of information and/or of support for victims").

seeking other types of assistance not of a coercive nature and not forbidden by the law of the requested State.[136]

It should be noted that, during this phase, the OTP may receive additional related information or develop additional insights while the OEM carries on its examination. The OTP will have the opportunity and, indeed, would be encouraged to share this information or these insights with the OEM during this period. Similarly, if the OEM has questions regarding the matters under examination, it can get in contact with the OTP to pose those questions. It could be, for example, that the OTP is working on an authorized investigation whose subject matter dovetails into an OEM preliminary examination. In such cases, to the extent no conflicting policies were implicated, it would promote both efficiency and investigatory coherence to allow the two offices to communicate with one another and share relevant information.

23.4.3.1.5. Stage 5: OEM Submission of a Dossier to the OTP

Analogous to the *modus operandi* in civil law jurisdictions and at the ECCC, the OEM would conclude its preliminary examination activities with submission to the OTP of a dossier announcing and supporting its conclusions. Where Phases 2 through 4 were satisfied, the OEM would certify to the OTP that the latter could file a request with the Pre-Trial Chamber to open a full-fledged investigation. If the conduct of the preliminary examination established failure to satisfy any of those phases, then the dossier would so indicate and advise terminating the matter without prejudice.

Thus, for instance, if the OEM concluded that the preliminary facts alleged suggested commission of crimes such as narcotics trafficking and terrorism not amounting to genocide, crimes against humanity or war crimes, it would recommend termination based on failure to satisfy Phase 2. To take another example, assuming Phase 2 were satisfied but the OEM concluded that the domestic jurisdiction was engaged in genuine justice

---

[136] Olásolo, 2005, p. 60, see *supra* note 6 ((1) identifying and locating persons or items; (2) questioning victims and witnesses on a voluntary basis on the territory of States Parties; (3) serving documents, including those of a judicial nature; (4) seeking records and documents, including those of an official nature; (5) inspecting places or sites; and (6) seeking other types of assistance not of a coercive nature and not forbidden by the law of the requested state).

efforts, thus signifying inadmissibility, then it could draft its dossier to recommend case closure.

23.4.3.1.6. Stage 6: OTP Follow-Up

On return of the case file to the OTP, the Prosecutor has a number of options depending on the recommendation. If the OEM finds each phase has been satisfied, and, upon receipt of the dossier, the Prosecutor is in accord with the recommendation to proceed to the next stage, she may apply to the Pre-Trial Chamber to open a full investigation (much as she would without the OEM dossier under the current system).

Alternatively, it is possible the Prosecutor could disagree. For example, she might have a different take on the Phase 4 determination regarding interests of justice. Significantly, the proposed new framework does not provide the OEM with the right of appeal – the decision of the Prosecutor not to request opening a full investigation must be accepted from the OEM perspective. This is part of the balancing of power between the OTP and the OEM, ultimately continuing to vest case strategy decisions with the OTP.

That said, in the case of a referral, per Article 53, at the request of the referring State or the Security Council, the Pre-Trial Chamber may review the Prosecutor's decision not to proceed. And the same would be true if the OEM recommends not proceeding and the Prosecutor accepts that decision – the new framework would not amend Article 53 in this regard.

Similarly, if closure is recommended by the OEM instead, the Prosecutor can accept that too. On the other hand, if she concludes closure is premature or unjustified, the restructuring proposed herein gives her options.

If she believes further probing is necessary, and there is still time on the preliminary examination clock (timing will be discussed below but an initial preliminary examination of 24 months is recommended), she could file a motion for reconsideration of case closure with the OEM. Based on a review of the dossier, that motion would require specifying the particular grounds for reconsideration – for example, internal inconsistencies in the dossier or receipt of new information casting doubt on the OEM's recommendation. The framework would allow for an appeal to the Pre-Trial Chamber if the OEM denied the motion for reconsideration.[137]

On the other hand, if case closure were recommended based on failure to satisfy one or more of Phases 2-4 (at the conclusion of the regular time frame), the OTP could apply for a 12-month extension to the Pre-Trial Chamber directly.[138] If such extension were granted, both offices could continue the preliminary examination activities outlined above as well as liaise with each other (as will be explained below).

In any event, were the OTP still resolved that the case should go forward against the OEM's recommendation and denial of the motion to extend by the Pre-Trial Chamber, the matter could be resubmitted as a new file to the OEM for a fresh preliminary examination if new facts or circumstances so warranted.

23.4.3.2. Timeline Parameters

23.4.3.2.1. Baseline Ceiling with Extension Mechanisms

Chronological considerations are key given the inconsistent timelines considered above. Thus, the new OEM framework proposes a fixed, baseline time-limit of 24 months to conduct the preliminary examination. At the end of that period, the OEM will need to submit a dossier to the OTP. If the preliminary examination can be completed in less time than that, the OEM is permitted to submit the dossier to the OTP at any point in advance (but not before the expiration of the initial mandatory six-month period, as set forth below).

---

[137] Appellate jurisdiction at the ICC is currently vested exclusively in the Appeals Division. See ICC Statute, Articles 81 and 82. The proposal herein would call for modifying the Rome Statute to give a limited appellate function to the Pre-Trial Division in reference to review of preliminary examination initiation, closure and extension decisions by the OEM. It is submitted that this works best as the OEM has a quasi-investigative function and the Pre-Trial Division considers requests for initiation of investigations.

[138] This application would go the Pre-Trial Chamber in the interests of efficiency. As set forth below, the OEM will also be eligible to apply for an extension (with a presumption that it will be granted as this will be effected through filing a notice of extension) – and that application would go the PTC. Presumably, if the OEM had determined that additional time had been needed, it would have applied on its own for an extension with the PTC in the first place. Having the OTP apply to the OEM, when it is likely the OEM has already determined that additional time is not needed, will most likely be a futile effort. Thus, having the OTP apply directly to the PTC makes more sense and promotes efficiency.

It is quite possible, of course, that either or both offices believe(s) more time is needed beyond the 24-month ceiling. First, as mentioned previously, the OTP can apply to the OEM for 12-month extensions. Second, the OEM can also file a notice of 12-month extension with the Pre-Trial Chamber. In such cases, the default will be acceptance of the extension. However, the OEM will be required to justify the extension in the notice via the Pre-Trial Chamber convening a show-cause hearing. If, pursuant to the show-cause hearing, the Pre-Trial Chamber believes the extension is not justified, it will have the power to terminate the preliminary examination.

Alternatively, the OEM may conclude at the end of the 24-month period that an investigation should not be opened. That conclusion, as well as the grounds for supporting it, will be communicated to the OTP via the dossier. However, the OTP may conclude that additional time is necessary. In that case, the OTP can file a motion to the Pre-Trial Chambers to extend the preliminary examination period for 12-months. If the motion is granted, upon expiration of the added 12-month period, the OTP can apply for another 12-month extension.

One can easily imagine how this might play out. In a country where a civil war appears to be winding down, the OEM might determine that, by the end of the 24-month default period, that the government has begun making genuine efforts to investigate and/or prosecute those most responsible for war crimes and crimes against humanity. Thus, admissibility would not lie and the case would fail at Phase 3. On reviewing the dossier, however, the Prosecutor might conclude that the government's justice efforts were ill-formed or too embryonic at that stage. It could thus request that the Pre-Trial Chamber grant the 12-month extension (and possibly new ones after expiration of the first).

23.4.3.2.2. Baseline Floor with Reduction Mechanism

At the other end of the spectrum, the OTP's record of relatively snap decisions regarding requests for investigation (for example, Libya – one month; DR Congo – two months; Sudan – three months; Central African Republic II – four months) mandate a minimum preliminary examination period as well. It is posited that a six-month minimum preliminary examination-period be established. If the OTP can show exigent circumstances (as supported by the OEM's transmittal dossier), then the six-month floor could be lifted upon successful motion to the Pre-Trial Chamber.

23.4.3.2.3. The Importance of Default Time Markers

It might be argued that the litigation activities surrounding departures from the proposed default timelines makes them more trouble than they are worth. But it is submitted that would not be the case. It is true that departures entail requests and/or notices and that appeals may flow from them. But that actually creates an incentive to finish the work within the default period. Besides, the suggested parameters are only advisory at this point and they could be adjusted with experience. But setting normative chronological points of repair will arguably affect internal work-clocks in a positive way that promotes greater efficiency and consistency. At the same time, in the truly difficult cases, the means for adjustment are available. This should give all the actors, as well as the international community, the benefit of greater consistency with the needed ability to inject flexibility into the process when truly called for.

23.4.3.3. Other Logistical Considerations

23.4.3.3.1. Public Communications during the Preliminary Examination Period

To date, the Prosecutor's public communications regarding preliminary examinations appear to be a double-edged sword. On the one hand, they may be said to help spur positive complementarity. On the other hand, especially in reference to the ICC's first Prosecutor, Luis Moreno-Ocampo, they arguably smack of grandstanding. It is submitted here that the visible presence of the OEM during on-site visits to the countries in question, along with outreach efforts to other stakeholders both internationally and in the region, should be a sufficient incentive for inspiring municipal justice efforts, deterring fresh violence or sparking peace negotiations. At the same time, perceptions of the integrity of the process, as well as an effort at depoliticization related to all preliminary examination activities, mandate prohibiting OTP public statements regarding the preliminary examination during the preliminary examination period. In an effort to further promote positive complementarity during this time, it is recommended that the new OEM continue the OTP's recent practice of publishing an annual report detailing preliminary examination activities for each open file.

23.4.3.3.2. Personnel and Resources

Although the precise details are beyond the scope of this chapter, it is worth commenting on the size and scope of the proposed OEM. Even if the proposal calls for only one Examining Magistrate to run the office and make final decisions, that judicial officer would be supported by a large staff with investigators, analysts and support staff. Presumably, a series of senior investigators would lead the examination of each individual matter, supported by teams of line investigators. The senior investigators would in turn report to the Examining Magistrate. The office would also have a Clerk, who would take care of all records, resource management, translators, and court staff (for depositions, hearings and related proceedings).

23.4.3.3.3. Examining Magistrate Selection and Placement within the ICC's Organizational Hierarchy

Although, to a certain extent, the OEM would work in tandem with the OTP and would have an investigative function, its primary nature would be as a judicial organ. The Examining Magistrate is conceived as a judicial officer who engages in preliminary examination-focused research and exercises a quasi-judicial function *vis-à-vis* the OTP. In this sense, it might be said that the Examining Magistrate is at the low-end of the ICC judicial hierarchy. Nevertheless, her office should be within the supervision and administration of the ICC's judicial branch.

The Court currently organizes itself into three divisions: Pre-Trial, Trial and Appeals Divisions. Pursuant to this chapter's proposal, the Court would be divided into four divisions, with the addition of the new 'Examining Magistrate Division'.

Finally, as a member of the judicial branch, the Examining Magistrate should be nominated by the President of the ICC and selected by majority vote of the Assembly of States Parties. She would be selected for a term of nine years and not eligible for re-election thereafter. She should have criminal investigation as well as judicial experience. And she should be chosen from among persons of high moral character, impartiality and integrity who possess the qualifications required for appointment to the highest judicial offices in her home jurisdiction.

23.5. Potential Advantages and Disadvantages to Integrating the OEM into the Existing Structure

23.5.1. An Analysis of Potential Advantages

In discussing the brief of the CIJs at the ECCC, Lise Reuss Muff has referred to the Ciorciari- Heindel framework of three objectives underlying the work at that institution: retributive justice, procedural justice and restorative justice.[139] That objectives-framework is effective for assessing this chapter's proposal to institute the OEM in the ICC's preliminary examination process.

23.5.1.1. Promoting Retributive Justice

Promoting retributive justice is essentially coextensive with laying the proper investigative/prosecutorial foundation in the interests of combating a culture of impunity in reference to atrocity crimes.[140] How is creation of the OEM, and its attendant framework modifications, advantageous in this regard? The answer lies primarily in specialization, concentration and efficiency. With respect to specialization, the proposed schema would establish an office focused exclusively on conducting preliminary examinations and thereby developing expertise to conduct them more effectively. This likely means more expeditious processing in terms of initial intake, better cultivation of research sources and skills consciously honed to verify background facts (thus, for example, creation of more effective general databases and NGO contacts), developing the most efficient protocols for preliminary examination-focused on-the-ground visits (consultations, inspections, etc.), and better sensitization to the reasonable basis standard in reference to various permutations of the ICC's core crimes.

Regarding concentration, the proposed time limits mean diving head first into the preliminary examination with a view to processing information to assemble a dossier that will serve as the bedrock for any future investigation or prosecution. Linked to this, of course, is efficiency – superior distillation through the compressed time frame and heightened

---

[139] Muff, 2011, pp. 23–24, *supra* note 128, citing John D. Ciorciari and Anne Heindel, *On Trial: The Khmer Rouge Accountability Process*, Documentation Centre of Cambodia, Phnom Penh, 2009, pp. 16–18.

[140] *Ibid.*, p. 24, noting that the "retributive aspect of justice deals with the punishment and condemnation of the offender [...]".

issue-spotting capability owing to refined expertise means the preliminary examination's fine points will not elude the OEM, while evidence will not grow stale nor witness memories fade.

And this, in turn, is linked to positive complementarity, deterrence and peace-promotion. Arguably, many preliminary examinations under the current system have turned into a metaphorical dance between the OTP and the State. The former dangles the threat of a full-fledged investigation while the latter does just enough to stave it off. We see this now in Colombia and Guinea, for example. With a dedicated Examining Magistrate and a 24-month ceiling, States will likely have better incentives for implementing domestic justice measures in a more timely and efficacious manner. And to the extent State actors may have a hand in atrocity crimes, the OEM schema will, for the same reasons, constitute a superior deterrence mechanism.

23.5.1.2. Promoting Procedural Justice

While retributive justice focuses on the *prosecutor*'s objective in seeking punishment, procedural justice centres on the potential *defendant*'s interest in fairness in terms of having his rights respected throughout the process.[141] While this may seem a bit amorphous at the preliminary examination stage (given that cases against specific defendants have not yet materialized), it still has important implications. For example, certain preliminary examinations are more limited in scope and clearly envisage the potential culpability of specific, identifiable high-level leaders. The Guinea preliminary examination, for instance, whose scope is limited to the 28 September 2009 Conakry Stadium massacre, necessarily contemplates the junta members in charge of the security forces that beat, raped and murdered civilians that day. This is especially true of junta leader Moussa Dadis Camara, who fled to Burkina Fasso soon after the massacre (in fact, domestic charges have been filed against Camara but the case has stalled).[142] In the meantime, as preliminary examinations languish, the proverbial Sword of Damocles hangs over these probable defendants. The proposed creation of the OEM, with its tight timelines and concentrated focus, would not allow such a cloud to hang over these actors indefinitely.

---

[141] Reuss Muff speaks broadly of "the procedural aspects [addressing] the holding of fair trials". *Ibid.*

[142] "Guinea Stadium Massacre: Former Ruler Camara Indicted", in *BBC News*, 9 July 2015.

On the flip-side, it would prevent the OTP from moving forward with an investigation, and thus immediately casting suspicion on certain suspects, straight after receipt of communications or referrals.

The other clear advantage in terms of procedural justice relates to equality of arms. Given that the current preliminary examination process largely tracks the adversarial model of investigation, the Prosecutor alone gathers evidence. True, the Rome Statute has her pay lip service to impartial investigation. As I have noted previously:

> [The] Prosecutor is not merely an adversarial party to the proceedings. As set forth in Article 54 of the Rome Statute, she is bound to search for, gather, and pass on to the defense both incriminating and exonerating evidence equally. In this sense, the Prosecutor acts as an "organ of justice" rather than just an opposing party in a contest.[143]

That said, I have also pointed out the imbalance that permeates the system, notwithstanding a nominally less adversarial role for the Prosecutor. In particular, "a predominately adversarial model invests the prosecution with a significant resource advantage over the defense and provides institutional channels of communication with governments, typically not available to the defense, that significantly facilitate collection of evidence". In light of this, and the more balanced calibration of forces in the inquisitorial system, I have called for a hybrid approach:

> A hybrid procedure might employ a specially designated pre-trial judge to participate in or oversee the collection of evidence. This would promote "equality of arms" by helping to facilitate defense collection of evidence abroad and ensure prosecutorial disclosure of exculpatory evidence. The ICC system, seeking to expand defendants' due process rights, already involves a certain degree of judicial pre-trial oversight of the prosecutor. A hybrid system extending that oversight to the collection of evidence would further level the playing field while preserving the inherent assiduousness of prosecutorial investigation.[144]

---

[143] Gregory S. Gordon, "Toward an International Criminal Procedure: Due Process Aspirations and Limitations", in *Columbia Journal of Transnational Law*, 2007, vol. 45, no. 3, p. 661.

[144] *Ibid.*, pp. 707–708.

The creation of the OEM, as proposed herein, entails the hybrid approach just described. It does so at the preliminary examination stage, thus dividing investigative responsibilities with the OTP early on in the life of the case and promoting equality of arms.

23.5.1.3. Promoting Restorative Justice

If retributive justice tends to be more prosecutor-oriented and procedural justice defence-oriented, restorative justice puts the emphasis on the victim.[145] In this sense, the inquisitorial nature of the proposed preliminary examination restructuring – via addition of the OEM – has two distinct advantages. First, as was true for potential defendants, the Examining Magistrate would proceed with a wider institutional mission and focus than the Prosecutor. Thus, the interests of victims in compiling the preliminary examination dossier would truly be on equal footing with that of the other juridical parties. As Daniel Shuman states: "Likely most individuals considering the possibility that they may find themselves in the role of the victim would see the benefits of the inquisitorial system that places the responsibility [for the matter] in the hands of a neutral judge".[146]

Second, given the neutral fact-gathering perspective, the OEM's inquisitorial features would better serve the victims' desire to understand what happened and memorialize the historical record. As explained by Lise Reuss Muff in the context of the ECCC:

> [The inquisitorial system has an advantage] as ascertaining the truth is seen as the ultimate goal. The introduction of investigating judges, whose sole purpose is to conduct an impartial investigation, examining all kinds of evidence regardless of its nature, is a better guarantee of the factual correctness of the findings than leaving the investigative responsibility with the respective parties. No facts will be hidden even though neither the defense nor the prosecutor might find a particular interest in them, and the final result and thereby the events found to have occurred should only to a very limited extent depend on the skills and capabilities of

---

[145] See Muff, 2011, pp. 24–25, see *supra* note 128.

[146] Daniel W. Shuman, "The Role of Legal Rules in Recollection of Trauma: An Overview and Introduction to the Legal Panel", in J. Don Read and D. Stephen Lindsay (eds.), *Recollections of Trauma: Scientific Evidence and Clinical Practice*, Springer Science, New York, 1997, p. 494.

the lawyers in question but instead reflect the reality. Rather than being viewed as a dispute between parties, the inquisitorial process is thought of as an official and thorough inquiry, and the vital role of the trial judge combined with the impartial investigation of the investigating judge ensures the best possible investigation of the virtual reality. Although [this arrangement] cannot serve restorative justice personally to each victim, [due] to the model of independent investigating judges, [it is] able to provide [victims] with a great understanding of the truth.[147]

23.5.2. An Analysis of Potential Disadvantages

In considering the possible downsides to this chapter's proposal, three main objections come to mind – creating unnecessary rigidity, restricting prosecutorial discretion, and detrimentally expanding the ICC's bureaucracy while increasing its expenses. Let us now consider each of these potential problems.

23.5.2.1. Creating Unnecessary Rigidity

The current framework is supple and allows for the preliminary examination to flow naturally according to the situation on the ground, the concern of the international community, as well as the available resources/manpower and enforcement priorities of the OTP at any given time. The new scheme requires the OTP to respond to communications, one way or the other, within a recommended period of six months (or any other designated reasonable time period). The proposal also sets a 24-month time limit on conducting the preliminary examination (albeit with the possibility of extensions). The OEM model also forbids the Prosecutor from making public comments about the preliminary examination during the OEM's work on the matter. To that extent, the flexibility or suppleness of the current framework is lost if this chapter's proposal is implemented.

23.5.2.2. Restricting Prosecutorial Discretion

Restricting prosecutorial discretion is very much linked to the rigidity issue but has its own dimension. In particular, beyond strict time frames and blanket speech limitations, the OEM proposal takes away much of the

---

[147] Muff, 2011, p. 25, see *supra* note 128.

freedom of action currently vested in the Prosecutor. The decision not to act on a communication, for example, is within the Prosecutor's prerogatives. But the proposed scheme allows that decision to be appealed to the OEM.

And then, beyond the ability to comment on a preliminary examination in public, a number of other prosecutorial privileges are curtailed given the role of the OEM – the collection of evidence, communications with players on the ground, and, most importantly, the decision about whether to open an investigation. Although the OTP can appeal OEM recommendations to the Pre-Trial Chamber, there will be a presumption in support of the OEM's conclusions and the OTP will have to overcome that presumption. To the extent experts believe that the Prosecutor is best situated to make conclusions about case processing at this stage, the OEM proposal would be seen as intrusive and problematic. Moreover, the public comments ban would deprive the Prosecutor of an effective forum to push for positive complementarity during the preliminary examination through the naming/shaming option.

Thus, some have "cautioned against regulation, arguing that the process should not be overly codified and that there was a virtue in prosecutorial discretion that should be preserved. Otherwise, preliminary examinations would lose some of their leverage".[148]

23.5.2.3. Ballooning Bureaucracy and Expenses

The ICC is already being criticized for excessive bureaucracy and costs. With 34 judges and over 700 staff,[149] one commentator has lambasted it for its "Kafkaesque bureaucracy" that is "hindering justice" and keeping the institution from "becoming [...] effective". Regarding the ICC's price tag for justice, by the end of 2014, Daniel Abebe could complain:

> A brief review of the ICC's operation suggests that it is failing. Since 2002, the court has spent over $1 billion, with a yearly budget of over $100 million, all for 36 indictments, two convictions and six acquittals, with several decisions pending. Two convictions hardly constitute a serious deter-

---

[148] Lieneke Louman, "Report: Preliminary Examination and Legacy/Sustainable Exit: Reviewing Policies and Practices – Part 1", in *Post-Conflict Justice*, 26 October 2015.

[149] David Davenport, "International Criminal Court: 12 Years, $1 Billion, 2 Convictions", in *Forbes*, 12 March 2014.

---

rent and one wonders if it is money well spent[…] Pouring more money into the ICC or expanding its powers won't overcome the constraints of international politics[…] In the end, if the supporters of the ICC really think it is necessary, they have the burden of explaining why two convictions from a flawed court are worth $1 billion.[150]

Of course, given the addition of a new office, with its own set of jurists, investigators, analysts and staff, this chapter's proposal necessarily entails adding to the ICC payroll and arguably creating more red tape. The larger bureaucratic edifice could be responsible for greater drags on efficiency and the higher costs could significantly hamstring an institution already challenged by the demands of bloated budgets. As Peter Cluskey pointed out in 2016:

[The] fact is that the court's finances too have been shaky. Just two years ago, the Dutch government averted a crisis by stepping in to pay the rent on the court's previous premises – because, it turned out, many of the countries that should have stumped up had become "reluctant" because of the financial crisis […] So the ICC as an institution is not without serious problems.[151]

23.5.3. A Net Positive Assessment

23.5.3.1. In Reference to Potential Inflexibility and Restricted Prosecutorial Discretion

Notwithstanding the potential disadvantages just considered, it is submitted that the OEM proposal is overall beneficial and should be adopted. With respect to inflexibility and prosecutorial discretion, the two main bugaboos identified boil down to limiting the Prosecutor in her efforts to promote positive complementarity/deterrence/peace and subjecting her decisions to judicial scrutiny.

---

[150] Daniel Abebe, "I.C.C.'s Dismal Record Comes at Too High a Price", in *New York Times*, 12 December 2014.

[151] Peter Cluskey, "International Criminal Court Opens Its 'Peace Palace'", in *Irish Times*, 19 April 2016.

23.5.3.1.1. Promoting Positive Complementarity

Regarding the former, the concern is exaggerated for two reasons. First, the key consideration in the preliminary examination is to inform the ICC as to "whether to initiate an investigation".[152] Thus, certain experts have expressed reservations regarding use of the preliminary examination for purposes of influencing the push toward transitional justice:

> It was noted that the use of [preliminary examinations] as leverage carries certain risks. It can conflate the judicial function of the Court with wider ambitions of restorative justice. Concerns were expressed that the ICC does not have the institutional capacity to exercise both functions, and that such engagement might entail a strain on the Court's resources. It was also argued the ICC intervention can cause certain critical side effects: a risk of derailing peace negotiations, rising victim expectations, or 'mimicking' of ICC processes at the national level.[153]

Moreover, even if the impact on positive complementarity were considered a priority, the proposed OEM framework can still be effective. The spectre of the preliminary examination and possible opening of an investigation still hangs over States, whether conducted by the OTP or the OEM. If anything, the OEM-conducted preliminary examination may have more of a positive impact on the ground given that States will be aware of the constricted timeline and seriousness of the inquiry – the awkward dance of half-measures followed by public OTP-nudging for greater action would be eliminated. And with public comments by the Prosecutor taken out of the equation, there would no longer be a perception of prosecutorial grandstanding as a possible motivation.

Another hindrance to prosecutorial discretion is the shortened timeline. But given the inconstancies chronicled in this chapter, setting limits has been proposed elsewhere. For example, some have recommended that preliminary examinations "should be concluded within one year, with the possibility for the Prosecutor to request the Pre-Trial Chamber to extend the time limit, if necessary".[154] The proposal herein actually provides greater flexibility than this by allowing for an initial 24-month prelimi-

---

[152] Louman, 2015, see *supra* note 146.
[153] *Ibid.*
[154] *Ibid.*

nary examination. Moreover, even if there were concerns about the time limit given "the complexity and fluidity of the situations [that] make it difficult to impose timelines" – such as "continuing or recurring violence [...] or when peace negotiations are ongoing or agreements have been reached and the OTP has to give the state time to proceed with its own investigations and prosecutions",[155] the possibility of open-ended year-long extensions exists.

23.5.3.1.2. Judicial Review

With regard to judicial review, that arguably exists in the current system to a certain extent. In particular, ICC judges can already review pre-preliminary examination legal issues via Regulation 46(3) of the Regulations of the Court, which governs the assignment of a "request or information not arising out of a situation assigned to a Pre-Trial Chamber".[156] This regulation has already been put to the test in the preliminary examination context. Regarding the July 2013 *coup d'état* that unseated Egyptian President Mohamed Morsi, Pre-Trial Chamber II denied Morsi's motion [filed together with the Freedom and Justice Party of Egypt] to review the Prosecutor's decision not to open a Preliminary Examination.[157] The Chamber held that "the decisions of the Prosecutor pursuant to Article 15(6) or 53(1) of the Statute may be subject to judicial review".[158] But it limited any potential review powers to Article 53(3)(b), which applies "only if the Prosecutor has taken her decision on the basis of the criterion of Article 53(1)(c) of the Statute, that is, if an investigation 'would not serve the interests of justice'".[159]

Similarly, as we saw earlier in the *Registered Vessels of the Union of the Comoros* matter, after initially opening a preliminary examination in that case, the Prosecutor terminated it, concluding that the conditions for

---

[155] *Ibid.*

[156] International Criminal Court, *Regulations of the Court*, adopted 26 May 2004, ICC-BD/01-01-04, Regulation 46(3) ('ICC Regulations') (http://www.legal-tools.org/doc/05fd20/).

[157] ICC, Pre-Trial Chamber, Decision on the 'Request for Review of the Prosecutor's Decision of 23 April 2014 not to Open a Preliminary Examination concerning Alleged Crimes Committed in the Arab Republic of Egypt, and the Registrar's Decision of 25 April 2014', 12 September 2014, ICC-RoC46(3)-01/14, para. 9 (http://www.legal-tools.org/doc/bfbb8f/).

[158] *Ibid.*, para. 7.

[159] *Ibid.*, para. 8.

opening an investigation into the situation had not been satisfied. Then, pursuant to a motion for review filed by the Comoros government, Pre-Trial Chamber I requested the Prosecutor to reconsider her decision. This decision was then upheld by the Appeals Chamber. So prosecutorial discretion is quite evidently already fettered by the prospect of judicial review.

Thus, the OEM proposal only modifies the way judicial review is conducted in relation to preliminary examinations, not the fact of judicial review itself. If anything, the proposal creates conditions of judicial review arguably more sensitive and receptive to the needs of the Prosecutor given that the Prosecutor and the Examining Magistrate can communicate with one another during the preliminary examination process. Moreover, given the Examining Magistrate's expertise in all things preliminary examination, it stands to reason that the she is in a position to better appreciate the Prosecutor's positions regarding the finer nuances of any situation that comes under review.

23.5.3.2. Bureaucracy and Budget

On the surface, it would appear that adding the OEM would entail additional bureaucracy and expense for the ICC. But on closer inspection, the added value of the proposal may result in a wash or even net gain for the ICC. In particular, as the time restrictions mean preliminary examinations should, in the main, be shorter and more efficient, this will enhance economies of scale. Even if it were argued that the OTP could still handle the preliminary examinations with the time restrictions and the same savings would result, that would be specious. The preliminary examination expertise and specialization of the OEM would likely result in even greater time savings and efficiencies.

23.5.3.3. The Other Advantages Already Considered

Not only can these potential criticisms be blunted or belied, but the other benefits considered above still pertain. Thus, in terms of retributive justice, the preliminary examination-expertise and efficiency that the OEM would cultivate ought to contribute to higher-quality investigations and prosecutions when a reasonable basis to proceed with a criminal investigation can be established. With respect to procedural justice, the OEM proposal would contribute toward removing the metaphorical Sword of Damocles hanging over the heads of potential defendants during prolonged preliminary examinations and remove the possibility of snap decisions to move forward with investigations. Additionally, it would help ensure equality of arms in evidence collection during what is essentially an inchoate version of an investigation. Finally, the proposal is friendly to the interests of victims. The neutral Examining Magistrate is better positioned to take victims' interests into account during the preliminary examination. And she is more likely to be guided by the interest in creating an accurate historical record for purposes of contributing to and preserving the victims' collective memory of the atrocities at issue. All this helps promote the interests of restorative justice.

23.6. Conclusion

The outsize expectations associated with history's first permanent global penal institution have saddled it with equally Brobdingnagian burdens. And those are unfair. The accumulated millennia of impunity cannot be erased in less than two decades. Instead, international criminal justice's baby steps ought to be seen as a working-out of proper protocol, not its perfection. Part of that exercise entails tinkering with its nascent phases. In its current iteration, the preliminary examination crawls on vestigial limbs born of adversarial DNA. In that sense, it is culturally cordoned off from the balance of ICC procedure, which bears the influence of an inquisitorial approach. From the investigation forward, judges play an integral role in the process – the Pre-Trial Chamber and later the Trial Chamber scrutinize the fruit of investigatory efforts, influence the direction of the case and thereby fulfil a quality control function.

But leading up to that point, the procedural landscape is quite different. The Prosecutor is given tremendous leeway – in time spent, resources devoted, communications made and conclusions drawn regarding the quality of evidence, the nature of any domestic efforts and the potential global impact of ICC proceedings. The proposal advanced herein cures many of the ills associated with the current preliminary structure.

Creation of the OEM helps inquisitorially hybridize what is now an essentially adversarial procedure. In doing so, it would fold into the early phase the necessary degree of judicial involvement and investigatory efficacy. Chronological points of repair would help regularize the timeline and ultimately conserve resources. Depoliticization through legislating a professional-responsibility-influenced confidentiality etiquette would highlight the solemnity and legal focus of the preliminary examination stage, while shielding the Prosecutor from accusations of untoward motives. That the current Prosecutor may be less driven by political or personal considerations does not mean the OTP may not be buffeted by such forces under future leadership. The institution's performance should not rise or fall strictly per the vagaries of the current office holder's personal virtues. And, in any event, the shield of procedural equanimity should be similarly effective for situationally-driven political heat, as opposed to the personality-driven version.

At the same time, the inherent truth-telling orientation of the inquisitorial jurist cum investigator would promote equality of arms *vis-à-vis* potential defendants, look after the possible interests of victims and more effectively track down incipient indicia of guilt. Regarding this last endeavour, this chapter's proposal envisages a crucible of preliminary examination experience that would whet examination instincts, concentrate examination knowledge, and ultimately create a repository of examination wisdom that, in the long run, would better serve the interests of justice and conserve the treasure of an increasingly resource-deprived ICC.

That the same office may provide the necessary degree of judicial oversight in reference to the Prosecutor's work at this stage only adds to the appeal of the proposal. The very reservoir of examination acumen just considered lends a normative advantage to the OEM's quality control function. Some might consider the Pre-Trial Chamber the more logical actor to assume this role as it already factors into the system. But that would deprive the enterprise of the OEM's anticipated expertise and situational sensitivity to any unfolding examination under consideration.

Of course, whereas this proposal considers remedying the ills of certain adversarial excesses on the international stage, it could certainly be adopted for domestic consumption too (just as the proposal itself was informed and inspired by certain domestic procedures). Consider the United States, for example. In his 2014 article "Lessons from Inquisitorialism", Christopher Slobogin observed that, as implemented in that country, "the adversarial system is a significant cause of wrongful convictions, wrongful acquittals, and 'wrongful' sentences".[160] And he added that "Empirical evidence suggests that a hybrid inquisitorial regime can reduce

---

[160] Christopher Slobogin, "Lessons from Inquisitorialism", in *Southern California Law Review*, 2014, vol. 87, no. 3, p. 699.

these erroneous results".[161] He then went on to propose that the American criminal justice process incorporate a series of inquisitorial mechanisms (including non-adversarial treatment of experts, and required unsworn testimony by the defendant).

It is beyond the scope of this chapter to consider those in detail. Although Slobogin's proposal dealt with the end-phases of the process, it is submitted that aspects of the proposal outlined herein could enhance American criminal procedure in its preliminary phases from both procedural and restorative justice perspectives. This could also be true for other adversarial jurisdictions, including England and Wales, Australia and Canada. If the ICC may be considered a laboratory for developing ideal hybrid procedures globally, why should municipal institutions not benefit from such experimentation domestically too?

In effect, as the ICC learns and adapts within the milieu of humanity's common jurisprudential heritage, so should the traditions that give rise to that heritage seek to learn and grow in return. Development at both levels, municipal and international, can reinforce one another and create greater goodwill for the ICC while advancing the latter's own efficacy. Thus, in this sense, the proposal for creation of the Office of the Examining Magistrate might only be considered a starting point, whose ripple effects could ultimately redound to the benefit of greater justice enterprises that still lie on the horizon.

---

[161] *Ibid.*

Part 4

**Transparency, Co-operation and Participation
in Preliminary Examination**

24

Deterrence or Withdrawals?
Consequences of Publicising
Preliminary Examination Activities

Ana Cristina Rodríguez Pineda[*]

24.1. Introduction

Preliminary examinations, the procedural step taken prior to determining whether or not to open an investigation, have become one of the International Criminal Court's ('ICC') principal and most controversial activities.[1] Notably, the Office of the Prosecutor ('OTP') is using the public announcement that a preliminary examination is underway to achieve the broader goals that underpin the Rome Statute, rather than fulfilling their statutory purpose. In this respect, publicising preliminary examination activities can be useful to the extent that it has an impact on the situation being considered before a decision to investigate is reached, including by creating pressure for national proceedings. Bearing in mind the limited capacity of the ICC, there is clear merit to the idea of extracting as much

---

[*]   **Ana Cristina Rodríguez Pineda** is the former Chef de Cabinet of the International Criminal Tribunal for the former Yugoslavia ('ICTY') President. Before joining the Tribunal, the author was the Deputy Permanent Representative and *Chargée d'Affaires* at the Permanent Mission of Guatemala to the United Nations ('UN') in New York. From 2006 she was the Permanent Mission's Legal Adviser and counselled on a wide array of political and legal issues at the UN with a focus on the Sixth Committee of the General Assembly, where she served as Vice-Chair, as well as in the Security Council, where she chaired the Informal Working Group on International Tribunals. She has facilitated several resolutions for the General Assembly, Security Council and the Assembly of States Parties to the Rome Statute. She is currently pursuing a Ph.D. on International Criminal Court ('ICC') preliminary examinations at Leiden Law School. This chapter was greatly improved by the contributions of those who commented on earlier versions, including Annelle Urriola, Gabrielle Macintyre, and Sergey Vasiliev.

[1]   See Office of the Prosecutor ('OTP'), Strategic Plan 2016–2018, 6 July 2015, para. 54 (https://www.legal-tools.org/doc/7ae957/). Preliminary examinations are one of the Office's three core activities that can positively impact on future investigations and prosecutions, in addition to their potential to obviate ICC intervention through prevention and complementarity.

---

preventive and deterrent value from preliminary examinations through publicity of the OTP's activities.

As part of its efforts towards ensuring transparency in its activities, as well as managing expectations, the OTP has developed the Policy Paper on Preliminary Examinations ('2013 Policy Paper').[2] The stated aim of this policy paper is to "promote clarity and predictability regarding the manner in which the OTP applies the legal criteria set out in the Statute for the conduct of a preliminary examination".[3] Although it offers some information on the procedures to be followed by the OTP, the policy paper does not provide a coherent methodology for deciding what gets publicised or when. This *ad hoc* approach to publicity surrounding preliminary examinations has left the OTP vulnerable to criticism concerning how it handles situations and impacted the credibility of the Office as an impartial organ of the Court.

The 2013 Policy Paper also promotes the idea of maximising the utility of preliminary examinations by encouraging genuine national proceedings and contributing towards the prevention of crimes. As a result, the first step in prosecutorial activity is not about applying a standard anymore – the reasonable basis standard – but about applying pressure on States involved in situations under consideration. While the OTP's efforts are laudable, purposefully using preliminary examinations in a different manner from what the Statute intended can run counter to the interests of the ICC as a whole.

This chapter takes stock of how the OTP has publicised its preliminary examination activities and the impact of those choices on the OTP's image and credibility. It begins with an overview of the preliminary examination regulatory framework, followed by an analysis of the consequences of publicity in general terms. It reviews the different approaches and practices developed by the OTP with regard to how specific preliminary examinations have been publicised. It then examines whether and how such publicity may influence or motivate a decision by a State under preliminary examination to halt its co-operation with the Court or in extreme circumstances withdraw from the Rome Statute. Furthermore, it contrasts

---

[2] OTP, *Policy Paper on Preliminary Examinations*, 1 November 2013, paras. 94–99 (http://www.legal-tools.org/doc/acb906/).

[3] *Ibid.*, para. 21.

the current practices of the OTP with those of other international bodies with investigative and fact-finding functions in terms of how their work products are publicised, if at all.

Having set the scene, this chapter also argues that prevention is not an appropriate policy objective for a preliminary examination, as such a focus leads the OTP to side-line its main statutory task: *determining whether or not there is a reasonable basis to proceed with an investigation.* This chapter posits that a much more careful balancing of different goals and objectives is required. In this regard, practical recommendations are presented to enhance and improve public communications of the OTP during preliminary examinations. Finally, it is suggested that the value of publicity should be reassessed in light of whether it serves to promote the OTP's prosecutorial strategy and the Court's credibility as a judicial institution.

When discussing the consequences of publicising preliminary examination activities, this contribution will focus mainly on examinations conducted under Article 15 of the Rome Statute.

24.2. General Framework of Preliminary Examinations[4]

The regime governing preliminary examinations raises legal and practical questions essential to the effective functioning of the ICC. The legal framework contains but a single reference to the wording "preliminary examination" in the entire Statute, in Article 15,[5] and no explicit mention at all in the Rules of Procedure and Evidence ('RPE').[6] According to the Pre-Trial Chamber ('PTC') Article 15 is one of the most delicate provi-

---

[4] For an overview on preliminary examinations see Pavel Caban "Preliminary Examinations by the Office of the Prosecutor of the International Criminal", in *Czech Yearbook of Public & Private International Law*, 2011, vol. 2.

[5] Statute of the International Criminal Court, 17 July 1998, Article 42(1) ('ICC Statute') (http://www.legal-tools.org/doc/7b9af9/): provides that the Office shall be responsible for 'examining' referrals and any substantiated information on crimes within the jurisdiction of the Court.

[6] Articles 15 and 53 of the Rome Statute are explicitly linked through [ICC], Rules of Procedure and Evidence, 2 September 2002, Rules 48 and 104 ('[ICC] RPE') (http://www.legal-tools.org/doc/8bcf6f).

sions of the Rome Statute.[7] Its origin resides in the compromise proposed by Germany and Argentina,[8] in response to intractable debates during the Rome Conference concerning the powers of the Prosecutor.[9]

This compromise succeeded in addressing several concerns relating to the scope of the Prosecutor's *proprio motu* powers.[10] In particular, leaving it up to Chambers to determine whether a matter should be pursued by the Prosecutor or dropped, in the absence of a referral from a State Party or the Security Council.[11] The compromise also introduced a procedural framework, which would prohibit the Prosecutor from initiating an investigation upon the mere receipt of a complaint. Through a preliminary examination, the Prosecutor would be required to first satisfy him or herself that enough information had been obtained to justify opening an investigation. In addition, the Prosecutor would have to consider whether the requirements necessary for the exercise of jurisdiction were present at the outset, avoiding a situation where the OTP would invest substantial resources only to discover that it could not exercise jurisdiction.[12]

A year after the entry into force of the Rome Statute in 2002, the OTP began developing policy papers on issues before it, including on preliminary examinations,[13] as well as some informal expert papers con-

---

[7]   ICC, Situation in Kenya, PTC, Decision pursuant to article 15 of the Rome Statute on the authorisation of an investigation into the situation in the Republic of Kenya, 31 March 2010, ICC-01/09-19, para. 17 (http://www.legal-tools.org/doc/338a6f/).

[8]   Proposal by Argentina and Germany, Article 46, Information submitted to the Prosecutor, A/AC.249/1998/WG.4/DP.35, 25 March 1998 (http://www.legal-tools.org/doc/896cf4/). This is the first time the term 'preliminary examination' appeared in the draft proposals and negotiations of the Preparatory Committee.

[9]   The current version of Article 15 is largely identical to the Argentine-German proposal, except that it leaves out the duty to assess admissibility. See Morten Bergsmo and Jelena Pejić, "Article 15", in Otto Triffterer (ed.), *A Commentary on the Rome Statute of the International Criminal Court*, C.H. Beck, Hart Publishing, p. 200.

[10] Summary of the Proceedings of the Preparatory Committee during the period 25 March–12 April 1996, A/AC.249/1, 7 May 1996, paras. 165–168 (Summary of the Proceedings of the Preparatory Committee) (https://www.legal-tools.org/doc/d7aad5/).

[11] Report of the Preparatory Committee on the Establishment of an International Criminal Court, Vol. 1, Proceedings of the Preparatory Committee during March–April and August 1999, A/51/22[Vol-I](Supp), 14 September 1996, para. 151 (https://www.legal-tools.org/doc/e75432/).

[12] Summary of the Proceedings of the Preparatory Committee, para. 168, see *supra* note 10.

[13] Paper on Some Policy Issues Before the Office of the Prosecutor, 5 September 2003 (https://www.legal-tools.org/doc/f53870/); Annex to the "Paper on some policy issues be-

---

cerning essential prosecutorial matters.[14] In 2009 the OTP issued its Regulations,[15] containing a section entitled "Preliminary examinations and evaluation of information".[16] These Regulations sought to flesh out the regulatory framework for the conduct of preliminary examinations. Subsequently, in 2010 the OTP released its first Draft Policy Paper on Preliminary Examinations,[17] which eventually was revised and resulted in the 2013 Policy Paper, which outlines a phased approach towards preliminary examinations[18] in accordance with Article 53(1).[19]

The 2013 Policy Paper suggests that preliminary examinations are *sui generis* to the ICC.[20] Drawing a distinction between the ICC and other *ad hoc* and hybrid tribunals, it stresses that, unlike the legal framework of these bodies, the Rome Statute does not have predefined specific situa-

---

fore the Office of the Prosecutor": Referrals and Communications, 5 September 2003 (https://www.legal-tools.org/doc/5df43d/); Draft paper on some policy issues before the Office of the Prosecutor for discussion at the public hearing in The Hague on 17 and 18 June 2003, 18 July 2003 (https://www.legal-tools.org/doc/abb9f7/).

14 Informal expert paper: Fact-finding and investigative functions of the office of the Prosecutor, including international cooperation, OTP-ICC 2003; Informal expert paper: The principle of complementarity in practice, OTP-ICC 2003. See Morten Bergsmo and SONG Tianying, "The Principle of Complementarity" and the Annexes thereto, in Morten Bergsmo, Klaus Rackwitz and SONG Tianying (eds.), *Historical Origins of International Criminal Law: Volume 5*, Torkel Opsahl Academic EPublisher, Brussels, 2017, pp. 739 ff. (http://www.toaep.org/ps-pdf/24-bergsmo-rackwitz-song).

15 ICC, Regulations of the Office of the Prosecutor, 23 April 2009, Regulations 25–31, Section 3 ('OTP Regulations') (http://www.legal-tools.org/doc/a97226/).

16 *Ibid.*, Regulation 28.

17 OTP, *Draft Policy Paper on Preliminary Examinations*, 4 October 2010 (http://www.legal-tools.org/doc/bd172c/).

18 OTP, *Policy Paper on Preliminary Examinations*, para.72, see *supra* note 2.

19 It should be noted that in Article 53(1) there is no reference to the trigger mechanisms. The Pre Trial Chamber ('PTC') has held consistently that the criteria of Article 53(1) of the Statute governing the initiation of an investigation by the Prosecutor equally inform the analysis under Article 15(3) and (4) of the Statute as they enable first the Prosecutor and then the Chamber to determine whether there is "a reasonable basis to proceed with an investigation". Situation in Kenya, Decision pursuant to article 15 of the Rome Statute on the authorisation of an investigation into the situation in the Republic of Kenya, paras. 21–22, see *supra* note 7; ICC, Situation in Côte d'Ivoire, Decision pursuant to article 15 of the Rome Statute on the authorisation of an investigation into the situation in the Republic of Côte d'Ivoire, 3 October 2011, ICC-02/11-14, paras. 17–18 (http://www.legal-tools.org/doc/7a6c19/). See also ICC RPE, Rules 48 and 105, see *supra* note 6.

20 OTP, *Policy Paper on Preliminary Examinations*, para. 24, see *supra* note 2.

---

tions for investigation. It is the ICC that ultimately determines when and where it should intervene in accordance with its statutory criteria. According to the OTP other courts are neither in a position to decide against investigating or with the jurisdictional capacity to expand their focus to other situations.[21] The comparison with other courts and tribunals is overstated. While it is true that concerned States or the Security Council defined the respective situations of other courts and tribunals, this was only for the purpose of conferring jurisdiction and not for determining its exercise. For example, Article 18 of the Statute of the International Criminal Tribunal for the former Yugoslavia ('ICTY') states that the Prosecutor "shall assess the information received or obtained and decide whether there is sufficient basis to proceed".[22] To some extent this assessment is similar to the one carried out by the ICC Prosecutor serving as a basis to determine whether or not to proceed with an investigation.[23]

Although the term 'preliminary examination' might not be universal or found in most jurisdictions, its fundamentals are certainly not new. The notion of a preliminary examination resonates within any domestic jurisdiction that deals on a daily basis with probabilities of criminal conduct and is required to probe and collect information to determine whether

---

[21] *Ibid.*

[22] Updated Statute of the International Criminal Tribunal for the former Yugoslavia, 25 May 1993, Article 18 ('ICTY' Statute) (http://www.legal-tools.org/doc/b4f63b/) concerning Investigation and preparation of indictment reads as follows: The Prosecutor *shall initiate investigations ex-officio or on the basis of information obtained from any source*, particularly from Governments, United Nations organs, intergovernmental and nongovernmental organisations. The Prosecutor *shall assess* the information received or obtained and *decide whether there is sufficient basis to proceed.*

[23] See also the Internal Rules of the Extraordinary Chambers in the Courts of Cambodia, 12 July 2007 (Rev.7), 23 February 2011 (http://www.legal-tools.org/doc/d6b146/) containing a provision on a pre-investigative phase. While this differs from a preliminary examination at the ICC in that it is not part of the formal stage of proceedings of the Court, it is still similar in two aspects, one both processes are preliminary steps of procedural nature, second their purpose is to establish whether crimes within the respective jurisdictions have been committed. Rule 50: Preliminary Investigations. "1. The Co-Prosecutors may conduct preliminary investigations to determine whether evidence indicates that crimes within the jurisdiction of the ECCC have been committed and to identify Suspects and potential witnesses. 2. Preliminary investigations may be carried out by Judicial Police officers or by Investigators of the ECCC only at the request of the Co-Prosecutors. The Judicial Police and Investigators may search for and gather relevant evidence including documents... [I]tems that are of no evidentiary value shall be returned without delay at the end of the preliminary investigation".

there is a basis to open an investigation.[24] Filtering procedures, together with a 'feasibility to collect evidence' or 'more likely than not' standard are common and necessary to avoid overwhelming the limited resources of police and prosecutor offices,[25] and to ensure that resources are directed towards cases where there is a likelihood of conviction. As rightly noted by Human Rights Watch, it would be entirely inappropriate for the Prosecutor to be expected to prove a *prima facie* case or probable cause at this stage, before initiating any investigation into the facts.[26]

The 2013 Policy Paper sets out a phased approach to determine whether a complaint warrants conducting a preliminary examination:

- Phase 1: Initial assessment;
- Phase 2: Subject matter assessment;
- Phase 3: Admissibility assessment; and
- Phase 4: Interests of justice assessment.

During Phases 1 and 2, the OTP must determine whether the available information provides a reasonable basis to conclude that a crime falling under the Statute has been committed, establishing that it would have jurisdiction over the alleged criminal conduct.[27] In Phase 3, it must consider if the situation would be admissible in terms of Article 17 of the ICC

---

[24] At the national level it is not clear when an investigation is commenced, who takes the decision to start it and what is the level of discretion to carry it out. Normally there is some form of initial information gathering done by the police, as well as mechanisms to file complaints but the decision to initiate proceedings for the most part rests with prosecutors. For this matter the distinction between civil law and common law systems is also relevant.

[25] The OTP reported that during the initial review of the communications received, approximately 80% of communications were found to be manifestly outside the jurisdiction of the Court. Of the approximately 20% of communications warranting further analysis, 10 situations have been subjected to intensive analysis. See OTP, Report on the activities performed during the first three years (June 2003 – June 2006), 12 September 2006 (http://www.legal-tools.org/doc/c7a850/). According to the latest OTP Report on Preliminary Examination activities, 14 November 2016, para. 18, the Office has received a total of 12,022 Article 15 communications since July 2002 (http://www.legal-tools.org/doc/f30a53/).

[26] Human Rights Watch ('HRW'), "Justice in the Balance, Recommendations for an Independent and Effective International Criminal Court", June 1998, p. 67.

[27] Temporal, material, and either territorial or personal jurisdiction.

Statute.[28] If these three phases are satisfied, the Prosecutor must then give consideration to the "interests of justice".[29]

Although a general duty to conduct a preliminary examination exists once the Prosecutor is seised of a matter, there are some procedural differences to bear in mind depending on the triggering mechanism.[30] Where the Prosecutor receives a referral, Article 53 provides that the Prosecutor shall initiate an investigation unless there is no reasonable basis to proceed under the Statute. In that circumstance, the decision to initiate an investigation is further simplified in that the PTC may only review the Prosecutor's determination not to proceed, but does not review an affirmative decision to proceed. However, when the Prosecutor receives a communication,[31] the test is the same but the starting point is reversed. In other words, the Prosecutor shall not seek to initiate an investigation without determining first that there is a reasonable basis to proceed and that decision to proceed is subject to authorisation of the PTC.[32]

24.2.1. Observations on Preliminary Examinations

The following basic features can be identified in every preliminary examination process:[33] (1) they apply routinely irrespective of whether the OTP receives a referral from a State Party, the Security Council, or acts on the basis of communications pursuant to Article 15;[34] (2) they are informal,

---

[28] This second factor involves examination of whether national courts are unwilling or genuinely unable to proceed; but it also involves an evaluation of the notion of "gravity".

[29] OTP, *Policy Paper on the Interests of Justice*, September 2007 (http://www.legal-tools.org/doc/bb02e5/).

[30] Article 15 is one of the three triggering mechanisms in the ICC Statute established under Article 13 in relation to the exercise of jurisdiction.

[31] The OTP has adopted the term 'communications' to describe information provided on the basis of Article 15. "The primary sources of such communications are individuals and non-governmental organisations", in William A. Schabas, *The International Criminal Court, A Commentary on the Rome Statute*, Oxford University Press, 2010, p. 320.

[32] Annex to the 'Paper of some policy issues before the Office of the Prosecutor', see *supra* note 13.

[33] A preliminary examination is not an end in itself, rather it constitutes a process serving as a precursor to potential investigations. This idea is explained further see *infra*, fn. 47.

[34] The author agrees with those considering that these procedural mandates create a general duty to conduct a preliminary examination. Jan Wouters, Sten Verhoeeven and Bruno Demeyere, "The International Criminal Court's Office of the Prosecutor: navigating be-

---

inconclusive and distinct from investigations;[35] and (3) their function is to determine whether or not a *reasonable basis exists* to proceed with an investigation.

24.2.1.1. Preliminary Examinations Apply Equally to All Triggering Mechanisms

Preliminary examinations are conducted routinely irrespective of whether the OTP receives a referral from a State Party, the Security Council, or acts on the basis of communications pursuant to Article 15. That said, most of the problems surrounding preliminary examinations only come into play when the Prosecutor acts *proprio motu*. This is explained by the fact that referrals by States or the Security Council are normally made public and the situation is immediately assigned to a PTC.[36] As there is no need for the OTP to seek authorisation to proceed with an investigation these preliminary examinations end up being fast-tracked.[37]

The OTP thereby treats preliminary examinations differently depending on whether they arise from a referral by a State or the Security Council, or at the Prosecutor's own initiative. This differentiated treat-

---

tween independence and accountability?", in *International Criminal Law Review*, 2008, vol. 8, para. 10.

[35] Situation in Kenya, Decision pursuant to article 15 of the Rome Statute on the authorisation of an investigation into the situation in the Republic of Kenya, paras. 32, 50 and 75, see *supra* note 7: "[t]he Prosecutor has limited powers which are not comparable to those provided for in article 54 of the Statute at the investigative stage" and the information available at such an early stage is "neither expected to be 'comprehensive' nor 'conclusive'. Furthermore, it should be noted that findings at the preliminary examination phase are not binding for the purpose of future investigations".

[36] In the case of an Article 15 *proprio motu* situation a PTC is assigned pursuant to Regulations of the Court, 26 May 2004, Regulations 45 and 46 (http://www.legal-tools.org/doc/2988d1/). The Prosecutor shall inform the President of the Court of: (1) the Prosecutor's determination that there is a reasonable basis to proceed with an investigation. Regulation 46, sub regulation 2 of the Regulations of the Court, pursuant to which "[t]he Presidency shall assign a situation to a Pre-Trial Chamber as soon as the Prosecutor has informed the Presidency in accordance with Regulation 45".

[37] Impetus is to make a decision quickly unless there is not a reasonable basis to proceed, Ignaz Stegmiller, *The Pre-Investigation Stage of the ICC, Criteria for Situation Selection*, Duncker & Humblot, GmbH, Berlin, 2011, p. 190.

---

ment results in fast track,[38] slow track,[39] and protracted[40] preliminary examinations.

To understand the preliminary examination process, it is important to properly construe Article 15 as a triggering mechanism that authorises the Prosecutor to initiate *proprio motu* investigations. It is not a provision dealing with the initiation of a preliminary examination *per se*, but rather a means through which the Prosecutor can initiate an investigation. The first step, which is compulsory, is the preliminary examination – the means by which the Prosecutor can decide whether or not to proceed with an investigation. It is thus an over-dramatisation for the OTP to announce to the world "the Prosecutor has decided to open a preliminary examination", since such a statement exaggerates what is merely a transitory step, not only in terms of what it is, but also what it can do.

24.2.1.2. Preliminary Examinations Do Not Constitute Investigations

Despite the OTP's best efforts of bringing clarity through its 2013 Policy Paper, it is in part responsible for creating the confusion that surrounds preliminary examinations and investigations. The OTP has consistently explained that a preliminary examination is not an investigation, but a process of examining the information available in order to reach a fully-informed determination on whether there is a reasonable basis to proceed

---

[38] Situations in Kenya, Libya, Guinea, Darfur, Democratic Republic of Congo, Uganda, Central African Republic II, Côte d'Ivoire and Mali. Preliminary examinations conducted expeditiously with Libya carried out in only five days. Investigations were opened in under two years.

[39] Preliminary examinations for the Situations in Honduras, Republic of Korea, Burundi, Nigeria, Gabon, Central African Republic I, Venezuela, Iraq/UK (2009), Ukraine, as well as the situation referred by Comoros were conducted for more than three years and less than five. The Situation in Central African Republic I eventually proceeded to an investigation. In five other situations the Prosecutor concluded the statutory requirements to proceed with an investigation had not been met, namely Honduras, Republic of Korea, Venezuela, Iraq/UK and the situation referred by Comoros. Regarding the most recent ones, in the Philippines and Venezuela, it is too early to know what pace they will take.

[40] Situations in Afghanistan, Colombia, Georgia, Palestine and Iraq/UK (2014). An investigation in Georgia was opened after nearly eight years under examination. Afghanistan and Colombia were ongoing for over a decade. At the time of writing the Prosecutor's request concerning Afghanistan was still pending review by the PTC. Palestine and Iraq/UK are still under subject-matter consideration.

---

with an investigation under the Rome Statute.[41] Yet, when speaking publicly of the preliminary examination process, it does so by referring to investigations instead of a precursor to a potential investigation.

Some authors[42] use imprecise terminology when referring to preliminary examinations,[43] such as pre-investigations.[44] Others contrast them with 'full' investigations or consider them part of the formal stage of ICC proceedings.[45] Although the Prosecutor requires an authorisation of

---

[41] ICC OTP, The Prosecutor of the International Criminal Court, Fatou Bensouda, opens a preliminary examination of the situation in Palestine, 16 January 2015, ICC-OTP-20150116-PR1083 (http://www.legal-tools.org/doc/1dcbe5/). *Idem.*, Statement of the Prosecutor of the International Criminal Court, Fatou Bensouda, on opening a Preliminary Examination into the Situation in Burundi, 25 April 2016 (http://www.legal-tools.org/doc/155b19/).

[42] Ignaz Stegmiller, 2011, pp. 26–27, see *supra* note 37. In a similar vein, Giuliano Turone, 'Powers and Duties of the Prosecutor', in Antonio Cassesse, Paolo Gaeta and John R.W.D Jones (eds.), *The Rome Statute of the ICC: A Commentary*, vol. II, Oxford University Press, 2002, pp. 1137, 1146; Jan Wouters, Sten Verhoeeven, Bruno Demeyere, 2008, para. 19, see *supra* note 34.

[43] Ignaz Stegmiller, 2011, see *supra* note 37. Ignaz Stegmiller explains that when referring to preliminary examinations as foreseen in Article 15(6) they take place before the (formal) investigation stage, in accordance with Article 54, begins. Thus, two different procedural stages regarding the ICC procedural law can be identified, namely the pre-investigation stage and the formal investigation stage. He goes on to underscore that these stages have to be distinguished carefully and provisions have to be tested as to whether they apply to pre-investigations or (full) investigations. The author dissents with this description because it splits the investigation stage in two. Preliminary examinations are not investigations and that imprecision remains with the use of the term 'pre-investigation'. There is also no such thing as a 'full' investigation. Investigating is either something you are doing or you are not. By contrast the author agrees that the investigation stage is formal and that preliminary examinations are informal and that the powers of the OTP in the course of 'formal' investigations go far beyond those during preliminary examinations (pre-investigations as referred to by Stegmiller).

[44] Ignaz Stegmiller, 2011, pp. 187–189, see *supra* note 37. Ignaz Stegmiller argues that the discretion meant by paragraph 1 [Article 15] covers the right of the Prosecutor to initiate pre-investigations only. He also states that one should speak of pre-investigations versus full investigations and that the terminology of Article 15(1) has to be interpreted, in light of Article 15(6) as referring to pre-investigation steps only.

[45] The ICC web site refers to the Legal Process of the Court as follows: *Stages of proceedings.* There are several stages of the ICC process. Where grave crimes occur, the OTP must first conduct a preliminary investigation before an investigation can begin. Investigations may lead to several cases, which may go through different stages including Pre-Trial stage, Trial stage and Appeals. See ICC web site, available at https://www.icc-cpi.int/about/how-the-court-works/Pages/default.aspx#legalProcess, last accessed on 8 May 2017. Luis Moreno-Ocampo considers preliminary examinations to be a formal process defined by Articles 12,

---

the PTC to initiate an investigation, this does not mean the power does not exist, only that the decision to investigate is not taken alone.[46] Accordingly, preliminary examinations constitute precursors to potential investigations,[47] since they either lead to an investigation or not. They are, nonetheless, a required precursor because all investigations commence with a preliminary examination, but not all preliminary examinations lead to an investigation.[48]

Preliminary examinations should therefore not be confused with investigations.[49] This is due to several other reasons, starting with the fact that Article 15, which governs preliminary examinations, is not a provision found in Part 5 of the Rome Statute relating to investigations and prosecutions.[50] Similarly, preliminary examinations fall outside of Part 9 relating to co-operation obligations. Moreover, Article 17 on admissibility is applied differently to preliminary examinations than to investigations, leaving the assessment of admissibility entirely to the discretion of the Prosecutor.[51] Further, the preliminary examination process is exempt from

---

15 and 53 of the Rome Statute. Luis Moreno-Ocampo, "The ICC's Afghanistan Investigation: The Missing Option", in *Lawfare*, 24 April 2017.

[46] The Prosecutor needs to convince the PTC that the standard of a reasonable basis to proceed has been met (Article 15(4) of the Rome Statute). The Chamber must be satisfied "that the case appears to fall within the jurisdiction of the Court", a determination that is without prejudice to subsequent determinations by the Court with regard to the jurisdiction or admissibility of a case.

[47] The term of preliminary examinations as precursors is borrowed from the Oxford University Press blog by Iain Macleod and Shehzad Charania, "Three challenges for the International Criminal Court", May 2011. The author modified the term by adding the word 'potential' to accurately reflect the possibility that not all preliminary examinations lead to investigations and has removed the word 'full' to maintain the clear distinction between the informal preliminary examination process and the formal stage of proceedings, which includes investigations.

[48] Just like not all investigations lead to prosecutions.

[49] Regarding terminology, William Schabas draws a differentiation between 'preliminary examinations' when the Prosecutor is acting *propio motu*, and the 'pre-investigative phase', when the matter results from a referral. See Schabas, 2007, p. 239, see *supra* note 31. In his Commentary on the Rome Statute, Schabas mentions that a distinction between a preliminary investigation and a full investigation has been suggested, with Article 15 governing the former and Article 53(1) the latter. *Idem*, pp. 659–660; Ignaz Stegmiller, 2011 see *supra* note 37.

[50] Schabas, 2010, p. 315, see *supra* note 31.

[51] Complementarity was established for States to protect themselves. During a preliminary examination, it is up for the OTP to assess admissibility. Some States possibly find this

---

judicial review or control,[52] and finally the information that is collected is not treated as evidence.[53] Even more problematic is that preliminary examinations lack defined parameters and methodologies in relation to the standard of proof, timelines, duration,[54] as well as publicity, which is the focus of this chapter.

24.2.1.3. The Main Function of Preliminary Examinations Is to Determine Whether or Not a *Reasonable Basis Exists* to Proceed with an Investigation

In 2009, Prosecutor Luis Moreno-Ocampo stated that the "preliminary examination of alleged war crimes in Afghanistan was 'exceedingly complex' and time-consuming because of the difficulty of gathering infor-

---

more convenient because in order to enjoy full rights pursuant to Article 17 of the ICC Statute the situation would have to be under investigation, which is less desirable given that it exposes States even more than during the preliminary examination.

[52] At least until Article 15(3) is prompted, prior to an authorisation by the PTC there is no judicial review. It is noticeable that the OTP has so far avoided submitting to the control by the PTC. For example, Article 53(3)(c)–interests of justice–has never been used by the OTP because that would trigger a *proprio motu* decision reviewable by the PTC, which would be imposing on the Prosecutor. Bergsmo and Pejić explain that the underlying purpose of the PTC check is to control for frivolous or politically motivated charges. See Morten Bergsmo and Jelena Pejić, 2008, see *supra* note 9. Stigen argues that the authorisation will presumably and in reality take the form of a "quality check" where the essential is to determine whether the Prosecutor's decision is made in good faith and according to the applicable procedures. See Jo Stigen, *The Relationship Between the International Criminal Court and National Jurisdictions: The Principle of Complementarity*, Martinus Nijhoff Publishers, 2008, p. 107.

[53] ICC, Situation on Registered Vessels of the Union of the Comoros, the Hellenic Republic and the Kingdom of Cambodia ('Situation referred by Comoros'), Decision on the request of the Union of the Comoros to review the Prosecutor's decision not to initiate an investigation, 16 July 2015, ICC-01/13-34, para. 13 (http://www.legal-tools.org/doc/2f876c/).

[54] The low standard of proof threshold purportedly should impact the duration of the preliminary examination. Neither the ICC Statute nor the RPE offers any significant guidance on how to conduct preliminary examinations. For years the OTP has maintained that there are no timelines provided in the ICC Statute for bringing a preliminary examination to a close. "Termination of Preliminary Examination. No provision in the Statute or the Rules establishes a specific time period for the completion of a preliminary examination". See OTP, *Policy Paper on Preliminary Examinations*, paras. 14 and 89, see *supra* note 2. The OTP has explained that due to its independence, holding rigid timetables on when to reach a "reasonable basis" determination is not in conformity with the statutory framework; Annex to the "Paper of some policy issues before the Office of the Prosecutor", see *supra* note 13.

---

mation".[55] While it is understandable that certain situations are more challenging than others, preliminary examinations have a low standard of proof.[56] It is therefore difficult to accept that a decade long preliminary examination is needed to determine whether the *reasonable basis* standard has been satisfied.[57] In this regard, the PTC in the situation relating to the Registered Vessels of Comoros, Greece and Cambodia expressed the following: "The question that is asked of the Prosecutor by article 53(1) of the Statute is merely whether or not an investigation should be opened. The Prosecutor's assessment of the criteria listed in this provision does not necessitate any complex or detailed process of analysis".[58]

The Rome Statute does not offer a definition of *reasonable basis*.[59] Providing a definition was left to the judges of the ICC. The PTC, dealing with the situation in Kenya, observed that to satisfy the requirements under Article 15, the material provided by the Prosecutor "certainly need not point towards only one conclusion",[60] nor does it have to be conclusive.[61]

---

[55] "Court to Probe Afghan War Crimes", in *BBC News*, 10 September 2009.

[56] Article 53 Rome Statute sets a reasonable basis standard, Article 58 of the Rome Statute sets a reasonable grounds standard and Article 66 of the Rome Statute sets a beyond reasonable doubt standard. During a preliminary examination there is no need to produce evidence. This is the crucial point in the decision concerning the Situation referred by Comoros in which the PTC affirmed that the OTP did not need much to start with an investigation in response to the argument that an investigation could not be opened because of the lack of clarity. See Situation referred by Comoros, Decision on the request of the Union of the Comoros to review the Prosecutor's decision not to initiate an investigation, see *supra* note 53.

[57] ICC Statute, Articles 15(6) and 53(1), see *supra* note 5.

[58] Situation referred by Comoros, Decision on the request of the Union of the Comoros to review the Prosecutor's decision not to initiate an investigation, see *supra* note 53.

[59] In the decision concerning the Situation in Kenya the PTC found that: "[t]he language used in both article 15(3) and (4) and in the chapeau of article 53(1) of the Statute is identical. The phrase "reasonable basis to proceed" in paragraph 3 regarding the Prosecutor's conclusion is reiterated in paragraph 4, which governs the Chamber's review of the Prosecutor's Request. Exactly the same language is also included in the opening clause of article 53(1) of the Statute. Thus, these provisions prescribe the same standard to be considered both by the Prosecutor and the Pre-Trial Chamber". See Situation in Kenya, Decision pursuant to article 15 of the Rome Statute on the authorisation of an investigation into the situation in the Republic of Kenya, para. 21, see *supra* note 7.

[60] *Ibid.*, para. 34.

[61] Situation in Côte d'Ivoire, Decision pursuant to article 15 of the Rome Statute on the authorisation of an investigation into the situation in the Republic of Côte d'Ivoire, para. 24, see *supra* note 19.

All that is necessary is that there "exists a sensible or reasonable justification for a belief that a crime falling within the jurisdiction of the Court has been or is being committed".[62] In that respect, the PTC provided the Prosecutor with some guidance in its decision on the situation referred by Comoros stating: "Even more, if, as stated by the Prosecutor, the events are unclear and conflicting accounts exist, this fact alone calls for an investigation rather than the opposite. It is only upon investigation that it may be determined how the events unfolded".[63]

The certainty of obtaining sufficient information to pass the statutory threshold is rarely uniform. However, the existing regulatory framework provides tools to enhance information-gathering capabilities of the OTP during a preliminary examination. Article 15(2) allows the Prosecutor to seek additional information from States, organs of the United Nations, intergovernmental or non-governmental organisations, or other reliable sources deemed appropriate, and may receive written or oral testimony at the seat of the Court.[64] Moreover, in the absence of any information provided by a third party, it would appear from public statements made by the Prosecutor that it is the OTP's policy to actively consider potential situations within the jurisdiction of the Court based on information in the public domain.[65]

With respect to how the Prosecutor considers information that comes before him or her, OTP Regulation 24 provides that in the analysis of information and evidence regarding alleged crimes, the Office shall

---

[62] *Ibid.*; Situation in Kenya, Decision pursuant to article 15 of the Rome Statute on the authorisation of an investigation into the situation in the Republic of Kenya, para. 35, see *supra* note 7; ICC, Situation in Georgia, Decision on the Prosecutor's request for authorisation of an investigation, 27 January 2016, ICC-01/15, para. 25 (http://www.legal-tools.org/doc/a3d07e/).

[63] Situation referred by Comoros, Decision on the request of the Union of the Comoros to review the Prosecutor's decision not to initiate an investigation, para. 36, see *supra* note 53.

[64] Article 15(2) of the Rome Statute allows for "written or oral testimony" received at the seat of the Court whereby the ordinary procedures for questioning shall apply and the procedure for preservation of evidence for trial may apply pursuant to Rule 47 of the RPE.

[65] This is compatible with the spirit of Article 15. The OTP has reported it "analyses all information on crimes within its jurisdiction", and that it received and analysed new Article 15 communications "relating to purported crimes during the reporting period [...] In parallel, the Office continued the proactive examination of open sources". See Report on the activities of the Court, 29 October 2008, ICC-ASP/7/25, paras. 63–64 (http://www.legal-tools.org/doc/055a93/).

develop and apply a consistent and objective method for the evaluation of sources, information and evidence.[66] Notwithstanding, the OTP has yet to explain what methodology it uses and what steps have been taken to operationalise this Regulation. For example, how does the OTP determine the authenticity and the reliability of sources and information? Remarkably, some domestic jurisdictions have adjudicated situations on the basis of open sources, particularly those found on the Internet through YouTube or Facebook pages.[67]

It is difficult to imagine that the OTP could rely on open sources without resorting to investigative or forensic techniques to ensure their veracity. In addition, it would seem indispensable to have State co-operation in order to examine the authenticity and reliability of sources. The Prosecutor has the capacity to shape the struggle for co-operation and opening more investigations can facilitate this.[68] Given this necessity, and bearing in mind the guidance provided by the PTC in the Comoros decision mentioned above, there would appear to be a bias in favour of having more preliminary examinations advance to the investigation stage. Not only would this be consistent with Article 53, which contains a presumption in favour of investigations, but it would also help the Prosecutor further the statutory duty to establish the truth.[69]

---

[66] Regulations of the Office of the Prosecutor, 2009, Regulation 24, see *supra* note 15: "Analysis of information and evidence. In the analysis of information and evidence regarding alleged crimes, the Office shall develop and apply a consistent and objective method for the evaluation of sources, information and evidence. In this context, the Office shall take into account inter alia the credibility and reliability of sources, information and evidence, and shall examine information and evidence from multiple sources as a means of bias control".

[67] In 2017 in Sweden, a Syrian Rebel was given a life sentence for a mass killing caught on *YouTube* video. Christina Anderson, "Syrian Rebel Gets Life Sentence for Mass Killing Caught on Video", in *New York Times*, 16 February 2017.

[68] Sub-goals within the OTP's 2016–2018 time period include: (1) further developing cooperation activities and networks related to preliminary examinations, (2) further enhancing complementarity at the preliminary examination stage, and (3) continuing to increase the transparency of and public information on preliminary examinations. OTP, Strategic Plan 2016-2018, para. 45, see *supra* note 1.

[69] ICC Statute, Article 54(1), see *supra* note 5. In the report of the Preparatory Committee, "[i]t was further stated that the Prosecutor's office should be established to seek the truth rather than merely seek a conviction in a partisan manner". Report of the Preparatory

24.3. Practices on Publicising Past and Present Situations

As explained previously, the Prosecutor's discretion is broad when conducting preliminary examination activities. Taking advantage of this leeway and considering resource constraints, the OTP has sought to use the preliminary examination process assertively for purposes other than what was originally intended in the Statute.[70] Indeed, the OTP has transformed the procedural step of preliminary examinations into an advocacy tool with a view to contributing towards some of the Rome Statute's overarching goals, namely ending impunity[71] and the prevention of future crimes.[72]

Despite the 2013 Policy Paper's aim of promoting clarity and predictability regarding the manner in which the OTP applies the legal criteria set out in the Statute, there is a growing gap between the Statute and the actual practice of preliminary examinations as developed by the OTP. This is illustrated by its publicity approach surrounding these activities, which is not properly regulated and is essentially selective. While this unfettered approach to publicity is problematic, publicising preliminary examinations has also become a crucial tool for the OTP in relation to its strategy of maximising utility. The frequent use of the media, public statements and other public relations devices by the OTP raises questions regarding what drives the decision-making process of the Prosecutor to publicise information concerning preliminary examination activities. Simply put, is it led by legal and political considerations, or is it simply a public relations exercise?

Publicity of preliminary examination activities was not seriously considered during the negotiations in Rome, though there are traces of the issue being discussed. In the Summaries of the Proceedings of the Preparatory Committee, the following reference is made in the context of the

---

Committee on the Establishment of an International Criminal Court, para. 46, see *supra* note 11.

[70] David Bosco, "The International Criminal Court And Crime Prevention: Byproduct Or Conscious Goal?", in *Michigan State Journal of International Law*, 2013, vol. 19, no. 2, p. 178.

[71] ICC Statute, Preambular paragraph 5, see *supra* note 5: "Determined to put an end to impunity for the perpetrators of these crimes and thus to contribute to the prevention of such crimes".

[72] OTP, *Policy Paper on Preliminary Examinations*, paras. 16–18 and 100–106, see *supra* note 2.

Chamber's power to decide whether an investigation should be initiated or not by the Prosecutor: "up to this point, the procedure would be *in camera* and confidential, thus preventing any publicity about the case and protecting the interest of the States".[73] This understanding was not crystallised in the Rome Statute or the RPE. In fact, if the practice of making announcements public concerning preliminary examinations had been foreseen during the drafting of the Rome Statute, it is probable that the interest of States in keeping these activities confidential would have been addressed. In any case, it is unlikely that negotiators in 1998 anticipated the amount of publicity given to preliminary examinations, including a preliminary examination list on the ICC's website even prior to the Prosecutor determining that a reasonable basis to proceed exists or seeking authorisation from the PTC to open an investigation.

The issue of public disclosure of preliminary examinations was explicitly regulated for the first time in 2009 in the OTP's Regulations.[74] Later it was included in the OTP's Prosecutorial Strategy (2009-2012) indicating that the Office would start to "regularly provide information about the preliminary examination process" and "issue periodic reports on the status of its preliminary examinations".[75] Both the Regulations, as well as some RPE provisions, conditionally allow for publicity of preliminary examinations, or at least do not prohibit it.[76] For example, the RPE require the Prosecutor to "analyse the seriousness of information received" but do not specify whether this can be done publicly or should be treated as a confidential exercise. The OTP's Regulations provide that "the Prosecutor *may* decide to make public the Office's activities in relation to the preliminary examination of information. In doing so, the Office *shall be guided inter alia* by considerations for the safety, well-being, and

---

[73] Summary of the Proceedings of the Preparatory Committee, para. 166, see *supra* note 10 (http://www.legal-tools.org/doc/d7aad5/); Report of the Preparatory Committee on the Establishment of an International Criminal Court, para. 150, see *supra* note 11.

[74] OTP Regulations, Regulation 28, see *supra* note 15.

[75] OTP, Prosecutorial Strategy 2009-2012, 1 February 2010, Objective 3 (http://www.legal-tools.org/doc/6ed914/). As an example, see also Situation in Palestine, Summary of submissions on whether the declaration lodged by the Palestinian National Authority meets statutory requirements, 3 May 2010 (http://www.legal-tools.org/doc/af5abf/).

[76] OTP Regulations, Regulations 21(1) and 28(1), see *supra* note 15; ICC RPE, Rules 46 and 49, Sub-rule 1, see *supra* note 6.

privacy of those who provided the information or others who are at risk".[77]

In addition, the OTP is required to send out acknowledgements of referrals and communications received and it may decide to make public such acknowledgement, *subject* to the Prosecutor's duty to protect the confidentiality of such information.[78] Rule 49 of the RPE requires the Prosecutor to promptly ensure that notice in accordance with Article 15(6) is provided, in a manner that prevents any danger to the safety, well-being and privacy of those who provided information, or the integrity of investigations or proceedings. The requirement to notify, however, only applies once a decision to investigate has been made,[79] and the Prosecutor therefore does not have to notify States when conducting preliminary examinations *proprio motu*.[80]

David Bosco notes that in 2010 certain court documents seemed to suggest that "the process of pre-investigation will normally be conducted without publicity and without public statements", noting further that generally, work in a situation does not become public knowledge until the Office opens an investigation.[81] However, the OTP's first publicised Draft Policy Paper on Preliminary Examinations in 2010 already evidenced a shift from such an approach by specifically providing for the regular publication of preliminary examination activities.[82] In the past, the Office

---

[77] The OTP Policy Paper on Preliminary Examinations sets forth that the Office may only publicly confirm receipt of a given communication if the sender has already made that fact public. The author believes this practice undermines the Prosecutor's discretionary powers in addition to exposing the Office to the personal agendas of external actors, including NGOs or individuals. As a general rule, communications are supposed to be confidential. See OTP, *Policy Paper on Preliminary Examinations*, para. 88, see *supra* note 2; OTP Regulations, Regulation 28(2), see *supra* note 15.

[78] OTP Regulations, Regulation 46, see *supra* note 15; ICC RPE, Rule 46, see *supra* note 6.

[79] ICC Statute, Article 18, see *supra* note 5.

[80] Article 15(6) requires the Prosecutor after concluding there is no reasonable basis to proceed to inform those who provided the information. The duty to notify those who provide information is a statutory obligation. Pursuant to Rule 49(1), such notification must be given promptly and must include reasons for the decision; Stigen, 2008, p. 126, see *supra* note 53.

[81] Bosco, 2013, p. 178, see *supra* note 70.

[82] OTP, *Draft Policy Paper on Preliminary Examinations*, para.15, see *supra* note 17: In order to promote transparency of the preliminary examination process the Office aims to issue regular reports on its activities and provides reasoned responses for its decision to ei-

handled internal reports for the consideration of the Executive Commit-tee[83] or the Prosecutor, containing general information on the volume, frequency and patterns of communications relating to particular situations, as well as analyses and recommendations in line with Article 53.

By 2011, in line with the 2010 Draft Policy Paper, public reporting on preliminary examination activities became more systematic with the introduction of annual reports on preliminary examination activities.[84] These reports were later complemented by situation-specific reports con-cerning the status of preliminary examination situations. Another report containing information on preliminary examinations is the annual report on Activities of the Court submitted every year to the Assembly of States Parties.[85]

---

ther proceed or not proceed with investigations. *Idem.*, para 20: The Office has made this policy paper public in the interest of clarity and predictability over the manner in which it applies the legal framework agreed upon by States Parties. Both these paragraphs were re-tained almost identically in the 2013 Policy Paper on Preliminary Examinations.

[83] The Executive Committee is composed of the Prosecutor and the Heads of the three Divi-sions of the Office. The Executive Committee provides advice to the Prosecutor, is respon-sible for the development and adoption of the strategies, policies and budget of the Office, provide strategic guidance on all the activities of the Office and coordinates them. OTP Regulations, Regulation 4, see *supra* note 15.

[84] Prosecutor Fatou Bensouda: "My Office began releasing these annual reports in 2011, making this the fifth such report we have published. *It is not a report to the ASP per se, but rather for the public at large*, and its publication is timed to coincide with the ASP. We adopted the practice of publishing these annual reports in order to promote public aware-ness and transparency regarding the Office's preliminary examination process. For this purpose, as of last year, I have also adopted the practice of notifying the report through a press release". Remarks by Prosecutor Fatou Bensouda at the Fourteenth Session of the Assembly of States Parties on the occasion of the Launch of the 2015 Annual *Report on Preliminary Examination Activities*, 5 November 2015 (http://www.legal-tools.org/doc/ 04c7bb/).

[85] ICC, Report on the Activities of the Court, ICC-ASP/3/10, 22 July 2004 (http://www.legal-tools.org/doc/3fb24f/). ICC, Report on the Activities of the Court, ICC-ASP/4/16, 16 Sep-tember 2005 (http://www.legal-tools.org/doc/678b4c/); ICC, Report on the Activities of the Court, ICC-ASP/5/15, 17 October 2006 (http://www.legal-tools.org/doc/afd592/); ICC, Report on the Activities of the Court, ICC-ASP/6/18, 18 October 2007 (http://www.legal-tools.org/doc/8f3363/); ICC, Report on the Activities of the Court, ICC-ASP/7/25, see *su-pra* note 65; ICC, Report on the Activities of the Court, ICC-ASP/8/40, 21 October 2009 (http://www.legal-tools.org/doc/95f2fc/); ICC, Report on the Activities of the Court, ICC-ASP/9/23, 19 November 2010 (http://www.legal-tools.org/doc/f45213/); ICC, Report on the Activities of the Court, ICC-ASP/10/39, 18 November 2011 (http://www.legal-tools. org/doc/c7389a/); ICC, Report on the Activities of the Court, ICC-ASP/11/21, 9 October

---

The OTP prepared its first public situation-specific report on preliminary examinations in December 2006.[86] This was in response to a motion filed by the Central African Republic ('CAR') challenging the lack of progress in the situation referred to the OTP in 2004.[87] In this respect, PTC III stated that "a preliminary examination of a situation pursuant to Article 53(1) of the Statute and Rule 104 of the Rules must be completed within a *reasonable time* from the reception of a referral by a State Party under Articles 13(a) and 14 of the Statute, regardless of its complexity".[88] It then requested the Prosecutor to provide the Chamber and the Government of CAR, no later than by 15 December 2006, with a report containing information on the current status of the preliminary examination of the CAR situation, including an estimate of when the preliminary examination would be concluded and a decision pursuant to Article 53(1) would be taken. The Prosecutor reluctantly complied with the request, in the interests of transparency,[89] while questioning the authority of the PTC to request such information, maintaining that no provision in the Statute or RPE established a definitive time-period for a preliminary examination. The OTP has yet to recognise the significance of PTC III's decision of 30 November 2006.

2012 (http://www.legal-tools.org/doc/2d3dda/); ICC, Report on the Activities of the Court, ICC-ASP/12/28, 21 October 2013 (http://www.legal-tools.org/doc/b22709/); ICC, Report on the activities of the International Criminal Court, ICC-ASP/13/37, 19 November 2014 (http://www.legal-tools.org/doc/8cdb8d/); ICC, Report on the activities of the International Criminal Court, ICC-ASP/14/29, 13 November 2015 (http://www.legal-tools.org/doc/42f05b/); ICC, Report on the activities of the International Criminal Court, ICC-ASP/15/16, 9 November 2016 (http://www.legal-tools.org/doc/144ca9/).

[86] ICC, Situation in Central African Republic, Prosecution's Report Pursuant to Pre-Trial Chamber III's 30 November 2006 Decision Requesting Information on the Status of the Preliminary Examination of the Situation in the Central African Republic,16 December 2006, ICC-01/05-7 (http://www.legal-tools.org/doc/1dd66a/).

[87] The Government of the Central African Republic pursuant to Article 13(a) and 14 of the Statute referred the situation in Central African Republic to the Prosecutor on 22 December 2004. The Prosecutor then made a public announcement in relation to said referral stating an analysis would be carried out in order to determine whether to initiate an investigation. On 27 September 2006 Central African Republic filed a motion before the PTC requesting information on the status of the preliminary examinations of the situation in the Central African Republic.

[88] ICC, Situation in Central African Republic, Decision Requesting Information on the Status of the Preliminary Examination of the Situation in the Central African Republic, 1 December 2006, ICC-01/05-6 (http://www.legal-tools.org/doc/76e607/).

[89] *Ibid.*, para. 11.

At the time of writing, 10 preliminary examinations were ongoing,[90] four were closed with a decision not to proceed,[91] and another 10 were completed with a decision to investigate,[92] bringing the total number of *official* preliminary examinations to 24 since 2002. It should be noted that this figure only covers official preliminary examinations that have, so to speak, been made public by the OTP. There are several other situations being monitored based on confidential communications. In that sense, what is publicly reported by the OTP or submitted to the Assembly of States Parties for the purposes of budgeting requirements does not fully reflect the number of preliminary examinations that are actually being conducted by the OTP.

It therefore follows that what determines a preliminary examination's official status is publicity. That is, a preliminary examination becomes official when its existence is made public. The 2013 Policy Paper indicates that the commencement of a preliminary examination will only become public in relation to activities under Phases 2 to 4.[93] Hence, those matters falling under Phase 1, the initial assessment phase, are undisclosed. This suggests that in practice the OTP conducts a *pre-preliminary* examination before a preliminary examination is announced to the public.

The confidential phase makes it difficult to ascertain when a preliminary examination actually commences once a situation comes to the attention of the Prosecutor on the basis of Article 15 communications.[94] The

---

[90]   See the Court's web site on preliminary examinations.

[91]   *Ibid.*

[92]   *Ibid.*

[93]   OTP, *Policy Paper on Preliminary Examinations*, para. 95, see *supra* note 2.

[94]   The examination of the situation in Afghanistan from 2006, was made public in 2007 and officially reported in 2011 in the OTP Report on Preliminary Examination of 13 December 2011 with the following mention: "The OTP has received 56 communications under article 15 of the Rome Statute between 1 June 2006 and 1 June 2011. The preliminary examination of the situation in Afghanistan became public in the course of 2007". However, in 2007 there was no mention of Afghanistan in the Prosecutor's report to the ASP or in the OTP's annual address to the Assembly. In fact, the wording purposefully stated that the "Office was currently analysing information on three continents" but only mentioned two situations, namely Colombia and Côte d'Ivoire. One would presume the third situation was in Afghanistan on the Asian continent. See OTP, *Report on Preliminary Examination Activities*, 13 December 2011 (http://www.legal-tools.org/doc/4aad1d/); Address of the OTP Prosecutor Luis Moreno-Ocampo to the Assembly of State Parties, 30 November 2007

OTP often alludes to the opening,[95] closing,[96] conclusion,[97] completion,[98] or re-opening of preliminary examinations.[99] This language underscores the perplexity between preliminary examinations and investigations, because only the latter are 'opened' in the strict sense of the Statute. Moreover, there are several incongruities regarding the start date of an examination. For instance, on 7 February 2014, the OTP announced the 'opening' of a preliminary examination in CAR II.[100] Prior to that date, the OTP had

---

(http://www.legal-tools.org/doc/c6de7d/); "ICC examines possible Afghan war crimes", in *Financial Times*, 10 September 2009.

[95] ICC OTP, "The Prosecutor of the International Criminal Court, Fatou Bensouda, opens a preliminary examination in Ukraine", 25 April 2014, ICC-OTP-20140425-PR999 (http://www.legal-tools.org/doc/e4a2b5/).

[96] For example, the ICC website indicates that the preliminary examination of the situation in Iraq, terminated on 9 February 2006, was re-opened on 13 May 2014 upon receipt of new information.

[97] ICC OTP, "Statement of the Prosecutor of the International Criminal Court, Fatou Bensouda, on the conclusion of the preliminary examination of the situation in the Republic of Korea", 23 June 2014, ICC-OTP-20140623-PR1019, 23 June 2014 (http://www.legal-tools.org/doc/8d0a96/).

[98] While the Press Release on the Situation in Honduras of 28 October 2015 refers to the conclusion of the preliminary examination, it is labeled both as a 'completed' and a 'closed' examination in the OTP, Report on Preliminary Examination activities, 12 November 2015 para. 19 (http://www.legal-tools.org/doc/ac0ed2/). Similarly, the ICC web site places the situation in Honduras under those completed without a decision to investigate, however once the webpage on the Situation in Honduras is accessed its status shows it as 'closed'.

[99] ICC OTP, "Prosecutor of the International Criminal Court, Fatou Bensouda, re-opens the preliminary examination of the situation in Iraq", 13 May 2014, ICC-OTP-20140513 (http://www.legal-tools.org/doc/d9d9c5/).

[100] The Prosecutor's Statement on a new preliminary examination in the Central African Republic asserts that following the Office's analysis of the jurisdictional parameters regarding the situation in the Central African Republic since September 2012, the Prosecutor concluded that the incidents and the serious allegations of crimes potentially falling within the jurisdiction of the ICC constitute a new situation, unrelated to the situation previously referred to the ICC by the Central African Republic authorities in December 2004. See ICC OTP, "Statement of the Prosecutor, Fatou Bensouda on opening a New Preliminary Examination in the Central African Republic", 7 February 2014 (http://www.legal-tools.org/doc/6b4438/). See also ICC, Situation in the Central African Republic II, Situation in the Central African Republic II Article 53 (1) Report, 24 September 2014 (http://www.legal-tools.org/doc/1ff87e/). On 30 May 2014, the transitional government of the Central African Republic referred to the Prosecutor, pursuant to Article 14 of the Statute. See referral of the Central African Republic II, *idem*, Annex 1 Decision Assigning the Situation in the Central African Republic II to Pre-Trial Chamber II, 18 June 2014, ICC-01/14-1-Anx1 (http://www.legal-tools.org/doc/1cfbfe/).

issued statements informing the general public that it was closely following the situation in CAR. These statements indicated that the Prosecutor had been doing so since the end of 2012. It therefore appears that prior to the public announcement of the preliminary examination, the OTP was monitoring the situation, but not examining it. The same occurred with the situation in Mali. On 18 July 2012, the OTP announced that it had been following the situation in Mali very closely since violence erupted there around 17 January 2012. However, the Prosecutor's press release indicates that it was only after receiving a referral from the Malian authorities on the same day, 18 July 2012,[101] that the Prosecutor publicly instructed the Office to immediately proceed with a preliminary examination of the situation in order to assess whether the Rome Statute criteria stipulated under Article 53(1) for opening an investigation were fulfilled.[102] A separate issue here is also trying to understand when a situation is being 'followed', as opposed to 'examined', or whether these activities all just fall under the OTP's inherent monitoring role.

When the Prosecutor determines to close a preliminary examination is also ambiguous because situations under examination never seem to truly shut down.[103] For instance, the public statements of the OTP in 2006 in relation to the situations in Iraq and Venezuela clearly refer to the Prosecutor's decision not to open an investigation, which is different from a decision to close a preliminary examination.[104] The language used for these two situations, where the Rome Statute requirements have not been met, has been more or less replicated on other occasions in which statutory requirements to open an investigation were not met, even though these statements were headlined as decisions to close a preliminary examination. A reading of these decisions reveal a caveat that the Office may reconsider its conclusion not to open an investigation and senders of relevant in-

---

[101] Referral Letter by the Government of Mali, 13 July 2012 (http://www.legal-tools.org/doc/06f0bf/).

[102] ICC OTP, "ICC Prosecutor Fatou Bensouda on the Malian State referral of the situation in Mali since January 2012", 18 July 2012, ICC-OTP-20120718-PR829 (http://www.legal-tools.org/doc/31525f/).

[103] "To close", in *Oxford Dictionary of English*: Bring or come to an end (available on its web site).

[104] ICC OTP, OTP response to communications received concerning Iraq, 9 February 2006 (http://www.legal-tools.org/doc/5b8996/); ICC OTP, OTP response to communications received concerning Venezuela, 9 February 2006 (http://www.legal-tools.org/doc/c90d25/).

formation are encouraged to continue to bring such information to the attention of the Prosecutor.[105] This is what occurred with the preliminary examination in Iraq when in May of 2014 the OTP publicly announced the 're-opening' of the examination under the new heading of Iraq/UK.[106] The language was slightly changed in the Comoros situation where the OTP stated the following: "Accordingly, the Office has determined that there is no reasonable basis to proceed with an investigation and has decided to *close* this preliminary examination. The referral and additional information submitted by the Comoros will be maintained in the Office's archives and the decision not to proceed may be reconsidered at any time based on new facts or information".[107]

There is also lack of clarity regarding what goes on after a situation is presumably closed or before it eventually gets 're-opened'. Could it be that the OTP remains 'seised of the matter' or is it that these situations pass on to an inactive status ready to be resumed once sufficient infor-

---

[105] *Ibid.* The last paragraph of the OTP response to communications received concerning Iraq reads as follows: "For the above reasons, in accordance with Article 15(6) of the Rome Statute, I wish to inform you of my conclusion that, at this stage, the Statute requirements to seek authorisation to initiate an investigation in the situation in Iraq have not been satisfied. This conclusion can be reconsidered in the light of new facts or evidence. I wish to remind you, in accordance with Rule 49(2) of the Rules of Procedure and Evidence, that should you have additional information regarding crimes within the jurisdiction of the Court, you may submit it to the Office of the Prosecutor. Bearing in mind the limited jurisdiction of this Court, as well as its complementary nature, effectively functioning national legal systems are in principle the most appropriate and effective forum for addressing allegations of crimes of this nature". See *idem*, OTP response to communications received concerning Iraq.

[106] Closed preliminary examinations resound to the OTP's equivalent: 'hibernated' investigations that can later be 'de-hibernated'. The OTP explains that not all investigations lead directly to a voluntary appearance, arrest, or surrender. Where there is a lapse in time between the end of an investigation and the apprehension or voluntary appearance of a suspect, a case is considered hibernated. The comparison would be with the lapse in time between the 'termination' of a preliminary examination and the emergence of new facts or evidence. See Report of the Court on the Basic Size of the Office of the Prosecutor, 17 September 2015 ICC-ASP/14/21, paras. 17 and 19 (http://www.legal-tools.org/doc/b27d2a/).

[107] A final decision not to proceed was communicated to the PTC on 29 November 2017. See also, ICC, Situation referred by Comoros, *Article 53 (1) Report*, 6 November 2014 (http://www.legal-tools.org/doc/43e636/); see also, ICC OTP, Statement of the Prosecutor of the International Criminal Court, Fatou Bensouda, on concluding the preliminary examination of the situation referred by the Union of Comoros: "Rome Statute legal requirements have not been met", 6 November 2014 (http://www.legal-tools.org/doc/e745a0/).

mation is obtained? Article 15(5) and (6) leaves the door open for the Prosecutor to consider whether new information gathered justifies re-evaluating the situation. The ICC website contains the following three categories of preliminary examinations: (1) ongoing preliminary examinations; (2) closed with a decision not to proceed and (3) completed with a decision to investigate.[108] Accordingly, the second category should also be referred to as completed rather than closed.[109] Terminology aside, this second category would appear to encompass those instances where the PTC refuses to authorise an investigation or rejects the Prosecutor's decision not to proceed.[110] In these circumstances, a preliminary examination cannot exactly be considered as completed.[111] The same can be said when the PTC requests the OTP to review a decision or the Prosecutor decides to reconsider it.[112] Following this reasoning, the Comoros situation should have been placed under the category of ongoing preliminary examinations until the OTP's reconsideration was finalised.

In 2009, the Palestinian Authority sought to accept the jurisdiction of the ICC. On 3 April 2012, after a three-year examination of the situation in Palestine, the OTP announced that the preconditions for the exercise of jurisdiction were not met.[113] This particular statement made no reference to the closing of the situation, although in subsequent documents it was described in those terms.[114] The OTP concluded it lacked

---

[108] Preliminary Examinations, ICC website, see *supra* note 90.

[109] The preliminary examination conducted in the Palestine situation between 2009–2012 belongs under the second category. In the 2012 OTP Report on Preliminary Examination Activities the situation is reported as completed. See OTP, *Report on Preliminary Examination Activities*, 22 November 2012, paras. 196–203 (http://www.legal-tools.org/doc/0b1cfc/).

[110] ICC Statute, Articles 15(4) and 53(1), see *supra* note 5; ICC RPE, Rule 105, see *supra* note 6.

[111] In the same way that the action of investigating may well continue through the proceedings and even at the appeals stage (or after, since many investigations can be opened in a same situation).

[112] ICC Statute, Article 53(4), see *supra* note 5; ICC RPE, Rule 107, see *supra* note 6.

[113] ICC, Situation in Palestine (embargoed until delivery 3 April 2012) (http://www.legal-tools.org/doc/f5d6d7/).

[114] OTP, *Report on Preliminary Examination Activities*, para. 196, see *supra* note 109 reads as follows: "On 3 April 2012, the Office issued a decision to close the preliminary examination of the situation in Palestine[…]". See also the OTP, *Report on Preliminary Examination Activities*, para. 48, see *supra* note 48: "*The Office previously conducted a preliminary*

---

jurisdiction due to Palestine's contested statehood, but the situation still required an examination to determine whether the statutory requirements had been met.[115] Technically, the lack of statehood should have led the OTP to declare the situation manifestly outside its jurisdiction. However, the Prosecutor's decision to consider this examination publicly resulted in greater polarisation of an already controversial matter and placed unnecessary pressure on the OTP to deliver results.[116] Notably in this situation, the Prosecutor determined that a fair process required that the Palestinian National Authority, as well as other interested parties be granted the opportunity to be heard and by so doing: "[T]he Office therefore ensured due process to all parties involved".[117] In the end, the Prosecutor conceded that the Rome Statute provides no authority for the Office to adopt a method to define the term "State" under Article 12(3).[118] What makes the Prosecutor's approach to the Palestinian matter exceptional is that due process considerations have not been a feature of any other preliminary examination process in any other situation.

---

examination of the situation in Palestine upon receipt of a purported article 12(3) declaration lodged by the Palestinian National Authority on 22 January 2009. The Office carefully considered all legal arguments submitted to it and, after thorough analysis and public consultations, concluded in April 2012 that Palestine's status at the UN as an "observer entity" was determinative, since entry into the Rome Statute system is through the UNSG, who acts as treaty depositary. The Palestinian Authority's "observer entity", as opposed to "non-member State" status at the UN, at the time meant that it could not sign or ratify the Statute. As Palestine could not join the Rome Statute at that time, the Office concluded that it could also not lodge an article 12(3) declaration bringing itself within the ambit of the treaty, as it had sought to do".

[115] The Office of the Prosecutor carefully considered all of the legal arguments put forth and concluded in April 2012, after three years of thorough analysis and public consultations that Palestine's status at the UN as "observer entity" was determinant – since entry into the Rome Statute system is through the UN Secretary-General, who acts as treaty depositary. The OTP's position was that the Palestinian Authority's "observer entity" status at the UN at that time meant that it could not sign up to the Rome Statute. As Palestine could not join the Rome Statute, Prosecutor Luis Moreno-Ocampo concluded that it could not lodge an Article 12(3) declaration bringing itself under the ambit of the treaty either, as it had sought to do.

[116] Palestine applied for Membership in the UN on 23 September 2011. The process was stalled in the Security Council, however on 31 October 2011 UNESCO's General Conference voted to admit Palestine as a Member State of the Organisation. In 2012, the General Assembly granted it a non-member observer State status, which was determinative.

[117] OTP, *Report on Preliminary Examination Activities*, para. 17, see *supra* note 94.

[118] OTP, *Report on Preliminary Examination Activities*, para. 201, see *supra* note 109.

The Palestine episode may provide some explanation of why the 2013 Policy Paper specifies that the commencement of a preliminary examination will not be publicised before entering Phase 2.[119] However, Phase 2 concerns jurisdiction as well. Consequently, preliminary examinations should not be publicised at all until jurisdiction has been established and ideally not before a decision to proceed or not with an investigation has been taken. It is not clear that the OTP could keep a preliminary examination confidential even if it wanted to, if senders of communications or States determine to make them public.[120] Regardless, the focus of this chapter is when the OTP purposefully publicises preliminary examination activities and takes public stances on situations under examination to influence change. In this respect, it would be preferable if the confidential nature of the examination process is maintained until a decision to investigate is taken. Making announcements before a determination to investigate can do more harm than good. Such is the case with situations under Phase 2 in which subject-matter jurisdiction is still being examined. At that point, the OTP is not even certain that crimes within the jurisdiction of the Rome Statute have been committed. What legitimate purpose, if any, does it serve to publicise the examination of activities that may not even end up constituting Rome Statute crimes? This can be observed in the Iraq/UK situation 're-opened' in 2014 and currently under Phase 2.[121]

Similarly, in the Honduras situation, after a nearly five-year long examination the conclusion was that "[t]he Prosecutor lacks a reasonable basis to proceed with an investigation and has decided to close this pre-

---

[119] OTP, *Policy Paper on Preliminary Examinations*, para. 95, see *supra* note 2.

[120] For example, news that the Prosecutor was examining crimes committed in Colombia became public in March 2005 when Colombian lawmakers released a letter from Luis Moreno-Ocampo requesting information on alleged crimes. See BBC News, "ICC probes Colombia on war crimes", 31 March 2005; School of the Americas, "War Crimes Tribunal Asks Colombia for Info" (available on its web site).

[121] Another question that arises is whether preliminary examinations should resume where they were left off, that is, when a situation is re-opened, previously finding there was subject-matter jurisdiction but that the alleged crimes were not of sufficient gravity. How is it that the Iraq/UK situation has remained under Phase 2 since its 're-opening' in 2014 when in 2006 the OTP had already confirmed jurisdiction over ICC crimes while concluding they were not of sufficient gravity, and collected information on national proceedings observing they had been initiated in respect to each incident. Currently it appears as though the OTP starts from scratch when re-opening situations.

liminary examination".[122] The OTP asserted that the situation in Honduras raised a number of issues that characterised it as a "borderline case",[123] without explaining why it reached this determination. Rather, it is left to interested stakeholders to infer that perhaps the complexity of the situation or the challenges of having to rely on information in different languages underpinned the Prosecutor's decision. Moreover, the OTP's open-ended practice to collect information over a long period of time prior to making any determination is neither pragmatic nor does it contribute to the efficiency of prosecutorial activity. In the Honduras situation, like with others, the Prosecutor continuously expanded the grounds for examination.[124] Preliminary examinations do not require the OTP to determine all aspects of a potential investigation, only to establish a reasonable basis to proceed with an investigation.

The Article 5 Report on the Situation in Honduras, which contains the reasoning for not proceeding with an investigation, is quite comprehensive and well-written. The report puts all the pieces together and lays bare the OTP's decision-making process. This approach reinforces holding off on putting out inconclusive or piecemeal information that can be misleading.[125] If we go back to the moment when the Honduras situation was made public, the OTP issued a newsletter referring to the recent announcement mentioning that, in "order to fulfil its mandate and maximize the preventative impact of its work, the Office will make public its preliminary examination activities when it assesses that this will have a posi-

---

[122] OTP, *Situation in Honduras: Article 5 Report*, 28 October 2015, paras. 31 and 143 (http://www.legal-tools.org/doc/54755a/).

[123] Unfortunately, the great majority of transnational organised crimes are outside the jurisdiction of the ICC. Attempts to include crimes such as trafficking in drugs into the ICC Statute were met by great opposition in Rome. See *ibid.*, paras. 30 and 93.

[124] The preliminary examination in Honduras was prompted by the 2009 coup that later expanded to post-electoral violence incidents and eventually led to a full analysis of links between the alleged crimes and the patterns of violence in the country affected by transnational organised crime.

[125] See OTP, Report on Preliminary Examination activities, see *supra* note 94; OTP, *Report on Preliminary Examination Activities*, see *supra* note 109; OTP, Report on Preliminary Examination activities, 25 November 2013 (http://www.legal-tools.org/doc/dbf75e/); OTP, Report on Preliminary Examination activities, 2 December 2014 (http://www.legal-tools.org/doc/3594b3/); OTP, Report on Preliminary Examination activities, see *supra* note 98; Report on the Situation in Honduras and Colombia 2 December 2014; OTP, *Situation in Honduras: Article 5 Report*, see *supra* note 122.

tive impact in stopping violence and preventing future crimes or when the senders of communications make them public".[126] Nevertheless, how can an assessment of positive impact occur before knowing if Rome Statute crimes have been committed? This is not to suggest that the idea is without merit. However, at such an early juncture, it would have been more prudent to simply confirm the receipt of communications and announce the OTP's commitment to seriously examine the information in accordance with the provisions of the Rome Statute. The fact that the Honduras situation deteriorated during the post-electoral period shows that, despite the OTP's best intentions, the announcement of the preliminary examination had little, if any, impact on preventing alleged crimes. It would therefore seem preferable to keep that process internal, in line with Article 53(1), until a reasonable basis decision is reached.

According to the 2013 Policy Paper, the Office will seek to publicise its preliminary examination activities in various ways, including through early interaction with stakeholders, dissemination of relevant statistics on Article 15 communications, public statements, periodic reports, and information on high-level visits to the concerned States.[127] If we were to group the different communication methods employed by the OTP to keep the public informed about situations under preliminary examination, we would find the following:

1. Media reports through press releases,[128] statements,[129] communications,[130] background notes,[131] and questions and answers;[132]

---

[126] ICC, OTP Weekly Briefing, 16–22 November 2010, Issue #64 (http://www.legal-tools.org/doc/0250bc/).

[127] OTP, *Policy Paper on Preliminary Examinations*, paras. 95–96, see *supra* note 2.

[128] ICC, "The Prosecutor of the International Criminal Court, Fatou Bensouda, issues her annual Report on Preliminary Examination Activities (2016)", 14 November 2016, ICC-CPI-20161114-PR1252 (http://www.legal-tools.org/doc/834809/).

[129] ICC, "Statement of the Prosecutor of the International Criminal Court, Fatou Bensouda, concerning referral from the Gabonese Republic", 29 September 2016 (http://www.legal-tools.org/doc/e0b4f6/).

[130] ICC-OTP, OTP response to communications received concerning Iraq, see *supra* note 104; *idem*, OTP response to communications received concerning Venezuela, see *supra* note 104.

[131] A background note on the situation in the Central African Republic and the OTP's work to date (http://www.legal-tools.org/doc/7ed1ee/).

2. Statements[133] and reports to the Assembly of States Parties, including on activities of the Court,[134] annual activities on preliminary examinations,[135] situation-specific reports,[136] Article 5 reports[137] and Article 53(1) reports;[138]

3. Reports[139] and statements to the United Nations;[140]

4. Filings by the OTP in relation to situations under preliminary examination;[141]

5. Policy Papers on preliminary examinations[142] and related matters;

6. OTP Weekly Briefings Newsletters;[143]

---

[132] Questions & Answers On the decision of the ICC Prosecutor to close the preliminary examination in Honduras, 28 October 2015 (http://www.legal-tools.org/doc/f0035a/).

[133] Address by Prosecutor Luis Moreno-Ocampo to the Third Session of the Assembly of States Parties to the Rome Statute of the International Criminal Court, 6 September 2004 (http://www.legal-tools.org/doc/0ada13/).

[134] ICC, Reports on activities of the ICC, see *supra* note 85.

[135] OTP, *Report on Preliminary Examination Activities*, see *supra* note 25.

[136] Rapport sur les activités menées en 2014 en matière d'examen préliminaire Situations en Guinée et République Centrafricaine, 2 December 2014 (http://www.legal-tools.org/doc/9cc819/); Informe sobre las Actividades de Examen Preliminar de 2014 Honduras y Colombia (Joint Reports Guinea/ and Honduras/Colombia) (http://www.legal-tools.org/doc/153076/).

[137] OTP, *Situation in Honduras: Article 5 Report*, see *supra* note 122; ICC, *Situation in the Republic of Korea: Article 5 Report*, 23 June 2014 (http://www.legal-tools.org/doc/ef1f7f/); OTP, *Situation in Nigeria: Article 5 Report*, 5 August 2013 (http://www.legal-tools.org/doc/508bd0/).

[138] *Situation referred by Comoros: Article 53(1) Report*, see *supra* note 107; *Situation in the Central African Republic II: Article 53 (1) Report*, see *supra* note 100.

[139] *Report of the International Criminal Court on its activities in 2015/16*, A/71/342, 19 August 2016 (http://www.legal-tools.org/doc/9606ac/).

[140] ICC, First Report of the Prosecutor of the International Criminal Court to the United Nations Security Council pursuant to UNSCR 1970 (2011), 4 May 2011 (http://www.legal-tools.org/doc/76ba00/); Statement by Prosecutor Luis Moreno-Ocampo to the United Nations Security Council on the situation in the Libyan Arab Jamahiriya, pursuant to UNSCR 1970 (2011), 4 May 2011 (http://www.legal-tools.org/doc/9bb5db/).

[141] Situation in the Central African Republic, Decision Requesting Information on the Status of the Preliminary Examination of the Situation in the Central African Republic, see *supra* note 88.

[142] OTP, *Policy Paper on Preliminary Examinations*, see *supra* note 2; OTP, Draft *Policy Paper on Preliminary Examinations*, see *supra* note 17.

[143] ICC, OTP Weekly Briefing, see *supra* note 126.

---

7. Lectures and speeches presented at seminars, conferences and training addressing or referring to preliminary examinations;[144] and

8. Diplomatic briefings.[145]

The above range of communication methods demonstrates the OTP's creativity and flexibility, as well as how it has evolved in its approach towards publicity in an effort to be more transparent about its activities.[146] At the same time, the range of communication methods also shows a case-by-case approach with no methodological system in place to understand when and what information is made public and for what reason. According to the 2013 Policy Paper, the Office has adopted a policy of issuing situation-specific reports to substantiate the Prosecutor's decision to 'close' a preliminary examination, or to proceed with an investigation.[147] Paradoxically, the rationale provided by the OTP is the same as in the 2009 OTP public responses to communications received concerning Iraq and Venezuela, both on decisions not to proceed with an investigation.[148]

There are two main types of situation-specific reports: Article 5 and Article 53(1).[149] Both reports attempt to explain the Prosecutor's reasons for 'closing' situations. However, Article 5 reports are limited to circumstances where subject-matter jurisdiction is not met. At least that was the basis for 'closing' the situation in Honduras and in relation to the Repub-

---

[144] The International Criminal Court and Africa: A Discussion on Legitimacy, Impunity, Selectivity, Fairness and Accountability, Keynote Speech of the Prosecutor - GIMPA Law Conference on the ICC and Africa, 17 March 2016 (http://www.legal-tools.org/doc/19ff9b/); Speech of the Prosecutor, International Seminar on the imperatives of the Observance of Human Rights and International Humanitarian Law Norms in International Security Operations, Seminar hosted by the Attorney General of the Federation and Minister of Justice of Nigeria, 24 February 2014 (http://www.legal-tools.org/doc/4cbd32/).

[145] Most of the texts of these briefings are available at the Court's web site under "Reports on activities", with search string "Diplomatic Briefing".

[146] OTP, *Report on Preliminary Examination Activities*, para. 14, see *supra* note 25.

[147] OTP, *Policy Paper on Preliminary Examinations*, para.97, see *supra* note 2.

[148] ICC-OTP, OTP response to communications received concerning Iraq, see *supra* note 104; *idem*, OTP response to communications received concerning Venezuela, see *supra* note 104.

[149] In addition to the joint reports referred to above, see *supra* note 137, the OTP has issued interim reports. In relation to the Interim Report on Colombia of 14 November 2012 the OTP explained the presentation of a more detailed report was exceptional in nature, in recognition of the high level of public interest generated by this examination.

---

lic of Korea. However, the Article 5 report relating to the situation in Nigeria addressed a different matter, namely why the OTP saw merit in moving the situation to Phase 3.[150] Not only is this a discrepancy regarding the purpose of Article 5 reports, but it also presents an inconsistency with regard to other situations that advanced to Phase 3, such as with the situation in Afghanistan. What this inconsistency underscores is the seemingly *ad hoc* and selective approach the OTP has adopted in relation to the publication of information about its preliminary examinations. If the OTP is committed to transparency in the preliminary examination process, then it needs to adopt a consistent approach. The fact that the OTP has to date failed to develop a coherent methodology that guides the publication of its preliminary examination activities is a matter that requires further scrutiny. Some of the possible reasons behind the OTP's publicity policies are examined below.

24.4. Reasons for Publicising Preliminary Examination Activities

The policy-making activity of the OTP has been regular and substantial, covering a wide array of topics.[151] According to the OTP's Regulations, the Office shall, as appropriate, make public policy papers that reflect the key principles and criteria of the prosecutorial strategy.[152] With respect to preliminary examinations, the OTP has from the outset been forthcoming about regularly fine-tuning its policies and practices. The 2013 Policy Paper stipulates it is a document reflecting an internal policy of the OTP that does not give rise to legal rights, and is subject to revision based on

---

[150] *Situation in Nigeria: Article 53(1) Report*, para. 131, see *supra* note 138 specifies the following: "Accordingly, the Prosecutor has decided to move the situation in Nigeria to Phase 3 of the preliminary examination with a view to assessing whether the Nigerian authorities are conducting genuine proceedings in relation to the crimes committed by Boko Haram".

[151] OTP, *Policy Paper on the Interest of Justice*, see *supra* note 29; *idem, Policy Paper on Victims' Participation*, 12 April 2010 (http://www.legal-tools.org/doc/3c204f/); *idem, Policy Paper on Preliminary Examinations*, see *supra* note 2; *idem, Policy Paper on Case Selection and Prioritisation*, 15 September 2016 (http://www.legal-tools.org/doc/182205/); *idem, Policy Paper on Sexual and Gender-Based Crimes and Policy*, 5 June 2014 (http://www.legal-tools.org/doc/7ede6c/); *idem, Policy on Children* (http://www.legal-tools.org/doc/c2652b/).

[152] OTP Regulations, 2009, Regulation 14(2), see *supra* note 15.

experience and in light of legal determinations by the Chambers of the Court.[153]

The OTP contends it has decided to put forward a policy paper that describes the relevant Rome Statute principles, factors and procedures applied by the Office in the conduct of its preliminary examination activities. It explains it has made the policy paper public in the interest of promoting clarity and predictability regarding the manner in which it applies the legal criteria set out in the Statute.[154] In this connection, the OTP produces annual reports on preliminary examination activities aimed at raising public awareness and promoting transparency regarding the Office's preliminary examination process and related activities.[155] Unlike other reports, these are promptly disseminated to the general public through press releases and promoted further through informal launch events during the sessions of the Assembly of States Parties.

24.4.1. Manifest Reasons

By and large, the OTP's practice of sharing information publicly has been well-received. At the same time, it is difficult not to find a political motive behind the profile-raising of the preliminary examination activities of the OTP when compared to equivalent procedures at the domestic level, where preliminary findings generally result from a confidential process that occurs away from the public eye. This is not to suggest the ICC does not need publicity. Quite the opposite, an international court requires a careful handling of its public image to maintain support for its activities from the international community.

24.4.1.1. Transparency

The *raison d'être* of having a public policy and reporting regularly is transparency. But what does transparency mean in the realm of preliminary examinations? It should not be just another buzzword to attract sup-

---

[153] This caveat is important and recognises the need to enhance preliminary examinations and to continue improving the process. Notwithstanding the OTP should abide as much as possible to its policy otherwise it can give the impression of applying double standards. See OTP, *Policy Paper on Preliminary Examinations*, para. 20, see *supra* note 2.

[154] *Ibid.*

[155] ICC, "The Prosecutor of the International Criminal Court, Fatou Bensouda, issues her annual Report on Preliminary Examination Activities (2016)", 14 November 2016 (http://www.legal-tools.org/doc/834809/).

---

port or gain legitimacy. For transparency to have a real impact, it must be meaningful, exemplifying appropriate communication and ensuring accountability. Transparency as an objective should also aim to give the OTP long-term coherence so that its activities become both predictable and credible. The 2013 Policy Paper associates transparency with access to information.[156] Paragraph 94 specifies that in order to promote a better understanding of the process of preliminary examinations and to increase predictability, the Office will regularly report on its preliminary examination activities.

There is a proper level of transparency that is unique for each organisation and for each of its processes. The OTP cannot be expected to share all the information in its possession with everyone who is interested in having access to it. What is important for the purpose of transparency is the accurate and timely disclosure of information to the appropriate recipient(s).

Despite the OTP's paramount and well-intentioned efforts to share information, concerns remain in the international community because its reporting on preliminary examination activities has not necessarily brought about greater transparency or understanding of the OTP's activities. Indeed, while some preliminary examinations move very quickly (Kenya), others seem to stagnate for years (Colombia and Afghanistan). It is also unclear why the Office conducts regular missions to some countries (Colombia, Guinea and Georgia) but not to others. In November 2016, the OTP reported that a final decision was "imminent" on whether to request the PTC authorisation to investigate the situation in Afghanistan.[157] This announcement naturally raised expectations. It took the Office a whole year to request the authorisation from the PTC, resulting in a loss of trust and credibility and clearly no sense of increased transparency in the activities of the OTP. The long-awaited justification of why such a statement was made at that time and the circumstances that caused it to be no longer true were not compelling, nor did they help to restore confidence in OTP reporting.[158]

---

[156] OTP, *Policy Paper on Preliminary Examinations*, paras. 94-99, see *supra* note 2.

[157] OTP, *Report on Preliminary Examination Activities*, para. 230, see *supra* note 25.

[158] In relation to the same situation compare the language in paragraph 4 of the ICC, Report on the activities of the International Criminal Court, see *supra* note 85 which reads as follows: "*[t]he Office began to gather information relevant for assessing whether there are*

Separately, it was also noticeable, after the PTC in July 2015 rejected the OTP's decision not to proceed with an investigation in the situation relating to the Registered Vessels of Comoros, Greece and Cambodia, that this important development was left out of the preliminary examination activities report of that same year.[159] In 2016, the situation was reintroduced in the preliminary examination activities report, listed as still under examination.[160] In that report, a new section was added entitled "situations under reconsideration" contending that the OTP was nearing completion of its review of all information gathered, prior to and since its initial report of 6 November 2014, and was preparing to issue the Prosecutor's final decision under Rule 108(3) in "the near future".[161]

The OTP's choice of terminology is once again at fault. The near future was somewhat distant from the 12 months it took the OTP to issue its decision. Moreover, it seems impossible to distinguish between an imminent decision and one that will be issued in the near future. The lack of updates between reports was also not helpful. The OTP should increase its efforts to provide more timely and accurate information, along with reliable forecasts. These examples serve to explain why transparency must be consistently demonstrated and statements supported by actions.

As we have seen, the OTP routinely reports on situations under examination even in the absence of a formal requirement. Although transparency is always desirable, it has to be the right kind and balanced out against other values such as the need to maintain confidentiality, the need to maintain credibility and the need to maintain the trust of States. If the intention of the OTP in publicising its preliminary examination activities is to send a particular message – to prevent crimes, encourage national prosecutions or to impact in some other way the situation that it is considering – then the OTP should reflect on what are the most appropriate

---

substantial reasons to believe that an investigation would not serve the interests of justice prior to making a decision on whether to seek authorization from the Pre-Trial Chamber to open an investigation". With just one week apart the 2016 OTP Report on Preliminary Examination Activities indicated convincingly that a final decision to seek authorisation to investigate in the situation in Afghanistan was 'imminent'.

[159] Although the OTP appealed the PTC decision it was still adjudicated before the issuance of the 2015 report.

[160] OTP, *Report on Preliminary Examination Activities*, para. 20, see *supra* note 25.

[161] OTP, *Report on Preliminary Examination Activities*, para. 331, see *supra* note 25.

---

means to achieve its goals. For example, resorting to quiet diplomacy. When it comes to reporting to the public at large the information should serve to update on the situation by presenting factual and legal findings that are relevant to the decision to proceed or not with an investigation. Anything different or divorced from reality is negligent and may even constitute a breach of the Prosecutor's duty of care as a global public figure.

During the preliminary examination stage, the OTP handles information that is both sensitive and inconclusive, making it premature to share with the general public given the adverse impacts for the States concerned. Under these circumstances, channels of communication should be limited to main stakeholders, such as the senders of information and concerned States, until the moment the OTP is truly in a position to announce its decision to proceed or not with an investigation. This should not be read as a statement against transparency. What the author is advocating for is a more meaningful transparency and that thoughtful consideration be given to what is publicised when a situation is under examination through a proper balancing of all the interests involved.

24.4.1.2. Raising Public Awareness

Structurally, within international courts or tribunals, external relations and raising public awareness about the work of the Court is a function that is mainly carried out by the Registry through outreach activities. However, prosecutors also have a valuable role to play in raising awareness and educating the public about their work, which is separate and independent from the work of the Court as such. Efforts must be made to ensure that the work of the Prosecutor is not only known but also understood by the societies on whose behalf he or she acts.

Under the regulatory framework of the Court, the OTP has a mandate relating to public information and outreach in general.[162] So far, the

---

[162] Pursuant to Regulation 15, the Office shall disseminate information on its activities to, and respond to enquiries from States, international organisations, victims, non-governmental organisations and the general public, with a particular focus on the communities affected by the work of the Office, as appropriate in coordination with the Registry. In doing so, the Office shall at all times ensure compliance with its statutory obligations and the decisions of the Chambers regarding confidentiality, and the safety and well-being of victims, witnesses, Office staff and other persons at risk on account of their interaction with the Court.

Office has focused most of its attention on increasing the visibility of its preliminary examination activities. On several occasions, the OTP has stressed the benefits that awareness of ICC scrutiny can have: "[T]he announcement of ICC activities can have a preventive impact. The mere monitoring of a situation can deter future crimes. It increases the risk of punishment even before trials begin. This effect is not limited to the situation under investigation but extends to all State Parties and reverberates worldwide".[163] However, this comes with particular challenges regarding the impartiality and role of the Prosecutor, as envisaged in the Rome Statute.

The Office is employing its monitoring of situations and subsequent public statements, as a form of targeted deterrence in situations where it appears that a recurrence of crimes is likely.[164] Promoting preliminary examination activities in this way can be counterproductive and to the detriment of the main functions of the OTP – investigations and prosecutions. Paragraph 95 of the 2013 Policy Paper underscores that "such information provided to the public will enable the Office to carry out its mandate without raising undue expectations that an investigation will necessarily be opened, while at the same time encouraging genuine national proceedings and contributing towards the prevention of crimes". The reality is that publicising this information has achieved the opposite. The policy of the Prosecutor to use preliminary examinations for other purposes is well intentioned but, as will be explained below, is simply not working.

It adds that the Office shall contribute to the Court's outreach strategies and activities. OTP Regulations, see *supra* note 15.

[163] Under ICC, Office of the Prosecutor, *Report on Prosecutorial Strategy*, 14 September 2006, p. 6 (http://www.legal-tools.org/doc/6e3bf4/): "The third principle [i]s to maximize the impact of the activities of the Office. As noted in the Preamble of the Statute, the Court has a role in contributing to the prevention of future crimes. The Office has to maximize the impact of each of its activities, from the analysis of the information, to the beginning of the investigation, to the trial and eventual conviction. Massive crimes are planned; the announcement of an investigation could have a preventative impact. The mere monitoring of a situation could deter future crimes from being committed. It increases the risk of punishment even before trials have begun. Interestingly, this effect is not limited to the situation under investigation but extends to different countries around the world".

[164] Bosco, 2013, p. 181, see *supra* note 70.

In 2009, the OTP incorporated into its Prosecutorial Strategy document the goal of prevention through public monitoring, indicating that the Office would "make preventive statements noting that crimes possibly falling within the jurisdiction of the Court are being committed" and "make public the commencement of a preliminary examination at the earliest possible stage through press releases and public statements".[165] This preventative goal is also one of the three policy objectives contained in the 2013 Policy Paper establishing that the Office may also issue public, preventive statements in order to deter the escalation of violence and the further commission of crimes, to put perpetrators on notice that they may be held to account.[166]

This policy objective has led the OTP to issue several 'early warnings' and strongly-worded statements directed to States and to perpetrators. In situations where conflict has broken out abruptly, the OTP has signalled to combatants that it is scrutinising events, a clear attempt to use its influence to alter the conduct of hostilities. When fighting erupted between Georgian and Russian forces in August 2008, the OTP released a statement indicating that it was analysing alleged crimes committed during combat operations.[167] Just two days after a massacre at a refugee camp in Uganda, the Prosecutor released a statement indicating his intent to investigate, which could also be seen as an effort to assure the affected Ugandan communities that revenge attacks were unnecessary and to thereby help prevent a spiral of violence.[168] The Prosecutor also condemned the killing of seven United Nations peacekeepers from Tanzania and the wounding of 17 military and police personnel of the African Union–United Nations Hybrid Operation in Darfur ('UNAMID') on 13 July 2013 in South Darfur. The statement provided a strong reminder that attacks against peacekeepers may constitute war crimes.[169]

---

[165] OTP, Prosecutorial Strategy 2009-2012, para. 39 see *supra* note 75.

[166] OTP, *Policy Paper on Preliminary Examinations*, para. 106, see *supra* note 2.

[167] ICC OTP, ICC Prosecutor confirms situation in Georgia under analysis, 20 August 2008, ICC-OTP-20080820-PR346 (http://www.legal-tools.org/doc/1e947b/).

[168] ICC OTP, Statement by the Prosecutor related to crimes committed in Barlonya Camp, Uganda, 23 February 2004 (http://www.legal-tools.org/doc/022076/).

[169] ICC OTP, Statement of the ICC Prosecutor: Attacks against peacekeepers may constitute war crimes, 19 July 2013 (http://www.legal-tools.org/doc/ac9487/).

The OTP has also adopted the practice of issuing statements related to electoral violence such as with Kenya, Guinea, CAR and Burundi.[170] Some of these statements have been pre-emptive and others *post-facto*. In Nigeria, the Prosecutor warned ahead of elections that: "Any person who incites or engages in acts of violence encouraging or contributing to the commission of crimes that fall within ICC's jurisdiction – is liable to prosecution; either by Nigerian Courts or by the ICC".[171] Conversely, when violence broke out in Côte d'Ivoire after a disputed election, the Prosecutor publicly warned one individual that his incitements to violence might be prosecuted.[172] On this point, the United Nations Secretary-General has recognised that carefully monitoring electoral processes in ICC situation countries may help prevent large-scale violence resulting from elections by putting would-be violators on notice that impunity is not assured.[173]

Another striking example where the OTP tried to exert pressure is in relation to the situation in the Philippines.[174] On 13 October 2016, the Prosecutor expressed concerns over alleged extra-judicial killings and vowed to closely follow developments "in the Philippines in the weeks to come and record any instance of incitement or resort to violence with a

---

[170] ICC OTP, Prosecutor reaffirms that the situation in Kenya is monitored by his office, 11 February 2009 (http://www.legal-tools.org/doc/acbb26); ICC OTP, Statement of the ICC Prosecutor Statement on the occasion of the 28 September 2013 elections in Guinea, 27 September 2013 (http://www.legal-tools.org/doc/96982f/); Statement of the Prosecutor of the International Criminal Court, Fatou Bensouda, ahead of general elections in the Central African Republic: "we will record any instance of violence or incitement to violence", 23 December 2015 (http://www.legal-tools.org/doc/b1e153/); ICC OTP, Statement of the Prosecutor of the International Criminal Court, Fatou Bensouda, regarding the recent pre-election violence in Burundi, 8 May 2015 (http://www.legal-tools.org/doc/db08e6/).

[171] ICC OTP, Statement by the Prosecutor of the International Criminal Court, Fatou Bensouda, ahead of elections in Nigeria: "I reiterate my call to refrain from violence", 16 March 2015 (http://www.legal-tools.org/doc/db08e6/).

[172] ICC OTP, Statement by ICC Prosecutor Luis Moreno-Ocampo on the situation in Côte d'Ivoire, 21 December 2010, ICC-OTP-20101221-PR617 (http://www.legal-tools.org/doc/3ffcf8/).

[173] Report of the Secretary-General, The rule of law and transitional justice in conflict and post-conflict societies, 23 August 2004, S/2004/616, para. 49 (http://www.legal-tools.org/doc/77bebf/).

[174] ICC OTP, Statement of the Prosecutor of the International Criminal Court, Fatou Bensouda concerning the situation in the Republic of the Philippines, 13 October 2016 (http://www.legal-tools.org/doc/bbc78e/).

view to assessing whether a preliminary examination into the situation of the Philippines needs to be opened". The statement expressly referred to high-level officials condoning or encouraging such actions, which included the Head of State of the Philippines. Interestingly it referred to a figure of over 3,000 deaths in three months, while clarifying that a preliminary examination had not yet taken place. Presumably, this alarming figure would be enough to conduct a preliminary examination in accordance with the duty to analyse the seriousness of the information communicated to the Office. How can the Prosecutor issue statements containing details it has not yet assessed? Why announce close scrutiny in the weeks to come to assess the need to conduct a preliminary examination, but then take 16 months - until February 2018 - to follow through?

The statement concerning the so-called Islamic State of Iraq and al-Sham/Greater Syria ('ISIS', also known as 'ISIL', 'Daesh' or 'IS')[175] was quite unique because it served as a clarification in response to criticism for not taking any action with respect to alleged crimes committed by this entity. After a careful reading of the statement, it seems to imply that a preliminary examination was carried out. In the statement, the Prosecutor claims to have jurisdiction but that the prospects of the OTP investigating and prosecuting those most responsible, within the leadership of ISIS, is limited because it involves nationals from two non-States Parties. The statement confirms the receipt of communications concerning the commission of crimes against humanity and war crimes by members of ISIS involving nationals from States Parties. The Prosecutor nevertheless concludes that: "[t]he jurisdictional basis for opening a preliminary examination into this situation is too narrow at this stage" taking into account OTP policy, which is to focus on those most responsible for mass crimes.[176]

---

[175] ICC OTP, Statement of the Prosecutor of the International Criminal Court, Fatou Bensouda, on the alleged crimes committed by ISIS, 8 April 2015 (http://www.legal-tools.org/doc/b1d672/).

[176] The contradiction lies in the OTP's reliance on its prosecutorial strategy as an obstacle to proceeding further. At that time the OTP in both Strategic Plans 2012–2015 and 2016–2018 had already shifted its policy through a strategy of gradually building upwards. By then the OTP had already recognised that it might need "first to investigate and prosecute a limited number of mid- and high-level perpetrators in order to ultimately have a reasonable prospect of conviction for the most responsible. Moreover that the Office would also consider prosecuting lower level perpetrators where their conduct has been particularly grave and has acquired extensive notoriety". The ISIS situation seems to fall within this policy

Unfortunately, this statement by the Prosecutor did not succeed in clarifying why not even a preliminary examination could be carried out, if indeed it had not been, given that the statement itself confirmed that there was enough information to do so. Instead the statement reads as an excuse for not fulfilling the Prosecutor's statutory duties. As well as an encouragement to those States Parties whose nationals allegedly committed crimes to fulfil their primary duty to investigate and prosecute.

The Prosecutor's strategy of issuing statements that threaten to 'open' a preliminary examination, or statements asserting that a situation is being monitored without a real intention to examine the situation, has muddied the waters further with respect to understanding the preliminary examination process. The Prosecutor is clearly using the powers to conduct preliminary examinations in ways that relate more to the OTP's policy objectives of prevention and deterrence or encouraging national proceedings, than to the task of determining whether a reasonable basis exists to open an investigation. Regardless of the Prosecutor's motives, any public statement issued by the Prosecutor should be strategically-framed if it is to be effective. Statements also present some advantages over reports, allowing for more timely and frequent messaging, whereas reports are lengthy and less adjustable given their annual cycles.

In 2015 the Prosecutor offered to assess the preventive impact of preliminary examination activities, though no methodology to do so has been developed so far.[177] Without convincing evidence that the Prosecutor's statements have a preventive or deterrent impact on crimes, it is premature to attribute so much value to this objective. It would be safer to collect more data in this regard.

---

and therefore should not have prevented the OTP from pursuing investigations or should have at least made the Prosecutor hesitate before issuing such a statement.

[177] OTP, Strategic Plan 2016-2018, para. 54(3), see *supra* note 1. "Preliminary examinations can also help deter actual or would-be perpetrators of crimes through the threat of international prosecutions. In accordance with its policy, the Office will seek to perform an early warning function by systematically and proactively collecting open source information on alleged crimes that could fall within the jurisdiction of the Court. The Office will also react promptly to upsurges or serious risks of violence by reinforcing early interaction with States, international, regional organisations and non- governmental organisations in order to fine-tune its assessment and coordinate next steps. Such steps may include field visits, public statements and media interviews. *The Office will further develop criteria for guiding such preventive activities*".

24.4.2. Secondary Reasons

It is conceivable that the OTP has secondary reasons for publicising its activities on situations under examination, for example, to mitigate criticism of perceived bias, insufficient workload or marginal outcomes, which will be considered in the following section.

24.4.2.1. To Counter Claims of Geographical Imbalance

The ICC has been consistently characterised by the African Union[178] as anti-African.[179] The alternative position is that the ICC is not unfairly targeting Africans; rather, it is simply and properly targeting alleged war criminals.[180] Pursuant to the 2013 Policy Paper, factors such as geopolitical implications or geographical balance are not statutory criteria or

---

[178] Of the 60 ratifications needed for the ICC to begin operations in 2002, 34 – of the continent's 55 nations – were African.

[179] Tense relations between African nations and the ICC likely began in 2005 when the UNSC referred the situation in Darfur to the ICC Prosecutor. The African Union called upon its Member States to adopt a policy of non-cooperation in relation to the ICC. See Decision on the Implementation of the Decisions on the International Criminal Court, Doc. EX.CL/639(XVIII), January 2011 (http://www.legal-tools.org/doc/2592b6/); Decision on the Implementation of the Assembly Decisions on the International Criminal Court, Doc. EX.CL/670(XIX), July 2011(http://www.legal-tools.org/doc/3b767f/); Decision on the Progress Report of the Commission on the Implementation of the Assembly Decisions on the International Criminal Court, Doc. EX.CL/710(XX), January 2012 (http://www.legal-tools.org/doc/d20b02/); Decision on the Implementation of the Decisions on the International Criminal Court- Doc. EX.CL/731(XXI), July 2012 (http://www.legal-tools.org/doc/76d96e/); Decision on International Jurisdiction, Justice and The International Criminal Court Doc. Assembly/AU/13(XXI) [Reservation by Botswana to the entire decision], May 2013 (http://www.legal-tools.org/doc/474c18/); Decision on the Progress Report of the Commission on the Implementation of the Decisions on the International Criminal Court Doc. Assembly/AU/13(XXII), January 2014 (http://www.legal-tools.org/doc/8fa4ae/); Decision on the Progress Report of the Commission on the Implementation of Previous Decisions on the International Criminal Court (ICC), Doc. Assembly/AU/18(XXIV), January 2015 (http://www.legal-tools.org/doc/263bf4/); Decision on the Update of the Commission on the Implementation of Previous Decisions on the International Criminal Court, Assembly/AU/Dec.586(XXV), June 2015 (http://www.legal-tools.org/doc/72bc7a/); Decision on the International Criminal Court Doc. EX.CL/987(XXIX), July 2016 (http://www.legal-tools.org/doc/e48950/); Decision on the International Criminal Court (ICC) – Doc. EX.CL/1006(XXX), January 2017 (http://www.legal-tools.org/doc/9645bf/). See also Decision on Africa's Relationship with the International Criminal Court adopted at the Extraordinary African Union Summit of 13 October 2013, *infra* note 188.

[180] W. Chadwick Austin and Michael Thieme, "Is the International Criminal Court Anti-African?", in *Journal Peace Review*, 2016, vol. 28, no. 3, p. 344.

---

relevant for a determination that a situation shall be investigated by the Court.[181] To examine the validity of allegations of racial selection, it is worth considering how cases make their way to the Court, the process used in selecting them, including whether or not the ICC has inappropriately refused to investigate other comparable offences committed on other continents, and finally, the motivations of those claiming a racial bias in the African Union.[182]

The majority of investigations and prosecutions concerning African States before the ICC have arisen from self-referrals by African States, including acceptance of the Court's *ad hoc* jurisdiction and Security Council referrals. Three African investigations have been initiated by the Prosecutor. Kenya was the first, and only after the Court ruled that domestic action by the Kenyan authorities was insufficient.[183] The 2008 post-election violence in Kenya was the subject of a preliminary examination for less than two years before the Prosecutor sought permission to open an investigation in November 2009.[184] During that period, the Prosecutor visited Kenya and made numerous public statements about the situation.[185] What followed during the investigation and prosecution stages

---

[181] OTP, *Policy Paper on Preliminary Examinations*, para.11 and 29, see *supra* note 2.

[182] On this last point see Austin and Thieme, 2016, pp. 342–343, see *supra* note 180.

[183] ICC, Situation in Kenya, Judgment on the appeal of the Republic of Kenya against the decision of Pre-Trial Chamber II of 30 May 2011 entitled 'Decision on the Application by the Government of Kenya Challenging the Admissibility of the Case Pursuant to Article 19(2)(b) of the Statute', 30 August 2011, ICC-01/09-01/11-307 (http://www.legal-tools.org/doc/ac5d46/).

[184] The situation in Kenya was under examination since 27 December 2007 until the moment the Prosecutor requested authorisation to proceed with an investigation on 26 November 2009. The *proprio motu* investigation was opened on 31 March 2010.

[185] The Prosecutor pledged that "[w]e will do justice, we will work together to avoid a repetition of the crimes [...] It has been two years since the post election violence in Kenya. In two years another election is planned. The world is watching Kenya and this Court". He later stressed that the court would try to proceed on a timetable that could maximise the chances for prevention. "Everyone is worried about the next election in Kenya in 2012", he told the press. "That's why I understand the importance of speed, and I am working to be sure that during 2010 – if the judges authorize investigations – we will be able to complete investigations and to define who are the suspects, who are the accused, that have to have justice in Kenya. And that will clean the situation [so] that you can have peaceful election [seasons] in 2011 and 2012". Voice of America News, "ICC Prosecutor Promises Speed in Kenya Proceedings", 7 November 2009.

---

with Kenya became one of the most political[186] and legally challenging cases at the ICC.[187] It also led to the Court's biggest confrontation and hostility with the African Union and its members.[188]

While the Kenya situation clearly demonstrated the politically volatile nature of cases dealing with international crimes, the predicament for the ICC is that every situation it is called upon to deal with will contain politically volatile elements. However, an overarching goal of international criminal courts is justice for victims of crimes, which should never be sacrificed at the altar of political expediency. On the dividing line between the political and the legal, the decision to investigate and prosecute is particularly sensitive. Time and again, ICC Prosecutors have strongly affirmed: "I follow the evidence not politics".[189] Sadly, the Prosecutor's actions have belied this assertion and what we have seen until recently is the OTP doing its best to avoid taking difficult decisions because of political sensitivities. In the early years, the OTP strongly relied on self-

---

[186] In 2013 the Security Council voted on a resolution presented by Rwanda calling for the deferral of the cases involving the President and Deputy President of Kenya. This resolution did not receive the necessary nine affirmative votes with seven members in favour and eight abstaining. This jurisdictional coup failed, but the attempt clearly demonstrated the concern of many African nations.

[187] See interview with Deputy Prosecutor, James Stewart, remarks on the Kenya cases in the *Justice in Conflict* blog, "A Test of Our Resilience – An Interview with the ICC Deputy Prosecutor", 10 August 2016.

[188] The 2013 Decision on Africa's Relationship with the ICC adopted the ruling of the Extraordinary Assembly of the African Union condemning the ICC's investigations of African political leaders and its impact on reconciliation and reconstruction efforts. First, the Assembly called for the cessation of any existing charges or future charges against any Serving African Union Heads of State or government. Second, that the trials of President Uhuru Kenyatta and Deputy President William Samoei Ruto should be suspended until they complete their terms of office. Third, that Kenya should send a letter to the UN Security Council seeking deferral, pursuant to Article 15 of the Rome Statute, of the proceedings against the President and Deputy President of Kenya; and fourth, that President Uhuru Kenyatta would not appear before the ICC until such concerns raised by the African Union and its Member States have been adequately addressed by the UN Security Council and the ICC.

[189] International Peace Institute, "Moreno-Ocampo: "I Follow Evidence, Not Politics"", 20 January 2012 (available on the Institute's web site). *BBC HARDtalk*, "ICC "following" Afghan war crimes claims", 29 June 2017: Fatou Bensouda stated, "I'm following the evidence, I'm following the law". See also interview with Prosecutor, Fatou Bensouda, in the *Justice in Conflict* blog, "Without Fear or Favour – An Interview with the ICC Prosecutor Fatou Bensouda", 15 October 2015.

---

referrals,[190] because it made it easier to open an investigation and in principle secure co-operation from the referring State. Indeed, for the most part, self-referrals from States are situations referred by States that are willing but not able to carry out their own investigations and prosecutions.[191] As such, these situations appeared obvious and initially no one questioned the Prosecutor's legitimacy in taking up these cases. Other situations have put the OTP's capabilities to the test, for example, the Iraq/UK situation involving a State Party that appears to be both willing and able to handle the situation. Under these circumstances, the legitimacy of the OTP's actions is questionable.

There is no doubt from the list of countries under preliminary examination that the Court has looked beyond Africa in the conduct of these activities. To exemplify the geographical diversity of situations under preliminary examination, the OTP has increased their publicity through statements, reports and other media related activities. This in turn has also highlighted the fact that some of these situations have been under preliminary examination for over a decade. The longer each non-African situation continues to languish in the preliminary examination stage, the more it becomes visible that situations arising from other geographical regions are treated in a vastly different fashion from those arising from Africa. African situations are dealt with swiftly while non-African cases remain stagnant. Disparate timelines between preliminary examinations also lead to the impression that the Prosecutor allocates time and resources unevenly among situations. Not only are unequal classes of preliminary examinations created, but it also makes the OTP come across as if it is the one that is not *willing and able* to move forward. Perhaps the Prosecutor is simply not willing, because it does not want the political backlash in circumstances where the ICC remains a fragile institution, and is unable, because it does not have the investigative capacity to do so. Ironically, in Rome the fears regarding the Prosecutor's *proprio motu* powers were based on

---

[190] The Draft Policy Paper on Preliminary Examinations encourages self-referrals. This explicit reference was not retained in the revised 2013 Policy Paper although it was not removed completely. OTP, *Draft Policy Paper on Preliminary Examinations*, paras. 16 and 76–78, see *supra* note 17.

[191] At least appearing to be willing. Uganda, a State Party used the Court for its own political purposes securing a one-sided investigation. However, it later withdrew its support for the Lord's Resistance Army investigation because of its impact on the peace process.

the belief that there would be too much activity.[192] And after more than 15 years of operations, victims of crimes falling under the jurisdiction of the Rome Statute in places other than Africa, in situations other than those arising from self-referrals, deserve more than public statements of concern with their plight. They deserve action.

Publicising information about preliminary examinations allows the Prosecutor to showcase geographical diversity. It is also a way of demonstrating that the Prosecutor is committed to following the evidence and is not primarily influenced by political sensitivities in the selection of situations. In this respect, the Prosecutor took bold steps in January 2016 by requesting the opening of its first non-African investigation into the situation in Georgia where the Russian Federation (non-Party) is involved.[193] Similarly, after more than a decade in November 2017, the OTP requested authorisation to open an investigation in Afghanistan, which includes alleged crimes committed by nationals from the United States (non-Party). If we then look at the list of situations under preliminary examinations we find it includes Iraq (non-Party) concerning the United Kingdom, and Palestine concerning Israel (non-Party). Currently it would appear that the OTP is prepared to take on powerful States, even very powerful non-Party States.

24.4.2.2. Perception of Productivity

According to the OTP, preliminary examination activities constitute one of the most cost-effective ways for the Office to fulfil the Court's mission.[194] It is unclear what the basis for this assertion is and how effective or productive preliminary examinations are in relation to their cost. It is also not apparent how the relative costs and outcomes of a preliminary examination compare to different courses of action undertaken by the OTP. On the ICC website, the OTP notes that it enjoys the following options

---

[192] Insofar as *proprio motu* investigations by the Prosecutor are concerned, both proponents and opponents of the idea feared the risk of politicising the Court and thereby undermining its "credibility". In particular, they feared that providing the Prosecutor with such "excessive powers" to trigger the jurisdiction of the Court might result in its abuse. See Report of the Preparatory Committee on the Establishment of an International Criminal Court, 1996, see *supra* note 11.

[193] Situation in Georgia, Decision on the Prosecutor's request for authorisation of an investigation, see *supra* note 62.

[194] OTP, *Report on Preliminary Examination Activities*, para. 16, see *supra* note 25.

when it comes to preliminary examinations:[195] (1) decline to initiate an investigation; (2) continue to collect information on crimes and relevant national proceedings in order to make a determination as to whether to initiate an investigation; or (3) initiate the investigation, subject to judicial authorisation as appropriate.

This is a generous interpretation of the Rome Statute given that the main function of a preliminary examination is to determine whether there is a reasonable basis to initiate an investigation. Notably, this determination results from the same analytical consideration and represents the potential outcome and not choices on how to proceed. Hence, to interpret the procedure of preliminary examinations as authorising the Prosecutor to monitor national proceedings or gather information for an indefinite period of time in order to amass the necessary legal and factual basis before making a determination is unsubstantiated. Under the Rome Statute, the Prosecutor has a positive duty to seriously examine all information that is communicated to it and the relatively low threshold that needs to be satisfied for the Prosecutor to make a determination cannot justify lengthy examinations. Nor does the long-term collation of information lend itself to cost-effectiveness. The OTP has at least a dozen dedicated analysts working exclusively on preliminary examinations and carries out several on-site missions to monitor situations. It is still hard to imagine what the Situation Analysis Unit can really do with the information received from the IEU[196] considering its limited non-investigative role.

Another aspect is how preliminary examinations are regarded in the context of the Prosecutor's functions.[197] The Prosecutor considers prelim-

---

[195] See OTP, "Preliminary Examinations" (available on the Office's web site).

[196] The Information and Evidence Unit ('IEU') is entrusted with preparing reports analysing the communications received. The reports are sent to Jurisdiction, Complementarity and Cooperation Division. The reports are supposed to identify: (a) those communications that manifestly do not provide any basis for the Office of the Prosecutor to take further action; (b) those communications that appear to relate to a situation already under analysis, investigation or prosecution; and (c) those communications warranting further analysis in order to assess whether further action may be appropriate.

[197] OTP, Strategic Plan 2016-2018, see *supra* note 1; see also remarks by Prosecutor Fatou Bensouda at the Fourteenth Session of the Assembly of States Parties on the occasion of the Launch of the 2015 Annual Report on Preliminary Examination Activities: "Preliminary examinations are one of my Office's three core activities, alongside investigations and prosecutions. It is an activity I am required to conduct under the Statute, through which I

---

inary examinations to be one of the Office's core activities. This is agreeable to the extent that preliminary examinations are conducted in accordance with how they are envisaged under the Rome Statute, that is, they can arguably be cost-effective if used to determine whether or not to open an investigation. But, when preliminary examinations are used for purposes beyond what was intended, then the notion that they are cost-effective withers. They actually increase the costs associated with them and make measuring their effectiveness impossible. Some of the recurring tensions between the Court and States Parties are due to a perceived disproportion between the growth of the Court's budget and its results. Undeniably, preliminary examinations allow the OTP to substantiate its workload in a manner that is discernible, complemented by comprehensive reports and frequent public statements. Preliminary examinations are also significant because they constitute the genesis of the OTP budget even though they are a poor basis for budget requests, given that not all preliminary examinations are made public and that some have remained stagnant for well over a decade.

The OTP maintains a public list on the ICC website with a fixed number of situations under examination. Once a preliminary examination advances to the investigation stage, another preliminary examination is added to the list. The tally currently stands at 10.[198] This idea of having a target number of preliminary examinations invites inaction, even where there is no reasonable basis to initiate an investigation. And keeping the list full allows for a perception of productivity.

In this regard, unless preliminary examinations are used more effectively and in the way intended by the Rome Statute, there is a risk that they will be seen as an instrument of perceived productivity to beguile States Parties. While there are many perspectives on how the OTP can demonstrate its productivity, at the very least it should be demonstrated in a way that resonates with the expectations of an international court. Under the Rome Statute, the Prosecutor is expected to establish the truth and to do so efficiently through the investigation and prosecution of cases based on solid evidentiary grounds. An efficient and focused approach to pre-

---

decide whether to open new investigations". Remarks by Prosecutor Fatou Bensouda at the Fourteenth Session of the Assembly of States Parties, 2015, see *supra* note 85.

[198] Preliminary Examinations, ICC website, see *supra* note 90.

liminary examinations, including reasonable time-frames for determining investigations in all situations, would be one step towards demonstrating concrete productivity. In those cases where productivity is contingent upon resource requirements, the onus lies on the OTP to be more forthcoming regarding its needs. It would then be up to States Parties to ensure the Office is equipped to deliver in a timely manner.

24.5. Consequences of Publicising Preliminary Examination Activities

It is generally accepted that preliminary examinations produce effects of their own and that they have had some unforeseen successes. We have seen this effect in the situation of Colombia where national authorities have demonstrated their commitment to the prosecution of their own nationals albeit under the constant watch of the Prosecutor. We have also seen this in the situation of Iraq where the United Kingdom was very quick to affirm its own commitment to the prosecution of its nationals following the Prosecutor's conspicuous announcement of a 're-opening' of the preliminary examination. Undeniably, there is some attractiveness about the idea that, as a result of extending preliminary examinations, States will undertake their own investigations, relieving the burden from the ICC, which is meant to be a court of last resort and is an institution of limited resources. However, the practice of protracted preliminary examinations reduces their impact, derogates from their intended purpose under the Rome Statute and undermines the trust of States Parties, especially those under the OTP's scrutiny.

As such, publicising preliminary examinations has consequences, intended and unintended, positive and negative. The OTP would do well to consider all the factors in play before making a decision to publish its intention to conduct a preliminary investigation.

24.5.1. Positive Consequences

While preliminary examinations do provide a potential avenue for the Court to have a greater impact outside the courtroom, any positive consequences can be undermined by an inconsistent approach to preliminary examinations.

24.5.1.1. Prevention and Deterrence

Prevention of serious international crimes is one of the Court's ancillary objectives.[199] As we have seen, the Prosecutor's public approach towards preliminary examinations broadens the sphere of influence outside the OTP's main function. Publicising preliminary examinations can increase the potential for progress regarding accountability for violations committed during situations of armed conflicts and internal disturbances, though this potential is not always realised. While the Court and the OTP are expected to contribute to the prevention of crimes, they do not to actually have to achieve it.[200]

Also, prevention is a much broader concept than deterrence; it is about sending messages to States not just perpetrators.[201] This is particularly relevant because the preliminary examination stage only entails a general analysis of situations. Whereas deterrence relates more closely to individuals, which are at the periphery of preliminary examinations. Some authors suggest that it is the increased likelihood of accountability, rather than the severity of the punishment, that deters criminal activity.[202]

Prevention and deterrence are intangible, which makes it extremely difficult to ascertain whether preliminary examinations effectively modify

---

[199] Beth Simmons and Allison Danner argue that the mere ratification of the Rome Statute by a government tends to be correlated with a pause in civil war hostilities. Accepting the Court's jurisdiction presents an opportunity for governments to make costly, credible commitments to peace. According to their research they have also found that the expectation of accountability is sufficient enough that some states will not join the Rome Statute in the first place. See Beth Simmons and Alison Danner, "Credible commitments and the International Criminal Court", in *International Organization*, 2010, vol. 64 no. 2, pp. 225–256.

[200] As the ICC's first President, Philippe Kirsch, said, "By putting potential perpetrators on notice that they may be tried before the Court, the ICC is intended to contribute to the deterrence of these crimes", in Courtney Hillebrecht, "The Deterrent Effects of the International Criminal Court: Evidence from Libya", in *International Interactions*, 2016, vol. 42, no. 4, p. 616.

[201] On the various stigmatizing features of international criminal law, see Frédéric Mégret, "Practices of Stigmatization", 2014 (on file with the author).

[202] Aaron Chalfin and Justin McCrary, "Criminal Deterrence: A review of the literature", in *Journal of Economic Literature*, 2017, vol. 55, no. 1, p. 5; Hunjoon Kim and Kathryn Sikkink, "Explaining the Deterrence Effect of Human Rights Prosecutions for Transitional Countries", in *International Studies Quarterly*, 2010, vol. 54, no. 4, p. 939–963. It should be noted that these authors focus on deterrence in relation to national criminal proceedings.

---

behaviour or prevent behavioural changes. To some, preliminary examinations act as buffers that stand in the way of ICC investigations, allowing some States to feel at ease with the *status quo*, thinking that nothing will change, particularly as time passes. Accordingly, no matter how powerful the effect of the ICC threat through an initial public statement, it is likely to diminish over time if the preliminary examination process does not lead to any outcome or is perceived as not leading to anything concrete. In fact, an informal proceeding intended to be preliminary that goes on for a protracted period runs contrary to any possible prevention/deterrent effect the institution may have. Unfortunately, protracted preliminary examinations that imply a threat to investigate more often than not simply contribute to perpetuating crimes and promoting impunity. This will likely be factored in by the State in question only if there is a credible threat to actually investigate.[203]

Due to the elusive nature of prevention/deterrence, the OTP would do well to accord less attention to it and focus on actually carrying out investigations where a preliminary examination suggests they should do so. This is mostly so given the difficulty in measuring whether changes in behaviour are attributable to actions or policies of the Court. The prevention/deterrence of crime does not rest on the shoulders of a single institution, much less a judicial one. Prevention should be viewed as a systemic and long-term goal, relying more on non-judicial institutions, such as the United Nations, the Office of the High Commissioner for Human Rights and NGOs.

If we take a look at the preliminary examination in Guinea, now under Phase 3, and ongoing since 14 October 2009 following the violent events of 28 September 2009, it seems to have produced some positive

---

[203] States Parties have addressed deterrence in the context of the peace and justice debate. "For justice to have an impact, the most important condition is that justice follows its own rules, without interference and without being subject to political considerations. Justice contributes to peace and prevention when it is not conceived as an instrument of either, and on condition that it is pursued for its own sake. If the ICC is contemplated simply as a lever, it will be undermined, as some will expect it to be turned on and off as political circumstances dictate. […]. The ICC would lose legitimacy, which is its strength, and be of little value to peace as perpetrators can also play the game of carrots and sticks. Certainty that law will be applied is the ultimate tool to ensure lasting peace". See Review Conference of the Rome Statute, "The Importance of Justice in Securing Peace", 30 May 2010, RC/ST/PJ/INF.3, paras. 26–27 (http://www.legal-tools.org/doc/5c0efe/).

effects. The national response was immediate prompting an investigation in 2010,[204] and with a trial in the horizon. The OTP moved this situation swiftly to Phase 3 without making public its Article 53(1) analysis. From the information publicly available, the OTP appears to have relied heavily on the findings of the United Nations Commission of Inquiry and the Guinean National Inquiry. Understanding the pace and rationale of the Guinean situation would provide more insight into the OTP's policy on preliminary examinations. Such is the case with the phased approach developed by the OTP. In the Guinea situation we can see it was applied in a linear fashion passing from one filtering phase to the next.[205] However, the Iraq/UK, Colombia and previously Burundi situations reveal a holistic application where the OTP simultaneously assesses subject-matter jurisdiction and admissibility in relation to alleged crimes.

To date, the OTP continues to assess the conduct of the preliminary examination and to encourage Guinean authorities to adhere to their commitment to complete the proceedings within the best possible deadline. It has also announced it will continue to engage with the international community and relevant partners to facilitate international assistance for the organisation of the trial phase.[206] This situation has remained under preliminary examination despite Guinea's significant steps in assuming its national responsibilities to investigate and prosecute the alleged crimes of 2009. For these reasons the situation in Guinea is considered by the OTP a successful example among preliminary examinations of their contribution to preventing/deterring the commission of crimes. Despite Guinea's positive response to the Prosecutor's preliminary examination, it is not evident that it is all due to the ICC. This can be explained by the fact that several accountability mechanisms have been involved in the situation from the

---

[204] On 8 February 2010, in accordance with the recommendations of the reports of the UN Commission and of the la Commission nationale d'enquête indépendante (CNEI), the Conakry Appeals Court General Prosecutor appointed three Guinean investigative judges to conduct a national investigation into the 28 September 2009 events. Considering the advanced stage of the investigation, during the reporting period, the Guinean authorities have publicly committed on several occasions their wish for a trial to take place in the near future, possibly early 2017.

[205] In the Nigeria Situation, the OTP's Article 5 Report is also useful in illustrating the phased approach applied in a linear fashion, see *supra* note 137.

[206] OTP, *Report on Preliminary Examination Activities*, para. 282–283, see *supra* note 25.

outset.[207] Naturally, if the ICC were to have a positive effect on national accountability efforts, it would be expected to be in relation to situations where the Court works with other actors.[208]

The Guinea situation seems ripe for removal from the list of situations under examination. This does not mean that the OTP should withdraw its support to the national authorities. It could remain engaged in other ways, just not under the umbrella of preliminary examinations.

24.5.1.2. Positive Complementarity

The Prosecutor has come to place particular emphasis on encouraging national investigations and prosecutions. The OTP adopted the term 'positive complementarity'[209] to describe the policy of actively encouraging investigations and prosecutions by national tribunals of crimes potentially falling under ICC jurisdiction.[210] The OTP has insisted for years that its

---

[207] For example, the UN International Commission of Inquiry for Guinea, CNEI set up by the Guinean authorities, and close follow-up by the UN Secretary-General, the UN Security Council, the European Union, the Economic Community of West African States and NGOs such as Human Rights Watch.

[208] For example, the ICC's involvement in Libya was also quite unique because it was initiated at the behest of the UN Security Council and accompanied by NATO-led military action against Qaddafi. Libya is also the only ICC situation in which significant international military intervention was contemporaneous to the ICC's investigations and indictments. These features set Libya apart from the other situations, but they also reflect the ICC's position within a larger international and national legal and political architecture meant to counter and deter atrocity crimes.

[209] See Address to the Assembly of States Parties 30 November 2007, Luis Moreno-Ocampo Prosecutor of the International Criminal Court: "States and NGOs have expressed an interest on what we call a positive approach to complementarity. My Office will shortly disseminate a concept paper based on our first years of experience". Also, the 2010 Draft Policy Paper on Preliminary Examinations asserts that 'positive complementarity' is based on the preamble and Article 93(10) of the Rome Statute and that this concept is distinct from the principle of complementarity set out in Article 17 of the Rome Statute: "At all phases of its preliminary examination activities, consistent with its policy of positive complementarity, the Office will seek to encourage where feasible genuine national investigations and prosecutions by the State(s) concerned and to cooperate with and provide assistance to such State(s) pursuant to article 93(10) of the Statute". The OTP noted that it had followed this approach with Colombia. OTP, *Draft Policy Paper on Preliminary Examinations*, paras. 93–94, see *supra* note 17.

[210] "The positive approach to complementarity means that the Office will encourage genuine national proceedings where possible, including in situation countries, relying on its various networks of cooperation, but without involving the Office directly in capacity building or

---

action in Colombia has been a determining factor in the fight against impunity in the country.[211] In political and academic events, Prosecutor Moreno-Ocampo presented the Colombian situation as an example of 'positive complementarity' in action.[212] Nevertheless, the preliminary examination in Colombia continues after more than a decade because national proceedings are ongoing and the Prosecutor has not finalised its assessment as to whether these proceedings are genuine. As mentioned previously, prolonged preliminary examinations weaken not only the Court's ability to deter crimes but also to encourage national proceedings.

The dynamic around admissibility, especially during a preliminary examination, is not always a positive one and can lead to tensions between governments and the Court. Occasionally one can also see an ironic parallelism between failings of the Court and failings in national proceedings. For example, if the Court is unable to protect witnesses in Kenya, then why should the Kenyan national authorities be expected to do so? If the OTP is permitted to sit on a preliminary examination for over a decade without opening an investigation, what is the standard of timeliness that State actions should be measured against? If the Court is unable to lead by example, then this inability impacts its effectiveness and the reasonableness of expectations it places upon national jurisdictions.

Similarly, it is not easy to establish causality when preliminary examination efforts are directed towards positive complementarity. In fact, it becomes quite challenging to gauge both short-term and long-term outcomes of the impact of preliminary examinations on national proceedings. Reforming national judicial systems takes time and is at odds with preliminary examinations, which are meant to be a transitory procedural step potentially leading to investigations. As for the need to wait for local developments to unfold, it does not seem practical, in the case of preliminary examinations, that the pace of local developments should determine

---

financial or technical assistance". See OTP, Prosecutorial Strategy 2009-2012, para.17, see *supra* note 75.

[211] Paul Seils, "Putting Complementarity in its Place", in Carsten Stahn (ed.), *The Law and Practice of the International Criminal Court*, Oxford University Press, 2015, p. 323. See also Keynote Speech by James Stewart, Deputy Prosecutor of the ICC, "Transitional Justice in Colombia and the role of the International Criminal Court", 13 May 2015 (http://www.legal-tools.org/doc/05d0ce/).

[212] OTP, *Report on Preliminary Examination Activities*, para. 84, see *supra* note 94.

the pace of ICC processes. Moreover, the ICC's long-term preliminary examination engagement in situation countries eventually results in the development of relationships with national authorities that may call into question the OTP's impartiality. It is therefore erroneous to believe that the longer the situation remains under examination, the greater the leverage of the OTP on the State in question.[213]

Not even the most advanced societies and legal systems in the world are fully equipped to deal with Rome Statute crimes.[214] States Parties accept that enabling States to prosecute these grave crimes is essential in the fight against impunity given the limited resources of the Court. However, there is no consensus that it is the role of the OTP or the Court to ensure States are equipped to do so. The ICC is not a development agency and, while it can provide technical assistance to States, it does not have a capacity-building mandate. Accordingly, rather than trying to pursue efforts beyond the scope of the Prosecutor's mandate, the Prosecutor should make more use of Article 18.[215] Pursuant to this article, if atrocity crimes have allegedly been committed, and the OTP determines through a preliminary examination that there is a reasonable basis to proceed with an investigation, it would first reach out to the States of jurisdiction in the matter to allow them to respond to those crimes and bring the perpetrators to justice. If the notified State fails to take action in response to the notification, the Prosecutor can take steps under Article 18 to investigate and

---

[213] The OTP has explained that it will engage with national jurisdictions provided that it does not risk tainting any possible future admissibility proceedings. First of all, it is difficult to ascertain how the OTP can truly assess admissibility when at that juncture the examination process is dealing with situations and not cases. Technically all that is needed is that the alleged crimes are at least being investigated. More importantly where does this relationship stand when the engagement with national authorities develops for several years? What criteria does the OTP use to objectively assess admissibility?

[214] For example, European States have a Network of focal points in respect of persons responsible for genocide, crimes against humanity and war crimes. The aim of the Network is to facilitate cooperation and assistance between the Member States' investigation and prosecution authorities and to exchange information on criminal investigation and prosecution of persons suspected of having committed or participated in the commission of these crimes. In this forum, the national authorities also share investigative, prosecutorial and trial experiences involved with these crimes, related methods and best practices.

[215] Where there has been either a State Party referral or a *proprio motu* Prosecutor investigation, the Prosecutor is required to "notify all States Parties and those States which, taking into account the information available, would normally exercise jurisdiction over the crimes concerned".

---

proceed to prosecute. A notification under Article 18 would send a stronger message to States than a long drawn out public preliminary examination, and is consistent with States' primacy in carrying out their own proceedings. Disappointingly, the 2013 Policy Paper undermines the potential of Article 18 in relation to preliminary examinations conducted under Article 15. According to the Policy Paper, once the OTP determines a reasonable basis to proceed to investigation exists, it will inform the relevant State(s) with jurisdiction of its determination and inquire whether they wish to refer the situation to the Court instead of resorting to Article 18's invitation to deal with the matter themselves.[216]

There is no doubt that the preliminary examination stage offers a first opportunity for the OTP to act as a catalyst for national proceedings. However, if the OTP is committed to stimulating credible national proceedings, it should avoid requesting States to refer the situation to it upon the determination that an investigation is warranted and as a means of securing 'easier' co-operation from that State in the conduct of ICC proceedings. If the OTP instead relied upon the provision of Article 18, the actual need for ICC intervention might be obviated. Such an approach would also underscore the nature of the ICC as a court of last resort, improve transparency and credibility, and foster co-operation with governments. It is envisaged that situation countries would certainly welcome an invitation pursuant to Article 18, which shows more respect for State primacy than a referral request.

24.5.2. Negative Consequences

The policy of using preliminary examinations as advocacy and political tools, along with their extensive publicity, has unfortunately produced unintended consequences, in part because of the dangers of publicising inconclusive results, but also due to the apparent absence of a communications strategy to guide the public profile of the OTP's work.

24.5.2.1. Withdrawals

In 2016, South Africa, Burundi and the Gambia initiated proceedings to withdraw from the Rome Statute.[217] For Burundi the public announcement

---

[216] OTP, *Policy Paper on Preliminary Examinations*, para. 98, see *supra* note 2.

[217] On 27 October 2016, Burundi deposited its instrument of withdrawal to the Rome Statute with the UN Secretary-General (http://www.legal-tools.org/doc/1bd37c/). On 12 October

that it was being placed under examination contributed to its decision to withdraw.[218] The three African States were joined on 16 November 2016 by the Russian Federation, a non-Party State, which said it was formally withdrawing its signature from the Rome Statute, a day after the OTP issued its preliminary examination activities report qualifying the Russian annexation of Crimea in 2014 as an occupation.[219] In 2018 the Philippines followed suit starting its withdrawal process after the OTP announced a preliminary examination was underway.

In the Burundi situation, it is difficult to assess what really drove this State to take such a measure. Taking into account the Burundian Government's decision to withdraw came at a time when the UN Human Rights Council adopted resolution 33/24, endorsing the United Nations Independent Investigation on Burundi ('UNIIB') report on "gross and abundant" human rights violations in the country between April 2015 and June 2016.[220] That same resolution also established a Commission of Inquiry on Burundi.[221]

2016, the Burundian Parliament voted in favour of Burundi's withdrawal from the Rome Statute and on 18 October, the President of Burundi signed off the bill. The Gambia also followed with a decision to withdraw on 10 November 2016 (http://www.legal-tools.org/doc/fa227a/). This action was later reversed on 10 February 2017 when the new Government took office that year, see Gambia: Withdrawal of Notification of Withdrawal (http://www.legal-tools.org/doc/5675c2/). South Africa was the first to deposit its instrument of withdrawal on 19 October 2016 (http://www.legal-tools.org/doc/9b2054/). On 7 March 2017, South Africa proceeded to withdraw its notification of withdrawal as well, see South Africa: Withdrawal of Notification of Withdrawal (http://www.legal-tools.org/doc/835fda/).

[218] South Africa's Declaratory Statement on the Decision to Withdraw submits that there is also "[t]he perception of inequality and unfairness in the practice of the ICC that do not only emanate from the Court's relationship with the Security Council, but also by the perceived focus of the ICC on African states, notwithstanding clear evidence of violations by others". See Declaratory Statement of the Republic of South Africa on the decision to withdraw from the Rome Statute of the International Criminal Court, see *supra* note 217.

[219] On 16 November 2016, the Russian Ministry of Foreign Affairs made the announcement on the orders of the President Vladimir Putin, saying the Court had failed to live up to hopes of the international community and denouncing its work as "one-sided and inefficient". See Russian Federation: Communication (http://www.legal-tools.org/doc/c9b51b/).

[220] On 20 September 2016, the final report of the United Nations Independent Investigation on Burundi (UNIIB), established pursuant to Human Rights Council resolution S-24/1 on 17 December 2015, was issued as document A/HRC/33/37 (http://www.legal-tools.org/doc/82b600/). The report covers violations and abuses of human rights from 15 April 2015 to 30 June 2016. The recommended actions included the immediate setting up of an interna-

According to the Burundian authorities, the ICC Prosecutor ignored its duty of neutrality in making multiple statements directed against the Government by announcing the "opening of a preliminary examination based on false reports,[222] violating the sacrosanct principle of complementarity by intervening without first informing the Government what the treaty basis for such intervention was, which had a high potential of compromising on-going encouraging efforts by the Government to investigate and prosecute all the crimes within its national territory".[223]

In October, at the time of Burundi's withdrawal, the preliminary examination was under Phase 2 subject-matter assessment. In the subsequent preliminary examination activities report, the OTP provided no further updates on subject-matter jurisdiction or admissibility, despite substantial findings in this regard by the UNIIB.[224] It is important to note that the findings by the UNIIB were established using the "reasonable grounds to believe" standard of proof,[225] a higher threshold than that applied by the OTP when conducting preliminary examinations. With the availability of the UNIIB findings it is difficult to comprehend why at that moment the OTP was still only assessing whether it had subject-matter jurisdiction.

During the Assembly of States Parties general debate in 2016, Burundi criticised the fact that no established ICC policy or process existed, and claimed that verifying the actual fulfilment of the right of complementarity was an "inescapable stage before any publicised intervention of

tional commission of inquiry, the involvement of other independent international judicial processes and reconsideration of Burundi's membership on the Human Rights Council.

221 The Burundian Government rejected the resolution as inapplicable in Burundi in a press communiqué dated 3 October 2016. Immediately after on 10 October, the Government declared the three experts of the independent investigation on Burundi *personae non gratae* in Burundi. Later, on 11 October, the Government announced the suspension of all cooperation and collaboration with the Office of the High Commissioner for Human Rights office in Burundi for 'complicity' in preparing the report of the independent investigation on Burundi.

222 Interview with the Burundi Ambassador to the Kingdom of the Netherlands, "Why Burundi has withdrawn from the Rome Treaty", in *Diplomat Magazine*, 5 November 2016.

223 *Ibid.*

224 UNIIB Final Report, paras. 101–117, see *supra* note 219. Also, Recommendation 154: "In light of the ineffectual accountability institutions set up by the Government, independent international judicial processes must consider whether international crimes were committed".

225 *Ibid.*, para. 17.

a preliminary examination".[226] Burundi pointed to the fact that "the November 2016 preliminary examination activities report did not contain any reliable information determining Burundi had failed to fulfil its complementarity obligations before a decision to begin a preliminary examination was taken". These arguments are not entirely unsubstantiated because in its report the OTP acknowledged receiving information on the work of investigative committees set up by the Burundian Prosecutor without saying a word regarding its significance. The report concludes by saying "the Office may also gather available information on relevant national proceedings at this stage of analysis".[227]

Surprisingly, the OTP offered comments to some parts of the UNIIB report, asserting that not all the killings could be attributed to Government security forces alone,[228] and that not all of the reported abuses and injuries could rise to the level of severity required to constitute other inhumane acts under Article 7(1)(k) of the Statute. The OTP noted also that "the legal qualification of the alleged conduct required further analysis in the context of the preliminary examination of the situation". Against this backdrop, the OTP went ahead with announcing it was considering moving forward with an investigation as a response to Burundi's withdrawal from the Rome Statute.[229]

The Burundi situation should not have been prioritised simply due to the State's withdrawal. Certainly, proceeding to request an authorisation is a clear signal that a State Party whose leaders might be defendants cannot avoid the ICC by withdrawing from the Rome Statute.[230] However, even if all factual and legal requirements were satisfied, which according to the 2016 report were not, Burundi's effective withdrawal, one year later negatively impacts the co-operation and enforcement stages. Unfortunately, under the current OTP policy, the feasibility of investigations only becomes relevant after the investigation stage at the moment of the selection

---

[226] Fifteenth Session of the Assembly of States Parties, Open Bureau Meeting, Relationship between the ICC and Africa, 18 November 2016, 15:00-1800 (copy on file with the author).

[227] OTP, *Report on Preliminary Examination Activities*, paras. 53 and 59, see *supra* note 25.

[228] *Ibid.*, para. 44.

[229] *Ibid.*, para. 60.

[230] The preliminary examination of the Burundi situation may also cover other crimes committed until such withdrawal becomes effective, namely one year after its notification to the Secretary-General of the UN.

of situations.[231] It is not a factor that is considered when determining whether to open an investigation.[232] The OTP rationale for this position is that weighing feasibility as a separate factor in the determination of whether or not to investigate could prejudice the consistent application of the Statute and might encourage obstructionism by States as a means of dissuading ICC intervention.[233] This logic has some merit, but ignoring this factor as relevant prior to the determination of whether or not to open an investigation may be at odds with the OTP's strategic goals of achieving high performance in relation to its mandate.[234]

Turning to the Russian Federation,[235] it became the focus of ICC activities through the preliminary examinations of the situations in Georgia and Ukraine. Initially, it was the 2016 preliminary examination activities report which sparked Russian backlash, with the reference to the annexation of Crimea as an "occupation" and by qualifying the situation between Russia and Ukraine as an "international armed conflict".[236] Later, in January 2016, the Russian Ministry of Foreign Affairs stated that in the light of the latest decision (the PTC's decision to authorise the investigation relating to the 2008 war between Russia and Georgia), the Russian Federation would be forced to fundamentally review its attitude towards the ICC.[237]

Indeed, the withdrawal of signature by Russia was a symbolic act and similar actions have already been carried out by Israel, the United States and Sudan. On a practical level, many believe such an action does

---

[231] Feasibility meaning where the OTP can conduct an effective and successful investigation leading to a prosecution with a reasonable prospect of conviction. OTP, *Policy Paper on Case Selection and Prioritisation*, see *supra* note 151.

[232] The OTP has expressed conflicting positions regarding feasibility. See OTP, Annex to the 'Paper of some policy issues before the Office of the Prosecutor', see *supra* note 13.

[233] OTP, Strategic Plan 2016-2018, para. 70, see *supra* note 1.

[234] *Ibid.*, paras. 4 and 40. Strategic goal 1: conduct impartial, independent, high quality preliminary examinations, investigations and prosecutions; Strategic goal 3: further improve the quality and efficiency of preliminary examinations, investigations and prosecutions.

[235] The Russian Federation signed the Statute on 13 September 2000. It is fair to say it co-operated with the ICC on an *ad hoc* basis. In addition, it was regularly in contact with the ICC's leadership in its capacity as a Permanent Member of the Security Council, which was seised of the two referrals to the ICC concerning Darfur and Libya.

[236] OTP, *Report on Preliminary Examination Activities*, para. 158, see *supra* note 25.

[237] "On the beginning of ICC's investigation of events in South Ossetia in August 2008", in "Briefing by Foreign Ministry Spokesperson Maria Zakharova Moscow", 29 January 2016 (http://www.legal-tools.org/doc/afeaf2/).

not make any difference.[238] However, it does matters in that it signifies that Russia no longer has any intention of joining the Rome Statute in the future. But more important is what this represents in terms of international co-operation – not only bilaterally in relation to the situations under preliminary examination, but also multilaterally as a Permanent Member of the Security Council and the impact the Russian position may have for effective follow-up of existing ICC referrals and on the possibility of any potential future referral.

The departure of any State Party is regrettable and contrary to the Rome Statute's overarching goal of universality. Notwithstanding, these situations carry lessons learned, especially for the OTP. They should serve as a warning sign that public statements at the preliminary examination stage may have negative consequences. To be successful in the discharge of its mandate the ICC needs to find more constructive ways to consolidate its authority and attract greater support for its activities. The current preliminary examination practice does not seem to be contributing towards this aim.

24.5.2.2. Undermining Future Investigations

The OTP's strategic decision to highlight and publicise preliminary examination activities could create complications for the methodical building of a case against perpetrators. A high degree of publicity about prosecutorial activities might lead perpetrators to cover up evidence, destroy documentation, and intimidate potential witnesses, steps that could complicate construction of a case for trial.

Publicity may also complicate the ultimate enforcement of any arrest warrant, as individuals who expect to be investigated may go into

---

[238] Mark Ellis, Director of the International Bar Association, said: "Russia's decision to 'withdraw' its signature from the Rome Statute will have little or no impact on the court. Contrary to the government's statement, Russia has never engaged with the court in any meaningful way and, in fact, has violated the prohibited crimes provisions of the Statute through its military actions in both Georgia and Ukraine. The more serious threat to the [ICC] is the withdrawal of African countries. Unless this alarming tide can be reversed, the court's own legitimacy will be in peril". Tanya Lokshina, the Russia Program Director at Human Rights Watch described the act as a: "[s]ymbolic gesture of rejection, and says a lot about Russia's attitude towards international justice and institutions". "Russia withdraws signature from international criminal court statute", in *The Guardian*, 16 November 2016 (http://www.legal-tools.org/doc/a01c8f/).

hiding or make preparations to do so. There is also a duty, albeit at the investigation stage, that measures must be taken to preserve evidence under Article 56(3) of the Statute, as well as to protect victims pursuant to Rule 87 of the RPE. The longer preliminary examinations run, the more pressing these duties become. Focusing on preliminary examinations as a means of deterrence rather than on whether there is a reasonable basis to proceed to investigation may also negatively eliminate the prospect of an investigation being brought forward as the passage of time impacts on memories of events, other evidence may deteriorate and relevant witnesses die.[239]

Overwhelmingly, it is the victims that stand to lose the most from this prosecutorial strategy of preliminary examinations as advocacy tools. Long delays in preliminary examinations without any indication of whether the ICC will initiate an investigation represent an offence to one of the Court's primary constituencies. Although one advantage of publicising preliminary examinations is that it may help with victims and witnesses coming forward with more information, this is not the most compelling argument, considering that evidence collection is not the priority at the preliminary examination stage.

A further risk of widely publicising information about situations under preliminary examination is that it may reveal the OTP's prosecutorial strategy. For example, the 2016 preliminary examination activities report states, for the first time, in relation to Afghanistan, that the alleged crimes were committed not only on the territory of Afghanistan, but also on the territories of Poland, Lithuania and Romania (all States Parties).[240] The OTP's suggestion that there could be investigations into crimes of

---

[239] OTP Regulations, Regulation 8, see *supra* note 15 establishes that the Investigations shall be responsible for: (a) the preparation of the necessary security plans and protection policies for each case to ensure the safety and well-being of victims, witnesses, Office staff, and persons at risk on account of their interaction with the Court, in adherence with good practices and in cooperation and coordination with the Registry, when required, on matters relating to protection and support; (b) the provision of investigative expertise and support; (c) the preparation and coordination of field deployment of Office staff; and (d) *the provision of factual crime analysis and the analysis of information and evidence, in support of preliminary examinations and evaluations, investigations and prosecutions.*

[240] OTP, *Report on Preliminary Examination Activities*, paras. 194, 199 and 200, see *supra* note 25.

torture by the CIA of detainees in these territories is reckless.[241] It is hard to believe that this is new information, which only surfaced in 2016. Also this expansion deflects attention from what should be the main focus of this situation and provides opportunities for more of those involved to cover their tracks.

24.6. Practical Recommendations to Enhance and Improve Public Communications of the OTP during Preliminary Examinations

From the preceding sections, it would appear to be a paramount necessity for the OTP to develop a coherent communications strategy. Indeed, a diverse array of practitioners and policy documents have advocated for a more strategic approach to public communication.[242] For the sake of consistency in communications, it is key to develop methodology that is adaptable to each situation, which restates the function of the preliminary examination process, sets out its limitations and what can be accomplished through the procedure in order to manage expectations. More careful thought should go into the messaging produced by the OTP and the terminology crafted to convey it. Having a strategy in place would help to mitigate selectivity in the OTP's publicity practices by having clear standards available.

Within the OTP, the Executive Committee makes the decision on when and how to make something public. In this regard, the Executive Committee should enhance its decision-making process by agreeing on guidelines addressing what the OTP should communicate publicly regard-

---

[241] *Ibid.*, para. 200 of the 2016 OTP *Report on Preliminary Examinations* states that the information available provides a reasonable basis to believe that at least some crimes within the Court's jurisdiction were committed on the territory of Poland prior to 1 May 2003 and would encompass not only alleged crimes committed in Afghanistan since 1 May 2003, but also other alleged crimes that are sufficiently linked to the situation in Afghanistan and that were committed outside of Afghanistan since 1 July 2002.

[242] For example, as an Office of the High Commissioner for Human Rights policy document states: "[I]t is important that the commission/mission discusses early on and decides on a media strategy, and does not simply react to events and media pressure". See Office of the High Commissioner for Human Rights, International Commissions of Inquiry and Fact-finding Missions on International Human Rights Law and International Humanitarian Law: Guidance and Practice, 2013 p. 94. The Siracusa Guidelines state that there is no "one size-fits-all strategy". See M. Cherif Bassiouni and Christina Abraham, (ed.), *Siracusa Guidelines for International, Regional and National Fact-finding Bodies*, Intersentia, 2013, pp. 37–38.

---

ing the preliminary examination process and what should remain internal, when the information should be communicated publicly and how the Office should do so. Clear parameters should be developed to present more accurate projections of when preliminary examination decisions will be taken instead of using words such as "imminent" and "in the near future". It should also identify what factors should shape OTP communications strategies and how these factors should influence the way in which reports and statements are drafted. A useful source in this connection is the Guidance and Practice document developed by the Office of the High Commissioner for Human Rights' which presents several factors to consider – ensuring that the public and relevant governments are informed about the mission's work, avoiding the perception of prejudged conclusions, countering misinformation, determining the likely impact of a public statement, and responding to key events.[243] Another relevant factor is clarifying the preliminary examination's uniqueness as a separate and distinct process from other accountability mechanisms, including commissions of inquiry.

In addition, the OTP should only make Article 53(1) reports public, refraining from publicising annual, interim or other-related reports. If the OTP continues to believe these other reports are useful, they should be produced for every situation and not just for some. If other reports, such as Article 5 reports, are to remain part of the practice, then they need to be more consistent. The OTP should also consider adopting a more discreet approach, either through full confidentiality or simply by providing limited factual information on a gradual basis.[244] Alternatively, the OTP could just use the Court's annual activities reports, complemented by periodic statements. Greater attention should be given to the announcement of next steps and there should be enough safeguards in place to ensure that the information publicised is accurate and realistic. More importantly, all the actors who have a role to play in the process should be kept well informed from start to finish.[245]

---

[243] International Commissions of Inquiry and Fact-finding Missions on International Human Rights Law and International Humanitarian Law: Guidance and Practice, p. 86, see *supra* note 242.

[244] Rob Grace, "Communication and Report Drafting in Monitoring, Reporting, and Fact-finding Mechanisms", July 2014, p. 12 (on file with the author). See *infra* note 248.

[245] *Ibid.*, pp. 11–17. Commissioners also sometimes use public engagement to pressure governments to cooperate with the mission, though this form of public advocacy has not prov-

Second, the OTP needs to improve the quality of its reporting with respect to their content, reporting cycles and their frequency. The OTP should avoid undermining its work through duplications in reports and inconsistencies. For instance, the OTP's preliminary examination activities report and the Court's annual activities reports contain overlaps and, more alarmingly, contradictions concerning the exact same situations. It appears that the drafters of these reports worked independently from each other and contradictions between reports evidence lack of a unified collaborative process. In relation to the content of reports and statements, the public information on preliminary examinations does not need to be detailed because, prior to the determination on whether to open an investigation, it will be mostly inconclusive information. During this initial step of preliminary examinations, it would suffice to include in reports the relevant statistics on Article 15 communications, overall and by year, how many of them are manifestly outside jurisdiction, what type of alleged crimes they cover and what regions are involved. For those situations under examination that are already public, it would be useful to know where and with what frequency missions are conducted. With respect to public statements, the OTP is quite swift in issuing early and loud calls for accountability, but less dynamic when it comes to moving forward. In this respect, public statements will be less effective if they are not followed up with swift and decisive action.

There is also a need to harmonise terminology used for public reports and statements. This would contribute to a better understanding of OTP policy and the application of the different phases of the preliminary examination process. More clarity should be brought to the use of terms referring to the supposed opening, conclusion, completion, re-opening and reconsideration of situations under examination. As it has already been explained, preliminary examinations are compulsory on the receipt of an Article 15 communication and it is therefore inaccurate to announce their opening as if they were investigations. The OTP's monitoring functions are also ambiguous and not easily detectable during the preliminary examination stage. Furthermore, when a situation does not meet the requirements of Article 53, the OTP should be more straightforward referring to the examination as completed with a decision not to investigate rather

---

en successful in terms of securing co-operation. Therefore, the danger always exists that public statements can backfire.

---

than closed. Ultimately, a decision not to investigate is a decision not to proceed. These situations would still remain 'on the books' and can be reverted to at a later time, when more information or facts arise as provided in Article 15 of the Rome Statute.

Third, the OTP should consider alternative ways to build trust. Although the field of criminal law investigations is unique, the OTP can benefit from looking at the established working methods and dynamics of monitoring, reporting and fact-finding ('MRF') missions,[246] as well as the confidentiality approach used by the International Committee of the Red Cross ('ICRC').[247] Notable research has been carried out relating to how, when and to what extent MRF mechanisms mandated to investigate alleged violations of international human rights and international humanitarian law should engage in public communication.[248]

In relation to monitoring,[249] reporting and fact-finding[250] mechanisms, these refer to bodies mandated to investigate alleged violations of

---

[246] Harvard Humanitarian Initiative, Research conducted by the Program on Humanitarian Policy and Conflict Research on monitoring, reporting, and fact-finding ('MRF') (available on the Initiative's web site).

[247] The ICRC is a humanitarian organisation established in Geneva, Switzerland, in 1863 that adheres strictly to the Fundamental Principles of neutrality, impartiality and independence in its operations. The ICRC's mandate is set out in the 1949 Geneva Conventions and in the 1977 Additional Protocols. See "The ICRC: Its Mission and Work", 2009 (available on its web site).

[248] This fascinating paper examines how MRF practitioners have responded to challenges such as what should be communicated publicly, what information should be kept private, when a mission does communicate publicly, how should practitioners do so? What factors should shape practitioners' communications strategies, and how should these factors influence the ways that practitioners approach drafting MRF reports. It also focuses on how fifteen MRF missions have dealt with these matters over the past decade, including some of the most politically sensitive ones. Grace, 2014, see *supra* note 244.

[249] Monitoring entails examining contextual information in search of patterns that indicate the potential perpetration of international law violations. Rob Grace and Claude Bruderlein, "Building Effective Monitoring, Reporting, and Fact-finding Mechanisms", Working Paper, Program on Humanitarian Policy and Conflict Research at Harvard University, 2012 (on file with the author).

[250] Fact-finding means any activity designed to obtain detailed knowledge of the relevant facts of a dispute or situation, which the competent UN organs need in order to exercise effectively their functions in relation to the maintenance of international peace and security. Fact-finding should be comprehensive, objective, impartial and timely. Declaration on Fact-Finding by the United Nations in the Field of the Maintenance of International Peace and Security, A/RES/46/5, 9 December 1991, paras. 2 and 3.

---

international human rights law and international humanitarian law.[251] MRF missions abide by three guiding principles: impartiality, neutrality and independence, that allow its technical and political aspects to operate in congruence with one another to further accountability and conflict resolution.[252] Similarly, the preliminary examination process is conducted in the context of the overarching principles of independence, impartiality and objectivity.[253] MRF missions have the potential to feed into investigations conducted by courts and tribunals, either by helping to generate political support for initiating an investigation or by gathering evidence that can be incorporated into different phases of future investigative and prosecutorial processes.[254]

According to some authors, monitoring and institutional fact-finding are the best way of bringing the weight of the community to bear on each Member State.[255] Indeed, MRF reports can directly influence the behaviour of government actors.[256] However, preliminary examination activities must not be managed as MRF mechanisms. While both preliminary examinations and MRF missions are announced to the public at the

---

[251] MRF emerge from various sources and assume multiple forms in areas such as UN peace operations, Security Council mandated commissions, sanctions committees, monitoring and expert groups, the UNHRC Special Procedures, truth commissions, regional organisation mechanisms, as well as the International Humanitarian Fact-finding Commission, established by Additional Protocol I to the Geneva Conventions in 1977.

[252] Grace and Bruderlein, 2012, p. 17, see *supra* note 249.

[253] OTP, Report on Preliminary Examination activities, paras. 25–33, see *supra* note 25.

[254] For example, UNHRC resolution S-19/1, the mandate specified that the mission should "preserve the evidence of crimes for possible future criminal prosecutions or a future justice process".

[255] Antonio Cassese, "Fostering Increased Conformity with International Standards: Monitoring and Institutional Fact-finding", in *Realizing Utopia: The Future of International Law*, Oxford University Press, Oxford, 2012, p. 303.

[256] As one article mentions of NGO fact-finding work: The strategy – promoting change by reporting facts – is almost elegant in its simplicity. And there is growing evidence that it works. Governments frequently have adopted reforms in response to critical reports by NGOs, and former political prisoners who had been subjects of Amnesty International letter writing campaigns have often attributed their release from detention to Amnesty International. Country reports prepared by the more prominent NGOs often receive front page news coverage abroad, and in the Untied States, such reports have prompted Congress to adopt legislation suspending foreign aid or conditioning future aid on a country's compliance with international human rights standards. See Diane F. Orentlicher, "Bearing Witness: The Art and Science of Human Rights Fact-Finding", in *Harvard Human Rights Journal*, 1990, vol. 84, p. 3.

---

outset, one difference is that the latter derive their mandates from governments, international and regional bodies or NGOs. In the case of preliminary examinations, unless they result from a referral by a State Party or the Security Council, it is really only the countries concerned and the sender(s) of communications who have a legitimate interest in being informed of the conduct and progress of a preliminary examination prompted *proprio motu*. At least until the moment that a decision has been taken and the OTP determines that a reasonable basis exists to proceed with an investigation.[257]

MRF missions take into account various factors in relation to public engagement while they carry out their mandates. Regarding what type of information to release to the public, most MRF mechanisms strive forcefully to bring the mission's findings to the public eye.[258] In this respect, some have argued that keeping reports confidential contributes to an environment of impunity.[259] As with the OTP's publication of preliminary examinations, disagreements have arisen in relation to what should be made public stemming from different perceptions about what the mission should aim to accomplish and how it should strategically pursue these ends. While NGOs see MRF reports as a way to publicly advocate at the national level, diplomats from donor governments are hesitant in this re-

---

[257] The OTP's work overlaps with several accountability mechanisms such as: the International Commission of Inquiry on Libya, the Secretary-General's Panel of Inquiry on the 31 May 2010 Flotilla Incident, the Independent, International Commission of Inquiry on Côte d'Ivoire, the International Commission of Inquiry for Guinea, the Independent International Fact-Finding Mission on the Conflict in Georgia, the United Nations Fact-Finding Mission on the Gaza Conflict, and the International Commission of Inquiry for Darfur.

[258] Either in accordance with their mandated reporting cycles or until the findings and recommendations are final.

[259] UN News & Media, "Council Hears Reports on Côte d'Ivoire and Syria, Holds General Debate on Human Rights Situations that Require its Attention", 15 June 2011 (http://www.legal-tools.org/doc/cd6612/). Also HRW, "Because They Have the Guns...I'm Left with Nothing: The Price of Continuing Impunity in Côte d'Ivoire", 2016, vol. 18, no. 4, p. 30 which states: "[T]he U.N. Security Council has yet to make public or discuss the findings of the report (Commission of Inquiry), which was handed to the U.N. Secretary General in November 2004 and transmitted to the Security Council on December 23, 2004. The failure to discuss the findings of the report, *let alone* act on them, sends the wrong signal to abusers". Conversely, the members of the Darfur Commission did little to no publicity upon the release of the mission's report. Regardless, the report wound up being quite impactful, since the mission was followed by a Security Council referral of the situation to the ICC, as the Darfur Commission's report recommended.

---

gard, believing that closed-door sessions with parties to the conflict are more effective.[260] The general trend is for MRF mechanisms to make their final reports public, to distribute them widely and ensure translations are available in the relevant languages. These missions are normally mandated to operate within prescribed timeframes contributing to a more expedient process of collecting and securing key information and potential evidence.

With respect to the ICRC, this body carries out a diverse range of activities that are mostly field-based. Yet, some parallels can be drawn: (i) the ICRC acquires and collects information that is relevant to proceedings of a judicial, quasi-judicial, public inquiry, fact-finding or similar nature; and (ii) the ICRC's activities have been described as "preventive"[261] which in turn is one of the OTP's policy objectives.[262]

ICRC policy dictates that in order to carry out its mandate and fully assume its operational role in the protection and assistance of victims in armed conflict and other situations of violence, confidentiality is an essential tool that allows them to build the necessary trust to secure access, open channels of communication, influence change and ensure the security of its staff.[263] Some critics argue that the organisation is too secretive and should share its findings publicly. When explaining why ICRC refuses to share its findings with the public, their representatives assert that "confidentiality does not equal complacency". The fact that they do not speak out publicly does not mean they are silent. Moreover, the ICRC

---

[260] Grace, 2014, p. 20, see *supra* note 244.

[261] ICTY, *Prosecutor v. Simić*, Decision on the Prosecution Motion Under Rule 73 for a Ruling Concerning the Testimony of a Witness, 27 July 1999, IT-95-9, paras. 76, 79 (http://www.legal-tools.org/doc/17bad5/): "The ICRC's activities have been described as 'preventive', while the International Tribunal [ICTY] is empowered to prosecute breaches of international humanitarian law once they have occurred. The same rational underpins the relationship with the ICC in which the OTP is empowered to establish the truth, while any preventive objective can only be aspirational but not operational". See also ICRC, 'The role of the ICRC in preventing armed conflict: its possibilities and limitations', 2001, no. 844, p. 923–946.

[262] OTP, *Policy Paper on Preliminary Examinations*, paras. 16, 93 and 104–106, see *supra* note 2.

[263] In this regard, the ICRC has developed a Memorandum that explains the rationale for and broad practical context of confidentiality as the ICRC's working method. See Memorandum on the ICRC's privilege of non-disclosure of confidential information, International Review of the Red Cross, 2016, 97 (897/898), pp. 433–444.

---

does not share confidential information with the media or other third parties, nor does it consent to the publication of such information, because there is always risk that their observations could be exploited for political gain or instrumentalised by one side or another. By discussing serious issues, such as abuse or ill-treatment, away from the glare of public attention, governments and non-State actors are often more likely to acknowledge problems and commit to taking action.[264] At the same time, they recognise that confidentiality is not unconditional and reserve the right to speak out or publish findings when their recommendations are not taken seriously and all other avenues of discourse have been exhausted.[265]

The ICRC's strategy is based on combining 'modes of action' and on selecting the appropriate activities depending on the approach(es) chosen.[266] Faced with an authority that has chosen to neglect or deliberately violate its obligations, persuasion (even with the mobilisation of support from influential third parties) may not be effective. In certain circumstances, therefore, the ICRC may decide to break with its tradition of confidentiality and resort to public *denunciation*. This mode of action is used only as part of the protection approach, which focuses on the imminent or established violation of a rule protecting individuals.[267]

24.7. Conclusion

As set out in this chapter, there are several issues with the OTP's policy on preliminary examinations. One of the most problematic relates to transparency and the Office's largely unregulated use of publicity during the preliminary examination process. The idea is not to encourage less transparency but rather, to advocate for the right type of transparency. Also, this contribution should not be read as being against publicity; instead it is suggesting less of it and handling it more strategically. The OTP

---

[264] Interview with ICRC Deputy Director of operations Dominik Stillhart, "Confidentiality: key to the ICRC's work but not unconditional", 20 September 2010 (available on ICRC's web site).

[265] *Ibid.*

[266] Modes of action are the methods or means used to persuade authorities to fulfil their obligations towards individuals or entire populations. Persuasion aims to convince someone to do something that falls within his area of responsibility or competence, through bilateral confidential dialogue. This is traditionally the ICRC's preferred mode of action. The ICRC: Its Mission and Work, 2009, p. 19, para. 1.a, see *supra* note 247.

[267] *Ibid.*, pp. 19–20 paras. 1 and 1.c.

will often be unable to satisfy all critics; still, the way it publicly communicates (or chooses not to publicly communicate) can mitigate and contain the effects of critiques that have the potential to inflict public perception damage on the ICC.[268] Support and buy-in for the preliminary examination process hinges on the OTP's ability to foster positive public perceptions of the Court's credibility as an impartial and independent institution committed to ensuring accountability for the worst crimes known to humankind.

While taking account of variations in mandates, the ICC could benefit from best practices on how other bodies handle the information they acquire or collect, including the advantages of not sharing inconclusive findings with the public and targeting only concerned parties in the sharing of that information. The Prosecutor should therefore adopt a gradual approach with regard to the disclosure of information before issuing public warnings or reporting prematurely findings in the context of preliminary examinations. No State likes to have a public finger pointed at it. States and other groups that are publicly under examination will naturally attempt to delegitimise the preliminary examination process by formulating critiques geared toward discrediting the Office if they have been publicly called out by the OTP at a time when the factual situation is less than clear. These critiques, credible or not, are harmful to the integrity of the Court as an institution and impact on the ability of the Court to achieve its mandate.

Purposefully using preliminary examinations in a different manner from what the Statute intended can be a legitimate means for the ICC Prosecutor to enhance the efficiency and effectiveness of his or her work. However, if the Prosecutor is afforded too much discretion in determining how to prioritise his or her duties under the Rome Statute, he or she may act in ways that, while arguably consistent with the Statute, do not fully take into account the interests of the ICC as a whole.

Although the OTP may not be facing a real 'deterrence or withdrawal' dilemma, some of the consequences discussed above should persuade it to review its preliminary examination process. This requires reconsidering fundamental aspects of its policy and practice. The OTP

---

[268] See Darryl Robinson, "Inescapable Dyads: Why the International Criminal Court Cannot Win", in *Leiden Journal of International Law*, 2015, vol. 28, pp. 323-347.

should advance more readily to investigations, instead of sitting on preliminary examinations for years. If the OTP's activities prevent future crimes or promote national accountability efforts, then these are side-effects, but should not be at the heart of ICC preliminary examinations, as they currently appear to be. The OTP should make the determination it is mandated to make, as efficiently as possible, and leave it in the hands of the judges to decide on the future of *proprio motu* investigations.

25

Objectivity of the
ICC Preliminary Examinations

Vladimir Tochilovsky[*]

25.1. Introduction

The quality of a preliminary examination in many regards depends on its objectivity. A one-sided approach inevitably affects the quality of the examination. It distorts the situation in general and the relevant facts in particular.

While the ICC Statute does not unequivocally require the Prosecution to examine the situation even-handedly, impartiality and objectivity are prerequisites of justice. In the Policy Paper on Preliminary Examinations, the Prosecutor emphasised that the preliminary examination process "is conducted on the basis of the facts and information available, and in the context of the overarching principles of *independence, impartiality and objectivity*".[1] The Policy Paper further explains that the principle of impartiality means that the Office will apply consistent methods and criteria, *irrespective of the States or parties involved or the person(s) or group(s) concerned.*[2] According to the document, the Office of the Prosecutor is to check "internal and external coherence, and considers information from *diverse and independent sources as a means of bias con-*

---

[*] **Vladimir Tochilovsky** was investigation team leader and trial attorney in the International Criminal Tribunal for the former Yugoslavia ('ICTY'), Office of the Prosecutor from 1994 to 2010; member (Vice-Chair) of the United Nations Working Group on Arbitrary Detention in 2010–2016; Deputy Regional Attorney for judicial matters, and District Attorney in the Ukraine from 1976 to 1994; and official representative of the ICTY to the United Nations negotiations for the establishment of the International Criminal Court ('ICC') from 1997 to 2001. He served as a member of two expert groups that prepared recommendations for the ICC Office of the Prosecutor ('OTP') in 2002–2003. He holds a Ph.D. and was a professor at Mechnikov National University, Ukraine in 1991–1994.

[1] OTP, *Policy Paper on Preliminary Examinations*, 1 November 2013, para. 25 (emphasis added) (https://www.legal-tools.org/doc/acb906/).

[2] *Ibid.*, para. 28 (emphasis added).

---

trol".[3] The Policy Paper concludes that the Prosecution "also seeks to ensure that, *in the interests of fairness, objectivity* and thoroughness, *all relevant parties are given the opportunity to provide information* to the Office".[4]

25.2. Two Categories of Situations

The situations under the preliminary examination can be divided, for the purpose of this chapter, into two categories. The first category includes situations involving a conflict between the situation-State and its non-State opponents. The second category comprises the conflicts where other States besides the situation-State are involved.

It is noteworthy that the preliminary examinations in the first category do not take long before the Prosecutor moves to the investigations stage. Examination of the situation in Congo lasted only two months, Côte d'Ivoire – five months, Uganda and Mali – six months each.

By contrast, in the second category, the preliminary examinations take years. Preliminary examination in Georgia situation took almost eight years. The situation in Afghanistan has been under the preliminary examination for ten years. The situation in Iraq has been under examination since 2014, and in Palestine – since 2015. This may be explained by reliance on the notion of positive complementarity (States' commitment to investigate) and the limited ICC resources. In fact, in these situations, the Prosecutor remains on standby mode for years. There might also be some political considerations behind the Prosecutor's unwillingness to trigger the investigation. In this regard, HRW in its Policy Paper on the meaning of the "interests of justice" states:

> A decision whether or not to initiate an investigation [...] must not be influenced by a) possible political advantage or disadvantage to the government or any political party, group or individual; and b) possible media or community reaction to the decision.[5]

---

[3] *Ibid.*, para. 32 (emphasis added).

[4] *Ibid.*, para. 33 (emphasis added).

[5] Human Rights Watch ('HRW'), "The Meaning of "the Interests of Justice" in Article 53 of the Rome Statute, Human Rights Watch Policy Paper", 1 June 2005, para. 3 (http://www. legal-tools.org/doc/4dc3b4/).

So far, only situations in the first category resulted in charges, arrests, and trials. Out of the six situations, five were submitted by the situation-States themselves under either Article 14 or Article 12(3) of the ICC Statute.[6] In fact, in these cases, the Prosecutor often encouraged the situation-States to submit the situations to the ICC. For instance, concerning situation in Congo, the Prosecutor stated:

> If necessary, [...] I stand ready to seek authorisation from a Pre-Trial Chamber to start an investigation under my *proprio motu* powers [...] [I]n light of the current circumstances in the field, the protection of witnesses, gathering of evidence and arrest of suspects will be extremely difficult without the strong support of national or international forces.

> Our role could be facilitated by a referral or active support from the DRC. The Court and the territorial State may agree that a consensual division of labour could be an effective approach. Groups bitterly divided by conflict may oppose prosecutions at each other's hands and yet agree to a prosecution by a Court perceived as neutral and impartial. The Office could cooperate with the national authorities by prosecuting the leaders who bear most responsibility for the crimes. National authorities with the assistance of the international community could implement appropriate mechanisms to deal with other individuals responsible.[7]

Soon after this statement, Congo referred the situation to the ICC. Indeed, in those situations, the States had been eager to investigate and prosecute those who were prosecuted by the ICC. Actually, these situations have been comparatively the easiest ones for the investigation as the Prosecutor enjoyed the full support of the situation-State and the eagerness of the Government to have its opponents prosecuted.

25.3. Risk of Manipulation

The first category of the situations under the preliminary examination often involve a conflict between the Government of the situation-State

---

[6] Côte d'Ivoire, Uganda, Congo, Mali, and Central African Republic.

[7] ICC, Second Assembly of States Parties to the Rome Statute of the International Criminal Court, Report of the Prosecutor of the ICC, Mr. Luis Moreno-Ocampo, 8 September 2003 (http://www.legal-tools.org/doc/8873bd/).

and its military or political opponents. This could be election-related violence like in Côte d'Ivoire or an armed conflict like in Congo and Uganda.

Formally, in such cases, the ICC Prosecutor has no obligation to examine crimes committed by all parties to the conflict. There is nothing in the law that would prevent the Prosecutor from focusing on only one party. This creates a risk of a one-sided ICC examination which adversely affects its objectivity.

In particular, the objectivity of the preliminary examination may suffer if it relies on the material received from the situation-State. The experience of the ICTY shows that such material may be of questionable credibility and reliability. It is difficult to ensure impartiality of the domestic investigations where the Government itself is a party to the conflict. The authorities are often reluctant or unwilling to investigate their own forces. Such investigations are considered damaging for the morale of the forces. This is also stigmatized as unpatriotic. One can hear arguments like "We cannot investigate people who defend our country".

25.3.1. Acceptance of Jurisdiction and Self-referrals

Incorporation of a one-sided, often biased, domestic investigation into the Prosecution's public report makes it a political tool used by the government both domestically and internationally.

This could be one of the reasons behind the acceptance of the ICC jurisdiction under Article 12(3) by a State that is not a party to the Statute. That is why, whenever the Court receives Article 12(3) declaration from a State, special attention should be paid to the actual intention of the Government. This should also apply to a self-referral by a State Party under Article 14.

Such declarations and self-referrals often reveal the intention of the governments to have the ICC to focus only on their opponents.

For instance, in the Uganda situation, the Prosecutor reported:

> In December 2003, I received a referral from the Government of Uganda, the first state referral in the history of the Court. In the referral letter the Government specifically mentioned the case of the Lord's Resistance Army, the LRA. We notified Uganda that we would interpret the referral as concerning all crimes under the Statute committed in Northern Uganda and that our investigation would be impartial. In a

July 2004 report to the Parliament the Government of Uganda confirmed their understanding of this interpretation.[8]

However, despite such commitment, the preliminary examination as well as the subsequent investigations and prosecution in this situation were limited to the offences committed by the opponents of the Government.

In Ukraine, the Parliament adopted the declaration "On the recognition of the jurisdiction of the International Criminal Court by Ukraine over crimes against humanity and war crimes committed by senior officials of the Russian Federation and leaders of terrorist organizations 'DNR' and 'LNR' [self-proclaimed entities]". The subsequent letter of the Minister for Foreign Affairs of Ukraine declaring acceptance of jurisdiction of behalf of Ukraine, however, was worded in accordance with Rule 44(2) of the ICC Rules of Procedure and Evidence. In particular, the letter does not contain any 'instruction' as to which particular parties to the conflict the ICC examination and investigations shall focused on. According to the letter, Ukraine accepted the jurisdiction of the Court "for the purpose of identifying, prosecuting and judging the perpetrators and accomplices of acts committed in the territory of Ukraine".[9]

Pursuant to Rule 44, a communication of the situation to the ICC under Article 12(3) of the ICC Statute has, as a consequence, the acceptance of jurisdiction with respect to the crimes referred to in Article 5 of relevance to the situation. It was emphasized in the *Gbagbo* case that: "Rule 44 of the Rules was adopted in order to ensure that States that chose to stay out of the treaty could not use the Court 'opportunistically'".[10] The Court further noted that: "there were concerns that the wording of Article 12(3) of the Statute, and specifically the reference to the acceptance of jurisdiction 'with respect to the crime in question', would allow the Court to be used as a political tool by States not party to the Statute who could

---

[8]   ICC, "Statement by the Chief Prosecutor on the Uganda Arrest Warrants", 14 October 2005, ICC-OTP-20051014-109 (http://www.legal-tools.org/doc/d9b3cb/).

[9]   ICC, "Declaration by Ukraine lodged under Article 12(3) of the Statute", 8 September 2015 (http://www.legal-tools.org/doc/b53005/).

[10]   ICC, *Prosecutor v. Laurent Gbagbo*, Pre-Trial Chamber, Decision on the "Corrigendum of the Challenge to the Jurisdiction of the International Criminal Court on the Basis of Articles 12(3), 19(2), 21(3), 55 and 59 of the Rome Statute Filed by the Defence for President Gbagbo (ICC–02/11–01/11–129)", 15 August 2012, ICC–02/11–01/11, para. 59 (https://www.legal-tools.org/doc/0d14c3/).

selectively accept the exercise of jurisdiction in respect of certain crimes or certain parties to a conflict".[11]

25.3.2. Publicity of the Preliminary Examination Reports

Such attempts of 'using' the ICC may also relate to the publicity of the Prosecutor's reports on preliminary examination.

Public awareness of the fact that the Prosecutor is conducting preliminary examination may by itself serve as a deterrent from further violations. However, the publicity of the Prosecutor's interim findings may also be counterproductive.

It is not only because in the interim findings the Prosecutor publicly 'designates' the 'guilty party' although no investigation has been conducted. Such publicity may also have a chilling effect on that party, discouraging it from co-operating, and may disturb peace negotiations and attempts of reconciliation.

Official reports of the ICC Prosecutor often have political ramifications. The preliminary character of the examination reports does not prevent governments from using them for political purposes. The reports are widely scrutinised by public and considered often as the authoritative source of the information on the situation in question. Such nuances in the report as terms "alleged" and "allegedly" are easily ignored in political discourse. In addition, publicity of the reports of one-sided examinations may serve as an incentive for other States to use the ICC against their opponents.

One may argue that, after preliminary examination and authorization, the Prosecutor may expand the scope of investigation beyond the events and parties covered by the report. In its request for authorisation of an investigation of situation in the Republic of Côte d'Ivoire, the Prosecution informed the Chamber:

> [F]or the purpose of the investigation and the development of the proceedings, [the Prosecution] is neither bound by its submissions with regard to the different acts alleged in its Article 15 application, nor by the incidents and persons identified therein, and accordingly may, upon investigation, take further procedural steps in respect of these or other acts, in-

---

[11] *Ibid.*

cidents or persons, subject to the parameters of the author-ised situation.[12]

However, in this case, as in other self-referred cases and cases of accepted jurisdiction, the subsequent investigations have been so far conducted mostly within the framework of the preliminary examination report.

25.4. Prosecutor's Policy and Nexus to Investigation

In 2005, the Prosecutor outlined his policy in the Uganda situation as follows:

> The criteria for selection of the first case was gravity. We analyzed the gravity of all crimes in Northern Uganda committed by the LRA and Ugandan forces. Crimes committed by the LRA were much more numerous and of much higher gravity than alleged crimes committed by the UPDF. We therefore started with an investigation of the LRA. [...] We will continue to collect information on allegations concerning all other groups, to determine whether the Statute thresholds are met and the policy of focusing on the persons most responsible is satisfied.[13]

In practice, however, this principle of focusing first on the party that committed the gravest crimes and then looking into the crimes committed by other parties turned out to be unworkable. In all the situations that were submitted by the situation-States, the Prosecutor got stuck with the first selection of accused. In the Uganda situation, after the warrants of arrest where issued for five members of the LRA in 2005, no perpetrators from the Government forces were charged.

If the ICTY Prosecutor had also focused only on a party that committed more numerous and the gravest crimes, Serbian and Croatian victims would have little chance to see justice. In this regard, HRW in its comments to the Prosecutor's draft policy paper noted:

> The International Criminal Tribunal for the former Yugoslavia [...] and the Special Court for Sierra Leone have prosecuted perpetrators from all of the major parties to the respec-

---

[12] ICC, Situation in the Republic of Côte d'Ivoire, Request for authorisation of an investigation pursuant to Article 15, 23 June 2011, ICC-02/11-03, p. 10, fn. 14 (http://www.legal-tools.org/doc/1b1939/).

[13] Statement by the Chief Prosecutor on the Uganda Arrest Warrants, see *supra* note 8.

tive conflicts. This contributed to their credibility among the communities most affected.[14]

HRW also expressed concerns in regard to ICC Prosecutor's policy:

> Because of the prosecutor's reliance on state cooperation to carry out his mandate, especially in those situations that have been voluntarily referred, we believe the prosecutor should be sensitive to the risks to his impartiality [...]

> The prosecutor's Policy Paper states that his office will investigate all groups in a situation "in sequence", suggesting that one group will be investigated at a time. After completion of an investigation of a particular group, the prosecutor's office examines whether other groups warrant investigation [...]

> We urge sensitivity to the implications of mechanically pursuing a policy of proceeding sequentially in all situations. In the context of the DRC, our field research suggests that this approach may have already undermined the perception of the ICC as an impartial institution. As such, to the greatest extent possible, we urge the prosecutor to avoid delays in investigating other groups alleged to have committed crimes within the ICC's jurisdiction.[15]

It was also opined in regard to the Prosecutor's policy in the Congo situation:

> In determining its potential role in the conflict in the Democratic Republic of Congo, the Office of the Prosecutor of the ICC must consider the stability of the country's government, [...] the ramifications of unequal justice for victims of the entire war, the feasibility of successful prosecutions, [...] *[T]here are various prisms through which the Court could consider the questions: it could think of itself first; it could think of the donor countries first; it could think of the Congolese government first, or it could think of the victims first. We hope that the victims will carry the day.*[16]

---

[14] HRW, "The Selection of Situations and Cases for Trial before the International Criminal Court. A Human Rights Watch Policy Paper", 26 October 2006 (http://www.legal-tools.org/doc/753e9b/).

[15] *Ibid.*

[16] Pascal Kambale and Anna Rotman, "The International Criminal Court and Congo", Crimes of War Project (emphasis added) (http://www.legal-tools.org/doc/7ed751/).

Later, the OTP, having adjusted its policy in the preliminary examination in accordance with jurisprudence of the Pre-Trial Chambers, asserted:

> [T]he consideration of admissibility (complementarity and gravity) will take into account potential cases that could be identified in the course of the preliminary examination based on the information available and that would likely arise from an investigation into the situation.[17]

As to the 'targets' of the preliminary examination, the Policy Paper referred to the following jurisprudence of the Pre-Trial Chambers:

> [A]dmissibility at the situation phase should be assessed against certain criteria defining a 'potential case' such as: (i) the *groups of persons involved that are likely to be the focus* of an investigation for the purpose of shaping the future case(s); and (ii) the *crimes* within the jurisdiction of the Court allegedly committed during the incidents that are *likely to be the focus* of an investigation for the purpose of shaping the future case(s).[18]

The Prosecution further reiterated its policy of "focussing on those bearing the greatest responsibility for the most serious crimes".[19] Accordingly, in the Uganda situation (Article 12(3) declaration), the Prosecution

---

[17] OTP, *Policy Paper on Preliminary Examinations*, para. 43, see *supra* note 1, with reference to ICC, Situation in the Republic of Kenya, Request for authorisation of an investigation pursuant to Article 15, ICC-01/09-3, 26 November 2009, paras. 51, 107 (http://www.legal-tools.org/doc/c63dcc/); ICC, Situation in the Republic of Kenya, Decision Pursuant to Article 15 of the Rome Statute on the Authorization of an Investigation into the Situation in the Republic of Kenya, 1 April 2010, ICC-01/09-19-Corr, paras. 50, 182, 188 (http://www.legal-tools.org/doc/f0caaf/).

[18] Situation in the Republic of Kenya, Decision Pursuant to Article 15 of the Rome Statute on the Authorization of an Investigation into the Situation in the Republic of Kenya, para. 50, see *supra* note 17; ICC, Situation in the Republic of Côte d'Ivoire, Corrigendum to "Decision Pursuant to Article 15 of the Rome Statute on the Authorisation of an Investigation into the Situation in the Republic of Côte d'Ivoire", 3 October 2011, ICC-02/11-14-Corr, paras. 190–191, 202–204 (emphasis added) (http://www.legal-tools.org/doc/7a6c19/).

[19] *Ibid.*, para. 45, with reference to Situation in the Republic of Kenya, Request for authorisation of an investigation pursuant to Article 15, see *supra* note 17; ICC, Situation in the Republic of Kenya, Prosecution's Response to Decision Requesting Clarification and Additional Information, 3 March 2010, ICC-01/09-16 (http://www.legal-tools.org/doc/1f1fec/); Situation in the Republic of Côte d'Ivoire, Request for authorisation of an investigation pursuant to article 15, see *supra* note 12.

---

focused both its preliminary examination and subsequent investigations and prosecutions on the offences committed by the opponents of the Government only. In this regard, it was noted:

> If the ICC wishes to establish and retain legitimacy, it must investigate all actors of possible atrocities, including the Ugandan government and the Ugandan People's Democratic Army (UPDF). "Just days before the ICC unsealed the warrants against the LRA leaders, HRW published a report in which it documented numerous instances in which the UPDF has been responsible for committing rapes, torture, killings, arbitrary arrests, and detentions of the civilian population in northern Uganda." [...] The investigation and prosecution of LRA members suspected of gross violations of international law must be accompanied by an equally robust investigation of government abuse.[20]

Furthermore, it was also reported:

> The ICC [...] made mistakes with the LRA case from the outset. When then chief prosecutor Luis Moreno-Ocampo announced the investigation in Uganda, he stood shoulder-to-shoulder in a London hotel with President Museveni. The court turned up with one of the parties to the conflict [...] effectively vindicating the Ugandan army – which also committed serious crimes – of responsibility in the Ugandan civil war.[21]

25.5. Safeguarding Objectivity of the Preliminary Examination

25.5.1. Sources of Information

Where the State is eager to investigate only its 'enemies', one of the reasons for the Prosecutor to step in should be the opportunity to ensure even-handed examination. In this regard, it is noteworthy that in its Policy Paper, the Prosecutor noted:

> In light of the global nature of the Court and the complementarity principle, a significant part of the Office's efforts at the

---

[20] David L. McCoy, "Fostering Peace and Ending Impunity: The International Criminal Court, Human Rights, and the LRA", in *International Affairs Review, Special Africa Edition 2007*.

[21] Jessica Hatcher-Moore, "Is the world's highest court fit for purpose?", in *The Guardian*, 5 April 2017 (http://www.legal-tools.org/doc/05813d/).

preliminary examination stage is directed towards encouraging States to carry out their primary responsibility to investigate and prosecute international crimes. The complementary nature of the Court requires national judicial authorities and the ICC to function together. [...] *Where national systems remain inactive or are otherwise unwilling or unable to genuinely investigate and prosecute, the ICC must fill the gap left by the failure of States to satisfy their duty.*[22]

Reliable information related to all parties to the conflict can be found in the reports of the OHCHR, UN Independent Commissions, UN Special Procedures, and NGOs. These sources are especially important in the situations where some parties to the conflict do not, for some reasons, co-operate with the ICC and do not provide the Prosecutor with any information. At the very least, the Prosecutor should not ignore these sources of information.

In the Uganda situation, the Prosecution limited its preliminary examination and subsequent investigation only to the offences of the opponents of the Government. And this was despite the repeated appeals from Human Rights Watch to look also into the serious offences, committed by the Government forces.

In particular, in 2004, Human Rights Watch reported that the violations committed by the Ugandan government troops include: "extrajudicial killings, rape and sexual assault, forcible displacement of over one million civilians, and the recruitment of children under the age of 15 into government militias".[23] HRW emphasised that: "the ICC prosecutor cannot ignore the crimes that Ugandan government troops allegedly have committed", and that the Government's referral "does not limit the prosecutor's investigation only to crimes allegedly committed by the LRA [...] The prosecutor should operate independently and has the authority to look at all ICC crimes committed in Uganda".[24] A year later, HRW reported again that soldiers in Uganda's national army have: "raped, beaten, arbi-

---

[22] OTP, *Policy Paper on Preliminary Examinations*, para. 100, see *supra* note 1 (emphasis added).

[23] HRW, "ICC: Investigate All Sides in Uganda. Chance for Impartial ICC Investigation into Serious Crimes a Welcome Step", 4 February 2004 (http://www.legal-tools.org/doc/dabb8d/).

[24] *Ibid.*

trarily detained and killed civilians in camps" and that "the Ugandan government has failed to pursue prosecutions of military officers before national courts that could put an end to such violations".[25] HRW once again urged the ICC to "thoroughly examine government forces' crimes against the civilian population as well as those committed by the rebels".[26]

Similarly, concerning the situation in Congo, HRW reported that: "both government soldiers and dissident forces have carried out war crimes in Bukavu, killing and raping civilians in their battle to control the eastern Congolese city [...] [C]ivilians have been targeted by all sides".[27]

The Prosecutor may also seek assistance from UNHCHR, UNHRC, ICRC, NGOs and others present in the field. Such assistance may include screening for identification of potential witnesses or seeking other types of information that may be relevant to the assessment of the situation.[28] Under Article 15(2) of the ICC Statute, the Prosecutor may receive written or oral testimony at the seat of the Court only. It was opined, however, that there is nothing barring the Prosecutor from asking States or organizations to obtain information from potential witnesses as part of 'seeking information', including through obtaining voluntary written statements. Furthermore, it was argued, that the Prosecutor may also be able to directly obtain information from witnesses as "other reliable sources" with the State's consent, provided these do not amount to "testimony", which must be taken "at the seat of the Court".[29]

---

[25] HRW, "Uganda: Army and Rebels Commit Atrocities in the North. International Criminal Court Must Investigate Abuses on Both Sides", 20 September 2005 (http://www.legal-tools.org/doc/dbcc41/).

[26] *Ibid.*

[27] HRW, "DR Congo: War Crimes in Bukavu", 11 June 2004 (http://www.legal-tools.org/doc/911fb5/).

[28] ICC, Informal Expert Paper: Fact-Finding and Investigative Functions of the Office of the Prosecutor, Including International Co-operation, 1 January 2003, para. 30 (http://www.legal-tools.org/doc/ba368d/). See also Morten Bergsmo and Vladimir Tochilovsky, "Fact-Finding and Investigative Functions of the Office of the Prosecutor, Including International Co-operation", in Morten Bergsmo, Klaus Rackwitz and SONG Tianying (eds.), *Historical Origins of International Criminal Law: Volume 5*, Torkel Opsahl Academic EPublisher, Brussels, 2017, chap. 44, pp. 695 ff. (http://www.toaep.org/ps-pdf/24-bergsmo-rackwitz-song).

[29] *Ibid.*, para. 31.

Some may argue that the even-handed approach may discourage the situation-States from co-operation with the ICC. However, the ICTY experience demonstrates that it is not impossible to investigate and prosecute perpetrators from all parties to the conflict despite of the lack of co-operation from some of them. Among those indicted and convicted by the Tribunal one can find perpetrators, including high-ranking ones, from all parties.

Indeed, in conducting preliminary examination, the Prosecutor should not pursue a 'fair balance' of number of perpetrators from all parties to the conflict at all costs. In the ICTY's early years, it had been criticised for perceived imbalance between the number of Serb and Croat defendants. The Prosecution was often criticized for an alleged ethnic bias. The imbalance was reduced to some extent at the end of 1995 when eight Croatian nationals were indicted in the *Kupreškić et al.* case. While this indictment temporarily improved the image of the ICTY, the subsequent outcome of the case was disastrous for the Prosecutor. Indictment against one defendant was withdrawn, another defendant was acquitted by the Trial Chamber, three others were acquitted by the Appeals Chamber, and one defendant died before the indictment was issued.[30]

25.5.2. On-site Visits

To address deficiency of one-sided domestic investigations, the Prosecution may seek access to the territory controlled by a non-State party to the conflict. Such visit to a self-proclaimed entity does not mean recognition of its legitimacy. It is a regular practice for the UN Special Procedures to visit such territories during country visits.

For instance, UN Special Rapporteurs visited Transnistrian region as a part of their visits to the Republic of Moldova. In July 2008, Special Rapporteur on torture and other cruel, inhuman or degrading treatment or punishment, visited the self-proclaimed 'Transnistrian Republic' (Transnistrian region of the Republic of Moldova) as part of his fact-finding

---

[30] Vladimir Tochilovsky, "Special Commentary: International Criminal Justice – Some Flaws and Misperceptions", in *Criminal Law Forum*, 2011, vol. 22, pp. 602–603.

visit to Moldova.[31] Similarly, Special Rapporteurs visited self-proclaimed entities in eastern part of Ukraine during country visits.

Similarly, in the *Ilaşcu and others v. Moldova and Russia* case, judges of the European Court of Human Rights visited Transnistria region of Moldova. The judges, in order to clarify, in particular, whether Moldova and/or the Russian Federation were responsible for the alleged human rights violations, conducted an on-site fact-finding mission in Moldova, including territory controlled by self-proclaimed Trans-Dniester Republic. They "took account of the numerous documents submitted by the parties and the Transnistrian authorities throughout the proceedings".[32] The Court also consulted certain documents filed by the authorities of the self-proclaimed entity through the OSCE mission.[33]

25.5.3. Role of Experts in National Investigations

The quality and objectivity of the domestic material relied upon in the ICC preliminary examination may be improved if it is collected with assistance of experts having experience in practical application of the international humanitarian law.

The NGOs and other members of the civil society conducting fact-finding investigations often lack the necessary legal expertise. Furthermore, even where the State investigators conduct investigations of the international crimes, they are not always properly equipped for the task. The States may have no shortage of investigators with experience in investigation of serious crimes such as murder or rape. However, the investigation of the same acts as international crimes is different. For the crimes against humanity, it is not only to prove elements of murders and rapes. The investigators shall also collect evidence that would demonstrate that those crimes were committed as part of a widespread or systematic attack; and that there was a State policy to commit the attack. The same is true for the investigation of war crimes. It does not happen often that States get involved in armed conflicts. As a result, in most countries it

---

[31] Report of the Special Rapporteur on torture and other cruel, inhuman or degrading treatment or punishment, Manfred Nowak, Mission to the Republic of Moldova, A/HRC/10/44/Add.3, 12 February 2009 (http://www.legal-tools.org/doc/f18040/).

[32] European Court of Human Rights, *Ilaşcu and Others v. Moldova and Russia*, [GC], Judgment, 8 July 2004, 48787/99, para. 16 (http://www.legal-tools.org/doc/f68a72/).

[33] *Ibid.*, para. 17.

is difficult to find investigators with experience in investigation of such crimes. Furthermore, in most jurisdictions, there are no experts and military analysts in the prosecution office.

Investigations of international crimes require additional skills and knowledge, including the knowledge of the international humanitarian law. Investigators with such skills and expertise are not always readily available in national jurisdictions. For this reason, domestic investigations of international crimes would usually require support and assistance of the experts with experience in practical application of the norms of the international humanitarian law to the facts of the case.

25.6. Conclusion

In the situations involving conflict between the Government of the situation-State and its non-State opponents, the Prosecutor often takes side of the Government that submitted the situation to the ICC. By contrast, the preliminary examinations in the situations involving other States besides the situation-State, seems to be conducted generally even-handedly. However, it would be premature to assess the objectivity of any ongoing preliminary examination before the examination is completed.

Declarations of acceptance of the ICC jurisdiction and self-referrals have the risk of having the Court used as a political tool by States. The situation-States are often unwilling to investigate crimes committed by their forces and eager to prosecute its opponents. In such cases, one of the reasons for the Prosecutor to step in should be the opportunity to ensure even-handed examination.

Preliminary examinations are unjust if they are one-sided. They are discriminatory if they ignore entire classes of victims. The reputation of the ICC suffers if it appears unjust and indifferent to victims. In the report on Uganda situation, the Coalition for the ICC noted:

> The ICC investigation has not yielded cases against government officials and armed forces. According to some civil society groups, the absence of such cases—or clear and public explanations as to why they are not being pursued—has left

too many victims without justice and undermined perceptions of the Court's independence and impartiality.[34]

The opponents in the conflict often do not care about the victims of the other side. The ICC must be different. The Prosecutor should not take or even seen as taking side in the conflict. By siding with the Government and turning a blind eye to the crimes committed by its forces, the Prosecutor ignores the victims of those crimes.

Decisions at this stage may have political ramifications on national and international levels. However, the Prosecutor should not be guided by political considerations in conducting examinations. An explicit pronunciation of the general Prosecution policy concerning objectivity of the preliminary examinations would be helpful to avoid any appearance of political bias in particular situations.[35] It should be made clear in a policy statement that the preliminary examination shall not be influenced by any perceived advantage by Governments.

---

[34] Coalition for the International Criminal Court, "Uganda" (available on the Coalition's web site).

[35] Informal Expert Paper: Measures available to the International Criminal Court to reduce the length of proceedings, 2003, 1 January 2003, para. 18 (http://www.legal-tools.org/doc/7eba03/).

26

The ICC's Interplay with UN Fact-Finding Commissions in Preliminary Examinations

Mutoy Mubiala[*]

26.1. Introduction

The Office of the Prosecutor of the International Criminal Court ('ICC-OTP') has on several occasions launched preliminary examinations preceding, coinciding with, or following the deployment of United Nations ('UN') Fact-finding Commissions ('UNFFCs') and human rights monitoring bodies and missions. This has been the case in most of the ICC situations in Africa. Despite their distinct nature (one outside and the other inside the criminal justice system), the two processes have experienced some levels of interaction. In its first section, this chapter examines this interaction, in light of three case studies on Darfur, Libya and the Central African Republic ('CAR'). In the second section, the chapter examines the issue of quality control of the information provided by the UNFFCs to the ICC-OTP in preliminary examinations and, subsequently, its implications for judicial review by the ICC Pre-Trial and Trial Chambers. The chapter concludes by formulating recommendations on ways and means to streamline UN fact-finding and ICC-OTP's preliminary examination.

26.2. Interaction between the ICC-OTP and UNFFCs in Preliminary Examination

Before reviewing the cases illustrating the interaction between the ICC-OTP and UNFFCs in preliminary examination, it is important to provide a

---

[*] **Mutoy Mubiala** has been working as a Human Rights Officer with the Office of the United Nations High Commissioner for Human Rights, in Geneva, since 1994. He holds a Ph.D. from the Graduate Institute of International and Development Studies, University of Geneva, Switzerland. He has served several UN Commissions of Inquiry whose findings were shared with the ICC-OTP in the context of preliminary examinations of African countries. The views expressed in this chapter do not necessarily reflect those of the UN.

brief overview of the legal and institutional framework of the co-operation between the ICC and the UN.

26.2.1. Legal and Institutional Framework of the Co-operation between the ICC and the UN

As provided by the ICC-OTP's Policy Paper on Preliminary Examinations, preliminary examinations rely on various sources of information, including international organisations, non-governmental organisations and testimonies received at the headquarters of the Court. In this regard, the ICC has signed several agreements with various entities, including with the UN on 4 October 2004.[1] Of particular importance are Articles 18 and 20 of the Agreement.

According to Article 18:

> 1. With due regard to its responsibilities under the Charter of the United Nations and subject to its rules, the United Nations undertakes to cooperate with the Prosecutor and to enter with the Prosecutor into such arrangements or, as appropriate, agreements as may be necessary to facilitate such co-operation, in particular when the Prosecutor exercises, under Article 54 of the Statute, his or her duties and powers with respect to investigation and seeks the cooperation of the United Nations in accordance with this Article.

> 2. Subject to the rules of the organ concerned, the United Nations undertakes to cooperate in relation to requests from the Prosecutor in providing such additional information as he or she may seek, in accordance with Article 15, paragraph 2, of the Statute, from organs of the United Nations in connection with investigations initiated *proprio motu* by the Prosecutor pursuant to that Article. The Prosecutor shall address a request for such information to the Secretary-General, who shall convey it to the presiding officer or other appropriate officer of the organ concerned.

> 3. The United Nations and the Prosecutor may agree that the United Nations provide documents or information to the Prosecutor on condition of confidentiality and solely for the purpose of generating new information shall not be disclosed

---

[1] Negotiated Relationship Agreement between the International Criminal Court and the United Nations, 4 October 2004 (https://www.legal-tools.org/doc/9432c6/).

to other organs of the Court or to third parties, at any stage of the proceedings or thereafter, without the consent of the United Nations.

4. The Prosecutor and the United Nations or programmes, funds and offices concerned may enter into such agreement, as may be necessary to facilitate their cooperation for the implementation of this article, in particular in order to ensure the confidentiality of information, the protection of any person, including former and current United Nations personnel, and the security or proper conduct of any operation or activity of the United Nations.[2]

Regarding the protection of confidentiality, Article 20 of the Agreement further provides:

If the United Nations is requested by the Court to provide information or documentation in its custody, possession or control which was disclosed to it in confidence by a State or an intergovernmental, international or non-governmental organisation or an individual, the United Nations shall seek the consent of the originator to disclose that information or documentation or where appropriate, will inform the Court that it may seek the consent of the originator for the United Nations to disclose that information or documentation. If the originator is a State Party to the Statute and the United Nations fail to obtain its consent to disclosure within a reasonable period of time, the United Nations shall inform the Court accordingly, and the issue of disclosure shall be resolved between the State Party concerned and the Court in accordance with the Statute. If the originator is not a State Party to the Statute and refuses to consent to disclosure, the United Nations shall inform the Court that it is unable to provide the requested information or documentation because of a pre-existing obligation of confidentiality to the originator.[3]

It is in the framework of the two above provisions that the UN bodies, in particular the Office of the High Commissioner for Human Rights ('OHCHR') and UNFFCs, have developed close co-operation with the ICC-OTP in relation to preliminary examinations.

---

[2] *Ibid.*, p. 7.

[3] *Ibid.*, pp. 7–8.

26.2.2. Case Studies

The Policy Paper also provides that preliminary examination consists of four phases, including:

1. the initial jurisdictional assessment of all information of the alleged crimes received;

2. the factual and legal analysis of information arising from referrals by a State Party to the Statute, the United Nations Security Council ('UNSC') and the open source information received at the seat of the Court, to assess whether there is a reasonable basis to believe that the alleged crimes fall within the subject-matter jurisdiction of the Court;

3. the admissibility of potential cases in accordance with Article 17 of the Rome Statute on complementarity, to assess the ability or willingness of the national authorities to prosecute the presumed authors of the alleged crimes; and

4. the examination of the interests of justice for the opening of an investigation.[4]

On the basis of this division, this section reviews three case studies illustrating the interaction between the ICC-OTP and UNFFC in preliminary examinations representing three scenarios: (1) the UNFFC's deployment *preceding* preliminary examination (Darfur); (2) the UNFFC's deployment *coinciding* with preliminary examination (Libya); and (3) the UNFFC's deployment *following* preliminary examination (CAR II). The work of each of the three UNFFCs deployed in the three countries contributed to the completion of one or several phases of the related preliminary examinations. The section focuses on one aspect of the contribution of each Commission:

1. the factual and legal analysis of the information and the identification of potential cases falling within the jurisdiction of the Court and of the presumed authors of international crimes (Phase 2) for the Darfur Commission;

2. the review of the subject-matter jurisdiction of the Court (Phase 2) for the Libya Commission; and

---

[4] OTP, *Policy Paper on Preliminary Examinations*, 1 November 2013, p. 19 (http://www. legal-tools.org/doc/acb906/).

---

3. the implementation of the principle of complementarity (Phases 1 and 3) for the CAR Commission and other fact-finding bodies and missions involved in the country.

26.2.2.1. Darfur

UNFFCs were particularly involved in the situation in Darfur. In April and May 2003, OHCHR deployed fact-finding missions in Darfur and Eastern Chad. The UN Human Rights Council's Special Rapporteur on Sudan and the UN Secretary-General's Special Representative on the situation of Internally Displaced Persons also visited Darfur during the same period. In October 2004, the UNSC established the International Commission on Darfur. The Darfur Commission, which operated from November 2004, submitted its final report to the UN Secretary-General on 31 January 2005.[5] This report was presented by the then High Commissioner Louise Arbour to the UN Security Council on 16 February 2005.[6] Based on the findings and recommendations of the Commission, the UNSC, by its resolution 1593 (2005) adopted on 31 March 2005, referred the situation in Darfur to the ICC.

Evaluating the outcome of the Darfur Commission, Philip Alston wrote the following:

> The Darfur Commission Report [...], even though miraculously completed in the space of only 90 days, was comprehensive in scope, assembled a very detailed factual account of the situation, evaluated the extent to which genocide had been involved, and succeeded in identifying by name 51 suspected perpetrators of various crimes. Another major accomplishment, with broader ramifications beyond this particular case, is its clarification of the legal principles applicable in such situations. The Report provides a careful and systematic analysis, written in clear and comprehensible language, of a number of complex legal issues which will arise in most comparable cases. They include issues such as the relationship between human rights and international humanitarian

---

[5]   Report of the International Commission of Inquiry on Darfur to the Secretary-General, UN doc. S/2005/60, 1 February 2005 (http://www.legal-tools.org/doc/1480de/).

[6]   United Nations, Statement by Ms. Louise Arbour, High Commissioner for Human Rights, to the Security Council on the International Commission of Inquiry on Darfur, New York, 16 February 2005, p. 1.

law ('mutually reinforcing and overlapping in situations of armed conflict', § 144), the extent and nature of customary law in this area (an analysis completed before the publication of the ICRC study) and the applicability of the relevant norms to non-state actors (an analysis based in part on general principles and partly on agreements accepted by the key actors in Sudan, §§ 172–174). It is significant that these legal analyses were not subject to any noteworthy criticisms or challenges in the Security Council or the Commission on Human Rights.[7]

The findings of the Darfur Commission have been heavily relied on by the ICC-OTP in preliminary examination on the situation in Darfur, as it was not on the ground. These findings and the list of the suspected authors of international crimes provided by the Commission, among other things, enabled the ICC-OTP to conclude to a reasonable basis to believe that war crimes and crimes against humanity were perpetrated in Darfur during the period under review,[8] leading to the opening of an investigation.

26.2.2.2. Libya

The UNSC referred the situation in Libya to the ICC on 15 February 2011. A few days after, on 25 February 2011, the UN Human Rights Council established the International Commission on Libya, which was granted access to Libya. The work and outcome of the investigations of the Libya Commission then became instrumental for the preliminary examination opened by the ICC-OTP, which had no access to Libya.

As this author has written elsewhere:

> Traditionally, international fact-finding commissions were tasked to investigate serious international human rights law and international humanitarian law violations. In many recent mandates, several hybrid commissions have been tasked to investigate international crimes as included in the ICC

---

[7] Philip Alston, "The Darfur Commission as a Model for Future Responses to Crisis Situations", in *Journal of International Criminal Justice*, 2005, vol. 5, no. 3, p. 604 (footnotes omitted).

[8] ICC, Synthesis Sheet: Situation in Darfur, February 2007.

Statute. This development has led to increased application of international criminal law by the hybrid commissions.[9]

As far as the Libya Commission is concerned, according to Philip Kirsch, who chaired it:

> International human rights law applied at all stages of the situation, i.e. both in peace and times of armed conflicts. Libya became a party over the years to a number of major United Nations Human Rights Treaties and is therefore bound by them, as well as by relevant customary international law. Non-state actors, including the NTC [National Transitional Council] at that time, are not formally bound by treaties but are increasingly seen, when occupying de facto control over territory, as having the obligation to respect fundamental rights of persons in that territory.
>
> When it comes to situations of non-international and international armed conflicts, international humanitarian law applies. Here again, Libya became a party to a number of applicable international instruments and is bound by them and by customary international law. However, it is not a party to other instruments which may be relevant to the situation at hand.
>
> In addition to the above, international criminal law also applies to the Libyan situation, by virtue of the referral by the Security Council to the International Criminal Court (ICC) of the situation in Libya even though Libya is not a party to the Rome Statute. The ICC can currently exercise jurisdiction on three categories of crimes, two of which, war crimes and crimes against humanity are relevant.[10]

The information provided by the Libya Commission to the ICC-OTP was instrumental in completing its preliminary examination and con-

---

[9] Mutoy Mubiala, "The Historical Contribution of International Fact-Finding Commissions", in Morten Bergsmo, CHEAH Wui Ling and SONG Tianying and YI Ping (eds.), *Historical Origins of International Criminal Law: Volume 4*, Torkel Opsahl Academic EPublisher, Brussels, 2015, p. 523 (http://www.toaep.org/ps-pdf/23-bergsmo-cheah-song-yi).

[10] Philippe Kirsch, "The Work of the International Commission of Inquiry for Libya", in M. Cherif Bassiouni and William A. Schabas (eds.), *New Challenges for the UN Human Rights Machinery: What Future for the UN Treaty Body System and the Human Rights Council Procedures?*, Intersentia, Antwerp, 2011, pp. 303–304 (footnotes omitted).

cluding that there was a reasonable basis to believe that crimes against humanity were perpetrated in Libya, leading to the opening of investigation, on 3 March 2011,[11] less than a month after the UNSC's referral.

26.2.2.3. Central African Republic II

The CAR Commission was established by the UN Secretary-General in accordance with the UNSC resolution 2127 (2013) adopted on 5 December 2013 to investigate the international crimes allegedly perpetrated in the country from 1 January to 31 December 2013 and to identify the presumed perpetrators of these crimes. The Commission started its work in March 2014. In the meantime, on 7 February 2014, the ICC Prosecutor, Fatou Bensouda, announced the opening of a preliminary examination of the same alleged crimes. Having an office in the CAR since the opening of the investigation into the alleged crimes perpetrated in the CAR in 2003, the ICC-OTP was in a better position to get the relevant information than the CAR Commission, which did not access some of the areas concerned by the investigation for security reasons. The latter then mainly relied on the open source information gathered by the OTP. They had meetings and co-operated in the exchange of information. In its preliminary report, the Commission recognised the ICC-OTP support:

> The Commission has also enjoyed the full support of the Office of the Prosecutor of the International Criminal Court, which has opened a preliminary examination in order to ascertain whether the criteria of the Rome Statute for opening an investigation into the alleged crimes committed in the Central African Republic, which fall within the jurisdiction of the Court, have been met. On 1 April 2014, the Commission sent a request to the Prosecutor to facilitate access to open-source material gathered by the Office of the Prosecutor, a broad selection of open-source material was subsequently provided to the Commission.[12]

In addition to the CAR Commission, other fact-finding mechanisms were deployed in the CAR by some UN bodies, including the UN Human

---

[11]   OTP, Report on the Preliminary Examinations Activities, 13 December 2011, p. 24 (http://www.legal-tools.org/doc/4aad1d/).

[12]   Preliminary Report of the International Commission of Inquiry on the Central African Republic, submitted pursuant to Security Council resolution 2127, S/2014/373, 26 June 2014, p. 10.

Rights Council Independent Expert on the situation of human rights in the CAR and the Human Rights Division of the Multidimensional Integrated Mission in the Central African Republic ('MINUSCA'). Their work also contributed to that of the ICC-OTP, as illustrated by its review of the admissibility of the situation in the CAR. In its Article 53(1) Report, the Prosecutor explicitly referred to the findings and recommendations of UNFFC:

> 245. During the mission of the Office to Bangui in May 2014, all of the CAR authorities whom the members of the mission met with indicated that the CAR judicial system is currently unable to investigate or prosecute individuals for crimes committed since 2012 that could fall under the ICC's jurisdiction. The main challenges raised by the authorities relate to the general lack of security and the specific dangers facing judicial personnel, as well as the lack of infrastructure and capacity at all levels of the criminal justice system, in Bangui and even more so in the provinces. [...]

> 246. The Office understands that both the general lack of security and the prevalence of political pressure are the main obstacles to conducting domestic proceedings. [...] In August 2014, the UN independent expert on the human rights situation in the CAR also came to the conclusion that security concerns, insufficient protection and political pressure are preventing magistrates and lawyers from doing their work. Similarly, a United Nations multidisciplinary team which visited the Central African Republic in 2014 confirmed "an almost total lack of capacity of national counterparts in the areas of police, justice and corrections" and found that "there are no guarantees that national magistrates can render justice in an impartial manner and without fear of political interference or physical violence."[13]

It is on the basis of these findings, including those by other UN fact-finding bodies and missions, that the ICC-OTP concluded the admissibility of the situation of CAR II, in accordance with Article 17 of the Rome Statute.

---

[13] ICC, *Situation in the Central African Republic II Article 53(1) Report*, 24 September 2014, ICC-01/14, paras. 245–246 (footnotes omitted) (http://www.legal-tools.org/doc/1ff87e/).

These three case studies illustrate the increased co-operation between the ICC-OTP and OHCHR, the UN supporting body of UNFFCs in preliminary examinations. As pointed out by the report of an international expert seminar on the "The Peripheries of Justice Intervention", jointly organised by the Grotius Centre for International Legal Studies and the Centre for International Law Research and Policy (CILRAP), held in The Hague, on 29 September 2015:

> 28. Further attention was given to the relationship between the ICC and other fact-finders. Participants identified points of convergence between PEs and the work of fact-finding bodies (e.g. in term of material jurisdiction, applicable standard – 'reasonable basis'/'reasonable grounds'). Participants stated that the work of fact-finding bodies can inform the OTP analysis and can be complementary to PEs. For example, Commissions of Inquiry (COIs) may have better access on the ground, while PEs remain remote, and their reports can inform the OTP about patterns of crimes. It was further pointed out that COIs have an important role in preserving evidence. These synergies should be used to 'break silos' between institutions and avoid that each institution needs to 're-invent the wheel'. At the same time, the sequencing of COIs and PEs might require attention.[14]

From the review of the above-mentioned three case studies (Darfur, Libya and CAR II), one can conclude that UNFFCs played a catalytic role in preliminary examinations of the ICC-OTP. This is why it is important to pay special attention to the quality control of the information provided by UNFFCs, which may be used for judicial purposes.

26.3. Quality Control in the Relationship between the ICC-OTP and UNFFCs in Preliminary Examination

The Phase-2 analysis of the statutory-based approach procedure is specified in the Policy Paper on Preliminary Examinations:

> 81. Phase 2 analysis entails a thorough factual and legal assessment of the crimes allegedly committed in the situation at hand with a view to identifying the potential cases falling within the jurisdiction of the Court. The Office will pay par-

---

[14] *Preliminary Examination and Legacy/Sustainable Exit: Reviewing Policies and Practices*, Grotius Centre for International Legal Studies, The Hague, 2015, p. 6.

ticular consideration to crimes committed on a large scale, as part of a plan or pursuant a policy. [...] Phase 2 leads to the submission of an 'Article 5 report' to the Prosecutor, in reference to the material jurisdiction of the Court as defined in article 5 of the Statute.[15]

One can therefore say that this phase represents the 'fact-finding' part of preliminary examinations, even though it normally falls outside the criminal justice system. Hence, it is important to determine how the two processes can influence each other in terms of quality control. The increased reliance of the preliminary examinations on UNFFCs has resulted in two trends: (1) the 'justiciability' of information and evidence provided by UNFFCs, and (2) the 'criminalisation' of UNFFCs. Before examining these two trends and evaluating their respective challenges, it is important to compare preliminary examination with both UNFFCs as well as the judicial review of the situations by the Pre-Trial Chambers.

26.3.1. Preliminary Examination between Fact-Finding and the Review by Pre-Trial Chambers

Items	UNFFCs	Preliminary Examination
1. Legal framework	International human rights law, international humanitarian law and the mandates of the UNFFC bodies.	International criminal law, in particular Article 53 of the Rome Statute.
2. Guiding principles	<ul><li>Do no harm;</li><li>Independence;</li><li>Impartiality;</li><li>Transparency;</li><li>Objectivity;</li><li>Confidentiality;</li><li>Credibility;</li><li>Visibility;</li><li>Integrity;</li><li>Professionalism;</li></ul>	<ul><li>Independence;</li><li>Impartiality;</li><li>Objectivity;</li><li>Transparency;</li><li>Confidentiality;</li><li>Complementarity;</li><li>Prevention.</li></ul>

---

15 OTP, *Policy Paper on Preliminary Examinations*, p. 19, see *supra* note 4.

	• Consistency.	
3. Methods of work	• Identification of the sources of information; • Determination of the modalities of the assessment or verification of information, including through field visits; • Formulation of the framework to ascertain the consent of sources on the judicial use of information collected. • **Applicable standard of proof:** 1. Fact-work: The reasonable ground threshold; 2. Account-work: The reasonable suspicion threshold (International Commission of Inquiry on Darfur)	• Review of information to consider whether: 1. It provides a reasonable basis to believe that a crime within the jurisdiction of the Court has been or is being committed; 2. The case is or would be admissible under article 17 of the Rome Statute; and 3. An investigation would serve the interests of justice. • Applicable standard of proof: The reasonable basis threshold.
4. Outcome	• Submission of a report to the mandating body, including findings on the allegations of violations of IHRL and IHL, as well as recommendations, including on judicial prosecution of the presumed authors of these violations; • Publication of the report; • Development and sealing of the list of the presumed authors of the violations of IHRL and IHL for their transmission, through the Office of the UN Secretary-General, to the competent judicial bodies, including and particularly the ICC.	• Article 53(1) report on the existence of a reasonable basis to proceed with an investigation or not; • Submission of the report to a Pre-Trial chamber of the ICC; • Review of the report by a pre-trial chamber and adoption of a decision to authorise or not an investigation on the situation of the concerned country (Article 15 of the Rome Statute).

Table 1: Fact-Finding and Preliminary Examination

Items	Preliminary Examination	Prosecutor/ Pre-Trial Chamber
1. Provision	Article 53(1) ("The Prosecutor shall, having evaluated the information made available to him or her, initiate an investigation unless he or she determines that there is no reasonable basis to proceed under this Statute")	Article 15 ("(3) If the Prosecutor concludes that there is a reasonable basis to proceed with an investigation, he or she shall submit to the Pre-Trial Chamber a request for authorisation of an investigation, together with any supporting material collected. Victims may make representations to the Pre-Trial Chamber, in accordance with the Rules of Procedure and Evidence. (4) If the Pre-Trial Chamber, upon examination of the request and the supporting material, considers that there is a reasonable basis to proceed with an investigation, and that the case appears to fall within the jurisdiction of the Court, it shall authorise the commencement of the investigation, without prejudice to subsequent determinations by the Court with regard to the jurisdiction and admissibility of a case.")
2. Source of information	Various sources, including reports of UNFFC bodies.	Article 53(1) reports and supporting material submitted by the ICC Prosecutor.
3. Standard of proof	The reasonable basis threshold.	The reasonable basis threshold.
4. Outcome	Request for authorisation to open an investigation into a situation.	Trial Chamber's Article 15 Decision on the authorisation of an investigation into a situation.

Table 2: Fact-Finding beyond Preliminary Examination and the Judicial Review of the Situations by the Pre-Trial Chambers

From the above comparisons, one can conclude that fact-finding outside criminal justice and preliminary examinations have similar methods of work, including a lower standard of proof than that applied by a criminal court. The main consequence of this similarity is the increased reliance by the ICC-OTP on the information collected by UNFFCs, in comparison with the other sources of information (States, non-governmental organisations, victims' representations, and so on). Therefore, preliminary examination plays the role of a 'Trojan horse' in the injection of information collected by UNFFCs in the judicial proceedings of the ICC. This is made easy by the fact that the Pre-Trial Chamber reviewing the Prosecutor's requests for authorisation to open an investigation proceeds from the same standard of proof (the reasonable basis threshold), as illustrated by the Table 2.

Commenting Article 53(1) in relation to Article 15 of the Rome Statute, an author rightly observes that:

> It follows from the wording of the chapeau of Article 53 that the threshold to start an investigation is the presence of a 'reasonable basis to proceed'. The same threshold is to be found in Article 15 (3), (4) and (6) ICC Statute and in Rule 48 ICC RPE, with regard to proprio motu investigations. A contextual interpretation clarifies that similar considerations underlie the 'reasonable basis to proceed' standard of Article 15 and 53. More precisely, it follows from Rule 48 ICC RPE that in determining whether there exists a 'reasonable basis to proceed' under Article 15 (3) ICC Statute, the Prosecutor shall consider the factors set out in Article 53 paragraph 1 (a) and (c)'.
>
> This was acknowledged by the Pre-Trial Chamber II, when it held that it would be illogical to dissociate the 'reasonable basis to proceed' standard in Article 15(3) and Article 53(1) (with respect to the Prosecutor) from the threshold provided for under Article 15(4) ICC Statute (with respect to the Pre-Trial Chamber) [...]. The Pre-Trial Chamber emphasised that these standards are used in the same or related Articles and that they share the same purpose: the opening of an investigation [...].
>
> With regard to Article 15(4) ICC Statute, ICC Pre-Trial Chamber III observed that the purpose of the 'reasonable ba-

sis to proceed' standard lies where it prevents "unwarranted, frivolous, or politically motivated investigations" [...].[16]

As will be demonstrated in the following section, the reliance of the ICC-OTP on the information from UNFFCs in preliminary examinations has legal and procedural implications for its review by the ICC Pre-Trial Chambers and, subsequently, Trial Chambers.

26.3.2. The 'Justiciability' of the Information Provided by the UNFFCs

With reference to the situation in Kenya and Côte d'Ivoire, this section examines the judicial consequences of the cross-cutting of fact-finding with preliminary examinations, as well as related issues and challenges.

26.3.2.1. Kenya

On 26 November 2009, the Prosecutor submitted a request for authorisation to open an investigation into the situation in Kenya relating to post-electoral violence occurred in the country in 2007 and 2008. In his submission, he recorded the sources of information he collected, where UNFFCs' reports are referred to, as follows:

> **Office of the High Commissioner for Human Rights (OHCHR), "Report from OHCHR Fact-finding Mission to Kenya" (6-28 February 2008)**
>
> 32. Between 6 and 28 February 2008, the UN Office of the High Commissioner for Human Rights (OHCHR) dispatched a fact-finding commission that investigated allegations of human rights violations. The ensuing 'Report from OHCHR Fact-finding Mission to Kenya, 6-28 February 2008' provides an analysis on the context, the patterns as well as a list of human rights violations. The OHCHR Mission conducted on-site visits to the affected areas and met with a wide range of actors in the Government, among the opposition, and met with victims, human rights defenders as well as the diplomatic community. The OHCHR Mission also analysed underlying civil, political, economic, social and cultural rights issues and formulated recommendations on possible accountability mechanisms.

---

[16] Karel De Meester, "Article 53", in Mark Klamberg (ed.), *Commentary on the Law of the International Criminal Court*, available in Lexsitus (www.cilrap-lexsitus.org).

Office of the Coordination of Humanitarian Affairs (OCHA) Humanitarian report updates

33. In response to the post-electoral violence in Kenya, the UN Office for the Coordination of Humanitarian Affairs (OCHA) has expanded the staff in their Kenya offices and has produced a series of publicly available humanitarian updates entitled "Humanitarian Report Updates for Kenya".

34. The Prosecution's application refers to 4 different Humanitarian Update volumes covering the periods between 21 and 28 January 2008; 11 and 15 February 2008; 23 and 27 February 2008 and 8 to 30 October 2009.

UNICEF, UNFPA, UNIFEM and Christian Children's Fund, 'A Rapid Assessment of Gender-Based Violence (GBV) during the post-election violence in Kenya' (Jan-Feb 08)

35. The report consists in an inter-agency gender based violence assessment carried out in January and February 2008 in selected sites in the North Rift Valley, South Rift Valley, the Coastal Region, Nairobi and Central Province. The assessment examined the nature and scope of sexual violence during flight [sic], as well as within the internally displaced persons (IDP) camps and alternative settlements.

Report of the UN Special Rapporteur on extrajudicial, summary or arbitrary executions "Mission to Kenya" (26 May 09)

36. Philip Alston, the UN Special Rapporteur on extrajudicial, summary or arbitrary executions visited the Kenyan provinces of Nairobi, Rift Valley Province (Nakuru, Eldoret and Kiambaa), Western Province Bungoma and Kapsokwony), Nyanza Province (Kisumu), and Central Province (Nyeri) from 16 to 25 February 2009 in order to: ascertain the types and causes of extra-judicial killings; investigate whether those responsible for such killings are held to account; and propose constructive measures to reduce the incidence of killings and impunity. The main focus was on extra-judicial killings by the police, violence in the Mt Elgon District, and killings in the post-election period. The Special Rapporteur concluded those responsible for the post-election violence, including those police responsible for extrajudicial

executions, and officials who organized or instigated violence, remain immune from prosecution.[17]

The mentioned reports and the information they provided were instrumental for the determination by the Prosecutor of the crimes against humanity falling under the jurisdiction of the ICC, including: murders, rape and other forms of sexual violence, deportation or forcible transfer of population and other inhuman acts. In addition, they also largely assisted in the identification of the persons or groups involved in these crimes, as well as in their legal characterisation as crimes against humanity.[18]

Anticipating the question on the probative value of the information provided in his application, the Prosecutor argued that:

> 102. The Prosecutor submits that the Court should proceed to authorise the investigation so long as it is satisfied that the Prosecutor's Application and supporting material reveal the existence of facts or information warranting investigation. The standard at this stage of the proceedings relates to the investigation of crimes of relevance to the situation as a whole and the existence of relevant information that provides a foundation to the request. It is not the opportunity to proceed with the identification of individual criminal liability.
>
> 103. The expression 'reasonable basis' in Article 15 indicates that a decision to authorize the commencement of an investigation shall be made pursuant to a lower standard than the one required for the issuance of a warrant of arrest or summons to appear. The test of reasonable basis is the lowest found in the Rome Statute, which applies four escalating tests for the progressive phases of the proceedings.[19]

While Pre-Trial Chamber II authorised the investigation on the basis of the information from UNFFC and non-governmental organisations,[20] Judge Hans-Peter Kaul provided an extensive dissenting opinion,

---

[17] OTP, Situation in the Republic of Kenya, Request for authorisation of an investigation pursuant to Article 15, 26 November 2009, ICC-01/09-3, pp. 13–14. (http://www.legal-tools.org/doc/c63dcc/).

[18] *Ibid.*, pp. 22–36.

[19] *Ibid.*, pp. 36–37 (footnotes omitted).

[20] ICC, Situation in the Republic of Kenya, Decision Pursuant to Article 15 of the Rome Statute on the Authorisation into the Situation in the Republic of Kenya, 31 March 2010, ICC- 01/09-19, 31 March 2010, p. 83 (http://www.legal-tools.org/doc/338a6f/).

in which he challenged the position of the majority on the characterisation of crimes against humanity based on reports of different sources, including UNFFCs. He pointed out the following:

> 19. [...] The decision whether or not the Prosecutor may commence an investigation rests ultimately with the Pre-Trial Chamber. Thus, the Pre-Trial Chamber's decision pursuant to article 15(4) of the Statute is not of a mere administrative or procedural nature but requires a substantial and genuine examination by the judges of the Prosecutor's Request. Any other interpretation would turn the Pre-Trial Chamber into a mere rubber-stamping instance. [...]

> 72. Indeed, crimes, such murder, rape, mutilations, looting, destruction of property, arson and eviction, seem to have occurred on the territory of the Republic of Kenya at least in the course of events between 28/29 December 2007 and 28 February 2008, commonly referred to as the post-election violence. Numerous abhorrent, brutal and vile incidents have been described in the reports upon which the Prosecutor based his determinations. But the point is not whether or not these crimes took place. The question is, whether those events reach the level of crimes against humanity *as defined under the Statute* and are thus subject to the jurisdiction of this Court. After having meticulously analysed the information contained in the supporting material and the victims' representations, I conclude that this threshold is not met.[21]

Contrary to this position, regarding the supporting material, as pointed out by two authors, "Pre-Trial Chamber II noted in its decision on Kenya that, due to the limited powers the Prosecutor has during the preliminary phase, the information available to the Prosecutor is not expected to be 'comprehensive' or 'conclusive', compared to evidence gathered during the investigation".[22]

---

[21] *Ibid.*, Dissenting Opinion of Judge Hans-Peter Kaul, pp. 11 and 38 (emphasis in original, footnotes omitted).

[22] Morten Bergsmo and Jelena Pejić, "Article 15 Prosecutor", in Otto Triffterer and Kai Ambos (eds.), *Rome Statute of International Criminal Court: A Commentary*, C.H. Beck, Hart, Nomos, Munich, 2016, p. 775.

26.3.2.2. Côte d'Ivoire

After the completion of the preliminary examination and the drafting of the Article 53(1) report, the Prosecutor submits a request for authorisation of an investigation pursuant to Article 175 of the Rome Statute. In the situation in Côte d'Ivoire, the Prosecutor submitted this request on 23 June 2011, which was then assigned to Pre-Trial Chamber III for review. There, in the examination of the available information, the Prosecutor started with the information provided by the UNFFC. These included: the press releases and reports of the United Nations Operation in Côte d'Ivoire ('UNOCI'); the Report of the Independent Commission of Inquiry on Côte d'Ivoire established pursuant to resolution 16/25 adopted by the UN Human Rights Council in May 2011 and released in June 2011; the progress reports of the UN Secretary-General on the situation in Côte d'Ivoire; other reports established and issued by OHCHR in February and June 2011; and the Office for the Coordination of Humanitarian Affairs ('OCHA') reports.[23]

In the Request, UNFFC was the main source of information of the Prosecutor. He referred to the materials of the various UN bodies involved for the particulars of the crimes (alleged crimes and statements of facts; identification of places of their alleged commission; their time period; the identification of the persons or groups involved), as well as for their legal characterisation (including the reasons that they fall within the jurisdictions of the Court).

Relying largely on such UNFFC-based information provided by the Prosecutor, Pre-Trial Chamber III authorised the opening of an investigation by its decision of 3 October 2011.[24] In her dissenting opinion, Judge Silvia Fernández de Gurmendi opined that believed the majority exceeded their supervisory role was their "fragmentary approach" to the supporting

---

[23] ICC, Situation in the Republic of Côte d'Ivoire, OTP, Request for Authorisation of an Investigation Pursuant to Article 15, 23 June 2011, ICC-02/11-3, pp. 11–12 (http://www.legal-tools.org/doc/1b1939/).

[24] ICC, Situation in the Republic of Côte d'Ivoire, Pre-Trial Chamber III, Decision Pursuant to Article 15 of the Rome Statute on the Authorisation of an Investigation into the Situation in the Republic of Côte d'Ivoire, 3 October 2011, ICC-02/11-14 (http://www.legal-tools.org/doc/7a6c19/).

material, which she thought should be taken holistically.[25] This raises the general issue of the scope of the Pre-Trial Chamber's assessment of the material, including UNFFC reports, contained in the Prosecutor's Request.

The case studies of Kenya and Côte d'Ivoire illustrate the extensive reliance of the Pre-Trial Chambers on UNFFC findings as channelled through the Prosecutor's requests for authorisation of an investigation. This trend raises methodological and legal issues. UNFFC has been plagued by several weaknesses, as identified by this author elsewhere:

> The basic challenge of international fact-finding commissions is the lack of a (common) regime. With a special emphasis on the creation and operation of international fact-finding commissions, this section examines the reasons for the origins of this gap and its main consequences on the quality of fact-work and account-work. [...]
>
> The multiplicity of the mandating bodies, their *ad hoc* approach and the lack of a legal framework relating to the establishment of international fact-finding commissions have caused the political, institutional and legal challenges faced by fact-finding in international human rights law, international humanitarian law and international criminal law. [...]
>
> The first challenge is caused by the *multiplicity* of the mandating bodies and the risk of competition [...] Also, depending on their decision-making process, the main mandating bodies are not in the same situation while establishing an international fact-finding commission. [...] [A]s demonstrated by participants in a workshop jointly organised by the Permanent Mission of Portugal (during its presidency of the Security Council) and the UN Office of the Coordination for Humanitarian Affairs in New York in November 2011, there is no consistent approach to fact-finding between the Security Council and the other UN mandating bodies. Moreover, even the practice of the Security Council itself is not coherent. [...] This is largely due to the political process of the decision-making. [...]

---

[25] ICC, Situation in the Republic of Côte d'Ivoire, Pre-Trial Chamber III, Corrigendum to "Judge Fernandez de Gurmendi's separate and partially dissenting opinion to the Decision Pursuant to Article 15 of the Rome Statute on the Authorisation of an Investigation into the Situation in the Republic of Côte d'Ivoire", 5 October 2011, ICC-02/11-15-Corr, pp. 13–16 (http://www.legal-tools.org/doc/eb8724/).

The other consequence of the multiplicity of the mandating bodies has been the *proliferation* of international fact-finding commissions. There has been a plethora of such commissions. Over the past two decades the OHCHR has provided support to 40 international fact-finding commissions established by various UN bodies. Some countries have hosted several international fact-finding commissions in a short period. For example, various UN bodies, including the Human Rights Council, the Secretary-General (at the request of the Security Council) and the OHCHR, have deployed five international fact-finding commissions in Côte d'Ivoire from 2002 to 2011. This proliferation is a serious challenge in international fact- finding.

On the *legal aspects*, international fact-finding commissions have been established on an *ad hoc* basis, mostly through the adoption of resolutions by the mandating bodies. Each international fact-finding commission has its legal framework and is mostly guided by the practice established so far by previous commissions.[26]

These observations are relevant to the case studies on Kenya and Côte d'Ivoire: diversity and multiplicity of the mandating bodies of UNFFCs, in their nature (commissions of inquiry, fact-finding missions, special procedures), composition (independent experts, international civil servants, governmental experts, etc.) and in their methods of work (the independent commissions of inquiry working on the basis of higher standards than OHCHR staff and political missions, like the UN Security Sanctions Committee). These weaknesses of UNFFCs have a potential to negatively impact on the quality of information collected and used in the context of preliminary examinations and, subsequently, in the review of the Pre-Trial Chambers, as mentioned in the two dissenting opinions. That said, so far, UNFFCs' reports have been used by the Court as sources of leads, rather than probative information. However, the judicial review of this information raises several issues, which will be further examined in the following section.

---

[26] Mubiala, 2015, pp. 536–38, see *supra* note 9 (emphasis in original, headings omitted).

26.3.2.3. Issues Relating to the Judicial Use of UNFFCs' Information by the ICC

As seen in the two dissenting opinions above, the judicial consideration of the information and evidence provided by the UNFFCs has brought a number of legal issues to which ICC jurisprudence has not yet coherently responded. As this author has written elsewhere:

> The ICC prosecutor has initiated preliminary investigations in some situations, based on the findings and recommendations of international fact-finding commissions. This has been the case in Guinea (2009) and in Mali (2012). In addition, the Office of the Prosecutor has also requested the OHCHR to provide it with documentation and material collected by international commissions of inquiry it has supported (for example, the 2004 International Commission of Inquiry on Côte d'Ivoire, whose report was not officially issued). This raises the question as to whether human rights fact-findings could be used for judicial purposes. The jurisprudence of the ICC on this is not coherent. While the ICC Trial Chamber in the *Katanga and Ngudjolo* case admitted the evidence provided by the UN Human Rights Field Office in the Democratic Republic of the Congo, the ICC Pre-Trial Chamber in the *Gbagbo* case did not attribute probative value to the materials provided by several sources, including United Nations reports.[27]

At the doctrinal level, the issue of the relationship between the ICC and UN fact-finding bodies was discussed during a Chatham House conference held on 22 January 2014:

> **PROBLEMS POSED BY INTERACTION BETWEEN FACT-FINDING AND INTERNATIONAL CRIMINAL LAW INVESTIGATIONS**
>
> The main problem that arises when fact-finding commissions 'hand over' to international criminal investigations is the multiple interviewing of witnesses. This inevitably entails conflicting statements, not because the witness is not truthful but owing to varying perspectives and standards of investigation. There is also the risk of taint of witnesses. Finally, the

---

[27] *Ibid.*, pp. 530–31 (italics in original, footnotes omitted).

---

collection of physical evidence and documents poses problems in terms of chain of custody and integrity of evidence.

The first prosecutor of the ICC was heavily criticized
for over-reliance on preceding investigations by NGOs and
commissions, as well as human rights reports. Such criticisms were voiced by both commentators and judges. Of late
there has been an effort within the prosecution to conduct investigations that are more thorough and to uncover higher-
quality, more reliable information. However, a problem is
posed by the court's reliance, at least for lead purposes, on
information emanating from other inquiries, and from states.
Further, this poses a risk that a certain narrative becomes
fixed early in the investigative process as to the course that
events took and the attribution of responsibility. This can be
difficult to rebut and test, and is another reason why fact-
finders should be of the highest possible quality.[28]

The last observation above explains the move of UN fact-finding towards
a 'criminalisation' of their methods of work.

26.3.3. The 'Criminalisation' of the UNFFCs' Methods of Work

The trend of the 'criminalisation' of UNFFCs started with the emergence
and development of the account-work by UNFFCs. This has resulted in
the extension of their subject matter to international criminal law and to
the adaptation of their methods of work in line with criminal justice.

26.3.3.1. The Extension of UNFFCs' Subject Matter to International Criminal Law

Since 1993, there has been a trend for the UN mandating bodies to task
UNFFCs with the identification of the perpetrators of the alleged violations of human rights and international humanitarian laws for their further
prosecution. An example is the International Commission on Central African Republic established in January 2014 following UNSC resolution
2127 (2013) of 5 December 2013, where the Council requested the Secretary-General:

---

[28] Sir Nigel Rodley and Alex Whiting (meeting summary by Shehara de Soysa), UN Fact-
finding and International Criminal Investigation, Chatham House, 22 January 2014, p. 4,
available on the web site of Chatham House.

> to rapidly establish an international commission of inquiry
> [...] in order immediately to investigate reports of violations
> of international humanitarian law, international human rights
> law and abuses of human rights in the Central African Re-
> public by all parties since January 2013, to compile infor-
> mation, to help *identify the perpetrators* of such violations
> and abuses, point out their possible *criminal responsibility*
> and to help ensure that those responsible are *held accounta-
> ble*.[29]

Despite the explicit reference to international human rights and international humanitarian laws, the Commission interpreted its mandate more
broadly to include international criminal law in the applicable law:

> **2. *Bodies of Applicable International Law***
>
> 102. The Commission has applied three bodies of interna-
> tional law to the situation in the CAR: international human
> rights law, international humanitarian law, and international
> criminal law.
>
> [...]
>
> **iii) International Criminal Law**
>
> 111. Although the Security Council resolution creating this
> Commission of Inquiry makes no specific reference to inter-
> national criminal law, this body of law is an essential com-
> plement to both international human rights law and interna-
> tional humanitarian law, in that it establishes individual
> criminal liability for serious violations of those other two
> bodies of law. The Central African Republic ratified the
> Rome Statute of the International Criminal Court on 3 Octo-
> ber 2001, thereby giving the Court jurisdiction over war
> crimes, crimes against humanity and genocide as defined in
> the Statute in relation to crimes committed on the territory of
> the CAR or by its nationals since 1 July 2002. On 30 May
> 2014 the transitional government of the CAR referred the
> situation on the territory of the CAR since 1 August 2012 to
> the Prosecutor of the ICC.[30]

---

[29] Emphasis added.

[30] International Commission of Inquiry on the Central African Republic, Final Report, Annex, UN doc. S/2014/928, 22 December 2014, pp. 37, 39.

This trend for UNFFCs to include international criminal law in their subject matter, as seen in the CAR example, has resulted in an increased co-operation between the ICC-OTP and UNFFCs. This is illustrated, for example, by the Standard Operating Procedures adopted by the ICC and the UN Department of Peacekeeping Operations for the provision of information collected by the human rights components of peacekeeping missions to the ICC-OTP. This co-operation raises the issue of the quality control of the information provided by UNFFC, in relation to criminal justice.

26.3.3.2. Quality Control in UN Fact-Finding in Relation to Criminal Justice

Based on the good practices developed during more than two decades, UNFFCs and OHCHR have improved the standard of proof in fact-work and account-work, developed criteria for information-sharing and taken initiatives for the professionalisation of UN fact-finding.

26.3.3.2.1. Standards of Proof for the Determination of the Facts

A field of special interest for the interaction between the ICC-OTP and UNFFCs in preliminary examinations is their respective methods of work. As already mentioned, the lower standard of proof of preliminary examination is close, if not similar, to that applied in UNFFC. As this author has written elsewhere:

> In principle and practice, international fact-finding commissions apply human rights methodology, in the context of which valuable information may be collected and contribute to the establishment of patterns for criminal investigations. Recently, the hybrid commissions have developed quasi-criminal methodological approaches. Influenced by the former or current judicial affiliation of their members and staff, some commissions of inquiry have adopted the "beyond a reasonable doubt" standard of proof, which is relevant to criminal investigations, rather than to fact-finding outside criminal justice. International fact-finding commissions should apply the "reasonable ground to believe" standard of

proof (fact-work), as well as the "reasonable suspicion" standard of proof (account-work).[31]

The Policy Paper, while providing that the ICC-OTP should indicate in its report on preliminary examination the persons involved (if identified) in the perpetration of the alleged crimes,[32] does not provide the applicable standard of proof. To be more relevant and useful for the ICC-OTP's preliminary examination, UNFFC should apply the 'reasonable suspicion' standard of proof. The criteria for the application of this standard of proof were articulated by the Darfur Commission. According to an author:

> The criteria of identifying perpetrators was first spelled out by the Darfur Commission of Inquiry, which decided that it could not comply with the standards adopted by criminal courts (proof of facts beyond a reasonable doubt), or with that used by international prosecutors and judges for the purpose of confirming indictments (that there must be a *prima facie* case). It concluded that the most appropriate standard was that requiring a reliable body of material consistent with other verified circumstances, which tends to show that a person may reasonably be suspected of being involved in the commission of a crime.
>
> The Darfur Commission also set the methodology of how to practically approach this issue. While it has collected sufficient and consistent material (both testimonial and documentary) to point to numerous (51) suspects, the Commission decided to withhold the names of these persons from the public domain. This decision was based on three main grounds: 1) the importance of the principles of due process and respect for the rights of the suspects; 2) the fact that the Commission has not been vested with investigation or prosecutorial powers; and 3) the vital need to ensure the protection of witnesses from possible harassment or intimidation. The Commission instead listed the names in a sealed file that was placed in the custody of the United Nations Secretary-General. The Commission recommended that this file be handed over to a competent Prosecutor (the Prosecutor of the

---

[31]   Mubiala, 2015, pp. 524–525, see *supra* note 9.

[32]   OTP, *Policy Paper on Preliminary Examinations*, p. 19, see *supra* note 4.

International Criminal Court, according to the Commission's recommendations), who may use that material as he or she deems fit for his or her investigations.[33]

The adoption of the 'reasonable suspicion' standard of proof by the UN Commission on Darfur was a milestone in the criminalisation of UNFFCs. Based on this practice, OHCHR has been developing guidance on "Attributing individual responsibility for violations of international human rights and humanitarian law in UN-mandated commissions of inquiry, fact-finding missions and other investigations", which was discussed at an experts' meeting convened in Geneva on 18 October 2016. The meeting discussed, among other things, issues relating to information sharing with the criminal justice system, including in particular the ICC.

26.3.3.2.2. Information-Sharing

In several situations under preliminary examination, the ICC-OTP has relied on information provided by UNFFC, including OHCHR field offices and human rights components of peace missions, where they exist, according to the 2004 UN-ICC Cooperation Agreement. This raises the issue of confidentiality. According to OHCHR's policy, prior and informed consent of victims and witnesses is required for the disclosure of information by the ICC. The concerned victim or witness must be informed that the information and/or documentation he/she provides could be used for judicial purposes and subsequently give informed consent. Sharing this information or documentation with the ICC-OTP or another jurisdiction is, therefore, subject to such consent.

In this regard, the challenges between the rules on the confidentiality of information and evidence gathered from the UN and the Prosecutor's power to disclosure have been pointed out:

> the UN and the Prosecutor may agree that the former will provide documents to the Prosecutor "on condition of confidentiality and solely for the purpose of generating new evidence," and that the documents "shall not be disclosed to other organs of the Court or to third parties… without the consent of the United Nations." The Prosecutor is expressly

---

[33] Mona Rishmawi, "The Role of Human Rights Fact-Finding in the Prevention of Genocide", Paper presented at the International Conference on the Prevention of Genocide, Brussels, 31 March–1 April 2014, p. 8 (on file with the author).

authorized to enter into such confidentiality agreements by Article 54(3)(e) of the Rome Statute, which authorizes the Prosecutor to "(a)gree not to disclose, at any stage of the proceedings, documents or information that the Prosecutor obtains on the condition of confidentiality and solely for the purpose of generating new evidence, unless the provider of the information actually consents…" At the same time, however, the Prosecutor is required under Article 67(2) of the Rome Statute to "disclose to the defence evidence in the Prosecutor's possession or control which he or she believes shows or tends to show the innocence of the accused, or to mitigate the guilt of the accused, or which may affect the credibility of prosecution evidence. The Prosecution is also obligated, under Rule 77 of the Rules of Procedure and Evidence, to "permit the defence to inspect any books, documents, photographs and other tangible objects in the possession or control of the Prosecutor, which are," *inter alia*, "material to the preparation of the defence."

Thus, there exists a tension between these provisions of the Rome Statute and the Rules, which allow the Prosecution to collect "lead" evidence on condition of confidentiality, on the one hand, and require the Prosecution to disclose or allow access to any potentially exonerating evidence, on the other. This tension came to a head in June 2008, when Trial Chamber I halted the trial against Thomas Lubanga Dyilo due to the Prosecution's failure to disclose potentially exculpatory documents obtained from the UN and other organizations on condition of confidentiality. […] the problem was ultimately resolved for purposes of the *Lubanga* trial, which commenced in late January 2009. However, given the fact that the Prosecution has admitted to relying heavily on confidential lead evidence obtained from the UN and various non-governmental organizations in its investigations in the Democratic Republic of Congo, and has potentially done the same in other situations under investigation by the ICC, it is likely that the tension between Article 54(3)(e) and 67(2) of the Rome Statute will become an issue before the Court again.[34]

The issue of information-sharing of fact-finding in relation to criminal justice system was thoroughly discussed by a Geneva experts' meeting in October 2016. Based on the outcome of this meeting, OHCHR has been preparing a guidance on "Attributing Individual Responsibility for Violations of International Human Rights and Humanitarian Law in UN-Mandated Commissions of Inquiry, Fact-Finding Missions and other Investigations". It is expected that the guidelines under finalisation will contribute to clarifying the issue of information-sharing by OHCHR and UNFFCs in relation to criminal justice system. Due to the increased reliance of the ICC-OTP on the information and material collected by the UNFFCs and in order to ensure a high quality of this information, OHCHR, in addition to developing methodological tools on fact-work[35] and account-work (on-going), has been doing efforts to professionalise UN fact-finding, in particular the staff servicing UNFFC mechanisms.

26.3.3.2.3. Towards the Professionalisation of UN Fact-Finding

A main weakness of UNFFC is the *ad hoc* character of its membership and staffing. This has led to inconsistent practice and diverse quality of information collected by UNFFCs and shared with the ICC-OTP. To address these challenges, OHCHR, as the supporting body to UNFFCs, has recently taken an initiative to put in place an arrangement for a dedicated staff to support UN human rights inquiries and fact-finding. If established, the proposed structure would contribute to streamline UNFFC and to develop coherence as well as institutional memory. Such a structure would also facilitate the operational relationship between UNFFC mechanisms/OHCHR and the ICC-OTP in preliminary examination.

---

[34] The Relationship Between the International Criminal Court and the United Nations, War Crimes Research Office, Washington College of Law, American University, August 2009, pp. 43–45 (footnotes omitted).

[35] OHCHR, *Commissions of Inquiry and Fact-Finding Missions on International Human Rights Law and International Humanitarian Law: Guidance and Practice*, United Nations, New York/Geneva, 2015.

26.4. Conclusion

As illustrated by the three case studies on Darfur, Libya and CAR II, UN Commissions of Inquiry and FFCs have contributed to preliminary examinations carried out by the ICC-OTP and the shared information has played a catalytic role in the opening of investigations by the latter into several situations. In turn, as seen in the situation of CAR II, UNFFCs have also benefited from the open source information gathered by the ICC-OTP in preliminary examinations. Overall, even when they have been deployed at the same time, the two entities have proceeded in a complementary, rather than competitive, manner. UN fact-finding and preliminary examinations are two cross-fertilizing and mutually reinforcing processes. In particular, preliminary examinations include a phase (the Phase 2 analysis), which involves factual and legal analyses similar to those of UNFFCs. As the two processes relate to two separate systems, namely non-criminal and criminal justice systems, their interaction raises the issue of quality control of the shared information, as illustrated by the case studies on Kenya and Côte d'Ivoire. This explains the on-going efforts by OHCHR to streamline and professionalise UN fact-finding, with a view to improving the quality of information provided to the ICC-OTP. In particular, high-quality information from UNFFCs could contribute to increasing its probative value before the ICC.

The interplay between UN fact-finding and preliminary examination provides, therefore, a good basis and an opportunity for the development of the co-operation between OHCHR and the ICC-OTP. Due to the limited capacity of the ICC-OTP, a more institutionalised co-operation with OHCHR can revitalise the interplay of UNFFCs with the ICC-OTP in preliminary examinations. The exchange of information between OHCHR, as the depository entity of the archives of UNFFCs, and the ICC-OTP has been based, so far, on the 2004 UN-ICC Cooperation Agreement. In this regard, this author recommends that the two entities agree on the adoption of standards of operating procedures (SOPs) similar to those existing between the ICC-OTP and the UN Department of Peace-keeping Operations, which are more specific and complementary to the 2004 UN-ICC Cooperation Agreement.

27

Non-States Parties and the Preliminary Examination of Article 12(3) Declarations

LING Yan*

27.1. Introduction

27.1.1. The Preliminary Examination of Situations

The duty of the Prosecutor of the International Criminal Court ('ICC') is different from that of national prosecutors and *ad hoc* tribunals. Prosecutors in national systems are responsible for investigating and prosecuting all crimes within national jurisdictions.[1] The jurisdiction of the two UN *ad hoc* tribunals (and the Residual Mechanism succeeding them) is limited to specific situations, namely, the former Yugoslavia and Rwanda. The Prosecutors there have no power to select situations other than cases to investigate. In contrast, the ICC is a permanent global criminal court facing situations and core international crimes which may be committed anywhere. Therefore, the Prosecutor of the ICC has broader powers to investigate both situations and cases.

The exercise of the ICC's jurisdiction may be triggered in three ways: (i) referral of a situation either by a State Party or (ii) by the UN Security Council, or (iii) by a decision of the Prosecutor to initiate an investigation *proprio motu*. In the last case, authorization by a Pre-Trial Chamber is required. Due to limited resources, the Prosecutor is unable to investigate and prosecute all crimes within the jurisdiction of the Court. The Prosecutor must select some situations for investigation and prosecu-

---

*   **LING Yan** has been a Professor at China University of Political Science and Law since 2004 and a Senior Researcher at Collaborative Innovation Centre for Territorial Sovereignty and Maritime Rights since 2014. Formerly, she worked as a legal officer for the International Criminal Tribunal for Rwanda (1998–2004).

1   William Schabas, "'O New World': The Role of the Prosecutor of the International Criminal Court", in *Die Friedens-Warte: Blätter für internationale Verständigung und zwischenstaatliche Organisation*, 2008, vol. 83, no. 4, p. 29.

---

tion. Article 15 of the Rome Statute provides that the Prosecutor is vested with the primary responsibility to determine whether there are reasonable grounds for initiating an investigation. In doing so, the Office of the Prosecutor ('OTP') should analyse the seriousness of the information it has obtained from various sources to ensure that they are reliable. Rule 48 of the Rules of Procedure and Evidence further states that "in determining whether there is a reasonable basis to proceed with an investigation under Article 15, paragraph 3, the Prosecutor shall consider the factors set out in Article 53, paragraphs 1(a) to (c)", including the jurisdiction of the Court, the admissibility and the interests of justice.

In short, the preliminary examination is a stage in which the Prosecutor identifies situations that meet the requirements of the Statute before proceeding with an investigation. Although Article 15 seems only to require a preliminary examination when the Prosecutor exercises its *proprio motu* power, reading Article 15 in conjunction with Article 53 and according to the Regulations of the OTP, the Prosecutor may initiate preliminary examinations on the basis of any information on crimes, a referral from a State Party or the Security Council. Even a declaration under Article 12(3) lodged by a non-State Party accepting the jurisdiction of the Court may also lead to a preliminary examination.[2]

27.1.2. Declarations under Article 12(3) of the Rome Statute

As a permanent international criminal institution established by an international treaty, the ICC has a mandate to complement national jurisdictions to effectively punish those responsible for the most serious international crimes so as to put an end to the culture of impunity and "thus to contribute to the prevention of such crimes".[3]

The jurisdiction of the ICC rests primarily on the consent of States Parties and on the basis of the principle of territorial and personal jurisdic-

---

[2]   Office of the Prosecutor ('OTP'), *Policy Paper on Preliminary Examinations*, 1 November 2013, para. 35 (http://www.legal-tools.org/doc/acb906/); International Criminal Court ('ICC'), Regulations of the Office of the Prosecutor, 23 April 2009, Regulation 25, para. 1 (http://www.legal-tools.org/doc/a97226/).

[3]   Statute of the International Criminal Court, 17 July 1998, Preamble ('ICC Statute') (http://www.legal-tools.org/doc/7b9af9/).

tions recognized in criminal law,[4] that is, when the "State on the territory of which the conduct in question occurred" or "the State of which the person accused of the crime is a national" is a party to the Rome Statute. A State Party *ipso facto* expresses its consent to accept the ICC's jurisdiction with respect to the core international crimes committed on its territory or committed by its nationals. As a result, the ICC also has jurisdiction over international crimes committed by nationals of a non-State Party to the Rome Statute on the territory of a State Party[5] (although countries like China and the United States have strongly objected to the exercise of such jurisdiction).[6] The ICC does not have jurisdiction over the situations in which a crime has been committed on the territory of a non-State Party unless the UN Security Council refers the situation to the ICC.[7]

Nevertheless, Article 12(3) provides opportunities for non-States Parties to use the ICC to punish perpetrators of core international crimes committed on their territories "without putting the States under pressures to accede to the Statute" themselves.[8] It provides that: "if the acceptance of a State which is not a Party to this Statute is required under paragraph 2, that State may, by declaration lodged with the Registrar, accept the exercise of jurisdiction by the Court with respect to the crime in question".

The provision existed as early as in the 1994 draft Statute of the International Law Commission.[9] There was no dispute when drafting the Statute on giving non-States Parties the opportunity to use the Court.[10] In

---

[4] Young Sok Kim, "The Preconditions to the Exercise of the Jurisdiction of the International Criminal Court: With Focus on Article 12 of the Rome Statute", in *Journal of International Law and Practice*, 1999, vol. 8, no. 1, p. 78.

[5] ICC Statute, Article 12(1) and (2), see *supra* note 3.

[6] "Guangya Wang talks about the Rome Statute of the ICC", in *Legal Daily* (《王光亚谈国际刑事法院罗马规约》，法制日报), 29 July 1998, p. 4; David Scheffer, "How to Turn the Tide Using the Rome Statute's Temporal Jurisdiction", in *Journal of International Criminal Justice*, 2004, vol. 2, no. 1, p. 28.

[7] ICC Statute, Article 12(3), see *supra* note 3.

[8] Carsten Stahn, Mohamed M. El Zeidy, and Hdctor Olasolo, "The International Criminal Court's and *ad hoc* Jurisdiction Revisited", in *American Journal of International Law*, 2005, vol. 99, no. 2, p. 422.

[9] International Law Commission, Draft Statute for an International Criminal Court with Commentaries *1994*, Article 22(4) (http://www.legal-tools.org/doc/390052/).

[10] Hans-Peter Kaul, "Preconditions to the Exercise of Jurisdiction", in Antonio Cassese, Paola Gaeta, John R.W.D. Jones (eds.), *The Rome Statute of the International Criminal Court: A Commentary*, Oxford University Press, 2002, vol. I, p. 610.

---

the discussions of the Bureau of Whole Committee at the Rome Conference, there was no substantive objection to this provision either. Views were positive as this provision would expand the scope of the ICC's jurisdiction.[11] The United States delegation also considered it a "useful and necessary provision".[12]

27.1.3. Declarations Lodged by Non-States Parties Accepting the Jurisdiction of the ICC

The Rome Statute entered into force on 1 July 2002. By the end of 2016, Uganda, Côte d'Ivoire, Palestine, Ukraine and Egypt had lodged Article 12(3) declarations.

27.1.3.1. Uganda

Uganda ratified the Rome Statute on 14 July 2002, which entered into force on 1 September 2002. Thus, Uganda was a non-State Party for a two-month period. On 16 December 2003, the President of Uganda referred the situation concerning the Uganda's LRA to the ICC.[13] On 17 June 2004, the Prosecutor informed the President of the Court of Uganda's self-referral and the declaration of provisional acceptance of the Court's jurisdiction over the two-month period.[14]

27.1.3.2. Côte d'Ivoire

Côte d'Ivoire signed the Rome Statute on 3 November 1998, but it had not ratified the Statute afterwards. It lodged a declaration in 2003 accepting the jurisdiction of the Court over the crimes committed on its territory since 19 September 2002 when a military coup occurred leading to a civil war, with no end date.[15] The Prosecutor did not take any immediate action

---

[11] Carsten Stahn *et al.*, 2005, p. 423, see *supra* note 8.

[12] William Schabas, *The International Criminal Court: A Commentary on the Rome Statute*, Oxford University Press, 2010, p. 288.

[13] ICC, Situation in Uganda, Warrant of Arrest for Joseph Kony Issued on 8 July 2005 as Amended on 27 September 2005, 27 September 2005, ICC-02/04-01/05-53, p. 9 (http://www.legal-tools.org/doc/b1010a/).

[14] ICC, Situation in Uganda, Decision Assigning the Situation in Uganda to Pre-Trial Chamber II, 5 July 2004, ICC-02/04-1, Annex (http://www.legal-tools.org/doc/b904bb/).

[15] Côte d'Ivore, *Déclaration de Reconnaissance de la Competence de la Cour Pénale Internationale* [Declaration recognizing the Jurisidiction of the International Criminal Court], 18 April 2003 (http://www.legal-tools.org/doc/036bd2/).

on this declaration until 2006. He said a working group would be sent to Côte d'Ivoire when security condition allowed.[16] The President of the ICC reported in 2006 to the United Nations General Assembly that five situations, including Côte d'Ivoire, had been under analysis.[17] By 2010, the Prosecutor had not yet announced a conclusion after seven years of preliminary examination.

In October and November 2010, Côte d'Ivoire held a presidential election, in which two candidates, Mr. Gbagbo and Mr. Ouattara, were announced to be elected by different authorities, leading to a nationwide armed conflict. On 14 December 2010, Mr. Ouattara, who was announced President-elect by the Independent Electoral Commission, sent a letter to the President, the Registrar and the Prosecutor of the ICC respectively confirming Côte d'Ivoire's acceptance of the Court's jurisdiction.[18] On 3 May 2011, when the Constitutional Council also announced his election, Mr. Ouattara sent another letter to the Prosecutor reiterating that Côte d'Ivoire had accepted the jurisdiction of the Court.[19] The Prosecutor then requested a Pre-Trial Chamber to authorize an investigation into the situation in Côte d'Ivoire on 23 June 2011,[20] which was approved on 3 October 2011.[21]

27.1.3.3. Palestine

Between December 2008 and January 2009, Israel carried out a three-week military operation against Hamas in the Gaza Strip in response to rocket and mortar attacks lunched by Hamas against Israeli civilians. The

---

[16] Sixth Diplomatic Briefing of the International Criminal Court, Compilation of Statements, 23 March 2006, p. 7 (http://www.legal-tools.org/doc/b65c5d/).

[17] Report of the International Criminal Court for 2005–2006, UN Doc. A/61/217, 3 August 2006, para. 32 (http://www.legal-tools.org/doc/11ef2c/).

[18] ICC, *The Prosecutor v. Laurent Koudou Gbagbo*, Judgment on the Appeal of Mr Laurent Koudou Gbagbo against the decision of Pre-Trial Chamber I on Jurisdiction and Stay of the Proceedings, 12 December 2012, ICC-02/11-01/11-321, para. 55 (Judgment on the Appeal) (http://www.legal-tools.org/doc/649ff5/).

[19] *Ibid.*, para. 56.

[20] ICC, Situation in the Republic of Côte d'Ivoire, Decision Pursuant to Article 15 of the Rome Statute on the Authorisation of an Investigation into the Situation in the Republic of Côte d'Ivoire, 3 October 2011, ICC-02/11-14, para. 2 (http://www.legal-tools.org/doc/7a6c19/).

[21] *Ibid.*

international community has condemned the violation of the law of armed conflict by both parties of the conflict, including States, non-State entities and individuals.[22] The United Nations Human Rights Council established a UN Truth Commission led by Justice Richard J. Goldstone, the former Prosecutor of the ICTY, to carry out investigations into the event.[23]

Before the 'Goldstone Report' was released, the Minister of Justice of Palestine lodged on 22 January 2009 a declaration with the Registrar of the ICC accepting the jurisdiction of the Court over crimes committed on the territory of Palestine since 1 July 2002.[24] Since neither Palestine nor Israel was a party to the Rome Statute, it would only be possible for the Court to exercise jurisdiction if Palestine lodged an Article 12(3) declaration, or if the UN Security Council referred the situation to the ICC.

It took three years for the Prosecutor to decide not to consider the declaration on the ground that he had no authority to determine whether Palestine was a "State" within the meaning of Article 12(3) that could accept the *ad hoc* jurisdiction of the Court.[25] Even when a majority resolution of the United Nations General Assembly granted Palestine the status of an observer State to the United Nations on 29 November 2012,[26] the Prosecutor insisted that the change in Palestine's status in the United Nations could not be applied retroactively and it cannot make the declaration valid because at the time when Palestine had lodged the declaration in 2009, it had no statehood.[27] On 31 December 2014, Mohammed Abbas, the President of the State of Palestine, lodged another Article 12(3) declaration with the Registrar of the ICC accepting the Court's jurisdiction

---

[22] Yaël Ronen, "ICC Jurisdiction over Acts Committed in Gaza Strip", in *Journal of International Criminal Justice*, 2010, vol. 8, no. 1, p. 4.

[23] UN Fact Finding Mission on the Gaza Conflict, Human Rights in Palestine and Other Occupied Arab Territories: Report of the United Nations Fact-Finding Mission on the Gaza Conflict, Human Rights Council, UN Doc A/HRC/12/48, 25 September 2009 (http://www.legal-tools.org/doc/ca9992/).

[24] Palestine, Declaration Recognizing the Jurisdiction of the International Criminal Court, 21 January 2009 (http://www.legal-tools.org/doc/d9b1c6/).

[25] ICC, Situation in Palestine, 3 April 2012 (http://www.legal-tools.org/doc/f5d6d7/).

[26] Status of Palestine in the United Nations, UN Doc. A/RES/67/19, December 2012 (http://www.legal-tools.org/doc/3a1916/).

[27] ICC, The State of Palestine accedes to the Rome Statute, 7 January 2015 (http://www.legal-tools.org/doc/59dd45/).

---

since 13 June 2014,[28] and deposited with the Secretary-General of the United Nations the instrument of accession to the Rome Statute on 2 January 2015.[29] Only on 16 January 2015 did the Prosecutor announce the start of a preliminary examination on Palestine.[30]

27.1.3.4. Ukraine

Ukraine signed the Rome Statute on 20 January 2000. The Government had not ratified the Rome Statute because the Constitutional Court of Ukraine declared that the Rome Statute was incompatible with the Constitution. From the end of 2013 to early 2014, anti-government demonstration took place in the Ukrainian capital, Kiev, and a fierce conflict occurred between the demonstrators and the riot police maintaining the order as well as internal security force soldiers, causing hundreds of casualties. On 25 February 2014, the Ukrainian Parliament passed a resolution declaring, in accordance with Article 11(1) and Article 12(2) and (3) of the Rome Statute, acceptance of the Court's jurisdiction over the crimes against humanity committed by senior Ukrainian national officials against Ukrainian nationals during their peaceful demonstrations between 21 November 2013 and 22 February 2014. The declaration also named the former President, the former Attorney General and the former Minister of the Interior of Ukraine to be held criminally responsible for the crimes.[31] On 17 April 2014, following the receipt of the declaration, the Prosecutor opened a preliminary examination of the situation with a view to ascertaining whether the criteria set out in the Rome Statute for initiating investigations had been met.[32] Further, on 8 September 2015, the Government of Ukraine lodged a second declaration accepting the Court's jurisdiction

---

[28] ICC Registry, Letter from ICC Registrar to President Mahmoud Abbas, 7 February 2015, 2015/IOR/3496/HvH (http://www.legal-tools.org/doc/3bea2d/).

[29] The State of Palestine Accedes to the Rome Statute, see *supra* note 27.

[30] ICC, "The Prosecutor of the International Criminal Court Fatou Bensouda opens a preliminary examination of the situation in Palestine", 16 January 2015 (http://www.legal-tools.org/doc/1dcbe5/).

[31] Ukraine, Declaration of the Verkhovna Rada of Ukraine to the International Criminal Court on the recognition of the jurisdiction of the International Criminal Court by Ukraine over crimes against humanity, committed by senior officials of the state, 25 February 2014 (http://www.legal-tools.org/doc/1a65fa/).

[32] ICC, "The Prosector of the International Criminal Court, Fatou Bensouda open up a preliminary investigation in Ukraine", 25 April 2014 (http://www.legal-tools.org/doc/8d811f/).

in relation to alleged crimes committed on its territory from 20 February 2014 onwards, with no end date.[33] Consequently, the Prosecutor decided to extend the temporal scope of the existing preliminary examination to include alleged crimes occurring after 20 February 2014.[34]

27.1.3.5. Egypt

In July 2013, after some large-scale protests, the Egyptian government of the first elected president, Morsi, was overthrown by the former Egyptian military leader and current incumbent President, Abdel Fattah al Sisi. Egypt is not a party to the Rome Statute. On 13 December 2013, an Egyptian lawyer representing the Liberty and Justice Party and others submitted a document signed on 13 August 2013 to the Registrar of the Court seeking to accept jurisdiction since 1 June 2013. However, the OTP concluded that the document was not submitted by the authorities with "full power" on behalf of the State of Egypt,[35] and therefore treated it as a 'communication' rather than an Article 12(3) declaration.

27.1.4. Purposes of Article 12(3) Declarations

Article 12(3) declarations have two main purposes. First, it allows the ICC to exercise jurisdiction over a non-State Party that may want to obtain the ICC Prosecutor's assistance in the investigation and prosecution of core international crimes in its territory. The declarations of Côte d'Ivoire and Ukraine as well as the unsuccessful declaration of Egypt fall into this type, sharing the same purpose as self-referrals by States Parties.[36]

The Palestinian declarations of 2009 and 2014 were slightly different, intending to enable the Court to investigate and prosecute crimes committed by Israeli nationals on its territory, including the Gaza Strip,

---

[33] Ukraine, Declaration by Ukraine lodged under Article 12(3) of the Rome Statute, 8 September 2015 (http://www.legal-tools.org/doc/b53005/).

[34] OTP, *Report on Preliminary Examination Activities 2015*, 12 November 2015, para. 80 (http://www.legal-tools.org/doc/ac0ed2/).

[35] ICC, The Determination of the Office of the Prosecutor on the Communication Received in Relation to Egypt, 8 May 2014 (http://www.legal-tools.org/doc/2945cd/).

[36] They are self-referral of situations in Uganda, Democratic Republic of Congo, the Central Africa Republic, Mali and Gabon.

although the declaration did not explicitly say so. Their purpose is similar to the referral by Comoros, a State Party.[37]

Another purpose is to extend the Court's temporal jurisdiction over a situation. This can be seen from the Palestine's declaration of 31 December 2014. Palestine deposited a document of accession with the Secretary-General of the United Nations on 2 January 2015. Pursuant to Article 126(2), the Rome Statute will enter into force on the first day of the month 60 days after the deposit of the instrument of ratification. Accordingly, the Rome Statute began to take effect in respect of Palestine on 1 April 2015. The Palestinian declaration extends the Court's temporal jurisdiction over the alleged crimes to 13 June 2014. Meanwhile, Uganda's declaration was lodged when Uganda was already a State Party. The declaration was merely for filling the temporal gap pursuant to Article 11(2), which states that:

> If a State becomes a Party to this Statute after its entry into force, the Court may exercise its jurisdiction only with respect to crimes committed after the entry into force of this Statute for that State, unless that State has made a declaration under article 12, paragraph 3.

Although there were discussions among scholars about whether a non-State Party can make an Article 12(3) declaration accepting the exercise of the Court's jurisdiction retroactively,[38] this has been confirmed by the Court.[39]

In addition to those purposes, however, some commentators considered that Article 12(3) is designed for the Prosecutor to promote the Court and the Rome Statute,[40] in light of the reference to "request of the Prosecutor" in Rule 44(1) of the Rules of Procedure and Evidence. This may happen where, having received information, "the Prosecutor invites or encourages a non-State Party to lodge a declaration so as to allow for a

---

[37] The situation in *Registered Vessels of Comoros, Greece and Cambodia* was referred by Comoros.

[38] Kevin Jon Heller, "Yes, Palestine Could Accept the ICC's Jurisdiction Retroactively", in *Opinio Juris*, 29 November 2012; Alexander Wills, "The ICC's Retroactive Jurisdiction, Revisited", in *Opinio Juris*, 29 January 2013.

[39] Judgment on the appeal, para. 83, see *supra* note 18.

[40] Carsten Stahn *et al.*, 2005, pp. 421–431 and 423, see *supra* note 8.

possible investigation and prosecution by the Prosecutor".[41] According to one commentator, an Article 12(3) declaration is required when a situation concerning a non-State Party has been referred to the ICC or investigation has been initiated by the Prosecutor.[42] The non-State Party may then make a declaration to accept the jurisdiction of the Court.

Nevertheless, while the original idea of Rule 44(1) may be specifically for this type of declaration, this has not happened in practice. So far, all declarations have been made on the States' own initiative without the Prosecutor's involvement. This type of declaration is certainly allowed by the Rome Statute. It has been well recognized that Article 12(3) is designed to extend the scope of the Statute's application by offering non-States Parties the opportunity to accept the Court's jurisdiction on an *ad hoc* basis when the crimes in question have been committed on its territory or by its nationals[43] and the situation has not been referred to or investigated by the ICC Prosecutor. To require that the Prosecutor must already have initiated an investigation with respect to a situation before a non-State Party lodged a declaration to accept the Court's jurisdiction will restrict the scope of Article 12(3)'s application.[44] It would also be illogical if the Prosecutor could take investigative steps *proprio motu* with regard to a situation in which crimes have been committed by nationals of a non-State Party on a territory of another non-State Party before the latter has accepted the jurisdiction of the Court.[45]

---

[41] Steven Freeland, "How Open Should the Door Be? Declarations by Non-States Parties Under Article 12(3) of the Rome Statute of the International Criminal Court", in *Nordic Journal of International Law*, 2006, vol. 75, no. 2, p. 222.

[42] Sharon A. Williams and William A. Schabas, "Article 12 Precondition to the exercise of jurisdiction", in Otto Triffterer (ed.), *Commentary on the Rome Statute of the International Criminal Court, Observer's Notes, Article by Article*, 2nd edition, C.M. Beck, 2008, p. 559.

[43] Carsten Stahn *et al.*, 2005, p. 423, see *supra* note 8.

[44] Carsten Stahn *et al.*, 2005, p. 425, see *supra* note 8.

[45] *Ibid.*, p. 426.

27.2. Procedure Applicable to Article 12(3) Declarations in the Preliminary Examination Stage

27.2.1. Applying the Same Procedure to Article 12(3) Declarations as the Procedure Applied to the Prosecutor's *Proprio Motu* Proceedings

Neither the Rome Statute nor the Rules of Procedure and Evidence expressly provide for the procedure following an Article 12(3) declaration. Carsten Stahn and others opine that the declaration may be treated "either as analogous to a state referral under Article 14 or as a *proprio motu* proceeding of the prosecutor under Article 15".[46] At first glance, they seem to favour the second procedural option because in the negotiation of the Rome Statute, it was considered that non-States Parties should not be entitled to refer a situation. To treat a declaration as a self-referral will entitle the non-State Party the privilege that a State Party enjoys.[47] In their view, an Article 12(3) declaration requires neither actions to be taken by the Prosecutor, nor the judicial review by the Court.[48]

The Appeals Chamber supported the above approach. It ruled in the *Gbagbo* case that as a member of the Assembly of States Parties, a State Party enjoys numerous rights including the right to refer situations,[49] while a non-State Party accepting the jurisdiction of the Court by lodging an Article 12(3) declaration is obliged to co-operate with the Court, but does not have all the rights or obligations of a State Party.[50]

Further, States' acceptance of the Court's jurisdiction is only a precondition for the Court to exercise its jurisdiction. In this regard, an Article 12(3) declaration is said to be similar to the practice of the International Court of Justice, which allows a State to accept the jurisdiction of the Court on an *ad hoc* basis in response to the allegation made by another State.[51] Therefore, an Article 12(3) declaration is only a precondition for

---

[46]   *Ibid.*, p. 424.

[47]   *Ibid.*, p. 425.

[48]   *Ibid.*, p. 423.

[49]   Judgment on the appeal, para. 72, see *supra* note 18.

[50]   *Ibid.*, para. 74.

[51]   Schabas, 2010, p. 289, see *supra* note 12.

the Court to exercise jurisdiction and it neither refers a situation, nor triggers the exercise of the Court's jurisdiction.[52]

The Pre-Trial Chamber and the Appeals Chamber have endorsed this view by ruling that an Article 12(3) declaration "could not be mistaken for a referral".[53] The Court indicated a distinction between Article 12 and Articles 13–15 of the Statute. The former sets out the preconditions for the exercise of jurisdiction, while the latter specify the trigger mechanism for such exercise.[54] The Appeals Chamber acknowledged that a declaration could involve in a specific situation, but "the question of whether a 'situation' exists becomes relevant only once the Court considers whether it may exercise its jurisdiction under Article 13 of the Statute".[55] Consequently, with the exception of Uganda's declaration as mentioned before, the rest of the declarations lodged by non-States Parties have been treated as *proprio motu* proceedings of the Prosecutor under Article 15.

In fact, the term "situation" appears throughout the Rome Statute and Rules of Procedure and Evidence without a definition therein. Articles 13 and 14 merely refer to a "situation in which one or more crimes appear to have been committed". Pre-Trial Chamber I has elaborated that situations are "generally defined in terms of temporal, territorial and in some cases personal parameters".[56] Therefore, a situation contains "broader parameters than that of a case and denotes the confines within which the Prosecutor is to determine whether there is a reasonable basis to initiate an investigation".[57]

---

[52] *Ibid.*, p. 289.

[53] ICC, *Prosecutor v. Laurent Koudou Gbagbo*, Decision on the "Corrigendum of the challenge to the jurisdiction of the International Criminal Court on the basis of articles 12(3), 19(2), 21(3), 55 and 59 of the Rome Statute filed by the Defence for President Gbagbo (ICC- 02/11-01/11-129)", 15 August 2012, ICC-02/11-01/11-212, para. 57 (Decision on the Jurisdiction) (http://www.legal-tools.org/doc/0d14c3/); Judgment on the Appeal, para. 58, see *supra* note 18.

[54] Decision on the Jurisdiction, para.57, see *supra* note 53.

[55] Judgment on the Appeal, paras. 81–82, see *supra* note 18.

[56] ICC, Situation in the Democratic Republic of the Congo, Decision on Applications for Participation in the Proceedings of VPRS-1, VPRS-2, VPRS-3, VPRS-4, VPRS-5, VPRS-6, 17 January 2006, ICC-01/04-101-tEN-Corr, para. 65 (http://www.legal-tools.org/doc/2fe2fc/).

[57] Rod Rastan, "What Is a Case for the Purpose of the Rome Statute?", in *Criminal Law Forum*, 2008, vol. 19 (3–4), p. 435.

Whereas the Rome Statute does not prevent a non-State Party from making an Article 12(3) declaration with a view to becoming a State Party in the future,[58] in reality, non-States Parties do so only to accept the exercise of the Court's jurisdiction over specific situations, for example, the Palestinian and the Ukrainian declarations. Having "temporal, territorial and in some cases personal parameters" contained in the Article 12(3) declarations, those non-States Parties have combined two steps: to express their consent to accept the jurisdiction of the Court and to refer their own situations to the Prosecutor.

So far, almost all situations referred by States Parties have concerned themselves.[59] This is likely because States rarely accuse foreign officials or nationals of serious international crimes.[60] By analogy, a non-State Party accepting the Court's *ad hoc* jurisdiction always with crimes committed on its territory or by its nationals in mind (not just to support the Court).

As mentioned, such a non-State Party will not "have all the rights or obligations of a State Party".[61] A State Party may involve in the decision on the "budget of the Court", "management oversight to the organs of the Court", and "matters relating to non-cooperation by States". In addition, it has "the right to refer situations to the Court" and "the right to nominate candidates for the elected offices of the Court". It may also propose amendments to the Statute and the Rules of the Court and has the right to vote on the amendments.[62]

In contrast, a non-State Party lodging an Article 12(3) declaration has none of those rights – not even the right to refer its own situation. On the other hand, the Rome Statute imposes obligations on the non-State Party to co-operate with the Court without any delay and exception in accordance with Part 9 just as a State Party. Does the phrase "without any delay and

---

58 Freeland, 2006, p. 223, see *supra* note 41.

59 Here, 'self-referral' is used to mean that a State Party refers a situation in which one or more crimes have been committed in its territory by its nationals. According to Darryl Robison, 'self-referral' is the term used "when a state party refers a situation on its own territory". See Darryl Robinson, "The Controversy over Territorial State Referrals and Reflections on ICL Discourse", in *Journal of International Criminal Justice*, 2011, vol. 9, no. 2, p. 357.

60 Antonio Cassese, *International Criminal Law*, Oxford University Press, 2008, p. 396.

61 Judgment on the Appeal, para. 74, see *supra* note 18.

62 *Ibid.*, para. 72.

exception" mean that such a State has to co-operate even on matters unrelated to the crimes on their territories – for example, to arrest and transfer a foreign national who was found in their country? If this is the case, the rights and obligations for an accepting State appear to be unbalanced.

It is argued that it is inappropriate to treat situations arising out of Article 12(3) declarations as the Prosecutor's preliminary examinations, because they are not the same. First, the situation was brought to the Prosecutor by a State publicly and formally, unlike information on crimes received from various undisclosed sources. In the latter case, the Prosecutor has discretion to decide whether to initiate a preliminary examination or not, as well as whether to make the situation arising out of the information public or not. In addition, Regulation 25 of the Regulations of the OTP also makes distinction between the two by listing "any information on crimes" in sub-paragraph (a) and an Article 12(3) declaration in sub-paragraph (c). To treat them with the same procedure applicable to the Prosecutor's *proprio motu* proceedings makes such separate categorization redundant.

Second, the wording of Articles 12 and 13 makes it clear that by becoming a State Party, the State only accepts the jurisdiction of the Court (Article 12(1)), which may exercise its jurisdiction if a criminal situation is referred by a State Party (Article 13(1)). Article 12(3) states that by lodging a declaration, a non-State Party accepts "the exercise of jurisdiction by the Court" rather than accepts the jurisdiction of the Court. Consequently, an Article 12(3) declaration has two implications. The accepting State accepts the *ad hoc* jurisdiction of the Court over the situation it may refer to the Court and the Court can exercise its jurisdiction with respect to the situation arising out of the declaration.

27.2.2. Application of the Procedure to Article 12(3) Declarations and Its Consequence

27.2.2.1. The Procedure Applied to Article 12(3) Declarations

While the OTP may initiate preliminary examinations on a referral by a State Party or the Security Council, any information on crimes or an Article 12(3) declaration, they are treated in two different ways. Regulation 45 of the Regulations of the Court requires the Prosecutor to "inform the Presidency in writing as soon as a situation has been referred to the Prosecutor by a State Party under article 14 or by the Security Council under article 13, sub-paragraph (b)". In contrast, this is not required for any information on crimes and an Article 12(3) declaration. The Registrar need not inform the Presidency of the declaration either, but shall merely inform the accepting State of the declaration's consequence.[63] Accordingly, whereas the Presidency shall assign a situation referred by a State Party or the Security Council to a Pre-Trial Chamber, which shall be responsible for any matters arising out of it, the Presidency can do nothing for an Article 12(3) declaration and must leave all matters arising from it to the Prosecutor.

Further, whereas the Prosecutor can directly investigate a situation referred by a State Party or the Security Council after preliminary examination, for an Article 12(3) declaration, he or she shall request the Pre-Trial Chamber's authorization if there is a reasonable basis to proceed with an investigation. It is only then and for that purpose that the Prosecutor will inform the Presidency of the situation concerned with the declaration.

27.2.2.2. Lack of Judicial Oversight as a Consequence of the Application

Due to the different procedures, while the Pre-Trial Chambers take charge of situations referred by States Parties,[64] there is little judicial oversight for preliminary examinations of the situations arising out of Article 12(3) declarations. The Prosecutor may protract or even terminate those preliminary examinations, which may not be challenged by the lodging State.[65]

---

[63] ICC, Rules of Procedure and Evidence, 9 September 2002, Rule 44(2).

[64] ICC, Situation in the Democratic Republic of Congo, Decision Assigning the Situation in the Democratic Republic of Congo to Pre-Trial Chamber I, 5 July 2004, ICC-01/04-01/06-10 (http://www.legal-tools.org/doc/65a7bb/); Situation in Uganda, Decision Assigning the Situation in Uganda to Pre-Trial Chamber II, see *supra* note 14; ICC, Situation in the Central African Republic, Decision Assigning the Situation in the Central African Republic to Pre-Trial Chamber III, 20 January 2005, ICC-01/05 (http://www.legal-tools.org/doc/5532e5/); ICC, Situation in Mali, Decision Assigning the Situation in the Republic of Mali to Pre-Trial Chamber II, 19 July 2012, ICC-01/12-1 (http://www.legal-tools.org/doc/f0774d/); ICC, Situation on Registered Vessels of the Union of the Comoros, the Hellenic Republic and the Kingdom of Cambodia, Decision Assigning the Situation on Registered Vessels of the Union of the Comoros, the Hellenic Republic and the Kingdom of Cambodia to Pre-Trial Chamber I, 5 July 2013, ICC-01/13-1 (http://www.legal-tools.org/doc/8e4e80/); ICC, Situation in the Central African Republic II, Decision Assigning the Situation in the Central African Republic II to Pre-Trial Chamber II, 18 June 2014, ICC-01/14-1 (http://www.legal-tools.org/doc/1cfbfe/); ICC, Situation in the Gabonese Republic, Decision assigning the Situation in the Gabonese Republic to Pre-Trial Chamber II, 4 October 2016, ICC-01/16-1, 4 October 2016 (http://www.legal-tools.org/doc/e5c5f8/).

[65] Freeland, 2005, p. 227, see *supra* note 41.

This can be observed from the treatment of Egypt's declaration. On 5 September 2014, Morsi and the Liberal Party requested the Court to review the Prosecutor's decision not to act upon the declaration. Pre-Trial Chamber II determined that the Prosecutor could take the initiative to deal with the information he or she had obtained and make the decision to initiate the investigation in accordance with Article 15 of the Rome Statute. The conditions for judicial review of the Prosecutor's decision vary depending on the triggering mechanism or the basis for Prosecutor's decision. The Pre-Trial Chamber may only review the decision only if its basis is solely that the investigation does not serve the interests of justice. Since the Prosecutor's refusal to open preliminary examination in Egypt was not on that basis, the Chamber could not review it.[66]

For a situation referred by a State Party, the assigned Pre-Trial Chamber can consider relevant matters very quickly. The referring State may also request the Pre-Trial Chamber to reconsider the decision of the Prosecutor not to proceed with an investigation. For example, in the Gaza Freedom Flotilla situation referred by Comoros on 14 May 2013,[67] following preliminary examination, the Prosecutor publicly announced her determination that there was no reasonable basis to proceed with an investigation.[68] Comoros applied to review that decision.[69] On 16 July 2015, Pre-Trial Chamber I decided on the request.[70] This is a safeguard against

---

[66] ICC, Decision on the 'Request for review of the Prosecutor's decision of 23 April 2014 not to open a Preliminary Examination concerning alleged crimes committed in the Arab Republic of Egypt and the Registrar's Decision of 25 April 2014', 22 September 2014, ICC-RoC46(3)-01/14, paras. 6–9 (http://www.legal-tools.org/doc/7ced5a/).

[67] ICC, Referral under Articles 14 and 12(2)(a) of the Rome Statute arising from the 31 May 2010, Gaza Freedom Flotilla situation, 14 May 2013 (http://www.legal-tools.org/doc/93705a/).

[68] ICC, Situation on Registered Vessels of Comoros, Greece and Cambodia, Article 53(1) Report, 6 November 2014 (http://www.legal-tools.org/doc/43e636/).

[69] ICC, Situation on Registered Vessels of the Union of the Comoros, the Hellenic Republic and the Kingdom of Cambodia, Public redacted version of application for Review pursuant to Article 53(3)(a) of the Prosecutor's Decision of 6 November 2014 not to initiate an investigation in the Situation, 29 January 2015, ICC-01/13-3-Red (http://www.legal-tools.org/doc/b60981/).

[70] ICC, *Situation on the Registered Vessels of the Union of the Comoros, the Hellenic Republic and the Kingdom of Cambodia*, Decision on the request of the Union of the Comoros to review the Prosecutor's decision not to initiate an investigation, 16 July 2015, ICC-01/13-34 (http://www.legal-tools.org/doc/2f876c/).

---

the abuse of power or inappropriate exercise of power by the Prosecutor.[71] The same safeguard should be provided to non-States Parties who have made declarations to accept the exercise of the jurisdiction of the Court.

27.2.2.3. Lack of Time Limits

Neither the Statute nor the Rules and Procedures of Evidence of the Court provide time limits for the Prosecutor to make a decision on preliminary examinations. The Prosecutor has also made similar statements.[72]

Schabas considers it "an entirely reasonable position",[73] because the Prosecutor needs time to evaluate the issue of complementarity that depends upon the conduct of the national justice system.[74] However, some commentators have noted that the Prosecutor has progressed with preliminary examination quickly in some situations, while "drawing out his analysis in others",[75] which may lead to an impression that the Prosecutor does not allocate time and resources evenly among preliminary examinations. It may also make the Prosecutor's work appear less credible.

In practice, preliminary examinations initiated *proprio motu* have generally taken a long time. The preliminary examination of the situation in Kenya that took about two years (from December 2007 to November 2009) was both fast and unique. The conclusion of the preliminary examination of the situation in Republic of Korea took three years and a half (December 2010–June 2014), Honduras five years (November 2010–October 2015), Georgia seven years (August 2008–October 2015) and Afghanistan nine years (2007–2016). The ongoing preliminary examination of the situations in Colombia, Guinea and Nigeria (opened in 2006, 2009 and 2010 respectively) have not yet been completed.

In contrast, preliminary examinations in situations referred by States Parties have been processed quickly. The shortest preliminary examination was that of the situation in the Democratic Republic of the

---

71   Freeland, 2005, p. 228, see *supra* note 41.

72   OTP, Report on preliminary examination, para. 13, see *supra* note 32.

73   Williams A. Schabas, *An Introduction to the International Criminal Court*, Cambridge University Press, 2017, p. 238.

74   *Ibid.*; "Updates from the International and Internationalized Criminal Courts", in *Human Rights Brief*, vol. 19, no. 2, 2012, p. 49 (on the International Criminal Court).

75   *Ibid.*

Congo, which took only two months from April to June 2004.[76] The longest one took two years and a half in the situation of the Central African Republic I from December 2004 to May 2007.[77] Even in the Gaza Flotilla situation referred by Comoros on 14 May 2013, it only took the Prosecutor about one year and a half to announce the conclusion of the preliminary examination on 6 November 2014.[78] This is partly because the Pre-Trial Chambers have overseen the situations.[79] For instance, Pre-Trial Chamber III said in the situation in Central African Republic:

> [T]he preliminary examination of a situation pursuant to article 53(1) of the Statute and rule 104 of the Rules must be completed within a reasonable time from the reception of a referral by a State Party under articles 13(a) and 14 of the Statute, regardless of its complexity.

Having noted that the preliminary examinations of the situations in the Democratic Republic of the Congo and Northern Uganda were completed within two to six months, the Chamber requested the Prosecutor to provide the Chamber and the Government of the Central African Republic with a report on the status of the preliminary examination on a certain date.[80]

Since situations specified in Article 12(3) declarations have been treated as Prosecutor's *proprio motu* proceedings, their preliminary examinations also took much longer. For example, after the government of Côte d'Ivoire made a declaration in 2003, it was only at the end of 2010 that the Prosecutor resumed analysing the situation. It concluded that the statutory criteria established by the Rome Statute for the opening of an investigation were met on 19 May 2011.[81] Also, more than three years

---

[76] Situation in the Democratic Republic of Congo (available on the Court's web site).

[77] Situation in the Central African Republic (available on the Court's web site).

[78] ICC, Statement of the Prosecutor of the International Criminal Court, Fatou Bensouda, on concluding the preliminary examination of the situation referred by the Union of Comoros: "Rome Statute legal requirements have not been met", 6 November 2014 (http://www.legal-tools.org/doc/e745a0/).

[79] William A. Schabas, *An Introduction to the International Criminal Court*, Cambridge University Press, 2007, p. 246.

[80] ICC, Situation in the Central African Republic, Decision Requesting Information on the Status of the Preliminary Examination of the Situation in the Central African Republic, 1 December 2006, ICC-01/05-6, pp. 4–5 (http://www.legal-tools.org/doc/76e607/).

[81] ICC, Situation in the Republic of Côte d'Ivoire, Decision Assigning the Situation in the Republic of Côte d'Ivoire to Pre-Trial Chamber II, 20 May 2011, ICC-02/11-1 (http://www.legal-tools.org/doc/aa6613/).

(from January 2009 to April 2012) had passed after the Palestinian authority made a declaration accepting the Court's jurisdiction before the Prosecutor decided that he could not determine whether Palestine had the right to lodge such a declaration.

27.3. Determination of the Validity of Article 12(3) Declarations

In preliminary examinations, according to Article 53 of the Rome Statute, the Prosecutor shall consider whether a crime within the jurisdiction of the Court has been or is being committed, the admissibility, gravity and the interests of justice. The Statute, Rules and jurisprudence of the Court have never envisaged that the Prosecutor shall determine whether a declaration is valid or not in the first place.

Nevertheless, the Prosecutor has examined the validity of the declarations made by Palestine and Egypt. In contrast, some scholars have questioned the validity of the Ukraine's declaration, which was neglected by the Prosecutor.

27.3.1. Authority to Determine Whether Palestine is Qualified as a State Capable to Make a Declaration

After receiving the declaration lodged by the Palestinian authority, the Prosecutor identified that the first step in the determination of jurisdiction was to ascertain whether the declaration meets statutory requirements,[82] namely the preconditions to the exercise of jurisdiction under Article 12. In other words, although the determination of jurisdiction involves analysing whether the situation fulfils the "temporal requirements; meets territorial or personal jurisdiction, and falls within the subject-matter jurisdiction of the Court",[83] the Prosecutor added one more step.[84] Between 2009 and 2012, the Prosecutor focused on the issue of whether Palestine was a "State" and thus entitled to make an Article 12(3) declaration at all. The Prosecutor endeavoured to collect opinions and views "from the Palestinian National Authority, the Israeli authorities, as well as from a variety of

---

[82]   ICC, Situation in Palestine, Summary of Submissions on Whether the Declaration Lodged by the Palestinian National Authority Meets Statutory Requirements, 3 May 2010, para.2 (Summary of Submissions) (http://www.legal-tools.org/doc/af5abf/).

[83]   OTP, *Draft Policy Paper on Preliminary Examinations*, 4 October 2010, para. 46 (http://www.legal-tools.org/doc/bd172c/).

[84]   Situation in Palestine, para. 3, see *supra* note 26.

experts, academics, international organizations and non-governmental organizations".[85] In the autumn of 2009, the Prosecutor suggested that Palestine should be accepted as a State if Palestine had the ability to enter into international agreements and to exercise criminal jurisdiction over Israeli nationals.[86] It gave an impression that his Office should address the issue.

However, whether Palestine qualified as a "State" for the purpose of the Rome Statute is controversial. After three years of consideration, the Prosecutor suddenly announced that he had no authority to make that determination,[87] because "the status granted to Palestine by the United Nations General Assembly is that of an observer, not as a non-member State".[88] It meant that Palestine could not sign the Rome Statute and could not declare its acceptance of the Court's jurisdiction.[89] He decided to leave the issue whether Palestine was a State to be resolved by competent organs of the United Nations or the Assembly of States Parties.[90]

Although the Prosecutor correctly acknowledged that he had no authority to define "State",[91] the solution of the legal issue by relying on the United Nations is questionable. The Prosecutor supported his conclusion by observing that States must deposit with the Secretary-General of the United Nations instruments of accession to the Statute under Article 125.[92] In case the statehood of the depositor is controversial or unclear to the Secretary-General, he will follow or seek directives from the UN General Assembly on the matter.[93] The Prosecutor therefore considered competent organs of United Nations had authority to determine whether Palestine is qualified as a "State" under Article 12(3) of the Statute.

However, the "Summary of Practice of the Secretary-General as Depositary of Multilateral Treaties" reveals that the Secretary-General

---

[85] Summary of Submissions, para. 16, see *supra* note 83.
[86] Michael Kearney, "The Situation in Palestine", in *Opinio Juris*, 5 April 2012.
[87] Situation on Palestine, see *supra* note 26.
[88] *Ibid.*, para. 7.
[89] ICC, Statement of the Prosecutor of the International Criminal Court, Fatou Bensouda: "The Public Deserves to know the Truth about the ICC's Jurisdiction over Palestine", 2 September 2014 (http://www.legal-tools.org/doc/e3fe6c/).
[90] Situation on Palestine, para. 8, see *supra* note 26.
[91] *Ibid.*, para.6.
[92] The State of Palestine accedes to the Rome statute, see *supra* note 27.
[93] Situation in Palestine, paras. 5–6, see *supra* note 26.

will need a complete list of the States provided by the General Assembly to implement the deposition only when the status of a State was controversial or unclear where "treaties adopted by the General Assembly were open to participation by 'all States' without further specifications".[94] There are multilateral treaties not adopted within the framework of the United Nations. The Rome Statute is one not adopted by the United Nations General Assembly, although it was adopted at a conference convened by the United Nations. It is doubtful if the Secretary-General would seek the General Assembly's directives if Palestine deposited the instrument of accession at the time it lodged the Article 12(3) declaration. In any event, since Palestine was admitted by UNESCO as a Member State on 30 October 2011, even if Palestine had deposited its instrument of accession to the Rome Statute with the Secretary-General in April 2012, the Secretary-General would not likely object.

Furthermore, the Prosecutor wrongfully confused the existence of a State with the recognition of a State and the admission of a State membership in an international organization. The United Nations has made its position very clear that:

> [T]he recognition of a new State or Government is an act that only other States and Governments may grant or withhold [...] The United Nations is neither a State nor a Government, and therefore does not possess any authority to recognize either a State or a Government.[95]

The conditions for the admission of any States to membership in the United Nations are that they are "peace-loving states which accept the obligations" contained in the Charter and are "able and willing to carry out these obligations".[96] Obviously, neither the General Assembly nor the Security Council has the authority to determine whether an entity is a State. Also, because of the veto power of the five permanent member States in the Security Council and for political reasons, some States had been excluded from the UN membership or had chosen not to join the UN.

---

[94] Summary of Practice of the Secretary-General as Depositary of Multilateral Treaties, prepared by the Treaty Section of the Office of Legal Affairs, UN doc. ST/LEG/7/Rev.1, 19 July 1994, para. 81 (http://www.legal-tools.org/doc/7749a6/).

[95] "About UN Membership" (available on the UN's web site).

[96] Charter of the United Nation, 26 June 1945, Article 4 (UN Charter) (http://www.legal-tools.org/doc/6b3cd5/).

It does not necessarily mean that they are not States. In short, the Prosecutor made a mistake to refer the legal issue to the United Nations, which is a political organization and does not possess an authority to determine whether Palestine is a State.

Instead, it is argued that the Chambers of the ICC have the authority to make an authentic interpretation of the term "State" in Article 12(3). The authentic interpretation is an "interpretation made by a body authorized to apply the law",[97] namely the Chambers.

Furthermore, according to the doctrine of competence-competence, each Court has "jurisdiction to determine its own jurisdiction",[98] which has been confirmed by the jurisprudence of the ICJ, the ICTY and the ICC itself.[99] Article 12(3) declarations concern the exercise of the jurisdiction of the Court. The judges of the Court shall therefore have authority to deal with the issue. Moreover, statehood is a legal issue with theories and criteria under international law. The Prosecutor should seek a legal resolution on this issue instead of relying on a resolution for an administrative matter from the Secretary-General and General Assembly of the United Nations.

That a Pre-Trial Chamber has not been assigned to deal with the issue does not excuse the Prosecutor from seeking the Chambers' determination. Article 19(3) of the Statute provides that "the Prosecutor may seek a ruling from the Court regarding a question of jurisdiction". Even if Article 19(3) does not apply to the stage of preliminary examination, the Regulations of the Court require the Prosecutor to "provide the Presidency with any other information that may facilitate the timely assignment of a situation to a Pre-Trial Chamber".[100] The Presidency shall assign a situation to a Pre-Trial Chamber or pass the information on to the President of the Pre-Trial Division, who could direct the situation to a Pre-Trial Cham-

---

[97] Malgosia Fitzmaurice, Olufemi Elias and Panos Merkouris (eds.), *Treaty Interpretation and the Vienna Convention on the Law of Treaties: 30 Years On*, Martinus Nijhoff Publishers, 2012, p. 115.

[98] ICC, *Prosecutor v. Duško Tadić*, Decision on the Defence Motion for Interlocutory Appeal on Jurisdiction, 2 October 1995, IT-94-1-AR72, para.18 (http://www.legal-tools.org/doc/866e17/).

[99] Carsten Stahn, *The Law and Practice of the International Criminal Court*, Oxford University Press, 2015, p. 189.

[100] Regulations of the Court, 26 May 2004, Regulation 45, see *supra* note 2 (http://www.legal-tools.org/doc/2988d1/).

ber to deal with "any matter, request or information not arising out of a situation assigned to a Pre-Trial Chamber".[101] Regrettably, the Prosecutor did not consider bringing the matter to the attention of the judges at all. Indeed, after receiving the declaration made by the Palestinian authority, the Registrar predicted that it was ultimately possible for the judges to resolve the issue.[102]

Alternatively, as the Prosecutor stated, the interpretation of the term "State" can be referred to the Assembly of States Parties. The Rome Statute being a treaty, "[i]t is for the power that imposed the law to interpret the law".[103] Article 31(2) and (3)(a)–(b) of the Vienna Convention on the Law of Treaties refer to "any agreement relating to the treaty which was made between all the parties in connection with the conclusion of the treaty" or "any subsequent agreement between the parties regarding the interpretation of the treaty or the application of its provisions" and so on for the interpretation of treaties, which "represent forms of authentic interpretation whereby all parties themselves agree on (or at least accept) the interpretation of treaty terms by means which are extrinsic to the treaty".[104] Therefore, the Assembly of States Parties may reach such an agreement on the interpretation of the term "State", though it may take a long time. Indeed, on 7 August 2009, a group of eminent international law scholars jointly wrote to the President of the Assembly of States Parties urging the inclusion of the issue on statehood of Palestine in the agenda of the eleventh annual conference of the Assembly (November 2012) to achieve international criminal justice and to maintain the Court's reputation.[105]

27.3.2. Authority to Determine a Government of a State

On 8 May 2014, the OTP rejected an Article 12(3) declaration made by Egyptian lawyers on behalf of the government of Egypt because they

---

[101] *Ibid.*, Regulation 46.

[102] Questions and Answers. para. 1 (http://www.legal-tools.org/doc/8cb916/).

[103] Seymour S. Peloubet, *A Collection of Legal Maxims in Law and Equity: With English Translations*, George S. Diossy, 1880, p.65; Gaetano Arangio Ruiz, *The United Nations Declaration on Friendly Relations and the System of the Sources of International Law*, Brill, 1979, pp. 81–83.

[104] Mark E. Villiger, *Commentary on the 1969 Vienna Convention on the Law of Treaties*, Martinus Nijhoff Publishers, 2009, p. 429.

[105] Dapo Akande, "ICC Assembly of States Parties Urged to Decide on Status of Palestine", in *EJIL: Talk!*, 24 September 2012.

lacked the requisite authority and full powers on behalf of Egypt.[106] First, the Prosecutor referred to the UN Protocol List to determine Dr. Mohamed Morsi was not the head of Egypt. Therefore, he could not deposit an instrument of accession on behalf of Egypt.[107] Second, under the 'effective control' test, Dr. Morsi no longer had the governmental authority with the legal capacity to incur new international legal obligations on behalf of Egypt.[108]

The Prosecutor's positions are controversial. In contrast to the statehood of Palestine, the Prosecutor believed that she was fully competent to determine the legitimacy of a government. The two tests that the Prosecutor adopted were also debatable. The first referred again to the views of the UN and depository of the Rome Statute. As for the second test of 'effective control', scholars disagreed on whether it is the only criterion on which recognition can be based.[109] Popular support, ability and will to fulfil international obligations, and legitimacy have been proposed additional criteria for recognition as a government. Legal scholars and policy-makers have also considered non-dependence on foreign support in the exercise of control and respect for human rights as additional criteria.[110]

Bearing in mind that the General Assembly and the Security Council are political organs, several cases reveal that effective control has been irrelevant in terms of the governmental representative accepted by the United Nations. For instance, the People's Republic of China was not awarded a seat in the United Nations until 1971 in spite of her effective control over most of China's territory since 1949. Also, Cambodia's contested seat in the United Nations was awarded to the Khmer Rouge throughout 1980s after it was overthrown in 1979, rather than to the People's Republic of Kampuchea, which gained *de facto* control of the country.[111] As has been observed: "although the new regime may be all too

---

[106] The Determination of the Office of the Prosecutor on the Communication Received in Relation to Egypt, see *supra* note 35.

[107] *Ibid.*, Point 3.

[108] *Ibid.*, Point 4.

[109] M.J. Peterson, *Recognition of Governments, Legal Doctrine and State Practice, 1815–1995*, Macmillan Press Ltd., p. 33.

[110] *Ibid.*, p. 77.

[111] Benny Widyono, "The Spectre of the Khmer Rouge over Cambodia", in *UN Chronicle*, April 2008, vol. 45, nos. 2 and 3.

clearly in effective control of the territory", "recognition may be withheld as a sign of political displeasure".[112] In short, determination of a government is a complicated issue. The 'effective control' test may not fully reflect the theory and practice of recognition of governments in international law. Some scholars have pointed out that ICC's jurisdiction might be most needed when a democratically elected president was ousted by a military coup.[113]

27.3.3. Representative to Sign the Declaration on Behalf of the State

A valid declaration must be signed and lodged by a person who is considered as representing his/her State. In view of their functions, Heads of State, Heads of Government and Ministers for Foreign Affairs are considered representing their State.[114] Although the Prosecutor mentioned "full power" when he determined the declaration made by Egyptian lawyers, he never questioned whether the declarations of Palestine and the Ukraine had been signed and lodged by the persons representing their States with "full power". Unlike Palestine's 2014 declaration, which was signed by the President of the State of Palestine, the 2004 declaration of Palestine was signed by the Minister of Justice for the Palestinian authority. Both the first and second declarations of Ukraine were signed by the chairperson of the Ukrainian parliament, although Article 106 of the Constitution of Ukraine conferring upon the Ukrainian President the power to represent the State in international relations and to conclude international treaties.[115] The first declaration can be explained on the ground that the chairperson of the parliament was also in his capacity as *ex officio* Head of State under Article 112 of the Constitution of Ukraine because the then President of Ukraine fled the country.[116] It is, however, questionable why the second declaration was not signed by the incumbent President.[117]

---

[112] Anthony Aust, *Handbook of International Law*, Cambridge University Press, 2005, p. 25.

[113] Eugene Kontorovich, Effective Control and Accepting ICC Jurisdiction, in *Opinio Juris*, 4 August 2014.

[114] Vienna Convention on the Law of Treaties, 23 May 1969, Article 7(2)(a) (http://www.legal-tools.org/doc/6bfcd4/). Stahn, 2015, pp. 201–202, see *supra* note 100.

[115] Iryna Marchuk, "Ukraine and the International Criminal Court: Implications of the *Ad Hoc* Jurisdiction Acceptance and Beyond", in *Vanderbilt Journal of Transnational Law*, 2016, vol. 49, no. 4, p. 362.

[116] *Ibid.*, p. 341.

[117] *Ibid.*, p. 362.

Determination on issues relevant to validity of Article 12(3) declarations involves several legal issues such as the criteria for statehood, legitimacy of government, persons representing States and so on, which should be resolved on a case-by-case basis. A declaration may be in conflict with a fundamental domestic law of the accepting State,[118] which may also affect the validity of the declaration in accordance with Article 46 of the Vienna Convention on the Law of Treaties. Present practice shows that leaving these issues in the hands of the Prosecutor without judicial oversight can be troublesome. While the Prosecutor is certainly "highly competent in and have extensive practical experience in the prosecution or trial of criminal cases",[119] he or she does not necessarily possess the requisite competence in international law. That is why the determination of the Prosecutor on validity of Article 12(3) declarations has some obvious flaws and has been challenged and criticized. As discussed above, in dealing with the 2004 declaration of Palestine, the Prosecutor not only wrongfully disregarded the ability of the Palestinian government in foreign relations with more than 130 States and international organizations, but also referred the issue to the United Nations, an international political body, rather than seeking the judicial resolution in the first place. That had inevitably damaged his image of independence.

Again, the issues on the validity of the declarations should be determined by Chambers because judges have competence in "relevant areas of international law".[120] They can decide the criteria for statehood, choose a proper approach to determining the legitimacy of governments and consider other legal obstacles in accordance with international law. As similar issues concerning the validity of Article 12(3) declarations may occur again, there should be a separate procedure regarding the validity of Article 12(3) declarations to be determined by a Pre-Trial Chamber when necessary, leaving other issues concerning the jurisdiction of the Court in the preliminary examination to be conducted by the Prosecutor.

---

[118] Ukraine did not ratify the Rome Statute because the Constitutional Court had decided that its Constitution would not allow its judicial functions to be delegated to other institutions or officials.

[119] ICC Statute, Article 42, see *supra* note 3.

[120] ICC Statute, Article 36, paragraph 3(b)(ii), see *supra* note 3.

27.4. Conclusion and Suggestions

So far, the Court and the Prosecutor has considered the Article 12(3) declaration as only a precondition for the exercise of jurisdiction and applied the same procedure as the Prosecutor's exercise of his/her *proprio motu* power in preliminary examinations. However, in reality, most Article 12(3) declarations are a combination of acceptance of jurisdiction and self-referrals of their own situations by non-States Parties. In so far as there were worries that an accepting State might intend to use the Court unilaterally against other States, the Pre-Trial Chamber's authorization understandably plays the necessary role of a gatekeeper. Nevertheless, one should not overlook the downside of this treatment. It took a longer time to process the preliminary examination of the situation arising out of the declaration, which made the results uncertain. In addition, the whole period of preliminary examination lacks judicial oversight, which is unfair to accepting States.

This chapter argues that the Article 12(3) declaration is different from communications and information obtained by the Prosecutor from undisclosed sources. A declaration is formally lodged by a non-State Party. The Prosecutor should inform the accepting State his conclusion on the relevant preliminary examination within a reasonable time as he does to the referrals of States Parties. In so doing, there needs to be "clear guidelines" and "a general timeline"[121] for the Prosecutor to conduct preliminary examination. The Prosecutor needs longer time for situations arising from received communications partly because he/she must determine whether there are already national proceedings covering the same conduct that would likely be the focus of an ICC investigation. This is usually not the case for Article 12(3) declarations if the situations merely involve their own nationals and territories. The preliminary examination of the situation in the Central African Republic that took two years and a half is the longest one among situations referred by States Parties. The preliminary examination of situations related to the Article 12(3) declaration should also take a similar time.

In the situation in Côte d'Ivoire, it seemed that the Prosecutor could not conclude that there was a reasonable basis to proceed with an investigation after two to three years of preliminary examination, but he did not

---

[121] "Updates from the International and Internationalized Criminal Courts", 2012, see *supra* note 74.

inform Côte d'Ivoire any conclusion. A declaration without an end-date does not mean that the Prosecutor should continue examining the situation until crimes are eventually committed many years in the future. For the purpose of saving resources, focusing on graver situations and enhancing efficiency, the Prosecutor should conclude the examination of a situation that does not meet the requirements to proceed with an investigation. The Prosecutor could reserve the right to reopen the preliminary examination later if necessary. By doing so, it can at least release the Chamber's burden to determine that the events occurred many years later in 2010-2011 and the previous mentioned events of 19 September 2002 in the 2003 declaration of Côte d'Ivoire is one and the same situation.[122]

Scholars have stressed that the treatment of the declarations require judicial involvement or monitor. Freeland points out that it would be of concern if a decision not to proceed with an investigation into a situation that a non-State Party cries for help by lodging the declaration "could be taken by the Prosecutor without recourse to judicial scrutiny under any circumstances".[123] CHAN James suggests "placing incoming declarations under preliminary oversight by the Pre-Trial Division" to ensure that "declarations are valid and sets guidelines for the OTP".[124] This chapter suggests that it should consider a separate procedure of determination of the validity of the declaration when such issues arise. The following provisions should be added to the Regulations of the Court:

> Upon receipt of a declaration under article 12(3), either the Prosecutor or the Registrar shall inform the Presidency the declaration. The Presidency shall assign a Pre-Trial Chamber to consider any issues with respect to the validity of the declaration at the request of the Prosecutor or when the Presidency considers necessary.

---

[122] Decision on the Jurisdiction, paras. 63–64, see *supra* note 53.

[123] Freeland, 2006, p. 231, see *supra* note 41.

[124] CHAN James, "Judicial Oversight over Article 12(3) of the ICC Statute", FICHL Policy Brief Series No. 11 (2013), Torkel Opsahl Academic EPublisher, Brussels, 2013, pp. 3–4 (http://www.legal-tools.org/doc/bc46c4/).

28

Making Sense of the Invisible:
The Role of the 'Accused' during
Preliminary Examinations

Dov Jacobs and Jennifer Naouri[*]

I am invisible, understand, simply because people refuse to
see me.

Ralph Ellison, *Invisible Man*

28.1. Introduction

International criminal justice deals with the most visible crimes receiving
international attention allegedly committed by people that are pre-
identified as responsible and perceived as guilty even before any proceedings are even remotely considered, especially when it comes to public
figures of a State. In other words, for most people, international crimes
are directly associated with known figures of international relations as
their perpetrators.

In the context of the actual criminal proceedings, consideration for
the accused, and more particularly his/her rights, are usually not very high
up on the list of priorities of the stakeholders of international criminal
justice. There are obvious reasons for that, which need not be developed
in the present chapter.[1] They include: (i) the collective nature of international crimes, which allows for a dilution of the consideration of an individual as a perpetrator; (ii) the increased focus on victims; and (iii) the

---

[*] **Dov Jacobs** is an Assistant Professor of International Law at Leiden University and Legal
Assistant at the International Criminal Court; **Jennifer Naouri** is Senior Legal Assistant on
the Defense team of Laurent Gbagbo at the International Criminal Court. All views expressed here represent solely the views of the authors and not the institutions they work for.
The authors thank more particularly Morten Bergsmo and Carsten Stahn for the opportunity to participate in this project and the reviewers for their valuable comments.
[1] Dov Jacobs, "A Tale of Four Illusions: The Rights of the Defense before International
Criminal Tribunals", in Colleen Rohan and Gentian Zyberi (eds.), *Defense Perspectives on
International Criminal Justice*, Cambridge University Press, Cambridge, 2017, p. 561.

---

moral stigma attached to international crimes, which leads to a desire to reach a guilty verdict for its symbolic and narrative effect. For many, observers and participants of the international justice project alike, a conviction is a 'victory for justice' while an acquittal is necessarily seen as a failure, especially for the victims.

While there are therefore reasons for ignoring the rights of the defence, it does create a sort of paradoxical cognitive dissonance: while outside the courtroom, the focus of the attention is symbolically on the perpetrator, inside the courtroom, the accused and his rights often does not have a central role in the procedure.

The result of this situation is that the rights of the accused, when they are taken into account, are always being balanced with other considerations, such as the costs of the proceedings, the rights of the victims, the interests of various stakeholders and overarching – and therefore necessarily vague – concepts such as the 'fight against impunity'.

While this assessment could apply at all stages of the process, one wonders if it applies equally throughout, especially for the present discussion, to preliminary examinations. A basic appraisal of the nature of a preliminary examination could lead to the conclusion that, until the preliminary examination moves to the next stage, and then cases are selected, there is technically no 'defendant' whose rights are to be protected and more generally who needs to be considered in the process. A preliminary examination could be seen as the Office of the Prosecutor ('OTP') simply gathering general information about a possible situation in order to decide whether a more formal investigation is required. One could say that this does not require precise identification of alleged perpetrators of crimes nor does it entail involving these alleged perpetrators in the process.

But the discussion does not end here. It is obvious that the OTP is going to be identifying during the preliminary examination not only contextual elements and details of the possible crimes, but also information relating to possible perpetrators. This is true from both a practical perspective (it is not possible to artificially distinguish between evidence relating to the crimes and evidence relating to the possible perpetrators of the crimes) and from a legal perspective (to the extent that during the preliminary examination the OTP is under an obligation to assess the admissibility of any future cases, there will necessarily be some assessment of potential defendants).

This chapter will highlight the ways in which alleged perpetrators are considered during the preliminary examination and what impact this might have for future practice of the OTP. The underlying idea is that potential defendants cannot simply be ignored during a preliminary examination. Experience has shown that the conduct of the preliminary examination, despite its preliminary nature, can affect the way the actual investigation and prosecution unfold. It is usually when the OTP starts developing its theory of the case, which will set in motion and influence a series of investigative choices, even many years down the road. If the initial direction is based on incomplete information or a general misunderstanding of the situation, it will be harder to correct at a later stage. Moreover, the understanding of the context and role of the protagonists in what are most of the time highly complex factual situations necessarily requires hearing what the alleged perpetrators (from the point of view of the OTP) have to say. In other words, the OTP cannot pretend that the potential defendant were invisible.[2]

Considering the 'accused', in a broad sense, during a preliminary examination, is therefore a fundamental component of ensuring the quality control of that particular phase of the process.

This chapter will start by providing some insight on how the authors approach the notion of 'quality control' in the context of preliminary examinations (Section 28.2.). The chapter will then move on to discuss 1) how the role of the Defendant comes into play in the legal assessment done under Article 53, namely whether there exists a reasonable basis to believe that a crime within the jurisdiction of the Court has been committed (Section 28.3.) and whether the case would be admissible (Section 28.4.), and 2) how the potential defendant might be treated and approached during the preliminary examination (Section 28.5.).

---

2   What we mean by 'invisible' here is not necessarily that the Office of the Prosecutor ('OTP') would not mention alleged perpetrators at all during the preliminary examination. As shown in subsequent sections of this chapter, the analysis of formal requests made by the OTP to open an investigation under Article 15 shows that the OTP generally does take into account, in more or less precise terms, possible perpetrators in the course of the preliminary examination, most notably when it comes to determining jurisdiction and admissibility. These alleged perpetrators are therefore not 'invisible' because they are not mentioned at all, but 'invisible' on a human level: they are reified as objects of study rather than considered as subjects that can be interacted with and whose input could provide the OTP with a better understanding of the situation it is examining.

28.2. Quality Control of the Preliminary Examination Phase: Some Basic Groundings

28.2.1. The Nature of a Preliminary Examination

28.2.1.1. The Legal Nature of a Preliminary Examination

The difficulty of establishing a framework to assess the quality of a preliminary examination is complicated by the uncertainty about the exact legal nature of a preliminary examination. While the language of the first sentence of Article 53(1) seems to suggest an obligation ("shall") to open an investigation, the legal framework surrounding preliminary examinations seems to suggest a large – and sometimes absolute – margin of discretion for the OTP for a finding that there is no reasonable basis to proceed.[3]

Indeed, a preliminary examination is not a formal 'judicial process' since it is not systematically subject to judicial review.[4] The only outcome of a preliminary examination that is necessarily subject to judicial review by a Pre-Trial Chamber is a decision to initiate an investigation *proprio motu* under Article 15.[5] Some decisions *may* be subject to review by a Pre-Trial Chamber: (1) the decision not to open an investigation after a State or UNSC referral (upon request from the referring State or the UNSC),[6] and (2) the decision not to proceed in the interests of justice (on the own initiative of the Pre-Trial Chamber).[7] In the first case, the Court

---

[3] For an interpretation along these lines, see "Decision on the request of the Union of the Comoros to review the Prosecutor's decision not to initiate an investigation" where the Pre-Trial Chamber ('PTC') claimed that Article 53(1) created a presumption in favour of opening an investigation: "In the presence of several plausible explanations of the available information, the presumption of article 53(1) of the Statute, as reflected by the use of the word "shall" in the chapeau of that article, and of common sense, is that the Prosecutor investigates in order to be able to properly assess the relevant facts" (International Criminal Court ('ICC'), Situation on registered vessels of the union of the Comoros, the Hellenic Republic of Greece and the Kingdom of Cambodia, Decision on the request of the Union of the Comoros to review the Prosecutor's decision not to initiate an investigation, 16 July 2015, ICC-01/13-34, para. 13 (http://www.legal-tools.org/doc/2f876c/).

[4] On the nature of the preliminary examination, see Hector Olasolo, "The Prosecutor of the ICC before the initiation of investigations: A quasi judicial or a political body?", in *International Criminal Law Review*, 2003, vol. 3, p. 87.

[5] Statute of the International Criminal Court, 17 July 1998, Article 15(4) ('ICC Statute') (http://www.legal-tools.org/doc/7b9af9/).

[6] ICC Statute, Article 53(3)(a), see *supra* note 5.

[7] ICC Statute, Article 53(3)(b), see *supra* note 5.

---

cannot compel the OTP to start an investigation, but can merely ask the Prosecutor to reconsider.[8] In the second case, while the language of the provision is ambiguous,[9] it appears from the Rules of Procedure and Evidence that if there is no confirmation from the Pre-Trial Chamber, the Prosecutor must proceed.[10] Some decisions are not subject to judicial review: the decision to open an investigation after a State or UNSC referral and a decision not to proceed further *proprio motu*.

What does this framework say of the nature of preliminary examinations? First, from a theoretical perspective, if Article 53 was thought of as providing a clear legalized process, then one would expect that judicial oversight would have been provided for in a systematic way. The fact that Article 53 is in the Rome Statute does not necessarily mean that it of itself creates any legal obligation or integrates the preliminary examination in the judicial process. In our view, the key consideration is whether there is judicial or quasi-judicial oversight. In the absence thereof, it makes no sense to speak of a legal process or even of an obligation in the abstract.

In the current state of affairs, it seems rather that Article 53 has, at best, a dual nature: on the one hand, it could be considered as providing an imperative legal framework to be followed by the Prosecutor during a preliminary examination in situations where his or her decision to proceed would be subject to judicial review; on the other hand, it could be considered as merely indicative of possible elements to take into consideration for the Prosecutor to decide to proceed or not, in situations where no judicial review is provided for.

Second, it is apparent that Pre-Trial Chambers can never force the OTP to initiate an investigation based on their own determinations on jurisdiction or admissibility. As noted previously, the only moment where judges have authority to trigger the commencement of an investigation is

---

[8]   ICC Statute, Article 53(3)(a), see *supra* note 5.

[9]   Article 53(3)(b) provides that: "the decision of the Prosecutor shall be effective only if confirmed by the Pre-Trial Chamber". It is however not clear what it means for a decision not to proceed to be "effective", given the fact that a decision not to proceed does not technically have any legal effect.

[10] ICC, Rules of Procedure and Evidence, 9 September 2002, Rule 110 ('[ICC] RPE'): "When the Pre-Trial Chamber does not confirm the decision by the Prosecutor referred to in sub-rule 1, he or she shall proceed with the investigation or prosecution" (http://www.legal-tools.org/doc/8bcf6f).

when the Prosecutor had decided not to proceed based on the interests of justice, but this is due to the particular nature of exercise on the evaluation of the "interests of justice", which only occurs when the Prosecutor has determined that the crimes would fall under the jurisdiction of the Court and that the case would be admissible.[11] As a consequence, it becomes clear that, whatever the language of Article 53(1) might suggest, decisions to investigate are largely – when not exclusively – within the realm of prosecutorial discretion.

This has an impact on evaluations of quality from a legal perspective. While all discretion can be subject to some control and oversight, there is always a margin of appreciation that escapes a rational and objective analysis. In this sense, calls for full transparency and control when it comes to the exercise of prosecutorial discretion when deciding to open a formal investigation are something of an illusion, especially given that the prosecution is unlikely to be open about certain criteria that come into play, for example: (i) the likelihood of co-operation by States, (ii) the likelihood of obtaining custody of potential defendants, (iii) the quality of evidence for certain crimes, which might explain a more focused charging strategy, and (iv) budgetary considerations, which might justify focusing resources on more promising investigations. These common-sense criteria for anyone closely following the workings of international criminal justice will always appear as unacceptable in the highly morally charged context of international criminal law where the fight against impunity is seen as the consideration that trumps all others.

28.2.1.2. The 'Investigative' Nature of a Preliminary Examination

It is clear from the wording of the Rome Statute, particularly in the context of *proprio motu* enquiries, that the preliminary examination is, at the very least, a pre-investigation. This is particularly clear in Article 15, where it is indicated that the OTP *can* rely on information the Office receives, but it also has the power to "seek additional information".[12] Therefore, the preliminary examination is not limited to an assessment of the information presented to the OTP. The moment the OTP decides to initiate

---

[11] For a recent discussion on the "interests of justice" in Article 53 of the Rome Statute, see Maria Varaki, "Revisiting the 'Interests of Justice' Policy Paper", in *Journal of International Criminal Justice*, 2017, vol. 15, p. 455.

[12] Cf. ICC Statute, Article 15(2), see *supra* note 5.

investigations based on information that crimes within the jurisdiction of the Court might have been committed, his or her work is to start building a case from evidence whatever the stage of the proceedings. One cannot artificially distinguish what it means to build a case at the different stages of the proceedings. The standard of proof can be different depending on the stage of the proceeding, which means that the assessment made of the evidence will be different, but this does not mean that there are different ways to build a case.

Moreover, the OTP should, from the moment it undertakes to build a case, bear in mind that as officers of the Court they have the duty to examine incriminating and exonerating circumstances equally.[13]

A policy of the OTP that would portray the preliminary examination as a mere 'assessment' of information provided to them and not an investigation or pre-investigation would mean forgetting about the purpose of a preliminary examination. To be able to decide whether to ask for the opening of a formal investigation, one has to take active steps to find out what happened in a given situation. The OTP cannot simply be at the mercy of the sources that volunteer information. Therefore, the Office itself also needs to seek information, which is *de facto* an investigative step. This means, concretely, that the OTP should, from very moment it starts analysing information presented to them, have a systematic approach of the evidence to set the ground work for building a case.

From the moment the prosecution starts a preliminary examination, it is their duty to: learn about the recent history of the country concerned by the situation, analyse facts, cross-reference information, interview political leaders, academics, journalists, lawyers, civil society leaders (including church leaders), local NGOs, take victims and/or witness statements, organize field mission, and so on. These steps constitute the core of an investigation regardless of the stage of the proceedings. And these steps are the first landmarks of building a legal case. This approach is exactly what distinguishes the Prosecutor of the ICC from an NGO or any other quasi-investigative bodies, such as UN commissions of Inquiry Any evidence collected (that may eventually be presented to the Pre-Trial Chamber) by the OTP must be the result of a neutral, unprejudiced, serious (pre-)investigation. If the OTP does not act independently and does

---

[13] ICC Statute, Article 54(1), see *supra* note 5.

not seek information on its own, the Office will never be able to assess the seriousness of the information it receives and thus the concrete need to open an investigation.

In sum, just because the preliminary examination is not legally a 'formal investigation' does not mean that the actions undertaken during a preliminary examination are essentially different from those in a formal investigation. The term 'formal' only means that the 'case' that the OTP has built during the preliminary examination is sufficient to move to a next step, when there is a referral from a State or the Security Council, or authorization by the Pre-Trial Chamber. Moreover, whereas in the latter case the judges will give the OTP a clearer picture of the scope of his or her investigation, this procedural step does not mean that the OTP had not been investigating as such. On the contrary, if the OTP has not built a proper case during a preliminary examination, it will be quite unlikely that authorization to open a formal investigation would be granted. This does not mean that at the end of a preliminary examination the investigations are finished – far from it. The investigations of the OTP, if a formal investigation is opened, will continue and the evidence collected will have to allow the OTP to prove the case to reach a higher standard of proof (for example, the OTP will collect more testimony, forensic evidence, consult experts, and so on).

Furthermore, the analysis made during a preliminary examination will set out the framework of a future formal investigation. This means that the factual narrative arising from and the potential perpetrators identified during a preliminary examination will be the factual foundation of the case to be further built during the OTP's formal investigation. This means, in practice, that because the OTP will be building a case from the very beginning, they are going to be identifying during the preliminary examination not only contextual elements and details of possible crimes, but also information relating to possible perpetrators.

The need to see preliminary examinations in the general context of investigations is summarized aptly by Carsten Stahn:

> the connection between preliminary examination and investigation needs to be improved. The Statute seems to imply that there is a clear-cut distinction between preliminary examination and investigation, according to which preliminary examination focuses on situation-related analysis while investigations involve the framing and testing of cases. Prac-

tice has shown that boundaries are more fluid. As part of the gravity test, the OTP has to make an assessment of hypothetical cases. There is a need to draw connections between incidents and suspects, even before the formal start of investigations. In 'hard cases', a preliminary examination may require onsite presence on the ground, and deeper engagement with the situational context. This would improve the quality of assessment and allow better hypotheses.[14]

28.2.2. The Temporal Dimension of Quality Control

There is also a temporal dimension to quality control. It is difficult to judge the quality of the preliminary examination, whatever the perspective, without considering the expected outcome of the process. Indeed, the preliminary examination phase is but the first step in a procedure that will have to go through various hurdles, such as the issuance of an arrest warrant, the confirmation of charges and the trial itself. What is expected of the preliminary examination necessarily depends on the expectations of these other phases. For example, the way the preliminary examination is conducted will likely have an impact on the nature and quality of evidence presented at later stages of the proceedings, even if the OTP does not have formal investigative powers at this stage nor do States have a duty to cooperate.

Also relevant from a temporal perspective is the extent to which the perspective of victims would be considered in presenting a complete, even if not necessarily detailed, overview of the nature, scope and diversity of the violence suffered.

28.2.3. Quality Control of the Preliminary Examination Phase: A Question of Perspective

These considerations come into play when considering the perspectives of the different participants of the criminal process.

More generally, there obviously cannot be a rigid objective definition of quality control of the preliminary examination phase, with boxes to be ticked, one that is universally applicable. Indeed, what one considers

---

[14] Carsten Stahn, "Damned if you do, Damned if you don't, Challenges and Critiques of Preliminary Examinations at the ICC", in *Journal of International Criminal Justice*, 2017, vol. 15, p. 413.

of 'quality' is necessarily contingent on the normative preferences of the various stakeholders in the process. Different stakeholders will have different objectives, which can range from financial efficiency to the quality of investigations. Others might approach the question from the perspective of the interaction with domestic jurisdictions, through concepts of 'positive complementarity'.[15] Under this approach, the quality of the preliminary examination might be assessed through a broader lens of how the OTP might contribute to domestic capacity-building and the conduct of their own investigations and prosecutions.

More specifically, three perspectives stand out as more particularly relevant for the evaluation of the quality of a preliminary examination.

From the perspective of the prosecution, the efficiency of the investigation is also not necessarily straight forward. Indeed, when you consider what strategy should be adopted towards evidence, should the OTP aim at securing minimal evidence to justify the formal opening of an investigation, which is, in the case of referrals by States Parties and the UNSC, not subject to judicial review, and in the case of a *proprio motu* investigation, subject to a fairly minimal oversight by pre-trial judges? Should the OTP see further and already try to assess, independently whether this evidence, when it comes under scrutiny, is likely to survive judicial debate?

From the perspective of victims, the objectives will not necessarily be aligned with those of the OTP. While victims of crimes looked at by the prosecution will be more likely to support the preliminary examination, victims which are not on the OTP radar – or who have suffered crimes that the OTP will not be looking at – will have a different agenda. For all victims wishing the ICC to intervene, one dimension which will affect their perception of the preliminary examination, whether it can be deemed as successful and as a criterion of 'quality control', is whether the outcome reflects their particular understanding of the situation in terms of responsibility. This puts a special burden on the prosecution, independently of its own desire to do so, to be seen as balanced.

---

[15] Carsten Stahn, "Taking Complementarity Seriously: On the sense and sensibility of 'classical', 'positive' and 'negative' complementarity", in Carsten Stahn (ed.), *The International Criminal Court and Complementarity*. Cambridge University Press, Cambridge, 2011, pp. 233–282.

From the defence's perspective, the situation is different. The quality of the preliminary examination will only have one yardstick of evaluation: whether it has respected the rights of the accused.[16]

What does this mean specifically in the context of the preliminary examination? The defence will ask that the prosecution take steps from the beginning to secure evidence in a way that can be later challenged, when it comes to chain of custody or authenticity.

As another corollary of the protection of the rights of the accused at the preliminary examination phase, the prosecution must take seriously its obligation to investigate exonerating and incriminating evidence equally. This is necessary not just as a legal obligation, but a practical one as well. First, a serious enquiry during the preliminary examination will ensure that the OTP builds strong cases in the future from the start. Second, such an approach might also elicit useful information for the defence, which likely has less capacity to investigate than the Prosecutor. It has fewer means and less access to relevant information, particularly in cases where the political opponents of the potential defendant will be in power. While States do not have a formal obligation to co-operate with the OTP during the preliminary examination, the OTP can use the institutional weight of the ICC to obtain relevant information, including for the defence. This is all the more crucial because the earlier evidence is secured, the better quality it is likely to be, whether it is eye-witness testimony or forensic evidence. Of course, this preliminary investigation by the prosecution cannot and should not replace the autonomous capacity of the defence to investigate, and any discussion on the adequacy of means provided for the defence in the international context. The prosecution cannot build a case for and against the defence at the same time. Instead, it should be continuously aware that during the preliminary examination it might be in a position to have access to evidence that might be useful for the defence

---

[16]   While this yardstick is presented from the 'perspective of the defence', it should not be confused with a 'defence perspective'. Indeed, the rights of the accused are enshrined in the Rome Statute. Referring to this criterion to assess the quality of a preliminary examination is therefore nothing other than applying the Rome Statute. Dov Jacobs, "A Tale of Four Illusions: The Rights of the Defense before International Criminal Tribunals", in Colleen Rohan and Gentian Zyberi (eds.), *Defense Perspectives on International Criminal Justice*, Cambridge University Press, Cambridge, 2017, p. 561.

and might not be available later on, and to take all necessary steps to secure this investigation.

28.3. Jurisdiction and the Potential Defendant

Under Article 53(1)(a), the first part of the OTP's evaluation is whether "the information available to the Prosecutor provides a reasonable basis to believe that a crime within the jurisdiction of the Court has been or is being committed".[17] While, technically, this provision refers specifically to the material (that is, subject-matter) jurisdiction of the Court and not, for example, its personal jurisdiction, this does not mean that individual involvement cannot be looked at in that context, as highlighted in the case law.[18]

As noted in the OTP Policy Paper on Preliminary Examinations, among the factors that could be looked into is the "alleged perpetrators, including the *de jure* and *de facto* role of the individual, group or institution and their link with the alleged crimes, and the mental element, to the extent discernible at this stage".[19] It should be noted, however, that given the collective and organizational nature of most international crimes, the persons prosecuted are often not the direct perpetrators of the alleged crimes. As a result, looking into alleged perpetrators does not necessarily mean identifying possible suspects for prosecution.

Such a determination of the role of individuals or groups makes sense both factually and legally. Factually, it would be somewhat artificial to distinguish between what is alleged to have happened and the authors of those acts, especially as sources used by the OTP during the preliminary examination are more than likely to provide some analysis of the authors of the alleged crimes. Legally, as a criminal court, as opposed to a human rights fact-finding commission, the ICC cannot avoid discussion of perpetratorship. An act is only technically a crime when both the *actus reus* and the *mens rea* are established. How can a finding, even of a pre-

---

[17] ICC Statute, Article 53(1)(a), see *supra* note 5.

[18] Morten Bergsmo, Pieter Kruger and Olympia Bekou, "Article 53", in Otto Triffterer and Kai Ambos (eds.), *Rome Statute of the International Criminal Court: A Commentary*, C.H. Beck, Hart, Nomos, 2016, p. 1372.

[19] OTP, *Policy Paper on Preliminary Examinations*, 1 November 2013, p. 10 (http://www.legal-tools.org/doc/acb906/).

liminary nature, of the possible commission of an international crime be made without some discussion of possible perpetrators and their intent?[20]

This section will first assess what it means to identify a potential perpetrator from a practical perspective, before looking at the current practice of the ICC.

28.3.1. Identifying a Potential Perpetrator during Preliminary Examination (from a Practical Perspective)

Building a case is not a theoretical exercise, which is why the Prosecutor will necessarily, by the time of the preliminary examination, have information at his or her disposal that relates to the alleged existence of a war or mass attack against civilians, to the alleged commission of crimes and to alleged perpetrators. This information will of course not be presented in such a systematic manner. There will not be one specific document indicating that a murder has been committed, another document that contains information that relates to a common plan of government to target civilians and a report that gives information on an alleged perpetrator. Each piece of evidence sent to the OTP will contain information of a different nature. When building a case, it is the task of the investigator assessing the evidence to try to establish the seriousness of the information to analyse the evidence, to organize it and to verify its authenticity, its credibility and supplement the information received with other sources of information. Only then, after having started building a case will the investigator be able to determine if the information available during the preliminary examination is sufficiently serious to establish that a crime within the jurisdiction of the Court may have been committed in a given situation.

One type of evidence that will be important is the testimony of victims (which can be included in NGO reports or taken directly by the OTP). This testimony will cover different facts. The victim often explains what he or she has suffered but also who attacked him or her, as well as the broader context of the attack. This means that specific testimony, even

---

[20] Interestingly, international criminal law has to some extent developed as a body of law where discussion of the perpetrators has somewhat taken a back seat as opposed to establishment of the commission of crimes, as can be seen from the structure of international judgments, notably at the *ad hoc* tribunals, where hundreds of pages are devoted to discussing the crimes, with minimal or no discussion of the actual intent of the direct perpetrators of the crimes, before the accused and his hypothetical *mens rea* is even considered.

anonymous, can provide both information on the alleged crime and on the alleged perpetrator. Every detail can be of importance.

In particular, the information about the potential perpetrator can be crucial because it can be cross-referenced with other available information. It is fundamental to keep in mind that when it comes to international crimes the perpetrator that the OTP might target for prosecution is usually not the alleged perpetrator of the crime reported by the witness. So the investigator of the OTP will have to find a link between the 'direct perpetrator' and the person that is responsible for him or on whose behalf the 'direct perpetrator' was acting. Therefore, all information in the victim statement can be an important lead and the information cannot be artificially logged into a specific category of information. For instance, the victim, in his/her statement, can explain in detail where the incident happened, at what time, who was present, and so on. This can be a lead to an assessment of the context of the crime but also to an investigation of the potential perpetrator. Indeed, if one cross-references just the information available in a statement where the victim describes the uniform or badge worn by the attacker, it may be possible for the investigator to have an idea of who the alleged perpetrator may be by ascertaining (1) what squad of the army wears the described uniform and (2) if members of that specific squad have been deployed at the location mentioned by the victim.

Additionally, this same victim statement found in an NGO report will also have to be cross-referenced with other evidence available: meeting with the author of the report, interviewing State officials, the military, members of civil society, other victims, and so on. If the investigator follows the leads of the anonymous victim statement and this lead is corroborated by other sources, the investigator will be in a position to identify an alleged perpetrator. This analysis also applies to any other type of information that might have been communicated to the OTP during a preliminary examination or that the OTP obtained during a preliminary examination.

As a consequence, if the OTP analyses the information during a preliminary examination and starts building a case, they will undoubtedly investigate the possible perpetrator of the alleged international crime. Not to mention that, in practice, most sources that reach out to the OTP concerning crimes that might have been committed will point in the direction of a person or persons that they consider to be responsible of those crimes.[21] This is why it is virtually impossible, from a practical perspective, to artificially distinguish between evidence collected relating to crimes and evidence relating to the possible perpetrators of crimes.

28.3.2. Current ICC/OTP Practice

The following analysis is based on the public redacted versions of OTP requests to open an investigation. It should be noted in that respect of all requests, the OTP has provided a confidential list of possible perpetrators that could be the target of future cases at following a formal investigation. This list is submitted under Regulation 49 of the Regulations of the Court which provides that the statement of facts in support of a request to be authorized to open an investigation should include: "The persons involved, if identified, or a description of the persons or groups of persons involved".[22] What one can note is first that this reference to "persons of groups of persons involved" was not included in the Rome Statute or the Rules of Procedure and Evidence, but added by the judges when drafting the Regulations of the Court. Second, there is no formal obligation to specifically identify individuals ("if identified"), merely a general description of the involvement of persons or groups of persons. Third, this obligation does not explicitly involve providing any information on modes of liability.

Moving on to the practice of the OTP in particular situations, one can note a number of differences, depending on the request.

In the request for authorization to open an investigation in Kenya,[23] discussion of alleged perpetrators and/or potential suspects is minimal. The OTP refers on occasion to the "perpetrators",[24] and mentions the fact that "political leaders, businessmen and others had enlisted criminal ele-

---

[21] ICC, Situation in Gabon, *Requête aux fins de renvoi d'une situation par un Etat partie auprès du Procureur de la Cour pénale internationale*, 20 September 2016 (http://www.legal-tools.org/doc/3b6e3e/).

[22] ICC, Regulations of the Court, 26 May 2004, Regulation 49(2)(c) (Regulations) (http://www.legal-tools.org/doc/2988d1/).

[23] ICC, Situation in the Republic of Kenya, Request for authorisation of an investigation pursuant to Article 15, 26 November 2009, ICC-01/09-3 (http://www.legal-tools.org/doc/c63dcc/).

[24] *Ibid.*, para. 57–58

ments and ordinary people to carry out attacks against specifically target-ed groups".[25] The section entitled "persons or groups involved" is com-posed of two paragraphs and refers to low level perpetrators who commit-ted the violence on the ground, "persons in position of power" who "ap-pear to have been involved in the organization, enticement and/or financ-ing of violence targeting specific groups", "political leaders of all sides", as well as the security forces. One can note that while there is some dis-cussion of the organized nature of the alleged crimes for the purposes of establishing the contextual elements of crimes against humanity, there is no direct discussion of modes of liability. Moreover, possible perpetrators or those that might end up being the target of a formal investigation are never named. One could therefore say that the OTP was very careful to remain very general in its request, in order to preserve the possibility for the formal investigation to yield more specific results.

The request for authorization to open an investigation in the situa-tion of the Ivory Coast[26] is very different. Within three paragraphs of the request, Laurent Gbagbo is named and the violence is described as being "pursuant to a policy to retain Laurent Gbagbo in power by all means",[27] and there is no mention of possible violence on both sides in the introduc-tion. Later on in the request, however, the Prosecutor mentions the exist-ence of a "list of persons or groups belonging to or associated with the pro-Gbagbo and pro-Ouattara sides that appear to bear the greatest re-sponsibility for the most serious crimes, with an indication of their specif-ic role".[28] Under the heading of "persons or groups involved", the possi-bility of both sides having committed crimes is also mentioned.[29] In the subsequent discussion on the crimes, the Prosecutor states that "pro-Gbagbo forces committed widespread and systematic attacks against civil-ians associated with his political opponent in pursuance of a policy of the State of Côte d'Ivoire under the leadership of former President Gbagbo to launch violent attacks against political opponents or persons perceived to

---

[25] *Ibid.*, para. 63.

[26] OTP, Situation in the Republic of Côte d'Ivoire, Request for authorisation of an investiga-tion pursuant to article 15, 23 June 2011, ICC-02/11-3 (http://www.legal-tools.org/doc/1b1939/).

[27] *Ibid.*, para. 3.

[28] *Ibid.*, para. 46.

[29] *Ibid.*, para. 70–71.

support the political opponents in order to retain power by all means".[30] While modes of liability are not directly referred to, this is the closest indication that the OTP did explore the intent of those who had allegedly organized the violence. In the next paragraph, the Prosecutor affirms: "the information currently available to the Prosecution does not suggest that there is a reasonable basis that crimes against humanity were committed also by pro-Ouattara forces".[31] This statement is striking because, of all four requests to open an investigation, this is the only where the OTP explicitly reaches a conclusion – be it preliminary – that one side of a conflict did not commit a particular crime. This makes sense, because there is no legal necessity to do so under Article 15 in order to obtain the opening of a formal investigation. Indeed, a decision authorizing the Prosecutor to open a formal investigation will not limit the scope of the investigation in terms of crimes or alleged perpetrators, irrespective of the evidence brought forward by the Prosecutor in his original request. There is therefore no need to explain what crimes were not committed, only explain what crimes were committed in order to justify the opening of an investigation.

The request to open an investigation in Georgia,[32] similarly to the request in the Kenya situation, does not go into much detail either on the direct perpetrators of the crimes or on those that might bear the greatest responsibility for the purposes of being identified as potential defendants. There is also no discussion of modes of liability. The only individual mentioned specifically in the section on "persons or groups involved" is President Eduard Kokoity, presented as the *de facto* President of South Ossetia[33] and later on in the request the holders of various positions of importance in the South Ossetian administration or military are also named,[34] as well as "a south Ossetian sniper, Oleg Galavanov".[35] Con-

---

[30] *Ibid.*, para. 74.

[31] *Ibid.*, para. 75.

[32] OTP, Situation in Georgia, Corrected Version of "Request for authorisation of an investigation pursuant to article 15", 16 October 2015, 17 November 2015, ICC-01/15-4-Corr, (http://www.legal-tools.org/doc/eca741/).

[33] *Ibid.*, para. 63.

[34] *Ibid.*, para. 94–95. It should be noted that these names are given not directly for the purposes of identifying possible perpetrators or potential accused, but to determine the institutional links between South Ossetian forces and Russia by showing that a number of senior figures in the South Ossetian army are also part of the Russian military.

versely, the structure of the Russian or Georgian military is not detailed, nor are specific military or civilian leaders of post holders mentioned.

In the report issued by the OTP when deciding to not open a formal investigation in the situation on registered vessels of Comoros, Greece and Cambodia, one can note that the Prosecutor provides a minimalist discussion of the alleged perpetrators, referring throughout to the "IDF", without any information on names, ranks or modes of liability.

In relation to the situation in Burundi which was opened on 25 October 2017 by a Pre-Trial Chamber,[36] while the OTP has not made available a public redacted version of its request, one can note in the decision itself that only the President of Burundi is explicitly named in the section concerning the assessment of jurisdiction.

Finally, in the request to open an investigation in Afghanistan, the Prosecutor, in a section entitled "persons or groups involved", provides some general discussion on groups that might have been implicated in the commission of the crimes, but does not indicate the role of specific individuals, other than mentioning their role as leaders of such or such group.[37]

28.3.3. Assessment of the OTP Practice

What conclusions can thus be drawn from OTP practice to date? First of all, none of the documents produced includes any direct discussion of modes of liability. One can note that the Kenya request is probably the most detailed in distinguishing the direct perpetrators of the violence and those who had organized it, financed it and incited it. Moreover, the Ivory Coast request is the only one that seems to indicate the existence of an

---

[35] *Ibid.*, para. 184.

[36] On the controversy surrounding the issuance of the decision, a mere two days prior to Burundi's withdrawal of the Rome Statute becoming effective, see Dov Jacobs, "Peek-A-Boo: ICC authorises investigation in Burundi, some thoughts on legality and cooperation", in *Spreading the Jam*, 11 November 2017.

[37] OTP, Situation in the Islamic Republic of Afghanistan, Public redacted version of "Request for authorisation of an investigation pursuant to article 15", 20 November 2017, ICC-02/17-7-Conf-Exp, paras. 53–71 (http://www.legal-tools.org/doc/db23eb/).

---

overall plan that could be linked with a mode of liability of indirect co-perpetratorship.[38]

One can wonder to what extent the increasingly flexible approach by judges in relation to modes of liabilities in the early stages of the proceedings and during trial affects the work of the OTP during the preliminary examination. Pre-Trial Chambers initially refused to confirm multiple modes of liability, considering that a person could not be considered to be both a direct perpetrator and an accomplice of the commission of a crime. For example, Pre-Trial Chamber II in 2011 held that: "Although the Prosecutor may generally charge in the alternative, he should be consistent throughout his Application about the actual mode(s) of liability that he intends to present to the Chamber. Moreover, the possibility for the Prosecutor to charge in the alternative does not necessarily mean that the Chamber has to respond in the same manner. In particular, the Chamber is not persuaded that it is best practice to make simultaneous findings on modes of liability presented in the alternative. A person cannot be deemed concurrently as a principal and an accessory to the same crime".[39] Starting with the *Ntaganda* confirmation of charges decision,[40] Pre-Trial Chambers started to accept that cumulative modes of liability could be confirmed. The consequence of this flexibility is that there is no incentive, from the prosecution perspective, to focus too much attention on modes of liability during the preliminary examination (this is equally true during the confirmation of charges hearing and even the trial).

To this situation must be added the pervasive use of Regulation 55 in most cases at the ICC thus far, which allows the Chamber to consider a legal re-characterization of the facts to fit another crime or mode of liability than the one charged. The result of this legal framework is that there is

---

[38] There is some indication of such an alleged coordinated plan in the Burundi decision of 25 October 2017, but it is unclear whether the Chamber has drawn such conclusions, or whether they were initially put forward by the OTP in its request.

[39] ICC, Situation in the Republic of Kenya, *Prosecutor v. William Samoei Ruto, Henry Kiprono Kosgey and Joshua Arap Sang*, PTC II, Decision on the Prosecutor's Application for Summons to Appear for William Samoei Ruto, Henry Kiprono Kosgey and Joshua Arap Sang, 8 March 2011, ICC-02/11-3, para. 36 (http://www.legal-tools.org/doc/6c9fb0/).

[40] ICC, Situation in the Democratic Republic of Congo, *The Prosecutor v. Bosco Ntaganda*, PTC II, Decision Pursuant to Article 61(7)(a) and (b) of the Rome Statute on the Charges of the Prosecutor Against Bosco Ntaganda, 9 June 2014, ICC-01/04-02/06-309 (http://www.legal-tools.org/doc/5686c6/).

less emphasis on the requirement for the prosecution to be specific about the modes of liability at any stage of the proceedings, which necessarily affects its work during the preliminary examination.[41] This is not merely a procedural development, it says something about how these trials and how the role of the alleged perpetrator are perceived. Indeed, to put it simply, modes of liability are often seen as a mere technical hindrance on the implementation of the principle that the perpetrators must have done something wrong. Again, given the possibility that Regulation 55 might be used up until the final stages of the proceedings, there is less need for the Prosecution to be precise in relation to modes of liability during the trial, which necessarily changes how these questions are approached during the preliminary examination.

A second takeaway from the OTP practice is that there does not seem to be a unified practice when it comes to identifying specific individuals within the request for authorization.[42] While no individual was named in the Kenya and Comoros situations, the same is not true in the Côte d'Ivoire and Georgia requests.

One can wonder if there should there be a unified practice at all? Possibly not, to the extent that the content of the request will depend on the availability of information on details of perpetrators in one situation but not another.

One risk of identifying certain possible perpetrators in the request, especially if they come from only one side of the conflict, is that it might suggest an imbalance in the approach of the OTP to the investigation, which might affect its credibility and legitimacy. The OTP could answer that this naming takes place in the context of a preliminary examination, and therefore does not provide any conclusion on the responsibility of the given individual. While technically true, this answer ignores the symbolic function of the work of the ICC and the disconnect between the legal na-

---

[41] Ironically, one of the justifications for Regulation 55 was that it would compel the OTP to be more precise in its charging policy. In fact, the exact opposite has occurred and the use of Regulation 55 has led to less specificity in both the charging policy and the charges confirmed. On Regulation 55, see Dov Jacobs, "A Shifting Scale of Power: who is in charge of the charges at the international criminal court", in William Schabas, Yvonne McDermott and Niamh Hayes, (eds.), *The Ashgate Research Companion to International Criminal Law*, Ashgate, 2013, p. 205.

[42] With the caveat that the analysis is based on publicly available documents.

---

ture of a procedure and the way it might be perceived from the outside. The fact that an official document issued by the OTP mentions a particular individual will necessarily give the impression that this individual is already the target of the OTP, as early as the preliminary examination. To avoid this risk, the OTP could possibly adopt a policy of generally not mentioning any names in the requests to open formal investigations, at least publicly.[43]

28.4. Admissibility and the Potential Defendant

Besides jurisdiction, another criterion to be taken into account during the preliminary examination is whether the case would be admissible under Article 17.[44] As part of this assessment, the Prosecutor is bound to verify whether domestic investigations and prosecutions exist, and, if they do, whether they are conducted in respect of certain individuals which could, at a later stage, be potential defendants before the ICC. Another aspect of the admissibility test is gravity and this might also involve the determination of potential defendants. This section will address these two aspects in turn, before providing a short critical assessment. It should be noted that the following discussion focuses exclusively on the core of this chapter, that is, whether potential perpetrators are identified during this phase of the proceedings. It does not purport to provide a general discussion of the admissibility test and how it is applied, which would be beyond the scope of this chapter.

28.4.1. Identifying alleged perpetrators when assessing complementarity.

This section will first highlight OTP official policy in that respect, before looking at how it applied in OTP requests to open an investigation and how the various Chambers have decided on the matter.

28.4.1.1. OTP Policy

In relation to complementarity, the OTP Policy Paper on Preliminary Examinations indicates that: "At the preliminary examination stage there is

---

[43] It should be noted here that the question here is whether potential perpetrators should be named in the request, not whether they should be the subject of the preliminary examination or even be approached in that context. As noted below, they should (Section 28.5.).

[44] ICC Statute, Article 53(1)(b), see *supra* note 5.

not yet a 'case', as understood to comprise an identified set of incidents, suspects and conduct. Therefore the consideration of admissibility (complementarity and gravity) will take into account potential cases that could be identified in the course of the preliminary examination based on the information available and that would likely arise from an investigation into the situation".[45]

The OTP later clarifies that: "Where there are or have been national investigations or prosecutions, the Office shall examine whether such proceedings relate to potential cases being examined by the Office and in particular, whether the focus is on those most responsible for the most serious crimes committed",[46] a statement corresponding to "its stated policy of focussing on those bearing the greatest responsibility for the most serious crimes".[47]

Nevertheless, nowhere in the policy paper is there any explanation as to what is meant by "those bearing the greatest responsibility", which is problematic given the somewhat subjective moral assessment that is required for such a determination. Does one focus on the direct perpetrators, or on those possibly higher up in the command structure, which seems to be a traditionally accepted way to understand the concept of "those bearing the greatest responsibility" in international criminal law?

The Regulations of the OTP do not shed light on the issue, merely indicating that: "The joint team shall review the information and evidence collected and shall determine a provisional case hypothesis (or hypotheses) identifying the incidents to be investigated and the person or persons who appear to be the most responsible".[48]

The 2016-2018 OTP Strategic Plan issued in 2016 provides the following explanation: "Where deemed appropriate, the Office will implement a building-upwards strategy by first investigating and prosecuting a limited number of mid- and high-level perpetrators in order to ultimately have a reasonable prospect of conviction for the most responsible. Pursuing this in-depth and open-ended approach, the Office will first focus on a wide range of crimes to properly identify organisations, structures and

---

[45] OTP, *Policy Paper on Preliminary Examinations*, para. 43, see *supra* note 19.
[46] *Ibid.*, para. 49.
[47] *Ibid.*, para. 45.
[48] Regulations, Regulation 34, see *supra* note 22.

---

individuals allegedly responsible for their commission. It will then consider mid- and high level perpetrators in its investigation and prosecution strategies to build the evidentiary foundations for subsequent case(s) against those most responsible. The Office will also consider prosecuting lower level perpetrators where their conduct was particularly grave and has acquired extensive notoriety".[49]

This explanation calls for two remarks. First, it shows a desire on the part of the OTP not to provide a clear and objective definition of who is considered to be the most responsible, even if the suggestion seems to be here that "most responsible" is somehow linked to the position of the perpetrator. Second, whatever is meant by "most responsible" it is not seen as a limiting criteria on who might actually be prosecuted, given that all levels of perpetrators might be a target for the OTP.[50]

The will on the part of the OTP to keep their options open is further confirmed in the Policy Paper on Case Selection and Prioritisation issued in 2016, where it is indicated that: "The notion of the most responsible does not necessarily equate with the *de jure* hierarchical status of an individual within a structure, but will be assessed on a case-by-case basis depending on the evidence. As the investigation progresses, the extent of responsibility of any identified alleged perpetrator(s) will be assessed on the basis of, *inter alia*, the nature of the unlawful behaviour; the degree of

---

[49] OTP, Strategic plan 2016–2018, 6 July 2015, p. 16 (http://www.legal-tools.org/doc/7ae957/).

[50] One could also question the fact that case selection might be based on the fact that conduct has "acquired extensive notoriety". This criterion, which makes prosecution partly dependent on whether a particular situation or case has received media attention, is difficult to justify in light of the complex dynamics which make certain issues newsworthy or not. In that respect, one can note that the Appeals Chamber rejected the idea that the "social alarm" created by a crime could be a relevant factor to be taken into account as part of the gravity assessment. However, more recently, it seems to have received some revival in the Comoros PTC decision, where the Majority expressed the following view: "As a final note, the Chamber cannot overlook the discrepancy between, on the one hand, the Prosecutor's conclusion that the identified crimes were so evidently not grave enough to justify action by the Court, of which the raison d'être is to investigate and prosecute international crimes of concern to the international community, and, on the other hand, the attention and concern that these events attracted from the parties involved, also leading to several fact-finding efforts on behalf of States and the United Nations in order to shed light on the events" (*Situation on registered vessels of the union of the Comoros, the Hellenic Republic of Greece and the Kingdom of Cambodia*, Decision on the request of the Union of the Comoros to review the Prosecutor's decision not to initiate an investigation, para. 51, see *supra* note 3).

their participation and intent; the existence of any motive involving discrimination; and any abuse of power or official capacity".[51]

28.4.1.2. OTP Practice

Does the practice of the OTP provide more clarity?

In the Kenya request, the OTP simply indicates that, "[b]ecause no national investigations or proceedings are pending against those bearing the greatest responsibility for the crimes against humanity allegedly committed, the Prosecutor submits that the cases that would arise from its investigation of the situation would be currently admissible".[52] There is, however, mention of a list of names of those bearing the greatest responsibility for the alleged crimes, established by the Waki Commission and provided in a sealed envelope to the OTP.[53]

In the Côte d'Ivoire request, the Prosecutor seems to have taken a more specific approach by providing a list of names of those it considered to bear the greatest responsibility: "the Prosecution has attached two confidential, ex-parte, annexes. Annex 1B presents a preliminary list of persons or groups belonging to or associated with the pro-Gbagbo and pro-Ouattara sides that appear to bear the greatest responsibility for the most serious crimes, with an indication of their specific role. As set out in the Office's Prosecutorial Strategy, the category of persons bearing the greatest responsibility includes those situated at the highest echelons of responsibility, including those who ordered, financed, or otherwise organized the alleged crimes".[54]

---

[51] OTP, *Policy Paper on Case Selection*, 15 September 2016, para. 43 (http://www.legal-tools.org/doc/182205/). The OTP refers in a footnote to Rules 145(1)(c) and 145(2)(b) of the Rules of Procedure and Evidence as guidance. These provisions relate to sentencing and aggravating circumstances and one can wonder to what extent they should logically be taken into account in the preliminary examination phase, particularly in assessing admissibility of the case. Indeed, if aggravating factors for sentencing are taken into account during case selection, what is the point of having aggravating factors at all in the Statute or RPE? This is true both for complementarity and for gravity, PTCs having themselves had recourse to such criteria in their determination of the gravity of the situation (see for example, Kenya decision, para. 62).

[52] Situation in the Republic of Kenya, Request for authorisation of an investigation pursuant to Article 15, para. 55, see *supra* note 23.

[53] *Ibid.*, para. 15.

[54] Situation in the Republic of Côte d'Ivoire, Request for authorisation of an investigation pursuant to article 15, para. 46, see *supra* note 26.

The mention of this list is, however, preceded by the following caveat: "The Prosecution's selection of the incidents or groups of persons that are likely to shape future case(s) is preliminary in nature and is not binding for future admissibility assessments, meaning that the Prosecution's selection on the basis of these elements for the purposes of defining a potential 'case' for this particular phase may change at a later stage, depending on the development of the investigation".[55] In other words, those which might be the target of a potential prosecution might be subject to change in the course of the actual investigation.

In the remainder of the request, the Prosecutor does not specify what is meant by "those who bear the greatest responsibility", simply concluding that: "Because no national investigations or proceedings are pending in Côte d'Ivoire against those bearing the greatest responsibility for the most serious crimes falling within the jurisdiction of the Court allegedly committed in Côte d'Ivoire since 28 November 2010, the Prosecution submits that the potential cases that would arise from its investigation of the situation would be currently admissible".[56]

In the *Mavi Marmara* report, the OTP provides no direct assessment of those it considered might bear the greatest responsibility for the crimes, although in subsequent proceedings regarding its report, it explained that, albeit in the context of gravity, "the Report shows that the Prosecution expressly considered key indicators in this regard in its gravity analysis – notably, that the available information did not suggest that the Identified Crimes were systematic or resulted from a deliberate plan or policy, having regard especially to the commission of the Identified Crimes on just one of the seven vessels of the flotilla and the manner in which those crimes were committed. These factors suggested that the potential perpetrators of the Identified Crimes were among those who carried out the boarding of the Mavi Marmara, and subsequent operations aboard, but not necessarily other persons further up the chain of command".[57] Further, as "the Report shows, the Prosecution's analysis did not support the view

---

[55] *Ibid.*, para. 45.

[56] *Ibid.*, para. 53.

[57] ICC, *Situation on registered vessels of the union of the Comoros, the Hellenic Republic of Greece and the Kingdom of Cambodia*, Public Redacted Version of Prosecution Response to the Application for Review of its Determination under article 53(1)(b) of the Rome Statute, 30 March 2015, ICC-01/13-14-Red, para. 60 (http://www.legal-tools.org/doc/0e4e4c/).

that there was a reasonable basis to believe that "senior IDF commanders and Israeli leaders" were responsible as perpetrators or planners of the apparent war crimes".[58]

This seems to suggest a rather straightforward approach to "those who bear the greatest responsibility" as being linked to the position within the military command.

In the Georgia request, the Prosecutor annexed an *ex parte* "preliminary list of persons or groups that appear to be the most responsible for the most serious crimes, with an indication of their specific role",[59] but does not provide specific information on this list in the request itself. The discussion on complementarity focuses exclusively on the absence of progress in domestic enquiries and lack of prosecutions.

The Prosecutor also provides a similar caveat as in the Côte d'Ivoire request: "The Prosecution's identification of the incidents or groups of persons that are likely to shape future case(s) is preliminary in nature and should not be considered binding for future admissibility assessments. Should an investigation be authorised, the Prosecution should be permitted to expand or modify its investigation with respect to these or other alleged acts, incidents, groups or persons and/or adopt different legal qualifications, so long as the cases brought forward for prosecution are sufficiently linked to the authorised situation".[60]

In the Afghanistan request, the Prosecutor apparently provided an *ex parte* list of persons or groups most likely to be the object of an investigation,[61] and explains, relying on the case law of the Court, that "as for the level of specificity and detail required to make an admissibility determination, the Prosecution has borne in mind the nature of the present stage, the low evidentiary threshold which applies, and the object and purpose of the article 15 stage".[62]

---

[58] *Ibid.*, para. 62.

[59] Situation in Georgia, Corrected Version of "Request for authorisation of an investigation pursuant to article 15", para. 276, see *supra* note 32.

[60] *Ibid.*, para. 277.

[61] Situation in the Islamic Republic of Afghanistan, Public redacted version of "Request for authorisation of an investigation pursuant to article 15", para. 264, see *supra* note 37.

[62] *Ibid.*, para. 263.

28.4.1.3. ICC Case Law

Given the approach taken by the OTP, it remains to consider how various Chambers have decided upon the issue.

In the 2010 decision to authorize an investigation in the Kenya situation, the Pre-Trial Chamber had to resolve the question of what the admissibility of a "case" could mean at the situation phase and found that: "since it is not possible to have a concrete case involving an identified suspect for the purpose of prosecution, prior to the commencement of an investigation, the admissibility assessment at this stage actually refers to the admissibility of one or more potential cases within the context of a situation".[63]

The Pre-Trial Chamber went on to specify that: "admissibility at the situation phase should be assessed against certain criteria defining a "potential case" such as: (i) the groups of persons involved that are likely to be the focus of an investigation for the purpose of shaping the future case(s); and (ii) the crimes within the jurisdiction of the Court allegedly committed during the incidents that are likely to be the focus of an investigation for the purpose of shaping the future case(s)".[64]

This test is picked up in subsequent case law,[65] but interestingly, no Pre-Trial Chamber has explicitly included in the complementarity branch of admissibility the question of "those bearing the greatest responsibility".[66]

Another interesting point to note in the case law, is that Pre-Trial Chambers are very careful to situate this complementarity assessment in

---

[63] ICC, Situation in the Republic of Kenya, PTC II, Decision Pursuant to Article 15 of the Rome Statute on the Authorization of an Investigation into the Situation in the Republic of Kenya, 31 March 2010, ICC-01/09-19, para. 48 (http://www.legal-tools.org/doc/338a6f/).

[64] *Ibid.*, para. 50.

[65] ICC, Situation in the Republic of Côte d'Ivoire, PTC III, Decision Pursuant to Article 15 of the Rome Statute on the Authorisation of an Investigation into the Situation in the Republic of Côte d'Ivoire, 3 October 2011, ICC-02/11-14, para. 191 (http://www.legal-tools.org/doc/7a6c19/). ICC, Situation in Georgia, PTC, Decision on the Prosecutor's request for authorization of an investigation, ICC-01/15-12, 27 January 2016, para. 37 (http://www.legal-tools.org/doc/a3d07e/).

[66] However, this criteria reemerges in the context of the gravity assessment (see *infra*, Section 24.4.2.).

the context of the preliminary nature of the examination, with the consequence that such assessment is not definitive.

For example, the Pre-Trial Chamber in the Kenya situation found that "the Prosecutor's selection of the incidents or groups of persons that are likely to shape his future case(s) is preliminary in nature and is not binding for future admissibility assessments. This means that the Prosecutor's selection on the basis of these elements for the purposes of defining a potential "case" for this particular phase may change at a later stage, depending on the development of the investigation".[67]

Similarly, the Appeals Chamber has remarked that: "For the purpose of proceedings relating to the initiation of an investigation into a situation (articles 15 and 53 (1) of the Statute), the contours of the likely cases will often be relatively vague because the investigations of the Prosecutor are at their initial stages. The same is true for preliminary admissibility challenges under article 18 of the Statute. Often, no individual suspects will have been identified at this stage, nor will the exact conduct nor its legal classification be clear".[68]

28.4.2. Assessing Gravity

The Regulations of the OTP provide little guidance on how potential defendants are taken into account in the gravity assessment, simply stating that: "In order to assess the gravity of the crimes allegedly committed in

---

[67] Situation in the Republic of Kenya, Decision Pursuant to Article 15 of the Rome Statute on the Authorization of an Investigation into the Situation in the Republic of Kenya, para. 50, see *supra* note 63. This approach was confirmed in the decision to open an investigation in the situation in Burundi: "The Chamber recalls that the Prosecutor's evaluation of these criteria is preliminary in nature and may change as a result of an investigation" (ICC, Situation in the Republic of Burundi, PTC I, Public Redacted Version of "Decision Pursuant to Article 15 of the Rome Statute on the Authorization of an Investigation into the Situation in the Republic of Burundi", 25 October 2017, ICC-01/17-X-9-US-Exp, para. 143 (http://www.legal-tools.org/doc/8f2373/)).

[68] ICC, Situation in the Republic of Kenya, *Prosecutor v. William Samoei Ruto, Henry Kiprono Kosgey and Joshua Arap Sang,* Appeals Chamber, Judgment on the appeal of the Republic of Kenya against the decision of Pre-Trial Chamber II of 30 May 2011 entitled "Decision on the Application by the Government of Kenya Challenging the Admissibility of the Case Pursuant to Article 19(2)(b) of the Statute", 30 August 2011, ICC-01/09-01/11-307, para. 39 (http://www.legal-tools.org/doc/ac5d46/).

the situation the Office shall consider various factors including their scale, nature, manner of commission, and impact".[69]

According to the 2013 policy paper: "The manner of commission of the crimes may be assessed in light of, *inter alia*, the means employed to execute the crime, the degree of participation and intent of the perpetrator (if discernible at this stage), the extent to which the crimes were systematic or result from a plan or organised policy or otherwise resulted from the abuse of power or official capacity, and elements of particular cruelty, including the vulnerability of the victims, any motives involving discrimination, or the use of rape and sexual violence as a means of destroying groups".[70]

This paragraph suggests that the conduct of the potential defendant could be taken into account in several ways: (1) "the degree of participation and intent of the perpetrator" and (2) "the abuse of power or official capacity". It is not entirely clear what these expressions mean, because there is no explanation of what a "degree of intent" is (presumably, there is either criminal intent, or no criminal intent) or what kind of intent would be more or less grave, nor is there a definition of what might constitute "abuse of power or official capacity". Moreover, the policy paper is very clear ("if discernible at this stage") that such determination of the conduct of the potential defendant is not a definitive prerequisite at this stage.

Also interesting to note is that the Prosecutor never puts forward as a distinct gravity criterion the fact that the person might "bear the greatest responsibility". In fact, the OTP, in the policy paper, relies on the case law of the Court to minimize this requirement: "The Appeals Chamber has dismissed the setting of an overly restrictive legal bar to the interpretation of gravity that would hamper the deterrent role of the Court. It has also observed that the role of persons or groups may vary considerably depending on the circumstances of the case and therefore should not be exclusively assessed or predetermined on excessively formulistic grounds".[71]

---

[69]   Regulations, Regulation 29(2), see *supra* note 22.

[70]   OTP, *Policy Paper on Preliminary Examinations*, para. 64, see *supra* note 19.

[71]   *Ibid.*, para. 60.

Indeed, in 2006, the Appeals Chamber had rejected the gravity criteria that the Pre-Trial Chamber had devised of focusing only on highest ranking perpetrators on the basis that: "The predictable exclusion of many perpetrators on the grounds proposed by the Pre-Trial Chamber could severely hamper the preventive, or deterrent, role of the Court which is a cornerstone of the creation of the International Criminal Court, by announcing that any perpetrators other than those at the very top are automatically excluded from the exercise of the jurisdiction of the Court. The particular role of a person or, for that matter, an organization, may vary considerably depending on the circumstances of the case and should not be exclusively assessed or predetermined on excessively formalistic grounds".[72]

Given the minimal importance given by the Prosecutor to the conduct of the potential defendant in the gravity assessment in light of the Appeals Judgment of 2006, it is unsurprising that there is little information on this aspect in the first request filed by the Prosecutor. There is therefore no mention of potential perpetrators in the gravity assessment part of the Kenya request.

However, despite the fact that this was not a criteria relied on by the OTP in its request, the Pre-Trial Chamber considered in the decision to open an investigation that: "As for the first element ["the groups of persons involved that are likely to be the object of an investigation for the purpose of shaping the future case(s)"], the Chamber considers that it involves a generic assessment of whether such groups of persons that are likely to form the object of investigation capture those who may bear the greatest responsibility for the alleged crimes committed. Such assessment should be general in nature and compatible with the pre-investigative stage into a situation".[73]

There is some indication of what is meant by "those who may bear the greatest responsibility" later on in the decision, where the Court notes

---

[72] ICC, Situation in the Democratic Republic of the Congo, Appeals Chamber, Judgment on the Prosecutor's appeal against the decision of Pre-Trial Chamber I entitled "Decision on the Prosecutor's Application for Warrants of Arrest, Article 58", 13 July 2006, ICC-01/04-169, paras. 75–76 (http://www.legal-tools.org/doc/8c20eb/).

[73] Situation in the Republic of Kenya, Decision Pursuant to Article 15 of the Rome Statute on the Authorization of an Investigation into the Situation in the Republic of Kenya, para. 60, see *supra* note 63.

that: "With respect to the first element concerning the groups of persons likely to be the focus of the Prosecutor's future investigations, the supporting material refers to their high-ranking positions, and their alleged role in the violence, namely inciting, planning, financing, colluding with criminal gangs, and otherwise contributing to the organization of the violence".[74] This seems to suggest that the high-ranking position of the potential defendant is a key element in the determination made by the Chamber. This appears, on the face of it, at odds with the Appeals Chamber decision from 2006 quoted previously. The fact that the Pre-Trial Chamber was applying the test at the "situation" phase rather than at the "case" does not affect this apparent discrepancy in the case law, because the underlying rationale of the Appeals Chamber was to avoid sending out a message that lower level perpetrators would not be prosecuted before the ICC, a rationale which applies whether at the situation phase or the case phase.

Following this decision, the OTP logically adopted the criteria as his own in subsequent requests,[75] noting each time that potential defendants were high-ranking officials, persons in position of command or persons with levels of responsibility in the commission of the crimes.[76] And all decisions authorizing an investigation so far have applied this criterion consistently.

One decision that stands out in that respect is the decision requesting the Prosecutor to reconsider its decision not to open an investigation in the *Mavi Marmara* situation. As noted above, the Prosecutor had indicated, in considering that the situation did not meet the gravity threshold, that no "'senior IDF commanders and Israeli leaders' were responsible as

---

[74] *Ibid.*, para. 198.

[75] Situation in the Republic of Côte d'Ivoire, Request for authorisation of an investigation pursuant to article 15, para. 55, see *supra* note 26; Situation in the Islamic Republic of Afghanistan, Public redacted version of "Request for authorisation of an investigation pursuant to article 15", para. 336, see *supra* note 37.

[76] Situation in the Republic of Côte d'Ivoire, Request for authorisation of an investigation pursuant to article 15, para. 57, see *supra* note 26; Situation in Georgia, Corrected Version of "Request for authorisation of an investigation pursuant to article 15", para. 337, see *supra* note 32; Situation in the Islamic Republic of Afghanistan, Public redacted version of "Request for authorisation of an investigation pursuant to article 15", para. 338, see *supra* note 37.

---

perpetrators or planners of the apparent war crimes".[77] The Pre-Trial Chamber did not find this determinative. It held instead that:

> Contrary to the Prosecutor's argument at paragraph 62 of her Response, the conclusion in the Decision Not to Investigate that there was not a reasonable basis to believe that "senior IDF commanders and Israeli leaders" were responsible as perpetrators or planners of the identified crimes does not answer the question at issue, which relates to the Prosecutor's ability to investigate and prosecute those being the most responsible for the crimes under consideration and not as such to the seniority or hierarchical position of those who may be responsible for such crimes. [...] there appears to be no reason, in the present circumstances and in light of the parameters of the referral and scope of the Court's jurisdiction, to consider that an investigation into the situation referred by the Comoros could not lead to the prosecution of those persons who may bear the greatest responsibility for the identified crimes committed during the seizure of the Mavi Marmara by the IDF.[78]

This decision seems to be at odds with prior case law of the assessment of gravity at the situation phase.[79] Moreover, the assertion that the investigation would lead to the prosecution of those who bear the greatest responsibility for the identified crimes, when stripped of any qualifier (such as rank), is somewhat empty. Indeed, it is obvious that, taken in its literal sense, an OTP investigation will focus on those most responsible for the commission of a crime (as opposed to those not responsible). That is not a gravity criterion, that is common sense. As a result, the Pre-Trial Chamber in the Comoros situation, rather than just doing away with the

---

[77] *Situation on registered vessels of the union of the Comoros, the Hellenic Republic of Greece and the Kingdom of Cambodia*, Public Redacted Version of Prosecution Response to the Application for Review of its Determination under article 53(1)(b) of the Rome Statute, para. 62, see *supra* note 57.

[78] *Situation on registered vessels of the union of the Comoros, the Hellenic Republic of Greece and the Kingdom of Cambodia*, Decision on the request of the Union of the Comoros to review the Prosecutor's decision not to initiate an investigation, paras. 23–24, see *supra* note 3.

[79] Interestingly, one Judge, Cuno Tarfusser, sat both on the PTC in the Kenya situation, where the high-ranking level of potential Accused was initially adopted as a gravity criteria, and on the Comoros Bench, which rejects it.

---

requirement that the investigation focus on "those who may bear the greatest responsibility", kept it, but emptied it of any meaning.

28.4.3. Critical Evaluation

In light of the current practice at the ICC, one could raise doubts on the opportunity of devolving so much time and resources to a determination of admissibility at such an early stage of the proceedings, during the preliminary examination.

28.4.3.1. Is a Determination of Admissibility a Legal Requirement during a Preliminary Examination?

It is not entirely clear from the Rome Statute that such an assessment is legally required. Of course, Article 53 does explicitly mention the question of future admissibility of a case as an element to take into account in deciding whether to open an investigation. However, this should not be equated with a *legal* requirement. Indeed, as noted previously, Article 53 has a dual nature in the Rome Statute depending on the existence of a judicial control over prosecutorial discretion. Moreover, it can be noted, specifically in the context of *proprio motu* investigations, that Article 15(4) tasks the Pre-Trial Chamber explicitly to verify "that there is a reasonable basis to proceed with an investigation, and that the case appears to fall within the jurisdiction of the Court", not to verify admissibility.[80]

What led to this situation is probably a confusion between, on the one hand, the OTP having to take into account whether a case would be admissible as a policy consideration in deciding whether to open an investigation, which is what the Statute says in our view, and on the other hand, the idea that opening an investigation actually requires a formal determination of admissibility, which, in our view is not the case. Indeed, it is not for the OTP to decide whether a case is admissible or not, it is part of the judicial function. This conclusion that an admissibility determination is in fact not a formal legal requirement to open an investigation also finds some support in the case law of the Court.

---

[80] In that respect, while beyond the scope of the current contribution, one can question how the PTC interpreted the Statute in order to determine that the language of Article 17 (relating to the admissibility of a "case") could somewhat be applied in the "situation" phase because the drafters somehow decided to let the Judges decide such an important matter.

For example, in deciding that the Pre-Trial Chamber decision for the Prosecutor to reconsider its decision not to open an investigation in the Comoros situation was unappealable, the Appeals Chamber clearly said that the impugned decision, even though it used the language of admissibility, was not strictly a decision on admissibility that could be appealed under Article 82(1)(a) of the Rome Statute.[81]

A more striking example is the decision allowing the Prosecutor to open an investigation in Georgia. In that decision, the Chamber was not in a position of making a definitive finding that potential cases that were being investigated in Russia would be admissible at the ICC. However, instead of either requesting further information or declaring the potential cases inadmissible, the Chamber allowed the Prosecutor to proceed, including on those contentious cases, pushing back to the formal determination of admissibility to a later stage: "It is therefore more appropriate to allow the Prosecutor to conduct her investigation, which will naturally extend to issues of admissibility, and for the question to be authoritatively resolved at a later stage if needed".[82]

Finally, it is difficult to argue that a determination of admissibility is a legal requirement to be satisfied to open an investigation, while at the same time accepting that, during the actual investigation, the OTP is free to completely change the parameters of potential cases, or even choose entirely different cases than the ones he put forward when deciding to open an investigation, which is the current situation today, as noted previously. If the determination of the admissibility of potential cases was legally decisive in deciding to open an investigation, then, at minimum, the OTP should be bound to stick to those potential cases during the formal investigations. This would obviously be contrary to prosecutorial discretion in choosing specific cases to pursue and therefore reinforces the conclusion that admissibility during the preliminary examination is at best a policy consideration.

---

[81] ICC, *Situation on registered vessels of the union of the Comoros, the Hellenic Republic of Greece and the Kingdom of Cambodia*, Appeals Chamber, Decision on the admissibility of the Prosecutor's appeal against the "Decision on the request of the Union of the Comoros to review the Prosecutor's decision not to initiate an investigation", 6 November 2015, ICC-01/13-51 (http://www.legal-tools.org/doc/a43856/).

[82] Situation in Georgia, Decision on the Prosecutor's request for authorization of an investigation, para. 46, see *supra* note 65.

28.4.3.2. Does a Discussion of Admissibility Have Any Practical Merit during a Preliminary Examination?

Even if one were to consider that a judicial determination, or at the very least a judicial discussion, of admissibility was required during a preliminary examination, one can wonder if it has any value in the current situation.

Indeed, given the OTP's discretion to determine the scope of potential cases, it will always be in a position to frame its request in order to make the situation as a whole admissible by focusing on those cases that – in the event that there are or have been relevant domestic prosecutions – are not being dealt with by domestic authorities. This applies equally to the gravity assessment because the Prosecutor simply has to claim to want to focus ultimately on those persons holding positions of responsibility within a State or organization.

Ultimately, as noted above, because the Prosecutor has full discretion to choose what cases to prosecute within a given situation, it does not seem to make much sense to devote so much time discussing the admissibility of 'potential cases' in the abstract during the preliminary examination.

Avoiding discussions on the admissibility of potential cases might also contribute to reducing the length of preliminary examinations, which is a common criticism. Indeed, the length of preliminary examinations to date seems to be in part due to, on the one hand, the difficulty in obtaining relevant information about domestic proceedings for the purpose of determining the admissibility of potential cases and, on the other, to the 'positive complementarity' approach adopted by the OTP in a number of situations, notably Colombia.[83]

28.5. The Status of the 'Accused' during a Preliminary Examination

As noted in Section 28.1., it is difficult to identify the exact position of the potential defendant during a preliminary examination, when alleged perpetrators are normally not the primary focus of the OTP's enquiry. The Rome Statute is silent on this issue, notably because the preliminary ex-

---

[83] Annie Pues, "Towards the 'Golden Hour': A Critical Exploration of the Length of Preliminary Examinations", in *Journal of International Criminal Justice*, 2017, vol. 15, p. 440.

amination is mostly not *per se* subject to the judicial process.[84] This does not mean that interaction with potential defendants cannot be subject to some judicial framework, even in this early phase of the proceedings, particularly through the operation of Article 55 of the Rome Statute. Moreover, taking things forward, there should be some thought into addressing the particular position of the potential defendant during the preliminary examination and providing some specific legal status for him or her to be heard by the OTP.

28.5.1. The Importance of Taking into Account the Potential Defendant during the Preliminary Examination

It is our opinion that from a policy perspective, the OTP could and should try to open lines of communication with possible perpetrators identified during a preliminary examination. This is a safeguard for the quality of a preliminary examination and further down the line for the quality of a formal investigation and for the proceedings as a whole.

If the OTP is allowed to reach out, in a defined framework, to a potential perpetrator during a preliminary examination,[85] it will inevitably spur the OTP do to so. Thus the OTP will be able, from the very beginning, to concretely assess the seriousness of the information received. Indeed, once the OTP has analysed all the information received from a broad spectrum of different sources, even from a potential perpetrator, it can have a clearer picture of what might have taken place in a specific country at a specific time and then the OTP can decide on solid grounds if it wishes to open an formal investigation or not. Plus, the OTP would be beyond reproach of any bias and there would be no doubt that starting from the preliminary examination it is examining incriminating and exonerating circumstances equally. Analysing a situation taking into account only 'one side of the story' bears an inherent risk of prejudice. This is why the OTP should always balance incriminating evidence that is presented to them with exonerating information at their disposal. To be beyond any reproach and fulfil their duty as officers of the Court, the OTP has to examine equally all obtainable information from the very start. It is the duty of the OTP on a policy and legal level to ensure that the rights of a poten-

---

[84] See *supra* Section 24.1.

[85] As we are going to explore the different statuses of a person who is targeted during a preliminary investigation we will refer to this person as a *potential perpetrator*.

tial perpetrator are respected from the very beginning. In doing so the right to a fair trial is also ensured from the beginning. The OTP cannot, especially at such an early stage, ignore the presumption of innocence of potential perpetrators. To build a case in an unprejudiced manner the OTP has to explore all the leads at their disposal and the potential perpetrator is undeniably one of those leads. Finally, it would benefit the Court as a whole because making sure a potential perpetrator can fully exercise his or her rights from the beginning of the proceedings is essential in giving meaning to rights that are enshrined in the Rome Statute and is essential to make sure that the ICC adheres to its own values.

More specifically, if a person is targeted during a preliminary examination because, for example, victims or NGOs are accusing him or her of being the perpetrator of a crime, he or she should have the opportunity to put forward his or her side of the story. This is even more so during a preliminary examination, which often occurs in a context broadly covered by the media and thus the opinion of the international community is usually already decided. In such a context, it is critical that the prosecution does not assume that the allegations presented to his or her office are well-founded. It is then the duty of the OTP to examine the situation impartially and seriously. Only then can the OTP decide if it is reasonable to open a formal investigation.

Article 15(2) provides: "The Prosecutor shall analyse the seriousness of the information received. For this purpose, he or she may seek additional information from States, organs of the United Nations, inter-governmental or non-governmental organizations, or other reliable sources that he or she deems appropriate, and may receive written or oral testimony at the seat of the Court". It is not because the Article does not expressly mention the potential defendant that he or she is not a reliable or appropriate source. Quite on the contrary, keeping a balance between opposing parties is crucial to maintain a non-biased approach to the situation at hand. In addition, not opening such lines of communication with all parties to a conflict, including possible perpetrators, might give rise to the question of whether the fact that the person that was targeted during a preliminary examination without having been heard or put in a position to defend him or herself is the reason why a formal investigation might have been opened in the first place. If the potential perpetrator that was targeted during a preliminary examination had been able to give valuable information to the OTP during a preliminary examination some or maybe all allegations might have appeared unfounded. In addition, denying the possibility to a potential perpetrator targeted during a preliminary examination to be heard may be counterproductive as suspicion of bias may arise.

But, of course, the question is now, in what capacity should he or she have been approached? A witness? A suspect? A defendant? One could consider that once a formal investigation is opened, his legal status will become clearer and so might his rights. But is it not too late? And how does the OTP have a clearer picture of the situation at hand if they do not reach out to one of the main actors of the situation they are investigating?

28.5.2. The Applicability and Scope of Article 55 during the Preliminary Examination

One provision of the Rome Statute which can arguable apply during the preliminary examination to provide some protection to the potential defendant is Article 55 which concerns the "rights of persons during an investigation" and provides that:

1. In respect of an investigation under this Statute, a person:

     (a) Shall not be compelled to incriminate himself or herself or to confess guilt;

     (b) Shall not be subjected to any form of coercion, duress or threat, to torture or to any other form of cruel, inhuman or degrading treatment or punishment;

     (c) Shall, if questioned in a language other than a language the person fully understands and speaks, have, free of any cost, the assistance of a competent interpreter and such translations as are necessary to meet the requirements of fairness; and

     (d) Shall not be subjected to arbitrary arrest or detention, and shall not be deprived of his or her liberty except on such grounds and in accordance with such procedures as are established in this Statute.

It is not entirely clear during what phase of the proceedings this provision applies. On the face of it, this provision seems to apply during "an investigation", which suggests that it would not apply during the preliminary examination. Such a reading, however, would lead to strange results.[86] Indeed, contrary to when a Pre-Trial Chamber authorizes the opening of an investigation under Article 15, there is no formal (that is, judicially controlled) moment when an investigation is opened, which would render the temporal scope of the protection of this Article ambivalent. Persons should have the same protection, irrespective of the trigger mechanism used. Moreover, a broad interpretation would be justified by the application of Article 21(3) of the Rome Statute which provides that: "the interpretation and the application of law pursuant to this article must be consistent with internationally recognized human rights".

There is little case law on the application of this article. However, it is interesting to note that in *Gbagbo*, the defence had argued that after his arrest on the 11 April 2011, Laurent Gbagbo had been detained without proper due process (access to courts, access to his lawyers) and that the circumstances of his detention constituted cruel and unusual punishment akin to torture, because he was held in poor facilities, in isolation and little access to the outside world, despite his dire health conditions.[87]

The defence argued that Laurent Gbagbo should benefit from the protection of Article 55 from his arrest up until his surrendering to the Court in November 2011.[88] This period covered the preliminary examination which was only transformed into a formal investigation in October 2011, with the decision of the Pre-Trial Chamber to authorize a formal investigation, following a request that was submitted in June 2011. In its decision, the Pre-Trial Chamber at least implicitly accepted that this provision could apply before the opening of a formal investigation. Indeed, it rejected the defence's claim that Article 55 applied, not on the basis that it did not apply during the preliminary examination, but because the defence had not, according to the Judges, established that the alleged violations of Laurent Gbagbo's rights could be linked to the OTP.[89] This suggests that

---

[86] Christopher K. Hall and Dov Jacobs, "Article 55", in Otto Triffterer and Kai Ambos (eds.), *Rome Statute of the International Criminal Court, A Commentary*, C.H. Beck, Hart, Nomos, 2016, p. 1397.

[87] ICC, Situation in Côte d'Ivoire, *The Prosecutor v. Laurent Gbagbo*, Corrigendum of the challenge to the jurisdiction of the International Criminal Court on the basis of articles 12(3), 19(2), 21(3), 55 and 59 of the Rome Statute filed by the Defence for President Gbagbo (ICC-02/11-01/11-129), 29 May 2012, ICC-02/11-01/11-129-Corr-tENG (http://www.legal-tools.org/doc/1a94c2/).

[88] *Ibid.*

[89] *Ibid.*, para. 97.

---

the Pre-Trial Chamber accepts that, on principle, the Article does apply during the preliminary examination.

If the provision applies, under what conditions can it be invoked? The *Gbagbo* case provides yet again some guidance in that respect. In that case, the defence had invoked a general obligation on the part of the prosecution to ensure that a person of interest for the OTP has his rights respected, for example, to enquire whether Laurent Gbagbo was detained under adequate conditions. The defence argued that Laurent Gbagbo was clearly held in custody for the purposes of being sent to the ICC and that this could be deduced easily from statements made by Ivorian officials at the time.[90] This was combined with the fact that, at the time, there was clear evidence that Laurent Gbagbo was already an identified target for the OTP.[91] The conclusion of the defence was therefore that Laurent Gbagbo fell under the protection of Article 55.

The Chamber adopted a stricter test than the one proposed by the defence and found that the protection of Article 55 only arose if it were established that the alleged human rights violations had been committed either by the OTP or by Ivorian authorities on the OTP's behest.[92]

In the case at hand, the reasoning of the Chamber was as follows: "With respect to the allegations of the Defence, the Chamber considers it decisive that the alleged violations of article 55(1) of the Statute were not perpetrated by the Prosecutor or by the Ivorian authorities on behalf of the Prosecutor or any organ of the Court. The Chamber in fact notes that Mr Gbagbo was arrested in the course of an operation carried out, as the Defence points out, by Mr Ouattara's forces. He was subsequently transferred to the north of Côte d'Ivoire and kept in detention there. Thus, the information provided shows that Mr Gbagbo was arrested and detained by

---

[90] *Ibid.*

[91] *Ibid.*, para. 236. See Section 24.5. *infra.* While the evidence might have been considered as circumstantial at the time, it is interesting to note that recent information seems to suggest more clearly that Laurent Gbagbo was indeed held by Ivorian authorities at the request of the Prosecutor of the ICC from the moment of his arrest (see Fanny Pigeaud, "Procès Gbagbo: les preuves d'un montage", in *Mediapart*, 5 October 2017).

[92] ICC, Situation in Côte d'Ivoire, *The Prosecutor v. Laurent Gbagbo*, PTC I, Decision on the "Corrigendum of the challenge to the jurisdiction of the International Criminal Court on the basis of articles 12(3), 19(2), 21(3), 55 and 59 of the Rome Statute filed by the Defence for President Gbagbo (ICC-02/11-01/11-129)", 15 August 2012, ICC-02/11-01/11-212, para. 9 (http://www.legal-tools.org/doc/0d14c3/).

the Ivorian authorities and subsequently charged with economic crimes in circumstances seemingly unconnected to the proceedings before the Court. Article 55(1) of the Statute is thus not applicable".[93]

The reasoning of the Chamber can be challenged on a number of levels. First, the emphasis of the Chamber on the way Laurent Gbagbo was arrested is misplaced given that his subsequent custody was, as noted previously, arguably entirely aimed at ultimately sending him to the ICC. There is no logical reason why the protection of Article 55 should depend on such a contingent factor as whether the Prosecutor has to officially ask for a person to be put in custody (which might trigger the protection of Article 55) or whether the person just happens to be in custody already (which would not trigger the protection of Article 55). Second, the fact that Laurent Gbagbo was being prosecuted domestically for economic crimes is not persuasive. Indeed, not only is that not incompatible with the fact that the person can also be the object of an investigation from the OTP, but in the Ivory Coast case, the Ivorian authorities explicitly excluded grave crimes to avoid any admissibility problems at the ICC.[94] It is thus somewhat ironic that the judges took into account the fact that Laurent Gbagbo was charged with economic crimes "in circumstances seemingly unconnected to the proceedings before the Court", when these charges were designed specifically with the proceedings before the Court in mind. Third, it seems rather restrictive to require that the Prosecutor directly commit or order others to violate a person's human rights. As noted elsewhere: "It is less than likely that the Prosecutor will directly order a person to be tortured. More likely, the person will be subject to mistreatment by national authorities without any formal link with the Prosecutor being established. In light of this, it would be more in conformity with the broad protection enshrined in article 55 for the Court to consider that once a person is under investigation, they fall under the protection of the ICC and that the Prosecutor has a duty to ensure that the

---

[93] *Ibid.*, para. 97.

[94] Situation in Côte d'Ivoire, Corrigendum of the challenge to the jurisdiction of the International Criminal Court on the basis of articles 12(3), 19(2), 21(3), 55 and 59 of the Rome Statute filed by the Defence for President Gbagbo (ICC-02/11-01/11-129), para. 245, see *supra* note 87.

rights of that person, especially if they are being detained, are respected by the local authorities".[95]

28.5.3. A New Formal Status for Potential Defendants?

On the one hand, opening lines of communication with a potential perpetrator could benefit the quality of the preliminary examination as it allows the OTP to conduct an unprejudiced preliminary examination. On the other hand, if one of the targeted perpetrators of a preliminary examination is interviewed, this might constitute a risk for him or her in the future. For example, what he or she might say could be used against him or her later in a formal investigation. The OTP may also argue that if one of their staff wants to meet with a potential perpetrator it might constitute a risk for them. And this might be true in some circumstances, because a person interviewed by the OTP during a preliminary examination can thereafter allege that he or she was coerced, that his or her rights might not have been respected, and so on. Safeguards for the OTP and the potential perpetrator are a necessity. This is why the status and thus the rights of these targeted perpetrators, which until now have been invisible, should be clarified. For example, if approached by the OTP, they should be informed in detail of the risks of meeting with the OTP, the risk of testifying and certainly the possibility to be assisted by counsel, just to mention some obvious rights.

Therefore, it is fundamental that if the lines of communication between the OTP and the potential perpetrator where to be opened more than they are today, this should occur in a defined legal framework. The person should have a specific status and the Rome Statute should guarantee his or her rights. Some will argue that the person may not be a suspect yet. But this really depends on the situation; from one preliminary examination to another it can be clear if a person is already targeted by the OTP. But assuming that we are in the situation in which a person is clearly under suspicion during a preliminary examination, we consider that it should be formally announced to that person. As a suspect, he or she should benefit from all the rights provided by Article 55 of the Rome Statute, waiting for a formal investigation is too late and is simply ignoring the power of the OTP during a preliminary examination.

---

[95] Christopher K. Hall and Dov Jacobs, 2016, para. 4, see *supra* note 86.

The rights provided by Article 55 of the Rome Statute can be considered roughly to be an equivalent of the 'Miranda rights'[96] in the United States. There, if a person is in police custody or is being interrogated by the police, he or she is considered a suspect and as a suspect he or she has to receive the *Miranda* warnings. The same situation should apply at the ICC.

Meeting with a suspect that is targeted during a preliminary examination must be feasible thus there must be a legal framework that allows the OTP to meet with that person. And we should emphasize that a preliminary examination by the OTP covers, by definition, potential grave crimes. In these circumstances it is even more crucial to protect the target of a preliminary examination if he or she would to be interviewed by the OTP. He or she cannot be simply treated as a 'person of interest' (who has no specific rights) or even a witness. There must be a balance between the benefits for the OTP to interview a target of their preliminary examination and the rights of that person.

The status of '*témoin assisté*'[97] (assisted witness) in France is an interesting example in helping to determine what the status of a person targeted during a preliminary examination might be. The *témoin assisté* is a person that is under investigation by an investigative judge[98] but that has not been indicted yet. This person is considered a *témoin assisté* because he or she has been specifically named either by a victim or in a criminal complaint.[99] The *témoin assisté* has more rights than a simple witness but

---

[96] United States Supreme Court, *Miranda v. Arizona*, Judgment, 13 June 1966, 384 U.S. 436:
You have the right to remain silent;
Anything you say can be used against you in a court of law;
You have the right to consult with a lawyer and have that lawyer present during the interrogation;
If you cannot afford a lawyer, one will be appointed to represent you;
You can invoke your right to be silent before or during an interrogation, and if you do so, the interrogation must stop.
You can invoke your right to have an attorney present, and until your attorney is present, the interrogation must stop.

[97] Code de Procédure Pénale, 2 March 1959, Article 113–1 ff (French Criminal Procedure Code) (http://www.legal-tools.org/doc/388101/).

[98] The investigative Judge in France (Juge d'instruction) is in charge of investigation only concerning crimes (not for felonies) (French Criminal Procedure Code, Article 79, see *supra* note 97) and he has to investigate incriminating and exonerating circumstances equally.

[99] French Criminal Procedure Code, Article 113–2, see *supra* note 97.

less than a person that has been indicted. For example, the *témoin assisté* has to be heard in the presence of his or her lawyer, the *témoin assisté* has the right to be confronted to the person that accuses him or her and the *témoin assisté* can see part of the evidence collected by the investigating judge. But the *témoin assisté* cannot request that investigative steps be undertaken. The *témoin assisté* does, however, have the ability to request to be indicted because then he would benefit from all the rights guaranteed to the defence (and not just some of them).[100] This is an interesting example, because during a preliminary examination it is unavoidable that victims or NGOs will expressly name some people as being perpetrators. Sometimes, it is also possible that a situation will be referred to by a State Party that will identify by name who they think are responsible.[101] Sometimes, it also possible that the Prosecutor him or herself makes it clear whom he or she is targeting during the preliminary examination (as in the Ivory Coast situation).[102] In those circumstances, if the Prosecutor, like the French investigative judge, would like to reach out to the potential perpetrator, he should be able to so in a determined legal framework that would guarantee the rights of the 'suspect' or the '*témoin assisté*'.

Acknowledging the existence of these potential perpetrators of a preliminary examination and his or her rights is also fundamental because sometimes the time lapse between a preliminary examination and a formal investigation can be short. Until now, in most cases, the time lapse between the two is quite long, but this is not always the case. In the *Gbagbo* case, for example, it went very quickly: three months. This short time-lapse is not surprising as the OTP was already making statements targeting Laurent Gbagbo just before its request to the Pre-Trial Chamber for leave to open a formal investigation. In the case, Laurent Gbagbo could already be considered a defendant more than a suspect or '*témoin assisté*'. In such a situation, it would have been beneficial to Laurent Gbagbo to be officially informed (not by the press) that he was a target of the OTP's preliminary examination. And if Laurent Gbagbo's status during the preliminary examination was recognized in some way, he and his lawyers could have chosen to act in a determined legal framework. Instead, he was

---

[100] French Criminal Procedure Code, Article 113-6, see *supra* note 97.

[101] See for example, Situation in Gabon, *Requête aux fins de renvoi d'une situation par un Etat partie auprès du Procureur de la Cour pénale internationale*, see *supra* note 21.

[102] *Infra*, Section 24.5.4.

---

identified as a target by the Prosecutor but invisible in the procedure. For example, what happened to the information and evidence his lawyers send to the OTP within the context of the preliminary examination? And maybe because there was no legal framework the Prosecutor never reached out to the Government of Laurent Gbagbo during the preliminary examination in the Ivory Coast situation. In this particular case, opening lines of communication between the Laurent Gbagbo and the OTP might have been beneficial to the OTP on two different levels: first, the OTP could have interceded with the Ivorian authorities concerning the detention of Laurent Gbagbo in Côte d'Ivoire, and second, the OTP could have obtained, from the very start, information about the rebels that had been active in Ivory Coast for over a decade and committed crimes in Abidjan and the rest of Ivory Coast during the post-electoral crisis.

The quality of the case that has been built during the preliminary examination cannot be stressed enough and the *Gbagbo* case is a clear example of the importance of a real investigation starting from the preliminary examination. Indeed, in the *Gbagbo* case, until now, only one of the two sides to the conflict has been prosecuted as such. What about the other side? The OTP has declared that they will investigate both sides.[103] Until now this has not been the case. During the preliminary examination the OTP exclusively focused on a few specific perpetrators and only on one side. This has impacted the whole proceedings. If, during the preliminary examination the OTP would have opened lines of communications with one of the persons they were targeting, they might have obtained more information about the situation and get a clearer picture of what had happened. Ignoring the potential perpetrator during a preliminary examination is a policy that is not sustainable anymore, especially as it is a reality that the OTP does target specific individuals as of a preliminary examination.

---

[103] ICC, *Prosecutor v. Gbagbo and Blé Goudé*, Transcripts of 28 January 2016, ICC-02/11-01/15-T-9-ENG, p. 42, lines 12–18: "Our investigations in the country are ongoing, but they do take time. And I encourage the people of Côte d'Ivoire to be patient, and I urge the national authorities to continue to cooperate with my office in its activities. My office will seek to ensure justice and accountability on all sides. This should be clear, my office is investigating both sides of the conflict. And this is what the office's legal mandate requires, this is what the victims deserve, and that is what the Prosecution is committed to and is working to achieve." (http://www.legal-tools.org/doc/73746b/).

28.5.4. Illustrating Differences in Approach: The Côte d'Ivoire and Gabon Situations

28.5.4.1. The Côte d'Ivoire Situation: Targeting an Individual with No Communication

In the *Gbagbo* case, it was clear that from the start that the OTP targeted Laurent Gbagbo and members of his government. As early as the preliminary examination, Laurent Gbagbo was presented by the Prosecutor of the ICC as a defendant more than a suspect or a potential target. As a matter of fact, it is our position that for a preliminary examination to be unprejudiced it is unavoidable, even indispensable, that from the moment that the OTP starts examining a situation they will examine who the potential perpetrator of the alleged crimes may be. As we already explained previously, it is hard to build a case or even assess the seriousness of situation where crimes have been committed without mentioning by whom they might have been committed.

During the Ivory Coast preliminary examination, ICC documents and press releases show that the OTP focused from the very beginning on a specific side and that the OTP had already targeted specific individuals during the preliminary examination. For example, in a press release from the OTP dated 21 December 2010, the Prosecutor Luis Moreno-Ocampo made the following statement on the situation in Côte d'Ivoire: "First, let me be clear: I have not yet opened an investigation. But, if serious crimes under my jurisdiction are committed, I will do so. For instance, if as a consequence of Mr. Charles Blé Goudé's speeches, there is massive violence, he could be prosecuted. Secondly, if UN peacekeepers or UN forces are attacked, this could be prosecuted as a different crime. I think African states play a critical role in this, to find a solution to the problem. But if no solution can be found and crimes are committed, African states could be willing to refer the case to my Office and also provide forces to arrest those individuals who commit the crimes in Côte d'Ivoire. Therefore, violence is not an option. Those leaders who are planning violence will end up in the Hague".[104]

The Prosecutor's press release in December 2010 explicitly pointing towards Charles Blé Goudé as a potential perpetrator occurred not

---

[104] ICC, *Statement by ICC Prosecutor Luis Moreno-Ocampo on the situation in Côte d'Ivoire*, 21 December 2010, ICC-OTP-20101221-PR617 (http://www.legal-tools.org/doc/3ffcf8/).

only at a very early stage of the proceedings but at the very beginning of the crisis in Ivory Coast, when there were no elements at the Prosecutor's disposal to determine what was actually going on in Ivory Coast.

After this press release it became clearer that the main target of the preliminary investigation of the OTP was Laurent Gbagbo. For example, during an interview with France 24 as early as January 2011, the Prosecutor warned the Gbagbo camp explicitly and exclusively of the risks of prosecution by the Court.[105] On 7 April 2011 – even before the capture of Laurent Gbagbo by the rebel forces – the Chief of the Situation Analysis Section of the OTP stated that Laurent Gbagbo "may be granted amnesty at the national level, in which case he will not be prosecuted in the national courts, but that will not shield him from prosecution at the international level".[106] This statement is also very clear: the OTP has already taken a stand: Laurent Gbagbo will be the main target of the OTP's preliminary investigation. One must keep in mind that at the moment this statement was made the war in Ivory Coast was not over,[107] so no one in Ivory Coast was in a position to decide if amnesty would be granted to Laurent Gbagbo. This premature statement made by the OTP shows that they had already pointed to Laurent Gbagbo and treated him as the main suspect of the post-electoral violence. Still in April 2011, during an interview in a Kenyan television documentary on Laurent Gbagbo's prosecution by the ICC, the Prosecutor responded to the question of whether Laurent Gbagbo would be prosecuted one day by saying that he would come to a "bad ending".[108] There is no doubt that the OTP clearly focused its examination on Laurent Gbagbo, even prior to its 23 June 2011 request to the Pre-Trial Chamber for leave to open a formal investigation into the situation in Côte d'Ivoire.[109]

---

[105] *France 24* video, "Le Procureur met en garde le camp Gbagbo", 27 January 2011.

[106] *Afrik.com*, "Côte d'Ivoire: 'pas d'amnistie qui tienne pour Gbagbo', selon la CPI", 7 April 2011.

[107] The legal qualification of the situation is still being discussed in the case *The Prosecutor v. Laurent Gbagbo and Charles Blé Goudé* but both the Prosecution and the Defense seem to agree on the fact that at least from the end of the crisis there is, at least, a non-international armed conflict in Ivory Coast. For this reason, we use the term 'war' here.

[108] *K24TV* video, "3 sides of a coin", 17 April 2011 (available on YouTube).

[109] Situation in the Republic of Côte d'Ivoire, Request for authorisation of an investigation pursuant to article 15, see *supra* note 26.

But based on what evidence did the OTP so openly target Laurent Gbagbo? It is certain that the circumspection inherent in the position of Prosecutor and respect for the presumption of innocence to which he is bound by the Court's Statute imply that he could not have reached such a conclusion without being privy to concrete facts to support his statements, and thus that he was in possession of evidence on which to base such an assertion. This means that during a preliminary examination a case was already being built and if a case was being built a potential perpetrator is identified.

28.5.4.2. The Gabon Situation: An Indication of Future Policy of the OTP towards a Potential Perpetrator?

In the Gabon situation it is even clearer that the OTP will be confronted during the preliminary examination with information provided by very different sources alleging that crimes within the jurisdiction of the Court might have been committed both by the State itself and by the political opposition; but more interestingly for us the OTP will be confronted with information that will clearly identify alleged perpetrators.

To understand how the Gabon situation can be a turning point concerning the place of a potential perpetrator targeted during a preliminary examination we have to briefly present the legal situation. On 21 September 2016, the OTP received a referral regarding the situation in Gabon since May 2016 with no end-date. The referral made by Gabon identifies as potential perpetrator Jean Ping. In their assessment of the evidence they sent to the OTP, Jean Ping would have committed the crime of incitement to commit genocide and the crime of persecution namely by setting fire to official buildings.[110] Three months later, on 15 December 2016, Jean Ping, leader of the Gabonese democratic movement, Gabonese civil society officials and victims of the repression led by the Gabonese authorities against the country's population together filed, through their Counsel Emmanuel Altit, a communication with the OTP.[111] The communication was the result of three months of investigations conducted in Gabon and abroad and had as goal to demonstrate the existence of crimes against

---

[110] Situation in Gabon, *Requête aux fins de renvoi d'une situation par un Etat partie auprès du Procureur de la Cour pénale internationale*, see *supra* note 21.

[111] "Crimes against humanity committed in Gabon by Security Forces/Communication filed at the International Criminal Court", in *Jean Ping* (personal web site), 15 December 2016.

---

humanity committed by the Gabonese authorities. According to the communication, the Gabonese security forces implemented, in particular on 31 August 2016 in Libreville, a planned attack against the population to enable the loser of the presidential election, Ali Bongo, to remain in power and prevent any democratic expression of the population.

Therefore, in the Gabon situation the OTP had to examine on the one hand a referral that identifies, by name, Jean Ping as a potential perpetrator and on the other hand a communication that identifies as potential perpetrators members of the Gabonese security forces.

During this preliminary examination the OTP could choose to open lines of communication with both the author of the referral and the author of the communication. In that scenario, the OTP could not be perceived as biased. But to be able to do so, the OTP would probably feel more comfortable to act within a legal framework. However, it can also act in good faith and with common sense and decide to meet with both parties while respecting the right established in Article 55. This is in light of the most important right both potential perpetrators benefit from: the presumption of innocence.

In the Gabon situation, the OTP went to Gabon between 20 and 22 June 2017 as part of its preliminary examination. During this mission they met with opposing parties. The OTP's new approach is very encouraging. In doing so the OTP can hope to obtain maximum co-operation during its pre-investigation while still maintaining a sense of balance between opposing parties to a conflict. But of course this has to be premised on an independent investigation, where the members of the OTP also act on their own or seek additional information from both parties. It cannot only be a public relations operation; it has to be followed by facts.

The Gabon situation is the perfect opportunity to put in place, during the preliminary examination, the examination of incriminating and exonerating circumstances equally but also to examine thoroughly the seriousness of the information received by the both parties in addition to information provided by victims, representatives of the civil society, organs of the United Nations, intergovernmental or non-governmental organizations, or other reliable sources. For example, the European Union Election observation mission on Gabon published a report on 12 December 2016 stating that anomalies in the electoral process call into question the integrity of the process of consolidating the results and the final result of the election.[112] It would make sense that the OTP also reach out the European Union Election observation mission on Gabon to obtain more information.

If a first effort is to be acknowledged it is not clear if the lines of communication timidly opened by the OTP will be pursued in the future. To be on the safe side, it would be best to create a framework that allows these lines of communication to be opened without any risk and also allows the OTP to be transparent about their pre-investigation as early as the preliminary examination.

28.6. Conclusion

On a concluding note, it would be mistaken to view this chapter as being merely a 'defence perspective' to be lumped in a one out of many factors to be shaken and stirred into the cocktail of quality control. Ignoring potential defendants, and more generally the 'other side', is not just detrimental to the rights of the accused, it is illustrative of a state of mind that undermines the quality of preliminary examinations at their core: that of a *de facto* investigation.

As highlighted throughout, making sure that no one, including potential defendants, is invisible during a preliminary examination and the subsequent investigations is a beneficial policy for everyone, not just for the potential defendant. Indeed, opening lines of communications with all parties to a conflict ensures the neutrality and impartiality of the OTP because they will be perceived as following the evidence, which is the foundation of any good case, rather than starting with a particular perpetrator in mind. It will also ensure the quality of the preliminary examination because the OTP will have access to all aspects of a situation and be in a better position to assess the evidence at its disposal.

Ultimately, this will enhance the quality of the investigation and facilitate the work of the judges in assessing the evidence and the fairness of subsequent proceedings.

The Prosecutor of the ICC is arguably the most visible figure of the Court and is often perceived as the voice of victims around the world and

---

[112] Cf. Rapport Final de la Mission d'observatoire électoral de l'Union Européenne en République Gabonaise, p. 4 (http://www.legal-tools.org/doc/1eb7f9/).

the beacon providing hope for justice for mass atrocities. This is of course an unreasonable and misguided weight to put on one organ of a complex institution. However, what is true is that, given its essential role in launching investigations, the OTP does have the key to making sure that all proceedings in a particular situation or subsequent case are fair and efficient, which contributes to the overall legitimacy of the system, and it all starts with the quality of the preliminary examination. Indeed, preliminary examinations conducted by the OTP are the first step towards ensuring the ICC is filling its expected role towards the international community as a whole, and it is fundamental that this first step is taken in the right direction.

29

Quality Control in the Preliminary Examination of Civil Society Submissions

Andreas Schüller and Chantal Meloni[*]

Pre-investigations within criminal justice systems have recently garnered much attention with regard to core international crimes. Careful scrutiny is warranted as this is one of the most sensitive stages of such proceedings, often characterized by a complex mixture of factors such as: broad prosecutorial discretion, limited public communication, delays, high public expectations, and political pressure.

Civil society organizations ('CSOs') involved in such proceedings as triggers of (pre-)investigations into egregious crimes and mass human rights violations have a unique vantage point in these proceedings. Those CSOs, which are usually in close contact with victims of such violations, are particularly well-placed to observe the pre-investigation stage of criminal proceedings, including experiencing how deficiencies in preliminary examinations can be fatal to the prosecutorial process.

This chapter aims to provide some observations and critical remarks drawn from the practical experience of the authors in their work as part of a CSO as well as from an academic standpoint, both (1) at the domestic level, specifically in Germany, and (2) at the International Criminal Court ('ICC').

[*] **Andreas Schüller** (LL.M. (adv.)) is a lawyer registered at the Berlin Bar and Head of the International Crimes and Accountability Program at the European Center for Constitutional and Human Rights ('ECCHR'). **Chantal Meloni** is Associate Professor at the University of Milan and Legal Advisor at the ECCHR. While working together on the whole paper, they contributed in particular to Section 29.1. and Section 29.2. respectively. The authors would like to thank Fiona Nelson for her valuable support and comments.

29.1. Quality Control at the Preliminary Examination Stage: The Role of Civil Society Submissions and Practice at the Domestic Level in Germany

In seeking criminal justice for core international crimes, the domestic level plays the most important role. According to the complementarity principle of the Rome Statute, it is primarily the responsibility of States to investigate and prosecute core international crimes. In addition, a number of human rights and international humanitarian law treaties include obligations for States to investigate and prosecute, for example, grave breaches of the Geneva Conventions or human rights crimes such as torture or enforced disappearance.

While the jurisdiction of the ICC depends on ratifications or declarations by States as well as referrals by States and the United Nations Security Council ('UNSC'), domestic courts can usually exercise jurisdiction if core international crimes have been committed on the State's territory, by a State's national, against a State's national or under the principle of universal jurisdiction. Universal jurisdiction means that a State can assume jurisdiction because the nature of the crime means it is of concern for the international community as a whole; there is no need for a link to the territory or a national of that State.[1]

The scope of the jurisdiction will depend on the particular State's legislation, which will, in the best case, be in full accordance with all international obligations. Especially with regard to universal jurisdiction, many States have limits to this form of jurisdiction such as the requirement that a suspect of a core international crime is present on the State's territory, not allowing for investigations against suspects resident outside the country, if no national of that State is involved.

For civil society, the jurisdictional requirements and the limitations that often apply are of utmost importance, especially for those expert groups that work transnationally in different jurisdictions as well as for CSOs that are seeking access to justice globally for a group of victims. Differences in jurisdictions often entail differences in litigation strategies. This is one of the most important factors when it comes to case strategies,

---

[1] TRIAL International with ECCHR, FIBGAR, FIDH and REDRESS, *Make way for Justice #4: Momentum Towards Accountability*, 2018, p. 101 (http://www.legal-tools.org/doc/b01bcf/).

in addition to political circumstances and access to witnesses and further evidence.

Besides the jurisdictional aspect, the criminal procedure of each State varies. Therefore, although the authors have experience with regard to jurisdictions and preliminary examinations in a number of European States and beyond, the following part focuses on the practice of preliminary examinations and the role of civil society in Germany (Section 29.1.2.). Turning to Germany, it is crucial to understand the general role of civil society in developing strategic criminal complaints before examining quality control of preliminary examinations of civil society submissions (Section 29.1.1.).

29.1.1. The Role of Civil Society in Developing Criminal Complaints: From Fact-finding to Submissions Triggering Preliminary Examinations

To understand the role of civil society submissions in preliminary examinations, both at the domestic and international level, it is important to analyse the processes leading up to the filing of a submission and the commencement of a preliminary examination.

Where large-scale human rights violations occur or in conflict situations, civil society plays a crucial role not only in documenting these violations, but also in developing ways to sanction them. Hence, victims, activists, lawyers, local CSOs and others often connect with international expert CSOs and jointly discuss strategies about how to achieve criminal justice.

The earlier local and international groups engage in the process, the better. A discussion process about strategies over months or years often leads to knowledge building and sharing on all sides whereby international experts learn about the specific conflict, culture and country while local groups learn about international law, jurisdiction and legal practice. Already at this stage, the usually intense discussions focus on selecting the best sets of cases for criminal complaints in a domestic transitional justice mechanism, third State or international jurisdictions. An early case selection strategy also impacts the way incidents are documented. In many conflicts, local groups focus on crime-based evidence, such as information about a specific aerial attack or a massacre, but no information is gathered about the perpetrators, units or the command system behind the crimes. Evidence on the latter is crucial for prosecutions, but it is in most instances the most difficult information to gather. With early focussed strategic discussions, the way can be paved for seeking information on perpetrator structures in combination with crime-based evidence for the coming years.[2]

In discussing case selection and litigation strategies, there are many factors to be considered. For instance, it is significant whether the focus lies on the gravest and most outrageous incidents or rather on the best-documented ones. The latter might have higher chances in terms of prosecutions, but the former might have a bigger impact in terms of justice for victims, enforcement of legal standards, or deterrence. Another option is to focus on groups of perpetrators and the policies behind the commission of the crimes and to seek information about incidents matching these policies. Within this case selection process, jurisdictional requirements play a significant role, as many States require a specific citizenship of a victim or perpetrator or the presence of the suspects in that State's territory. This means that considerations in case selection may include potential travel movements of suspects as well as the nationality of victims or perpetrators.

Thus, there is often a long and intense phase before filing a submission and entering preliminary examinations in order to present the best cases of interest to affected communities and societies with realistic chances of leading to full criminal investigations. This process also requires the best possible documentation of incidents as well as the attribution to specific groups of perpetrators. Case selection based on the demands of local groups and victims often has more value in terms of the impact of prosecutions than prosecutor-driven case selection within preliminary examinations, in which more technical, evidence-based considerations tend to prevail over interests of victims. Civil society submissions in preliminary examinations can thus contribute to a stronger case selection with improved long-term impact as compared with what tends to be a short-term, merely prosecution-focused, case selection.

Taking, for example, the cases of international crimes committed in Syria and parts of Iraq since 2011, factors for strategic discussions for a

---

[2] See, especially taking a (self-)critical view on power dynamics between international NGOs and local communities, our ECCHR-colleagues' article, Wolfgang Kaleck and Carolijn Terwindt, "Non-Governmental Organisation Fact-Work: Not Only a Technical Problem", in Morten Bergsmo (ed.), *Quality Control in Fact-Finding*, Torkel Opsahl Academic EPublisher, Florence, 2013, pp. 403–26 (http://www.toaep.org/ps-pdf/19-bergsmo).

---

criminal complaint in Germany – in which the authors' organization is involved – included choosing sets of cases from crimes committed in the context of detention, chemical attacks, attacks on city centres, sexualized violence, and genocidal attacks against minorities such as the Yazidis. In addition, jurisdictional requirements played a crucial role in case selection discussions. Whereas Germany has 'pure' universal jurisdiction and thus can investigate international crimes regardless of whether or not there is a link to Germany, other States require the presence of a suspect on its territory or for the victim to be one of its citizen. As such, case selection in the context of Syria often also depends on the nationality of a victim or information about the whereabouts of suspects. These factors certainly limit the case selection options and make it much more dependent on the chance occurrence of such links as compared with the more comprehensive investigations available from jurisdictions like Germany. Here it is more feasible to further discuss in which cases suspects at the top of a chain of command are known, can be named by 'linkage witnesses' (witnesses with insider knowledge), and thus become targets for arrest warrants. At this point, civil society can assist in finding linkage witnesses through networks of local activists or refugee communities, but at the same time they can also arrange for a lawyer to advise key witnesses who do not want to talk for security or political reasons.

In addition, the communication strategy around the presentation of a submission is crucial. There are situations in which there is no public communication to avoid risking the loss of evidence if suspects are publically informed that they might soon be under criminal investigation. On the other hand, many cases depend on a strong communication strategy in which messages by victims, local activists, lawyers and expert CSOs reach different audiences to build support. This aims at garnering public support for the cases, reaching out to other potential witnesses and victims and helping war crimes units within prosecution authorities to internally secure the allocation of further resources given the public attention and importance of the cases, but also at building public pressure on prosecutors to act on the cases and begin investigations.

Finally, by submitting a case and making it public, CSOs involved in such proceedings as triggers of (pre-)investigations often experience both foreseen and unforeseen developments. With a filing of a criminal complaint and public communication around it, if it is done in a professional way, groups gain a lot of trust within communities as they are publically standing up for the victims and affected communities and supporting their quest for justice. This often leads to more victims and witnesses approaching the groups for advice and potentially joining the complaint and related activities.

Thus, when CSOs present submissions within already existing preliminary examinations or in order to initiate them, there is often a longer process with numerous strategic discussions in order to present cases with the biggest impact for the affected communities and on the groups of perpetrators involved. This differentiates civil society submissions from preliminary examinations initiated by a prosecution service. The latter often focus on a rather technical case selection for prosecutions or are merely opportunistic – even though still necessary in terms of fighting impunity – for example, when low-level suspects reside on a State's territory.

29.1.2. Preliminary Examinations in Germany and the Role of Civil Society Submissions

Once a criminal complaint has been filed, the next phase starts, often with an initial period of preliminary examinations. In Germany, examinations and investigations can be differentiated in three types: (1) monitoring procedure (without investigatory powers); (2) structural investigation (with full investigatory powers); (3) formal investigation of a specific case against known or unknown suspects.[3]

Only the first type is comparable to preliminary examinations under the Rome Statute. Unlike the Office of the Prosecutor ('OTP') of the ICC with its Policy Paper on Preliminary Examinations, giving this phase a certain structure in terms of content as well as decision-making, the monitoring procedure in Germany has neither transparent policies nor structure.[4] It basically serves as an opportunity, even before examining jurisdictional questions, to gather a pool of publically available information

---

[3] See, for the German laws and practice of preliminary examinations, Matthias Neuner, "German Preliminary Examinations of International Crimes", in Morten Bergsmo and Carsten Stahn (eds.), *Quality Control in Preliminary Examination: Volume 1*, Torkel Opsahl Academic EPublisher, Brussels, 2018, chap. 6. See also the article of two German Federal Public Prosecutors, Thomas Beck and Christian Ritscher, "Do Criminal Complaints Make Sense in (German) International Criminal Law?", in *Journal of International Criminal Justice*, 2015, vol. 13, no. 2, pp. 229–35.

[4] Office of the Proscutor ('OTP'), *Policy Paper on Preliminary Examinations*, 1 November 2013 (http://www.legal-tools.org/doc/acb906/).

which includes submissions from CSOs in order for the Federal Public Prosecutor General (*Generalbundesanwalt*) to be in a position to react in case a suspect enters German territory and thereby making the exercise of universal jurisdiction obligatory. At any point in time, the Federal Public Prosecutor General can also move from the monitoring procedure to a structural or formal investigation.

The standard required under German criminal procedural law for this step is one of 'initial suspicion' that a crime has been committed. In the case of a suspect or a victim of German nationality or the presence of a suspect on German territory, the Federal Public Prosecutor General is legally obliged to open formal investigations. In pure universal jurisdiction cases, the Federal Public Prosecutor General has discretion as to whether to proceed to the investigatory phase, for example, in order to secure evidence.[5]

The discretionary decision must be based on factors laid down in Article 153 lit. f of the German Code of Criminal Procedure. Hence, the prosecutor can refrain from pursuing a case if no suspect is present or expected to be present on German territory, there are no victims of German nationality or there is a pending prosecution in another State or before an international court.

CSOs formally only have the right to submit criminal complaints, just as every person or legal entity can submit information to a prosecutor or police station. Other more specific rights, such as receiving information about decisions during investigations, access to files and the right to file appeals against decisions, are reserved only for the victims.

In Germany, there are a number of uncertainties and shortcomings in the practices of preliminary examinations and monitoring procedure by the Federal Public Prosecutor General.

29.1.2.1. Selection Criteria in Universal Jurisdiction Cases

There is no transparency on the criteria for opening structural investigations on a general situation in which core international crimes have been committed. This step is the most important one, moving from a monitoring procedure to an investigation with full investigatory powers. The im-

---

[5]   Strafprozeßordnung, StPO, 7 April 1987, last amendment 30 October 2017, Section 153f ('German Code of Criminal Procedure') (http://www.legal-tools.org/doc/f7d369/).

portance of starting investigation proceedings is briefly explained in the following section as it is crucial to examine the preliminary examination part of the process.

In recent years, the Federal Public Prosecutor General relied on the concept of anticipatory mutual legal assistance as a criterion for opening structural investigations.[6] This means that the Federal Public Prosecutor General secures evidence in order to be prepared to act upon requests by other States or international courts in the future. In order to be prepared and not to lose evidence over time, testimonies can also be taken and stored.

At the same time this evidence can also be used in case a suspect of a crime of the same situation enters Germany. In the past cases occurred in which suspects came to Germany but left before the Federal Public Prosecutor General took action, although civil society had informed the office about the presence of the suspect and provided access to evidence.[7]

Furthermore, if sufficient evidence is gathered during structural investigations, the Federal Public Prosecutor General can separate individual investigations from the structural ones and request the issuance of an arrest warrant against a suspect at the Federal Supreme Court. The suspect does not have to be present in Germany at any point in this process, but could then be wanted internationally. A trial *in absentia* is not possible in Germany. Examples exist from the local Nuremberg-Fuerth prosecutor's office with regards to Argentinean torture perpetrators.[8] These cases were opened before Germany's Code of Crimes against International Law (including universal jurisdiction) entered into force in 2002 and were based on the passive personality principle as a number of victims were Germans. After five years of investigations, the district court in Nuremberg issued arrest warrants against former members of the military junta Jorge Rafael

---

[6] Martin Böse, "Das Völkerstrafgesetzbuch und der Gedanke 'antizipierter Rechtshilfe'", in Florian Jeßberger and Julia Geneuss (eds.), *Zehn Jahre Völkerstrafgesetzbuch*, 2013, pp. 167–76; Wolfgang Kaleck, "Strafverfolgung nach dem Völkerstrafgesetzbuch: Ein kurzer Blick in die Zukunft – ein Kommentar zum Beitrag von Martin Böse", in Florian Jeßberger and Julia Geneuss (eds.), *Zehn Jahre Völkerstrafgesetzbuch*, 2013, pp. 177–84.

[7] ECCHR, "Criminal complaint against Zakir Almatov" (available on the ECCHR's web site).

[8] ECCHR, "Argentinean Dictatorship Cases: the German "Coalition against Impunity" to Press Criminal Charges" (on file with the author).

Videla and Emilio Eduardo Massera. Germany officially requested their extradition, which was denied, but the accused later faced prosecutions in Argentina as a result of collective efforts of civil society in Argentina, Germany and other States. In this process, the role of civil society in many different countries and judicial fora was crucial to push for prosecutions in the territorial State in which the crimes had been committed.

Whereas in the last years several structural investigations have been opened, including one on Libya and two on Syria and Syria/Iraq, in other cases that has not happened. Certainly, given the large numbers of victims and witnesses living in Germany from areas in which international crimes have been and are being committed (for example, from Syria, Iraq, Afghanistan, Yemen, Libya, Bahrain, Iran, Turkey, Egypt, Eritrea, Ethiopia, Sudan as well as Sri Lanka, Chechnya and Uzbekistan), not all testimonies can be taken and preserved. Thus, it is paramount to secure evidence from linkage witnesses and to cluster cases. In many cases it is not foreseeable at an early stage, whether there will be sufficient evidence accessible in Germany in order to request arrest warrants, whether a suspect will ever enter German territory, or whether there will be legal assistance requests from other States or international courts in the future. However, civil society can support demands of affected groups to focus on their cases, to open a monitoring procedure in order to collect open-source information, to further submit information from different sources and to inform the Federal Public Prosecutor General about available key witnesses, sources of evidence as well as travel plans of suspects, so that structural investigations will be opened to secure evidence and prepare cases.

One emblematic case that has not yet led to the opening of structural investigations is the case of war crimes committed by United States ('US') officials in overseas detention facilities such as Guantánamo Bay. Although victims and crime-based witnesses are living in Germany, their testimonies have not been secured. In addition, a number of other crime-based and linkage witnesses offered to provide testimonies in Germany to the Federal Public Prosecutor General on detainee treatment by the US in specific detention centres. Thanks to the publication of large numbers of internal documents through Freedom of Information Act litigation, further evidence is available to prove the connection of the relevant structures in the US military, the CIA and the US government to the alleged crimes. Taking together all these sources of accessible evidence, which have been presented by CSOs to the Federal Public Prosecutor's Office,[9] there would be a higher likelihood than in other situations that investigations would lead to the issuance of arrest warrants by the Federal Supreme Court. Given the criteria formulated by the prosecutors themselves, that "one can assume that such media reports [about situations of relevance for international criminal law] containing enough information as to the potential commission of international crimes will lead to the initiation of an investigation procedure and to the lodging of a formal investigation",[10] the opening of investigations into US war crimes based on the information and analysis provided by civil society – which far exceeds information from regular media reporting – is long overdue. However, no reason has been given on the failure to do so.

The selection criteria of the Federal Public Prosecutor General remains opaque as to why in some situations preliminary examinations continue while in others structural and/or formal investigations have been opened. On the one hand, the situation in Syria and Iraq and the comparably large number of witnesses currently living in Germany certainly justified the opening of structural investigations in this situations in 2011 and 2014 respectively. On the other hand, cases are selected for structural investigations when evidence is secured from witnesses in Germany on international crimes committed in Libya, whereas investigative leads with regard to US war crimes are not followed, although in both cases there are only a small number of relevant witnesses in Germany.[11] This leads to the public perception of double standards in international criminal justice.

29.1.2.2. Duration of Preliminary Examinations

In other cases, where there was no prosecutorial discretion but instead a legal obligation to investigate, the Federal Public Prosecutor General failed to open formal investigations within a reasonable time by keeping cases in the monitoring procedure phase.

---

9   See for submissions, ECCHR, "Germany: CIA director Gina Haspel should face arrest on travelling to Europe" (available on the ECCHR's web site).

10 Beck, Ritscher, 2015, p. 233, see *supra* note 3.

11 On double standards in international criminal justice, see Wolfgang Kaleck, *Double Standards: International Criminal Law and the West*, Torkel Opsahl Academic EPublisher, Brussels, 2015 (http://www.toaep.org/ps-pdf/26-kaleck).

In cases such as the one of an airstrike ordered by a German colonel in Afghanistan in September 2009, killing about 100 people, preliminary examinations took almost six months, despite the legal obligation to open an investigation as a German national was the suspect. After six months, the formal investigation was opened for four weeks, during which two suspects and two witnesses were heard, before the case was closed.

In another case of international crimes, in which a German citizen was killed by a US drone strike in Pakistan in October 2010, preliminary examinations took about 20 months before a formal investigation was opened in order to question a witness who had been extradited to Germany. Eleven months later, this investigation was closed. During preliminary examinations, the Federal Public Prosecutor General reviewed a number of reports, by experts and the Federal Intelligence Service, for example, but did not formally request information from Pakistan or the United States, nor take testimonies of witnesses present in Germany.

Steps such as ordering expert reports or asking other States through diplomatic channels for information can certainly be considered as part of an investigation, as they are examined in light of the question whether there is an initial suspicion whether a crime was committed. However, by keeping this process part of preliminary examinations, the Federal Public Prosecutor General has avoided any form of transparency or public scrutiny and deprived the victim of his or her right to access the files or to further contribute to the investigation. In such cases, CSOs can exercise public pressure in order to enforce the victims' rights or advise victims on how to challenge delays before domestic courts or the European Court of Human Rights.

29.1.2.3. Transparency and Public Outreach

As addressed in the previous section, there is no transparency in preliminary examinations and generally also no public outreach. Victims cannot access files and the Federal Public Prosecutor General usually does not publicize about the opening of a preliminary examination, but will in certain situations confirm, on request, that one exists.

CSOs can ask members of parliament to pose questions to the Government in order to get some information about activities by the Federal Public Prosecutor General. With such information, CSOs can then inform the public or interested persons and groups on specific requests.

As there is also no public outreach about activities within preliminary examinations, the public and especially the victims do not know what activities are being conducted, in which direction the focus on a situation might go and whether or not CSOs can even confidentially contribute information on specific parts of a conflict. In terms of quality control of preliminary examinations, civil society could make an important contribution to the monitoring procedure if basic information would be made public. In addition, the impression often prevails that German law enforcement authorities are not acting at all on international crimes cases, which is inaccurate as well. This criticism is based on a lack of information and transparency which leads to less support of those authorities in charge of international crimes investigations. More quality control here could also mean more support and also more political discussion around case selection, which is important in terms of quality control and addressing double standards in international criminal justice.[12]

29.1.2.4. Limited Rights of Victims to Appeal a Decision

If the Federal Public Prosecutor General does not open investigations, victims – but not CSOs – have a limited right to appeal the decision. CSOs can support victims in exercising their rights before the courts, including with activities to gather new facts that could prompt the re-opening of an investigation.

The limitation of German criminal procedure lies in the fact that a complaint mechanism is foreseen only at the end of investigations, but not at the end of preliminary examinations or if an investigation is terminated at an early stage.[13] This mechanism is meant to provide the relevant aspects of the investigation file to the Appeals Court so that the judges can determine whether the Federal Public Prosecutor General has made the right decision not to indict a suspect based on the results of the full investigation. In order to exercise this right, the victim also needs access to the full file, otherwise the case cannot be fully presented to the Court. However, in many of the aforementioned cases, a full investigation was never conducted, nor was a decision made not to indict a suspect.

---

[12] German Federal Public Prosecutors also see some value in public outreach during preliminary examinations under specific circumstances, see Beck, Ritscher, 2015, p. 235, see *supra* note 3.

[13] German Code of Criminal Procedure, Section 172, see *supra* note 5.

In the case of the airstrike in Afghanistan, investigations were first delayed and then closed within a month without giving the victim the right to express his views on the evidence gathered at the point of the decision. The case on the drone strike in Pakistan was also closed at a very early stage, similarly without the possibility for the victims' relatives to comment on the content of the investigation file. This would have been particularly important as the decision was based on a number of controversial facts, for instance, concerning the nature of local groups and their alleged involvement in the conduct of direct hostilities, as well as legal findings of importance on questions of international humanitarian law. As the case was never fully investigated, there was no avenue to lodge a complaint to a court whereby judges could review the prosecutor's decision whether to indict the suspect or not. As it stands, the factual and legal findings of the Federal Public Prosecutor General remain unchallenged by a court, thus it is the prosecutor who sets interpretation of international humanitarian law norms, but not judges after hearing at least two parties in a proceeding. Without a full judicial review, there is no quality control of preliminary examinations nor investigations of international crimes cases possible in Germany.

29.1.3. Conclusions on Quality Control of Preliminary Examinations in Germany through Civil Society Submissions

Civil society submissions play a key role in preliminary examinations. As shown above, those submissions are often based on intense discussions and selection processes, involving different key players, such as victims' groups, experts on criminal and transitional justice or local civil society of a concerned country. Thus, civil society submissions can reflect not only single individual cases of victims of core international crimes, but a comprehensive submission on the most emblematic cases within a context of systematic human rights or international humanitarian law violations. Civil society is in the best position to present such comprehensive submissions, as individual submissions will often lack the discussion of the political context of an affected group whereas submissions by other States or political groups will potentially serve political interests more than the interests of criminal justice.

CSOs conduct their own research with regard to information about the commission of core international crimes. As a result, civil society can identify patterns and systems of core international crimes committed as part of a conflict or in the context of repression. At the same time, CSOs can establish contact with victims, witnesses and perpetrators of these crimes and thus provide useful links for future evidence gathering.

Moreover, many CSOs are victims' representation groups. Such groups have larger networks of victims and witnesses which can contribute to criminal justice. As those groups are often self-founded, they have the trust and confidence of other victims as well as the necessary contacts to other CSOs that can provide expertise with regard to substantive law. At the same time, they can speak and represent victims' voices and demands – something that is of paramount importance in the process of transitional justice, of which criminal justice mechanisms form only one part.

CSOs can also provide political support for investigations and prosecutions. Those offices of a prosecution service dealing with international crimes can then benefit from this overall support, in seeking more financial support from the government in order to be able to fulfil their tasks. At the same time, civil society can also shift the focus and argue why certain investigations are of greatest importance, even if politically more controversial.

Civil society submissions often contribute to the quality control of preliminary examinations. On the one hand, they support the competent prosecutor's office with valuable information and analysis; on the other hand, they support victims' rights to get their cases heard and challenge the authorities if they refuse, in violation of their obligations, to pursue investigations.

29.2. Quality Control in the Preliminary Examination: Civil Society Submissions at the International Criminal Court

As in domestic systems, the ICC must take questions of efficiency into consideration to ensure its proper functioning. The limited resources of the Court require that the Prosecutor carefully select investigations cases to pursue. The way in which the Prosecutor evaluates the myriad of communications and victims' complaints alleging the commission of crimes within the Court's jurisdiction and selects which investigation to pursue or not, is currently one of the most critical issues before the ICC. Undoubtedly, the improper exercise of the discretional power in this regard can have tremendous consequences for an institution, such as the ICC, which is, to a certain extent, still seeking to establish its legitimacy.

Unlike at the domestic level (as discussed above), the preliminary examination phase at the ICC is now regulated and heavily 'procedural-ized'. In fact, despite the lack of specific provisions in the Rome Statute and its related documents, which do not even mention the term 'preliminary examination', over the years the OTP has refined its *modus operandi* with regard to the initial phase of the proceedings, and in particular, with regard to decisions whether to open an investigation. The outcome has been published in subsequent documents: the first draft was published in 2010,[14] followed by a November 2013 Policy Paper on Preliminary Examinations ('Policy Paper').[15] In respect of transparency,[16] the Prosecutor decided to make public the OTP's activities in relation to preliminary examinations. The OTP has indicated that it will regularly report on its preliminary examinations activities,[17] which has indeed been done since 2013 through yearly reports.[18] Thus, not only is the commencement of preliminary examinations made public but the OTP also provides updates on the activities in respect of the various phases of its analysis.[19] This move towards transparency, an absolute pre-condition for the effective participation of victims, non-governmental and CSOs in ICC proceedings, is welcome. However, as will be discussed, several points remain problematic in the way the ICC deals with this delicate phase of proceedings, in particular, from the point of view of CSOs which, representing the victims, have been involved for many years in a constructive dialogue with the Court.

Firstly, although the OTP must heavily rely on victims' communications and CSO submissions in deciding whether, pursuant to Article 15(3) of the Rome Statute, there is a "reasonable basis to proceed with an investigation",[20] victim and CSO participation in preliminary examinations is

---

[14]   OTP, *Draft Policy Paper on Preliminary Examinations*, 4 October 2010 (http://www.legal-tools.org/doc/bd172c/).

[15]   OTP, *Policy Paper on Preliminary Examinations*, see *supra* note 4.

[16]   ICC, *Regulations of the Office of the Prosecutor*, 23 April 2009, Rule 28(2) ('Regulat-ions') (http://www.legal-tools.org/doc/a97226/).

[17]   OTP, *Policy Paper on Preliminary Examinations*, para. 94, see *supra* note 4.

[18]   OTP, *Report on Preliminary Examination Activities*, 14 November 2016 (http://www.legal-tools.org/doc/f30a53/).

[19]   OTP, *Policy Paper on Preliminary Examinations*, para. 95, see *supra* note 4. The OTP has also indicated there that it will seek to early interact with stakeholders, for example, on Article 15 communications.

[20]   See *ibid.*, paras. 34–71, for OTP's interpretation of the standard.

very restricted. More precisely, there appears to be a gap in the ICC-designed system of preliminary examinations with regard to the tools victims and CSOs have at their disposal to defend their interests at this early stage of the proceedings *vis-à-vis* the broad prosecutorial discretion. In particular, this becomes clear when the Prosecutor fails to make any decision on whether to open an investigation and keeps the preliminary examination ongoing for years.

The latter is also illustrated by the OTP's Policy Paper that highlights that neither the Rome Statute, nor the Rules of Procedure and Evidence ('RPE') mentions a specific time period for the completion of preliminary examinations.[21] Thus, the OTP is not obliged to indicate a time limit for preliminary examinations. The rationale is to ensure that the OTP's analysis is adjusted to the specific features of each particular situation instead of being confined by arbitrary time limits.[22] Furthermore, the Policy Paper mentions that examinations must be continued until the information provides clarity on whether or not a reasonable basis for an investigation exists. This could include assessing national proceedings over an extensive period of time, as epitomized in the Colombia situation.[23] Even though the Policy Paper outlines a transparency policy by the OTP in the preliminary examination phase, the decision of whether or not to share information with CSOs and other stakeholders seems to be at the OTP's discretion.

Moreover, over the years, as the practice of the ICC developed, the amount of resources that the ICC poured into the analysis of data and information in this pre-investigative stage has grown exponentially. Notably, many elements (for instance, gravity and complementarity) which are reviewed during a preliminary examination are those which, according to the Rome Statute, shall also be reviewed, eventually, during the investigation phase. Thus, the question is whether it is useful to double the analysis in terms of both resources and expediency of proceedings, especially considering that the OTP has far fewer powers during preliminary examinations, in which it basically only relies on open source material and on

---

[21] *Ibid.*, para. 89.

[22] *Ibid.*

[23] *Ibid.*, para. 90.

what States or CSOs submit.[24] In other words, it is questionable whether doubling the analysis (before and after opening the investigation proper) can be seen as waste of resources, a source of delays and a ground for ineffectiveness of the ICC proceedings. Both the never-ending preliminary examination of the Colombia situation and the stalled one of the UK/Iraq situation, for instance, indicate these difficulties.

29.2.1. A Preliminary Observation

Before getting into the discussion of the above-mentioned points, it can be observed that the current practice of the ICC shows that it is much more unlikely that an investigation be opened in the absence of a State or UNSC referral. Article 13 of the Rome Statute provides three trigger mechanisms for an investigation to be opened at the ICC: (1) upon referral by a State Party; (2) upon referral by the UNSC, acting pursuant to Chapter VII of the UN Charter; and (3) *proprio motu*, that is, on the Prosecutor's initiative. With regard to this last triggering mechanism, Article 15 of the Rome Statute specifies that: "the Prosecutor may initiate investigations *proprio motu* on the basis of information on crimes within the jurisdiction of the Court". Here, CSO submissions and victims' communications play a major role as a source of information pointing at the commission of crimes under the ICC's jurisdiction.

Regardless of the source of the information received, the Prosecutor is never obliged to proceed with an investigation: in fact, the Rome Statute always leaves the decision whether to open such an investigation in the sphere of the Prosecutor's discretion. Undoubtedly a referral, either by a State or by the UNSC, does not automatically imply the opening of an investigation: the power to decline the opening of an investigation into a situation even when the Court has received a State or UNSC referral lies at the heart of the independence of the ICC Prosecutor and ultimately of the ICC. Thus, the Prosecutor is always tasked with the responsibility to determine whether a situation meets the legal criteria established by the Rome Statute to warrant an investigation by the Court, pursuant to Article 53(1). Such an analysis is carried out according to the four phases that

---

24   Carsten Stahn, "Damned if you do, Damned if you don't: Challenges and Critiques of Preliminary Examinations at the ICC", in *Journal of International Criminal Justice*, 2017, vol. 15, no. 3, p. 413.

have been outlined by the OTP in its successive policy documents and seem now to have been crystallized in its yearly reports published so far.[25]

The Prosecutor also clarified from the outset that: "the Office's preliminary examination activities will be conducted in the same manner irrespective of whether the Office receives a referral from a State Party or by the Security Council or acts on the basis of information of crimes obtained pursuant to article 15".[26] Thus, in theory, the analysis is the same regardless of the source of the information received, but in practice, the chances of the examination moving into the investigative phase are much greater for situations referred to the Court.[27] If one examines the various situations currently under investigation as well as under preliminary examination at the ICC, it is apparent that most of the investigations were in fact opened upon referral either by the UNSC (for example, Sudan and Libya) or by a State (for example, Uganda, the Democratic Republic of Congo, the Central African Republic ('CAR'), and Mali) – or at least with tacit agreement of the State involved, for instance, via *ad hoc* acceptance of ICC jurisdiction under Article 12(3) (for example, Ivory Coast),[28] or otherwise (as it was the case with Kenya, where the former Prosecutor had engaged in an exercise of 'positive complementarity').[29]

Thus, it appears that 'pure' *proprio motu* investigations are very rare; and (at least for now) they do not get very far. Moreover, with just the one exception illustrated below, all situations which have been referred to the

---

[25] See, for instance, the already mentioned most recent *Report on Preliminary Examination Activities*, see *supra* note 18. The Prosecutor shall consider in particular: jurisdiction; admissibility (complementarity and gravity); and the interests of justice.

[26] OTP, *Draft Policy Paper on Preliminary Examinations*, 2010, para. 12, see *supra* note 14.

[27] *Ibid.* "In all circumstances, the office will analyse the seriousness of the information received and may seek additional information from States, organs of the United Nations, intergovernmental and non-governmental organizations and other reliable sources that are deemed appropriate. The Office may also receive oral testimony at the seat of the Court."

[28] "The procedural mechanism under Article 12(3) is based on the general idea of reciprocity referring to a structural balance of rights and obligations of states parties and third states under the ICC as a treaty system". Carsten Stahn, Mohamed M. El Zeidy and Hector Olasolo, "The International Criminal Court's *Ad Hoc* Jurisdiction Revisited", in *American Journal of International Law*, 2005, vol. 99, no. 2, p. 422.

[29] Chantal Meloni, "Kenya and the ICC: A Boomerang Effect?", in *ISPI Analysis*, no. 245, May 2014; ICC, Situation in Kenya, Request for authorization of an investigation pursuant to Article 15, 26 November 2009, ICC-01/09-3, para 9–11, 20–22 (http://www.legal-tools.org/doc/c63dcc/).

Court (either by a State or by the UNSC) have triggered an investigation. Indeed, the 'Flotilla situation'[30] represented the first time the ICC Prosecutor decided *not to open* an investigation after having received a referral by a State Party. Significantly, this gave, for the first time, the opportunity for the judges to review the decision not to open an investigation pursuant to Article 53(3)(a) of the Rome Statute. Notably, this also appears to be the only case so far where the referral by the State was not a pure 'self-referral' – concerning crimes committed by nationals on its own territory – but it did concern alleged crimes committed by foreigners (members of the Israeli army) on the territory of the referring State (the vessel flying the Comoros' flag) and on third States' territory (the vessels flying the Cambodian and the Greek flags). It is an open question whether the latter element played a role in the assessment of the situation by the Prosecutor, who could have applied restraint given the critical circumstances.[31]

Conversely, a UNSC referral not only exponentially increases the likelihood of an investigation, but also appears to influence the expeditiousness of the (positive) decision: upon receipt of a UNSC resolution, the decision to open an investigation into the Libya situation was made in a matter of days.[32]

It would be naïve to think it is mere coincidence that most investigations – and open cases – so far have emerged from referrals. One of the reasons for this state of affairs could be that the procedure envisaged by the Rome Statute for the opening of an investigation *proprio motu* is more complex than in the case of a State or UNSC referral: only in the first case, in fact, does the Prosecutor need to request an authorization by the Pre-Trial Chamber ('PTC'), and thus the decision is subjected to judicial scrutiny, which could complicate matters. At the same time, it should be noted

---

[30] The Situation of the Registered Vessels of Comoros, Greece and Cambodia was under reconsideration by the OTP at the time of writing, OTP, *Report on Preliminary Examination Activities*, pp. 69 ff., see *supra* note 18.

[31] Please see on this Chantal Meloni, "The ICC preliminary examination of the Flotilla situation: an opportunity to contextualise gravity", in *Questions of International Law*, 30 November 2016.

[32] For the whole ICC documentation, including the decision of 2 March 2011 to open the investigation in Libya upon referral received on the 26 February 2011 by the United Nations Security Council ('UNSC'), see ICC, "Situation in Libya", ICC-01/11 (available on the Court's web site).

that, so far, every request by the Prosecutor for authorization to open an investigation has been granted swiftly by the PTC.

Despite what the Prosecutor argued in the 2010 draft policy paper, there is a difference in the analysis of the information received depending on its source.[33] Notably, such a difference would have a statutory basis: with regard to a situation which has been referred to the Court, either by a State or the UNSC, the Prosecutor is obliged to initiate an investigation unless: "he or she determines that there is no reasonable basis to proceed under this Statute", pursuant to Article 53(1);[34] whereas in case of *proprio motu* preliminary examinations, the Prosecutor is obliged to proceed with a full-fledged investigation only if he or she concludes that: "there is a reasonable basis to proceed, according to Article 15(3) of the Statute".[35] Thus, "as regard the threshold to initiate an investigation the policy of the OTP differentiates between referrals (by a State Party of the Security Council) and the Prosecutor's *proprio motu* authority".[36]

Such a preliminary observation, as outlined above, is telling of the difficult role played by CSOs and victims, whose communications are

---

[33] See also Matthew Cross, "The Standard of Proof in Preliminary Examinations", in Morten Bergsmo and Carsten Stahn (eds.), *Quality Control in Preliminary Examination: Volume 2*, Torkel Opsahl Academic EPublisher, Brussels, 2018, chap. 22.

[34] An interesting recent interpretation of this can be found in the Pre Trial Chamber ('PTC') decision that reviewed the OTP Comoros decision closing the preliminary examination: "The presumption of Article 53(1) of the Statute, as reflected by the use of the word "shall" in the chapeau of that article, and of common sense, is that the Prosecutor investigates in order to be able to properly assess the relevant facts". The judges also affirmed that, "[m]aking the commencement of an investigation contingent on the information available at the pre-investigative stage being already clear, univocal and not contradictory creates a short circuit and deprives the exercise of any purpose". Thus: "[i]f the information available to the Prosecutor at the pre-investigative stage allows for reasonable inferences that at least one crime within the jurisdiction of the Court has been committed and that the case would be admissible, the Prosecutor shall open an investigation, as only by investigating could doubts be overcome", ICC, Situation on Registered Vessels of the Union of the Comoros, the Hellenic Republic and the Kingdom of Cambodia, PTC I, Decision on the request of the Union of the Comoros to review the Prosecutor's decision not to initiate an investigation, 16 July 2015, ICC-01/03-34, para. 13 (http://www.legal-tools.org/doc/2f876c/).

[35] Pavel Caban, "Preliminary Examinations by the Office of the Prosecutor of the International Criminal Court", in *Czech Yearbook of Public & Private International Law*, 2011, vol. 2, p. 203.

[36] *Ibid.*

---

generally the source of the information for the Prosecutor to act *proprio motu* and who have an interest in the prompt opening of the investigation by the ICC. Thus, the question is: how can such actors participate, influence and counter-balance the broad prosecutorial discretion in this early phase of proceedings? Moreover, what are the tools (if any) at the disposal of victims and CSOs to undertake quality control of the activities carried out by the Prosecutor before the opening of an investigation?

29.2.2. Can CSOs and Victims Effectively Participate and Counter-balance Prosecutorial Discretion before the Opening of an Investigation?

The participation of victims and CSOs in preliminary examinations is very restricted. Nevertheless, there are some ways in which the victims and the organizations representing their interests can attempt to influence how preliminary examinations are conducted and, in particular, the ensuing decisions of the Prosecutor. In the first place, victims and CSOs can of course submit communications and observations to the OTP to trigger a *proprio motu* investigation or to provide information to the OTP. In this sense, victims can participate in a request by the Prosecutor for authorization to initiate an investigation. Moreover, both victims and CSOs can make requests to the PTC in relation to Article 53(3)(b) reviews, pursuant to Article 68(3) of the Rome Statute and Rule 103 of the RPE and seek leave from the PTC to submit their observations.

However, perhaps the thorniest issue with regard to victims and CSO participation at the pre-investigation stage concerns the lack of means for them to challenge a decision of the Prosecutor not to initiate investigations under Article 15(6). In fact, the Rome Statute provides very limited means to push the Prosecutor to undertake an action he or she is not willing to undertake. Indeed, as the preparatory works of the Rome Statute show, most of the attention back then was focused on (limiting) the powers of the Prosecutor when deciding *to open an investigation*. At Rome, the debate over the Prosecutor's powers was essentially a fight over the proper scope of the Prosecutor's discretion: in particular, whether it should extend to the decision to initiate an investigation.[37] Maybe less

---

[37] The initial draft prepared by the International Law Commission in fact did not include the *proprio motu* power of the Prosecutor to initiate an investigation; for the negotiating history of the provision: see Allison Marston Danner, "Enhancing the Legitimacy and Account-

attention was devoted to the opposite scenario, that is, to the limits of discretion permitted with regard to a decision of the Prosecutor *not to open an investigation*. However, during these first years of activity of the ICC, the issue has already surfaced several times and it appears to be one of the most controversial ones facing the Court.[38]

As will be shown, in answering to what extent it is possible to push the Prosecutor to pursue an investigation into a situation or case, one needs to differentiate whether the preliminary examination was triggered by a referral, or was a *proprio motu* one. Once more, it is especially with regard to this latter scenario that victims and CSOs face major problems given the lack of remedies at their disposal.

29.2.2.1. The Submission of Communications

Victims and CSOs play a crucial role at the preliminary examination phase. In fact, when the OTP decides to pursue an investigation *proprio motu*, it must rely on information provided by victims and CSOs, who are the main actors and stakeholders that can submit communications to the OTP. It is important for victims to be able to participate, including through CSOs, in the preliminary examination phase, as it is in their interest that an official investigation be pursued.[39] In the first place it is thus necessary that CSOs and victims be properly informed on the progress of the analysis. However, it has been noted that there was a lack of information on the progress of the analysis by the Prosecutor.[40] The situation improved after the decision to periodically publish the OTP report on preliminary examination activities. However, such reports of course are focused on the scope of the examination as it has been determined and limited by the OTP itself, which does not necessarily include the whole pic-

---

ability of Prosecutorial Discretion at the International Criminal Court", in *American Journal of International Law*, 2003, vol. 97, no. 3, pp. 510–52, 513 ff.

[38] See, for instance, the attempts done both by CSO and victims as well as by the judges, to have information on OTP pre-investigation activities and have certain crimes included in the situations under investigation, in Uganda and Democratic Republic of Congo just to mention two.

[39] Cécile Aptel, "Prosecutorial Discretion at the ICC and Victims' Right to Remedy: Narrowing the Impunity Gap", in *Journal of International Criminal Justice*, 2012, vol. 10, no. 5, pp. 1367–68.

[40] FIDH, *Victims' Rights before the ICC: A Guide for Victims, their Legal Representatives and NGOs*, 2007, at p. 20.

---

ture as communicated by the CSOs and victims; thus not all who have submitted communications are necessarily informed on whether these are being analysed, what the progress of the investigations is, whether further information is required, and what the results of the analysis are.[41] There is no provision in the Rome Statute, the RPE or Regulations of the OTP that obliges the Prosecutor to respond to communications he or she receives. Due to this shortage of information, those who have submitted communications have fewer possibilities to challenge the Prosecutor's analysis and any eventual decision not to investigate.[42] In addition, less transparency by the Prosecutor in preliminary examinations could also lead to the Prosecutor not considering certain crimes, or certain areas, or dismissing those as he or she does not possess sufficient information on. More transparency would enable victims and CSOs to provide substantial and better tailored information to the Prosecutor. Furthermore, it would provide victims and CSOs with the opportunity to shed light on other crimes that have occurred, but that might be overlooked by the Prosecutor.

29.2.2.2. Representations during Authorization to Open an Investigation

As already noted, a decision of the PTC is needed in order for the Prosecutor to initiate an investigation into those situations where no referral – either by the UNSC or by a State Party – has been received. The judicial authorization to open *proprio motu* investigations was introduced to provide a check on the Prosecutor's discretion at a very early stage, in the absence of other 'legitimacy tools' (the aforementioned referrals).[43] The requirement to get the authorization by the PTC puts an additional burden on the OTP's shoulders, in order to establish before the judges in a very early phase of the proceedings that there is a "reasonable basis to proceed with an investigation" pursuant to Article 15.

Interestingly, such a need for an authorization provides victims with an initial opportunity to make representations before the PTC.[44] Accord-

---

[41] *Ibid.*

[42] *Ibid.*

[43] Thoroughly on this point, see Allison Marston Danner, 2003, p. 515, see *supra* note 37.

[44] On the contrary, in the event of preliminary examinations based on a state referral or a referral by the UNSC, the Prosecutor does not need to seek authorization from the PTC to proceed and thus there is also no stage for the victims to make representations.

ing to the Rome Statute, when the Prosecutor requests authorization from the PTC to initiate an investigation, he or she must also inform the victims of his or her intention to seek authorisation;[45] in accordance with Article 15(3) of the Rome Statute and Rule 50(1) of the RPE, victims may then make representations to the PTC.[46] It shall be noted that the first quality control of a preliminary examination can be done by those who personally experienced the alleged crimes and brought them to the attention of the Prosecutor.

29.2.2.3. Intervention during the Judicial Review of the Decision Not to Open an Investigation

If, upon completion of the preliminary examination, the Prosecutor determines that there is no reasonable basis to proceed with an investigation, the Rome Statute provides for some limited possibility of judicial review. Interestingly, the mechanism of review differs depending on whether the Prosecutor acted *proprio motu* or upon referral.[47]

1. Where the preliminary examination was opened upon a referral, Article 53(3)(a) provides that the PTC may review a decision of the Prosecutor 'not to proceed' at the request of the State making the referral or the UNSC.[48] However, there is no express right for victims or CSOs to make such a request to the PTC.[49] Notably, the judges can never oblige the Prosecutor to pursue a specific investigation: at most they can "request the Prosecutor to reconsider that decision"

---

[45] Rome Statute of the International Criminal Court, 17 July 1998, Article 15(3) ('ICC Statute') (http://www.legal-tools.org/doc/7b9af9/).

[46] *Ibid.*, William A. Schabas, *The International Criminal Court: A Commentary on the Rome Statute*, Oxford University Press, 2010, p. 322.

[47] Hector Olasolo, "The Prosecutor of the ICC before the Initiation of Investigations: A Quasi-Judicial or a Political Body", in *International Criminal Law Review*, 2003, vol. 3, no. 87, 2003, pp. 101–04.

[48] In the Gaza situation referred by the State of Comoros, the PTC requested the Prosecutor to reconsider her decision not to initiate an investigation, based on her assessment of gravity, ICC, Situation on Registered Vessels of the Union of the Comoros, the Hellenic Republic and the Kingdom of Cambodia, PTC I, Decision on the request of the Union of the Comoros to review the Prosecutor's decision not to initiate an investigation, 16 July 2015, ICC-01/03-34, see *supra* note 34.

[49] Susana SaCouto and Katherine Cleary, "Victims' Participation in the Investigations of the International Criminal Court", in *Transnational Law and Contemporary Problems*, 2008, vol. 17, no. 73, p. 94.

(not to open an investigation).[50] Moreover, as the PTC noted: "the Chamber's competence under Article 53(3)(a) of the Statute [...] is triggered only by the existence of a disagreement between the Prosecutor (who decides not to open an investigation) and the referring entity (which wishes that such an investigation be opened), and is limited by the parameters of this disagreement".[51]

2. In the event that, when acting proprio motu, the Prosecutor decides not to initiate an investigation, the PTC may, on its own initiative, only review such a decision if based solely on the "interests of justice" pursuant to Article 53(3)(b).[52] Article 53 of the Rome Statute does not provide for a right of victims or other stakeholders to participate in the review of the decision of the Prosecutor not to proceed. However, Article 68(3) could be interpreted to allow victims to present their views and concerns with regard to the decision of the Prosecutor not to proceed with an investigation (also taking into account Rules 89, 92(2), and 93 of the RPE).[53] Furthermore, it shall be noted that victims, their legal representatives and CSOs can seek leave from the PTC in accordance with Rule 103 of the RPE to submit their observations on any issue; CSOs, for instance, could request leave from the PTC to submit an amicus curiae brief.[54]

---

[50] However, it shall be noted that according to the wording of Article 53(3)(b), when the Prosecutor's decision not to investigate/prosecute is based solely on the interests of justice and the PTC reviews it on its own initiative, "the decision of the Prosecutor shall be effective only if confirmed by the Pre-trial Chamber".

[51] ICC, Situation on Registered Vessels of the Union of the Comoros, the Hellenic Republic and the Kingdom of Cambodia, PTC I, Decision on the request of the Union of the Comoros to review the Prosecutor's decision not to initiate an investigation, 16 July 2015, ICC-01/03-34, para. 9, see *supra* note 34.

[52] ICC Statute, Article 53(3)(b), see *supra* note 45.

[53] Rule 93 Rules of Procedure and Evidence ('RPE') sets out that the Chamber may seek the views of the victims or their legal representatives at any time in relation to issues referred to in Pules 107, 109, 125, 128, 136, 139 and 191. Subsequently, Rule 107 RPE provides for a possibility to make a request for a review of a decision by the Prosecutor not to initiate an investigation or not to prosecute in writing, supported with reasons.

[54] Brianne McGonigle Leyh, *Procedural Justice? Victim Participation in International Criminal Proceedings*, Intersentia, 2011, at p. 237. With regard to CSO participation see ICC, Situation in the Democratic Republic of the Congo, PTC I, Decision on the Request submitted pursuant to Rule 103(1) of the RPE, 17 August 2007, ICC-01/04-373, para. 5 (http://www.legal-tools.org/doc/b9775f/).

3. In the other cases, namely if the decision of the Prosecutor is not based solely on the interests of justice,[55] and there is no request by the referring State or by the UNSC, there is no mechanism for the victims, CSOs or other stakeholders that provided information to the OTP.[56] It must be noted that in the event that the PTC decides not review the Prosecutor's decision, or does not order the Prosecutor to reconsider her decision not to proceed, there are no provisions through which victims, CSOs or other stakeholders can challenge these decisions.

29.2.2.4. Lack of Powers with Regard to a Decision Not to Open an Investigation Based on Article 15(6)

Where the Prosecutor concludes that there is no reasonable basis to proceed with the investigation, based on Article 15(6) of the Rome Statute and Rule 49(1) of the RPE, the Prosecutor needs to inform those who provided information in relation to the preliminary examinations.[57] However, different than the situation under Article 15(3) (where there *is* a reasonable basis to proceed), victims may not make representations to the PTC to challenge the decision of the Prosecutor not to prosecute since the Rome Statute does not provide victims with an express right to do so.[58]

For example, the first preliminary examination of the Iraq situation was opened on the basis of a number of communications pointing to the

---

[55] "In absence of a definition of the expression 'interests of justice' in the Statute and the RPE, Article 53 practically gives the prosecutor the broadest possible scope of political discretion in order to decide whether or not to proceed with an investigation", see Olasolo, 2003, p. 111, see *supra* note 47 (also differentiates between inherent discretion arising from the principle of legality and political discretion).

[56] See in this sense also the ICC, PTC II, Decision on the request for review of the Prosecutor's decision of 23 April 2014 not to open a preliminary examination concerning alleged crimes committed in the Arab Republic of Egypt, and the Registrar's Decision of 25 April 2014, 12 September 2014, ICC-RoC46(3)-01/14-3 (http://www.legal-tools.org/doc/bfbb8f/).

[57] To allow victims to apply for participation in the proceedings in accordance with Rule 89, the Court notifies victims concerning the decision of the Prosecutor not to initiate an investigation or not to prosecute pursuant to Article 53 of the ICC Statute. Such a notification shall be given to victims or their legal representatives who have already participated in the proceedings or, as far as possible, to those who have communicated with the Court in respect of the situation or case in question. The Chamber may order the measures outlined in sub-rule 8 if it considers it appropriate in the particular circumstances.

[58] SaCouto, Cleary, 2008, p. 94, see *supra* note 49.

---

commission of grave crimes by UK armed forces. On 9 February 2006, the OTP informed those who submitted communications of the fact that it would not pursue investigations.[59] There was, however, no possibility for victims and CSOs to challenge this decision before the PTC, as the Rome Statute does not foresee such a right for victims to challenge an Article 15(6) decision of the Prosecutor when acting *proprio motu*.

The fact that, under the Rome Statute, there is no review mechanism that can be triggered in such circumstances by those who provided the information deserves strong criticism. In fact, the issue was debated during the drafting of the Rome Statute, as in many domestic systems, it is possible to challenge a decision of a Prosecutor not to initiate investigations. During the negotiations of the Rome Statute, delegates from France argued that victims have the right to review a decision from the Prosecutor not to initiate an investigation.[60] Other delegates disagreed, stating that this as well as review possibilities by the Court, would affect the Prosecutor's independence.[61] The current system reflects a compromise, as the Court has been granted the possibility to review on certain occasions and victim participation has been restricted.[62]

29.2.3. Challenging the Prosecutor's Failure to Open Investigations in the absence of a Decision Not to Open an Investigation

With regard to the possibility of CSOs, victims and other stakeholders carrying out quality control on preliminary examination, the thorniest issue is that the Prosecutor, instead of taking a formal decision not to investigate (or not to proceed), often simply leaves the preliminary examination (or the investigation) open indefinitely. As a consequence, the Prosecutor's (non-)decisions cannot be challenged.[63]

---

[59] ICC, OTP response to communications received concerning Iraq, 9 February 2006 (http://www.legal-tools.org/doc/5b8996/).

[60] Leyh, 2011, p. 265, see *supra* note 54.

[61] *Ibid.*

[62] Based on Article 53(3)(a) and 53(3)(b) of the Rome Statute, the Court may review certain decision of the Prosecutor not to initiate an investigation or to prosecute.

[63] Redress, *The Participation of Victims in International Criminal Court Proceedings, a Review of the Practice and Considerations for the Future*, October 2012, p. 46. This policy of suspension or indecisiveness by the Prosecutor is also illustrated by a request lodged by victims in 2010 in relation to the Situation in the Democratic Republic of Congo. In 2010 in respect of the Situation in the Democratic Republic of Congo, based on Article 68(3) of

An interesting case in this regard is what happened in the situation of the CAR, which could also perhaps be relied on by CSOs and victims to obtain information and challenge the (non-)decisions of the OTP.

In 2006, the CAR Government attempted to obtain information on the status of the preliminary examination in respect of the situation that the Government itself had referred to the OTP in December 2004.[64] The Government filed a request to the PTC requesting: "that the Prosecutor provide information on the alleged failure to decide, within a reasonable time, whether or not to initiate an investigation pursuant to Rules 105(1) and 105(4) of the Rules of Procedure and Evidence".[65] The OTP submitted that it is under no obligation to submit information to the PTC absent decisions pursuant to Article 53 of the Rome Statute. Nevertheless, the request was followed by a decision of the PTC requesting the Prosecutor to provide the Chamber with an update on the status of the preliminary examination, as: "the State which referred the situation has the right to be informed by the Prosecutor and therefore to ask the Chamber to request that the Prosecutor provide the said information".[66] Eventually, the OTP

---

the Rome Statute victims requested the PTC to review the alleged decision of the Prosecutor not to proceed against Bemba in relation to certain crimes. However, the PTC declared that "to date no decision on 'interest of justice' grounds not to proceed against Mr Bemba with respect to crimes allegedly committed in Ituri has been taken" and thus that there is "[...] no decision for the Chamber to review and there is, accordingly, no basis for it to exercise its powers under article 53(3)(b) of the Statute", see ICC, Situation in the Democratic Republic of Congo, PTC I, Decision on the designation of a Single Judge of Pre-Trial Chamber I, 25 October 2010, ICC-01/04-583, paras. 4–5 (http://www.legal-tools.org/doc/c84b80/). This decision does imply that in a case where the Prosecutor has decided not to proceed with the investigation or to prosecute based on Article 53(1)(c) or 53(2)(c), victims can request the PTC to review the decision by the Prosecutor, Leyh, 2011, p. 267, see *supra* note 54 (http://www.legal-tools.org/doc/c84b80/).

64 The Government of the Central African Republic ('CAR') submitted its referral of the situation in the CAR to the OTP pursuant to Article 13 and 14 of the Rome Statute on 22 December 2004.

65 Schabas, 2010, p. 668, see *supra* note 46, referring to Situation in the Central African Republic (ICC-01/05), Transmission par le Greffier d'une Requête aux Fins de Saisine de la Chambre Préliminaire de la Coeur Pénale Internationale et Annexes Jointes, 27 September 2006, ICC-01/05-5-Anx2 (http://www.legal-tools.org/doc/cdd070/).

66 ICC, Situation in the Central African Republic, PTC III, Prosecution's report pursuant to Pre-Trial Chamber III's 30 November 2006, Decision Requesting Information on the Status of the Preliminary Examination of the Situation in the Central African Republic, 15 December 2006, ICC-01/05-07 (http://www.legal-tools.org/doc/1dd66a/). The Court also

---

provided the PTC with the report, though explicitly stating that it was under no obligation to do so, as no decision under Article 53(1) had been made, and thus there was no exercise of prosecutorial discretion subjected to judicial review by the Chamber.[67] Nowadays, 10 years after the facts in question, the OTP is of course much more transparent with regard to the activities undertaken in the course of its preliminary examinations, as reflected in the OTP Policy Paper. Nevertheless, as already noted before, the OTP's yearly reports on preliminary examinations do not necessarily cover the whole spectrum of communications received and do not necessarily address all the requests raised by victims and CSOs.

Thus, even though the OTP's preliminary examinations into the Situation in the CAR were based on a State Party referral, the case might be significant in order to argue that in the case of *proprio motu* preliminary examinations by the OTP, victims and CSOs that provided information on the alleged crimes can request that the PTC order the OTP to provide information on its activities. In other words, it could be argued that similar to a State Party that has referred a situation, those victims and CSOs who have 'referred' a situation to the OTP by way of communications also have "the right to be informed by the Prosecutor and therefore to ask the Chamber to request that the Prosecutor provide the said information".

29.2.4. Conclusions on Preliminary Examinations before the ICC

The preliminary examination of the situation in Colombia has been ongoing for over a decade: the OTP acknowledges receipt of 181 communications pursuant to Article 15.[68] However, since CSOs and victims' participatory rights are limited in the preliminary examination phase, there seem to be few methods available for victims or CSOs to influence these preinvestigations or to obtain information on the proceedings. ICC practice and the OTP's Policy Paper indicate that the Prosecutor is not bound to time limits in respect of the preliminary examinations. Furthermore, even though the OTP has a transparency policy in relation to preliminary examinations, the Prosecutor is not obliged to respond to communications by victims or CSOs or to inform them of the status of the investigations. In-

---

requested the Prosecutor to provide an estimate of when the preliminary examination of the CAR situation would be concluded.

[67] *Ibid.*, para. 1; Schabas, 2010, p. 668, see *supra* note 46.

[68] OTP, *Report on Preliminary Examination Activities*, para. 52, see *supra* note 18.

deed, until the Prosecutor has made a decision whether or not to seek authorization from the PTC in accordance with Article 15(3), there are few if any means for victims or CSOs to further this process. Moreover, no means are available for victims or CSOs to challenge a decision of the Prosecutor not to initiate investigations based on Article 15(6) of the Rome Statute.

Moreover, it shall be noted that even if the preliminary examination of the situation in Colombia has been ongoing for more than 10 years, without investigation powers, it is difficult for the OTP to receive the necessary information, for example, about policies at highest governmental level and their connection to sets of crimes that fall under crimes against humanity. The case of Colombia shows that the OTP granting too much time to allow for legislative and judicial developments in a country – while crimes continue – undermines the objectives of Rome Statute. This is because while there may be positive domestic legislative and judicial developments, the policies potentially linked to international crimes remain in place.

Similarly, the (new) preliminary examination of the situation in Iraq, which focuses on the responsibility of UK military personnel, strongly points to the need for the opening of an investigation at this stage of the proceedings. In the face of grave crimes committed in that context, which have been confirmed by several sources,[69] the preliminary examination proves to be ineffective and causes grave delays in the administration of justice.

In this regard, for the OTP to establish subject-matter jurisdiction under the Rome Statute, and confirm the credibility of witness statements received, conducting its own investigations and witness interviews would be more effective in order to make its own assessment of the allegations presented. Examining the methodology behind some witness statements taken by lawyers and CSOs is of course necessary to assess their credibility, but the focus must remain on the content of the information provided, which can be corroborated by different sources, such as official documents, including domestic decisions confirming the allegations, as well as evidence presented in individual cases through videos and photographs.

---

[69] Nicholas Mercer, "The truth about British army abuses in Iraq must come out", in *Guardian*, 3 October 2016.

The "reasonable grounds to believe" requirement should not be interpreted as setting an overly high standard of proof at this stage. This would shift the burden of conducting fact-finding investigations – with all the resources required for this – from the OTP to CSOs. Beyond this, it also exposes those CSOs to intense scrutiny by the State under examination. Such organizations may end up becoming subject to extreme domestic political, legal and economic backlash, potentially leading to a chilling effect for other organizations that would not serve the interests of justice. In this sense, a full-fledged investigation by the ICC, thus giving the OTP investigative powers – rather than a mere preliminary examination which is based on open source materials and information provided by third parties – would be much more effective to overcome obstacles within situations such as Iraq/UK or Colombia and avoid arbitrariness and double standards.

30

Civil Society Participation in
Preliminary Examinations

Sarah Williams[*]

30.1. Introduction

The role of civil society in the negotiations for the Rome Statute of the International Criminal Court ('Rome Statute') is a significant illustration of the increasing civil society influence on the development of international law and the design of international institutions.[1] Civil society actors, under the umbrella organization of the Coalition for the International Criminal Court, assisted States to prepare for negotiations for the first permanent international criminal court and played a vital role in developing the Court's institutional, procedural and substantive framework.[2] Civil society also argued for broader rights of participation in the new International Criminal Court ('ICC') compared to other international institutions, including previous international criminal tribunals. The inclusion of both victim participation in proceedings and a framework for delivering reparations to victims of ICC crimes was an important victory for civil society actors, albeit an outcome also supported by many State delegations participating in the negotiations.

A more controversial, and harder won, victory was the inclusion of an independent prosecutor capable of initiating an investigation *proprio*

---

[*]   **Sarah Williams** is Professor, Faculty of Law, UNSW Sydney and Associate, Australian Human Rights Centre. This research was supported under Australian Research Council's *Discovery Projects* funding scheme (project DP 140101347). The views expressed herein are those of the author and are not necessarily those of the Australian Research Council. She would like to thank Professors Bergsmo and Stahn for the invitation to participate in this project and Natalie Hodgson and Emma Palmer for their research assistance.

[1]   See, for example, Alan Boyle and Christine Chinkin, *The Making of International Law*, Cambridge University Press, 2007.

[2]   See, for example, Benjamin Schiff, *Building the International Criminal Court*, Cambridge University Press, 2008; Michael Struett, *The Politics of Building the International Criminal Court: NGOs, Discourse and Agency*, Palgrave, 2008.

motu in the absence of a referral from a State or the UN Security Council. The possibility of independent action by the Prosecutor is linked to an important avenue for civil society participation in the ICC, namely, the ability under Article 15 of the Rome Statute for the Prosecutor to receive information from various actors, including individuals and non-governmental organizations, as to whether ICC crimes have occurred within a situation country. This provides a novel avenue for civil society to influence future ICC investigations as, by providing information to the Prosecutor, civil society may draw the Prosecutor's attention to a particular situation and may ultimately prompt the Prosecutor to initiate an investigation. The potential influence of civil party 'communications' to the Prosecutor under Article 15 through the preliminary examination phase is clear. Broader engagement with civil society is supported by notions of enhanced transparency and representativeness in decision-making, which ultimately contributes to the legitimacy of the Office of the Prosecutor ('OTP') and the ICC.

As the resources of the Prosecutor are limited, and the number of situations demanding attention increases, civil society are increasingly seeking ways to influence the Prosecutor to act. However, this chapter will demonstrate that the Article 15 communication mechanism is not best suited to this role. Despite the volume of communications received by the Prosecutor pursuant to Article 15, it is not clear how, if at all, such communications have actually influenced the Prosecutor's decision to proceed to an investigation or to close a preliminary examination. Nor is it evident that the ability to file a communication provides civil society with sufficient means to participate in key decisions during the preliminary examination phase, in particular those decisions concerning the exercise of prosecutorial discretion in this essential phase. While there is a system for judicial review of prosecutorial decisions concerning the initiation of investigations, it is designed to protect the Court (and ultimately States) from an overly political or overreaching prosecutor, not to prompt a reluctant prosecutor to act.

Another mechanism of civil society participation in ICC proceedings and potential avenue of influence is the *amicus curiae* brief, discussed in Rome and incorporated in the ICC Rules of Procedure and Evidence. Unlike Article 15 communications, *amicus curiae* is not a novel mechanism invented for the ICC, but is found in the rules of other international criminal tribunals and international institutions, as well as in many national legal systems. It too is justified by the need for transparency and broader participation in judicial decision-making, as enabling *amici* submissions allows judges to reach better decisions and thus enhances the legitimacy of the institution. A study of ICC *amici* practice reveals that civil society actors do use the mechanism to participate in ICC proceedings; moreover, there is some evidence that submissions have influenced judicial decision-making and legal outcomes.[3] It thus appears to be a successful mechanism for civil society influence. Yet its application to the preliminary examination phase and its influence on prosecutorial (as opposed to judicial) decision-making is limited. This chapter suggests that if civil society desires greater influence in preliminary examinations, actors must look for other methods of influence instead.

This chapter first provides an overview of civil society participation in the preliminary examination phase. It then details the limited influence of civil society on key prosecutorial decisions during preliminary examinations and highlights the potential for manipulation of the Article 15 process by civil society actors. It concludes that Article 15 does not support general rights of participation for civil society actors, nor does it overcome the absence of a right to trigger judicial review of prosecutorial decisions in the preliminary examination phase. However, the chapter argues that introducing legal standing for civil society actors is not feasible or necessarily desirable.

Next, the chapter briefly outlines the practice of the ICC regarding civil society *amici* before considering whether the *amicus curiae* mechanism has any potential to enhance civil society influence at the preliminary examination stage or whether alternative mechanisms are required. The chapter concludes by suggesting two possible measures for enhancing civil society participation during preliminary examinations: (1) a call for focused submissions by the OTP at key stages of a preliminary examination – a 'friend of the prosecutor' type model; and (2) a staged approach to Article 15 communications, with an initial communication format, followed by more detailed information after the OTP has determined the information to be credible and that the situation may fall within the ICC's jurisdiction. Moreover, the chapter argues that the OTP should provide

---

3   Sarah Williams and Emma Palmer, "Civil Society and Amicus Curiae Interventions in the International Criminal Court", in Sarah Williams and Hannah Woolaver (eds.), *Acta Juridica*, 2016, p. 40.

greater information and transparency concerning: the communications it receives (even if limited to the nature of submitter and the type of information provided due to confidentiality concerns); the manner in which it assesses such information; and the need to manage so-called strategic communications.

30.2. Civil Society, Preliminary Examinations and Article 15 Communications

30.2.1. The Nature of Preliminary Examinations and the Role of Article 15 Communications

The preliminary examination phase is unique to the ICC. Its purpose is to decide whether there is a reasonable basis to proceed with an investigation into a situation.[4] Pre-Trial Chamber II has interpreted this as requiring that "there exists a sensible or reasonable justification for a belief that a crime falling within the jurisdiction of the Court 'has been or is being committed'".[5] This test requires consideration of whether the legal criteria set out in the Rome Statute have been satisfied, namely: jurisdiction (temporal, territorial or personal, and substantive); admissibility (complementarity and gravity); and the interests of justice.[6] The Prosecutor may initiate a preliminary examination process on the basis of: (a) a referral from a State Party or the United Nations Security Council; (b) a declaration by a State accepting the jurisdiction of the Court under Article 12(3) of the Rome Statute; or (c) information provided by individuals or groups, States, intergovernmental or non-governmental organizations ('NGOs') pursuant to Article 15 of the Rome Statute.[7] Regardless of the basis for a preliminary examination, prosecution activities during the preliminary examination phase are conducted in the same manner. The OTP has no independent investigative powers during the preliminary examinations process; rather the OTP may receive and request additional information on the situation

---

4 Rome Statute of the International Criminal Court, adopted 17 July 1998, entry into force 1 July 2002, Article 53 ('ICC Statute') (http://www.legal-tools.org/doc/7b9af9/).

5 ICC, Situation in the Republic of Kenya, Pre-Trial Chamber, Decision Pursuant to Article 15 of the Rome Statute on the Authorisation of an Investigation into the Situation in the Republic of Kenya, 31 March 2010, ICC-01/09-19, para. 35 (http://www.legal-tools.org/doc/338a6f/).

6 Office of the Prosecutor, *Policy Paper on Preliminary Examinations*, 1 November 2013 (http://www.legal-tools.org/doc/acb906/).

7 *Ibid.*, para. 73.

---

from States, UN organs, intergovernmental organizations, NGOs and "other reliable sources that are deemed appropriate".[8] The OTP's decision is therefore based on the facts and information made available to it and is, in this sense, preliminary and subject to revision where new facts or evidence are presented. The OTP has indicated that it adopts a filtering process involving four phases (an initial assessment; jurisdiction; admissibility and interests of justice; and final recommendation).[9]

The preliminary examination phase is thus an essential one that determines the situations, and ultimately the cases, that will be investigated and prosecuted before the Court. It is also a phase that endows the Prosecutor with considerable discretion; even though the Rome Statute sets out clear legal criteria for the initiation of an investigation, there is much scope in how these criteria are interpreted and applied within a given context. This chapter addresses the important issue as to whether Article 15 enables civil society sufficient influence in respect of decisions to proceed or not to proceed to an investigation.

There is limited judicial review of prosecutorial decisions taken in the preliminary examination phase: the Pre-Trial Chamber is only required to review a decision to initiate an investigation where the Prosecutor exercises her *proprio motu* power under Article 15.[10] Further, the Pre-Trial Chamber is only required to review a decision *not* to proceed to an investigation in two circumstances. First, regardless of how the situation came before the Court, the Pre-Trial Chamber must review a decision not to proceed where the Prosecutor has declined to proceed on the basis of the interests of justice criterion.[11] Second, where the decision not to proceed to an investigation is based on other criteria in the Statute (that is, jurisdiction, gravity and complementarity), the UN Security Council or the State that referred the situation to the Court may request a review by the Pre-Trial Chamber.[12] There is no right of review where the preliminary examination was triggered by communications received under Article 15 and the decision not to proceed is based on criteria other than the interests

---

[8]   *Ibid.*, para. 85.

[9]   *Ibid.*; Office of the Prosecutor, *Paper on Some Policy Issues Before the Office of the Prosecutor*, 5 September 2003 (http://www.legal-tools.org/doc/f53870/).

[10] ICC Statute, Article 15(3), see *supra* note 4.

[11] *Ibid.*, Article 53(3)(b).

[12] *Ibid.*, Article 53(3)(a).

of justice. Those submitting a communication will be informed about the decision not to proceed, but have no standing to seek a review of that decision.

Similarly, victims have limited procedural standing in a preliminary examination. While the regulations applicable to the Prosecutor require the OTP to address the interests of the victims at all stages of proceedings, and victims can pass on information to the Prosecutor during the preliminary examination phase,[13] the only express right victims have is to make representations where the Prosecutor requires authorization to initiate an investigation under Article 15(3) and where jurisdiction or admissibility is challenged under Article 19(3). Therefore, victims do not have standing to request a review of *any* decision taken by the Prosecutor during the preliminary examination phase. In addition, ICC judges have to date refused to recognize an inherent jurisdiction of the Court to conduct a *proprio motu* judicial review of the Prosecutor's decisions during the preliminary examination and investigation stages, outside the limited avenues for review expressly indicated in the Rome Statute.[14]

30.2.2. Do Article 15 Communications Influence the Prosecutor?

As noted above, the ability of the Prosecutor to initiate investigations based on information provided by civil society without necessarily having the support of relevant States was a major victory for those at Rome in favour of an independent and responsive Prosecutor. The ability of civil society, including victims, to submit information to the OTP in the form of communications under Article 15 is a novel form of civil society participation, at least in the context of international judicial institutions. Moreover, the Article 15 process is also available for situations referred by a

---

[13] OTP, *Regulations of the Office of the Prosecutor*, 23 April 2009, ICC-BD/05-01-09, Regulation 16 (http://www.legal-tools.org/doc/a97226/).

[14] ICC, Pre-Trial Chamber, Decision on the 'Request for Review of the Prosecutor's Decision of 23 April 2014 Not to Open a Preliminary Examination Concerning Alleged Crimes Committed in the Arab Republic of Egypt, and the Registrar's Decision of 25 April 2014', 12 September 2014, ICC-RoC46(3)-01/14-3 (http://www.legal-tools.org/doc/bfbb8f/); ICC, Pre-Trial Chamber, Decision on a Request for Reconsideration or Leave to Appeal the "Decision on the 'Request for a Review of the Prosecutor's Decision of 23 April 2014 Not to Open a Preliminary Examination Concerning Alleged Crimes Committed in the Arab Republic of Egypt, and the Registrar's Decision of 25 April 2014'", 22 September 2014, ICC-RoC46(3)-01/14-5 (http://www.legal-tools.org/doc/7ced5a/).

State or the Security Council, so it is potentially a valuable route to place information before the OTP, including materials which may not be in the interest of the referring State to provide. Article 15 may thus be said to enhance the legitimacy of OTP decision-making by making the process more representative as various views and sources of information can be considered. Yet it appears that civil society does not desire merely to provide information, but also to have a say in the decision whether or not to proceed to an investigation, as will be discussed below.

Submitting an Article 15 communication has certainly proven to be a popular mechanism. As at September 2016, the OTP had received a total of 12,022 communications made pursuant to Article 15 since July 2002.[15] Yet, filing a communication under Article 15 is not a right of formal participation, even in the limited sense in which *amici* participate (see Section 30.3. below). It also appears to be mostly ineffective in bringing about an investigation, as the Prosecutor has only initiated four investigations under Article 15, namely the situations in Kenya, Georgia, Burundi and Côte d'Ivoire. In Kenya, the investigation was only initiated following the failure of domestic authorities to agree to proceed at the national level and the main sources of information came from the preceding investigative commission. The situation in Côte d'Ivoire was arguably more like a referral by the Government, which accepted jurisdiction under Article 12(3) as a non-State Party at the time. The investigation into the situation in Georgia appears to be the first genuine '*proprio motu*' exercise of power; however, it was also preceded by an investigation commission that provided the evidence and impetus to move to an investigation. In the Prosecutor's requests to the Pre-Trial Chamber for approval to initiate an investigation in these three situations, it is striking that the Prosecutor does not appear to rely on information contained in Article 15 communications; rather, the evidentiary basis for the request is in each case information obtained from previous non-judicial investigations, media sources and public source documents.[16] The decision concerning Burundi, which

---

[15] Office of the Prosecutor, *Report on Preliminary Activities 2016*, 14 November 2016 (http://www.legal-tools.org/doc/f30a53/).

[16] ICC, Situation in the Republic of Kenya, Pre-Trial Chamber, Request for Authorisation of an Investigation Pursuant to Article 15, 26 November 2009, ICC-01/09-3 (http://www.legal-tools.org/doc/c63dcc/); ICC, Situation in the Republic of Côte d'Ivoire, Pre-Trial Chamber, Request for Authorisation of an Investigation Pursuant to Article 15, 23 June 2011, ICC-02/11-3 (http://www.legal-tools.org/doc/1b1939/); ICC, Situation in Georgia,

was linked to the entry into force of Burundi's withdrawal from the Rome Statute, is the second.

There is an extensive role for civil society actors in this sense. In the request under Article 15 concerning the situation in Georgia, for example, the Prosecutor's request relies largely on reports by NGOs such as Human Rights Watch and Amnesty International.[17] This information was not provided as formal communications but rather information contained in ordinary fact-finding and context analysis activities performed by such organizations. The decision not to rely expressly on Article 15 communications may be due to the OTP's policy concerning the confidentiality of communications, but the practice suggests that individual communications are perhaps less influential than public source reports by credible, large and international NGOs.

Of the twelve situations currently in the preliminary examination phase (as at March 2018), eight arise from Article 15 communications.[18] Whether to open an investigation in these situations will depend on the exercise of the Prosecutor's *proprio motu* powers and is subject to approval by the Pre-Trial Chamber. In two further situations, although the jurisdiction is based on Article 12(3) declarations, the opening of an investigation will require the Prosecutor to exercise her discretion under Article 15 (as Article 12(3) declarations are not considered to be the equivalent of State referrals).[19] Thus, the current preliminary examinations, if they lead to investigations, may change the perception of some civil society actors and commentators that the Article 15 mechanism has little impact.

Perhaps the clearest example of the potential influence of Article 15 communications we have seen to date is the reopening of the preliminary

---

Pre-Trial Chamber, Request for Authorisation of an Investigation Pursuant to Article 15, 13 October 2015, ICC-01/15-4 (https://www.legal-tools.org/doc/460e78/).

[17] See, for example, *ibid.*, paras. 32, 63.

[18] These are the situations in Afghanistan, Burundi, Colombia, Guinea, Iraq, and Nigeria, OTP, 2016, see *supra* note 15. Note that the Prosecutor announced in February 2018 that her office would open preliminary examinations in respect of the Philippines and Venezuela. A decision on the Prosecutor's Article 15 request to open an investigation concerning the situation in Afghanistan was pending at the time this chapter was finalised (early March 2018).

[19] These are the situations in Ukraine and Palestine. *Ibid.*

examination into Iraq. Former Prosecutor Moreno-Ocampo received several communications concerning alleged war crimes committed by UK forces in Iraq. However, in 2006 he declined to proceed to an investigation, stating that, while there was some evidence crimes within the jurisdiction of the ICC had been committed, these crimes did not appear to be of sufficient gravity to be admissible before the ICC.[20] In 2014, Prosecutor Bensouda reopened the preliminary examination based on a communication received from two civil society actors – the European Center for Constitutional and Human Rights together with the Public Interest Lawyers. That communication, which was made publicly available by the organizations themselves, comprised both factual evidence and legal analysis.[21] The Prosecutor expressly based her decision to reopen the preliminary examination on the information provided in the communication.[22] Thus the Iraq preliminary examination demonstrates the potential of civil society communications to influence prosecutorial decisions. It also emphasizes that preliminary examination is a process and that a decision not to proceed is not necessarily final and can be revisited if fresh information becomes available.

The Iraq preliminary examination also illustrates the potential risk for the Prosecutor (and the ICC) in basing key prosecutorial decisions on information obtained from civil society. In 2017, the Law Society of England and Wales removed Phil Shiner, the main lawyer for Public Interest Lawyers, from the roll of solicitors after finding him responsible for multiple professional misconduct offences, including dishonesty concerning false witness accounts tendered to a national inquiry into allegations committed by UK personnel in Iraq.[23] While the charge was related to

---

20 Office of the Prosecutor, *OTP Response to Communications Received Concerning Iraq*, 9 February 2006 (http://www.legal-tools.org/doc/5b8996/).

21 See European Center for Constitutional and Human Rights and Public Interest Lawyers, *Communication to the Office of the Prosecutor of the International Criminal Court: The Responsibility of Officials of the United Kingdom for War Crimes Involving Systematic Detainee Abuse in Iraq from 2003-2008*, 10 January 2014, (http://www.legal-tools.org/doc/8d151d/).

22 OTP, "Prosecutor of the International Criminal Court, Fatou Bensouda, Re-opens the Preliminary Examination of the Situation in Iraq", 13 May 2014 (http://www.legal-tools.org/doc/d9d9c5/).

23 Solicitors' Regulation Authority, "Professor Phil Shiner and the Solicitors Disciplinary Tribunal", 2 February 2017 (http://www.legal-tools.org/doc/c95b3a/); Owen Bowcott,

domestic proceedings, this same evidence might well have been incorporated into the Article 15 communication and thus might have directly influenced the Prosecutor's decision to reopen the preliminary examination. The implications of this national disciplinary action for the current ICC preliminary examination are not clear, with the Prosecutor having made no reference to the incident.

There are also signs that the Prosecutor has become more responsive to certain communications by highlighting the preventative role of the OTP in responding to alleged ICC crimes. A number of communications or prospective communications have appeared to trigger a direct response from the Prosecutor. For example, the Prosecutor issued a statement concerning alleged crimes in the Philippines,[24] in a climate where various actors were preparing and at least one eventually did file an extensive communication.[25] Yet many other communications have not triggered a response from the Prosecutor, including those submitted in relation to Australia's asylum and detention policy. This may suggest that in certain circumstances the OTP was already looking at a situation and would have acted independently of Article 15 communications, which appears to be the case with the Philippines. It is also possible that the Prosecutor reserves her strong public statements for 'serious' situations where there are on-going violations and which appear to fall clearly within the purview of the ICC.

Dugard suggests that other factors may also influence the Prosecutor's reliance on Article 15 communications as a basis for opening an investigation, in particular the preference both Prosecutors have given to securing referrals from States so that co-operation is more likely – although not guaranteed – to eventuate.[26] This means that civil society communications concerning alleged crimes committed by a government

---

"Phil Shiner: Iraq Human Rights Lawyer Struck Off Over Misconduct", in *The Guardian*, 3 February 2017 (http://www.legal-tools.org/doc/4f6a4d/).

[24] OPT, "Statement of the Prosecutor of the International Criminal Court, Fatou Bensouda Concerning the Situation in the Republic of the Philippines", 13 October 2016 (http://www.legal-tools.org/doc/bbc78e/).

[25] Clare Baldwin and Stephanie van den Berg, "Lawyer for Philippines Hit-man Files Complaint Against Duterte at ICC", in *Reuters*, 24 April 2017.

[26] John Dugard, "International Criminal Law, the International Criminal Court, and Civil Society", in Linda van de Vijver and Hugh Corder (eds.), *Acta Juridica*, 2006, p. 3.

---

still in power are unlikely to result in an investigation, unless the Prosecutor believes the authorities will co-operate. Moreover, Dugard refers to the significance the OTP places on effective control of the affected territory where authority for the territory is disputed. Where an authority is not in effective control of the territory, then that authority is unlikely to be able to co-operate and an investigation may not be feasible.

In current practice, it therefore appears that, while Article 15 communications allow some influence to civil society actors, that influence is not extensive and will generally not lead directly to a request to open an investigation. This is particularly so where there are concerns regarding co-operation with any investigation, such as where the communication concerns an incumbent government or a situation where authorities lack effective control over territory. However, if the current situations under preliminary examination are considered, the number of investigations that follow from the Prosecutor's *proprio motu* power and which are based on Article 15 communications may increase. Existing practice also highlights the challenges for the Prosecutor in relying on evidence provided by third parties, both in terms of quantity and quality.

30.2.3. Quality of Article 15 Communications and Standard of Review

Is there any explanation as to the current low rate of Article 15 communications leading to investigations? For instance, does it suggest that Article 15 communications are not of a high standard? There is no information as to the type or standard of information that should or can be submitted to the OTP. The OTP has no formal filter mechanism, initially accepting all communications filed. There is no guidance as to the content, focus, length, quantity or quality of the communications, nor is there any indication as to how the OTP will deal with the information, other than that it will be verified. The Prosecutor generally does not make communications public, although as noted above there have been instances where she has issued a statement based on information submitted in a communication. However, the information provider is not precluded from making public both the fact of its submission and the content of that communication. The confidential nature of the process makes collating data on information submitted to the OTP challenging and means that researchers must rely on an information provider making public the communication and at least a summary of its contents, usually through a press release. This skews analysis of the practice in this area, but without access to full OTP database of communications, it is impossible to map the communications, their provider, content and eventual impact.

It is clear from those communications that have been publicized that the information provided ranges from vague allegations and assertions with little proof or analysis to detailed factual and evidentiary material supported by extensive legal analysis. The fact that the vast majority of communications are dismissed as "manifestly outside of the Court's jurisdiction" suggests that they fall within the former extreme, and probably include unreliable information or display a fundamental misunderstanding of the basic jurisdictional and other limits of the Court.[27] This is in contrast to the *amicus curiae* mechanism (discussed below), where accepting submissions is within the discretion of the Chamber and the *amici* are limited to certain questions or issues, and face strict page limits. Moreover, the fact that many *amicus* briefs are submitted by organizations that engage lawyers to draft submissions or have experience in submitting *amicus* submissions in the ICC and other courts, or by experienced academics, means that the submissions are generally of good quality. This is not to say that Article 15 communications should be subject to the same tight levels of control as *amici*, as this would be inconsistent with the aim of enabling broader access to the Court. Many civil society organizations do employ lawyers with experience in international criminal law or engage their own in-house legal teams to prepare Article 15 communications. The practice on *amici*, where 'repeat players' appear to have greater influence, suggests that such an approach may well explain the 'success' of those communications that are not rejected outright and may then influence the Prosecutor. For example, local actors in Cambodia engaged Richard Rogers, a legal consultant and defence counsel at the Extraordinary Chambers in the Courts of Cambodia, to draft communications submitted to the Prosecutor.[28] The OTP should perhaps look for ways to encourage communications filed by qualified and experienced organizations, using legal advisors familiar with the ICC's jurisdictional framework. However, the

---

[27] For figures on how many communications are categorised as being "manifestly outside of the Court's jurisdiction", see, for example, OTP, 2016, see *supra* note 15.

[28] International Federation for Human Rights, "Cambodia: ICC Preliminary Examination Requested into Crimes Stemming from Mass Land Grabbing", 7 October 2014 (available on its web site).

large proportion of rejected communications does suggest that the 'image' of Article 15 enabling wider participation in or influence on OTP decisions is a false one for many of those submitting communications. Such 'failed' communications raise concerns about the wasted resources of the OTP and the submitting actors, as well as the prospect of creating false expectations of the OTP and the Court amongst victim groups.

Another suggestion as to why Article 15 communications are not as effective as civil society actors might hope is that they may be held to a higher standard than evidence obtained from other sources.[29] The non-public nature of decisions as to what weight is given to Article 15 communications contributes to a lack of transparency around the preliminary examination process. While this has been partially addressed by the annual preliminary examination report and situation specific reports, as well as specific policy papers, there is still insufficient information as to what happens to communications, the verification process and the standard(s) against which they are assessed. The OTP indicates that it evaluates sources of information according to a consistent methodology, based on criteria such as relevance, reliability, credibility, and completeness. It also endeavours to corroborate information provided to it against information obtained from open and other reliable sources.[30] In its request for approval to open an investigation in the situation in Georgia, for example, the Prosecutor highlighted the treatment of information that may be subject to "possible bias and interests from parties to the conflict" and how it "focused its examination on allegations corroborated by credible third parties".[31]

Thus there is no suggestion that the OTP assesses information provided by civil society differently to that received from States or international organizations, at least not as reflected in its stated policy. The OTP seems to be aware that those submitting Article 15 communications may have other motives, be biased and have their own interests to advance and thus the information must be verified and corroborated. This may lead to certain civil society communications being treated more favourably than

---

[29] Dugard, 2006, see *supra* note 26.

[30] OTP, 2013, paras. 30–31, see *supra* note 6.

[31] ICC, Situation in Georgia, Pre-Trial Chamber, Request for Authorisation of an Investigation Pursuant to Article 15, 13 October 2015, ICC-01/15-4, para. 46 (http://www.legal-tools.org/doc/460e78/).

others, for example, those from organizations that have a 'repeat' history of submitting communications in one or more situations and large international NGOs with established reputations. It also partly explains why the sources used to support Article 15 requests tend to be public source reports from reputable, large NGOs or investigative commissions. However, these risks also arise in relation to information provided by States and other actors with an interest in the outcome of the preliminary examination.

30.2.4.   What is the Aim of Article 15 Communications?

The large proportion of rejected communications may suggest that the Article 15 process is being used for instrumental reasons, rather than to make a genuine contribution to the preliminary examination process. Fairlie labels such communications as "strategic communications".[32] There have certainly been several examples of 'strategic communications' that have been submitted to the OTP and widely publicized, with perhaps no real prospect of 'success'. These include the communication filed by the Center for Constitutional Rights on behalf of the Survivors Network of those Abused by Priests ('sNAP') concerning alleged crimes against humanity perpetrated by members of the Catholic Church,[33] and the communication filed concerning US President G.W. Bush and senior members of his administration.[34] Both were accepted to have no chance of triggering an OTP investigation, but were widely publicized and used as a part of publicity and litigation strategies intended to draw attention to the alleged crimes.

There is, generally speaking, a closer and more evident link between certain Article 15 communications and domestic politics than is seen in *amici* submissions. Civil society actors often submit communications to achieve broader policy goals of the organizations concerned. While an *amicus* submission may also be part of a broader long-term

---

[32]   Megan A Fairlie, "The Hidden Costs of Strategic Communications for the International Criminal Court", in *Texas International Law Journal*, 2016, vol. 51, no. 3, p. 281.

[33]   Survivors Network of those Abused by Priests and Centre for Constitutional Rights, "Clergy Sex Victims File International Criminal Court Complaint: Case Charges Vatican Officials with 'Crimes Against Humanity'", 13 September 2011.

[34]   Francis A. Boyle, "International Criminal Court Complaint Filed Against Bush, Cheney, Rumsfeld, Tenet, Rice, Gonzales", in *Global Research*, 20 January 2010.

strategy for many organizations, there is greater judicial control and guidance. Submissions are limited to specific, mainly legal, issues, thus minimizing the waste of judicial and party resources. *Amicus* briefs are public and, if accepted, form part of the case file. It is thus easier to measure the content and quality of submissions and to identify any other interests or goals served by filing the brief.

This is where a more detailed breakdown of the identity and type of those submitting Article 15 communications would be useful, as would information of what motivates actors to submit communications. It appears that the range of actors submitting communications is far broader than those seeking to participate as *amici*, which tends to be dominated by larger, international NGOs, or actors that pursue a specific legal or policy objective rather than objectives focused on a particular situation. For example, Women's Initiatives for Gender Justice ('WIGJ') has used the *amicus* brief to advocate for advances on women issues[35] and REDRESS aims its interventions largely at reparations and victim participation.[36] The participation of such international NGOs can be assumed to involve a range of strategic considerations, including: an assessment of their ability to contribute important expertise; whether they were invited; internal policy requirements; time, resource considerations and other priorities; the availability of alternative avenues for influencing proceedings; and the potential to co-ordinate the submissions of a range of internal agencies. However, both actors have a long-term commitment to the ICC and the project of international criminal justice generally, thus are less likely to risk damaging the ICC by making politically motivated communications with no chance of success.[37]

The approach of such actors, who are all 'engaged' in the ICC system, can be contrasted with communications that aim to publicize crimes beyond the Court's jurisdiction, to push for accountability (either in the

---

[35] For discussion of the role of WIGJ on such issues, see Louise Chappell, *The Politics of Gender Justice at the International Criminal Court: Legacies and Legitimacy*, Oxford University Press, 2015.

[36] See, for example, the filings by REDRESS in the Katanga reparations phase: ICC, Situation in the Democratic Republic of the Congo, *The Prosecutor v Germain Katanga*, Trial Chamber, Redress Trust Observations Pursuant to Article 75 of the Statute, 15 May 2015, ICC-01/04-01/07-3554 (https://www.legal-tools.org/doc/de6097/).

[37] Fairlie, 2016, see *supra* note 32.

ICC or other fora) or to shift national or international public opinion.[38] A much greater risk of 'lawfare' type concerns arises with Article 15 communications than in the context of *amici* submissions, thus increasing the risk of undermining the legitimacy of the process and wasting OTP resources. Many credible civil society actors thus eschew the Article 15 process entirely, in favour of detailed reports or statements, or other forms of influence. This is evidenced in the interviews conducted with civil society for our project on civil society and international criminal justice, where NGO representatives have revealed that they did send reports and analysis to the OTP.[39] One explained that "we do have a role in researching human rights violations and we do, in a number of contexts, call for the ICC to step in and investigate or to open preliminary examinations on those issues".[40] However, at least one NGO drew a distinction between general advocacy and making Article 15 submissions, suggesting that "basically I feel like Article 15 [is] saying, 'You should open this investigation'" whereas "we, actually, don't call for that many investigations for a variety of reasons. It has to be a really extreme [...] because we're also aware that this court is already very overloaded so we have a very high threshold".[41] This actor explained that "we'd be more likely to call on a government to refer" a situation to the ICC because "you don't see a lot of action on Article 15 whereas [...] if a state refers, [the ICC Prosecutor has] been pretty quick" to respond.[42]

A representative of another international NGO explained that "we haven't done any Article 15s to date but I don't think we would rule it out in some circumstances [...] we realize it's really important that we're not criminal investigators [...] and we don't want to be perceived as such because that raises risk issues", especially in terms of protecting the security of sources.[43] Indeed, a lack of clarity about the OTP's use of Article 15 information has been a barrier to making use of this avenue, since it is recognized that "this information [...] will, eventually, be handed over to

---

[38] *Ibid.*

[39] "We send all of our reports to them. Not every report but [...] we send reports", and "We do a lot to try to influence the prosecutor", Interview CT2 (on file with the author).

[40] Interview SY7 (on file with the author).

[41] Interview CT2 (on file with the author).

[42] *Ibid.*

[43] Interview SY7 (on file with the author).

investigators if there's an investigation".[44] Article 15 communications thus represent only one available, but relatively narrow, option for international criminal justice advocacy that many credible organizations choose not to use.

30.2.5. The Absence of Standing for Judicial Review in Preliminary Examinations

Civil society organizations do raise a fundamental concern with the preliminary examination process, and what they argue is an unfortunate omission in the Article 15 procedure. That is, the need for judicial review of *all* decisions to proceed or not to proceed to an investigation, with standing for civil society actors, in particular those who have submitted an Article 15 communication, to trigger a review in the same way as a referring State or the Security Council. Instead, as is evident from Rome Statute negotiations, the judicial review process is designed to stop a rouge prosecutor (a State concern) and not to encourage a reticent prosecutor to proceed with an investigation (a victims' and civil society concern).

As the number of situations before the Court has increased, and the OTP's budget has been reduced, the issue of reviewing decisions *not* to proceed has taken on greater importance. A decision not to investigate has serious consequences: it will preclude international criminal accountability at the international level and possibly also the national level; it denies a level of recognition to those victims affected, and also their potential to participate or be represented in proceedings; and it precludes access to reparations under the Rome Statute and assistance pursuant to the Trust Fund's assistance mandate. Yet, while the significance of decisions taken by the OTP in the preliminary examination stage is clear, the ability of civil society to influence such decisions is less certain and there is little scope for formal participation in decision-making processes. This in turn may be said to contribute to a lack of participation, transparency and accountability, thus raising concerns for the legitimacy and effectiveness of the OTP and the Court itself.

As at August 2017, three preliminary examinations based on Article 15 communications had been closed without proceeding to an investiga-

---

[44] *Ibid.*; "We've had some disclosure challenges... there's supposed to be this provision that, basically, allows you to provide information that leads to investigation, confidentially, but it doesn't really work that way", Interview *CT2* (on file with the author).

tion (Honduras, Republic of Korea and Venezuela). In each situation, the decision not to proceed to an investigation was based on jurisdictional criteria so there was no prospect of Pre-Trial Chamber review. The initial preliminary examination into Iraq, which was also based on Article 15 communications, was closed in 2006 due to the finding that the alleged crimes were of insufficient gravity, thus providing no prospect of review by the Pre-Trial Chamber. As at March 2018, the Prosecutor had not declined to proceed to an investigation based on the interests of justice, so there has been no review by a Pre-Trial Chamber of a decision not to proceed on this basis. Thus, judicial review of decisions not to investigate has been limited to two situations.

The first concerned the situation referred to the ICC by the Government of the Union of the Comoros, concerning an incident on a humanitarian aid flotilla bound for the Gaza Strip. The incident occurred against and on vessels registered to Comoros, Greece and Cambodia (all party to the Rome Statute), and thus the referral triggered the Court's jurisdiction based on Articles 12(2)(a) and 14 of the Rome Statute. The Prosecutor opened a preliminary examination, but in November 2014 announced that the preliminary examination had been closed based on her finding that there was insufficient gravity.[45] Comoros, as the referring State, requested a review by the Pre-Trial Chamber of the decision not to open an investigation.[46] The Pre-Trial Chamber revealed different views as to the role of the Chamber and the scope and standard of review of the Prosecutor's decision. A majority determined that the Prosecutor had erred in her assessment of gravity.[47] The Appeals Chamber declined to hear the Prosecutor's appeal, leaving unresolved the issue as to how the Pre-Trial

---

[45] OTP, "Statement of the Prosecutor of the International Criminal Court, Fatou Bensouda, on Concluding the Preliminary Examination of the Situation Referred by the Union of the Comoros: 'Rome Statute Legal Requirements Have Not Been Met'", 6 November 2014 (http://www.legal-tools.org/doc/e745a0/).

[46] ICC, Situation on the Registered Vessels of the Union of the Comoros, the Hellenic Republic and the Kingdom of Cambodia, Pre-Trial Chamber, Application for Review Pursuant to Article 53(3)(a) of the Prosecutor's Decision of 6 November 2014 not to Initiate an Investigation in the Situation, 29 January 2015, ICC-01/13-3-Red (http://www.legal-tools.org/doc/b60981/).

[47] ICC, Situation on the Registered Vessels of the Union of the Comoros, the Hellenic Republic and the Kingdom of Cambodia, Pre-Trial Chamber, Decision on the Request of the Union of the Comoros to Review the Prosecutor's Decision Not to Initiate an Investigation, 16 July 2015, ICC-01/13-34 (http://www.legal-tools.org/doc/2f876c/).

Chamber should approach its role.[48] Thus, even where the Pre-Trial Chamber is involved in a review of a decision made during the preliminary examination process, the standard and scope of such a review is not clear. In any event, the outcome of a successful judicial review is to remit the situation back to the Prosecutor to reach a further decision, a further exercise of her discretion.

The second situation concerned the attempted referral of the situation in Egypt (a State not party to the Rome Statute) to the ICC. This example aptly illustrates the limits of the Article 15 communication and the lack of standing. In December 2013, lawyers acting on behalf of the Freedom and Justice Party, the political wing of the Muslim Brotherhood, sought to trigger the jurisdiction of the ICC by filing an instrument with the Registry that purported to be a declaration under Article 12(3) of the Rome Statute.[49] The instrument included evidence of alleged crimes including murder, unlawful imprisonment, torture, persecution, and enforced disappearances. In a statement issued in May 2014, the Prosecutor determined that the communication was not submitted by a person possessing the requisite authority to make an Article 12(3) declaration and thus did not constitute consent by Egypt to the exercise of ICC jurisdiction.[50] The complaint was thus considered as a communication under Article 15 and, as the allegations fell outside the Court's territorial and personal jurisdiction, the Prosecutor would not proceed to open a preliminary examination.

Lawyers on behalf of the ousted President Morsi and the Freedom and Justice Party then requested the Pre-Trial Chamber to appoint a Chamber specifically to review the decision by the Prosecutor not to open

---

[48] ICC, Situation on the Registered Vessels of the Union of the Comoros, the Hellenic Republic and the Kingdom of Cambodia, Appeals Chamber, Decision on the Admissibility of the Prosecutor's Appeal Against the "Decision on the Request of the Union of the Comoros to Review the Prosecutor's Decision Not to Initiate an Investigation", 6 November 2015, ICC-01/13-51 (https://www.legal-tools.org/doc/a43856/).

[49] ICC, "Communication Seeking to Accept the ICC's Jurisdiction over Egypt", 13 December 2013. For further discussion see Hossam El Deeb, "An Attempt to Prosecute: The Muslim Brotherhood's Communication to the International Criminal Court Relating to the Alleged Crimes in Egypt", in *International Criminal Law Review*, 2015, vol. 15, no. 4, p. 733.

[50] OTP, "The Determination of the Office of the Prosecutor on the Communication Received in Relation to Egypt", 8 May 2014 (http://www.legal-tools.org/doc/2945cd/).

a preliminary examination.[51] The request was based on Regulation 46(2) or in the alternative Regulation 46(3), which enables matters arising out of a situation to be directed to a Pre-Trial Chamber. It is the first attempt by an actor that has submitted an Article 15 communication to trigger a review of a decision by the Prosecutor not to conduct a preliminary examination. The original request was rejected by the Presidency, but was re-filed before the President of the Pre-Trial Division, who assigned the matter to Pre-Trial Chamber II.[52] However, that Chamber then dismissed the request for review *in limine*, finding that Regulation 46(3) was a purely administrative provision and did not create substantive rights. Moreover, consideration of the request should not be viewed as recognizing any right of standing on the part of the applicant.[53] A subsequent attempt to seek reconsideration of this decision, or alternatively a request to appeal the decision,[54] was denied.[55] The application(s) argued that the judges should exercise an inherent right of review of the Prosecutor's decision not to open an examination, as review was essential to promote the integrity and

---

[51] ICC, Situation in the Arab Republic of Egypt, Pre-Trial Division, Re-Filing Before the President of the Pre-Trial Division of the 'Request for Review of the Prosecutor's Decision of 23 April 2014 Not to open a Preliminary Examination Concerning Alleged Crimes Committed in the Arab Republic of Egypt, and the Registrar's Decision of 25 April 2015', 1 September 2014, ICC-RoC46(3)-01/14-2 (http://www.legal-tools.org/doc/7ce712/).

[52] ICC, Pre-Trial Division, Decision Assigning the 'Request for Review of the Prosecutor's Decision of 23 April 2014 Not to Open a Preliminary Examination Concerning Alleged Crimes Committed in the Arab Republic of Egypt, and the Registrar's Decision of 25 April 2014' to Pre-Trial Chamber II, 10 September 2014, ICC-RoC46(3)-01/14-1 (http://www.legal-tools.org/doc/51f209/).

[53] ICC, Pre-Trial Chamber, Decision on the 'Request for Review of the Prosecutor's Decision of 23 April 2014 Not to Open a Preliminary Examination Concerning Alleged Crimes Committed in the Arab Republic of Egypt, and the Registrar's Decision of 25 April 2014', 12 September 2014, ICC-RoC46(3)-01/14-3, see *supra* note 14.

[54] ICC, Pre-Trial Chamber, Request for Reconsideration of, and Alternatively, Leave to Appeal Against the "Decision on the 'Request for Review of the Prosecutor's Decision of 23 April 2014 Not to Open a Preliminary Examination Concerning Alleged Crimes Committed in the Arab Republic of Egypt, and the Registrar's Decision of 25 April 2014'" of 12 September 2014, 18 September 2014, ICC-RoC46(3)-01/14-4 (http://www.legal-tools.org/doc/cd87ac/).

[55] ICC, Pre-Trial Chamber, Decision on a Request for Reconsideration or Leave to Appeal the "Decision on the 'Request for a Review of the Prosecutor's Decision of 23 April 2014 Not to Open a Preliminary Examination Concerning Alleged Crimes Committed in the Arab Republic of Egypt, and the Registrar's Decision of 25 April 2014'", 22 September 2014, ICC-RoC46(3)-01/14-5, see *supra* note 14.

---

transparency of the ICC. The Chamber did not enter into the substance of these arguments, finding instead that the procedural framework of the ICC does not permit a broad motion for reconsideration. Further, as the applicant was not a party to proceedings, it was not entitled to appeal. These proceedings show the difficulty in obtaining review of decisions taken by the Prosecutor where no right of review is set out in the Rome Statute.

Another issue is where the OTP does not take a decision whether to open or not to open an investigation. The OTP may keep examinations open without taking a formal decision to end a preliminary examination and not to move to an investigation, meaning there is no decision that could then be reviewed. Here, it is very difficult to force the OTP to make a decision. The Central African Republic, as the referring State, attempted to do so by filing a request with the Pre-Trial Chamber asking for information on the alleged failure to decide, within a reasonable time, whether or not to open an investigation. This application was successful, with the Pre-Trial Chamber requesting the Prosecutor to provide information.[56] The OTP complied "in the interests of transparency" but has consistently refused to acknowledge any legal obligation to do so or a time limit on the exercise of its discretion in the preliminary examination stage.[57] Instead, its practice has been to suspend, rather than close, the preliminary examination or investigation. For example, in *Lubanga*, the OTP suspended investigation of charges other than those concerning child soldiers, thus limiting the availability of judicial review. In relation to the Kenya cases, where investigations remain suspended, Ferstman suggests that this is one tactic used by the OTP to avoid judicial review of prosecutorial discretion.[58] There, the Common Legal Representative for Victims sought judi-

---

[56] ICC, Situation in the Central African Republic, Pre-Trial Chamber, Decision Requesting Information on the Status of the Preliminary Examination of the Situation in the Central African Republic, 30 November 2006, ICC-01/05-6 (http://www.legal-tools.org/doc/76e607/).

[57] ICC, Situation in the Central African Republic, Pre-Trial Chamber, Prosecution's Report Pursuant to Pre-Trial Chamber III's 30 November 2006 Decision Requesting Information on the Status of the Preliminary Examination of the Situation in the Central African Republic, 13 December 2006, ICC-01/05-7, para. 11 (http://www.legal-tools.org/doc/1dd66a/).

[58] Carla Ferstman, "Prosecutorial Discretion and Victims' Rights at the International Criminal Court: Demarcating the Battle Lines", in Sarah Williams and Hannah Woolaver (eds.), *Acta Juridica*, 2016, p. 17.

cial review, arguing that the lack of action should be construed as a decision by the Prosecutor not to proceed "because it has concluded that further investigation or prosecution would be futile, and therefore would not be in the interests of justice".[59] The OTP opposed the application, arguing that the victims lacked standing. The PTC confirmed that victims did have standing to file the application, stating that it "considers that one of the valid forms of victims' participation in the proceedings of a situation is to prompt the Chamber to consider exercising its *proprio motu* powers with respect to a specific issue affecting the victims' personal interests".[60] Despite allowing the application, the Pre-Trial Chamber declined the request on the merits, finding that there had been no decision not to investigate on the basis of the interests of justice. Moreover, the Chamber was clear that its right to review decisions of the Prosecutor is set out in Article 53, "as well as the boundaries of the exercise of any such competence".[61]

This chapter does not suggest that civil society actors should be given standing to trigger judicial review of a decision not to open a preliminary examination or to proceed to an investigation, even for those actors who have submitted an Article 15 communication. Given the evidence of strategic communications, and the volume of communications received, to do so would likely cripple the OTP and further increase the strategic use of Article 15 communications, ultimately undermining the legitimacy of the ICC itself. States would certainly not condone amendments to the Rome Statute to accommodate such rights of standing. Instead, the next section explores the *amicus curiae* mechanism as a possible option to prompt the Prosecutor to act or to call for judicial review, a mechanism that falls short of recognizing such broad rights of standing.

---

[59] ICC, Situation in the Republic of Kenya, Pre-Trial Chamber, Victims' Request for Review of Prosecution's Decision to Cease Active Investigation, 3 August 2015, ICC-01/09-154, para. 10 (http://www.legal-tools.org/doc/aa057e/).

[60] ICC, Situation in the Republic of Kenya, Pre-Trial Chamber, Decision on the "Victims' Request for Review of Prosecutions' Decision to Cease Active Investigation", 5 November 2015, ICC-01/09-159, para. 7 (http://www.legal-tools.org/doc/18b367/).

[61] *Ibid.*, para. 18.

30.3. The *Amicus Curiae* and the Potential to Influence and Regulate Prosecutorial Discretion

30.3.1. The *Amicus Curiae*

The traditional notion of the *amicus curiae* is a friend of the court, an impartial actor with knowledge or expertise relevant to the proceedings who – at the discretion of the court – is given permission to participate in a limited form in proceedings. The *amicus* was thus a highly flexible, and relatively undefined, legal mechanism that allowed judges to overcome some of the disadvantages of the adversarial process that does not easily allow for the participation of third parties. In various national jurisdictions, this role has now expanded – in some situations renamed – and allows broad rights of third party or public interest intervention, with *amici* or interveners frequently providing legal analysis of factual evidence to support a particular legal outcome. The rationale is that such participation will lead to better judicial decision making by permitting additional sources of information to be placed before the court and, in some circumstances, to ensure fair proceedings by allowing the representation of interests affected by proceedings that are not otherwise represented. With the exception of the International Court of Justice, which remains primarily linked to the participation of States, and not other interest groups, many other judicial institutions have enthusiastically endorsed intervention by expert or interest groups (for example, the European Court of Human Rights) or are experimenting with the benefits and limitations of intervention (such as the World Trade Organization and in investment arbitration). What is clear is that *amicus* or third-party participation is equated with broader theories concerning the need for representation, transparency and other 'democratic values' in the judicial decision-making process.[62]

International criminal tribunals have not been immune to the pressure to enable broader participation. The *amicus curiae* mechanism was found in the rules of procedure and evidence of the International Criminal Tribunal for the former Yugoslavia ('ICTY') and the International Criminal Tribunal for Rwanda ('ICTR') and other internationalized and hybrid tribunals. It is also found in Rule 103 of the ICC Rules of Procedure and

---

[62] The discussion in this section is based on material included in Sarah Williams, Hannah Woolaver and Emma Palmer, *The Amicus Curiae in International Criminal Justice*, Hart Publishing, forthcoming 2018.

Evidence. Although the decisions on applications can be brief, it is clear that *amicus* intervention is a discretionary measure. Chambers have recognized the necessarily limited role of the mechanism, particularly in a criminal trial, where the Court must respect the rights of the defence to a fair and expeditious trial. The practice shows civil society contributors, including large international NGOs, international organizations, smaller national NGOs, academics and associations have been permitted to intervene.[63] What is clear from the practice is that there is not a particularly permissive judicial approach to allowing *amicus* intervention and that the *amicus curiae* mechanism has not been used to generate a flood of public interest type interventions in ICC proceedings, as has been seen in some national jurisdictions. Moreover, ICC judges are less likely to accept *amici* submissions addressing, or engaging in arguments concerning, the broader political or social implications of their decisions than some of their national counterparts. Victim participation in proceedings may also remove the need for *amici* submissions on social impact of decisions. Therefore, within the ICC, the *amicus* is a constrained mechanism.

30.3.2. Using the *Amicus Curiae* Mechanism to Influence the Prosecutor?

As outlined above, civil society actors, including those who have submitted an Article 15 communication to the Prosecutor, do not have standing to seek review of decisions to proceed to an investigation. Nor do they have standing to participate in the hearings concerning a request by the Prosecutor to open an investigation under Article 15. Thus formal avenues for participation in, and possibly influence, these key decisions do not appear to exist. Does the *amicus curiae* mechanism offer an alternative way to influence the Prosecutor?

The greatest restriction on the use of the *amicus curiae* to address decisions concerning the exercise of prosecutorial discretion is that an

---

[63] Williams and Palmer, 2016, see *supra* note 3. See also Mark Ellis, "NGO Intervention in Court Proceedings Through Amicus Curiae Briefs", in Linda E Carter, Mark S Ellis and Charles Chernor Jalloh (eds.), *The International Criminal Court in an Effective Global Justice System*, Edward Elgar, 2016, p. 264; Avidan Kent and Jamie Trinidad, "The Management of Third-party Amicus Participation before International Criminal Tribunals: Juggling Efficiency and Legitimacy", in *International Criminal Law Review*, 2017, vol. 17, no. 4, p. 728; Chatham House, "Shaping the Law: Civil Society Influence at International Criminal Courts", 25 January 2016 (available on its web site).

---

amicus is a friend of the Court, not of the Prosecutor. Under Rule 103 of the ICC Rules of Procedure and Evidence, it is the Chamber that authorizes an *amicus* submission, which can occur "at any stage in proceedings", thus suggesting that judicial proceedings must have been initiated. This then raises the question as to when judicial proceedings start. In the context of victims' participation, the Appeals Chamber has held that:

> What emerges from the case law of the Appeals Chamber is that participation can take place only within the context of judicial proceedings. Article 68 (3) of the Statute correlates victim participation to "proceedings", a term denoting a judicial cause pending before a Chamber. In contrast, an investigation is not a judicial proceeding but an inquiry conducted by the Prosecutor into the commission of a crime with a view to bringing to justice those deemed responsible. [...] The initial appraisal of a referral of a situation by a State Party, in which one or more crimes within the jurisdiction of the Court appear to have been committed as well as the assessment of information reaching the Prosecutor and in relation to that the initiation by the Prosecutor of investigations *proprio motu* are the exclusive province of the Prosecutor.[64]

Thus, other than the specific rights to make representations regarding Article 15 requests or on jurisdiction or admissibility challenges, victims have no general standing to make submissions during the investigation phase as there are no judicial proceedings. This would apply by extension to the preliminary examination phase. Instead, the Appeals Chamber indicated:

> there is ample scope within the statutory scheme of the Statute for victims and anyone else with relevant information to pass it on to the Prosecutor without first being formally accorded "a general right to participate". For example under Article 15 (2) the Prosecutor is authorised to receive information from, inter alia, any "reliable source" - including victims. He is similarly authorised under article 42 (1) to re-

---

[64] ICC, Situation in the Democratic Republic of the Congo, Appeals Chamber, Judgment on Victim Participation in the Investigation Stage of the Proceedings in the Appeal of the OPCD Against the Decision of Pre-Trial Chamber I of 7 December 2007 and in the Appeals of the OPCD and the Prosecutor Against the Decision of Pre-Trial Chamber I of 24 December 2007, 19 December 2008, ICC-01/04-556, paras. 45, 51 (http://www.legal-tools.org/doc/dca981/).

ceive and consider "any substantiated information on crimes within the jurisdiction of the Court". Victims may thus make representations to the Prosecutor on any matter pertaining to the investigations and to their interests.[65]

The same approach would likely be applied to civil society actors seeking to make *amici* submissions concerning a preliminary examination or investigation in the absence of judicial proceedings. That is, *amici* submissions could not be accepted where there is no 'judicial proceeding' on foot, which would preclude attempts to file a submission concerning the preliminary examination phase.

However, *amici* have occasionally been permitted – or even invited – to make submissions during the pre-trial phases. For example, Pre-Trial Chamber I invited Louise Arbour and Antonio Cassese to provide information to the ICC about their investigations into events in Darfur in Sudan,[66] in their capacities as High Commissioner of the Office of the United Nations High Commissioner for Human Rights and Chairperson of the International Commission of Inquiry on Darfur, respectively. In doing so, the Chamber recalled that the UN Security Council had referred the situation in Darfur to the ICC Prosecutor, but that the Prosecutor's investigation had apparently been inhibited by the security situation within Darfur. The Chamber therefore sought further information about "the protection of victims and the preservation of evidence".[67] Although the Chamber did not mention this in the invitation, Arbour was a former ICTY Prosecutor and Cassese the first President of the ICTY Chambers. The *amici* were arguably invited to make submissions in the hope that they would propose actions that would progress the Prosecutor's stalled investigations.[68] The stated reasons for inviting (or proposing) civil society *amicus curiae* submissions may not always be apparent from the call or decision allowing their observations, but in this case allowed UN officials with prosecutorial experience to share that expertise with the ICC and

---

[65] *Ibid.*, para. 53.

[66] ICC, Situation in Darfur, Pre-Trial Chamber, Decision Inviting Observations in Application of Rule 103 of the Rules of Procedure and Evidence, 24 July 2006, ICC-02/05-10 (http://www.legal-tools.org/doc/657682/).

[67] *Ibid.*

[68] Lyal S Sunga, "How Can UN Human Rights Special Procedures Sharpen ICC Fact-Finding?", in *International Journal of Human Rights*, 2011, vol. 15, no. 2, p. 187.

---

appeared to be a direct or indirect attempt by the Pre-Trial Chamber to influence the Prosecutor's investigation via an *amicus* submission.

There seems to be no reason why *amici* would be precluded from seeking to make submissions in proceedings where the Prosecutor has requested authorization to open an investigation. Two academics did seek to participate as *amici* in the Article 15 proceedings in the Kenyan situation, arguing that the novel nature of the issues to be determined and the effectively *ex parte* nature of the proceedings warranted the Chamber hearing from *amici*.[69] The Chamber rejected the application on the basis that the proposed submissions would not help it to "reach a proper determination on the Prosecutor's Request".[70] One of the suspects ultimately charged by the Prosecutor, William Ruto, also sought to appear as *amicus* via his legal counsel after the Pre-Trial Chamber had authorized the Prosecutor to open the investigation, arguing that he could provide a different perspective on the investigation and that he had been misrepresented in key sources relied upon by the Prosecutor in the Article 15 request.[71] The Chamber rejected the request, arguing that a suspect under investigation is not a category of person able to submit observations as *amicus curiae*, as Rule 103 refers to the right of the defence to respond to any observations.[72] No requests to participate as *amicus curiae* were formally received in connection with the Article 15 proceedings concerning the situations in Georgia, Côte d'Ivoire or Burundi.

Similarly, civil society actors should in principle be able to seek leave to participate as *amici* in proceedings for review by a Pre-Trial Chamber of a decision *not* to open an investigation. There was no applica-

---

69   ICC, *Situation in the Republic of Kenya*, Pre-Trial Chamber, Request by Professors Max Hilaire and William A. Cohn to Appear as Amicus Curiae, 11 January 2010, ICC-01/09-8 (http://www.legal-tools.org/doc/8329d7/).

70   ICC, *Situation in the Republic of Kenya*, Pre-Trial Chamber, Decision on Application to Appear as Amicus Curiae and Related Requests, 3 February 2010, ICC-01/09-14, para. 8 (https://www.legal-tools.org/doc/af0e44/).

71   ICC, *Situation in the Republic of Kenya*, Pre-Trial Chamber, Transmission by the Registry of an Application Communicated by Katwa & Kemboy Advocates, Commissioners for Oaths on Behalf of Applicant, William Ruto, 21 December 2010, ICC-01/09-32 (http://www.legal-tools.org/doc/91e729/).

72   ICC, *Situation in the Republic of Kenya*, Pre-Trial Chamber, Decision on Application for Leave to Submit Amicus Curiae Observations, 18 January 2011, ICC-01/09-35 (http://www.legal-tools.org/doc/773abe/).

---

tion to submit an *amicus* brief in the Pre-Trial Chamber's review of the Prosecutor's decision in the Comoros situation. However, one civil society organization, the European Centre for Law and Justice, sought leave to submit submissions as *amicus curiae* in the appellate proceedings, in support of the Prosecutor's request to appeal.[73] The proposed submissions, which were appended to the request for leave, concerned the issue of jurisdiction in respect of a nationals of a State that is not a party to the Rome Statute, the basis of the Pre-Trial Chamber's review of the Prosecutor's evidence, and the proper role of review under Article 53 of the Rome Statute. As the Appeals Chamber ultimately rejected the Prosecutor's appeal, the request to participate as *amicus* was never determined.[74] This shows that there is potential for *amicus curiae* to participate in proceedings under Article 15 and reviews under Article 53, although it may be a challenge to convince the Chamber that the submissions will assist it to make a proper determination.

Yet, *amicus curiae* submissions will not assist where there is no right to call for a review under Article 53 or the referring State or Security Council does not use this option. Arguably, a civil society actor, particularly one who had filed a communication with the Prosecutor under Article 15, could seek leave to make submissions under Rule 103 as part of the situation. However, it is unlikely to be granted, as ICC judges have appeared to be reluctant in expanding the rights of review (and the participation in the review) of prosecutorial decisions. This was demonstrated clearly by the decisions concerning the Egypt situation, where an *amicus curiae* request would have been unlikely to result in a different outcome. Thus, given there would be no standing to trigger judicial proceedings, an *amicus* submission, as an attempt to trigger and participate in judicial proceedings, would also fail.

---

[73] ICC, Situation on Registered Vessels of the Union of the Comoros, the Hellenic Republic of Greece and the Kingdom of Cambodia, Appeals Chamber, Request for Leave to Submit Amicus Curiae Observations Pursuant to Rule 103 of the Rules of Procedure and Evidence, 7 August 2015, ICC-01/13-44 (http://www.legal-tools.org/doc/d13172/).

[74] ICC, Situation on Registered Vessels of the Union of the Comoros, the Hellenic Republic of Greece and the Kingdom of Cambodia, Appeals Chamber, Decision in Relation to Request for Leave to Submit Rule 103 Observations, 14 August 2015, ICC-01/13-46 (http://www.legal-tools.org/doc/2da258/).

However, it may sometimes be possible for *amicus curiae* to address pre-trial issues once proceedings commence. One of the most frequently mentioned cases of civil society *amicus curiae* influence concerned the sexual violence charges prosecuted by the ICTR in *Akayesu*. A group of women's organizations – the Coalition for Women's Human Rights in Conflict – submitted an *amicus curiae* brief arguing that the ICTR Trial Chamber could and should correct the Prosecutor's failure to charge rape in the *Akayesu* case. It thus addressed an issue of charging that generally arises at the pre-trial or prosecutorial investigation stage of a trial,[75] which in turn impacted on the proceedings.[76]

Yet similar attempts in the ICC have failed, and in practice civil society actors cannot submit an '*amicus*' brief to the ICC Prosecutor when she is exercising her discretion to lay charges (as there are not yet 'proceedings'). For example, in August 2006, WIGJ attempted to expand the charges brought at the ICC against Lubanga to include sexual violence by writing to the ICC Prosecutor, in vain. The next effort by WIGJ was to apply to appear as *amicus curiae* in Lubanga's Article 61 confirmation of charges hearing, seeking to make submissions on the proper role of the Pre-Trial Chamber in the determination of charges. WIGJ argued that there was a broad supervisory duty on the part of the Pre-Trial Chamber, which could ask the Prosecutor to include other crimes. The organization also argued for broader definition of victim and thus participation at Article 61 proceedings (not just linked to those crimes on the arrest warrant), and wanted the Prosecutor to investigate sexual and gender-based violence and include it in the charges. The Prosecutor and defence counsel for Lubanga opposed the request.

The Pre-Trial Chamber declined WIGJ's application because, by this stage, the case against Lubanga was "confined to the alleged enlist-

---

[75] International Criminal Tribunal for Rwanda, *The Prosecutor Versus Jean-Paul Akayesu*, Trial Chamber, Amicus Brief Respecting Amendment of the Indictment and Supplementation of the Evidence to Ensure the Prosecution of Rape and Other Sexual Violence within the Competence of the Tribunal, 17 June 1997 (http://www.legal-tools.org/doc/9017af/). For a discussion of the probable influence of this brief, see Anne-Marie de Brouwer, *Supranational Criminal Prosecution of Sexual Violence: The ICC and the Practice of the ICTY and the ICTR*, Intersentia, 2005, pp. 294–95; Rhonda Copelon, "Gender Crimes as War Crimes: Integrating Crimes Against Women into International Criminal Law", in *McGill Law Journal*, 2000, vol. 46, no. 1, p. 217.

[76] de Brouwer, 2005, see *supra* note 74; Copelon, 2000, p. 225, see *supra* note 74.

ment, conscription and active use in military operations of children under the age of fifteen; and [...] therefore, the Request has no link with the present case".[77] Instead, the Pre-Trial Chamber invited WIGJ "to re-file their request for leave to submit observations in the record of the DRC situation".[78] In other words, the Chamber suggested that WIGJ apply to act as *amicus curiae* within the broader pre-trial process, rather than in the *Lubanga* case specifically, where charges had already been laid. WIGJ obliged, but this request was also opposed by the OTP and ultimately rejected.[79] On the relevant point concerning the "role of the Pre-Trial Chamber in supervising prosecutorial discretion when the Prosecutor decides 'not to prosecute a particular person or not to prosecute a person for particular crimes'", the Pre-Trial Chamber found that "investigations in the Situation in the DRC are ongoing and the Prosecutor has not taken any decision not to investigate or prosecute".[80] Thus it was not an appropriate time to file *amicus* submissions.

A similar situation arose in 2015 when Uganda Victims Foundation attempted to provide *amicus curiae* submissions regarding victim participation and the scope of the charges in the *Ongwen* case. As noted above, the Appeals Chamber has held that victims generally cannot participate in an investigation; rather, they can participate in judicial proceedings only where their personal interests are affected. Otherwise, victims do not have standing before the Court to seek the Prosecution to take any action. Given the lack of standing, the applicant *amicus* in *Ongwen* attempted to file submissions seeking to widen the rights of participation and concerning the charges. However, Pre-Trial Chamber II noted that since there were not yet victims participating in the case and "prosecution, including the identification of which crimes to charge, is exclusively in the hands of the Prosecutor, [...] the issues raised by the applicant are not live issues in the

---

[77] ICC, Situation in the Democratic Republic of the Congo, *The Prosecutor v Thomas Lubanga Dyilo*, Pre-Trial Chamber, Decision on Request Pursuant to Rule 103(1) of the Statute, 26 September 2006, ICC-01/04-01/06-480 (https://www.legal-tools.org/doc/826ac5/).

[78] *Ibid.*

[79] ICC, Situation in the Democratic Republic of the Congo, Pre-Trial Chamber, Decision on the Request Submitted Pursuant to Rule 103(1) of the Rules of Procedure and Evidence, 17 August 2007, ICC-01/04-373 (https://www.legal-tools.org/doc/b9775f/).

[80] *Ibid.*, para. 5.

---

case".[81] Thus it remains unclear as to when might be the appropriate time to make *amicus* submissions concerning charges.[82]

This discussion shows that there are no – or very limited – opportunities for victims and civil society to use the *amicus* brief to trigger or participate in reviews of key decisions made by the Prosecutor as part of the preliminary examination phase. There are opportunities to participate as an *amicus* concerning the *outcomes* of the preliminary process only, namely where there are requests to authorize an investigation or decisions not to open an investigation, but only where other actors – referring States or the Security Council – trigger the review mechanism under Article 53 or where the decision is based on the interests of justice criterion. In other circumstances, the *amicus* mechanism does not offer an alternative approach to seek judicial review of decisions not to open a preliminary examination in the first place or to not proceed to an investigation at the end of the process. While a civil society actor and victims can submit communications to the OTP in these situations under Article 15, their interests may well be different from those of the OTP, yet there will never be a formal judicial proceeding that may allow them to present their views to the Pre-Trial Chamber.

Even where the *amicus* mechanism may be available, it is discretionary and ICC judges will not grant leave unless the submissions would assist them to make their decision. Moreover, under Rule 103, the parties to proceedings are permitted to respond to both an application for leave to make submissions as *amicus curiae* and to the submissions themselves. Thus, the Prosecutor will always have the opportunity to object to any attempts to use the *amicus* mechanism to step outside the formal restrictions on review of the exercise of prosecutorial discretion. It should be expected that the Prosecutor would strongly oppose any attempt to expand standing via the *amicus curiae* brief. As indicated in the Prosecution brief in the Kenya case, the Prosecutor's firm view is that

---

[81]   ICC, Situation in Uganda, *The Prosecutor v Dominic Ongwen*, Pre-Trial Chamber, Decision on an Application by the Uganda Victims Foundation to Submit Amicus Curiae Observations, 15 April 2015, ICC-02/04-01/15-221, para. 2 (http://www.legal-tools.org/doc/b38fcf/).

[82]   For further discussion regarding *Lubanga*, see Emily Haslam, "Subjects and Objects: International Criminal Law and the Institutionalization of Civil Society", in *International Journal of Transitional Justice*, 2011, vol. 5, no. 2, pp. 221, 236.

participants should not be permitted to circumvent the rules on standing by asserting a general right to request a Chamber to take action *proprio motu*. This would generally allow victims an open-ended right to make legal submissions on any topic in the absence of a judicial proceeding, provided those submissions are couched as a request for a Chamber to intervene.

Participants here would certainly also include *amici*. Thus, efforts to secure greater rights of participation and ultimately review of prosecutorial decisions in preliminary examinations must be sourced elsewhere.

30.4. Conclusions

The preceding discussion demonstrates that options for triggering reviews of prosecutorial decisions during the preliminary examination phase and then for formal participation in review proceedings are limited. Civil society actors may call for judges to recognize standing for civil society actors to trigger a review of decisions not to proceed to an examination or investigation. This could – but need not be – limited to those actors who have submitted a communication. However, this development is unlikely to occur without a change to the Statute, as negotiators in Rome expressly excluded broader rights of standing for civil society and rights of review for other Prosecutorial decisions. The Prosecutor would also likely (and correctly) object strongly to any such proposals. The ICC Prosecutor is in a very different position to prosecutors in national systems where rights of judicial review of prosecutorial decisions are more extensive. The practice on Article 15 communications shows that many address crimes that are manifestly outside the jurisdiction of the ICC or are not substantiated or credible. Given the volume of such communications, and the implication on quality, allowing any actor who has filed a communication standing to trigger or participate in a review would be unmanageable. This is particularly so if we accept that many of the communications filed are for strategic reasons, with no real expectation that the ICC would act. Extending standing to trigger a review would perpetuate such strategic and politicized use of Article 15.

Nor is there a need for a mechanism that would enable civil society actors to submit information during a preliminary examination – this is exactly what Article 15 is intended to do. There is already a considerable amount of information flowing to the Prosecutor, although there are concerns about the volume and the quality of that information. What may offer a useful development would be a more targeted strategy to obtain good quality and relevant legal or factual material that may be more likely to assist the Prosecutor in her decisions and would also improve transparency and representation. In the same way as a Chamber may issue a call for *amicus* submissions, the Prosecutor could issue a call for specific submissions focusing on particular issues that will influence the decision to open or not to open an investigation – a limited 'friend of the Prosecutor' model. This would have the benefit of attracting submissions from a range of civil society actors, including those who do not generally file Article 15 communications but may have considerable expertise on the legal issues in question and experience in drafting *amicus* and other legal submissions. Submissions could also be limited by a page or word count to minimize the impact on resources, both of the OTP and the civil society actor. The timing of such calls could be linked to key phases of the examination, for example, shortly before issuing a report on jurisdiction or admissibility.

There is precedent for this type of action. The former Prosecutor adopted a similar approach in relation to the first attempt to trigger the ICC's jurisdiction in relation to Palestine. In 2009, the Palestinian Authority had attempted to trigger the jurisdiction of the ICC by filing an Article 12(3) declaration. The legal issue for the OTP was whether Palestine constituted a "State" that could make such a declaration. Before making its decision, the Prosecutor sought the views of several actors (including the representatives of Palestine), considered a number of reports and received submissions from experts, academics and NGOs.[83] The submissions were made public, a summary of the submissions was released,[84] and the OTP sought supplementary submissions to address specific issues or to respond to arguments raised. Although the OTP ultimately decided not to proceed and closed the preliminary examination after the jurisdiction phase,[85] this shows that the OTP can seek and accept more focused expert submissions, in much the same way a Chamber can using the *amicus curiae* mechanism.

---

[83] OTP, *Report on Preliminary Examination Activities 2012*, 22 November 2012, para. 199 (http://www.legal-tools.org/doc/0b1cfc/).

[84] OTP, Situation in Palestine: *Summary of Submissions on Whether the Declaration Lodged by the Palestinian National Authority Meets Statutory Requirements*, 3 May 2010 (http://www.legal-tools.org/doc/af5abf/).

[85] OTP, "Situation in Palestine", 3 April 2012 (http://www.legal-tools.org/doc/f5d6d7/).

This process, which has not been repeated in any other preliminary examination, was more transparent and allowed the Prosecutor to make a decision fully informed by arguments from various perspectives. It is suggested here that the OTP should consider formalizing such a mechanism.

Separate to this proposed mechanism, there is also a need to restrain the strategic use of Article 15 communications by organizations not necessarily committed to the ICC and the aims of international criminal justice process. As outlined above, strategic communications have the potential to drain vital prosecutorial resources, raise false expectations for victims and undermine confidence in and the legitimacy of the OTP and the ICC. One issue that has not been canvassed and may offer some promise is the role of ethics in the filing of communications. Civil society actors often hold professional ethical or disclosure obligations in their respective fields. For instance, academics need to comply with university or national research ethics policies, lawyers are members of bar associations, and NGOs may have reporting obligations for donors or under domestic (including charity) legislations. However, *amicus curiae* before the ICC hold additional ethical obligations under the Code of Conduct although many *amici* may not be aware of its potential application to them. It may be worth considering what ethical responsibilities should attach to those actors submitting information to the OTP – an issue raised directly by the domestic proceedings concerning Phil Shiner.

The Article 15 communication process may also be able to learn something from the experience with the *amicus curiae*. The OTP could provide greater guidance as to what might be useful, the types of information sought and the quality of information requested. It may also be possible to introduce a staged information process, whereby a civil society actor submits a limited initial overview of the material they intend to submit under Article 15, with the OTP then able to request a fuller submission if the situation in question is within the jurisdiction of the ICC and further material (both factual or legal) may be useful. Here, again, the OTP could ask for specific issues to be addressed. This appears to be what the OTP is already doing in its field visits and other interactions. It would also be useful, and consistent with the policy on confidentiality, to publish a breakdown of the type of actors submitting material to the OTP under Article 15. Of course, any attempt to tighten the Article 15 process must not unduly restrict the mechanism, which is still important to allowing access to the Court for a broader range of participants despite its limits.

Part 5
Thematicity in Preliminary Examination

31

Quality Control in Preliminary Examination of Rape and Other Forms of Sexual Violence in International Criminal Law: A Feminist Analysis

Usha Tandon, Pratibha Tandon and Shreeyash U. Lalit[*]

31.1. Introduction

Though the International Criminal Court ('ICC') is currently facing huge criticism,[1] preliminary examinations of the ICC have become one of the most significant instruments of Court practice[2] and have been acquiring growing importance for the last few years.[3] However, in the context of sexual and gender-based crimes, it is disheartening that many allegations of rape and other forms of sexual violence against women do not make it beyond preliminary examination; hence the effective investigation and prosecution of such offences against women simply do not take place.

More disturbingly, though the practice of mass rapes is well established in certain situations, the ICC Office of the Prosecutor ('OTP') has failed to charge the accused like Thomas Dyilo Lubanga[4] with sexual and

---

[*]   **Usha Tandon** is Professor and Head, Campus Law Centre, University of Delhi; **Pratibha Tandon** is Research Associate, National Law University, Delhi; and **Shreeyash U. Lalit** is LL.M. student, University of Cambridge.

[1]   Valerie V. Suhr, "Feminism and the International Criminal Court – Still an Issue?", in *Völkerrechtsblog*, 19 April 2017. "It is, facing its biggest crisis with member states withdrawing, from it. Recently, some African states have publicly declared their intended withdrawal from the International Criminal Court (ICC) over the past month. The court has repeatedly been criticized by African states as an inefficient, neo-colonial institution of the Western powers to try African countries".

[2]   Carsten Stahn, "How Fair Are Criticisms of the ICC?", in *OUPblog*, 23 November 2015.

[3]   Lieneke Louman, "Report: Preliminary Examination and Legacy/Sustainable Exit: Reviewing Policies and Practices – Part 1", in *Post-Conflict Justice*, 26 October 2015.

[4]   ICC, Situation in the Democratic Republic of the Congo, *Prosecutor v. Thomas Lubanga Dyilo*, Trial-Chamber, Judgment pursuant to Article 74 of the Statute, 14 March 2012, ICC-01/04-01/06-2842, para. 142 (http://www.legal-tools.org/doc/677866/) ('Lubanga

---

gender-based violence. From a feminist perspective,[5] this 2012 judgment of the ICC was a great disappointment.[6] The acquittal of Germain Katanga[7] is a glaring instance that illustrates the failure of the OTP to secure a conviction for sexual crimes. The first-instance conviction of Jean-Pierre Bemba for rape and sexual violence was the first and the only conviction so far at the ICC, before it was overturned on appeal.[8] Furthermore, Guinea and Colombia have proven to be negative examples depicting the deficiency in the quality of the OTP's preliminary examinations in so far as

---

Judgment'); see also Appeals Chamber, Judgment on the appeal of Mr Thomas Lubanga Dyilo against his conviction, 1 December 2014, ICC-01/04-01/06-3121-Red, para. 447 (http://www.legal-tools.org/doc/585c75/.)

[5] Feminist legal theory is one of the most dynamic fields in the law. Feminism is based on two premises: one, women's and men's position in society is the result of social and not natural factors. Two, women's perspectives and interest are not inferior to those of men. Feminist Jurisprudence or the feminist analysis of law examines and challenges the laws that have excluded or restricted women from enjoying the benefits of law. It explores the understanding of the complex interrelationship between gender and law and highlights the issue of gender discrimination in law. Feminist scholars believe that law has been a potent weapon for women subordination and oppression. The law is formulated by men for men and the point of view of women, who have been silenced and misrepresented has been ignored. The feminist scholars seek a reinterpretation of legal theory from a new perspective, which involves rejection of a theory in which the subordination of women to men is taken to be a part of an unalterable scheme of things. Through various approaches, legal feminists have identified gender components and gender complications of seemingly neutral laws and practices See generally Hillaire Barnett, *Sourcebook on Feminist Jurisprudence*, Cavendish Publishing, London, 1997; Catherine MacKinnon, *Towards a Feminist Theory of the State*, Harvard University Press, 1989; Nancy Levit and Robert R.M. Verchick, *Feminist Legal Theory*, NYU Press, 2016; Maxine Molyneux, "Analysing Women's Movement", in *Development and Change*, April 1998, vol. 29, no. 2, pp. 219–45; Cynthia Grant Bowman and Elizabeth M. Schneider, "Feminist Legal Theory, Feminist Lawmaking, and the Legal Profession", in *Fordham Law Review*, 1998, vol. 67, no. 2, p. 249.

[6] Suhr, 2017, see *supra* note 1.

[7] ICC, Situation in the Democratic Republic of the Congo, *The Prosecutor v. Germain Katanga and Mathieu Ngudjolo Chui*, Appeals Chamber, Judgment on the Appeal of Mr. Germain Katanga against the Oral Decision of Trial Chamber II of 12 June 2009 on the Admissibility of the Case, 25 September 2009, ICC-01/04-01/07-1497 ('Katanga Judgment') (http://www.legal-tools.org/doc/ba82b5/).

[8] ICC, Situation in the Central African Republic, *The Prosecutor v. Jean-Pierre Bemba Gombo*, Trial Chamber, Judgment pursuant to Article 74 of the Statute, 21 March 2016, ICC-01/05-01/08-3343 (http://www.legal-tools.org/doc/edb0cf/); Appeals Chamber, Judgment on the appeal of Mr Jean-Pierre Bemba Gombo against Trial Chamber III's "Judgment pursuant to Article 74 of the Statute", 8 June 2018, ICC-01/05-01/08-3636-Red (http://www.legal-tools.org/doc/40d35b/).

---

they have failed to accurately apply the principle of complementarity, or even understand and challenge the gender biases against women in the domestic legal systems.

The feminist critics argue that the failure of the ICC to respond to women's experiences, both in responding to the past and in installing peace and stability, has made it ineffective.[9] Although the Rome Statute establishes the substantive law regarding sexual and gender-based crimes, the ICC is far from achieving true gender justice and serving as a deterrent for sexual and gender-based crimes against women.[10] Hence, feminist critique is more important than ever in the current political situation to ensure further progress and prevent regression in the prosecution of sex crimes in international law.[11]

Xabier Agirre Aranburu, an experienced practitioner, recounts how officials have refused to deal with allegations of sexual violence in several occasions. When drafting an indictment for an international tribunal in the late 1990s, his attempt to include a reference to sexual violence as a crime against humanity was stopped by two senior attorneys. Later, when he discussed the issue with one of them, they explained that prosecutors in their country always avoided sexual violence because it was annoyingly difficult to prove. He also mentions that while lecturing a group of experienced judges and prosecutors visiting The Hague, the reference to sexual offences was met with laughter and mocking signs.[12]

This chapter argues that the proper processing and analyses of facts, communication and situations of the rape and other forms of sexual violence require a feminist approach to enhance their quality. It is also necessary to conduct a thorough evaluation of the reliability of the sources and

---

9   Martha L. Minow, "Taking Up the Challenge of Gender and International Criminal Justice: In Honor of Judge Patricia Wald", in *International Criminal Law Review*, 2011, vol. 11, no. 3, p. 366.

10   Laurie Green, "First-Class Crimes, Second-Class Justice: Cumulative Charges for Gender-Based Crimes at the International Criminal Court", in *International Criminal Law Review*, 2011, vol. 11, no. 3, p. 529.

11   Suhr, 2017, see *supra* note 1.

12   Xabier Agirre Aranburu, "Beyond Dogma and Taboo, Criteria for the Effective Investigation of Sexual Violence", in Morten Bergsmo, Alf Butenschøn Skre and Elisabeth J. Wood (eds.), *Understanding and Proving International Sex Crimes*, Torkel Opsahl Academic EPublisher, Beijing, 2012, p. 269 (http://www.toaep.org/ps-pdf/12-bergsmo-skre-wood).

the credibility of the information received, to determine whether there is a reasonable basis to initiate investigation.

This chapter is divided into seven sections. The second section seeks to thematise the offences of sexual violence from a feminist perspective, whereas Section 31.3. provides a brief overview of the feminist struggle in incorporating gender-sensitive provisions into the Rome Statute. The fourth section deals with various aspects of quality control in preliminary examinations from a feminist perspective, including the principles of complementarity, gravity and interests of justice. Next, the OTP Policy Papers on Sexual and Gender-Based Crimes (2014) and on Preliminary Examinations (2013) will be examined. Section 31.5. will highlight the positive steps undertaken by the OTP under these two Policy Papers and suggest areas of further development. After the current status of preliminary examinations has been briefly dealt with in Section 31.6., the Conclusion paves the way for future academic inquiries arguing for 'feminization' of the ICC by invoking the principle of 'shared complementarity'.

31.2. Understanding the Feminist Perspective in Sexual Violence

31.2.1. Reasons for Targeting Women

Women are more likely to be subjected to sexual violence than men in armed conflicts. Traditional attitudes to women's subordinate position in society augment their vulnerability to sexual crimes during armed conflict.[13] The gender biases as well as violence against women in peacetime provides the context for targeted violence against women in armed conflict and war. Sexual violence against women is inflicted during armed conflict to humiliate,[14] dominate,[15] or terrorize[16] the members of a com-

---

[13] Brigid Inder, *Gender in Practice: Guidelines and Methods to Address Gender based Crimes in Armed Conflicts*, Women's Initiatives for Gender Justice, Hague, 2005, p. 5.

[14] "During the war army men made my father sleep with me and when he refused they tied him up with ropes and put a pistol to his head and made him lie down on me. He tried to penetrate me but he could not as the army men pierced me down below with a pistol and he saw the blood and lost desire. They took my father aside and shot him with a bullet in his chest and he died." Cited in Ruth Ojiambo Ochieng, "The Consequence of Armed Conflicts to Women's Health; The Case of Africa", p. 5 (on file with the author).

[15] "They brought her fourteen-year-old son and forced him to rape her [...] On [another] occasion, I was raped with a gun by one of the three men [...] in the room [...] Others stood watching. Some spat on us. They were raping me, the mother and her daughter at the

munity or ethnic group. Such sexual violence is either expressly authorized by military policy or impliedly condoned by superiors to reward or
re-energize exhausted fighters. Violence against women thus remains inherent to situations of lawlessness as a cruel extension of the pervasive
gender subordination already endemic worldwide in times of relative
peace and security.

From a feminist perspective, the victim suffers from double discrimination of not only the conflict but the pre-existing gender inequality
in society. Thus, patriarchal norms play an important role in explaining
why women become the victims of heinous crimes in times of conflict. In
societies where gender biases against women are deep-rooted and women
are identified by association to their male counterparts, sexual violence
against women is perpetrated as acts of dishonour to the family, especially
male members of family.[17] Thus, sexual crimes against women are not

---

same time. Sometimes you had to accept ten men, sometimes three [...] I felt I wanted to
die [...] The Serbs said to us, "Why aren't you pregnant?" [...] I think they wanted to
know who was pregnant in case anyone was hiding it. They wanted women to have children to stigmatize us forever. The child is a reminder of what happened". Cited in Barbara
Bedont and Katherine Hall Martinez, "Ending Impunity for Gender Crimes under the International Criminal Court", in *Brown Journal of World Affairs*, 1999, vol. 6, no. 1, p. 65.

16   "Under-age children and elderly women were not spared. Other testimonies mention cases
of girls aged between 10 and 12. Pregnant women were not spared. Women about to give
birth or who had just given birth were also the victims of rape in hospitals. Their situation
was all the more alarming in that they were raped by members of the militias some of
whom were AIDS virus carriers. Women who had just given birth developed fulminating
infections and died. Women who were "untouchable" according to custom (e.g. nuns) were
also involved and even corpses, in the case of women who were raped just after being
killed". Report on the Situation of Human Rights in Rwanda Submitted by René Degni-
Ségui, Special Rapporteur of the Commission on Human Rights, UN Doc.
E/CN.4/1996/68, 29 January 1996, para. 17 (http://www.legal-tools.org/doc/fa034c/), cited
in United Nations, Department of Social and Economic Affairs, Division for the Advancement of Women, *Sexual Violence and Armed Conflict: United Nations Response*, 1998, pp.
16–17.

17   Meger, in her exploration of sexual violence in the Congolese society, points out that "the
aim of this is twofold: firstly, it is regarded 'as a direct attack on an individual woman as a
representative of her gender or her community'; and, secondly, it should be treated as a
'symbolic gesture, sending a message to a second target, be it the woman's husband, father,
or other men of her community'". See Sara Meger, "Rape of the Congo: Understanding
Sexual Violence in the Conflict in the Democratic Republic of Congo", in *Journal of Contemporary African Studies*, 2010, vol. 28, no. 2, p. 130.

committed in a vacuum, and the pre-existing patriarchal norms provides the basis for these crimes.

Then, the social and cultural constructs of sexual violence to women's bodies augment the trauma that women suffer during conflicts. The cultural constructs of sexual violence to women's bodies have differing social meanings in the context of war. Understanding this core dimension to sex-based abuse helps in appreciating the prevalence and forms of sex-based violence. It also helps explain the public and ritualised experiences of rape for many victims. Perpetrators understand that public sexual violence is a form of communication of power, and not only a sexual act. Hyper-masculinity plays out in graphic form in these settings, where men communicate to other men their relative positions of power and helplessness.[18]

It also demonstrates the continual hold that the notion of female purity and the value it exudes in communal setting and confirms the double victimization that many women experience once the violence ends.[19]

31.2.2. Health Impairments of Sexualized Violence

Women are not only targeted for reasons different than men, but also suffer in health in a different manner. After the commission of rape, for a woman, there is the added risk of pregnancy. The permanent damage to the reproductive system, which often results from sexual violence, has different implications for women than for men.[20] Survivors of sexualized violence in war suffer from numerous health impairments.[21] Many women

---

[18] See generally Barnett, 1997, see *supra* note 5; MacKinnon, 1989, see *supra* note 5.

[19] See generally Naomi Cahn, Fionnuala Ni Aoláin and Dina Haynes, "Masculinities and Child Soldiers in Post-Conflict Societies", in Frank Cooper and Ann C. McGinley (eds.), *Masculinities and Law: A Multidimensional Approach*, New York University Press, 2011.

[20] "Although the militia had burnt my house and took away all the property, I did not become sad as I felt when I witnessed the militia when they were attacking and raping our people [...] we hid among the trees and watched what was going on with three women all pregnant [...] they were first badly beaten [...] then all of them raped [...] until one of them aborted [...] then they were left. We went to save them [...] then another aborted [...] by afternoon all of them passed away, so we buried them [...] it was a very hard experience [...] I will never forget", cited in Ochieng, "The Consequence of Armed Conflicts to Women's Health; The Case of Africa", pp. 6–7, see *supra* note 14.

[21] Ingeborg Joachim, "Stress and Risk Factors Resulting from Confrontation with the Trauma of War-related Sexualized Violence in a Professional Context", in Medica Mondiale (ed.), *Violence Against Women in War: Handbook for Professionals Working with Traumatised*

---

suffer severe physical injuries with irreversible secondary injuries and
functional losses. Furthermore, numerous functional disturbances occur in
the hormonal and vegetative systems. The women's physical and psychological exhaustion makes them more vulnerable to infectious diseases.[22]
In addition, during rape women may be infected with venereal diseases or
HIV/AIDS. Injuries and functional impairment of the genital organs may
also lead to complications later during pregnancy and childbirth, and may
also cause infertility.

31.2.3. Effects of Gendered Stigma

Female victims of sexual violence occupy very different positions in society than that of men, and are treated differently as a result of sex crimes.
In 2002, Human Rights Watch published a report that detailed the stigma
experienced by women and girls who had experienced rape and sexual
violence in Eastern Congo. The report explains that such women are frequently shunned and ostracized by wider community for loss of virginity
or chastity. Married women are abandoned by their own husbands on the
presumption of their consent to rape. If rape victims are tolerated to stay
home, their husbands take other wives, reducing those victims to a subordinate and oppressive position. Widows who have been raped are rejected
by family of their husbands and are often accused of being accomplices in
their husband's deaths because they have survived. Further, if rape victims
become pregnant, husbands and families are reluctant to take responsibilities that would be involved in raising the child. Carrying on with their
pregnancy, they are often compelled to take whatever job is available to
them, however dangerous and low-paying. The unmarried woman who
became pregnant as a result of rape loses the chance of getting a husband
in the future.[23] Rejection by husbands and families of rape victims often
leads to homelessness and delinquency for such women.

Women, Medica Mondiale, Koln, 2005, pp. 72–78, cited in Inder, 2005, p. 53, see *supra*
note 13.

[22] *Ibid.*

[23] "One doctor estimated that a woman who gave birth to a child of rape had only a 20%
chance of becoming married. Despite the stigma attached to having a child while unmarried, young women usually gave birth, as abortion is illegal in the predominantly Catholic
DRC and not condoned culturally, even in the case of rape. Those who did decide to end
pregnancies often sought abortions from unqualified practitioners, rather than doctors."

31.3. Feminist Engagements with the Rome Statute

Although the 1990s were a time of hope and achievement for international women's movements, the feminists' issues could not attract much attention during the early stages of the drafting of the Rome Statute.[24] In 1997, a group of women's rights activists founded the Women's Caucus for Gender Justice in the ICC with the objective of ensuring a gendered perspective throughout the Statute. In many ways, it was the ripe time to campaign for a 'gendered' statute for the ICC.[25] States Parties' obligations to address violence against women had already been taken up by international human rights treaties.[26] Human rights at the international level had travelled from general to specific areas of attention.[27] The Convention on

---

See Human Rights Watch, *The War Within the War: Sexual Violence Against Women and Girls in Eastern Congo*, New York, 2002.

[24] "Feminist engagements with international criminal law can be traced back to the 1990s when activists and practitioners worked to ensure sexual violence crimes were included in the statutes of the Yugoslav and Rwandan Tribunals. This early phase of feminist engagement with international criminal law in the 1990s, appeared focused on four main objectives, many of which remain of current concern. First, there was and still is a need to establish the gendered and sexualized forms of to denote how conflict has gendered impacts. The fact that women experience wartime violence in ways particular to them as women was largely disregarded in the post-1945 period. Feminist activists thus needed to address an immediate gap in knowledge about, and political commitment to addressing, sexual violence in conflict situations. This objective was closely linked to a second one: making the connection between gendered and sexualized harm and the definition of crimes under international law, particularly genocide. The decisions in Akayesu and Kunarac, were early steps in achieving this objective. Third, feminists identified at the outset the importance of situating wartime rape within a broad socio-political context to recognize that violence against women in wartime is shaped and made possible in large measure by violence and inequality in so-called 'peacetime'. A fourth objective was to ensure that rape remains visible as a gendered crime, not just or only a crime against an ethnic/racial/religious community. The task then was and is to ensure the ongoing visibility of the gendered nature of the harm women face in conflict, while maintaining recognition of the political, social and economic complexity of violence and conflict." Doris Buss, "Performing Legal Order: Some Feminist Thoughts on International Criminal Law", in *International Criminal Law Review*, 2011, vol. 11, no. 3, pp. 412–13.

[25] Bedont and Martinez, 1999, pp. 65–85, see *supra* note 15.

[26] United Nations, Department of Economic and Social Affairs, Division for the Advancement of Women, *Handbook for Legislation on Violence Against Women*, New York, 2010, p. 5.

[27] See United Nations Development Fund for Women, South Asia Regional Office, *CEDAW: Restoring Rights to Women*, Partners for Law in Development, New Delhi, 2004, chap. 1.

Elimination of All Forms of Discrimination against Women 1979[28] had
established that discrimination is at the core of and encompassed any form
of violence against women.[29] The Committee on the Elimination of Discrimination against Women, in its general recommendation no. 19 (1992)
had confirmed that "under general international law and specific human
rights covenants, States may be responsible for private acts, if they fail to
act with due diligence to prevent violations of rights or to investigate and
punish acts of violence, and for providing compensation".[30] The condemnation of gender-based violence against women in war situations at the
World Conference on Human Rights held in Vienna in 1993,[31] and the
Fourth World Conference on Women, held in Beijing in 1995,[32] provided
legitimacy to the Women's Caucus to Gender Justice[33] for continuing its
struggle for integrating gender issues in Rome Statute. Furthermore, the
two *ad hoc* tribunals – the International Criminal Tribunals for the former
Yugoslavia ('ICTY') and for Rwanda ('ICTR') – took cognizance of mass
rapes committed during those conflicts.[34] The issue of sexual violence

---

[28] Convention on the Elimination of All Forms of Discrimination Against Women, adopted
18 December 1979, entry into force 3 September 1981 (http://www.legal-tools.org/doc/
6dc4e4/).

[29] Fausto Pocar, "Foreword", in Morten Bergsmo, Alf Butenschøn Skre and Elisabeth J.
Wood (eds.), *Understanding and Proving International Sex Crimes*, Torkel Opsahl Academic EPublisher, Beijing, 2012, p. iii (http://www.toaep.org/ps-pdf/12-bergsmo-skre-
wood).

[30] Committee on the Elimination of Discrimination against Women, General Recommendation No. 19: Violence against Women, 1992, para. 9 (http://www.legal-tools.org/doc/
f8d998/).

[31] Vienna Declaration and Programme of Action, adopted 25 June 1993, part I, paras. 18 and
28; part II, para. 37 (http://www.legal-tools.org/doc/5fdaa4/).

[32] Beijing Declaration and Platform for Action, adopted 15 September 1995, para. 142(b)
(http://www.legal-tools.org/doc/098c5d/).

[33] "Women's Initiatives for Gender Justice" is now the successor of "Women's Caucus for
Gender Justice".

[34] The International Tribunal for Rwanda ('ICTR') in the landmark case of *Prosecutor v.
Jean Paul Akayesu*, (Chamber I, Judgment, 2 September 1998, ICTR-96-4-T (http://www.
legal-tools.org/doc/b8d7bd/)) recognized rape and sexual violence as constituting acts of
genocide and of rape as a form of torture. Askin describes its significance, in terms of the
law developed, as "unparalleled". Kelly Dawn Askin, "Gender Crimes Jurisprudence in the
ICTR: Positive Developments", in *Journal of International Crime Justice*, 2005, vol. 3, no.
4, p. 1012. Copelon observes that the International Criminal Tribunals were an "important
foundation for the codification of sexual violence in the Statute". Rhonda Copelon, "Gen-

---

against women in war had therefore received much attention by the time the Statute was negotiated and going to be adopted in July 1998[35] at the United Nations Diplomatic Conference of Plenipotentiaries at Rome.[36]

Though most States at the Rome Conference supported the integration of gender provisions in the Statute,[37] some delegations considered gender issues as a threat to their religious beliefs. The resistance to gender justice was mainly on two issues. Firstly, those States were determined on undermining the inclusion of the crime of forced pregnancy due to misleading linkages to the issue of the legalization of abortion. Secondly, those States opposed the use of the term 'gender' anywhere in the statute.[38] The Women's Caucus preferred the term 'gender' as opposed to 'sex' because the latter is restricted to the biological differences between men and women, whereas gender includes differences between men and women because of their socially constructed roles. Similarly, 'gender

---

der Crimes as War Crimes: Integrating Crimes against Women into International Criminal Law", in *McGill Law Journal*, 2001, vol. 46, p. 231.

[35] "On 17 July 1998, the Rome Statute was adopted by a vote of 120 to 7, with 21 countries abstaining. Because the way each delegation voted was officially unrecorded, there is some dispute over the identity of the seven countries that voted against the treaty. It is certain that the People's Republic of China, Israel, and the United States were three of the seven because they have publicly confirmed their negative votes; India, Indonesia, Iraq, Libya, Qatar, Russia, Saudi Arabia, Sudan, and Yemen have been identified by various observers and commentators as possible sources for the other four negative votes, with Iraq, Libya, Qatar, and Yemen being the four most commonly identified." Stephen Eliot Smith, "Definitely Maybe: The Outlook for U.S. Relations with the International Criminal Court During the Obama Administration", in *Florida Journal of International Law*, 2010, vol. 22, no. 2, p. 160.

[36] Though it was adopted on 17 July 1998, it entered into force on 1 July 2002. See Rome Stature of the International Criminal Court (http://www.legal-tools.org/doc/7132fd/).

[37] "The States that indicated their support during the Opening Plenary for including provisions in the Statute to enable the Court to prosecute sexual (and where indicated gender) violence crimes included: Australia, Austria, Bangladesh, Bosnia and Herzegovina, Botswana, Canada, Costa Rica, Cyprus, Denmark, European Union (gender crimes), Finland, Georgia, Ghana, Israel (gender crimes), Korea (gender-related violence), Kuwait, Lithuania, Luxembourg, Mexico, New Zealand, Norway, Philippines, Portugal, Russian Federation, Samoa, Slovenia (gender-related crimes), South Africa (for SADC), Spain, Sweden (gender-related crimes), Trinidad and Tobago, Uganda, USA, and Zambia." See Bedont and Martinez, 1999, fn. 5, see *supra* note 15.

[38] "The states that made statements opposing the term "gender" included: Qatar, Libya, Egypt, Venezuela, Guatemala (but flexible), United Arab Emirates, Saudi Arabia, Kuwait, Syria, Turkey, Sudan, Bahrain, Iran, Yemen, Brunei, and Oman. The delegates who led the negotiations for this group were from Syria and Qatar." See *ibid.*, fn. 7.

---

crimes' were preferred to 'sexual violence', because it included crimes
which are targeted because of the gender roles which may or may not
have a sexual element. Ultimately, the following provision was negotiated:
"it is understood that the term 'gender' refers to the two sexes, male and
female, within the context of society. The term 'gender' does not indicate
any meaning different from the above".[39] Accordingly, the term 'gender'
was used at many places in Rome Statute instead of the narrower terms
'sex' and 'sexual violence'. The scholars opine that though this definition
is far from clear, it provides space for broader interpretation for including
the sociological and cultural differences between men and women.[40]

The inclusion of 'gendered' provisions in Rome Statute was a great
victory for the women activists. The Women's Caucus proved to be an
essential catalyst in ensuring the integration of a gendered perspective
throughout the Rome Statute. The merit of the Rome Statute lies in the
fact that it is a treaty that creates a permanent international court, whereas
other international instruments, including the Vienna Conference's Programme of Action and the Beijing Conference's Platform for Action, are
non-binding human rights instruments.

Thus, although sexual violence and gender-based crimes were
largely overlooked in the initial drafts of the Rome Statute, most delegations accepted the necessity of including certain 'gendered' aspects of
crimes in the Statute by the time the final version of the Statute was being
debated.[41] The drafting history of the Statute also reveals that, while there
were serious differences over certain aspects of the provisions relating to
gender and sexual violence, there was general consensus among delegations on the recognition of these crimes as serious international crimes in
the Statute.

From a feminist perspective, the notable provisions of Rome Stature
are contained in Part 2,[42] which deals with crimes falling within the juris-

---

39 Rome Statute for the International Criminal Court, adopted 17 July 1998, Article 7(3)
    ('ICC Statute') (http://www.legal-tools.org/doc/7b9af9/).
40 Suhr, 2017, see *supra* note 1.
41 Susana Sacouto and Katherine Cleary, "The Importance of Effective Investigation of Sex-
    ual Violence and Gender-Based Crimes at the International Criminal Court", in *American
    University Journal of Gender, Social Policy & the Law*, 2009, vol. 17, no. 2, pp. 3–4.
42 ICC Statute, Part 2 ("Jurisdiction, Admissibility and Applicable Law") runs into 17 arti-
    cles, from Article 5 to Article 21, see *supra* note 39.

diction of the ICC. Gender-specific crimes are mentioned in Articles 7 and 8 dealing with crimes against humanity and war crimes. Among 11 offences listed in the former and 26 crimes listed in the latter, one relates to:[43] "rape, sexual slavery, enforced prostitution, forced pregnancy, enforced sterilization and any other form of sexual violence of comparable gravity".[44] It also includes within its ambit "any other sexual violence constituting a grave breach of the Geneva Conventions regarding war crimes".[45] The sexual violence crimes are included under the definition of war crimes for both "international and non-international armed conflict". Two other gender-specific crimes have been enumerated under crimes against humanity, that is, "persecution against any identifiable group or collectivity" on various grounds including gender,[46] and the crime of enslavement defined as "the exercise of any power attaching to the right of

---

[43] *Ibid.*, Article 7(1)(g).

[44] "While rape had previously been included in three of five international war crime statutes, additional forms of sexual violence had never been explicitly defined. The statutes of the international tribunals for Rwanda and SFRY did not list crimes of sexual violence other than rape. In direct contrast, the Rome Statute specifies gender-based crimes including sexual slavery, enforced prostitution, forced pregnancy, enforced sterilization, and any other form of sexual violence of comparable gravity. This is an important recognition of the varied forms that gender-based crimes may take; their specific enumeration highlights them as among the most serious. With regard to war crimes the definition stems from the Geneva Conventions, where serious crimes are listed as 'grave breaches', however, rape and sexual violence are not included. The improvement on this position witnessed in the Rome Statute is that it specifically enumerates both rape and different forms of sexual violence as war crimes." Sophie O'Connell, "Gender Based Crimes at the International Criminal Court", in *Plymouth Law Review*, 2010, vol. 3, pp. 69, 70.

"Another important difference is that the Rome Statute, unlike the Geneva Conventions, does not link sexual violence to an attack on a woman's honor. The Geneva Conventions refer to rape and sexual violence in terms of 'family honor and rights', which is a characterization that has reinforced the secondary importance as well as the shame and stigma of victimized women. By characterizing rape and sexual violence in this way, the crime becomes an offence against male dignity and an attack on their property. The Rome Statute cites rape and other forms of sexual violence as crimes in their own right, thereby emphasizing the serious and egregious nature of the crimes, rather than reinforcing stereotypes of shame and honor." See Copelon, 2001, see *supra* note 34; see Bedont and Martinez, 1999, p. 70, see *supra* note 15.

[45] ICC Statute, Article 8(2)(xxii), see *supra* note 39.

[46] *Ibid.*, Article 7(1)(h).

---

ownership over a person, including in the course of trafficking in persons, in particular women and children".[47]

Other significant provisions of the Statute, from a feminist angle, relate to the composition of the Court that provides for the inclusion of women with special emphasis of appointing women and men with specific expertise in dealing with sexual and gender violence.[48] It also incorporates provisions safeguarding the right of victims of sexual violence.[49] The Gender and Children's Unit was established to provide advice and assistance to the OTP activities, including sexual and gender-based crimes, during all phases, right from the pre-analysis phase. It is worth mentioning that the OTP has appointed Professor Catharine MacKinnon, who is seen as a radical feminist, as a Special Gender Adviser.[50]

Though the Rome Statute was applauded as a progressive international instrument from the point of view of women, it is regretful that, there are either no charges for sexual crimes against women (as in *Lubanga*), or the charges are not comprehensive to include sexual crimes.[51] Some feminists lament that "despite the extensive provision in the Rome Statute, the ICC is failing to advance the prosecution of gender-based crimes".[52]

31.4. Quality Control in Preliminary Examinations

A preliminary examination is a process of examining the information on the alleged crimes available to the OTP, in order to arrive at a fully informed decision on whether there is a reasonable basis to proceed with an investigation. During preliminary examinations, the main task of the OTP[53] is to determine whether to open an investigation by analysing the

---

[47] *Ibid.*, Article 7(2)(c).

[48] *Ibid.*, see Articles 36, 42, 43 and 44.

[49] *Ibid.*, see Article 68.

[50] See ICC-OTP, "The ICC Prosecutor Appoints Prof. Catharine A. MacKinnon as Special Advisor on Gender Crimes", 26 November 2008, ICC-OTP-20081126-PR377 (http://www.legal-tools.org/doc/866eda/).

[51] Lubanga Judgment, see *supra* note 4.

[52] For a detailed criticism of these cases, see O'Connell, 2010, see *supra* note 44.

[53] "The Office of the Prosecutor (OTP) is an independent organ of the Court. It is responsible for examining situations under the jurisdiction of the Court where genocide, crimes against humanity and war crimes appear to have been committed, and carrying out investigations and prosecutions against the individuals who are allegedly most responsible for those

available information before it.[54] The findings of the OTP are preliminary in nature and may be reconsidered in the light of new facts or evidence.[55] It should be recalled that the OTP does not enjoy investigative powers at this stage. In the conduct of its preliminary examination activities, the OTP seeks to contribute to its two main goals of the Rome Statute, that is, "ending of impunity", and the "prevention of crimes".

Thus, to pass from the stage of documentation to criminal investigation one must cross the bridge of preliminary examinations which involve some of the hardest questions and choices facing the ICC.[56] Preliminary examination activities also constitute one of the most cost-effective ways for the OTP to fulfil the ICC's mission.[57] Though, it is a moot point, whether preliminary examinations are mainly a gateway to investigations, or whether they have objectives and functions of their own, irrespective of ICC investigations, several scholars believe that preliminary examinations have a certain intrinsic value that goes beyond investigations. They argue that preliminary examinations could be used to facilitate choices in relation to peace and justice. It facilitates several goals, like prevention of atrocity crimes, shaping the agenda of peace negotiations, or serving as catalyst for complementarity or transitional justice. Preliminary examinations could also have a certain deterrent effect due to their element of surprise, their 'watchdog function' and the structural relationship between the

---

crimes. Like the judges of the Court, the Prosecutor and Deputy Prosecutor are elected by the ASP for a non-renewable mandate of nine years. The OTP is composed of three main Divisions: 1. the Jurisdiction, Complementarity and Cooperation Division conducts preliminary examinations, provides advice on issues of jurisdiction, admissibility and cooperation, and coordinates judicial cooperation and external relations for the OTP; 2. the Investigation Division is in charge of providing investigative expertise and support, coordinating field deployment of staff and security plans and protection policies, and providing crime analysis and analysis of information and evidence; 3. the Prosecution Division prepares the litigation strategies and conducts prosecutions, including through written and oral submissions to the judges." The current Prosecutor is Ms. Fatou Bensouda from The Gambia (since 15 June 2012). Before that she served as a Deputy Prosecutor in charge of the Prosecutions Division of the ICC since 2004. See ICC, "Office of Prosecutor" (available on its web site).

[54] ICC Statute, see Part 5 "Investigation and Prosecution", see *supra* note 39.

[55] ICC-OTP, *Report on Preliminary Examination Activities 2016*, p. 3 (http://www.legal-tools.org/doc/f30a53/).

[56] Louman, "Report: Preliminary Examination and Legacy/Sustainable Exit: Reviewing Policies and Practices – Part 1", 2015, see *supra* note 3.

[57] *Ibid.*, p. 5.

OTP and the State concerned that is, monitoring, putting pressure, providing reward for behaviour, hence make preliminary examinations a powerful instrument of the ICC.[58]

Be that as it may, the very purpose to conduct a preliminary examination is to decide whether there is a reasonable basis to initiate an investigation. In doing so, the OTP is required to assess and verify a number of legal criteria as set in the Rome Statute for jurisdiction, admissibility, complementarity, and gravity.

31.4.1. Initiation of Preliminary Examinations

Where crimes within the ICC's jurisdiction appear to have been committed, preliminary examinations may be initiated by the OTP by receiving information from: 1. individuals; 2. group of individuals; 3. States; 4. inter-governmental organizations; 5. non-governmental organizations; and 6. other reliable sources.[59] The information to the OTP may include referrals from States Parties[60] or the United Nations Security Council,[61] or declarations accepting the exercise of jurisdiction by ICC lodged by a State which is not a party to the Statute.[62] After the authorization of the judges, the OTP may open an investigation on her own initiative.[63] The Prosecutor, however, cannot, on her own motion, initiate investigations with respect to non-States Parties, unless the matter involves nationals of States Parties involved in the alleged crimes, on the territory of the non-State Party in question.

---

[58] *Ibid.*

[59] ICC-OTP, *Regulations of the Office of the Prosecutor*, 23 April 2009, ICC-BD/05-01-09, chap. 3, Subsection 3, Regulation 25(1)(a) ('Regulations, 2009') (http://www.legal-tools. org/doc/a97226/). "To date, the OTP has received more that 10,000 of such communications, which can form the initial basis of the Office's preliminary examinations". ICC, "Office of Prosecutor", see *supra* note 53.

[60] Regulations, 2009, Regulation 25(1)(b), see *supra* note 59; ICC Statute, Article 13(a) and Article 14, see *supra* note 39. "This was the case for the Democratic Republic of the Congo, Uganda, Central African Republic on two occasions, and Mali". See ICC, "Office of the Prosecutor", see *supra* note 53.

[61] Regulations, 2009, Regulation 25(1)(b), see *supra* note 59; ICC Statute, Article 13(b), see *supra* note 39. "To date, this possibility has materialized with respect to the situations of Darfur and Libya", see ICC, "Office of the Prosecutor", see *supra* note 53.

[62] Regulations, 2009, Regulation 25(1)(c), see *supra* note 59.

[63] "This was the case for Kenya, Côte d'Ivoire and Georgia". ICC, "Office of the Prosecutor", see *supra* note 53.

The receipt of the information, referral or a declaration by the OTP will not automatically lead to the opening of preliminary examinations. The OTP will open a preliminary examination, only on the basis of Article 15, when the alleged crimes appear to fall within the jurisdiction of the Court.

31.4.2. Jurisdiction

The first principle in conducting preliminary examinations ensures that the Court has jurisdiction and the case is admissible. The Prosecutor must ascertain if there is a reasonable basis to believe that a crime within the jurisdiction of the Court has been committed.[64] There are three jurisdictional requirements[65] namely, 'temporal jurisdiction', 'subject-matter jurisdiction', and 'territorial or personal jurisdiction'. As per the requirements of 'temporal jurisdiction', the purported crime must have taken place after coming into force of the Rome Statute for the nation under consideration.[66] Accordingly, the ICC has no jurisdiction with respect to events which occurred before the coming into force of the Statute on 1 July 2002.[67] If a State becomes a party to the Statute after 1 July 2002, the ICC cannot exercise its jurisdiction retroactively, unless that State has made a declaration accepting retroactive ICC jurisdiction.[68] However, the ICC cannot exercise jurisdiction with respect to events which occurred before 1 July 2002. For a new State Party, the Statute enters into force on the first day of the month after the 60th day following the date of the deposit of its instrument of ratification, acceptance, approval or accession or personal jurisdiction.

The 'subject-matter jurisdiction' of the Court[69] extends to the "crime of genocide",[70] "crimes against humanity",[71] "war crimes"[72] and

---

[64] ICC Statute, Article 53(1)(a), see *supra* note 39. In accordance with Article 15(4), the Pre-Trial Chamber must also consider whether "the case appears to fall within the jurisdiction of the Court". *Ibid.*, Article 15(4).

[65] *Ibid.*, Articles 12 and 13(b).

[66] *Ibid.*, Articles 11 and 24.

[67] *Ibid.*, Article 11(1).

[68] *Ibid.*, Article 11(2).

[69] *Ibid.*, Article 5.

[70] *Ibid.*, Article 6.

[71] *Ibid.*, Article 7.

---

the "crime of aggression".[73] To satisfy the 'territorial or personal jurisdiction' of the ICC, "the accused must be a national of a country that has accepted the ICC's jurisdiction, or the crime must have taken place within the borders of a country that accepts the ICC's jurisdiction".[74] A State not party to the Statute may decide to accept the jurisdiction of the ICC by lodging a declaration accepting the exercise of jurisdiction by the Court.[75] Further, the conditions of 'territorial or personal' jurisdiction do not apply when the Security Council refers a situation to the OTP.[76]

As mentioned above, the Rome Statute comprehensively deals with the list of sexual violence crimes that are considered "crimes against humanity" and "war crimes", including "sexual slavery", "enforced prostitution", "enforced sterilization" and "forced pregnancy". Further, unlike the ICTR and the ICTY, which merely prohibited persecution on the basis of "religion, politics or race", the ICC also prohibits persecution based on "gender".[77] In addition, the ICC has recognized that rape can constitute genocide by causing "serious bodily or mental harm" committed with the intent to "destroy" a particular population, thus, codifying the holding in *Akayesu*.[78]

Further, the Rome Statute explicitly declares that military commanders and other superiors can be held responsible for the acts of the subordinates under their authority and control under certain circumstances.[79] This is important, from a feminist perspective, as those who physically commit rape and other sexual offences are often relatively low in the hierarchy of command and thus fall outside the ICC's mission to ensure accountability at the highest levels. Furthermore, the liability for military

---

[72]   *Ibid.*, Article 8.

[73]   *Ibid.*, Article 5(2).

[74]   *Ibid.*, Article 12(2).

[75]   *Ibid.*, Article 12(3).

[76]   *Ibid.*, Article 13.

[77]   *Ibid.*, Article 7(1)(h).

[78]   ICTR, *The Prosecutor v. Jean-Paul Akayesu*, Chamber I, Judgment, 2 September 1998, ICTR-96-4-T, see *supra* note 34. See also ICC Statute, Article 6(b), see *supra* note 39. See also Alexa Koenig, Ryan Lincoln and Lauren Groth, *The Jurisprudence of Sexual Violence*, Human Rights Centre, University of California, Berkeley, 2011, p. 19.

[79]   ICC Statute, Article 28(a), see *supra* note 39.

chiefs also correct the patriarchal notion of recognizing sexual violence as a tool of warfare, encouraged directly or indirectly by leaders.

31.4.3. Admissibility

The second requirement, that the OTP has to satisfy in the process of preliminary examinations, is regarding the principle of 'admissibility'. As set out in Article 17(1) of the Statute, 'admissibility' requires an assessment of "complementarity and gravity". Domestic jurisdictions bear the primary responsibility to investigate and prosecute the alleged offenders under Rome Statute. The OTP will initiate the situation for investigation only when the domestic authorities fail to uphold this primary responsibility and there is absence of genuine domestic proceedings.[80] The Court's Appeals Chamber has elucidated this requirement, explaining that there is a twofold test to establish 'complementarity': "[T]he initial questions to ask are (1) whether there are ongoing investigations or prosecutions, or (2) whether there have been investigations in the past and the state having jurisdiction has decided not to prosecute the person concerned".[81] If the answer to these two questions is in affirmative and the State under consideration is unwilling or unable to prosecute the accused, then the ICC can exercise jurisdiction.

31.4.3.1. Complementarity

In contradistinction to the UN's *ad hoc* tribunals such as the ICTY and the ICTR, which were given primacy over domestic jurisdiction, the Rome Statute does not preclude States from prosecuting international crimes. The rationale behind this is said to be, that "the ICC's success would not only be determined by the number of cases reaching the ICC, but also the number of effective and efficient disposals by the national courts".[82]

Since, the jurisdiction of the ICC shall be complementary to national criminal jurisdictions, this implies that domestic jurisdictions have an

---

[80] *Ibid.*, Article 17(1)(a).

[81] Katanga Judgment, see *supra* note 7.

[82] Mark Drumbl, "Policy through Complementarity: The Atrocity Trial as Justice", in Carsten Stahn and Mohamed M. El Zeidy (eds.), *The International Criminal Court and Complementarity: From Theory to Practice*, Cambridge University Press, Cambridge, 2011.

---

important role to play in punishing atrocities within their jurisdiction,[83] and the function of the ICC is to act as a Court of last resort.[84] The principle of "complementarity" is implemented by the Court through Articles 17 and 53, which deal with the conditions for a specific case to be admissible at the ICC. This principle is perceived to be the foundation of the Rome Statute.[85] The justification of the principle seeks to balance the competing considerations of international justice *vis-à-vis* State sovereignty. The idea of complementarity has vastly evolved with time. Scholars have identified the "big idea of complementarity"[86] wherein the ICC's function is primarily associated with galvanizing efforts at the domestic jurisdictional level.[87] This big idea has the ultimate objective to incentiv-

---

[83] As far as India's position is concerned, it has not signed the ICC Statute. It has, however enacted Geneva Convention Act, 1960, as it had ratified it in 1950. India's legal regime to tackle international crimes lacks vitality. The process of pre-investigation and investigation for prosecution of rape and sexual offences under Indian criminal justice system differs from that of ICC. Under the domestic criminal justice system, though the registration of First Information Report (FIR) is compulsory, however, after registration, the officer in charge of the concerned police station is allowed to file a closure report to the Magistrate, if she or he feels that the evidence is deficient. However, even if the police attempt to file a closure report, the Magistrate may demand further investigation, after taking cognizance under Criminal Procedure Code. The role of prosecutor in India differs from that of the OTP at ICC primarily due to the reason that in India, investigation and prosecution of offences are performed by different institutions. Prior to 1973, public prosecutors were attached to the police department. However, after the new Code of Criminal Procedure came into force in 1973, the prosecution wing has been totally detached from the police department. Fact finding, pre-investigation and investigation of offences are the prerogative of police. The prosecution wing in the State is headed by an officer designated as Director of Prosecution that is responsible for prosecution of cases in the Magisterial Courts. Furthermore, India follows common law system, whereas ICC follows predominantly civil law.

[84] ICC Statute, paragraph 10 of the Preamble, reads as follows: "Emphasizing that the International Criminal Court established under this Statute shall be complementary to national criminal jurisdiction", see *supra* note 39.

[85] Ben Bathos, "The Evolution of the ICC Jurisprudence on Admissibility", in Carsten Stahn and Mohamed M. El Zeidy (eds.), *The International Criminal Court and Complementarity: From Theory to Practice*, Cambridge University Press, Cambridge, 2011.

[86] Sarah M.H. Nouwen, *Complementarity in the Line of Fire: The Catalysing Effect of the International Criminal Court in Uganda and Sudan*, Cambridge University Press, Cambridge, 2013.

[87] William Schabas, *An Introduction to the International Criminal Court*, Cambridge University Press, Cambridge, 2011; Jann K. Kleffner, "Complementarity and Auto Referrals", in Carsten Stahn and Göran Sluiter (eds.), *The Emerging Practice of the International Criminal Court*, Brill, Leiden, 2009; Carsten Stahn, "Complementarity: A Tale of Two Notions", in *Criminal Law Forum*, 2008, vol. 19, no. 1, pp. 87–113.

ize States to reciprocally adopt the Rome Statute crimes into penal provisions at the domestic level, thereby catalysing the prosecution of such crimes at the domestic jurisdictional level.[88] Then there is a "narrow idea" of complementarity,[89] which is concerned with the jurisdictional conflict surrounding States and the ICC and the provision relating thereto. Article 17 lays down the criteria for assessing the admissibility of a case to the ICC, namely "inaction", "unwillingness" and "inability" on behalf of the State supposed to prosecute the alleged offenders.

The first test which is undertaken to determine, by the OTP, admissibility is the 'action' test. This test entails an assessment of the action undertaken by a State to investigate or prosecute a case over which the domestic courts have jurisdiction. Upon inaction of the State, the 'case' may be rendered admissible to the ICC. Over the years, the ICC has applied the 'same-person, same-conduct' rule in construing the definition of 'case', which includes proceedings against the same person with whom the OTP is concerned and for the 'same conduct' the OTP is charging. The ICC, however, has confirmed through cases that the State is not mandated to investigate or prosecute the perpetrator in relation to any specific international crimes so long as a contemporaneous provision governing the 'same conduct' is existent in the domestic penal code.[90] Even if the 'action' test is satisfied, the case may still be inadmissible to the ICC if it does not fulfil the 'unwilling or unable' test. This test requires that the cases must be proceeded with genuinely, with the 'willingness' coupled with the 'ability' of the State. Since these tests are disjunctive, therefore either test needs to be satisfied to attract admissibility of the case concerned. Further guidance is available in the Statute in so far as the construction of 'unwillingness' is concerned, including whether the national proceedings are being machinated to protect the perpetrator from liability, or whether the proceedings have been deliberately protracted to prejudice

---

[88] Frédéric Mégret, "Too Much of a Good Thing? ICC Implementation and the Uses of Complementarity", in Carsten Stahn and Mohamed M. El Zeidy (eds.), *The International Criminal Court and Complementarity: From Theory to Practice*, Cambridge University Press, Cambridge, 2011.

[89] See Stahn, 2008, see *supra* note 87; Nouwen, 2013, see *supra* note 86.

[90] Louise Chappell, Rosemary Grey and Emily Waller, "The Gender Justice Shadow of Complementarity: Lessons from the International Criminal Court's Preliminary Examinations in Guinea and Colombia", in *International Journal of Transitional Justice*, 2013, vol. 7, no. 3, p. 460.

the case, or whether independence or impartiality is severely wanting within the proceedings.[91] The definition of 'unwillingness' is not exhaustive,[92] which advances the likelihood of alternative constructions of 'unwillingness', while not precluding an interpretation which is 'gendered'.

If there is a substantial degradation in the judicial system or if the State is unable to obtain the accused or the necessary evidence or testimony, then the same would attract the 'inability' test.[93] This test may refer to considerations which are completely pragmatic, such as "a lack of judicial personnel, an insecure environment or a lack of essential cooperation by other states", or legal factors, including "amnesty or immunity laws, the lack of the necessary extradition treaties, or the absence of jurisdiction under domestic law".[94]

At the stage of preliminary examinations, the OTP is first confronted with the application of these tests to the information collected, that may help to assess if there is a "reasonable basis" to open an investigation after considering the principle of complementarity. Preliminary examinations such as the ones in Guinea and Colombia offer a lot of insight into the application of these tests. During this stage, the OTP has made it clear that while its primary objective may be to make this assessment, it also considers this stage as an opportunity wherein domestic authorities can be incentivized and persuaded to investigate and prosecute perpetrators domestically.[95]

31.4.3.1.1. Feminist Shadow of Complementarity

From a feminist perspective, the principle of 'complementarity' provides a strict limitation on the fulfilment of the goal of the ICC to end impunity to sexual crimes. The provisions in the Rome Statute relating to complementarity have been found to have no nexus with feminist principles. Given the protection of victims and appointment of Court personnel, this ab-

---

[91] ICC Statute, Article 17(2), see *supra* note 39.

[92] Chappell, Grey and Waller, 2013, see *supra* note 90.

[93] ICC Statute, Article 17(3), see *supra* note 39.

[94] Sarah M.H. Nouwen, "Fine-tuning Complementarity", in Bartram S. Brown (ed.), *Research Handbook on International Criminal Law*, Edward Elgar, Cheltenham, 2011, p. 214.

[95] ICC-OTP, *Policy Paper on Preliminary Examinations*, 2 November 2013 (http://www.legal-tools.org/doc/acb906/).

sence of a link is baffling.[96] The OTP's initial inquiry to assess State's willingness and ability to prosecute sexual crimes should include an examination of gender biases against women in domestic legal systems. The case of Kosovo is in hand, where its judicial system failed to investigate and prosecute sexual violence crimes, despite extensive documentation by women's groups, nongovernmental organizations and NATO of rape and other crimes of sexual violence committed on a large scale during the conflict in Kosovo.[97]

The critics have analysed the preliminary examinations in Guinea and Colombia to argue that the OTP's apparent inattention to gender biases underpinning domestic legal systems has left impunity for perpetrators of sexual violence intact and the victims of these crimes unrecognized.[98]

The 'action' test using the 'same person same conduct' rule precludes any opportunity to address gender biases in domestic jurisdiction. For example, if there were a situation where mass rape would have been inflicted on several sections of the women population, it would not be necessary for States to reflect the Rome Statute crimes into their domestic penal code. All that would be necessary to see would be whether the same conduct could be brought under the umbrella of the domestic penal code. Thus, if an individual concerned were to be prosecuted, all that this test would require is to ascertain if the State can prosecute the said individual under a domestic penal provision, *albeit* the said domestic provision may not necessarily rectify the patriarchal connection between sexual violence against women and armed conflict which is considered to be inherent in a war crime or armed conflict.

31.4.3.2. Gravity

The second criterion, that the OTP has to apply in 'admissibility' while conducting Preliminary Examinations, is whether the case is of "sufficient gravity" to justify the ICC's involvement.[99] The 'gravity' of the offence is measured both in terms of 'quantity' and 'quality'. For instance, the quantitative scale of 'gravity' can be established by a huge number of victims

---

[96] Chappell, Grey and Waller, 2013, see *supra* note 90.

[97] Amnesty International, *Kosovo (Serbia): The Challenge to Fix a Failed UN Justice Mission*, 2008, pp. 23 and 63 (http://www.legal-tools.org/doc/0dccb4/).

[98] Chappell Grey and Waller, 2013, see *supra* note 90.

[99] ICC Statute, Article 17(1), see *supra* note 39.

---

of war crimes. However, it is not just the number of victims that matters, but the existence of aggravating or qualitative factors attached to the commission of crime that make it a grave crime.[100] Various factors that can be used to consider whether a crime is sufficiently grave from a qualitative perspective include the geographical and temporal intensity of the alleged crimes, the nature of the alleged crimes, manner of committing the crimes, and the impact on victims and their families.[101] Before initiating the investigation, the OTP considers the seriousness of the crimes including sexual and gender-based crimes; the factual context and the groups and individuals that appear most responsible for those crimes.

31.4.3.2.1. The Patriarchal Mindset of the OTP

The patriarchal mindset of the OTP had considered rape and other forms of sexual violence less serious than crimes resulting in death. History is a witness to the fact, that there is an almost inevitable tendency for treating rape and sexual violence against women to be treated of secondary importance.[102] For centuries, the rape and sexual abuse of women associated with the enemy were considered an inevitable by-product of war and thus dismissed as a natural consequence of war.[103] Where gender violence was condemned, humanitarian law, which primarily reflected the male experience with armed conflict, conceptualized such conduct as an offense against a woman's dignity or a family's honour.[104] Women were considered the property of men, and accordingly, rape was condemned as a property crime and a crime against dignity and honour, not a crime of violence.[105] Such classifications reinforced traditional stereotypes that rape was solely a woman's crime, masked the violent nature of rape, and

---

[100] *Ibid.*

[101] *Ibid.*

[102] Copelon, 2001, pp. 217, 220, see *supra* note 34.

[103] See Susan Brownmiller, *Against Our Will, Men, Women and Rape*, Ballantine Books, 1975, p. 2.

[104] See Beth Van Schaack, "Obstacle on the Road to Gender Justice: The International Criminal Tribunal for Rwanda as Object Lesson", in *American University Journal of Gender, Social Policy & the Law*, 2009, vol. 17, no. 2, p. 364.

[105] *Ibid.*

perpetuated the view that rape was a secondary crime in relation to other offences.[106]

The decisions not to charge perpetrators with the full range of crimes available for acts of sexual and gender-based violence, despite sufficient evidence, runs the risk of marginalizing and systematically excluding such charges as too difficult to prove or non-essential.[107] Post-World War II trials failed to charge a single defendant with sex crimes despite abundant evidence that such crimes had occurred.[108] The trial before the International Military Tribunal for the Far East in Tokyo, though included some prosecutions for sexual violence, the crimes were not appropriately labelled, but rather prosecuted under such euphemistic rubrics as "inhumane treatment" and "failure to respect family honour and rights".[109] Before the 1990s, gender crimes were largely invisible or trivialised.[110] In the early 1990s, when international criminal prosecutions were resumed, there was again initial resistance to investigation and prosecution of sex crimes. Investigators of the ICTY and the ICTR were instructed to consider sex crimes as less serious than crimes involving killing, that should not be pursued.[111] Defence counsel questioned the appropriateness of international jurisdiction over sex crimes, contending that they are insufficiently serious.[112]

Scholars have examined primary philosophical bases advanced for international prosecutions – retribution, deterrence, expressivism, and

---

[106] See Catherine N. Niarchos, "Women, War, and Rape: Challenges Facing the International Tribunal for the Former Yugoslavia", in *Human Rights Quarterly*, 1995, vol. 17, no. 4, pp. 649, 674.

[107] Schaack, 2009, see *supra* note 104.

[108] See Margaret M. deGuzman, "Giving Priority to Sex Crime Prosecutions: The Philosophical Foundations of a Feminist Agenda", in *International Criminal Law Review*, 2011, vol. 11, no. 5, p. 511, at p. 517.

[109] *Ibid.*

[110] Copelon, 2001, p. 219, see *supra* note 34.

[111] See Peggy Kuo, "Prosecuting Crimes of Sexual Violence in an International Tribunal", in *Case Western Reserve Journal of International Law*, 2002, vol. 35, no. 3, p. 310.

[112] Julie Mertus, "When Adding Women Matters: Women's Participation in the International Criminal Tribunal for the Former Yugoslavia", in *Seton Hall Law Review*, 2008, vol. 38, no. 4, p. 1307; see also Jenny S. Martinez, "International Law at The Crossroads: The Role of Judge Patricia Wald", in *International Criminal Law Review*, 2011, vol. 11, no. 3, pp. 391–400.

---

restorative justice – to determine how they inform decisions whether to give priority to sex crime prosecutions and argue that 'retribution' and 'deterrence' support such selections at least some of the time, and 'expressivist' and 'restorative justice' provide an even stronger foundation for giving priority to sex crimes.[113]

31.4.3.2.2. Feminist Advocacy

Feminist scholars have worked hard to change such attitudes, urging that sex crimes should be selected for prosecution even at the expense of prosecuting other serious crimes, including crimes resulting in death. As a result of feminist advocacy work, there is now widespread agreement that international criminal courts should give higher priority on prosecuting sex crimes than they have in the past. This agreement is manifested in the Rome Statute of the ICC and in policy statements of the OTP. Unlike prior international court statutes, the Rome Statute mandates that in exercising the Prosecutor's duties, he or she must consider "the nature of the crime, in particular where it involves sexual violence, gender violence or violence against children". The Statute further requires that hiring decisions at the court take into account the need to include personnel with expertise in sexual and gender violence.[114] Moreover, as a policy matter, the OTP has pledged that in selecting cases it will pay particular attention to sexual and gender-based crimes. Other international prosecutors have also begun to emphasise the particular need to prosecute sex crimes. In 2010, a number of current and former international prosecutors issued a declaration urging States to ensure the appropriate investigation and prosecution of gender crimes.[115]

Despite all these efforts, the impetus to address sexual and gender-based violence envisioned in the Rome Statute does not appear to have completely transferred to the practice of the ICC. The historical tendency of international criminal tribunals to treat rape and sexual violence as secondary crimes has led to the ICC Pre-Trial Chamber's recent misapplication of "cumulative charging practices" in *Prosecutor v. Jean-*

---

[113] deGuzman, 2011, p. 515, see *supra* note 108.

[114] *Ibid.*, p. 518.

[115] *Ibid.*, p. 519.

Pierre Bemba Gombo (*'Bemba'*).[116] This decision reflects the failure of the ICC to recognize the distinctive nature of rape versus other crimes and leads to discriminatory and marginalizing treatment of sexual and gender-based violence victims.[117]

31.4.4. Interests of Justice

The criteria of "interests of justice" is considered by the OTP during preliminary examinations, only where the requirements of 'jurisdiction' and 'admissibility' are fulfilled. While the requirements for 'jurisdiction' and 'admissibility' are positive requirements, the "interests of justice" is a negative requirement that may furnish a reason for not proceeding further.[118] As such, the OTP is not required to establish that an investigation serves the "interests of justice". On the other hand, the OTP will have to prove that, having fulfilled the 'jurisdiction and admissibility' criteria, it still must be in the "interests of justice" to initiate an investigation.

It deals with those circumstances in which a situation otherwise qualified for initiation for investigation by the OTP is not pursued on the ground that the investigation would not serve the "interests of justice".[119]

The issue of the "interests of justice", as it appears in Article 53 of the Rome Statute, represents one of the most complex aspects of the Statute.[120] However, it is safe to state that the concept of "interests of justice"

---

[116] ICC, Situation in the Central African Republic, *The Prosecutor v. Jean-Pierre Bemba Gombo*, ICC-01/05-01/08, see *supra* note 8.

[117] Green, 2011, p. 530, see *supra* note 10.

[118] Article 53(1) of the Statute addresses the initiation of an investigation. "If the Prosecutor is satisfied that there is a reasonable basis to believe that the case is within the jurisdiction of the Court and is or would be admissible under Article 17 of the Statute, he must determine whether, taking into account the gravity of the crime and the interests of the victims, there are nonetheless substantial reasons to believe that an investigation would not serve the interests of justice." Article 53(2) addresses the initiation of a prosecution. It indicates that, "upon investigation, the Prosecutor may conclude that there is not sufficient basis to proceed because it is not in the interests of justice, taking into account all the circumstances, including the gravity of the crime, the interests of victims and the age or infirmity of the alleged perpetrators, and his or her role in the alleged crime".

[119] ICC-OTP, *Policy Paper on the Interests of Justice*, September 2007 (http://www.legal-tools. org/doc/bb02e5/).

[120] The phrase "in the interests of justice" appears in several places in the ICC Statute and Rules of Procedure and Evidence, but it is never defined. Thorough reviews of the preparatory works on the treaty also offer no significant elucidation. See *ibid.*, p. 2.

cannot be referred to include issues relating to international peace and
security, as Article 16 of the Rome Statute recognizes a specific role for
the United Nations Security Council in matters affecting international
peace and security. The OTP Policy Paper on the Interests of Justice clarifies that "in particular, the 'interests of justice' provision should not be
considered a conflict management tool requiring the Prosecutor to assume
the role of a mediator in political negotiations: such an outcome would
run contrary to the explicit judicial functions of the Office and the Court
as a whole. In terms of whether effective investigations are operationally
feasible, the Office notes that feasibility is not a separate factor under the
Statute when determining whether to open an investigation. Weighing
feasibility as a separate self-standing factor, moreover, could prejudice the
consistent application of the Statute and might encourage obstructionism
to dissuade the ICC from intervention".[121]

The Policy Paper on the Interests of Justice tries to explain the understanding of this concept by stating that the criteria for the "interests of
justice" is determined by taking into consideration circumstances such as
gravity of the crime, the interests of the victims, the age or infirmity of the
accused, and his or her role in the alleged crimes.[122] It cautions, however,
that it is possible, that an individual deemed by the OTP to be most responsible person for the alleged crimes may not be prosecuted in the "interests of justice". The rationale of this principle seeks to command respect for the ICC in considering the interests of alleged accused. For example, international justice may not be served by the prosecution of a
terminally ill defendant or a suspect who has been the subject of abuse
amounting to serious human rights violations, as is the practice in many
national legal systems.[123] The OTP Policy Paper on the Interests of Justice
emphasizes that the "exercise of the Prosecutor's discretion under Article
53(1)(c) and 53(2)(c) is exceptional in its nature and there is a presumption in favour of investigation or prosecution".[124] Similarly, the OTP Policy Paper on Preliminary Examinations clarifies that the decision not to
proceed on the grounds of the interests of justice would be highly exceptional. It emphasizes that considering the mandate of the OTP and the

---

[121] *Ibid.*, p. 1.

[122] *Ibid.*, p. 6.

[123] *Ibid.*, p. 7.

[124] *Ibid.*, p. 1.

object and purpose of the Statute, "there is a strong presumption that investigations and prosecutions will be in the interests of justice, wherever the criteria established in Article 53(1)(a) and (b) or Article 53(2)(a) and (b) have been met".[125]

31.4.5. The Lack of Concrete Time Frame

The Rome Statute as well as the Rules of Procedure and Evidence do not prescribe any definitive time period[126] during which the preliminary examination has to be completed by OTP. The time and length for conducting preliminary examination is entirely left on the facts and circumstances of different situations before the OTP. The Prosecutor is obliged to continue with the examination until such time as the information shows that there is, or is not, a reasonable basis for an investigation. An examination of various situations reveals that there is absolutely no principle for regulating the duration of preliminary examinations with the result that in some situations, it took many years to initiate the investigation by the OTP. In the case of exercising *proprio motu* powers of the Prosecutor, the duration of a preliminary examination is even longer, for instance, in the case of Colombia, the lack of progress in the situation referred to the OTP was challenged by the Central African Republic in 2005 before the Pre-Trial Chamber. The Chamber said[127] that the "preliminary examination of a situation must be completed within a reasonable time from the reception of a referral by a State Party, and requested the Prosecutor to submit a report on the status of the preliminary examination, including an estimate of when the preliminary examination will be concluded". The OTP reacted by challenging the authority of the Pre-Trial Chamber to request this information, arguing that "the Pre-Trial Chamber is, under Art. 53(3), entitled only to review a decision by the Prosecutor not to proceed with an investigation [...]".[128] The OTP submitted the requested report, but ex-

---

[125] ICC-OTP, *Policy Paper on Preliminary Examinations*, 2013, p. 17, see *supra* note 95.

[126] *Ibid.*, p. 3.

[127] See ICC, Situation in the Central African Republic, Pre-Trial Chamber III, Decision Requesting Information on the Status of the Preliminary Examination of the Situation in the Central African Republic, 30 November 2006, ICC-01/05-6 (http://www.legal-tools.org/doc/76e607/).

[128] See ICC, Situation in the Central African Republic, Pre-Trial Chamber III, Prosecution's Report Pursuant to Pre-Trial Chamber III's 30 November 2006 Decision Requesting In-

pressly reserved its interpretation of Article 53(1) and the prerogatives of
the Prosecutor in this respect that is, saying that "it is hoped that a decision can be made in the near future".[129]

From a feminist angle, a wide discretion with the OTP whether to
initiate investigation, or continues to assess relevant national proceedings,
or to gather more information to establish a sufficient basis for a decision
on further steps without any timeline results in slow justice for victims of
sexual crimes and this way justice delayed results in justice denied for the
victims of sexual violence.

31.5. OTP Policy Papers

This section will briefly summarize the Policy Paper on Preliminary Examinations and the Policy Paper on Sexual and Gender-Based Crimes
before analysing their feminist dimensions.

31.5.1. Policy Paper on Preliminary Examinations, 2013

With the objective of ensuring transparency and objectivity in applying
the legal criteria to assess whether a situation warrants investigation, the
OTP released, in November, 2013, the Policy Paper on Preliminary Examinations, dealing with various aspects of policy and practice in the conduct
of preliminary examinations.[130] It describes various principles, factors and
procedures applied by the OTP in the conduct of its preliminary examinations. It draws special attention to the two overarching goals of Rome
Statute that is, ending of impunity, by encouraging genuine national proceedings, and the prevention of crimes.[131] Thus, while describing the
Rome Statute System, it highlights the primary responsibility of national
jurisdictions to investigate and prosecute the crimes listed in the Rome

---

formation on the Status of the Preliminary Examination of the Situation in the Central African Republic, 15 December 2006, ICC-01/05-7 (http://www.legal-tools.org/doc/1dd66a/).

[129] William A. Schabas, *The International Criminal Court: A Commentary on the Rome Statute*, Oxford University Press, 2010, p. 659, at pp. 667–68.

[130] ICC, *Policy Paper on Preliminary Examinations*, 2013, p. 5, see *supra* note 95. "The paper
is based on the Rome Statute ("Statute"), the Rules of Procedure and Evidence ("Rules"),
the Regulations of the Court ("RoC"), the Regulations of the Office of the Prosecutor, the
Office's prosecutorial strategy and policy documents, and its experience over the first
years of its activities."

[131] *Ibid.*, p. 5.

Statute.[132] The Policy Paper outlines the General Principles of "independence", "impartiality" and "objectivity" to be applied by the OTP while conducting the preliminary examination on the basis of available facts and information.[133] The legal framework and various statutory factors, as prescribed in Article 53(1), that are applied by OTP at the stage of preliminary examination to determine reasonable basis to proceed with an investigation are also examined in the Policy Paper. While examining the obstacles of jurisdiction, admissibility and interests of justice, to reach investigation, it clarifies that these factors, are applied to all situations, irrespective of whether the preliminary examination was initiated on the basis of information received by a referral, or by a declaration lodged pursuant to Article 12(3),[134] or on the basis of information obtained pursuant to Article 15.[135] The Policy Paper further makes it clear that there are no other statutory criteria for conducting the preliminary examinations by OTP. It particularly emphasizes, that factors like geographical or regional balance are not statutory criteria for determining investigated by the ICC.[136] The Policy Paper very nicely described the 'phased approach' followed by the OTP while conducting the preliminary examinations. It details four phases of filtering process to distinguish those situations that warrant investigation from those that do not require any investigation. It acknowledges that no timelines are provided in the Statute for bringing a preliminary examination to a close. Huge discretion is invested with OTP to initiate an investigation or to continue to collect information on crimes and relevant national proceedings in order to establish a sufficient factual and legal basis to render a determination.[137] One of the laudable objectives of the Policy Paper is to promote transparency of the preliminary examination process, for which the OTP will provide public information on reasoned decisions either to proceed or not to proceed with investiga-

---

[132] *Ibid.*, pp. 5–6.

[133] *Ibid.*, pp. 7–8.

[134] *Ibid.*, pp. 8–9.

[135] *Ibid.*, p. 3.

[136] *Ibid.*

[137] *Ibid.*, p. 21.

tions, and will issue regular reports on its activities including annual reports on its preliminary examination activities.[138]

31.5.2. Policy Paper on Sexual and Gender-Based Crimes, 2014

The OTP faced a considerable "gendered criticism",[139] in March 2014,
when it failed to secure conviction at the ICC against Germain Katanga[140]
for rape and other sexual violence as crimes against humanity and as war
crimes.[141] Taking serious cognizance of this criticism, three months thereafter, in June 2014, OTP released the Policy Paper on Sexual and Gender-
Based Crimes, affirming its commitment to the prosecution of sexual and
gender-based crimes.[142] The Policy Paper declares that the issue of sexual
and gender-based crimes, is recognized in its Strategic Plan 2012-2015, as
one of its key strategic goals. It expresses its commitment to integrate a
gender perspective and analysis into all of its work, right from preliminary
examinations to investigation and from investigation to prosecution of
these crimes. The Policy Paper also promises gender sensitive training for
its staff, a victim-centric approach for victims, witnesses, families and
communities.[143]

One of the sections[144] of the Policy Paper exclusively devoted to
preliminary examinations emphasizes that, at the stage of analysing information, OTP will examine the general context within which the alleged
sexual and gender-based crimes have been committed within its jurisdic-

---

[138] *Ibid.*, p. 22.

[139] Women's Initiatives for Gender Justice, "Statement: Appeals Withdrawn by Prosecution
and Defence: *The Prosecutor vs. Germain Katanga*", 26 June 2014 (available on its web
site).

[140] Katanga Judgment, see *supra* note 7. See also ICC, Situation in the Democratic Republic
of the Congo, *The Prosecutor v. Germain Katanga*, Case Information Sheet, 20 March
2018, ICC-PIDS-CIS-DRC-03-014/18_Eng (http://www.legal-tools.org/doc/7649d0/).

[141] Katanga was convicted by a majority of the Trial Chamber as an accessory to the war
crimes of directing an attack against a civilian population, pillaging, and destruction of
property, as well as murder as a war crime and a crime against humanity, however the
Chamber unanimously acquitted Katanga as an accessory to rape and sexual slavery as war
crimes and crimes against humanity.

[142] ICC-OTP, *Policy Paper on Sexual and Gender-Based Crimes*, June 2014 (http://www.
legal-tools.org/doc/7ede6c/).

[143] *Ibid.*, p. 5.

[144] *Ibid.*, sect. IV running into paras. 38–47.

tion.[145] Since the principle of "admissibility", consisting of "complementarity" and "gravity", is an important criteria to be considered by OTP to reach a determination whether there is a reasonable basis to initiate an investigation, the Policy Paper explains that where sexual and gender-based crimes have been identified, the OTP will seek to encourage genuine national investigations and prosecutions by the State. In this context, it will pay special attention to the discriminatory attitudes and gender stereotypes in domestic substantive law as well as procedural law. It also depicts its commitment, while examining the absence of genuine national proceedings by seriously taking into consideration the "lack of political will which may be reflected in official attitudes of trivialization or denial of these crimes, and the deliberate focus of national proceedings on low-level perpetrators, despite evidence against those who may bear greater responsibility".[146]

As explained earlier, one of the criteria of "admissibility" determination relates to the "sufficient gravity" of crimes to justify initiation of investigation. In assessing the "gravity" of the crimes, factors such as scale, nature, manner of commission, and impact are considered. It is heartening to mention that the Policy Paper recognizes that sexual and gender-based crimes are amongst the gravest under the Statute and the OTP will pay due attention to the multi-faced character of such crimes including the impact of such crimes, in assessing the gravity of these crimes.[147]

31.5.3. Feminist Dimensions of the Policy Papers

The OTP Policy Paper on Preliminary Examination, 2013, while describing the relevant Rome Statute principles, factors and procedures applied by the OTP in its conduct during preliminary examination is completely silent on the feminist sensitivity that is required to handle the sexual offences against women resulting in poor execution by the OTP in dealing with such offences. The overarching principles, regulating the preliminary examination process, talking about independence, impartiality and objec-

---

[145] *Ibid.*, p. 22.

[146] *Ibid.*, p. 23.

[147] *Ibid.*, pp. 23–24.

---

tivity, do not include 'gender feminist sensitivity' with which sexual crimes against women need to be analysed to improve its quality control.

The Policy Paper on Sexual and Gender-Based Crimes appears to respond, fairly, to the criticism raised by feminist scholars and NGOs on the acquittal of Germain Katanga of rape and sexual slavery. It depicts the broad commitment of OTP for gender-conscious analysis of crime by outlining relevant policies and providing victims with safety and support measures.[148]

While the OTP released the Policy Paper on Sexual and Gender-Based Crimes in 2014, the interaction between the complementarity provisions in the Rome Statute and gender biases is in a fairly grey area. Thus, there is plenty of scope and opportunity for the OTP to determine the level of gender discrimination against women in a domestic legal system while it applies the complementarity tests at the stage of preliminary examinations.

It is interesting to note that the 2014 Policy Paper begins with the definition of certain key terms such as 'gender', [149] 'gender-based crimes',[150] 'gender perspective'[151] and 'gender analysis'.[152] However, the definitions only manifest the gendered understanding of the OTP in this

---

[148] "The Office of The Prosecutor of the ICC, Policy Paper on Sexual and Gender Based Crimes", in *Harvard Law Review*, 2014, vol. 128, no. 2, p. 797.

[149] ICC-OTP, *Policy Paper on Sexual and Gender-Based Crimes*, 2014, p. 2, see *supra* note 142. ""Gender", in accordance with Article 7(3) of the Rome Statute, refers to males and females, within the context of society. This definition acknowledges the social construction of gender, and the accompanying roles, behaviours, activities, and attributes assigned to women and men, and to girls and boys."

[150] *Ibid*. ""Gender-based crimes" are those committed against persons, whether male or female, because of their sex and/or socially constructed gender roles. Gender-based crimes are not always manifested as a form of sexual violence. They may include non-sexual attacks on women and girls, and men and boys, because of their gender."

[151] *Ibid*. ""Gender perspective" requires an understanding of differences in status, power, roles, and needs between males and females, and the impact of gender on people's opportunities and interactions. This will enable the Office to gain a better understanding of the crimes, as well as the experiences of individuals and communities in a particular society."

[152] *Ibid*. ""Gender analysis" examines the underlying differences and inequalities between women and men, and girls and boys, and the power relationships and other dynamics which determine and shape gender roles in a society, and give rise to assumptions and stereotypes. In the context of the work of the Office, this involves a consideration of whether, and in what ways, crimes, including sexual and gender-based crimes, are related to gender norms and inequalities."

Policy Paper which lacks feminist sensitivity. The Policy Paper simply acknowledges the differences in status, power, roles, needs between men and women to better understand the experiences of victims, families and communities, but do not challenge these differences. The principles of the text of this Policy Paper are based on 'gender' perspective and lacks the 'feminist' perspective.

While the success of both Policy Papers remains to be seen and will certainly depend on the extent to which the OTP is able to implement these policies, the Paper's endeavours that address the structural and societal aspects of its prosecutions may be significant in terms of 'gender' perspective, but certainly lacks the focused feminist angle.

Thus, it is important to juxtapose the Policy Papers of 2013 and 2014 to feminist issues to determine the true policy objective of the OTP against sexual crimes at the stage of preliminary examinations. This has to be viewed in light of the lack of timelines that are established as well as the complementarity principle which enables or disables international prosecution of the sexual crimes.

31.6. Current Status of Preliminary Examinations *vis-à-vis* Sexual Offences

This section briefly deals with the status of preliminary examinations focusing on rape and other sexual offences under the alleged 'war crimes' or 'crimes against humanity'. As on 31 May 2017, the OTP has made public its preliminary examination of 23 situations. While three situations[153] have been closed with decision not to investigate; ten situations have been completed with decision to investigate[154] and in another ten situations preliminary examinations are still ongoing.[155]

---

[153] Honduras, Republic of Korea, Venezuela, see ICC, "Preliminary Examinations" (available on the Court's web site).

[154] Central African Republic, Central African Republic II, Côte d'Ivoire, Darfur, Sudan, Democratic Republic of Congo, Georgia, Kenya, Libya, Mali, Uganda, *ibid.*

[155] Afghanistan, Burundi, Colombia, Gabon, Guinea, Iraq/UK, Nigeria, Palestine, Registered Vessels of Comoros, Greece and Cambodia, Ukraine, *ibid.*

31.6.1. Ongoing Preliminary Examinations

During the conduct of preliminary examinations, the OTP examines various situations in three phases.[156] In Phase 1, OTP analyses the seriousness of the information received and eliminates that information on offences that are outside the ICC's jurisdiction. In Phase 2, it officially starts the examination to assess the pre-conditions to the subject matter of the ICC over the alleged crimes as required under Article 12 of Rome Statute. Phase 3 assesses the 'admissibility' criteria in terms of 'complementarity' and 'gravity'. Five of the situations are in the second phase; four are in the last stage of preliminary examinations while one situation, previously dismissed, is now under consideration.[157]

Among ongoing preliminary examinations, the communications on alleged crimes of rape and other forms of sexual violence are received by OTP, for the situations in Burundi, Ukraine, Colombia, Guinea and Nigeria. In the situation of Burundi, where political crisis between ruling party and opponents began with the announcement on 25 April, 2015, of Mr. Pierre for a third presidential term, the OHCHR found 18 cases of sexual violence against women allegedly committed by the security forces, in the areas perceived as supportive of the opposition. The women who fled the country were sexually abused during their flight by armed men and border guards. Many women related to men perceived as political dissidents, became the targets of sexual violence including sexual mutilation, by the security forces, border guards and unidentified armed men.[158] The situation in Ukraine that has been under preliminary examination since April 2014, the gender sensitivity of OTP is reflected in acknowledging the underreporting of sexual crimes against women due to the social and cultural stigma.[159] In the situation of Colombia that has long been experiencing an armed conflict, between government forces and rebel armed groups, the preliminary examination is in Phase 3. In the on-going 'admissibility' analysis, the OTP has observed that the national criminal proceedings relating to sexual and gender-based crimes are little and only one convic-

---

[156] See ICC-OTP, *Report on Preliminary Examination Activities 2016*, pp. 4–5, see *supra* note 55.

[157] *Ibid.*, parts II–IV.

[158] *Ibid.*, p. 11.

[159] *Ibid.*, p. 40.

tion of a low-level army member has been rendered.[160] In the situation in Guinea, that witnessed widespread and systematic attacks by the ruling power against civilian population, the OTP has concluded that the information available provides a reasonable basis to believe that the crimes of rape and sexual violence including sexual mutilations and sexual slavery were committed in the national stadium where people had gathered to celebrate the Independence day of Guinea on 28 September, 2009 and its aftermath.[161] Though, the OTP is hopeful that Guinean authorities will set the stage of trial soon, to provide justice to the victims, however, no specific mention of sexual violence has been made in its report. A critical analysis of the gender biases in domestic legal system of Guinea and Colombia has already been made in Section 31.4. of this chapter.

Further, though, in pursuance to its Policy Paper on Sexual and Gender Based Crimes, the OTP has conducted analysis of rapes, sexual slavery and other sexual offences in the situation of Nigeria, but, sadly, the result of such analysis, has been missing in its report on preliminary examinations.[162]

31.6.2. Completed with Decision to Investigate

Coming to the situations that have been completed by the OTP, with the decision to investigate, in the situation in Central African Republic II, in opening the investigation in September 2014, the OTP stated that the information available furnished a reasonable basis to believe that 'war crimes' and 'crimes against humanity' including rape have been committed. In the post-election violence in Kenya, noting the gravity and scale of violence, the OTP stated that over 900 acts of rape and sexual violence, several acts of gang rape forcing family members to watch, genital mutilation have been committed. Similarly, in the situations of Côte d'Ivoire,[163] Democratic Republic of Congo,[164] Mali[165] and Uganda,[166] the OTP, in-

---

[160] *Ibid.*, p. 56.

[161] *Ibid.*, pp. 60, 61.

[162] *Ibid.*, p. 65.

[163] ICC, Situation in the Republic of Côte d'Ivoire, ICC-02/11.

[164] ICC, Situation in Democratic Republic of Congo, ICC-01/04.

[165] ICC, Situation in the Republic of Mali, ICC-01/12.

[166] ICC, Situation in Uganda, ICC-02/04.

cluded rape, sexual slavery, genital mutilation and so on under the alleged
'war crimes' and 'crimes against humanity'.

31.6.3. Closed with Decision Not to Investigate

As stated above, three situations have been closed by OTP with the decision not to investigate. Out of those three situations, the situation in Honduras is quite relevant. In 2010, the OTP announced preliminary examination in the situation of Honduras after having received communications on
the crimes committed following the 2009 coup and during post-2010 election period,[167] till 2014.[168] In March 2009, when José Manuel Zelaya, the
elected President of Honduras adopted a controversial decree, it was heavily criticized as beyond constitutional limits by opposition as well as national authorities. In June 2009, when Zelaya was arrested following an
arrest warrant issued by the Supreme Court of Justice, the National Congress passed a resolution removing Zelaya from Presidency and appointing Roberto Micheletti Baín, as President of Honduras. In July 2009, a
'crisis room' was established on the premises of the presidential palace for
coordinating police and military operations and many times curfews were
imposed through executive decrees, which were denounced by the international community as an illegal *coup d'état*. In opposition to this coup
frequent demonstrations were held by the supporters of former President,
which were met with resistance and violence by State security forces.

Since there was no armed conflict in this situation, the legal analysis of subject matter of OTP focused on alleged 'crimes against humanity'
including rape and other acts of sexual violence. In the course of exploring contextual elements of 'crimes against humanity', the OTP noted that
the *chapeau* of Article 7(1) of Rome Statute prescribes that "for the purpose of this Statute, 'crime against humanity' means any of the following
acts when committed as part of a *widespread or systematic attack directed
against any civilian population,* with knowledge of the attack" Article
7(2)(a) stipulates that "'attack directed against any civilian population'
means a course of conduct involving the multiple commission of acts referred to in paragraph 1 against any civilian population, pursuant to or *in
furtherance of a State or organizational policy to commit such attack*"

---

[167] ICC-OTP, *Situations in Honduras: Article 5 Report*, October 2015, p. 14 (http://www.
legal-tools.org/doc/54755a/).

[168] *Ibid.*, p. 5.

(emphasis added). In the situation of Honduras, the OTP found that though it may be said that the *de facto* regime has formed a plan to take over power and assume control over the country, it cannot be said, that the design of the plan contained a policy to attack the civilian population in a systematic manner, hence the information available does not provide a reasonable basis to believe that acts were committed as part of an attack pursuant to or in furtherance of a State policy to commit such attack, and therefore these acts do not constitute crimes against humanity within the scope of Article 7 of the Statute. The OTP further noted that there was no evidence that the alleged attacks were either widespread or systematic; the scale of victims of alleged crimes was relatively small.[169] The alleged crimes were not committed in the context of an attack that can be considered to be "massive, frequent, carried out collectively with considerable seriousness and directed against a multiplicity of victims".[170] It also noted that though, violence in Honduras escalated sharply following the 2009 coup, but it was also a result of the proliferation of drug trafficking and organized crimes, the massive growth of weapons, and the armed forces' involvement in matters of citizen security.[171]

31.7. Conclusion

In the context of the preliminary examination of rape and other forms of sexual violence against women, the quality control in the assessment and admissibility of such offences involve many challenges peculiar to these crimes. After the adoption of the Rome Statute, many envisioned the ICC as almost 'feminist' due to its statutory emphasis on 'gender'. Now, almost 20 years later, it is time to consider whether this has been proved right.[172] This chapter has revealed that the Rome Statute in recognizing sexual and gender-based crimes, as acts of 'crimes against humanity' as well as 'war crimes', incorporates and integrates 'gender' perspective with 'feminist' perspective. The OTP Policy Paper on Preliminary Examinations of 2013, while describing the relevant Rome Statute principles, factors and procedures applied by the OTP in its conduct during prelimi-

---

[169] "[A]cts of rape (two to eleven cases) and other acts of sexual violence (approximately 23)". *Ibid.*, p. 7.
[170] *Ibid.*
[171] *Ibid.*, p. 8.
[172] Suhr, 2017, see *supra* note 1.

nary examination, is completely silent on the feminist sensitivity that is required to handle the sexual offences against women resulting in poor quality in dealing with such offences. The overarching principles, regulating the preliminary examination process, independence, impartiality and objectivity, do not include 'gender feminist sensitivity' with which sexual crimes against women need to be analysed to improve its quality control.

The chapter explains that the proper processing and analyses of facts, communication and situations of the rape and other forms of sexual violence require a feminist approach to enhance quality control, while conducting a thorough evaluation of the reliability of the sources and the credibility of the information received, to determine whether there is a reasonable basis to initiate investigation. The information received and collected on sexual offences against women should be, legally and factually, analysed from the point of view of women's norms and experience to bring in it better quality control.

Gender-based crimes may be sexual or non-sexual crimes and sexual crimes may be committed against women as well as against men. This chapter argues that for higher quality control in prosecution and investigation of rape and other forms of sexual crimes, such offences cannot be lumped into one category using 'gender' without a 'feminist' perspective. Thus, to augment quality control, in dealing with such situations, it is pertinent to understand their different experiences, especially at the stage of preliminary examination, when the OTP decides whether to proceed a with full investigation.

However, it is heartening to note that in the wake of heavy criticism of *Katanga*, the OTP came out with the Policy Paper on Sexual and Gender-Based Crimes, however, this Policy Paper is also based on 'gender' perspective and lacks the 'feminist' perspective. This chapter stresses that the 'gender' analysis considers and explains discrimination and differences in male and female behaviour but does not challenge existing social, economic, political or cultural inequalities. A 'feminist' analysis on the other hand challenges the inequalities and the power dynamics that produce them. In the context of preliminary examination of rape and other forms of sexual offences, the gender analysis, for instance, may take into account under-reporting or non-reporting of such crimes and the stigma attached to the victims, but the feminist analysis, will question as to why there is under reporting or non-reporting of sexual crimes against women. Similarly, a feminist perspective and analysis in preliminary examination confronts the stigma attached to the female victims of sexual crimes; the social, cultural and religious norms that govern the gender roles of men and women in society. To prove rape, the emphasis on lack of consent on the part of victim may be shifted to the lack of coercion on the part of perpetrator. Thus, the Policy Paper of June 2014 incorporates gender analysis without 'feminist' perspective in considering lack of readily available evidence; lack of forensic or other documentary evidence; and inadequate or limited support services at national level in such cases. A feminist perspective will surely improve the quality control in preliminary examination to help the OTP office to assess the gravity of the offence qualitatively and quantitatively and the interests of victims. The poor quality in preliminary examination of rape and the sexual offences direct-ly affects the legitimate expectations of justice, particularly from the point of view of victims. Further the 'feminist' argument would make the deci-sion of OTP not to proceed on the grounds of "interests of justice" highly improbable, further enriching the quality control in preliminary examina-tion of such cases.

High hopes are being raised from the current female Chief Prosecu-tor, Fatou Bensouda,[173] who believes that such crimes should no longer be accepted as inevitable consequences of war and conflict. Her commitment in seriously dealing with these crimes is manifested in her efforts in re-leasing the Policy Paper on Sexual and Gender-Based Crimes in 2014 and elevating these crimes in the strategic goals.[174] Despite a progressive Chief Prosecutor, however, the ICC record with respect to the investiga-tion of sexual violence and gender-based crimes has not been encouraging in the last few years. The conviction in *Bemba* in July 2016 for sexual crimes may a notable achievement for feminists, but the October 2016, judgment in *Al Mahdi*[175] for not charging him for sexual and gender-based crimes, even though credible reports suggest these crimes occurred, is another setback for feminists. To conclude, two things may be stated. First,

---

[173] See ICC, "Office of Prosecutor", see *supra* note 53.

[174] Fatou Bensouda, "The Prosecution of Sexual and Gender-Based Crimes by International Courts", 16 July 2016 (http://www.legal-tools.org/doc/fe0045/).

[175] ICC, Situation in the Republic of Mali, *The Prosecutor v. Ahmad Al Faqi Al Mahdi*, ICC-01/12-01/15.

it is the right time to re-examine the ICC from a feminist perspective,[176] moving beyond the 'gender' perspective. Second, the principle of 'complementarity' in preliminary examinations, though applicable for other alleged crimes, should be inapplicable for the crimes of rape and sexual violence, as it is proving to be defeating the main objective of the ICC to end impunity to sex crimes in armed conflicts. In this context, a new concept of 'shared complementarity' may be invoked by OTP to end impunity to sexual crimes against women, to improve the quality in preliminary examination of such offences.

---

[176] Valerie V. Suhr, "The ICC's Al Mahdi Verdict on the Destruction of Cultural Heritage: Two Steps Forward, one Step Back?", in *Völkerrechtsblog*, 3 October 2016.

32

Preliminary Examinations and Children: Beyond Child Recruitment Cases and Towards a Children's Rights Approach

Cynthia Chamberlain[*]

32.1. Introduction

On November 2016, as the International Criminal Court ('ICC') advanced into adolescence, the OTP ('OTP') adopted its Policy on Children.[1] After a difficult childhood (during its first cases), the OTP recognised that it could reclaim the ICC's objective to work "for the sake of present and future generations".[2] With the adoption of the Policy on Children, the OTP showed a strong commitment to go beyond child recruitment cases, in order to include a child-sensitive approach in all its current and future work.

However, a policy is just that: a set of ideas or a plan of what to do in particular situations that has been agreed to officially.[3] It is therefore crucial to determine how the OTP will use and employ the ideas and plans adopted in its Policy on Children.

This chapter will focus on how the Policy on Children can be interpreted and applied as regards preliminary examinations. Preliminary ex-

---

[*] **Cynthia Chamberlain** is a Costa Rican lawyer who has worked as a Legal Officer in the Chambers of the International Criminal Court ('ICC') since 2006. She has a Ph.D. from Leiden University and a Master (DEA) from Universidad Autónoma and Universidad Complutense, Madrid. She obtained her law degree from the University of Costa Rica, where she also worked as an assistant lecturer. The opinions expressed in this chapter reflect the personal views of the author and do not reflect the views of the International Criminal Court.

[1] OTP ('OTP'), *Policy on Children*, November 2016 (http://www.legal-tools.org/doc/c2652b/).

[2] Rome Statute of the International Criminal Court, 17 July 1998, preamble (http://www.legal-tools.org/doc/7b9af9/) ('Rome Statute'). Quoted in paragraph 1 of the *Policy on Children*.

[3] "Policy", in *Cambridge Dictionary* (available on its web site).

aminations are the gateway to trials at the ICC, as they trigger investigations and lead to selection of cases against individuals for specific crimes. Ultimately, they may result in convictions, sentences and reparations. If the initial steps exclude children from the equation, they will most likely not benefit from judicial redress.

32.2. The Prosecutor's Policy on Children

The Policy on Children follows the OTP's previous thematic policies on Interests of Justice, Victims' Participation, Preliminary Examinations, Case Selection and Prioritisation and Sexual and Gender Based-Crimes.[4] During the first years of its work, the OTP focused mainly on the crime of enlistment, conscription and use of children to actively participate in armed forces or groups. Thus, early policies referred to children mainly as victims and witnesses of crimes.[5] Hence, albeit having focused on child-specific crimes at the outset,[6] and referring to the protection of child victims and witnesses in these cases,[7] the OTP still lacked a general approach to mainstream children's rights in its mandate. The Policy on Children is both a remedial strategy given the lessons learnt from these first trials, but also an undertaking to comprehensively integrate children's rights perspective in the OTP's work.

---

[4] OTP, *Policy Paper on the Interests of Justice* (http://www.legal-tools.org/doc/bb02e5/); *idem, Policy Paper on Victim's Participation* (http://www.legal-tools.org/doc/3c204f/); *idem, Policy Paper on Preliminary Examinations* (http://www.legal-tools.org/doc/acb906/); *idem, Policy Paper on Case Selection and Prioritisation* (http://www.legal-tools.org/doc/182205/); and *idem, Policy Paper on Sexual and Gender-Based Crimes* (http://www.legal-tools.org/doc/7ede6c/).

[5] OTP, "Report on the activities performed during the first three years (June 2003-June 2006)" (http://www.legal-tools.org/doc/c7a850/); OTP, "Prosecutorial Strategy 2009-2012" (http://www.legal-tools.org/doc/6ed914/).

[6] The first three cases included charges of child recruitment. See ICC, *The Prosecutor v. Thomas Lubanga Dyilo*, ICC-01/04-01/06, Warrant of Arrest, 10 February 2006 (http://www.legal-tools.org/doc/59846f/); ICC, *The Prosecutor v. Germain Katanga*, ICC-01/04-01/07, Warrant of Arrest, 2 July 2007 (http://www.legal-tools.org/doc/53f65c/); ICC, Situation in Uganda, ICC-02/04-01/05, Warrant of Arrest for Joseph Kony issued on 8 July 2005 as amended on 27 September 2005, 27 September 2005 (http://www.legal-tools.org/doc/b1010a/).

[7] OTP, "Report on the activities performed during the first three years (June 2003-June 2006)", pp. 12, 24, see *supra* note 5. See *idem*, "Strategic Plan June 2012-2015", para. 60 (http://www.legal-tools.org/doc/954beb/).

The adoption of the Policy on Children is the first palpable step of a plan that started in 2013, when the OTP turned its attention to child victims and witnesses beyond child recruitment cases.[8] The adoption of a Policy on Children was hence long overdue and its absence became more evident with the *Lubanga* judgment, where the Trial Chamber reproached the Prosecution's approach towards child witnesses and its use of intermediaries.[9]

Already in its Prosecutorial Strategy 2009-2012, the OTP identified crimes against children as one of the main issues to be addressed,[10] in respect of its own investigations, but also with reference to the positive complementarity principle and the duty for States Parties to investigate and prosecute crimes of genocide, crimes against humanity and war crimes committed against children.[11]

As with all other previous policies, the Policy on Children is aimed at providing greater clarity and transparency to the work of the OTP. In the case of preliminary examinations, the Rome Statute has left considerable room for prosecutorial discretion. Therefore, the OTP adopted a Policy Paper on Preliminary Examinations,[12] to promote clarity and predictability in the manner in which it applies the Rome Statute's sometimes-nebulous legal criteria. As regards children, the Rome Statute's provisions are also quite general,[13] hence the pressing need to adopt a more specific work plan. In light of this, the Policy on Children should be read together with the OTP's other previously adopted policies. For the purpose of this chapter, and in relation to preliminary examinations, it is evident that the Policy on Children must be interpreted and applied consistently with the policy on preliminary examinations.

---

[8] OTP, "Strategic Plan June 2012-2015", para. 63, see *supra* note 7. See OTP, *Policy Paper on Sexual and Gender-Based Crimes*, para. 8, see *supra* note 4.

[9] ICC, *The Prosecutor v. Thomas Lubanga Dyilo*, ICC-01/04-01/06, Judgment pursuant to Article 74 of the Statute, 14 March 2012, paras. 479–484 (http://www.legal-tools.org/doc/677866/).

[10] OTP, "Prosecutorial Strategy 2009-2012", p. 8, see *supra* note 5.

[11] *Ibid.*, p. 14.

[12] OTP, *Policy Paper on Preliminary Examinations*, see *supra* note 4.

[13] See, for example, Rome Statute, Article 68, see *supra* note 2; Rules of Procedure and Evidence of the International Criminal Court, 9 September 2002, rule 86 (http://www.legal-tools.org/doc/8bcf6f/) ('Rules of Procedure and Evidence').

32.3. The Relevant Legal Framework

At the outset, it is significant to note that the Policy on Children adopts a child-sensitive approach, which should be distinguished from a children's rights or child-centred approach.[14] In fact, the Convention on the Rights of the Child is referred to as one of the "applicable treaties",[15] in apparent reference to Article 21(1)(b) of the Statute. Accordingly, the OTP interprets the Convention, including its core principles, as subsidiary and optional sources of law, instead of "international recognised human rights" of compulsory application pursuant to Article 21(3) of the Statute.

Nonetheless, as will be explained below, the present chapter is based on the relevant provisions of the Rome Statute and the Rules of Procedure and Evidence, interpreted and applied pursuant to internationally recognised children's rights.[16]

Regardless of whether the applicable law is internal (Article 21(1)(a) and 21(2)) or external and subsidiary (Article 21(1)(b) and (c)), Article 21(3) of the Rome Statute establishes two interpretative principles that must be involved throughout all proceedings before the ICC. That is, interpretation and application of the law must be (a) non-discriminatory and (b) in accordance with internationally recognised human rights:[17]

---

[14] Cynthia Chamberlain, *Children and the International Criminal Court: Analysis of the Rome Statute Through a Children's Rights Perspective*, Intersentia, Antwerp, 2015, pp. 39–40.

[15] OTP, *Policy on Children*, para. 11, see *supra* note 1. In fact, the Policy includes other international human rights instruments of quasi-universal application within this same narrow definition of 'applicable treaties'. See, for example, Convention No. 182 concerning the Prohibition and Immediate Action for the Elimination of the Worst Forms of Child Labour, 17 June 1999 (http://www.legal-tools.org/doc/4a7509/) ('Convention No. 182'); and the Convention on the Elimination of All Forms of Discrimination against Women, 18 December 1979 (http://www.legal-tools.org/doc/6dc4e4/) ('Convention on the Elimination of All Forms of Discrimination against Women').

[16] Gerhard Werle, *Tratado de Derecho Penal Internacional*, Tirant lo blanch, Valencia, 2005, pp. 98–100.

[17] ICC, *The Prosecutor v. Thomas Lubanga Dyilo*, Judgment on the Appeal of Mr Thomas Lubanga Dyilo against the Decision on the Defence Challenge to the Jurisdiction of the ICC pursuant to Article 19(2)(a) of the Statute of 3 October 2006, 14 December 2006, ICC-01/04-01/06, paras. 37–38 (http://www.legal-tools.org/doc/1505f7/); Mikaela Heikkilä, "Article 21", in Mark Klamberg (ed.), *Commentary on the Law of the International Criminal Court*, Torkel Opsahl Academic EPublisher, Brussels, 2015, fn. 255 (http://www.toaep.org/ps-pdf/29-klamberg).

The application and interpretation of law pursuant to this article *must* be consistent with internationally recognized human rights, and be without any adverse distinction founded on grounds such as gender as defined in article 7, paragraph 3, *age*, race, colour, language, religion or belief, political or other opinion, national, ethnic or social origin, wealth, birth or other status. [emphasis added]

Rule 86 of the Rules of Procedure and Evidence also provides a general interpretation and application principle that is binding to all organs of the Court, and refers specifically to the needs of children:

A Chamber in making any direction or order, and other organs of the Court in performing their functions under the Statute or the Rules, shall take into account the needs of all victims and witnesses in accordance with article 68, in particular, *children*, elderly persons, persons with disabilities and victims of sexual or gender violence. [emphasis added]

Nonetheless, as mentioned above, these interpretative principles are general (including children within a broad category of victims and witnesses requiring special consideration) and should be analysed in view of specific "internationally recognised human rights" – in the instant case, children's rights, and more specifically those protected in the Convention on the Rights of the Child.[18] Although the ICC is not bound by the Convention on the Rights of the Child (not being a party thereto), it must apply norms of similar or identical content of customary international law or general principles of law as enshrined in Article 21(3) of the Rome Statute.[19] Moreover, considering that children may also be part of other protected groups (for example, persons with disabilities and/or girls), other international human rights treaties that crystallise these other internationally recognised human rights are also applicable.

For the purpose of this chapter, the core principles of the Convention on the Rights of the Child are considered as "internationally recognised human rights" pursuant to Article 21(3) of the Rome Statute. The

---

[18] Convention on the Rights of the Child, 20 November 1989 (http://www.legal-tools.org/doc/f48f9e/) ('Convention on the Rights of the Child').

[19] Chamberlain, 2015, p. 43, see *supra* note 14; Rebecca Young, "Internationally recognised human rights before the International Criminal Court", in *International & Comparative Law Quarterly*, 2011, vol. 60, no. 1, pp. 190, 199, 204–205.

Convention on the Rights of the Child enjoys nearly universal ratification[20] and its core principles have been recognised as the general requirements for children to enjoy all other rights contained in the Convention.[21]

Article 2 [Non-Discrimination]

1. States Parties shall respect and ensure the rights set forth in the present Convention to each child within their jurisdiction without discrimination of any kind, irrespective of the child's or his or her parent's or legal guardian's race, colour, sex, language, religion, political or other opinion, national, ethnic or social origin, property, disability, birth or other status.

2. States Parties shall take all appropriate measures to ensure that the child is protected against all forms of discrimination or punishment on the basis of the status, activities, expressed opinions, or beliefs of the child's parents, legal guardians, or family members.

Article 3 [Best Interests of the Child]

1. In all actions concerning children, whether undertaken by public or private social welfare institutions, courts of law, administrative authorities or legislative bodies, the best interests of the child shall be a primary consideration.

2. States Parties undertake to ensure the child such protection and care as is necessary for his or her well-being, taking into account the rights and duties of his or her parents, legal guardians, or other individuals legally responsible for him or her, and, to this end, shall take all appropriate legislative and administrative measures.

3. States Parties shall ensure that the institutions, services and facilities responsible for the care or protection of chil-

---

[20] To date, 140 ratifications. Likewise, very few reservations refer to the articles of the Convention on the Rights of the Child containing these four core principles, and in fact do not question the principles themselves. See Convention on the Rights of the Child, entry into force 2 September 1990 (http://www.legal-tools.org/doc/f48f9e/); Susanna Greijer, "Thematic Prosecution of Crimes Against Children", in Morten Bergsmo (ed.), *Thematic Prosecution of International Sex Crimes*, Torkel Opsahl Academic EPublisher, Beijing, 2012, p. 140 (http://www.toaep.org/ps-pdf/13-bergsmo).

[21] Committee on the Rights of the Child ('CRC'), "General Comment No. 5 (2003): General measures of implementation of the Convention on the Rights of the Child (arts. 4, 42 and 44, para. 6)", 2013, para. 12 (http://www.legal-tools.org/doc/69c527/) ('GC No. 5').

---

dren shall conform with the standards established by competent authorities, particularly in the areas of safety, health, in the number and suitability of their staff, as well as competent supervision.

Article 6 [Right to Life, Survival and Development]

1. States Parties recognize that every child has the inherent right to life.

2. States Parties shall ensure to the maximum extent possible the survival and development of the child.

Article 12 [Right to be Heard]

1. States Parties shall assure to the child who is capable of forming his or her own views the right to express those views freely in all matters affecting the child, the views of the child being given due weight in accordance with the age and maturity of the child.

2. For this purpose, the child shall in particular be provided the opportunity to be heard in any judicial and administrative proceedings affecting the child, either directly, or through a representative or an appropriate body, in a manner consistent with the procedural rules of national law.

As regards preliminary examinations at the ICC, these are mainly regulated by Article 15 and Article 53 of the Rome Statute. While Article 15 provides the jurisdictional trigger mechanism allowing *proprio motu* investigations, Article 53 provides the criteria that must be evaluated by the Prosecutor when taking her discretionary prosecutorial decision.

Article 15

1. The Prosecutor may initiate investigations *proprio motu* on the basis of information on crimes within the jurisdiction of the Court.

2. The Prosecutor shall analyse the seriousness of the information received. For this purpose, he or she may seek additional information from States, organs of the United Nations, intergovernmental or non-governmental organizations, or other reliable sources that he or she deems appropriate, and may receive written or oral testimony at the seat of the Court.

3. If the Prosecutor concludes that there is a reasonable basis to proceed with an investigation, he or she shall submit to the Pre-Trial Chamber a request for authorization of an investigation, together with any supporting material collected. Vic-

tims may make representations to the Pre-Trial Chamber, in accordance with the Rules of Procedure and Evidence.

[...]

6. If, after the preliminary examination referred to in paragraphs 1 and 2, the Prosecutor concludes that the information provided does not constitute a reasonable basis for an investigation, he or she shall inform those who provided the information. This shall not preclude the Prosecutor from considering further information submitted to him or her regarding the same situation in the light of new facts or evidence.

Article 53

1. The Prosecutor shall, having evaluated the information made available to him or her, initiate an investigation unless he or she determines that there is no reasonable basis to proceed under this Statute. In deciding whether to initiate an investigation, the Prosecutor shall consider whether:

(a) The information available to the Prosecutor provides a reasonable basis to believe that a crime within the jurisdiction of the Court has been or is being committed;

(b) The case is or would be admissible under article 17; and

(c) Taking into account the *gravity of the crime* and the *interests of victims*, there are nonetheless substantial reasons to believe that an investigation would not serve the *interests of justice*.

[...]

2. If, upon investigation, the Prosecutor concludes that there is not a sufficient basis for a prosecution because:

[...]

(c) A prosecution is not in the *interests of justice*, taking into account all the circumstances, including the *gravity of the crime*, the *interests of victims* and the age or infirmity of the alleged perpetrator, and his or her role in the alleged crime; [...].[emphasis added]

On the basis of the above legal framework, the Prosecutor must endeavour to conduct preliminary examinations in accordance with internationally recognised children's rights. For the purpose of this chapter, particular attention will be given to how the Convention on the Rights of the Child should be taken into consideration in the interpretation and application of the concepts of "gravity", "interests of victims" and "interests of justice". Although preliminary examinations are, in essence, within the discretionary realm of the Prosecutor, this power has intrinsic responsibilities and boundaries. As stated above, in respect of internationally recognised human rights there is no room for discretion. This was determined by the Appeals Chamber of the ICC at the outset of the Court's first trial: "[h]uman rights underpin the Rome Statute; every aspect of it, including the exercise of jurisdiction of the International Criminal Court".[22] These human rights include the rights of the accused person, but also the rights of victims and witnesses of crimes within the jurisdiction of the Court.

32.4. Quality of Communications

Pursuant to Article 15(1) of the Rome Statute, the Prosecutor may initiate investigations on the basis of information received. This information can be provided by victims themselves, but also by human rights and other organisations. Unless communications relate specifically to children (that is, child recruitment cases), it is foreseeable that in the more 'general' communications, children – as an often 'misinformed and misrepresented' group in an adult-centred system – will not be automatically included in the information received by the Prosecutor pursuant to Article 15 (for example, communications related to a situation of post-election violence). The same stands as regards State or UN Security Council referrals, which will most likely focus on what happened or is happening 'in general' within the territory of a State, and may exclude specific reference to children within the affected population. Children as a group have less ability than adults to present Article 15 communications in their own interests. Thus, if the interests of children are not highlighted in general information submitted to the Prosecutor, they will be overlooked.

However, children represent almost half of the refugee population worldwide,[23] and it is well documented that armed conflict has a destructive impact on education, which ultimately affects children's development

---

[22] ICC, *The Prosecutor v. Thomas Lubanga Dyilo*, ICC-01/04-01/06, Judgment on the Appeal of Mr Thomas Lubanga Dyilo against the Decision on the Defence Challenge to the Jurisdiction of the ICC pursuant to Article 19(2) (a) of the Statute of 3 October 2006, 14 December 2006, para. 37 (http://www.legal-tools.org/doc/1505f7/).

[23] UNICEF, "Protecting against abuse, exploitation and violence: children affected by armed conflict" (http://www.legal-tools.org/doc/f44dd4/).

and future.[24] Hence, excluding the children's perspective is not an option. If information received pursuant to Article 15(1) of the Rome Statute lacks the children's perspective, the analysis of the OTP pursuant to Article 53 of the Rome Statute may result in an incomplete and partial application of its mandate.

It is therefore important to maintain the highest children's rights standards as undertaken in the Policy Paper. To achieve this, the OTP must create a network with children's rights organisations already involved in States where the OTP is carrying out preliminary examinations, but also with other international organisations dealing with children's rights (for instance, United Nations Children's Fund). Only if such a network is created, will the OTP be able to receive communications that duly inform about the crimes committed against children or affecting their interests as part of multi-generational communities.[25]

Moreover, in creating this network with children's rights organisations, the OTP's interaction with them should be two-fold. First, the OTP should receive from organisations and other information providers views on a given situation that is child-sensitive. Second, it would be useful if these organisations would have appropriate tools and training so that communications are relevant for potential international criminal proceedings. Although this is not necessarily the mandate of the OTP or even the ICC, the Prosecutor has continuously referred to 'positive complementarity' as one of its main strategies. Within this concept of positive complementarity, the OTP has mentioned the need for capacity building at a national level, even if it has referred to it only indirectly.[26]

Just like OTP must endeavour to receive information that sees all sides of a conflict or situation, it should also endeavour to include all members of the affected communities, and among them, children. Information provided under Article 15 should also include different groups within children (for instance, minority groups, young children and youth, and girls).

---

[24] UNICEF, "The State of the World's Children 2016: A fair chance for every child", p. 53 (http://www.legal-tools.org/doc/7cf2c6/).

[25] OTP, *Policy on Children*, para. 3, see *supra* note 1. See also OTP, "Strategic Plan 2016-2018", pp. 11, 44 (http://www.legal-tools.org/doc/7ae957/).

[26] OTP, "Prosecutorial Strategy 2009-2012", para. 17, see *supra* note 5.

In other words, it is not only about receiving Article 15 communications or information about crimes affecting children (*quantity* of information), but these communications should also meet minimum standards so that they are useful to the work of the OTP (*quality* of the information).

Partial information under Article 15(1) that is not further complemented by impartial and inclusive information pursuant to Article 15(2) may result in incomplete and unfair decisions by the OTP in the context of preliminary examinations.

To achieve this impartiality and non-discrimination pursuant to Article 21(3) of the Statute, the OTP's interaction with NGOs must also be organised and duly regulated, and most importantly, kept under careful and continuous scrutiny.

The analysis under Article 15(2) of the Rome Statute pertaining to the "seriousness of the information", does not only refer to the truthfulness of the material received, but should also evaluate whether the information encompasses information that may ultimately result in a determination of the truth (not a partial determination that excludes a certain group of the population, that is, children). The OTP should therefore require from these organisations complete and impartial information. Nonetheless, in order to achieve this 'quality control' in the information received, organisations co-operating with the ICC must be knowledgeable of the statutory provisions, not only *vis-à-vis* child victims, but also the rights of the accused and to a fair trial. Therefore, training of information providers in the field is essential.

Moreover, from the receiving point of view, the OTP should have specialised and trained staff that will be able to adequately process information received so that the children's perspective is not 'lost' in the process.[27] Moreover, if the OTP's staff is duly trained, they will also seek

---

[27] Staff should also be well-trained in order to make the assessment under the OTP Policy on Children, particularly *vis-à-vis* the best interests of the child. In this regard, the CRC has stated the following: "Facts and information relevant to a particular case must be obtained by well-trained professionals in order to draw up all the elements necessary for the best-interests assessment" (CRC, "General comment No. 14 (2013) on the right of the child to have his or her best interests taken as a primary consideration (art. 3, para. 1)", 2013, p. 10 (http://www.legal-tools.org/doc/18a4c1/) ('GC No. 14'). See Comisión Interamericana de Derechos Humanos, El derecho del niño y la niña a la familia: Cuidado alternativo poniendo fin a la institucionalización en las Américas, 2013, para. 158.

further information when children's rights views are absent. Pursuant to Articles 15(2) and 21(3) of the Rome Statute, discriminatory or biased information should be considered as not 'serious' and should be supplemented with additional information.

Otherwise, this biased and partial information sometimes may reach the investigation and pre-trial phase and exclude children. For example, as regards communications transmitted to the Pre-Trial Chambers in both the Kenya and Côte d'Ivoire situations, victims' representations were in their majority from middle-aged men. Although these communications were made for purposes of Article 15(3) of the Rome Statute (request for authorisation to open an investigation), it is reasonable to conclude that the Prosecutor could have had similar information for the purpose of its Article 15(2) analysis (information received on crimes). For example, in the Kenya situation, there were no victims' representations of children (the youngest was a 19-year-old person). The average age of the persons who made individual representations was 44 years old and 60% of the victims were men. In the Côte d'Ivoire situation, out of 655 individual representations received, a limited number (20) were from persons aged below 20 years old, while the majority (232) were 31-50 years old. Of these representations (655), 423 were men and 179 were women, while 53 did not specify gender.[28] One could think that perhaps the views of children were transmitted to the Court via adult persons. However, this has not been the case.

Such numbers are not positive *vis-à-vis* children's rights (nor as regards gender). Ultimately, children are being excluded or restricted, on the basis of their age and sex (girls). Although this is clearly not the *purpose* of the OTP, the Registry (who transmits Article 15 communications to Pre-Trial Chambers) or of organisations co-operating with the ICC, this is the *result* (which impairs or nullifies the recognition, enjoyment and exercise of children's rights to judicial redress).[29] Consequently, this is mani-

---

[28] ICC, Situation in the Republic of Kenya, ICC-01/09, Public Redacted Version Of Corrigendum to the Report on Victims' Representations (ICC-01/09-17-Conf-ExpCorr), 29 March 2010, paras. 40–45 and annexes 1 and 5 (http://www.legal-tools.org/doc/b9ce79/); ICC, Situation in the Republic of Côte d'Ivoire, ICC-02/11, Report on Victims' Representations, 29 August 2011, paras. 35–36 (http://www.legal-tools.org/doc/5dd52b/).

[29] The right to non-discrimination is not a passive obligation, prohibiting all forms of discrimination in the enjoyment of rights under the Convention, but also requires appropriate proactive measures taken by the State to ensure effective equal opportunities for all chil-

festly contrary to the principle of non-discrimination, enshrined in Article 21(3) of the Rome Statute.[30]

With the adoption of the Policy on Children, these numbers should shift and more reference should be made to the plight of children living in the current and future situations under scrutiny by the OTP. Otherwise, the OTP would be failing to meet its pledge that "any information received is subject to critical analysis and evaluation". It is not only, as stated in its Policy on Children, to pay "particular attention to information received on crimes against or affecting children",[31] but to proactively seek additional information when these are missing from information received.

32.5. Analysing the Article 53 Test from a Children's Rights Perspective

Although the OTP's Policy on Children adopted a child-sensitive approach (that is where children's best interests are taken into consideration but not necessarily prevail over other interests),[32] it should apply and interpret the law pursuant to internationally recognised children's rights (Article 21(3)).

Therefore, as noted above, in its application and interpretation of the statutory texts, including Article 53 of the Rome Statute, the OTP shall respect, at a minimum, the four guiding principles of the Convention on the Rights of the Child: (a) the best interests of the child; (b) the right to life, survival and development; (c) respect for the views of children according to their age and maturity; and (d) the right to non-

---

dren to enjoy the rights under the Convention. This may require positive measures aimed at redressing a situation of real inequality (GC No. 14, p. 6, see *supra* note 27). See also, Convention on the Elimination of All Forms of Discrimination against Women, Article 1, see *supra* note 15, which defines what is meant as 'discrimination': "For the purposes of the present Convention, the term 'discrimination against women' shall mean any distinction, exclusion or restriction made on the basis of sex which has the effect or purpose of impairing or nullifying the recognition, enjoyment or exercise by women, irrespective of their marital status, on a basis of equality of men and women, of human rights and fundamental freedoms in the political, economic, social, cultural, civil or any other field".

[30] OTP, *Policy Paper on Preliminary Examinations*, para. 28, see *supra* note 4.

[31] OTP, *Policy on Children*, para. 53, see *supra* note 1.

[32] *Ibid.*, para. 22.

---

discrimination.[33] However, on a case-by-case basis, the OTP may also be guided by other internationally recognised human rights contained in the Convention on the Rights of the Child, for example, the right to education, freedom of religion, prohibition of sexual abuse and ill-treatment, among others.[34] Moreover, the OTP should also bear in mind other general or specific internationally recognised human rights and the impact that the Prosecutor's actions could have on children's enjoyment of these rights. For example, the right to reparations,[35] gender equality,[36] and the rights of children with disabilities.[37]

---

[33] CRC, "General Comment No. 12 (2009): The Right of the Child to be Heard", 2009, para. 2 (http://www.legal-tools.org/doc/8c2532/).

[34] Convention on the Rights of the Child, arts. 14, 19, 28, see *supra* note 18.

[35] See Permanent Court of Arbitration, *Chorzow Factory Case (Germany v. Poland)*, Judgment, 13 September 1928, Series A, No. 17, p. 47 (http://www.legal-tools.org/doc/b2ff98/); International Court of Justice ('ICJ'), *Military and Paramilitary Activities in and against Nicaragua (Nicaragua v. United States of America)*, Merits, 27 June 1986, I.C.J. Reports 1986, General List No. 70, p. 114 (http://www.legal-tools.org/doc/046698/); ICJ, *Corfu Channel Case (United Kingdom v. Albania)*, Merits, 9 April 1949, I.C.J. Reports 1949, General List No. 1 (http://www.legal-tools.org/doc/861864/); ICJ, *Reparations for Injuries Suffered in the Service of the United Nations*, Advisory Opinion, 11 April 1949, I.C.J. Reports 1949, General List No. 4, p. 184 (http://www.legal-tools.org/doc/f263d7/); ICJ, *Interprétation des traités de paix conclus avec la Bulgarie, la Hongrie et la Romanie (deuxième phase)*, Avis Consultatif, 18 July 1950, I.C.J. Report 1950, General List No. 8, p. 228 (http://www.legal-tools.org/doc/5a4014/). See also International Law Commission, "Draft Articles on Responsibility of States for Internationally Wrongful Acts", Article 1 (http://www.legal-tools.org/doc/10e324/) ("Every internationally wrongful act of a State entails the international responsibility of that State").

[36] Convention on the Elimination of All Forms of Discrimination against Women, see *supra* note 15, Article 1 defines discrimination against women (this is applicable to interpret the principle of non-discrimination in the CRC and ultimately in the Rome Statute): "the term 'discrimination against women' shall mean any distinction, exclusion or restriction made on the basis of sex which has the effect or purpose of impairing or nullifying the recognition, enjoyment or exercise by women, irrespective of their marital status, on a basis of equality of men and women, of human rights and fundamental freedoms in the political, economic, social, cultural, civil or any other field".

[37] Convention on the Rights of Persons with Disabilities, 6 December 2006, Article 7 (http://www.legal-tools.org/doc/06e036/) ('Convention on the Rights of Persons with Disabilities'): "States Parties shall ensure that children with disabilities have the right to express their views freely on all matters affecting them, their views being given due weight in accordance with their age and maturity, on an equal basis with other children, and to be provided with disability and age-appropriate assistance to realize that right". This article allows for a specialised, cross-sector interpretation of the Convention on the Rights of the Child, Article 12, see *supra* note 18.

The following criteria of Article 53 of the Statute will now be analysed pursuant to the children's rights framework previously mentioned.

32.5.1. Gravity

As regards gravity, the Policy on Children states that in general, crimes committed against or affecting children are particularly grave. In fact, it is stated that the OTP will ensure that an assessment of the impact of the alleged crimes on children is incorporated into its analysis of the gravity of potential cases.[38] This affirmation and assurance of the OTP is in accordance with the guiding principle of children's right to life, survival and development. Most (if not all) crimes within the jurisdiction of the Court will infringe this core principle of the Convention on the Rights of the Child. The fact that information received by the OTP refers to crimes against or affecting children is relevant for the gravity analysis. For example, scale of the crime (number of children that directly or indirectly suffered harm), nature (crimes committed against children),[39] and manner (cruelty standards are different in respect of children and adults)[40] are all relevant for the gravity analysis under Article 53 of the Statute.

Gravity also examines the impact of crimes on victims and communities.[41] Thus, analysing the impact of crimes *vis-à-vis* children in a community will most likely shift the balance in favour of gravity (and thus

---

[38] OTP, *Policy on Children*, paras. 57–58, see *supra* note 1.

[39] OTP, *Policy Paper on Preliminary Examinations*, para. 63, see *supra* note 4. The nature of the crimes refers to the specific factual elements of each offence, including crimes committed against of affecting children (OTP, *Policy Paper on Case Selection and Prioritisation*, para. 39, see *supra* note 4).

[40] OTP, *Policy Paper on Preliminary Examinations*, para. 64, see *supra* note 4. See OTP, *Policy Paper on Case Selection and Prioritisation*, para. 40, see *supra* note 4: "The manner of the commission of the crimes may be assessed in light of, inter alia, the means employed to execute the crime, the extent to which the crimes were systematic or resulted from a plan or organised policy or otherwise resulted from the abuse of power or official capacity, the existence of elements of particular cruelty, including the vulnerability of the victims, any motives involving discrimination held by the direct perpetrators of the crimes, the use of rape and other sexual or gender-based violence or crimes committed by means of, or resulting in, the destruction of the environment or of protected objects".

[41] OTP, *Policy Paper on Preliminary Examinations*, para. 65, see *supra* note 4; Roisin Burke, "UN Military Peacekeeper Complicity in Sexual Abuse: The ICC or a Tri-Hybrid Court", in Morten Bergsmo (ed.), *Thematic Prosecution of International Sex Crimes*, Torkel Opsahl Academic EPublisher, Beijing, 2012, p. 354 (http://www.toaep.org/ps-pdf/13-bergsmo).

---

opening an investigation), as harm caused to children has long-lasting effects in their lives and may be easily passed down to entire generations. For example, the Policy on Children refers to the notion of a child's life plan,[42] which is not only relevant for the analysis of the impact of the crime for gravity purposes, but also for future reparations.

32.5.2. Interests of Victims

When analysing the element of "interests of victims", Articles 3 and 12 of the Convention on the Rights of the Child are essential. While Article 3 enshrines the principle of "best interests of the child", Article 12 contains the complementary principle of the right of children to be heard.[43]

A preliminary examination is without a doubt an action that will concern children of the affected communities,[44] and as such, the "best interests of the child" shall be a primary consideration. As explained by the Committee on the Rights of the Child, this concept, far from being abstract and general, is a "dynamic concept that requires an assessment appropriate to the specific context".[45] This guiding principle requires all actors to engage in securing the holistic integrity of the child and promote his or her human dignity.[46] Thus, in assessing a situation under Article 53 of the Rome Statute, the OTP should consider the three-fold nature of this principle. *Firstly*, the OTP must assess and give primary consideration to

---

[42] OTP, *Policy on Children*, fn. 78, see *supra* note 1. OTP, *Policy Paper on Case Selection and Prioritisation*, para. 41, see *supra* note 4: "The impact of the crimes may be assessed in light of, inter alia, the increased vulnerability of victims, the terror subsequently instilled, or the social, economic and environmental damage inflicted on the affected communities. In this context, the Office will give particular consideration to prosecuting Rome Statute crimes that are committed by means of, or that result in, inter alia, the destruction of the environment, the illegal exploitation of natural resources or the illegal dispossession of land". See Elisabeth Schauer, "The Psychological impact of child soldiering" (http://www.legal-tools.org/doc/ccb0d2/).

[43] The CRC has noted that articles 3 and 12 have an inextricable link. Article 12 provides the methodology for hearings the views of children, including the child's best interests (GC No. 14, 2013, p. 6, see *supra* note 27). See Comisión Interamericana de Derechos Humanos, 2013, para. 249, see *supra* note 27.

[44] The CRC has stated that the principle applies to situations directly concerning children, but also other measures that have an effect on children, even if they are not the direct targets of the measure (GC No. 14, 2013, p. 4, see *supra* note 27).

[45] *Ibid.*, pp. 2, 5. The CRC has stated that the concept is flexible and adaptable, and should be adjusted and defined according to specific circumstances.

[46] *Ibid.*, p. 2.

---

the interests of children of the situation at hand.[47] *Secondly*, if two or more interpretations of a legal provision are possible (for example, regarding the principle of complementarity in Article 17 or the threshold in the context of crimes against humanity under Article 7), the OTP should favour the interpretation which most effectively serves children's best interests. *Thirdly*, in its decision-making process in general pursuant to Article 53 (including the Prosecutor's discretion), an evaluation of the possible impact (positive or negative) of the decision on children concerned must be included.[48]

As regards this last point, the adoption of the Policy on Children is not enough, and general reference to it in a decision under Article 53 will be insufficient. The OTP must show in its decision under Article 53 that the right has been explicitly taken into account and explain how the right has been respected in its decision (which criteria it is based on and how the interests of children were weighed against other competing interests).[49]

---

[47]   *Ibid.*

[48]   *Ibid.*

[49]   *Ibid.* This may be difficult to achieve as the Policy (OTP, *Policy on Children*, para. 32, see *supra* note 1) establishes an approach which foresees decisions that are contrary to the best interests of the child. However, the CRC also foresees this, although exceptionally, and provides some further guidance that could be useful in situations where the OTP has to choose other competing interests. The CRC has stated: "In order to demonstrate that the right of the child to have his or her best interests assessed and taken as a primary consideration has been respected, any decision concerning the child or children must be motivated, justified and explained. The motivation should state explicitly all the factual circumstances regarding the child, what elements have been found relevant in the best-interests assessment, the content of the elements in the individual case, and how they have been weighted to determine the child's best interests. If the decision differs from the views of the child, the reason for that should be clearly stated. If, exceptionally, the solution chosen is not in the best interests of the child, the grounds for this must be set out in order to show that the child's best interests were a primary consideration despite the result. It is not sufficient to state in general terms that other considerations override the best interests of the child; all considerations must be explicitly specified in relation to the case at hand, and the reason why they carry greater weight in the particular case must be explained. The reasoning must also demonstrate, in a credible way, why the best interests of the child were not strong enough to be outweigh the other considerations. Account must be taken of those circumstances in which the best interests of the child must be the paramount consideration" (GC No. 14, 2003, p. 11, see *supra* note 27). See Comisión Interamericana de Derechos Humanos, 2013, para. 157, see *supra* note 27.

But how can the OTP determine what the best interests of children in a specific ICC situation are? One of the methods is self-evidently to seek the children's views, which is where Article 12 of the Convention on the Rights of the Child becomes imperative. However, one could think, on the other hand, that given the initial stages of the proceedings, it would be counterproductive to expose children to international criminal proceedings. Thus, the OTP must apply Articles 3 and 12 of the Convention on the Rights of the Child in a manner that is also consistent with its obligation to protect the safety, physical and psychological well-being, dignity and privacy of victims and witnesses as provided for in Article 68(1) of the Rome Statute. Children's direct participation with the OTP at this early stage of the proceedings may not be opportune. However, interaction with local children's rights organisations or youth groups could enable the OTP to gather the views of children, while at the same time preserving their security, safety and well-being.

In relation to Article 12 of the Convention on the Rights of the Child, the Committee on the Rights of the Child has established that views should be weighed in accordance with the child's age and maturity (evolving capacities); and taking into consideration the diversity among children (including their social and cultural differences and needs).[50] It must be noted that as regards these cultural or religious values, when these are incompatible with other rights (for instance, non-discrimination or sexual and reproductive rights) they should never be regarded as 'in the best interests' of children.[51]

Just as the "best interests of the child" should be interpreted broadly (direct and indirect), the term 'matters affecting the child' pursuant to Article 12 of the Convention on the Rights of the Child should also be defined as involving all ICC situations, as these all relate to traumatic social processes in a community (genocide, crimes against humanity, armed conflict) that will certainly deeply affect children's lives.

---

[50] Comisión Interamericana de Derechos Humanos, 2013, paras. 252, 258, see *supra* note 27; GC No. 12, 2009, paras. 21, 74, see *supra* note 33; GC No. 14, 2013, para. 43, see *supra* note 27.

[51] For example, the fact that sexual violence against girls is considered as taboo or stigmatised in a given society is not a reason not to investigate these crimes (to prevent the victims from being embarrassed, harassed or ostracized).

And how does the OTP seek the views of children (that is, children of a situation under scrutiny) according to Article 12 of the Convention on the Rights of the Child? Article 12 applies to one child but also to a group of children in general,[52] which will most likely be the case of preliminary examinations.

Article 12 is not a 'momentary act' (that is, one consultation meeting), but a process, and should be the "starting point for an intense exchange" between children of a situation and the OTP.[53] Moreover, the OTP needs to be active ("shall assure") to ensure the right of children to express their interests/views.[54] The OTP cannot presume that children or persons acting on their behalf will present their views in the context of preliminary examinations. Thus, measures must be taken so that preliminary examinations are child-friendly (accessible and age appropriate), but also appropriate to the particular characteristics of children within a given situation.

As stated above, children's views should be sought for the purpose of preliminary examinations, but in a manner that is consistent with Article 68(1) of the Rome Statute. Children must be informed about the right to be heard, but most importantly, their right to live free of violence (as some of them may have been born into violence already).[55] Likewise, participation of children in preliminary examinations should avoid putting them at risk and therefore a child-protection strategy is necessary.[56] The Policy on Children already gives some indications that the OTP already has, at least, a general strategy. However, the Policy refers more to the stages after the start of an investigation, and not to the preliminary examination stage.[57] This is logical, since individual children will most likely not participate at this early stage of the proceedings. However, this does

---

[52] GC No. 12, 2009, paras. 87–88, see *supra* note 33; Comisión Interamericana de Derechos Humanos, 2013, paras. 151–153, see *supra* note 27.

[53] GC No. 12, 2009, para. 13, see *supra* note 33.

[54] GC No. 14, 2013, p. 19, see *supra* note 27; Comisión Interamericana de Derechos Humanos, 2013, para. 251, see *supra* note 27.

[55] GC No. 12, 2009, para. 120, see *supra* note 33.

[56] The Policy on Children already gives some indications that the OTP already has some strategy set-out, but these refer more to the stages after the start of an investigation, and not to the Preliminary Examination stage.

[57] OTP, *Policy on Children*, paras. 62 ff., see *supra* note 1.

not mean that the OTP will not be able to consider their views. It can always do so indirectly, as noted above, through organisations working with affected children.

The creation of some kind of ombudsperson within the OTP, that monitors children's legal rights but also maintains communications between children from a situation and the OTP could be a possible mechanism to guarantee that a children's rights policy is correctly implemented at all stages, including the preliminary examinations. Another solution could be that of creating a monitoring mechanism (for example, with the Committee on the Rights of the Child, United Nations Children's Fund or another specialised agency). Such a joint venture could provide needed feedback and expertise to the OTP but also to organisations in the field that work with affected communities. As regards preliminary examinations, this ombudsperson or the specialised agency/organisation could make child-rights impact assessments on how a certain investigation by the OTP could affect children and their enjoyment of rights.[58] Although the Gender and Children Unit within the OTP already fulfils some these duties, it may not necessarily have the autonomy to carry out such impact assessments,[59] which may sometimes clash with broader prosecutorial strategy.

32.5.3. The Interests of Justice

In its analysis under Article 53 of the Statute, the Prosecutor must also evaluate the "interests of justice". However, this concept must also be understood from the perspective of the best interests of the child and the interests of child victims, as members of affected communities.

The Convention on the Rights of the Child provides that children shall be heard in any judicial and administrative proceeding affecting the child.[60] The preliminary examinations carried out by the OTP are the eve of judicial proceedings before the ICC, but they also will inevitably have an impact on both judicial and administrative procedures, including domestic and international non-judicial transitional justice mechanisms.

---

[58] GC No. 14, 2013, p. 11, see *supra* note 27.

[59] GC No. 12, 2009, paras. 129–131, see *supra* note 33. The CRC has encouraged networking among organisations working with children to increase opportunities for shared learning and collective advocacy.

[60] Convention on the Rights of the Child, Article 12, see *supra* note 18.

Thus, an analysis of Article 53(1)(c) from a human rights perspective (something required pursuant to Article 21(3) of the Rome Statute), obliges the Prosecutor to balance competing interests. In the case at hand, the Prosecutor must take into consideration recognised human rights of child victims of an alleged crime but also children of a situation country in general. Such analysis, depending on each situation, could lead the OTP to consider a wider approach to the concept "interests of justice",[61] for example, in favour of non-judicial or traditional justice mechanisms that could address some of the previously mentioned human rights in the "best interests of children". For example, a non-judicial justice mechanism that will address the crimes more expeditiously or in a more child-friendly manner could have an impact on the analysis of "interests of justice". However, this would have to be assessed carefully and on a case-by-case basis, taking into account all the other elements addressed above, as well as other competing obligations of the Prosecutor, such as its primary obligation to avoid impunity.

Another important consideration is that of time. The Committee on the Rights of the Child has established that the passing of time is not the same for children and adults and has affirmed that delays in or prolonged decision-making have particularly adverse effects on children as they evolve.[62] Hence, a non-decision or delayed decisions under Article 53 of the Statute (that is, situations that are still under analysis for years) may be contrary to the best interests affected children. Thus, effects on children should be considered when the OTP extends a preliminary examination for a prolonged period of time.

The Policy on Children affirms that there is a strong presumption that investigations and prosecutions of crimes affecting children are in the interests of justice.[63] This commitment of the OTP to give serious consideration to crimes committed against children not only entails the investigation and prosecution of such crimes, but also the prompt determination of preliminary examinations, and eventual investigations and prosecutions. When the OTP receives information about crimes affecting children, pre-

---

[61] Talita de Souza Dias, "'Interests of justice': Defining the scope of Prosecutorial discretion in Article 53(I)(C) and (2)(C) of the Rome Statute of the International Criminal Court", in *Leiden Journal of International Law*, 2017, p. 3.

[62] GC No. 14, 2013, p. 10, see *supra* note 27.

[63] OTP, *Policy on Children*, para. 59, see *supra* note 1.

liminary examinations should be dealt with expeditiously. From a prose-cutorial point of view, this is necessary in order to preserve the relevant evidence. As proven in *Lubanga*,[64] with the passing of time all evidence depreciates, but particularly if it relates to children. Also, from an "inter-ests of victims" perspective, the passing of time is also of essence, as rep-arations for child victims should be granted in a timely manner, preferably when they are still children and measures such as rehabilitation can still be meaningful.[65] Given their age and vulnerability, the adage "justice de-layed is justice denied" is strikingly applicable.

Finally, as part of this broader system of protection of human rights (because although criminal in nature, the ICC was established to protect human beings from heinous crimes), if and when the OTP decides not to open an investigation, it could still transmit that the information received to other appropriate mechanisms that could still address victims. For ex-ample, as regards information received on children's rights violations, the Prosecutor could still transmit the information to other relevant fora, such as the Committee on the Rights of the Child or regional human rights courts. This is important, as the OTP may receive information about hu-man rights violations that although not within the jurisdiction of the Court, they could be within the jurisdiction of other mechanisms.[66] Such actions are within the general mandate and the objects and purpose of the Court to combat impunity against the most heinous crimes (even if, for example, these crimes are outside the Court's material, temporal or territorial juris-diction).

32.6. Conclusions

The Policy on Children is a welcome development, but now the OTP has to put in place a formal process, with procedural safeguards, designed to assess and determine whether it is following its undertaking consistently with internationally recognised children's rights.[67]

---

[64] ICC, *The Prosecutor v. Thomas Lubanga Dyilo*, ICC-01/04-01/06, Judgment pursuant to Article 74 of the Statute, 14 March 2012, paras. 479–484 (http://www.legal-tools.org/doc/677866/).

[65] In *Lubanga*, the victims that were aged 10–14 at the time of the events (2002–2003) are currently 25–30 years old. To date, reparations for these victims are still pending.

[66] Gerhard Werle, 2005, pp. 99–101, see *supra* note 16.

[67] GC No. 14, 2013, p. 10, see *supra* note 27.

Although there is ample prosecutorial discretion in preliminary examinations, internationally recognised human rights underpin the entirety of proceedings before the ICC and are of compulsory application. Hence, the Convention on the Rights of the Child, and its core principles must guide all prosecutorial actions, including preliminary examinations. The OTP equally needs to create a network with children's rights organisations and children rights experts, so that a child-centred perspective can be truly mainstreamed in the Court's prosecutorial mandate.

With the adoption of the Policy on Children the OTP should not only pay particular attention to information received regarding children, but also seek this information when it is missing in adult-centred communications. An analysis of victims' interests and interests of justice that excludes the child population is partial and discriminatory. Accordingly, the views of children must be taken into consideration, balancing between the often-conflicting rights of children to express their views and the eminent security risks that may arise when they interact with the Court. Measures should be taken to guarantee that their views are considered in a manner that safeguards children well-being. However, excluding them due to their vulnerability alone is not a valid reason.

The adoption of the Policy on Children cannot be seen as a goal. It is only the first step in a process that requires careful and co-ordinated implementation on all those involved in the OTP, beginning at the first stages of the preliminary examinations and until the conclusion of judicial proceedings. If child victims, survivors of crimes within the jurisdiction of the Court are excluded from the preliminary examinations, they will be excluded from the 'determination of the truth' after trial proceedings, and ultimately be excluded from eventual reparations in case of conviction.

33

Casting a Larger Shadow:
Premeditated Madness,
the International Criminal Court,
and Preliminary Examinations

Mark Kersten[*]

33.1. Introduction: Shadow Politics and the International Criminal Court

It has been repeatedly put forward that that the International Criminal Court ('ICC') has a 'shadow'. This notion has been regularly and increasingly invoked in scholarship on the ICC. In their 2012 article entitled *Kenya in the Shadow of the ICC*, Chandra Lekha Sriram and Stephen Brown ponders "whether the shadow of the ICC is likely to deter future atrocities".[1] Kevin Jon Heller has offered an analysis of the "shadow side of complementarity" – the effects of the Court "on the likelihood that defendants will receive due process in national proceedings".[2] Louise Chappell and others have described what they see as the institution's "gender justice complementarity shadow", an effect they argue results from the lack of linkage between the gender justice provisions under the Rome

---

[*]   **Mark Kersten** is a postdoctoral research fellow at the Munk School of Global Affairs, University of Toronto. This chapter draws on a presentation given by the author on the occasion of the conference, *The Peripheries of Justice Intervention: Preliminary Examination and Legacy/Sustainable Exit*, which took place at the Peace Palace in The Hague, on 29 September 2015. The author wishes to express his gratitude to the inestimable Carsten Stahn for the generous opportunity to present at the conference and write this chapter. He would also like to thank Alex Whiting for his generous and helpful comments during the early stages of planning this chapter.

[1]   Chandra Lekha Sriram and Stephen Brown, "Kenya in the Shadow of the ICC: Complementarity, Gravity, and Impact", in *International Criminal Law Review*, 2012, vol. 12, no. 2, pp. 219–44.

[2]   Kevin Jon Heller, "The Shadow Side of Complementarity: The Effect of Article 17 of the Rome Statute on National Due Process", in *Criminal Law Forum*, 2006, vol. 17, no. 3, pp. 255–80, p. 255.

Statute and the Court's foundational principle of complementarity.[3] Even ICC Chief Prosecutor, Fatou Bensouda, has spoken of the Court's shadow, which she describes as its "capacity to set precedents that would meet the global challenges of our times" and something that "should be considered as the most important impact of the court".[4]

This chapter is likewise concerned with the shadow cast by the ICC – but from an altogether different angle. The focus of this chapter is on identifying and exploring novel strategies at the preliminary examination stage of ICC interventions, strategies that could enlarge the ICC's shadow.[5] Above all, it is argued that the Office of the Prosecutor ('OTP') should consider deploying more intrepid strategies at the preliminary examination phase in order to positively influence the behaviour of the Court's potential targets. But what is meant by the ICC's 'shadow'?

Given the diverse use of the term 'shadow' in international criminal law and justice scholarship, it is worthwhile briefly outlining what this chapter means by it. 'Shadow' here is taken to entail the *indirect impression* and *impact* that the ICC has on various actors and, in particular, on those whose behaviour the Court seeks to affect through its actions and decisions. These effects and impressions can exist at any time and at any stage of the Court's interventions – including prior to the opening of an official investigation.

There are two related reasons reason that likely explain the growing interest in the ICC's shadow rather than a myopic focus on its direct effects. First, the limits of the Court's effects on key issues such as deterring mass atrocities, successfully concluding cases, and ending impunity, are increasingly evident.[6] The ICC's 'bite' has not been as threatening or ef-

---

[3] Louise Chappel, Rosemary Grey and Emily Waller, "The Gender Justice Shadow of Complementarity: Lessons from the International Criminal Court's Preliminary Examinations in Guinea and Colombia", in *International Journal of Transitional Justice*, 2013, vol. 7, no. 3, pp. 455–75.

[4] See remarks by Fatou Bensouda, Council on Foreign Relations, "The International Criminal Court: A New Approach to International Relations", 21 September 2012 (http://www.legal-tools.org/doc/100ce0-1/).

[5] This chapter employs a broad conception of intervention, wherein the OTP's decision to open a preliminary examination into a given situation already constitutes an intervention on the part of the ICC.

[6] See, for example, Nick Grono, "Justice in Conflict: The ICC and Peace Processes", in Nicholas Waddell and Phil Clark (eds.), *Courting Conflict? Justice, Peace and the ICC in*

fective as some had originally hoped and others had feared.[7] Instead, concern seems to be focused on whether the Court bit off more than it could chew and thus created an expectations gap in what justice and accountability the institution can deliver. Second, there has been something of a 'complementarity turn' in the field of international criminal justice, with scholars and practitioners focusing on how the ICC can galvanize and stimulate domestic and regional accountability processes as a primary motivation of the Court's mandate.[8] As a result, there is a palpable focus on how to increase the shadow of the ICC.

Of course, and as we know from famous childhood stories such as *Peter Pan*, shadows are real but can neither be caught nor physically grasped. They are impressions of light upon surfaces. Importantly, the size and shape of a shadow changes with the angle of the light upon the object casting it. If one were to take a flashlight and point it at a toy-house from a small angle above, the house's shadow will appear diminutive. Increase the angle, and the edifice's impression upon the floor becomes elongated and increasingly striking. At the core of this chapter is an assertion that the ICC's strategies are the light that determines how long and striking the Court's shadow is and can be. Changing the focus of those strategies can have an impact on how effective the Court is at casting its shadow and, ultimately, in achieving desired outcomes.

Africa, Royal African Society, 2008, pp. 13–20; Human Rights Watch, *Unfinished Business: Closing Gaps in the Selection of ICC Cases*, 15 September 2011 (http://www.legal-tools.org/doc/738f10/); Mark Kersten, "The ICC and its Impact: More Known Unknowns", in *Open Global Rights*, 5 November 2014; Mark Kersten, *Justice in Conflict: The Effects of the International Criminal Court's Interventions on Ending Wars and Building Peace*, Oxford University Press, 2016.

[7] See discussion of US antagonism to the ICC below, see *infra* Section 33.4.2.

[8] See, among others, Carsten Stahn and Mohamed M. El Zeidy (eds.), *The International Criminal Court and Complementarity: From Theory to Practice*, Cambridge University Press, 2011; Sarah M.H. Nouwen, *Complementarity in the Line of Fire: The Catalysing Effect of the International Criminal Court in Uganda and Sudan*, Cambridge University Press, 2014; Mark Kersten, "The Complementarity Turn in International Criminal Justice", in *Justice in Conflict*, 30 September 2014; Kirsten Ainley, "The Responsibility to Protect and the International Criminal Court: Counteracting the Crisis", in *International Affairs*, 2015, vol. 91, no. 1, pp. 37–54.

33.1.1. Overview

The chapter proceeds as follows. The second section of the chapter outlines the orthodox view of preliminary examinations that sees this stage of an ICC intervention as a 'legal checklist'. It is posited that this classical understanding has neglected to view the preliminary examination phase as a unique stage during which the OTP can deploy strategies to affect and influence actors in the contexts under examination – namely to induce domestic judicial activity and to deter and prevent mass atrocities. In the second section, the chapter explores four key assumptions that should constitute the foundation for thinking through how to deploy preliminary examinations effectively: 1) that the ICC is predisposed to intervening in ongoing and active conflicts; 2) that the Court is a political, as well as legal, institution; 3) that, generally, the ICC's preference is to have domestic authorities – and not the Court – prosecute international crimes; and 4) that the strategic imperatives and incentives of warring actors and potential targets of ICC interventions are unique at the preliminary examination stage. Together, these assumptions should inform how the OTP deploys preliminary examination strategies as a means to expand the shadow of the Court.

In the third section that follows, the chapter draws on recent historical revelations pertaining to strategies developed by Richard Nixon and Henry Kissinger as an analogy for one particular strategy that should be considered in the OTP's preliminary examination 'toolbox': the 'madman theory' of preliminary examinations, wherein the OTP deploys a brazen communication strategy in order to give the impression that all actors alleged to have committed mass atrocities may be targeted for indictment. It is argued that the 'madman theory' should be employed in the most politically sensitive and precarious contexts. It is further demonstrated that the embers of such a policy can already be seen in how the OTP's 2014 and 2015 preliminary examination reports covered allegations of torture perpetrated by US officials in Afghanistan.

How the ICC can leverage preliminary examinations to affect State behaviour is discussed in the penultimate section of the chapter. Section 33.4. subsequently outlines and discusses relevant weaknesses and drawbacks to the madman approach to preliminary examinations. The chapter concludes by arguing for the need to think creatively about how the preliminary examination stage can be strategically deployed in order to have intended and desired effects on the behaviour of warring parties and the pursuit of accountability. Doing so might not only increase the likelihood of the Court incurring positive outcomes but also bolster the independence and legitimacy of the institution.

33.2. An Orthodox Understanding of Preliminary Examinations

As a distinctive strategic stage of an ICC intervention, the preliminary examination phase has not received sufficient or sustained scholarly scrutiny.[9] Research on the Court has generally been focused on the institution's impacts. These are typically identified and measured following the opening of an official investigation, once a preliminary examination has already been terminated.[10] Compounding the lack of scholarship on preliminary examinations, the OTP has only begun releasing detailed information regarding its preliminary examinations since 2011.[11] In addition, insofar as it has described them, its orthodox understanding of a preliminary examination presents it as a generally unremarkable 'legal checklist'. According to the OTP itself:

> The preliminary examination process is conducted on the basis of the facts and information available. The goal of this process is to reach a fully informed determination of whether there is a reasonable basis to proceed with an investigation.[12]

Scholars have tended to view the preliminary examination similarly. Pavel Caban, for example, describes preliminary examinations as "the activities of the OTP carried out in order to determine whether a situation, brought to the attention of the OTP, meets the legal criteria established by

---

[9] By way of example, a recently published, impressive and authoritative volume on the ICC includes only three mentions, and no sustained analysis of, the preliminary examination stage. See Carsten Stahn (ed.), *The Law and Practice of the International Criminal Court*, Oxford University Press, 2015.

[10] There are notable and increasingly common exceptions to this general rule, including the decision on the part of Palestine to join the ICC and the OTP's subsequent to open a preliminary examination into alleged crimes perpetrated in Gaza since June 2014. Another example is the preliminary examination in Colombia.

[11] See David Bosco, "The Preliminary Examination Procedure of the ICC Prosecutor", in *American Journal of International Law*, 2015, vol. 109, no. 4.

[12] International Criminal Court OTP, *Report on Preliminary Examination Activities 2014*, 2 December 2014, para. 11 (http://www.legal-tools.org/doc/3594b3/).

---

the Rome Statute to warrant investigation by the ICC".[13] Carsten Stahn has described this conceptualization of preliminary examinations as a "narrow functional/institutional view" which singularly and exclusively sets out "to serve as a means to decide whether or not to open an ICC investigation… that is, the conception of [preliminary examinations] as gateway[s] to investigations".[14]

This legal checklist can be summarized as follows. Prior to preceding to an official investigation, the OTP must ascertain during the preliminary examination stage whether or not three criteria are met: 1) whether the Court has temporal, material, territorial and personal jurisdiction in the situation under examination; 2) whether an official investigation and any consequent prosecutions would be admissible before the Court, based on the principles of complementarity and gravity; and 3) whether the opening of an official investigation is in the "interests of justice".[15]

In addition, the preliminary examination stage is itself divided into four phases used as a "filtering process" to determine which situations should proceed to official investigation. These sub-phases correspond, roughly, to the criteria outlined above. In Phase 1, the OTP must ascertain whether the alleged crimes fall within its jurisdiction. In the second phase, the OTP must consider the evidence provided by relevant actors and "determine whether the preconditions to the exercise of jurisdiction under article 12 [of the Rome Statute] are satisfied and whether there is a reasonable basis to believe that the alleged crimes fall under the subject matter jurisdiction of the Court". In Phase 3, the OTP assesses complementarity and gravity relating to the situation under preliminary examination. Finally, in Phase 4, the OTP must make a determination as to whether proceeding to an official investigation would serve the "interests of justice". As of writing, the OTP currently has seven ongoing preliminary examinations. These are divided amongst Phase 2 (Iraq, Palestine, and Ukraine) and Phase 3 (Afghanistan, Colombia, Guinea, and Nigeria).

---

[13] Pavel Caban, "Preliminary Examinations by the Office of the Prosecutor of the International Criminal Court", in *Czech Yearbook of Public & Private International Law*, 2011, vol. 2, pp. 199–216, p. 199.

[14] Concept Note for Expert Meeting, "The Peripheries of Justice Intervention: Preliminary Examination and Legacy/Sustainable Exit", 29 September 2015 (on file with the author).

[15] International Criminal Court, "Preliminary Examinations" (available on the Court's web site).

Based on this checklist approach, the OTP has, in essence, three options with regards to preliminary examinations: 1) to proceed to opening an official investigation, which it has done, most recently, in the case of the 2008 war in Georgia; 2) close a preliminary examination, which was the decision made in Comoros (2014),[16] Honduras (2015)[17] and Venezuela (2006), and the Republic of Korea (2014);[18] or 3) leave a preliminary examination in some 'half-way house', long-term 'purgatory', which the OTP appears to have done in the case with Afghanistan, under preliminary examination since 2007 (see below).

The approach outlined above also represents a highly legalistic conception of what a preliminary examination is. It is a simplistic outlook neglecting, as Christopher Stone observes, that "a preliminary examination is a complex, carefully structured stage of activity".[19] However, preliminary examinations are heavily imbued with politics – and political potential. Indeed, there is an increasing recognition that the legal vocabulary upon which preliminary examinations are based permits the OTP to deploy legal terminology as a means to justify political decision-making. Unpacking these terms unveils the political and un-immutable elements of preliminary examinations. Examples include how the OTP determines admissibility across situations, how it imagines the gravity principle across contexts and through time,[20] and what, precisely, counts as or is meant by, the "interests of justice".[21] For some scholars, such as William

---

[16] See International Criminal Court, "Registered Vessels of Comoros, Greece and Cambodia" (available on the Court's web site).

[17] See International Criminal Court, "Honduras" (available on the Court's web site).

[18] See International Criminal Court, "Republic of Korea" (available on the Court's web site).

[19] Christopher Stone, "Widening the Impact of the International Criminal Court: The Prosecutor's Preliminary Examinations in the Larger System of International Criminal Justice", in Martha Minow, C. Cora True-Frost and Alex Whiting (eds.), *The First Global Prosecutor: Promise and Constraints*, University of Michigan Press, Ann Arbor, 2015, pp. 297–308, p. 290.

[20] Alana Tiemessen, "Defying Gravity: Seeking Political Balance in ICC Prosecutions", Justice in Conflict, 22 April 2013.

[21] See, among others, Human Rights Watch, *Human Rights Watch Policy Paper: The Meaning of "the Interests of Justice" in Article 53 of the Rome Statute*, 1 June 2005; Linda M. Keller, "Comparing the "Interests of Justice": What the International Criminal Court Can Learn from New York Law", in *Washington University Global Studies Law Review*, 2013, vol. 12, no. 1, p. 1–40; Priscilla Hayner, "Does the ICC Advance the Interests of Justice?", in *Open Global Rights*, 4 November 2014.

Schabas, the lack of definitional clarity of these legal concepts provides a veneer for the OTP to act politically. For Schabas, the language of gravity, for example, "strikes the observer as little more than obfuscation, a laboured attempt to make the determinations look more judicial than they really are [...] to take a political decision while making it look judicial".[22] Stahn concurs, observing that the lack of clarity of such terms "has provided an opportunity to the Prosecutor to shape the meaning of the concepts and to develop prosecutorial discretion outside the realm of legal thresholds".[23]

Moreover, a restricted view of preliminary examinations denies what Stahn sees as "the broader analytical features of assessment and the link between [preliminary examinations] and goals of the Statute".[24] These goals, according to the OTP, are two-fold:

> In the course of its preliminary examination activities, the Office will seek to contribute to the two overarching goals of the Rome Statute: the ending of impunity, by encouraging genuine national proceedings, and the prevention of crimes.[25]

Crucially, these are not legal but political goals, insofar as they reflect an aim to shape the decision-making of *political* actors to both initiate "genuine national proceedings" as well as deterring and preventing crimes. Thus, from this brief analysis, we can conclude that the OTP seeks to use preliminary examinations as a means to influence the behaviour of its potential targets. Doing so effectively requires smart – and political – strategies that can expand the reach of the ICC's shadow. But before delving into how this can be achieved, it is worth outlining key assumptions regarding the Court's interventions, interests, and desired impacts that should inform any strategy brought to bear in a preliminary examination.

---

[22] William A. Schabas, *Unimaginable Atrocities: Justice, Politics, and Rights at the War Crimes Tribunals*, Oxford University Press, 2012, p. 89.

[23] Carsten Stahn, "Judicial Review of Prosecutorial Discretion: Five Years On", in Carsten Stahn and Göran Sluiter (eds.), *The Emerging Practice of the International Criminal Court*, Martinus Nijhoff Publishers, Leiden, 2009, pp. 247–80, p. 267.

[24] See Concept Note for Expert Meeting, *supra* note 15.

[25] International Criminal Court OTP, *Policy Paper on Preliminary Examinations*, November 2013 (http://www.legal-tools.org/doc/acb906/).

33.3. Preliminary Examinations and Assumptions about the ICC's Desired Impact and Interests

In order to fully appreciate and understand how the ICC can achieve desirable effects through preliminary examinations, it is important to outline key assumptions about the Court's intended impacts and interests. This section delineates four assumptions to consider.

The first assumption is that the ICC is predisposed to intervening in ongoing and active conflicts.[26] The vast majority of situations in which the ICC intervenes in are active wars or very recently concluded conflicts. Moreover, the institution is increasingly expected to act as a 'first responder' in conflicts characterized by atrocities and human rights abuses. In line with its own identified aims noted above, the Court thus has an interest in affecting the behaviour of actors engaged in political violence to refrain from the perpetration of international crimes (that is, prevention and deterrence) as well as taking the prosecution of international crimes seriously – either as an element of conflict resolution itself or as part of its post-conflict transitional justice measures.

A second assumption is that the ICC is a political body. This has already been made clear in the above analysis. Going further, it should be assumed that that the Court must make political decisions that reflect its institutional interests.[27] In particular, the OTP has an interest in taking decisions that are likely to result in: 1) effective co-operation from relevant political actors that allow the OTP to build cases based on strong evidence; 2) the enforcement of any arrest warrants it subsequently issues; and 3) a contribution to its standing in international relations and politics. However, the OTP must negotiate these institutional interests with the political actors upon which it depends for co-operation and relevance. How it negotiates its interests with those actors will determine how it proceeds with its mandate and, importantly, *whom* it targets for prosecution in any given context.[28] The Court's record to date indicates a clear pattern as a consequence of this negotiation: self-referrals by States have solely

---

[26] See Mark Kersten, 2014, see *supra* note 6.

[27] *Ibid.*

[28] See also Kenneth A. Rodman, "Justice as a Dialogue Between Law and Politics Embedding the International Criminal Court within Conflict Management and Peacebuilding", in *Journal of International Criminal Justice*, 2014, vol. 12, no. 3, pp. 437–69.

resulted in non-State actors and government adversaries being targeted by the ICC, whilst UN Security Council referrals have almost exclusively led to the targeting of State/government actors.[29]

The third assumption is that, in general, the ICC would prefer to prosecute as seldom as possible and that this is particularly true in situations where major political powers are involved. As the Court's first Chief Prosecutor, Luis Moreno-Ocampo, regularly insisted during his tenure, an ideal outcome for the ICC would be to have no case before its judges because States were able and willing to mete justice for international crimes themselves. In addition to this long-term ideal, a more recent issue contributes to the institution's recalcitrance to expand its prosecutorial workload, namely the scarcity of resources offered to the institution. Financing the ICC has become a permanent feature at the yearly Assembly of States Parties' conferences.[30] Moreover, as the OTP's recent report on the Court's 'basic size' suggests, the Office simply does not have sufficient resources to match the worldwide demands and expectations for international criminal justice. The goal of avoiding prosecutions wherever possible is further evidenced in the ICC's apparent turn to positive complementarity as a central objective of the Court's interventions. This is apparent the OTP's reports on preliminary examinations which refer explicitly to effective examinations "obviating the need for the Court's intervention".[31] In short, in both principle and practice, the institution's predilection is to prosecute as seldom as possible by galvanizing States to conduct prosecutions themselves.

The fourth assumption guiding this analysis is that the strategic imperatives and incentives of actors during the preliminary examination stage are substantially different from those that exist once the OTP proceeds to the official investigation stage. This final assumption is worth unpacking.

---

[29] Alana Tiemessen, "The International Criminal Court and the Politics of Prosecutions", in *International Journal of Human Rights*, 2014, vol. 18, no. 4–5, pp. 444–61; see also Mark Kersten, 2014, see *supra* note 6.

[30] See Human Rights Watch, *Human Rights Watch Briefing Note for the Fourteenth Session of the International Criminal Court Assembly of States Parties*, November 2015 (http://www.legal-tools.org/doc/001993/); Elizabeth Evenson and Jonathan O'Donohue, "The International Criminal Court at Risk", in *Open Global Rights*, 6 May 2015.

[31] International Criminal Court OTP, *Report on Preliminary Examination Activities (2015)*, 12 November 2015, para. 16 (http://www.legal-tools.org/doc/ac0ed2/).

The lack of clarity regarding whom, if anyone, the ICC will target is most pronounced in the preliminary examination stage. In contrast, once an official investigation is open, the Chief Prosecutor is likely to become locked into a particular prosecutorial strategy and, in some cases, even make clear his or her intentions to prosecute particular sides of a conflict.[32] During the preliminary examination stage, warring parties cannot know *with certainty* whom the ICC will target. It is a stage where anything – and nothing – can happen. States and relevant actors may surmise that the ICC's record of targeting non-State actors following self-referrals and government actors following Security Council referrals will continue to hold true. Crucially, however, they cannot establish beyond doubt whether or not the Court will receive effective co-operation, effective access to relevant territories and evidence, and whether or not they themselves are in danger of being targeted by the ICC. In other words, uncertainty is elevated in the preliminary examination stage. Paradoxically, then, the most likely phase in which the Court could have a significant effect on the behaviour of warring actors may be the preliminary examination stage.

Consider the example of deterrence, an oft-stated aim of the ICC during the preliminary examination stage as well as more broadly.[33] There are poignant critiques of whether deterrence is a logical and possible outcome of ICC decision-making. But let us assume that specific deterrence – the deterrence of potential targets of the ICC – is a worthy aspiration and feasible by-product of ICC action.[34] If there is to be any deterrent effect, it seems likely that it will be heightened during a preliminary examination because of the inherent phase's unpredictability and the OTP's concomitant flexibility in whom to ultimately target. Warring actors and perpetrators cannot know whether or not they will be targeted for prosecution. As a result, they can respond to the signal sent, or the 'shadow' cast,

---

[32] In the case of Libya, for example, Moreno-Ocampo announced his intended and primary targets – Gaddafi regime officials – almost immediately following his opening of an investigation. This was raised as an issue by defence counsel at the ICC.

[33] See Kate Cronin-Furman, "Managing Expectations: International Criminal Trials and the Prospects for Deterrence of Mass Atrocity", in *International Journal of Transitional Justice*, 2013, vol. 7, no. 3, pp. 434–54.

[34] On specific deterrence versus general deterrence, see Payam Akhavan, "Justice in The Hague, Peace in the Former Yugoslavia? A Commentary on the United Nations War Crimes Tribunal", in *Human Rights Quarterly*, 1998, vol. 20, no. 4, pp. 737–816, p. 746.

by the ICC in the preliminary examination stage by ceasing the perpetration of international crimes. If they do so, it is within the Prosecutor's
discretion via, for example, an argument relating to the "interests of justice", not to proceed to the official investigation stage and/or not target
those actors who responded 'positively' to the impetuses of the OTP's
preliminary examination. This is in sharp contrast to the incentives that
exist once an arrest warrant has been issued for a particular target. At this
point, there is no logical means by which ICC targets can be deterred because the warrants cannot be revoked as a reward for improved behaviour.
As David Mendeloff argues, "for coercive threats to be effective they
must be accompanied by credible assurances that the threat will be removed in the face of compliance".[35] The judicial sanctions issued via ICC
arrest warrants, however, cannot be revoked in exchange for positive
changes in the behaviour of targeted actors. The Court's warrants can only
expire with the acquittal, conviction or death of the accused.

The potential for a preliminary examination to induce 'positive
complementarity', that is, instigating relevant and genuine judicial processes domestically, is less clear.[36] Some suggest that the shadow of the
ICC has been effective in galvanizing domestic accountability in situations such as Colombia.[37] In other instances, like Georgia, authorities have
been clear that, despite having a functioning judiciary, they will not investigate or prosecute crimes relevant to the Court's jurisdiction, leaving the
OTP with little choice but to proceed with an official investigation. In yet
other instances, States appear to be interested in outsourcing some of their
ICC targets to The Hague whilst prosecuting others domestically. This has
been the case in Ivory Coast where the current government of Alassane
Ouattara approved the surrender of ousted former President Laurent

---

[35] David Mendeloff, "Punish or Persuade? The ICC and the Limits to Coercion in Cases of
Ongoing Violence", 2014 (draft paper on file with the author).

[36] See William W. Burke-White, "Implementing a Policy of Positive Complementarity in the
Rome System of Justice", in *Criminal Law Forum*, 2008, vol. 19, no. 1, pp. 59–85;
Nouwen, 2014, see *supra* note 8; see also International Criminal Court OTP, *ICC Prosecutorial Strategy 2009-2012*, 1 February 2010, para. 17 (http://www.legal-tools.org/doc/
6ed914/).

[37] See, for example, Amanda Lyons and Michael Reed-Hurtado, "Colombia: Impact of the
Rome Statute and the International Criminal Court", May 2010 (http://www.legal-tools.
org/doc/17ec15/).

Gbagbo but has fought to ensure that former First Lady Simone Gbagbo is prosecuted and incarcerated domestically.

Still, it should be noted that there is no evidence that the Court is better at galvanizing genuine domestic judicial processes during official investigations than it is in the preliminary examination stage. Even in relatively stable situations where the Court has intervened, judicial actions are beset by serious problems. In Kenya, despite promises to investigate and prosecute allegations of crimes against humanity perpetrated during the 2007-2008 post-election violence via the established of an International and Organized Crimes Division, it has become clear that such crimes will not be investigated.[38] In Uganda, the government of Yoweri Museveni created an International Crimes Division which has prosecuted one (non-ICC indicted) senior commander of the Lord's Resistance Army, Thomas Kwoyelo. The trial has faced serious allegations of unfairness and impropriety.[39] When Caesar Achellam, an Lord's Resistance Army commander of similar seniority, came into the custody of Ugandan officials, he was amnestied and given residence in the military's Gulu-based barracks.[40] Moreover, the government decided that Dominic Ongwen, who had been indicted by the ICC, would not be prosecuted in the International Crimes Division and instead approved his transfer to The Hague.[41]

Based on the above assumptions, it is evident that the preliminary examination stage presents a unique, if under-theorized, opportunity to potentially affect the behaviour of conflict and post-conflict actors. Consequently, there is a need to dedicate more scrutiny as to what strategies the OTP can employ to help to ensure that preliminary examinations are

---

[38] The author worked during 2014 on a project with the Wayamo Foundation, training potential investigators, prosecutor and members of the judiciary who would be involved and staff the International and Organized Crimes Division. During this time, it was made clear that the Division would not investigate or prosecute crimes relating to the 2007–08 post-election violence.

[39] See, for example, Alexis Okeowo, "Thomas Kwoyelo's Troubling Trial", in *The New Yorker*, 20 July 2012; see also Mark Kersten, "Uganda's Controversial First War Crimes Trial: Thomas Kwoyelo", in *Justice in Conflict*, 12 July 2011.

[40] See Scott Ross, "A Rebel's Escape – An LRA Commander Tells His Story", in *Justice in Conflict*, 31 July 2013.

[41] See "Uganda: International Criminal Court to Prosecute Alleged Perpetrator of Uganda War Crimes", in *UN News Service*, 20 January 2015.

more effective in affecting potentially positive behavioural responses from warring actors. This is particularly important with regards to strategies that can be deployed in the most politically contentious ICC situations – those in which major power interests are involved. One such case, as described below, is Afghanistan.

33.4. A 'Madman Theory' of Preliminary Examinations

33.4.1. Nixon, Kissinger and ICC Preliminary Examination Strategies

The lack of clarity in what the OTP will do, if anything, as well as whom, if anyone, the Court will target is most pronounced in the preliminary examination stage of an ICC intervention. Yet the classical approach to preliminary examinations views the examination phase as a 'waiting room' wherein the OTP performs a legalistic diagnosis and then, after some indeterminate period of time that could range from days to decades, decides between doing nothing and issuing arrest warrants. Instead of this narrow interpretation of preliminary examinations, it would be useful to think through how the OTP can capture and capitalize on the unpredictable nature of preliminary examinations in order increase the likelihood of it having a positive impact on the situations under its purview. One such approach, which this section elaborates and proffers, is an adaptation of the 'madman theory' of former US President Richard Nixon and his national security advisor Henry Kissinger.

In 1969, Nixon was failing in his election promise of ending the US' engagement in Vietnam – either via military means or through peace negotiations. As a result, Nixon and Kissinger began crafting a policy of 'premeditated madness'. As Jeremy Suri writes:

> Frustrated, Nixon decided to try something new: threaten the Soviet Union with a massive nuclear strike and make its leaders think he was crazy enough to go through with it. His hope was that the Soviets would be so frightened of events spinning out of control that they would strong-arm Hanoi, telling the North Vietnamese to start making concessions at the negotiating table or risk losing Soviet military support.

Codenamed 'Giant Lance', Nixon's plan was the culmination of a strategy of premeditated madness he had developed with national security adviser Henry Kissinger. The details of this episode remained secret for 35 years and have never been fully told. Now, thanks to documents released through the Freedom of Information Act, it is clear that Giant Lance was the leading example of what historians came to call the 'madman theory': Nixon's notion that faked, finger-on-the-button rage could bring the Soviets to heel.[42]

Nixon and Kissinger's plan was 'mad' because in threatening the communist bloc with a nuclear attack, the US putting its own existence at risk. The policy flew directly in the face of Mutually Assured Destruction, the principle whereby the capacity of two or more States to obliterate each other creates a high-tension equilibrium wherein none attacks the other for fear of certain annihilation. James Rosen and Luke A. Nichter usefully summarize the US President's position: "Nixon wanted to impress upon the Soviets that the president of the United States was, in a word, mad: unstable, erratic in his decision-making, and capable of anything".[43]

The OTP can and should consider adapting and bringing to bear such a madman strategy in its preliminary examinations. This would require the OTP to convincingly demonstrate that it was willing to target any and all relevant actors in a conflict: even those with significant political power, even those who are patrons of Western States, and even those who referred the situation to the ICC in the first place. It would also require a willingness on the part of the OTP to convincingly demonstrate it was mad enough to target these actors even if doing so would, on its face, undermine the Court's institutional interests.

As suggested above, the outcomes of referrals, from the opening of preliminary examinations to the issuance of arrest warrants, currently follow predictable trends. Self-referrals translate into the ICC targeting non-State actors and government enemies; Security Council referrals result in government figures being targeted. This leads to the danger of States and the Security Council manipulating the ICC to target only their adversaries, a risk that has received increasing scrutiny as well as condemnation.[44] A madman approach would disrupt this predictability. By

---

[42] Jeremi Suri, "The Nukes of October: Richard Nixon's Secret Plan to Bring Peace to Vietnam", in *Wired*, 25 February 2008.

[43] James Rosen and Luke A. Nichter, "Madman in the White House: Why looking crazy can be an asset when you're staring down the Russians", in *Foreign Policy*, 25 March 2014.

[44] See, for example, comments by Louise Arbour, "Are Freedom, Peace and Justice Incompatible Agendas?", in *International Crisis Group*, 17 February 2014; see also the report by David Kaye, "The Council and the Court: Improving Security Council Support of the In-

demonstrating a sincere willingness to target any and all warring parties, it would also give the Court the impression a being more independent institution.

While the OTP *should* consider invoking a 'madman strategy' in some situations, attention needs also to be paid to how it could do so. Such a policy would have to be carefully planned and executed through the yearly preliminary examination reports in combination with timely and well-placed communications to the media, to embassies, civil society, and other relevant actors. Notably, there are growing signs that the OTP is willing to embrace a bolder approach to preliminary examinations.

33.4.2. Growing Older, Growing Bolder: The ICC and Preliminary Examinations

Beginning in 2014, the OTP began to "shed new light on a process that has been opaque for much of the court's existence and that has attracted relatively limited scholarly and specialist attention".[45] Indeed, the OTP's 2014 and 2015 preliminary examination reports indicate an increasing willingness on the part of prosecutors to confront an especially thorny issue: allegations of international crimes perpetrated by Western States and, in particular, alleged abuses by US forces, in Afghanistan. This represents a marked change on the part of the ICC in its approach to the US, which has tended to be cautious, if not deferential.[46] This section briefly outlines the historical relationship between the ICC and Washington before demonstrating how the most recent preliminary examination reports signal an increasingly brazen strategy on the part of the OTP towards allegations of US war crimes in Afghanistan.

The issue that dominated the Court's first years of existence was its tumultuous relationship with the United States. While former US President Bill Clinton decided to sign the Rome Statute as one of his last acts in office, the administration of George W. Bush pursued policies to active-

---

ternational Criminal Court", 2013, University of California, Irvine, School of Law Research Paper No. 2013-127.

[45] Bosco, 2015, see *supra* note 11.

[46] David Bosco, *Rough Justice: The International Criminal Court in a World of Power Politics*, Oxford University Press, 2014.

---

ly undermine and isolate the Court.[47] The amount of attention and legislation that focused on the ICC during the Bush administration's first tenure
is illustrative of just how actively the administration sought to undercut
the Court's prospects. The American Service-Members' Protection Act
(2002), pejoratively referred to as the "Hague Invasion Act", provided the
US President with the ability to deploy "any necessary measures" to free
any American citizen detained and surrendered to The Hague.[48] The US
also threatened approximately 100 States that it would rescind provisions
of aid if they did not sign so-called Bilateral Immunity Agreements.[49]
Those agreements drew on Article 98 of the Rome Statute, which prohibits the ICC from issuing "a request for surrender or assistance which
would require the requested State to act inconsistently with its obligations
under international law with respect to the State or diplomatic immunity
of a person or property of a third State". The most dramatic act of antagonism towards the Court, however, came in May 2002 when John R. Bolton, an American diplomat, later National Security Advisor, delivered a
notice to the UN Secretary General, 'un-signing' the Rome Statute. Bolton
later called it his "happiest moment" at the US State Department.[50]

These antagonistic policies were often justified by invoking fear
that the Court would unfairly target American officials and troops who
were disproportionally engaged militarily in contexts where other States
either refused to or were unable to intervene. In other words, the Court
was painted as an unfair and unnecessary threat to American political interests. In response, there appears to have been some consensus within the
Court that if the institution was to survive, it would need to demonstrate
that it did not pose a direct threat to the US and that a co-operative relationship with the Court was in Washington's interests.

---

[47] See William A. Schabas, "United States Hostility to the International Criminal Court: It's
All About the Security Council", in *European Journal of International Law*, 2004, vol. 15,
no. 4, pp. 701–20; Jason Ralph, *Defending the Society of States: Why America Opposes the
International Criminal Court and its Vision of World Society*, Oxford University Press,
2007.

[48] US, American Service-Members' Protection Act, 30 July 2003 (http://www.legal-
tools.org/doc/b48688/).

[49] See Kingsley Chiedu Moghalu, *Global Justice: The Politics of War Crimes Trials*, Stanford
University Press, 2008, p. 138.

[50] See "U.S. Letter to U.N. Secretary-General Kofi Annan", in *CNN*, 6 May 2002.

In its first years, the ICC demonstrated a policy of 'accommodation' to the US, evidenced, if not by admission of the Prosecutor Luis Moreno-Ocampo than in his decision-making as well as the Court's record.[51] This could be achieved by honing in on situations where US interests were few and by refraining from opening investigations independent of the explicit request of States or the United Nations Security Council. As part of this policy of accommodation towards the US, the ICC initially focused primarily on receiving self-referrals from its States Parties. Such self-referrals were useful for the new Court. In order to encourage self-referrals, "the OTP shifted emphasis from a legalistic approach to a somewhat more political-diplomatic one".[52] Pursuing self-referrals had certain key advantages. At the Rome Conference, many States, including the US, had been wary of establishing a Court with a Prosecutor that was too independent and who would run roughshod in the pursuit of justice. The Prosecutor and his staff were not oblivious to these fears and sought to assuage them. This was achieved, according to former senior ICC staff, by not flexing the Prosecutor's *proprio motu* powers but instead working to receive invitations to intervene from ICC States Parties.[53] In accepting self-referrals from States, the Court could demonstrate that it was sensitive to US interests as well as have a small footprint on the relatively novel conceptualization of the relationship between sovereignty and international criminal justice. After all, a self-referral requires the State in question to voluntarily cede at least partial sovereignty over its jurisdiction for atrocity crimes to the Court.

In many respects, the ICC was successful in tempering Washington's antagonism towards the Court. In sharp contrast to the Bush administration's concerns, "the ICC appeared to be working in ways broadly consistent with American interests".[54] In its first two years, the OTP accepted three such self-referrals: Uganda (2003), the Democratic Republic of the Congo (2004) and the Central African Republic (2004). None was in States where major powers have vested interests and that all were States where the UN had been deeply involved prior to the ICC's inter-

---

[51] Bosco, 2014, see *supra* note 46.

[52] Benjamin Schiff, *Building the International Criminal Court*, Cambridge University Press, 2008, p. 225.

[53] Confidential interviews cited in Kersten, 2016, see *supra* note 6.

[54] Bosco, 2014, see *supra* note 46, p. 107.

vention. One aim in selecting these situations appears to be to improve relations between the US and the Court. If the more co-operative and closer relationship that the ICC has enjoyed with the United States since Bush's second term is any indication, the Prosecutor was certainly able to achieve just that.[55]

But the improvement of the Court's relationship with the US coincided with deteriorating relations with other States. At precisely the same time as relations between Washington and the ICC began to improve, allegations arose that the Court was biased against African States.[56] Until the OTP opened an official investigation into Georgia in late 2015, no State outside the African continent had been investigated by the Court. While assessing the validity of the criticism of the ICC as a biased institution is beyond the scope of this chapter, it is important to note that there has been increased pressure on the ICC in recent years to investigate not only situations outside of Africa but situations in which citizens of Western States have allegedly perpetrated war crimes and crimes against humanity. A number of public international groups have, for example, prepared what they see as a 'devastating dossier' implicating senior British officials in human rights abuses and international crimes in Iraq.[57] In response, the OTP re-opened a preliminary examination in 2014.[58] In addition, after more than eight years, the OTP has been under pressure to finally decide whether its ongoing preliminary examination in Afghanistan, which includes assessing whether abuses perpetrated by US forces amount to war crimes prosecutable by the Court, should proceed to an official investigation.

---

[55] See, for example, Marlise Simons, "U.S. Grows More Helpful to International Criminal Court, a Body It First Scorned", in *New York Times*, 2 April 2013.

[56] See, for example, Charles Chernor Jalloh, Dapo Akande and Max du Plessis, "Assessing the African Union Concerns about Article 16 of the Rome State of the International Criminal Court", in *African Journal of Legal Studies*, 2011, vol. 4, no. 1, pp. 5–50; Kurt Mills, "Bashir is Dividing Us: Africa and the International Criminal Court", in *Human Rights Quarterly*, 2012, vol. 34, no. 2, pp. 404–47.

[57] See Jonathan Owen, "Exclusive: Devastating Dossier on 'Abuse' by UK forces in Iraq goes to International Criminal Court", in *The Independent*, 12 January 2014.

[58] International Criminal Court OTP, "Prosecutor of the International Criminal Court, Fatou Bensouda, Re-Opens the Preliminary Examination of the Situation in Iraq", 13 May 2014 (http://www.legal-tools.org/doc/d9d9c5/).

Perhaps responding to this pressure, for the first time in 2014, the OTP's preliminary examination report included a reference to the alleged "enhanced interrogation techniques" waged by US officials in Afghanistan against anti-government forces (who are also under examination by the Court).[59] Indicative of the interests and politics at play, according to a former OTP staff member, the inclusion of the reference to enhanced interrogation techniques was negotiated over a period of several weeks.[60] US diplomats reacted coolly in response to the inclusion of the ICC examining torture allegations, insisting that the Court could not prosecute citizens of States that had not assented to the Rome Statute.[61]

In its 2015 report, the Prosecutor went even further. There, the OTP essentially challenged US officials to open genuine investigations and prosecutions into allegations of torture – those being examined by the ICC as well as those outlined in the so-called 'Torture Memos'. While the report took note of the judicial activity taking place against US citizens allegedly responsible for perpetrating torture in Afghanistan, it also signalled that those efforts have been wholly insufficient and would thus leave the allegations admissible before the Court. Specifically, the report points out that two cases that involved the deaths of detainees in CIA custody "did not result in any indictments or prosecutions" and that 13 Department of Defence investigations "were administrative enquiries rather than criminal proceedings".[62] The message was clear: American officials were not taking accountability for alleged abuses in Afghanistan sufficiently seriously and, if this continues to be the case, the OTP will eventually have little choice but to proceed to an official investigation.

However, in perhaps its most bold and most terse paragraph, the report suggested that it was no longer questioning whether war crimes had been committed by US forces but was focusing on how systematic those crimes were:

---

[59] International Criminal Court OTP, *Report on Preliminary Examination Activities 2014*, 2014, para. 94, see *supra* note 12.

[60] Confidential conversation with former OTP staff member.

[61] See David Bosco, "The War Over U.S. War Crimes in Afghanistan Is Heating Up", in *Foreign Policy*, 3 December 2014.

[62] OTP, *Report on Preliminary Examination Activities (2015)*, 2015, see *supra* note 31, paras. 128–29.

The Office is assessing information relevant to determine the scale of the alleged abuse, as well as whether the identified war crimes were committed as part of a plan or policy. The information available suggests that victims were deliberately subjected to physical and psychological violence, and that crimes were allegedly committed with particular cruelty and in a manner that debased the basic human dignity of the victims. The infliction of "enhanced interrogation techniques," applied cumulatively and in combination with each other over a prolonged period of time, would have caused serious physical and psychological injury to the victims. Some victims reportedly exhibited psychological and behavioural issues, including hallucinations, paranoia, insomnia, and attempts at self-harm and self-mutilation.[63]

In short, the OTP has reprimanded the US for not doing enough in pursuing accountability for alleged abuses committed by its citizens in Afghanistan and, taking a step further, has suggested that the perpetration of torture in Afghanistan may not have been the work of 'bad apples' but a *plan or policy* orchestrated at senior levels of the Bush administration.

The 2014 and 2015 reports indicate a growing maturity on the part of the OTP and an evident willingness to challenge major powers via the medium of preliminary examinations. This may not yet reach the level of a strategy of 'premeditated madness' but it is certainly inching in that direction.

33.5. Strategies in the Preliminary Examination 'Toolbox': Thinking through Drawbacks

The above analysis raises important questions: Can the ICC truly leverage preliminary examinations in order to positively influence State behaviour? If so, where does this influence come from and how can it be harnessed? More specifically, can the OTP's bolder strategy with regards to allegations of abuses by US troops in Afghanistan have the intended effect of galvanizing domestic judicial action? If not, how long can the OTP invoke a strategy of premeditated madness without actually pursuing all sides to a conflict before its bluff is called? When should such a policy apply – and when should it be avoided?

---

[63] *Ibid.*, para. 130.

The argument set out in this chapter should not be read as being applicable across cases or, in and of itself, a full-proof strategy. Whatever form they take, preliminary examination strategies need to be carefully managed and calibrated to through time and to specific cases. This penultimate section first outlines how the ICC might leverage preliminary examinations to shape State behaviour. It subsequently and briefly explores three limitations or shortcomings that need to be considered when deploying the madman strategy, or indeed any sophisticated strategy to preliminary examinations.

It is increasingly evident that States have a diverse diaspora of positions concerning their engagement with the ICC. Some choose to become States Parties whilst other remain outside of the Rome Statute system. Within those subsets, some are more proactively engaged than others. Moreover, as the relationship between the US and the ICC, as well as that of many African States with Court, clearly demonstrate, the engagement of States with the institution is dynamic and changes with time. Consequently, identifying which States that are potentially receptive to pressures exerted by the ICC via its preliminary examinations would be a useful and necessary endeavour prior to deploying the madman, or any other preliminary examination, strategy.

The ICC is most likely to be able to achieve leverage in the preliminary examination over States that are concerned with the reputational costs of coming under the Court's microscope. Many States, including Western States such as the US and the UK, would likely seek to avoid such judicial scrutiny and political labelling from the Court – what Mahmood Mamdani might call "a perverse version of the Nobel Prize".[64] Importantly, and as demonstrated by the defence of Israel by the US, Canada, and the UK against an ICC intervention into alleged crimes perpetrated in Gaza, States are not only concerned about their own reputations, but those of their allies.

This, of course, still does not mean that the attention placed on States during the preliminary examination stage, even if it does affect their reputation, will necessarily encourage them to act. Alone, the ICC is unlikely to be able to instigate judicial activity or a cessation of atrocities.

---

[64] Mahmood Mamdani, "The Politics of Naming: Genocide, Civil War, Insurgency", in *London Review of Books*, 8 March 2007.

What is needed is the development and entrenchment of strategic partnerships and engagements between the ICC and international and domestic civil society groups, widely respected diplomats and political leaders, human rights advocates, journalists, as well as other bodies such as the United Nations, in order to establish modalities of indirect leverage. To some degree, this is already part of the ICC's embryonic strategies for preliminary examinations. As Stone observes: "By terming these 'preliminary examinations,' disclosing many of them publicly, and publishing updates about them weekly, the prosecutor is inviting others to leverage the OTP's attention to these situations into broader pressure for domestic action".[65] Crucially, pressure should be exerted from multiple outlets: from the OTP towards States under preliminary examination; by external, non-States Parties towards the ICC to ensure that preliminary examinations progress; and from those eternal actors towards States under examination. Fostering such a system of pressure would increase the probability of States under preliminary examination responding to the ICC with genuine investigations. It would also, potentially, lessen the possibility of those States responding by attempting to isolate or undermine the institution.

Nevertheless, even with such a system of pressures, at least three possible issues that a madman approach to preliminary examination raises need to be considered. First and foremost, it is worth repeating: the madman strategy should not be applied to all situations. Some situations will require more restraint while others may instigate a need for the OTP to act hastily. An example of the former is Colombia, where the Court's patient policy appears to have been fruitful in bringing about at least some significant positive outcomes regarding justice and accountability. In other cases, such as Libya, a fast-developing crisis and a clear and looming threat to civilian life, led the OTP to judge it necessary to speedily conduct and conclude its preliminary examination so that it could quickly open an official investigation, capture global attention, and attempt to have an impact 'on the ground'.[66]

Secondly, the more brazen approach encompassed in the madman theory of preliminary examinations should only be applied in those situations that meet two key criteria: 1) there is strong evidence of crimes per-

---

[65] Stone, 2015, see *supra* note 19, p. 293.
[66] See Kersten, 2016, see *supra* note 6.

petrated by major powers, and 2) these powers are likely to take the Court's examinations seriously and potentially respond to them by taking judicial action or changing the behaviour of their personnel engaged in warfare. Moreover, the OTP should not go from 'zero-to-sixty', deploying the premeditated madness approach immediately when it opens a preliminary examination. Rather, as indicated by the 2014 and 2015 reports *vis-à-vis* allegations of enhanced interrogation techniques in Afghanistan, the OTP should begin with implicit warnings and only become increasingly intrepid if its signals are ignored.

This second condition also highlights an important limitation, namely that some belligerents and actors will not care about what the ICC does or does not do – at *any stage* of an ICC intervention. A feasible response by States as well as non-State actors to coming under ICC scrutiny is to simply ignore the Court altogether. More broadly, there is an ever-present danger in viewing the ICC as more potent than it actually is. Preliminary examination strategies should be tailored not only to specific situations, but also to the *types* of actors the Court is attempting to affect or influence.

Finally, there is at least some risk of crying wolf and having the OTP's bluff called if the madman theory is deployed but States fail to respond positively to ICC signals and the Court never actually targets those it has threatened. This is the most significant potential drawback of this approach to preliminary examinations and would have to be managed by the OTP from the very outset of the preliminary examination.

These issues and potential limitations can and should be taken into account as part of a broader toolkit for preliminary examinations, one that would be managed and applied contextually with the aim of positively affecting conflicts and the behaviour of belligerents rather than just acting as a legal checklist. In other words, strategies should be developed to enhance the shadow cast by the ICC. The analysis and recommendations within this chapter may inspire more questions than answers. But, at the very least, the OTP should consider the madman approach as a viable strategy against which it can measure the merits of other types of approaches. This would help increase the sophistication of strategies employed in the preliminary examination phase in and across various contexts.

33.6. Conclusion: An Opportunity to Think of Preliminary Examinations Creatively

Limiting our understanding of preliminary examinations to a legal check-list whereby the OTP simply determines whether or not to open an official investigation is unsatisfactory. There is a need to think more strategically about how preliminary examinations can help to induce positive effects in the situations where the ICC intervenes. Thinking through how this might be done requires examining key assumptions regarding the Court's impacts and interests. This chapter has outlined four: 1) that the ICC is predisposed to intervening in ongoing or very recently concluded conflicts; 2) that the Court is a political body with its own institutional interests determining the situations in which it intervenes and whom the ICC targets; 3) that, for a diversity of reasons, the institution would prefer that States take the responsibility for prosecuting international crimes; and 4) that the unpredictable nature of the preliminary examination stage of an ICC intervention creates unique incentives for warring parties and potential ICC targets. These assumptions should be considered when crafting strategies to promote what the OTP sees as its two primary (and *political*) objectives in the preliminary examination stage: galvanizing genuine domestic judicial action and preventing/deterring mass atrocities. One such strategy that should, at the very least, receive greater consideration is the madman theory whereby the OTP makes clear, via its yearly reports as well as communications to relevant actors, that it is willing to investigate and prosecute *any and all* parties to a conflict, irrespective of whether doing so undermines its own institutional interests. The OTP has already shown signs of doing so with regards to allegations of US torture in Afghanistan. This holds some promise in alleviating the widespread perceptions of the ICC is anything but an impartial and independent institution.

Much has been written about the bias of the ICC in favour of the powerful over the weak. Whether this is a perception, a reality, or some combination of the two, the Court's seeming selection bias against African States affects the institution's legitimacy as a criminal court as well as an independent international institution. If the ICC is to retain its standing within the broader international community, it seems increasingly clear that the Court will need to take on the alleged crimes perpetrated by officials of powerful States. To this end, Schabas has written of the Court's need for what he calls a "Pinochet moment":

> One of the great and defining moments of international justice in recent times was the arrest of Augusto Pinochet in London in October 1998. Occurring only a few months after the adoption of the Rome Statute, it sent a message that even the friends of the most powerful could be brought to book if a genuinely independent and impartial justice system was in operation [...] Fifteen years later, international criminal justice is focussed on global pariahs like Charles Taylor, Saif Gaddafi and Hissene Habre. The friends of the rich and powerful are nowhere to be seen. There are no more Pinochets in the dock [...]
>
> [T]he ICC has now become far too deferential to the established order. Mostly it does not operate under a direct mandate from the Security Council, but that may be more illusory than real, because it never strays from the comfort zone of the permanent members [...]
>
> Right now international justice needs more Augusto Pinochets [...][67]

But what if the Court could both avoid the inevitable political confrontation of issuing arrest warrants for high level, powerful actors *and* receive the benefits of affecting accountability for crimes perpetrated by great powers and their allies? If this is indeed a possibility, expanding the size and veracity of the ICC's shadow by formulating creative, smart, and proactive preliminary examination strategies should be a priority of the OTP.

---

[67] William A. Schabas, "The Banality of International Justice", in *Journal of International Criminal Justice*, 2013, vol. 11, no. 3, pp. 550–51

34

Open Source Fact-Finding in Preliminary Examinations

**Alexa Koenig, Felim McMahon, Nikita Mehandru
and Shikha Silliman Bhattacharjee**[*]

34.1. Introduction

In national and international criminal jurisdictions, preliminary examination refers to a pre-investigative stage of prosecution during which available information is examined to determine whether a threshold for further engagement is met. In the context of the International Criminal Court ('ICC'), the Office of the Prosecutor ('OTP') makes an informed determination about whether there is enough information to proceed to a full investigation.

Article 15(3) of the Rome Statute sets the threshold for determining whether the available evidence is sufficient, requiring a "reasonable basis" to advance to investigation.[1] In making this determination, the OTP must grapple with all of the information at its disposal, including both tradi-

---

[*]   **Alexa Koenig** (J.D., Ph.D.) is the Executive Director of the Human Rights Center and Lecturer-in-Residence at the UC Berkeley School of Law; **Felim McMahon** (M.A.) is the Technology and Human Rights Program Director at the UC Berkeley School of Law; **Nikita Mehandru** (B.A., Claremont McKenna College) and **Shikha Silliman Bhattacharjee** (J.D., Ph.D. candidate) are researchers affiliated with the Human Rights Center. The authors thank Caitlin Hoover and Michelle Lee for their research support and Lindsay Freeman for her feedback on earlier drafts of this chapter.

[1]   Office of the Prosecutor ('OTP'), International Criminal Court ('ICC'), *Policy Paper on Preliminary Examinations*, 2013 ('OTP 2013'), para. 24 (http://www.legal-tools.org/doc/acb906/). As explained in the introductory remarks, the Paper "describes the OTP's policy and practice in the conduct of preliminary examinations, that is, how the Office applies the statutory criteria to assess whether a situation warrants investigation. The paper is based on the Rome Statute [...], the Rules of Procedure and Evidence [...], the Regulations of the Court [...], the Regulations of the Office of the Prosecutor, the Office's prosecutorial strategy and policy documents, and its experience over the first years of its activities. [The Paper reflects] an internal policy of the OTP. As such, it does not give rise to legal rights, and is subject to revision based on experience and in light of legal determinations by the Chambers of the Court" (paras. 19, 20).

---

tional and newer forms of evidence. Such data streams include a wide range of digital sources that can be accessed through open source investigations – that is, online investigations that involve combing through publicly accessible resources for information related to potential crimes.[2]

Since the OTP does not have full investigative powers at the preliminary examination phase,[3] rigorous collection and analysis of open source information can play a significant role in shaping preliminary examination outcomes. Open source investigation and analysis can be used to authenticate existing information and discover new materials and sources.[4]

According to the OTP, preliminary examinations are governed by established internal standards, including standard formats for analytical reports, specific methods of source evaluation, consistent practices for measuring internal and external coherence, and a commitment to using information from diverse and independent sources as a means of bias control.[5] As information ecologies evolve, these standards must continuously adapt to the range and scale of available open source materials.

The OTP routinely uses open source information in preliminary examinations and, accordingly, has taken steps to grapple with a rapidly evolving context. These measures include engaging in meetings, workshops, and bilateral conversations with human rights organizations to discuss the range of scientific and digital technologies that can assist the Office in its use of open source materials. Among other considerations, these conversations have focused on harnessing data via remote sensing and satellite imaging, as well as how to manage the 'coming storm' of potential evidence from social media – a storm that has arguably arrived.[6]

---

[2]   For the purposes of this chapter, 'open sources' include news media, academic publications, public reports, social media as well as online video and image sharing services. Clive Best, "Open source intelligence", in Françoise Fogelman-Soulié (ed.), *Mining massive data sets for security: advances in data mining, search, social networks and text mining, and their applications to security*, IOS Press, Amsterdam, 2008, pp. 331-344.

[3]   OTP 2013, para. 12, see *supra* note 1.

[4]   Alexa Koenig, *The New Forensics: Using Open Source Information to Investigate Grave Crimes*, Human Rights Center, 2018 (forthcoming).

[5]   OTP 2013, para. 32, see *supra* note 1.

[6]   Human Rights Centre, UC Berkeley School of Law, "Beyond Reasonable Doubt: Using Scientific Evidence to Advance Prosecutions at the International Criminal Court" (http://www.legal-tools.org/doc/a95842/). *Idem*, "Digital Fingerprints: Using Electronic Evidence to Advance Prosecutions at the International Criminal Court" (http://www.legal-tools.org/

The ICC is far from alone in these conversations. In this digital age, methodologies for discovering, verifying and analysing information from open sources have changed rapidly, including in the context of journalism, policing, and government intelligence. Investigative journalists are experimenting with more efficient ways of using social media and embracing new technologies to monitor global events. Human rights organizations like WITNESS are training activists in how to document atrocities with an eye to maximizing court admissibility and the weight of any videos they produce.[7]

Reflecting these recent developments, the question at the heart of this chapter is: "how can evolving practices around the use of online open source information be harnessed to improve the quality of preliminary examinations at the ICC?". This issue, which resides at the intersection of international criminal justice, human rights, and law and technology scholarship, has yet to be adequately addressed in legal and academic analysis. Finding an answer, we argue, is particularly important in the context of our rapidly expanding digital information ecosystem, in which information sources and transmission practices are continuously evolving.

Bringing together international criminal justice and human rights scholarship and practice, this chapter raises critical issues, including quality control, related to the use of open source information in preliminary examinations. Section 34.2. of this chapter outlines the historic use of open source information to show how the comparatively recent use of such data by the OTP fits into the larger context of information gathering for effective prosecution. This section describes shifts in available types of open source information and maps the transition from military, political, and diplomatic uses of open source intelligence – with governments as the primary agents of retrieval, extraction, and analysis – to our contemporary context. This context is driven by the relatively recent proliferation of smartphones, social media, and other networked public repositories as civil society has increasingly emerged as an agent in both intelligence gathering and information generation.

---

doc/84e097/). *Idem*, "First Responders: An International Workshop on Collecting and Analyzing Evidence of International Crimes" (http://www.legal-tools.org/doc/bf0b24/). *Idem*, "The New Forensics: Using Open Source Information to Investigate Grave Crimes" (http://www.legal-tools.org/doc/e7b0b9/).

7   WITNESS, "Video as Evidence Field Guide" (https://www.legal-tools.org/doc/a1c088-1/).

Section 34.3. discusses the factors the OTP weighs when using information derived from open sources to support preliminary examinations and explains how open source material can strengthen the preliminary examination process. It opens by discussing three core principles that are supposed to guide that process: (1) independence, (2) impartiality, and (3) objectivity.[8] Next, consistent with the Policy Paper on Preliminary Examinations released by the OTP in 2013, the section considers three statutory factors that guide preliminary examination processes: (1) jurisdiction, (2) admissibility, and (3) the interests of justice. Finally, this section addresses the implications of open source information for three policy objectives at the preliminary examination phase: (1) transparency, (2) ending impunity through positive complementarity, and (3) the prevention of crimes. In the context of each of these factors, this chapter discusses the implications of open source information gathering for quality control standards in preliminary examination. We argue that effective methods for gathering and rigorously analysing open source information are essential to the preliminary examination process and, if optimally conducted, present significant opportunities to improve associated outcomes.

34.2. The Rise of Open Source Investigations for Intelligence Gathering and Human Rights Monitoring

Governments have long utilized open source information in military, political, and diplomatic contexts to shed light on events happening at a distance. Significant shifts in the types of open source information collected by governments have occurred with the proliferation of new information technologies, often motivated by and thus concurrent with periods of political unrest and war. Three distinct eras in the evolution of open source intelligence include: (1) newspaper-based intelligence gathering during the Crimean War (1853–1856); (2) the use of journals and foreign broadcasts during World War II (1939–1945); and (3) the mining of print, radio, television and telephonic communication during the Cold War, and later for human rights monitoring.

A fourth and more recent stage in the evolution of open source information gathering has been driven by the relatively recent proliferation of smartphones, social media, and other networked public repositories –

---

[8] OTP 2013, p. 7, see *supra* note 1.

including academic and legal communities on portals such as Academ-
ia.edu and LinkedIn, as well as social media sites such as Facebook,
YouTube, and Twitter. This stage is distinct from the first three because
private actors, rather than governments, have emerged as dynamic players
in both information generation and intelligence gathering. This expansion
of access to the production, dissemination, and collection of open source
information has disaggregated and arguably democratized information
production and usage.

This history is instructive for at least two reasons. First, the evolving nature of open source information calls for similarly evolving strategies for information collection and verification. Thus, developing rigid
policies that cannot accommodate new forms of media will be counterproductive. Second, this history suggests that existing practices governing
authentication of open source information that were developed in relation
to government-dominated phases of open source intelligence may need
rethinking.

34.2.1. Brief History of Open Source Intelligence: 1853 to Present

The Crimean War (1853–1856) – provoked by Russian expansion into the
Danube principalities then under Turkish control – positioned Russia
against Britain, France, the Ottoman Empire, and Sardinia. Historians of
the Crimean War have marked the legacies that this conflict left for future
international conflicts. They note the role of nationalism in driving such
conflicts, the forming of alliances between world powers, the widespread
use of railways as supply lines, and the use of modern warfare, including
trench warfare and machine guns.[9]

Equally important, the Crimean War was also the first major global
conflict to be covered by wartime correspondents and photojournalists.[10]
Thus, this period witnessed the birth of the modern military-media relationship, a distinction largely attributed to the work of British journalist
William Howard Russell from *The Times*. Prior to the Crimean War, junior army officers filtered information about wartime activities from battle-
fronts through letters to newspaper editors. Conversely, Russell, a civilian
reporter, unleashed unbridled criticism of the war directly from his posi-

---

[9]   "The Crimean War", in *BBC News*, 29 March 2011.
[10] *Ibid.*

tion on the frontlines, revealing the awful living conditions of soldiers and the occasional incompetency of army leadership. Coverage of sinking troop morale and experiences by embedded journalists like Russell provided an early source of open intelligence. With Russian and British spies using newspapers to track what was happening around the world, Russell's war coverage became a valuable source of information. This shift in the military-media relationship and the stream of information it produced led then-Russian Emperor Nicholas I to remark: "I have no need of spies, I have the *Times* of London".[11]

A second significant moment in the evolution of open source information occurred during World War II when the United States government systematically invested in developing open source intelligence capacity. As early as 1939, the Princeton School of Public and International Affairs developed the Foreign Broadcast Monitoring Service, which was brought under the ambit of the Federal Communications Commission. On 25 February 1941, President Franklin Delano Roosevelt designated $150,000 from his emergency fund to monitor foreign broadcasts for intelligence purposes.[12] Following the attack on Pearl Harbor in December 1941, the Foreign Broadcast Monitoring Service was renamed the Foreign Broadcast Intelligence Service, responsible for tracking foreign short-wave radio signals to extract intelligence.[13]

Meanwhile, the Roosevelt administration had also established the Office of the Coordination of Information, tasked with analysing information collected abroad.[14] In June 1942, the Office of the Coordination of Information became the Office of Strategic Services, directed to conduct both espionage against the Axis powers and in-depth research and analysis on designated national enemies and their capabilities.[15] The Office's Research and Analysis Branch collected newspaper clippings, journals, and radio broadcast reports from around the world that could provide valuable

---

[11] David Murphy, *Ireland and the Crimean War*, Four Courts Press, Dublin, 2014, p. 174.

[12] Central Intelligence Agency, "Early Beginnings" (http://www.legal-tools.org/doc/0c9562/).

[13] Central Intelligence Agency, "Impact of Pearl Harbor Attack" (http://www.legal-tools.org/doc/669689/).

[14] Central Intelligence Agency, "A Look Back ... Gen. William J. Donovan Heads Office of Strategic Services", 31 December 2009 (available on the Agency's web site).

[15] Central Intelligence Agency, "A Look Back ... Gen. William J. Donovan Heads Office of Strategic Services", see *supra* note 16.

---

intelligence.[16] Obituaries of soldiers or navy officers in German newspapers, for instance, could include images of battleships and bomb craters that facilitated an understanding of German technologies, some of which were reverse engineered for American use.[17]

In 1946, following the war's conclusion, first the Office of Strategic Services and then the Foreign Broadcast Intelligence Service were dissolved. Their respective roles were concentrated in the Central Intelligence Agency ('CIA'), established under President Truman by the National Security Act.[18]

During this period, the Soviet Union gained parity with intelligence operations in the United States. The Ministry of State Security (MGB) was one of the USSR's many iterations of intelligence agencies, and played a prominent role during World War II. It was succeeded by the Committee for State Security (KCG), which served as the Community Party's watchdog, with the added objective of monitoring domestic counterintelligence efforts.[19]

In addition to the expanded *number* of organizations collecting open source information, the Cold War era witnessed an explosion of new *means* for intelligence gathering, specifically radio, television, and real time phone communication. It was towards the end of this third era, in the late 1980s, that the US military first coined the term 'OSINT' to reference open source intelligence.[20] Scrutiny of foreign press, propaganda, and radio initiated during World War II was extended and expanded, not only by the United States but by all other major national government players.[21] One inside source at the time remarked in response to this enormous growth that, "in aggregate, open sources probably furnish the greater part

---

16 Cameron Colquhoun, "A Brief History of Open Source Intelligence", in *Bellingcat*, 14 July 2016.

17 *Ibid.*

18 Central Intelligence Agency, "A Look Back ... Gen. William J. Donovan Heads Office of Strategic Services", see *supra* note 16.

19 Encyclopedia Britannica, "KGB" (available on its web site).

20 Florian Schaurer and Jan Störger, "The Evolution of Open Source Intelligence (OSINT)", in *Intelligencer: Journal of U.S. Intelligence Studies*, vol. 19, no. 3, Winter/Spring 2013 (available on AFIO's web site).

21 Stephen Mercado, "Sailing the Sea of OSINT in the Information Age", in *CSI Studies*, vol. 48, no. 3, 14 April 2007 (available on the Agency's web site).

---

of all information used in the production of military intelligence on the Soviet Union".[22]

These public information sources provided near real time access to sites of conflict and other remote events. In the United States, the CIA developed innovative approaches to intelligence gathering, including the use of overhead surveillance systems to collect images of weapons and operational sites.[23] Signal intelligence ('sIGINT') collectors eavesdropped on military exercises, and were deployed covertly in the air, under sea, and within the USSR.[24] The Council of Ministers of East Germany for State Security mined 1,000 Western magazines, hundreds of books, and twelve hours of West German daily radio and television programming.[25] The US publication *Aviation Week* served as a particularly valuable source, fueling East German intelligence gatherings of recent US developments in aerospace.[26] New media forms not only expanded government use of open source intelligence during the Cold War era but facilitated the creation, collection, and use of visual documentation by a variety of stakeholders seeking accountability for government misconduct – including ever-increasing numbers of human rights advocates.

Reflecting on US-North Korea relations at the time, Donald P. Gregg explained, "it is a well-known phenomenon in the field of intelligence that there often comes a time when public political activity proceeds at such a rapid and fulminating pace that secret intelligence, the work of agents, is overtaken by events publicly recorded".[27] Gregg's assessment of the immediacy of press coverage anticipated the next stage in the evolution of open source intelligence, when nongovernmental actors emerged as participants in both information generation and intelligence gathering.

---

[22] *Ibid.*

[23] Clarence E. Smith, Central Intelligence Agency, "CIA's Analysis of Soviet Science and Technology", in Gerald K. Haines and Robert E. Leggett (eds), *Watching the Bear: Essays on CIA's Analysis of the Soviet Union*, 2003, chap. 4 (available on the CIA's web site).

[24] *Ibid.*

[25] Schaurer and Störger, see *supra* note 23.

[26] Mercado, see *supra* note 24.

[27] Donald P. Gregg, "A Long Road to P'yongyang", in *Korea Society Quarterly*, Spring 2002, vol. 3, no. 1, p. 7.

This third era is marked by the accelerated creation of visual and print- based documentation of human rights abuses by organizations such as the New York Civil Liberties Union, American Civil Liberties Union ('ACLU'), Amnesty International, and Helsinki Watch – a precursor to Human Rights Watch. For instance, in order to document police violence, ACLU staff, armed with movie cameras, posted themselves in buildings overlooking protest sites during the Vietnam war. Aryeh Neier, former director of the ACLU and founder of Human Rights Watch, recalled that when he began working at the ACLU in the mid-1960s, protestors "could not produce witnesses or evidence other than their bruises to support [police brutality] complaints". Addressing this evidentiary gap, lead attorney for the New York Civil Liberties Union, Police Practices Project, Paul Chevigny, used a 'moviola' film editing tool to comb through footage, frame by frame, and capture police abuses. In one instance, Chevigny used segments from a film to clear charges against approximately 600 demonstrators, establishing that police who claimed to have arrested activists were, in fact, providing false testimony against those activists. These practices, developed at the New York Civil Liberties Union, were embraced by the ACLU in the early 1970s. In a landmark case, the ACLU used activist footage to clear charges against 13,000 demonstrators and to secure damages.[28]

Amnesty International similarly used open source information to support their investigations and produce publicly accessible data for use by others. Established in Britain in 1961 to provide amnesty for prisoners of conscience, by 1963, Amnesty International had founded an international secretariat and expanded its mandate to include global engagement.[29] The Amnesty staff, comprised almost entirely of volunteers, "regularly scanned [foreign newspapers] for information about those imprisoned", developed detailed reports, and filed prisoner-specific information on index cards. During their first year in operation, Amnesty volunteers, many housed in universities, produced approximately 1,200 prisoner histories. These histories were made available to the press and other interest-

---

[28] Aryeh Neier, *Taking Liberties: Four Decades In The Struggle For Rights*, Public Affairs, New York, 2003, p. 19.

[29] For a brief overview of the transition from the domestic orientation of the United States based civil rights movement into an international human rights endeavour, see *ibid.*

ed bodies,[30] a practice that facilitated frequent partnerships between Amnesty and news outlets, including the BBC.[31] Amnesty International also published research in journals and newsletters.[32] Now operating in around 70 countries, Amnesty International both consumes and produces publicly-accessible data for use in a range of human rights campaigns and initiatives.[33]

By 1978, production of publicly accessible data was directed at monitoring compliance with international agreements and legal standards. Helsinki Watch was established in 1978 to support citizen groups formed throughout the Soviet bloc to monitor government compliance with the 1975 Helsinki Accords.[34] Helsinki Watch later morphed into a series of regional 'Watches' to monitor abusive governments in disparate parts of the world, eventually collectivizing into Human Rights Watch. The Human Rights Watch mandate, to monitor and document abuse, expanded in the 1990s to tracking violations of humanitarian law.[35] Today, the Human Rights Watch International Justice programme works closely with the ICC, other international and hybrid tribunals, and national courts to bring justice to perpetrators who have committed war crimes and crimes against humanity.[36]

By the late 1980s, in concert with the rise of these large non-governmental organizations, smaller civil society organizations had also begun using still and video cameras to document human rights abuses. In 1988, while on a humanitarian tour with a group from Amnesty International, activist and musician Peter Gabriel used his Sony Handycam to record survivor stories. A few years later, in 1991, a bystander captured the brutal beating of Rodney King, an African-American male, by Los Angeles police. The footage hit television and sparked condemnation and riots that lasted days. In 1992, inspired by these two events, Gabriel established the non-governmental organization WITNESS to train activists

---

[30] Amnesty International, *First Annual Report 1961-1962*, Temple, London, 1962, p. 5.

[31] *Ibid.*, p. 11.

[32] *Ibid.*, p. 10.

[33] Amnesty International, "Who We Are" (available on its web site).

[34] Human Rights Watch, "History" (available on its web site).

[35] *Ibid.*

[36] Human Rights Watch, "International Justice" (available on its web site).

---

around the world in the effective use of video documentation for human rights purposes.[37]

By this time, the Internet had dramatically changed the accessibility of a wide range of public information. In military information gathering contexts, an emergent pool of information online necessitated a fresh look at the use of non-classified information for military purposes. Increasingly, videos, photographs and satellite imagery, including images collected through remote sensing by drone, were being used not only for military, political and foreign policy purposes,[38] but to support legal accountability. One particularly notable example is the use of perpetrator footage in the now-infamous Skorpions case at the International Criminal Tribunal for the former Yugoslavia ('ICTY').[39] The footage was passed along from activists to ICTY prosecutors, and ultimately used to help establish the killings that were alleged to have occurred, who committed them, and how.[40] Increasingly, video content generated in conflict zones began to be used as evidence in war crimes cases around the world. As that content began to flood the internet, new opportunities emerged for both accessing and analysing such resources.

34.2.2.   The Shifting Nature of the Internet: Web 1.0 to Web 2.0

The fourth era in the evolution and use of open source information – the one we are in today – is meaningfully distinct from the first three stages in part because individual (as opposed to organizational) actors have emerged as central participants in both the process of information generation and intelligence gathering. This is largely due to the availability of open source information on the Internet. This evolution can be described as a transition from exploiting the first generation of Internet-based re-

---

[37]   Peter Gabriel, "WITNESS", available at *PeterGabriel.com*.

[38]   Steven Livingston, *Clarifying the CNN Effect: An Examination of Media Effects According to Type of Military Intervention*, Joan Shorenstein Centre on the Press, Politics and Public Policy, John F. Kennedy School of Government, Harvard University, 1997.

[39]   Alexa Koenig, Keith Hiatt, and Khaled Alrabe, "Access Denied? The International Criminal Court, Transnational Discovery, and The American Servicemembers Protection Act", in *Berkeley Journal of International Law*, 2018 (forthcoming) (discussing the use of video as evidence in international courts).

[40]   *Ibid.*

sources on Web 1.0 (the 'readable' phase of the Internet) to discovering materials available during its next, 'writable' stage: Web 2.0.[41]

During the early years of the Internet, Web version '1.0' was a relatively static place from which users could access information from a limited number of sources. While version 1.0 facilitated access to news reports, public statements and official websites, academic articles, and human rights reports, these sources – available at a comparatively limited scale – tended to be relatively stable and attributable to particular national or international sources, and therefore more easily authenticated. While Web 1.0 made it quicker and easier to find information related to an investigation when compared with analogue sources, the type of information available online was not radically different from what could otherwise be found in a physical library. The ways in which Web 1.0 data and resources were used were also similar to engaging with traditional information sources.

The Internet has since evolved to become a more dynamic environment, one that permits significant interaction between users and sites, and features a greater diversity of resources, including citizen journalism, social media, and data derived from social science to hacktivism to leaks. Referred to as 'Web 2.0', this writable world of expanded online open source information presents new opportunities and challenges. Web 2.0 is marked by an exponential expansion of online content that includes "profile pages, public messages, digital photographs, video, chat transcripts, [and] private messages"[42] and the enabling of two-way communication between user and platform, and between user and user.

This next generation of the Internet was driven in part by the proliferation of smartphones, social media, and networked public repositories, such as digital archives, during the first two decades of the twenty-first century. Today, Web 2.0 open sources are increasing exponentially. For instance, as of early 2017, there were reportedly more hours of citizen footage documenting the Syrian war than had taken place during the war

---

[41]   Riaan Rudman and Rikus Bruwer, "Defining Web 3.0: opportunities and challenges", in *The Electronic Library*, 2016, vol. 34, no. 1, pp. 132–154 (discussing the evolution of Web 1.0 to 2.0 as well as the emergence of later versions).

[42]   Christopher Boehning and Daniel Toal, "Authenticating Social Media Evidence", in *New York Law Journal*, 2002, vol. 248, no. 65, p. 2.

itself.[43] In addition to volume challenges, this next generation requires new approaches to assessing veracity, since sources may be transitory, manipulated and/or lack attribution. Importantly, the repeat sharing of content hinders the potential to identify an incident's veracity by potentially obscuring its source. Since metadata – information about the content – can be stripped away, it may be difficult to corroborate critical information about the videographer, uploader, time, date and place. These features of Web 2.0 sources require new modes of retrieval, extraction and analysis – including new methods for source verification and credibility assessment.

Importantly for legal accountability, version 2.0 has also facilitated access to information about human rights abuses and alleged war crimes. For example, in 2007, rising fuel prices in Myanmar combined with decades of political oppression and human rights abuses by the Burmese government triggered massive demonstrations.[44] Termed the 'Saffron Revolution', civilian video footage documented daily protests despite government attempts to suppress Internet access.[45] In 2009, the Green Revolution in Iran was marked by millions of young Iranians sharing real-time videos from Tehran.[46] Twitter and Facebook served as platforms to document the revolution and encourage international observers to stand in solidarity. The movement helped instigate the advent of citizen journalism, with news from civilians reaching the masses before many, if not most, traditional media outlets.[47] While citizen journalism and mobilization through networked public repositories was perhaps most visible during this Arab Spring period of democracy building,[48] around the same time

---

[43] Andy Greenberg, "Google's New YouTube Analysis App Crowdsources War Reporting", in *Wired*, 20 April 2016.

[44] Human Rights Watch, "Crackdown: Repression of the 2007 Popular Protests in Burma" (http://www.legal-tools.org/doc/058507/).

[45] "Burmese Government Clamps Down on Internet", in *New York Times*, 28 September 2007.

[46] Cameron Colquhoun, "A Brief History of Open Source Intelligence", see *supra* note 19.

[47] Jared Keller, "Evaluating Iran's Twitter Revolution", in *The Atlantic*, 18 June 2010.

[48] Philip N. Howard and Muzammil M. Hussain, *Democracy's Fourth Wave? Digital Media and the Arab Spring*, Oxford University Press, New York, 2013. Gadi Wolfsfeld, Elad Segev, and Tamir Sheafer, "Social Media and the Arab Spring: Politics Comes First", in *International Journal of Press/Politics*, 2013, vol. 13, no. 2, pp. 115-137 (finding that social media activity tends not to lead political protest activity but to follow it).

'user generated content' was also streaming out of South and Central America, Africa and Asia.

A rise in citizen journalism has been evident even in countries that lag in access to technology. Midia Ninja in Brazil, for example, has been challenging traditional media outlets that have historically been monopolized by powerful Latin American families. Promoting independent journalism, in June 2013 Midia Ninja's citizen journalists were on the ground with citizens protesting Brazilian government spending and education policies.[49] YouTube quickly became one of the primary platforms for sharing relevant video and providing a counter narrative to that disseminated by major broadcasting corporations.

Compared with Web 1.0 open sources, which are relatively static, Web 2.0 sources are dynamic, may be transitory, lack attribution, and/or may increase or spread quickly. By August 2017, as many as 300 hours of video footage were being uploaded to YouTube every minute, a number that continues to rise.[50] Thus, the challenge for activists has become less about how to get information about what is happening in various regions of the world, than to find *relevant* data – to separate the 'signal' from the 'noise.'[51]

By the start of the second decade of the twenty-first century, video footage was not only being increasingly uploaded, but sent from human rights activists directly to courts with the objective of strengthening prosecutions, including at the ICC.[52] Simultaneously, OTP investigators began meeting with human rights organizations to discuss the range of scientific and digital technologies that could assist the court in generating the critical lead, linkage and corroborative evidence needed to identify witnesses, strengthen witness testimony, and pursue successful prosecutions. These conversations focused on harnessing data via remote sensing and satellite

---

[49] Hivos, "Ninja, the rise of citizen journalism in Brazil", 13 August 2013.

[50] Danny Donchev, "37 Mind Blowing YouTube Facts, Figures and Statistics – 2017", Fortunelord.

[51] For a discussion of source verification and spatial relevance of YouTube footage on the Syrian war, see Michael Storm, Nadine Fattaleh, and Violet Whitney, "Conflict Urbanism: Aleppo Seminar Case Study, Spatializing Syria's YouTube War" (available on the web site of Columbia University).

[52] For an overview of the various kinds of evidence that video footage can provide, see WITNESS, "Video as Evidence Field Guide", see *supra* note 10.

imagery, as well as how to manage vast quantities of potential evidence derived from smartphones and social media.[53]

Responding to challenges associated with source verification and credibility assessment, groups like WITNESS and Videre est Credere began training activists in how to document atrocities with an eye to maximizing the court admissibility and weight of any video they produced.[54] Investigative journalists also began experimenting with how to use new technologies, including social media, to monitor global events. For example, the founders of Storyful in Ireland figured out how to scoop major media outlets by collecting open source information from Twitter, Facebook, and other social media platforms, and then systematically verifying and authenticating the information they harvested to maximize its reliability. Human rights activists and legal investigators have since adopted many of these methods to more effectively search publicly accessible resources,[55] sometimes using crowdsourcing to conduct the labor intensive work of digital discovery, verification, and authentication of online open sources.[56]

34.3. The Use of Open Source Information to Advance Preliminary Examinations at the ICC

The preliminary examination process at the ICC is rooted in Article 15 of the Rome Statute, which describes the powers of the Prosecutor. A preliminary examination can be initiated in three ways: (1) on the basis of information sent to the court about crimes within its jurisdiction;[57] (2) via a declaration lodged by a State accepting the exercise of jurisdiction by the

---

[53] Human Rights Centre, UC Berkeley School of Law, "Beyond Reasonable Doubt: Using Scientific Evidence to Advance Prosecutions at the International Criminal Court", "Digital Fingerprints: Using Electronic Evidence to Advance Prosecutions at the International Criminal Court", "First Responders: An International Workshop on Collecting and Analyzing Evidence of International Crimes", and "The New Forensics: Using Open Source Information to Investigate Grave Crimes", see *supra* note 9.

[54] WITNESS, "Video as Evidence Field Guide", see *supra* note 10.

[55] Bellingcat, "About" (available on its web site). Amnesty International, "Digital Verification Corps-Citizen Evidence Lab", available at https://citizenevidence.org.

[56] In this context, verification refers to investigating the accuracy of the information while authentication refers to verifying whether the item is what it claims to be.

[57] Rome Statute of the International Criminal Court, 17 July 1998, in force 1 July 2002, Article 14 ('ICC Statute') (http://www.legal-tools.org/doc/7b9af9/).

Court;[58] or (3) based on a referral from a State Party[59] or the United Nations Security Council acting under Chapter VII of the United Nations Charter.[60] In the case of a declaration or a referral, the preliminary examination process begins immediately. Otherwise, the Prosecutor is acting *proprio motu,* or on her own initiative based on information about crimes within the jurisdiction of the court.[61]

The Policy Paper on Preliminary Examinations, released by the OTP in 2013, details how a preliminary examination may be initiated, describes its phased approach, and outlines the activities that the Office may carry out during the process. It sets out general principles that are required of the Office in the conduct of its preliminary examination: independence, impartiality and objectivity. It also addresses jurisdiction, admissibility, and the interests of justice – three statutory factors that guide the preliminary examination process.[62] Finally, the Paper identifies three policy objectives for the Office in conducting its preliminary examinations: enhancing transparency, ending impunity, and preventing crimes.[63]

The ultimate objective of the preliminary investigation is to determine whether there is a basis to proceed to a full investigation. ICC judges have interpreted the standard of proof required to open an investigation as a "sensible or reasonable justification" to believe that a crime falling within the jurisdiction of the Court "has been or is being committed".[64] Judges have furthermore indicated that not all of the information available to the Prosecutor must "point towards only one conclusion", adding that such information cannot be expected to be comprehensive or conclusive during a preliminary examination.[65]

---

[58] *Ibid.*

[59] *Ibid.*

[60] *Ibid.*

[61] OTP 2013, para. 4, see *supra* note 1 (laying out the various ways in which a preliminary examination can be initiated).

[62] ICC Statute, Article 53(1)(a)–(c), see *supra* note 62.

[63] OTP 2013, paras. 93–106, see *supra* note 1.

[64] ICC, Situation in the Republic of Kenya, Corrigendum of the Decision Pursuant to Article 15 of the Rome Statute on the Authorization of an Investigation into the Situation in the Republic of Kenya, ICC-01/09-19-Corr, 31 March 2010, paras. 34, 35 (http://www.legal-tools.org/doc/f0caaf/).

[65] OTP 2013, para. 11, see *supra* note 1.

Article 15(1) of the Rome Statute leaves open the types of data that can be relied upon during the preliminary examination phase, noting simply that such data should comprise "information on crimes within the jurisdiction of the Court". The 2013 Policy Paper reiterates the breadth of information upon which the Office may rely, stating that it may initiate a preliminary examination "taking into account *any* information on crimes within [its] jurisdiction".[66]

Similarly, the Statute does not limit the sources from which information can be received or solicited. Such information can come "from States, organs of the United Nations, intergovernmental and non-governmental organizations, or other reliable sources".[67] While the 2013 Policy Paper does not specifically mention individuals, unaffiliated persons could also be relied upon by the OTP insofar as they are reliable sources. Additionally, the Prosecutor "may receive written or oral testimony at the seat of the Court" in assessing the "seriousness" of information already in her possession. The OTP can therefore receive, gather or solicit information from almost any source during the preliminary examination phase. This provides the Office with a wide scope and strong incentive to use open source information.

Regardless of how a preliminary examination is initiated, the effective gathering and rigorous analysis of open source information is essential to the process. Since the Office does not "enjoy full investigative powers"[68] during preliminary examination, it is limited in the methods it can employ. The Office may send requests for information to reliable sources and may conduct field missions with the aim of analysing information, but these visits must be limited to collecting further information.[69] Accordingly, the value of open source information in the overall information-seeking context is at its apex at this point in the proceedings. Furthermore, optimum gathering and processing of open source information

---

[66]   *Ibid.*, para. 73 (emphasis added).

[67]   ICC Statute, Article 15(2), see *supra* note 62.

[68]   OTP 2013, paras. 12–13, see *supra* note 1.

[69]   For instance, field missions were conducted in Colombia, Guinea, Nigeria, and elsewhere. See Ignaz Stegmiller, "Article 15(2)-Additional information", in *Commentary on the Law of the International Criminal Court*, available at https://cilrap-lexsitus.org/clicc/content/15-2-additional-information (citing ICC, *Report of the Activities of the Court*, 21 October 2013, ICC-ASP/12/28, paras. 72, 74, 77 (http://www.legal-tools.org/doc/b22709/)).

has a greater relative impact during the preliminary examination phase than during the investigation phase, when the full spectrum of State co-operation measures can be activated.

The Office's policy and practice is therefore especially well developed with regard to the use of open source information during preliminary examination, during which open-source approaches are used to gather information about possible crimes, assess information in the Office's possession, and identify further sources of information. The degree to which the Office can rely on open source information does not seem to be limited by either the Rome Statute or Court policy or practice. This wide ambit reinforces the idea that open source information can play a positive role in both triggering and determining the outcome of a preliminary examination.[70]

34.3.1. Guiding principles

The use of open source information in preliminary examination is bound only by the necessity to analyse the information in line with the principles of independence, impartiality and objectivity. These general principles,[71] derived respectively from articles 42, 21(3), and 54(1) of the Rome Statute, define how such information is to be assessed.

34.3.1.1. Independence

Article 42 of the Statute states that the Office shall "act independently of instructions from any external source" and "shall not be influenced or altered by the presumed or known wishes of any party".[72] In the case of a State Party or United Nations Security Council referral, and in relation to

---

[70] Although not explicitly stated in the Policy Paper, it seems theoretically possible for a preliminary examination to be initiated entirely on the basis of information collected from open sources by the Office of the Prosecutor. In practice, it would be extremely rare for a situation to become the subject of an investigation, a preliminary examination, or a preventive statement without the office receiving any related communications or interacting with an external actor. However, the Rome Statute and Policy Paper do not rule out the possibility that the Office might open a preliminary examination, or even a full examination, on the basis of information derived entirely from its own open source collection and analysis, nor does it limit the degree to which the Office may rely on such information in issuing preventive statements.

[71] OTP 2013, para. 25, see *supra* note 1.

[72] *Ibid.*, para. 26.

Article 15 communications, the Office "is not bound or constrained by the information" it receives. It may seek further information from "reliable sources" and all information is "subject to critical analysis and evaluation".[73]

In practice, Article 42 not only permits but reinforces the importance of effectively using open source information to corroborate existing information and to identify further sources. The principle of independence also requires the Office to develop and apply consistent and defensible standards in analysing and evaluating information received from outsiders, supplementary information received at the request of the Office, and information gathered from open sources.

34.3.1.2. Impartiality

The principle of impartiality is rooted in Article 21(3) of the Statute, which states that the Court shall interpret and apply the law "without any adverse distinction founded on grounds such as gender, age, race, colour, language, religion or belief, political or other opinion, national, ethnic or social origin, wealth, birth, or other status".[74] According to the Policy Paper, this requires the Office to "apply consistent methods and criteria, irrespective of the states or parties involved or the person(s) or group(s) concerned".[75] The principle of impartiality thus reinforces the need to develop and apply a methodology around open source information and information collection more generally that does not unfairly disadvantage persons or groups based on unequal access to modern information and communication technologies.

In developing preliminary examination methodologies in relationship to a wide range of open source information, impartiality as a governing principle requires continued attention to ensuring that the use of open source information does not disadvantage persons on the basis of their being on the wrong side of the digital divide or otherwise poorly represented. The Policy Paper states that the OTP "seeks to ensure that [...] all relevant parties are given the opportunity to provide information".[76] The

---

[73] *Ibid.*, para. 27.
[74] *Ibid.*, p. 7, fn. 15.
[75] *Ibid.*, para. 28.
[76] *Ibid.*, para. 33.

principle of impartiality and the wider requirements of Article 21(3) therefore stand as a corrective to an over-reliance on digitally derived open
source information.

The principle of impartiality also points to the importance of governmental organizations, the UN system, non-governmental organizations,
civil society, and other 'first responders' in rendering situations and their
complexities visible to criminal jurisdictions. Further, it reinforces the
importance of systematically accessing mass communication platforms
associated with modern information communication technologies that are
increasingly being used by underrepresented groups in order to identify
and integrate their experiences and perspectives.

34.3.1.3. Objectivity

The 2013 policy paper derives the principle of objectivity from Article
54(1), which provides that the Office will "investigate incriminating and
exonerating circumstances equally". The Paper notes that, because the
information assessed in preliminary examinations is mainly from external
sources, the OTP will pay "particular attention to the assessment of the
reliability of the source and the credibility of the information".[77]

Today, organizations seeking to make objective use of all available
resources must assess information from a diverse range of sources including information from State organs, political and military actors, professional news organizations, media activists, hacktivists, citizen journalists,
ordinary citizens and untrained eyewitnesses. A far richer and more diverse stream of information is available than ever before, including detailed real-time information. This presents a challenge not just in terms of
source evaluation, but also in terms of source identification and the corroboration and verification of available data.

The Policy Paper notes that "the Office uses standard formats for
analytical reports, standard methods of source evaluation, and consistent
rules of measurement", checking "internal and external coherence" and
"drawing information from diverse and independent sources as a means of
bias control".[78] As discussed in the previous section, methodologies
around the discovery, verification and analysis of relevant information

---

[77] Ibid.
[78] Ibid.

from open sources have changed rapidly in the context of journalism, policing and in the world of intelligence. As the information ecosystem evolves, the formats, methods, and rules of the Office will need to adapt to respond to those changes. It is thus incumbent upon the Office to equip itself with the latest skillsets in terms of handling data streams from open sources.

In service of the principle of objectivity, the Office is also presented with an opportunity and a challenge in relation to the volume, variety, and relatively unstable nature of open source information. Online investigations require fact gatherers to grapple with ever larger quantities of information, while valuable information often appears, disappears, or is replicated in real time, with varying degrees of fidelity. In ensuring that the use of open source information is in line with the principle of objectivity, the OTP can draw on the experience and activities of a range of actors outside the Court, including from the fields of journalism, human rights, and law enforcement.

34.3.2. Statutory Factors

The OTP analyses three statutory factors when determining whether to proceed with an investigation: jurisdiction, admissibility, and the interests of justice.[79] Each analysis can benefit from open source information to varying degrees. The 2013 Policy Paper examines each of the factors in turn and situates them within a four-phase filtering process. For analytical purposes, each stage focuses on a distinct statutory factor. Following this framework, the remainder of this section explores how open source information can inform an assessment of whether statutory factors are met.

34.3.2.1. Phases 1 and 2: Jurisdiction

Phase 1 – the "pre-preliminary examination phase"[80] – consists of an assessment of information received via Article 15 communications whereby outsiders send information to the court for consideration.[81] This sifting of material during the Article 15 process distinguishes between communications related to matters manifestly outside the jurisdiction of the Court,

---

[79] Each factor is set out in ICC Statute, Article 53(1)(a)–(c), see *supra* note 62.

[80] Amitis Khojasteh, "ICC Statute Article 15", Centre for International Law Research and Policy (https://www.cilrap.org/cilrap-film/15-khojasteh/).

[81] In 2016, the OTP received nearly 600 Article 15 submissions. *Ibid.*

which are dismissed, and those pertaining to matters already under preliminary examination, under full investigation, or forming the basis of an existing prosecution, which are forwarded to the relevant team.[82] Those that do not fit in these two categories are then subject to an "independent and objective" two-step analysis, the first step being factual and the second legal, to see if the alleged crimes potentially fall within the jurisdiction of the Court and thus whether further engagement is warranted. According to the 2013 Policy Paper, "[those situations] deemed to require further analysis will be the subject of a dedicated analytical report which will assess whether the alleged crimes appear to fall within the jurisdiction of the Court and therefore warrant proceeding to the next phase. Such communications shall be analysed in combination with open source information such as reports from the United Nations, non-governmental organisations and other reliable sources for corroboration purposes".[83]

Between mid-2012 and mid-2017, situation analysts produced nearly 40 such reports, each of which relied on information derived from open sources. Of them, two resulted in investigations, including allegations against United Kingdom forces in Iraq and an inquiry into the situation in Burundi. As of summer 2017, analysts were considering Article 15 submissions that focused on allegations as varied as forceful evictions in Cambodia, the ill treatment of asylum seekers in Australia, and extrajudicial killings in the Philippines.[84]

The reports ultimately provide the basis for moving to phase 2, "the formal commencement of a preliminary examination". Phase 2 includes those Article 15 submissions that survive phase 1 analysis, as well as any referrals from a State Party, referrals from the United Nations Security Council, or declarations by non-State Parties. In addition to any infor-

---

[82] The final category is for matters that are not manifestly outside the jurisdiction of the Court or subject to ongoing examination, investigation or prosecution and which therefore warrant further analysis and thus may provide the basis for a preliminary examination. Communications deemed to be manifestly outside the Court's jurisdiction may be revisited in light of new information or circumstances, such as a change in the jurisdictional situation, so these are retained. Amitis Khojasteh, *ibid.*

[83] OTP 2013, para. 79, see *supra* note 1. This third category of submissions that 'warrant further analysis' are known as 'WFA communications'. They are not subject to the "reasonable basis" standard; instead, the applied standard is whether any alleged crimes "appear to fall within the jurisdiction of the court". Khojasteh, see *supra* note 80.

[84] Khojasteh, *ibid.*

mation provided by these external actors, the phase 2 process can be supported by testimony received at the seat of the Court and open source information.[85] Like phase 1, phase 2 aims to identify whether potential cases fall within the Court's jurisdiction.

Findings from phase 2 are documented in an 'Article 5 report' to the Prosecutor that clarifies the Court's jurisdiction. When considering whether the Court has jurisdiction, the Office must consider temporal, territorial or personal and subject-matter jurisdiction over crimes that have been or are being committed. In accordance with Article 53(1), the required standard of proof during phase 2 is a "reasonable basis" to believe that such crimes have occurred.[86] Open source information, as touched on below, can be helpful in analysing whether the requisite standard can be met.

34.3.2.1.1. Temporal Jurisdiction

The temporal jurisdiction of the Court applies from the date of the Rome Statute's entry into force (1 July 2002); the date of entry into force for a particular State Party (when ratified later); the date specified in a United Nations Security Council referral; or a declaration by a State pursuant to Article 12(3) accepting the exercise of the Court's jurisdiction.

Given the clarity of these options, it is difficult to imagine a situation where the Office might have to rely on open-source information to make an assessment of its temporal jurisdiction. Summaries of the application of this statutory factor *tend* to be short and refer only to legal facts such as the date a State deposited its instrument of ratification of the Rome Statute, or the dates specified in a United Nations Security Council referral or State declaration.

34.3.2.1.2. Territorial or Personal Jurisdiction

Territorial or personal jurisdiction is determined by whether a crime specified in Article 5 has been committed "on the territory or by a national of a state party".[87] In most instances, establishing a person's nationality and analysing the statutory factor of personal jurisdiction can be done with

---

85 OTP 2013, paras. 79–80, see *supra* note 1.

86 *Ibid.*, para. 36.

87 *Ibid.*, para. 40.

reference to official records and will not require the Office to rely on open sources.

However, the role of foreign fighters acting as combatants can complicate this assessment. In such instances, open source information may play a role. For example, social media sources were specifically mentioned by the Prosecutor in her 2015 statement on alleged crimes committed by ISIS, which focused on the question of the Court's personal jurisdiction over foreign fighters in Iraq and Syria who were nationals of State Parties. In her statement on the alleged crimes committed by ISIS, the Prosecutor noted that: "A few [foreign fighters] have publicised their heinous acts through social media".[88] In this particular assessment, there was a wealth of open source information on the role of foreign fighters from States Parties in Iraq and Syria, including videos of French nationals who joined ISIS in burning their passports and videos of atrocities.

In this particular situation, since ISIS was primarily led by nationals of Iraq and Syria, which are not States Parties, the Office concluded that the jurisdictional basis for prosecuting those most responsible was too narrow to proceed. However, in other instances, it is entirely possible for open source research to indicate that State Party nationals are in fact those most responsible for atrocity crimes in a situation *not* covered by territorial jurisdiction. For instance, it may be possible to use open source information to establish the facts around the involvement of foreign fighters in specific incidents and perhaps even their place within command structures. In other words, it is conceivable that open source information could, in the future, be instrumental not only in gathering information about the crime base but also in throwing light on leadership structures in complex organizations for purposes of ascertaining personal jurisdiction.

In addition to the type of investigation described above, there are other instances where open source information collection and analysis could inform determinations of territorial jurisdiction. For example, geolocation techniques can be used to anchor and verify the locations depicted in videos that show troop movements or alleged criminal activity. Geolocation is now a standard means to corroborate a video obtained from

---

[88] ICC, "Statement of the Prosecutor of the International Criminal Court, Fatou Bensouda, on the alleged crimes committed by ISIS", 8 April 2015 (http://www.legal-tools.org/doc/b1d672/).

open sources and can contribute heavily towards both source and content evaluation.[89]

34.3.2.1.3. Subject-Matter Jurisdiction

With regard to subject-matter jurisdiction, the Court is limited to assessing the crimes set out in Article 5: genocide, crimes against humanity, war crimes, and the crime of aggression. An analysis of whether there is a reasonable basis to believe that such crimes have been committed will consider "underlying facts and factors", "contextual circumstances", "patterns of similar conduct [...] aimed at a protected group", alleged perpetrators, the "role of the individual, group or institution" and their "link with the alleged crime", as well as the mental element of any alleged crime(s).[90] While a detailed assessment is beyond the scope of this chapter, the potential for open sources to support each of these factors is worth exploring in further research.[91]

34.3.2.2. Phase 3: Admissibility

Phase 3 of the preliminary examination process focuses on admissibility, and whether discovered data supports the necessary gravity and complementarity assessments.[92] At this stage, the Office will continue to collect information relating to its subject-matter jurisdiction, in particular where new or ongoing crimes are alleged to be taking place.

---

[89] Craig Silverman, *Verification Handbook: A definitive guide to verifying digital content for emergency coverage*, European Journalism Centre, Maastricht, 2014, p. 39 (discussing use of satellite imagery for verification). Sam Dubberley, "In the Firing Line: How Amnesty's Digital Verification Corps changed official narratives through open source investigation", in *Medium*, 18 May 2017.

[90] OTP 2013, paras. 38–39, see *supra* note 1.

[91] In a June 2017 presentation in The Hague, a situation analyst from the OTP suggested the value of information provided by external actors, such as survivors and non-governmental organizations, to the second phase of the preliminary examination process. She noted how helpful it would be for those actors, when sending information to the ICC or posting online, to provide the "who, what, when, where, and how" underlying a particular atrocity, as opposed to focusing on the impact of any alleged crimes. In addition, she stressed that those external actors could improve the quality of information for ICC purposes by using and declaring a clear and consistent method of information collection and analysis, as well as preserving and providing primary sources. Matilde Gawronski, "ICC Statute Article 15", Centre for International Law Research and Policy (https://www.cilrap.org/cilrap-film/15-gawronski/).

[92] OTP 2013, para. 42, see *supra* note 1.

In determining admissibility, the Office must consider three things: gravity, complementarity, and the interests of justice in the context of specific cases that might be pursued.[93]

Two questions for defining potential cases have been identified by the Pre-Trial Chambers: (1) What groups or persons involved in a situation; and (2) What alleged crimes are likely to become the focus of a future investigation? In practice, the Office has made its admissibility assessment based on an assessment of which persons or organizations bear the "greatest responsibility for the most serious crimes"[94] related to a situation. As discussed below, open source data can inform an analysis of the crimes that may have been perpetrated, who was involved, and whether the national system – under the complementarity process – has jurisdiction instead of the ICC.

34.3.2.2.1. Complementarity

A complementarity assessment is concerned with determining whether the relevant national system is willing and/or able to investigate and prosecute the potential cases identified by the OTP in its preliminary examination, in which case the ICC does not have jurisdiction. First, the Office looks at whether national proceedings are taking place in relation to the potential cases it has identified. If they are, the Office asks whether "the focus is on those most responsible for the most serious crimes committed"[95] and whether the proceedings are "vitiated by an unwillingness or an inability to genuinely carry out the proceedings". In assessing any potential unwillingness to conduct genuine national proceedings, the Court asks whether the investigation or prosecution is being undertaken to shield somebody from ICC jurisdiction; whether there has been an unjustified delay; and whether national proceedings are being conducted independently and impartially.

Much of this information may be obtained through a careful review of online, public sources. For example, the OTP can obtain useful information via open sources about the ability of a national justice system to carry out proceedings, including whether a "substantial collapse or una-

---

[93] *Ibid.*, para. 43.

[94] *Ibid.*, para. 45.

[95] *Ibid.*, para. 49.

vailability" means it is incable of being successful.[96] In making such an assessment, the 2013 Policy Paper indicates that the Office will consider evidence of a lack of adequate protection systems for victims; the absence of a legislative framework; and a general paucity of resources.

34.3.2.2.1.1. National Investigations that Shield Alleged Perpetrators

Even when a national investigation has commenced, complementarity is not satisfied if the Office concludes that the investigation is a sham, for example, if it was commenced to shield one or more alleged perpetrators. The OTP's 2013 Policy Paper lists indicators that suggest a person at the heart of a potential ICC case is being deliberately shielded by a State. These include manifestly insufficient steps taken towards prosecution; deviations from standard practices and procedures; ignoring evidence or giving it insufficient weight; intimidation; findings that are irreconcilable with the evidence; inadequacies in charging and in the application of modes of liability; flawed forensic examinations; failures related to disclosure; fabricated evidence; manipulated or coerced witness statements; undue admission or non-admission of evidence; lack of resources; and failure to co-operate with the Court.[97]

Open source investigative techniques can provide information on many of these indicators. For instance, information on the more difficult-to-ascertain, such as deviations from procedure or intimidation, may be available via national non-governmental organizations. Open source monitoring can supplement such sources. Given that potential ICC cases tend to be high-profile, there is likely to be significant reporting and other online information available to the OTP in near real time.

In the absence of information from a local non-governmental organization, assessing whether there has been an unjustified delay can be greatly assisted with open source information. For example, open sources can help the Office understand the context in which a potential case is playing out as well as the actors involved and their relationships. In addition, official government information accessed through open information portals can feed into an assessment of the national process, including the

---

[96] *Ibid.*, para. 56.
[97] *Ibid.*

allocation of resources and other organizational factors, even in the absence of co-operation with the ICC.

34.3.2.2.1.2. Independence and Impartiality of National Proceedings

Indications of the independence of national proceedings include the involvement of State organizations or personnel in alleged crimes; the structure of the criminal justice system; appointments and dismissals impacting on proceedings; the application of immunities and privileges; and political interference and corruption. The *indicia* of impartiality can include connections between the accused persons and the authorities charged with proceedings and "public statements, awards, sanctions, promotions or demotions, deployments, dismissals or reprisals in relation to [the] investigative, prosecutorial or judicial personnel concerned".[98]

Open sources, especially news reports, but also information publicly available via social media, can shed light on negative indicators regarding the independence and impartiality of those involved in national proceedings. In the absence of the collation of such information by national actors or other relevant organizations, or in a situation where there is no co-operation from local authorities, the OTP can access much relevant information online.

34.3.2.3. Phase 4

If the admissibility and jurisdiction requirements are met, the preliminary examination moves to phase 4, during which the OTP considers the interests of justice and produces what is known as an Article 53(1) report.[99] There is a presumption that any investigation will be in the interest of justice "unless there are specific circumstances which provide substantial reasons to believe that the interests of justice are not served by an investigation at that time".[100] As part of this assessment, the OTP is particularly charged with considering the gravity of the alleged crimes and the interests of victims, as well as the views of "community, religious, political or tribal leaders, States, and intergovernmental, and non-governmental or-

---

[98] *Ibid.*

[99] *Ibid.*, para. 80. See also OTP, *Policy Paper on the Interests of Justice*, 2007 (http://www.legal-tools.org/doc/bb02e5/).

[100] OTP 2013, para. 67, see *supra* note 1.

ganisations".[101] Assuming there is no justice-based reason to prevent moving to an investigation, the resulting report will include an initial legal characterization of the alleged crimes within the jurisdiction of the Court and a basic statement of the facts, detailing the places the alleged crimes took place, the time or time period in which they took place, and the persons or groups involved.

Open source information may be quite helpful to both the interests of justice assessment and the Article 53(1) report. In the CILRAP-conference in The Hague in June 2017 titled "Quality Control in Preliminary Examination: Reviewing Impact, Policies and Practices", an OTP analyst emphasized the importance of thinking through what both the OTP could do internally – and what modifications external actors could make – to enhance the quality of the preliminary examination process. She noted the potential value of systematically soliciting the impressions of survivors and other stakeholders as to what they perceive as satisfying the needs of 'justice' in a particular situation in order to determine whether a case at the ICC would potentially compete with (and/or support) those interests. While she proposed creating a survey to gather those perspectives, a systematic combing of open source materials could fulfill a similar function and/or be used to support any survey that might be employed.[102]

34.3.3. Policy Considerations

In addition to contributing to decisions around whether to launch a full investigation, the 2013 Policy Paper mentions other potential uses of open source information. Specifically, the Paper outlines an "early warning function" as within the Office's mandate, noting that the OTP "systematically and proactively collect[s] open source information on alleged crimes that appear to fall within the jurisdiction of the Court" in order to gauge potential spikes in violence around the world.[103] The monitoring of open sources is thus seen as central to the Office fulfilling not only its mandate to combat impunity but to prevent future violence, with the Policy Paper noting that such monitoring will "allow the Office to react promptly to upsurges in violence by reinforcing early interaction with States, interna-

---

[101] *Ibid.*, para. 68.

[102] Gawronski, "ICC Statute Article 15", see *supra* note 94.

[103] OTP 2013, para. 104, see *supra* note 1.

tional organisations and non-governmental organisations in order to verify information on alleged crimes, to encourage genuine national proceedings and to prevent reoccurrence of crimes". Thus, the Policy Paper foresees that open source information may be used in preparing and issuing "public, preventive statements"[104] that put perpetrators 'on notice' and encourage national jurisdictions to act.

34.4. Conclusion

As indicated above, significant changes in the means of information dissemination, especially online, have facilitated the sharing of data related to core international crimes. Much of this information is publicly accessible. The growing quantity and quality of online sources – and practices of harvesting information derived from those sources – has considerable potential to strengthen the quality of information feeding into the preliminary examination stage of situations that are being considered by the ICC. Ultimately, open source-derived information is an under-utilized resource that is quickly expanding in importance. When considering standards and initiatives for improving the quality of preliminary examinations, a careful look at the open source fact-finding process is essential.

---

[104] *Ibid.*

35

ICC Preliminary Examinations and National Justice: Opportunities and Challenges for Catalysing Domestic Prosecutions

Elizabeth M. Evenson[*]

The International Criminal Court ('ICC') is a court of last resort. Under the principle of complementarity, the ICC can only take up cases where national authorities do not; these national authorities have the primary responsibility under international law to ensure accountability for atrocity crimes. Where States have an interest in avoiding the ICC's intervention, they can do so by conducting genuine national proceedings. This means that the leverage of the Court's Office of the Prosecutor ('OTP') with national authorities to press for domestic proceedings can be significant in countries where it is considering whether to open an investigation, that is, in what are known as 'preliminary examinations'.

The OTP has recognized this opportunity. In policy and in practice, the OTP is committed, where feasible, to encouraging national proceedings into crimes falling within the ICC's jurisdiction in preliminary examinations. This makes the OTP an important actor in what has come to be known as 'positive complementarity' – that is, the range of efforts by international partners, international organizations, and civil society groups to assist national authorities to carry out effective prosecutions of interna-

---

[*] **Elizabeth M. Evenson** is Associate International Justice Director, Human Rights Watch. Her research and advocacy centres on the International Criminal Court, monitoring the court's institutional development and conducting advocacy toward court officials and its member countries. Previously, she was a Leonard H. Sandler fellow in the Africa division of Human Rights Watch, focused on Uganda. From June to August 2012, Evenson served as a civil society program officer with No Peace Without Justice's Libya Project. She was a visiting scholar from March to April 2014 at the Human Rights Center at the University of California Berkeley School of Law. She holds a B.A. from the University of Chicago, an M.Phil. from the University of Nottingham, and a J.D. from Columbia Law School.

---

tional crimes. These efforts include legislative assistance, capacity building, and advocacy and political dialogue to counter obstruction.

Translating this commitment into successful practice is far from easy. Domestic prosecutions of international crimes face a number of obstacles. Political will of national authorities to support independent investigations is needed, but often in short supply given that these prosecutions will likely touch on powerful interests opposed to accountability. Prosecutions of mass atrocity crimes also require specialized expertise and support, including witness protection, but countries are often ill-equipped to meet these challenges. The OTP, like other complementarity actors, needs to have strategies geared towards bridging these two pillars of 'unwillingness' and 'inability'.

As challenging of a task as it may be, the stakes for the OTP's success in this area are no less profound. In the long term, bolstering national proceedings is crucial in the fight against impunity for the most serious crimes and is fundamental to hopes for the ICC's broad impact.

Indeed, the demands for justice for atrocity crimes have far outstripped the capacity of the ICC; the number of situations in which the ICC could and should act simultaneously are probably far more than what the Court's founders envisioned. And this is not likely to improve any time soon, with a multiplication of human rights crises and an all-too-limited appetite on the part of ICC States Parties to fund a court that can go beyond a handful of investigations in any given year.

The OTP's commitment to encouraging national proceedings in situations under preliminary examination therefore holds out significant potential to meet victims' rights to access justice, by bridging some of this capacity gap. Prospects for success should be realistically understood and appraised, however.

As a follow-up to our 2011 briefing paper on the OTP's approach to situations under analysis, "Course Correction",[1] Human Rights Watch undertook fresh research between 2015 and 2017 on aspects of national proceedings in situations in four countries that are or were the subject of OTP preliminary examinations – Colombia, Georgia, Guinea, and the

---

[1] Human Rights Watch, *Course Correction: Recommendations to the Prosecutor for a More Effective Approach to "Situations under Analysis"*, 16 June 2011 (http://www.legal-tools.org/doc/43aefb/).

United Kingdom. Our research aimed to understand both the limits of what the OTP can reasonably be expected to accomplish through its preliminary examinations when it comes to catalysing national justice and areas where the OTP could strengthen its impact in future practice. We did not seek to evaluate numerous other aspects of the OTP's approach to preliminary examinations, which, of course, have as their primary aim the determination of whether or not to open a full ICC investigation. Catalysing national proceedings is only a secondary aim.

Our case studies in these four countries are the subject of a forthcoming Human Rights Watch report, to be published in 2018. This chapter does not deal with the findings of the research. Instead, it provides the conceptual background against which these case studies were carried out. It first looks at the OTP's approach to positive complementarity in its preliminary examinations, and then identifies the key challenges that run across efforts to implement this policy commitment in practice. This chapter is an expanded version of a background section to be published as an appendix in the forthcoming Human Rights Watch report. Some of these observations have also previously been set out in "Course Correction", cited above.

It is important to note that regarding most, if not all, of the challenges referenced below, the OTP has relevant strategies. The absence of reference to these strategies in this chapter should not be understood to suggest that the OTP is unaware of or not actively seized of these issues. Our full report assesses the OTP's approaches and strategies, and makes recommendations as to how the OTP and other complementarity actors can strengthen practice.

35.1. Overview of the Preliminary Examination Process

'situations under analysis' or 'preliminary examinations' are a specific set of events in a given country that the OTP is assessing to determine whether to open a formal ICC investigation.[2] It is important to note that the

---

[2] ICC jurisdiction can be triggered in one of three ways: ICC member states or the Security Council can refer a specific set of events – known as a situation – to the ICC prosecutor or the ICC prosecutor can seek to open an investigation on their own initiative (*'proprio motu'*) with the authorization of an ICC pre-trial chamber. See Rome Statute of the International Criminal Court (hereinafter 'Rome Statute'), U.N. Doc. A/CONF.183/9, 17 July 1998, entered into force 1 July 2002, Article 13. Regardless of how the Court's jurisdiction is triggered, however, the Office of the Prosecutor first analyses the information it has be-

OTP's approach to the preliminary examination process has been consolidated over a number of years; the approach described below reflects current practice and dates to 2013, when the OTP issued a revised policy on preliminary examinations.[3]

Information about possible crimes falling within the ICC's jurisdiction first comes to the OTP through one of two channels: communications and referrals. These channels relate to the three mechanisms that can trigger ICC jurisdiction: *proprio motu* investigations (Rome Statute, Articles 13(c) and 15), Security Council referrals (Article 13(b)), and State Party referrals (Article 13(a)).

'Communications' are information received by the OTP under Article 15 of the Rome Statute, which permits the prosecutor to open an investigation *proprio motu* ("on one's own initiative") with the authorization of a pre-trial chamber. Not all such communications, however, will lead to a preliminary examination. Instead, and consistent with Article 15(2)'s instruction that the prosecutor "analyse the seriousness of information received", the OTP first filters out information regarding crimes manifestly outside the ICC's jurisdiction. This is known as Phase 1. Situations that survive this initial filter then enter Phase 2 and become formally 'situations under analysis'.[4]

By contrast, situations referred to the ICC prosecutor by the Security Council or a State Party are automatically considered to be situations under analysis and directly enter Phase 2. In addition, the prosecutor has indicated that situations directly enter Phase 2 when a declaration has been lodged under Article 12(3), which permits a State to temporarily accept the jurisdiction of the ICC.[5] This is the case even though an investigation opened following an Article 12(3) declaration is done so pursuant to the prosecutor's *proprio motu* powers under Article 15.

Beginning with Phase 2 – which marks the formal start of a preliminary examination – the OTP, through its Situation Analysis Section with-

---

fore it regarding a situation to determine whether there is a reasonable basis for initiating a formal investigation. This process is known as 'preliminary examination'.

[3]   Office of the Prosecutor, ICC, *Policy Paper on Preliminary Examinations*, November 2013 (http://www.legal-tools.org/doc/acb906/).

[4]   *Ibid.*, para. 80.

[5]   *Ibid.*

in the Jurisdiction, Complementarity and Cooperation Division, examines the factors listed in Article 53(1) of the Rome Statute that control the prosecutor's determination as to whether to initiate an investigation. Those are:

- whether there is "a reasonable basis to believe that a crime within the jurisdiction of the Court has been or is being committed" (Article 53(1)(a));

- whether "the case is or would be admissible under article 17" (Article 53(1)(b)); and

- whether "taking into account the gravity of the crime and the interests of victims, there are nonetheless substantial reasons to believe that an investigation would not serve the interests of justice" (Article 53(1)(c)).[6]

Admissibility – assessed in Phase 3 of the examination – has two components, consistent with the requirements of Article 17 of the Rome Statute. First, a potential case must be of sufficient gravity to justify further action by the ICC. Second, the principle of complementarity must be satisfied; that is, national authorities are not conducting national proceedings or, if they are, they are unable or unwilling to carry out genuine investigations and prosecutions.[7]

At the conclusion of Phase 2 and, again at the end of Phase 3 should the examination proceed, the Situation Analysis Section prepares an internal report – an Article 5 report for Phase 2, referring to the Rome Statute article governing the ICC's subject matter jurisdiction, and an Article 17 report for Phase 3, referring to the Rome Statute provision governing admissibility – assessing the relevant criteria and submits the report to the prosecutor. If the examination proceeds further, at the conclusion of Phase 4, the Situation Analysis Section submits an Article 53(1) report. The de-

---

6   *Ibid.*, paras. 34–71, 80–83.

7   Given that at the pre-investigation stage there are no cases (understood to mean an "identified set of incidents, individuals, and charges"), the Office of the Prosecutor examines the admissibility of "potential cases that could be identified in the course of the preliminary examination based on the information available and that would likely arise from an investigation into the situation". *Ibid.*, para. 43.

cision of the prosecutor as to whether to open an investigation – or to seek authorization to investigate, as needed – is based on this report.[8]

Phases 2 through 4 are conducted sequentially, although there may be a certain fluidity in the OTP's approach, given that information relevant to more than one phase may be received by the OTP at any point.

Only decisions not to proceed with investigations following a State or Security Council referral, or where the OTP has based its decision solely on the interests of justice, are subject to judicial review. Review of the former must be requested by the State or Security Council, while the latter may be reviewed at the initiative of the Pre-Trial Chamber, and if reviewed, will only be effective if confirmed by the judges.[9]

35.2. Overcoming Inability and Unwillingness through Positive Complementarity

There are often several obstacles to effective national investigations and prosecutions of mass atrocity crimes. Tracking the language of the Rome Statute in Article 17, these challenges can be described as falling into one of two categories: unwillingness on the part of national authorities to genuinely investigate and prosecute, or an inability to do so.

Unwillingness refers to an absence of political will by national authorities to support genuine proceedings. Unwillingness, of course, can result in no proceedings at all. Where there are proceedings, Article 17(2) of the Rome Statute refers to the following aspects of unwillingness to conduct genuine proceedings: proceedings undertaken to shield the person concerned from justice; unjustifiable delay in proceedings that is inconsistent with an intent to bring the person concerned to justice; or proceedings lacking independence or impartiality, and conducted in a manner inconsistent with an intent to bring the person concerned to justice. The OTP has articulated several indicia it considers in assessing these different dimensions of unwillingness, ranging from too limited investigations to witness intimidation to political interference with investigations.[10]

Inability refers to a lack of capacity within a national jurisdiction to conduct genuine proceedings. The Rome Statute in Article 17(3) defines

---

[8]   *Ibid.*, paras. 81–83.
[9]   Rome Statute, Article 53(3)(a)–(b).
[10] Office of the Prosecutor, ICC, 2013, paras. 50–55, see *supra* note 3.

inability by reference to "a total or substantial collapse or unavailability of its national judicial system" that renders the State "unable to obtain the accused or the necessary evidence and testimony or otherwise unable to carry out its proceedings". The OTP has also developed a limited set of indicia for assessing inability; they are, among other things, "the absence of conditions of security for witnesses, investigators, prosecutors and judges or lack of adequate protection systems; the existence of laws that serve as a bar to domestic proceedings in the case at hand, such as amnesties, immunities or statutes of limitation; or the lack of adequate means for effective investigations and prosecutions".[11]

The definitions or indicia of 'unwillingness' and 'inability' contained in the Rome Statute and elaborated on in the OTP's policy statements are there to guide the court's exercise of its jurisdiction, that is, to determine which cases remain admissible before the ICC, and which, because of genuine national activity, are inadmissible.

It is important to note that difficulties encountered or imposed by national authorities and which may need to be addressed to ensure credible justice may go beyond the Rome Statute definitions of 'unwillingness' and 'inability'. The ICC appeals chamber, for example, in assessing an admissibility challenge mounted in the Abdullah Al-Senussi case by the government of Libya noted that the ICC "is not primarily called upon to decide whether in domestic proceedings certain requirements of human rights law or domestic law are being violated"; rather, in its view, admissibility is concerned with guarding against sham proceedings that lead to the evasion of justice. While violations of fair trial rights are not irrelevant to the court's consideration of admissibility, the appeals chamber held that only "violations of the rights of the suspect [that] are so egregious that the proceedings can no longer be regarded as being capable of providing any genuine form of justice to the suspect" will be, in the language of Article 17(2), "inconsistent with an intent to bring that person to justice".[12]

In addition, admissibility before the ICC is case-specific; the existence of national proceedings that could preclude ICC jurisdiction is de-

---

[11] *Ibid.*, paras. 56–57.

[12] See ICC, *Prosecutor v. Saif Al-Islam and Abdullah Al-Senussi*, Judgment on the appeal of Mr Abdullah Al-Senussi against the decision of Pre-Trial Chamber I of 11 October 2013 entitled "Decision on the admissibility of the case against Abdullah Al-Senussi", 24 July 2014, para. 230 (http://www.legal-tools.org/doc/ef20c7).

termined by reference to an actual (or, at the situation phase, potential) case, defined by the person charged (or groups of persons who could be charged) and the conduct charged (or the kinds of conduct that may be charged). Admissibility assessments before the ICC are "not a judgement or reflection on the national justice system as a whole".[13]

Nonetheless, the concepts of "unwillingness" and "inability" contained in the Rome Statute have been useful to broader efforts to map and address obstacles to national justice.[14] Such efforts to encourage and assist national investigations and prosecutions – which range from legislative assistance with capacity building to political dialogue for countering obstruction – have come to be known collectively as 'positive complementarity'. The first ICC prosecutor, Luis Moreno-Ocampo, introduced the concept of 'positive complementarity' – although he did not use that term – at a public hearing when he took office in June 2003, referring specifically to the role of the ICC.[15] The term has since evolved, particularly leading up to and after the 2010 ICC review conference in Kampala, Uganda. While momentum has been difficult to sustain since Kampala, the term has come to encompass initiatives by a range of actors to encourage national prosecutions of international crimes.[16]

---

[13]   Office of the Prosecutor, ICC, 2013, para. 46, see *supra* note 3.

[14]   See, for example, Open Society Justice Initiative, *International Crimes, Local Justice: A Handbook for Rule-of-Law Policymakers, Donors, and Implementers*, Open Society Foundations, New York, 2011; High Representative of the European Union for Foreign Affairs and Security Policy and European Commission, "Joint Staff Working Document on Advancing the Principle of Complementarity: Toolkit for Bridging the gap between international and national justice", SWD(2013)26final, 31 January 2013; Assembly of States Parties, ICC, "Report of the Bureau on Stocktaking: Complementarity", ICC-ASP/8/51, 18 March 2010.

[15]   Statement made by Mr. Luis Moreno-Ocampo, Ceremony for the solemn undertaking of the Chief Prosecutor of the International Criminal Court, The Hague,16 June 2003, p. 3; see also Office of the Prosecutor, ICC, "Paper on some policy issues before the Office of the Prosecutor", September 2003, p. 5 (http://www.legal-tools.org/doc/f53870/); Silvana Arbia, "The Three Year Plans and Strategies of the Registry in Respect of Complementarity for an Effective Rome Statute System of International Criminal Justice", Consultative Conference on International Criminal Justice, 2009 conference.

[16]   See Morten Bergsmo, Olympia Bekou, and Annika Jones, "Complementarity After Kampala: Capacity Building and the ICC's Legal Tools", in *Goettingen Journal of International Law*, 2010, vol. 2, pp. 793–803; Olympia Bekou, "The ICC and Capacity Building at the National Level", in Carsten Stahn (ed.), *The Law and Practice of the International Criminal Court*, Oxford University Press, Oxford, 2015, pp. 1252–54.

The ICC is now considered just one actor in this landscape, which also includes assistance between States, international organizations, and civil society groups.[17] Indeed, some ICC States Parties – citing budgetary or mandate concerns – have steered the ICC away from taking on a more robust role on positive complementarity.[18] To be sure, successfully shifting the political will and capacity to permit national prosecution of international crimes, particularly in circumstances of entrenched impunity, is likely to require strategic alliances between a number of different stakeholders. The ICC is not a development agency, and does not have resources to contribute directly to rule-of-law programming.

And yet, the role of the ICC could be central to positive complementarity in situations pending before the court.[19] In these situations, the OTP's engagement around justice with a range of domestic actors promises to be a powerful catalyst for national proceedings. Human Rights Watch's previous reporting and ongoing monitoring of situations under analysis, as well as its broader work on complementarity, suggest a few possible pathways in this regard. These relate to both overcoming political obstruction and addressing capacity gaps, and include:

- Focusing public debate through the media and within civil society on the need for accountability;

---

[17] This approach is clear from reports of the Assembly of States Parties facilitation on complementarity issued since the Kampala review conference. See, for example, Assembly of States Parties, ICC, "Report of the Bureau on stocktaking: Complementarity", 2010, see *supra* note 14.

[18] Unfortunately, the Assembly of States Parties – a natural ally – has not taken up this role. See Elizabeth Evenson and Alison Smith, "Completion, Legacy, and Complementarity at the ICC", in Carsten Stahn (ed.), 2015, p. 1274, see *supra* note 16.

[19] The Office of the Prosecutor's commitment in practice to positive complementarity has been much more evident in its preliminary examinations. But in ICC situations under investigation, the Court's clear knowledge of what is needed to try grave crimes coupled with its understanding of the capacity limitations in countries where it is active means it is well placed to help donor states efficiently identify existing gaps and target their assistance to strengthening national prosecutions. Court staff can also directly lend expertise and, subject to protecting witnesses and other vulnerable sources, the Office of the Prosecutor may be able to share information gathered during investigations, including non-confidential material and broad pattern analysis of crimes. Field-based staff, in particular, may be particularly well-placed to broker positive complementarity efforts through relationships between national authorities and rule-of-law actors.

- Serving as a source of sustained pressure on domestic authorities to show results in domestic proceedings;

- Highlighting to international partners the importance of including accountability in political dialogue with domestic authorities;

- Equipping human rights activists with information derived from the OTP's analysis, strengthening advocacy around justice; and

- Identifying weaknesses in domestic proceedings, to prompt increased efforts by government authorities and assistance, where relevant, by international partners.[20]

---

[20] Other authors have also addressed strategies available to the Office of the Prosecutor to advance positive complementarity, including several authors in this volume. William Burke-White's article was among the first on positive complementarity, although not specific to the preliminary examination phase, see William Burke-White, "Proactive Complementarity: The ICC and National Courts in the Rome System of International Justice", in *Harvard International Law Journal*, 2008, vol. 49, pp. 53–108; see also Carsten Stahn, "Complementarity: A Tale of Two Notions", in *Criminal Law Forum*, 2008, vol. 19, pp. 87–113; Carsten Stahn, "Taking Complementarity Seriously", in Carsten Stahn and Mohamed M. El Zeidy, *The International Criminal Court and Complementarity: From Theory to Practice*, Cambridge University Press, Cambridge, 2011, pp. 233–82; Justine Tiller, "The ICC Prosecutor and Positive Complementarity: Strengthening the Rule of Law?", in *International Criminal Law Review*, 2013, vol. 13, pp. 507–91. Mark Kersten and Thomas Obel Hansen have sought to further theorize the mechanisms through which the Office of the Prosecutor can influence national actors in preliminary examinations, whether to bring about proceedings or to deter abuses. Of them, Kersten emphasizes, as we do, the importance of strategic alliances and the Office of the Prosecutor taking a bolder approach with governments, under certain circumstances: see Mark Kersten, "Casting a Larger Shadow: Premeditated Madness, the International Criminal Court, and Preliminary Examinations", in Morten Bergsmo and Carsten Stahn (ed.), *Quality Control in Preliminary Examination: Volume 2*, Torkel Opsahl Academic EPublisher, Brussels, 2018, chap. 33; Obel Hanson, whose study of the Iraq/United Kingdom situation is also included in this volume, while citing some exceptions, notes that, generally, there have been "few existing studies [to] examine the extent to which this goal is being effectively pursued by the Office of the Prosecutor at the preliminary examination phase and how ICC preliminary examinations may affect national authorities' commitment to domestic accountability processes and otherwise impact the scope, nature, and conduct of such process", see Thomas Obel Hansen, "The Policy Paper on Preliminary Examinations: Ending Impunity Through 'Positive Complementarity'?", Transitional Justice Institute Research Paper No. 17-01, 22 March 2017 (on file with the author). One of the exceptions cited by Hansen is Christine Björk and Justine Goerbertus, "Complementarity in Action: The Role of Civil Society and the ICC Ruel of Law Strengthening in Kenya", in *Yale Human Rights and Development Journal*, 2014, vol. 14, pp. 205–29. Other authors have examined what approach the Office of the Prosecutor should take to its legal analysis during the preliminary examination in order to advance complementarity. See Paul Seils, "Putting Complementarity in its Place", in

While these strategies are shared, for the most part, with other complementarity actors, the OTP's leverage – that is, that it can open investigations where national authorities fail to act and where it has jurisdiction – is unique.

35.3. OTP's Approach to Encouraging National Proceedings in Preliminary Examinations

As already indicated above, during its preliminary examinations, "[w]here potential cases falling within the jurisdiction of the Court have been identified, the Office [of the Prosecutor] will seek to encourage, where feasible, genuine national investigations and prosecutions by the States concerned in relation to these crimes".[21]

As the language makes clear, this is not an unqualified commitment to encouraging national proceedings in every circumstance. The OTP's practice is to do so "where feasible", and, in addition, to focus, for the most part, on situations in Phase 3, that is, only after the OTP has concluded in Phase 2 that a reasonable basis exists to believe that crimes within the ICC's jurisdiction have been committed. This current statement of policy and practice reflects an evolution in the OTP's approach, part of its overall consolidated practice in situations under analysis, memorialised in its 2013 "Policy on Preliminary Examinations".[22]

Where it does seek to encourage national proceedings, the OTP has identified a number of different forms of engagement: "report[ing] on its monitoring activities, send[ing] in-country missions, request[ing] information on proceedings, hold[ing] consultations with national authorities as well as with intergovernmental and non-governmental organisations, participat[ing] in awareness-raising activities on the ICC, exchang[ing] lessons learned and best practices to support domestic investigative and

---

Carsten Stahn (ed.), 2015, pp. 305–27, see *supra* note 16. Seils has also written a handbook with guidance for national prosecutors seeking to avoid an ICC intervention, see International Center for Transitional Justice, *Handbook on Complementarity: An Introduction to the Role of National Courts and the ICC in Prosecuting International Crimes*, 2016, p. 79.

21 Office of the Prosecutor, ICC, 2013, para. 101, see *supra* note 3.

22 See also Office of the Prosecutor, ICC, "Results of the Strategic Plan (June 2012-2015)", annex 1 to "Strategic Plan 2016-2018", 6 July 2015, para. 18 (http://www.legal-tools.org/doc/7ae957/).

prosecutorial strategies, and assist[ing] relevant stakeholders to identify pending impunity gaps and the scope for possible remedial measures".[23]

35.4. Key Challenges

Our observation of the OTP's practice and our research for our forthcoming report highlight several consistent challenges in strengthening the influence of the OTP with national authorities.

35.4.1. Context Matters

It is clear that context will influence the likelihood of successful positive complementarity activities by the OTP. Context here includes the underlying alleged crime base; public demand for accountability, where high public interest providing more fertile ground for engagement; the availability of other partners on complementarity, particularly among international donors; and, most significant of all, the posture of national authorities. The OTP can take steps to influence context – in fact, that is the entire premise of positive complementarity strategies – but there will be objective challenges to its ability to do so. To a certain extent, it has to take situations as it finds them.

That context matters is an obvious point, but it may have some implications for practice.

In Human Rights Watch's 2011 report on OTP practice in preliminary examinations, we criticized the appearance of inconsistent treatment of situations, which tended to undermine the OTP's credibility with potential complementarity partners and its leverage with national authorities. Inconsistency can be problematic, but when it comes to having an impact on national justice efforts, differences in context mean that there may be

---

[23] Office of the Prosecutor, ICC, 2013, para. 102, see *supra* note 3. A number of the Office of the Prosecutor's activities during the preliminary examination – in particular, collecting information and consultations with national authorities and other stakeholders with an informed perspective on the commission of crimes or the status of national proceedings – relate to the primary aim of the preliminary examination, that is, the determination as to whether or not an ICC investigation in a given situation is warranted. Regular reporting also leads to increased transparency, which serves an important end: responding to interests of affected communities in knowing the status and eventual outcome of the Office of the Prosecutor's preliminary examination. Increased public understanding of the criteria guiding the Office of the Prosecutor's decision-making process also should help combat accusations of selectivity or bias in the court's investigations.

differences in the OTP's approach. How the OTP can navigate the need for tailored approaches that give rise to perceptions of inconsistent treatment and, therefore, raise credibility risks may be a significant challenge.

35.4.2. Importance of Strategic Alliances

Given the steep obstacles to national justice, it is likely that the OTP cannot go alone and will have more influence where its efforts are amplified by others, including local and international non-governmental actors, international donors, and intergovernmental partners, like the UN or regional organizations. Under some circumstances, the OTP's engagement with these other actors can stimulate collective efforts; in other circumstances, these actors may need to proactively develop approaches that take into account the potential to make us of the preliminary examination as a pressure point on national justice efforts. Depending on context, the media, too, can be an important source of attention to the issue of accountability.

35.4.3. Passive v. Active Effects

To what extent does the OTP need active strategies around positive complementarity or is the existence of the preliminary examination itself sufficient for impact? The emphasis in our research is on the former – what steps the OTP can take to actively increase its impact. But this is not to overlook the possibility of more passive effects.

The strength of such passive effects may have some implications for assessing the OTP's current phased approach to preliminary examinations. The OTP's current focus on encouraging national proceedings largely after moving from Phase 2 to Phase 3 has significant advantages, in that it limits the appearance of OTP engagement as amounting to an empty threat, a concern we had raised in our 2011 report.[24] At the same time, a delay may also have opportunity costs, given uncertainty as to how long moving from Phase 2 to Phase 3 may take (on the absence of timelines, see below). To the extent there are passive effects even in the absence of active strategies, however, this may provide a greater flexibility and momentum on complementarity than the division between Phase 2 and Phase 3 suggests.

---

[24] See Human Rights Watch, 2011, Part III.D, see *supra* note 1.

35.4.4. Effects of the ICC's Admissibility Regime and OTP's Prosecutorial Policies

As noted above, the ICC is a court of last resort. Under the principle of complementarity, cases are only admissible before the ICC where national authorities have not conducted genuine domestic proceedings.

On the one hand, that the ICC's jurisdiction is complementary to domestic jurisdiction is what, in the first place, makes space available during the preliminary examination to seek to catalyse national proceedings. Where States have an interest in avoiding the ICC's intervention, they can do so by conducting national proceedings. This can mean that the OTP's leverage over national authorities is or can be made to be significant.[25]

On the other hand, however, the ICC's complementary jurisdiction means that the OTP will need to be prepared to prove to the judges that there are no national proceedings that would render potential cases inadmissible. Efforts by the OTP to stimulate national proceedings can produce domestic activity that will make it more difficult for the OTP to meet this burden. Where that activity leads to genuine national proceedings, this is positive. But there is an equal risk of domestic authorities producing a certain amount of activity – opening of case files and limited investigative steps – to starve off ICC intervention, but without following through to prosecutions.

In this scenario, the preliminary examination period may be manipulated by national authorities, leaving it in limbo: the domestic activity may be too much to warrant OTP actions, but too little to close out the preliminary examination in deference to genuine national proceedings. As a result, ICC action could be delayed where it is ultimately needed, both making it more difficult to investigate long after crimes are committed and deferring the access of victims to justice.

---

[25] It is important to note, however, that the degree to which states care about avoiding an ICC intervention is highly contingent on context. ICC states parties through their membership in the ICC may have a stronger incentive to carry out national prosecutions than non-states parties that are the subject of Security Council referrals. ICC states parties may even already have relevant national legislation (laws embodying the provisions of the Rome Statute through 'implementation' of the treaty) and, through the ratification and implementation processes, pro-accountability constituencies within parliament or civil society.

This catch-22 applies, primarily, to situations where the OTP would need to act *proprio motu* under Article 15 to open investigations. For these investigations, the OTP needs to seek authorization from the court's judges, which includes a positive determination that there are no national proceedings that would render potential cases inadmissible. The judges' remit to look at the admissibility of potential cases – which has been defined as the "groups of persons involved that are likely to be the focus of an investigation for the purpose of shaping the future case(s); and ... the crimes within the jurisdiction of the Court allegedly committed during the incidents that are likely to be the focus of an investigation for the purpose of shaping the future case(s)"[26] – means that there is a wide scope of national investigative activity that could be deemed to render ICC action impermissible.[27] Again, where this serves to promote genuine national cases, this is a strength of the ICC system. But it can offer national authorities space to manipulate the admissibility regime.

This was perhaps a particular risk in the court's earliest years. As with many aspects of the Rome Statute system, the court's case law on complementarity is a work in progress. It may have been difficult for the OTP to predict just what it would need to show the judges to satisfy the statute's admissibility requirements. It was only with the first Article 15 investigation, in Kenya in 2010, where judges had the opportunity to clarify what admissibility would look like at this phase of proceedings, namely, that it would be measured with regard to potential cases, rather than a more abstract assessment of the situation as a whole. The requisite gravity of potential cases – the other admissibility requirement – continues to be debated.[28]

---

[26] ICC, Situation in the Republic of Kenya, Decision Pursuant to Article 15 of the Rome Statute on the Authorization of an Investigation into the Situation in the Republic of Kenya, 31 March 2010, para. 50 (http://www.legal-tools.org/doc/338a6f/).

[27] Once specific charges are pressed against specific individuals, the court's case law invokes a 'same person, same conduct' test, requiring a successful challenge to admissibility to show domestic activity with regard to the same incidents and persons against whom the prosecutor seeks to press charges. For an overview of the ICC's case law on complementarity, see Seils, 2016, Part V, see *supra* note 20; see also, Carsten Stahn, "Admissibility Challenges Before the ICC: From Quasi-Primacy to Qualified Deference", in Stahn (ed.), 2015, pp. 228–59, see supra note 16.

[28] See, for example, ICC, *Situation on the Registered Vessels of the Union of the Comoros et al.*, Decision on the request of the Union of the Comoros to review the Prosecutor's decision not to initiate an investigation, 16 July 2015 (http://www.legal-tools.org/doc/2f876c/).

The OTP needs to carefully determine when deferring to national authorities and deploying positive complementarity strategies is the right choice, and when this will only delay ICC action without any reasonable prospect of national justice. Getting that call right and avoiding instrumentalization is perhaps the OTP's paramount challenge when it comes to encouraging national proceedings in situations under analysis.

Finally, as indicated above, ICC judges have not interpreted the court's admissibility regime in a manner that seeks to safeguard the quality of national justice. Their examination of the 'genuineness' of proceedings aims at ensuring that proceedings are not undertaken to shield perpetrators from justice, rather than a concern for protecting the fair trial rights of defendants, in all but the most egregious circumstances. Whether the OTP ought to consider increasing its focus on the quality of these proceedings as a matter of policy may be a relevant question for future consideration.

35.4.5. Absence of Timelines

The ICC's legal texts do not prescribe any timeline for taking decisions regarding preliminary examinations. The absence of timelines can provide a helpful flexibility to the OTP, when it comes to carrying out its analysis, as well as implementing its policy commitment to encourage domestic proceedings; the time necessary to catalyse national proceedings is likely to vary greatly depending on context.[29]

---

[29] The Office of the Prosecutor has provided some generic guidance on the length of Phases 1–2 and 4, but when it comes to Phase 3, has stated that the phase "often entails the assessment of national proceedings which inevitably makes it impossible to establish a definite duration of this phase". See Assembly of States Parties, ICC, "Resource justification for mandated activities", annex 2 to "Report of the Court on the Basic Size of the Office of the Prosecutor", ICC-ASP/14/21, 17 September 2015, p. 37. Human Rights Watch has previously recommended that the Office of the Prosecutor develop general guidance on how long preliminary examinations can be expected to take. A certain flexibility, of course, is also necessary for the primary purpose of the preliminary examination, that is, to reach a decision as to whether an ICC investigation is merited because the time required for assessing the article 53(1) factors is likely to vary from situation to situation. For example, information about alleged crimes may be difficult to obtain. And a determination as to complementarity may be more straightforward where there is a complete absence of national proceedings as opposed to where there are proceedings that need to be evaluated for their relevancy and genuineness. See Human Rights Watch, 2011, Part III.C, IV, see *supra* note 1.

The absence of timelines, however, could exacerbate some of the risks identified above. That is, the OTP cannot resort to pre-set timelines in order to put national authorities under pressure to produce real results, nor can it rely on these timelines to help it make crucial and difficult determinations regarding whether prospects for national investigations are sufficient to justify deferring ICC action. In addition, the OTP's ability to influence national authorities can be amplified through civil society actions. But civil society groups may lose confidence in the OTP's process due to the prolonged nature of preliminary examinations. Strategies to increase transparency with these key partners may be critical to addressing this challenge.

35.4.6. Maintaining Leverage and the Use of Publicity

While the fact that a situation may come before the ICC can initially provide an incentive for national authorities to start their own investigations, that leverage is likely to wane with the passage of time. Authorities can become desensitized to impending ICC action. And with a number of pending situations being analysed simultaneously by the OTP, with limited resources (see below) national authorities may judge that the chances a situation will be selected for investigation do not warrant changes in behaviour.

In our 2011 report, following a period in which the OTP sought to raise the public profile of preliminary examinations, Human Rights Watch welcomed increased transparency, but expressed some concern that certain kinds of publicity could actually undermine, rather than sustain leverage with national authorities.[30] One risk we noted is that where the OTP's preliminary examination is protracted, as has often been the case, repeated public statements but no apparent action on investigations can give rise to perceptions of the ICC as a paper tiger, lessening the weight future statements of possible ICC action may carry.[31]

---

[30] We also noted that there were limits to the resources the Office of the Prosecutor had available, and therefore it needed to strike a proper balance between the primary aim of reaching a decision as to whether or not to open an investigation, and efforts, including increased publicity aimed at positive complementarity. This increase in publicity also related to potential deterrent effects. *Ibid.*, Part II.

[31] *Ibid.*, Part IV.

Publicity can be a powerful and important medium to maximize leverage on national authorities, and to a certain extent, these risks are inherent to its use. At the time, we recommended a few steps the OTP could take in its public statements on preliminary examinations to mitigate these risks. First, we called on the OTP to increase its regular reporting on its substantive assessment of the Article 53(1) factors – including admissibility – in pending situations under analysis. Among other things, we thought this would help demonstrate more credibly that the OTP is actually proceeding with the analysis, and could have helped counteract perceptions of what appeared at that time to be an inconsistent treatment of different situations, with some receiving considerable public attention or public missions by the OTP, and others comparatively little. Second, we recommended that public statements provide additional context about the preliminary examination process, and not go beyond where the OTP's own examination stands, in order to inform and manage expectations as to the prospects of ICC action. Third, we recommended that the OTP take care to avoid improperly publicizing aspects of a possible investigation – such as the names of possible suspects – in a manner that could undermine the due process rights of potential accused or the reputation of others and call into question the impartiality of any subsequent investigation.[32]

The OTP's current approach to publicity in preliminary examinations has since changed, and incorporates some of these recommendations.

First, while the OTP issued a draft policy on preliminary examinations in 2010, it finalized the policy in 2013, setting out in detail the principles and processes governing situations under analysis. It also now publicly identifies on the ICC's website and other public materials where a situation falls in the four-phased approach, which is also explained in that policy paper.[33]

Second, it has also increased substantive reporting on its preliminary examinations. In December 2011, the OTP issued its first annual report spanning all preliminary examination activities over the previous year. These annual reports have become increasingly more detailed with

---

[32]   *Ibid.*, Part IV.
[33]   See ICC, "Preliminary Examinations" (available on its web site).

each year. In 2012, the OTP also issued a lengthy 'interim report' on Colombia, covering both subject matter and admissibility issues.[34]

The OTP has also made public an internal Article 5 report when moving from one phase to the next (Nigeria, Phase 2 to Phase 3). Decisions not to move a situation under analysis forward into the next phase or to open an investigation – because the OTP considers that the legal criteria are not met – are also communicated publicly, and since 2013 have been accompanied by publication of the relevant report (to date, an Article 5 report for South Korea and Honduras, and an Article 53(1)) report for Comoros). Decisions to open investigations in non-*proprio motu* cases have been accompanied by a public Article 53(1) report since 2013 (Mali and CAR II).

35.4.7. Limited Resources

At this writing, there are 13 staff members within the Situation Analysis Section. Of these 13 positions, two are at the P-1 level, six are at the P-2 level, four are at the P-3 level, and one position is at the P-5 level. This staffing size falls below the 17 staff members the OTP has indicated ought to be the "basic size" of the Situation Analysis Section.[35]

But even with 17 staff members, by the OTP's calculations this would translate into an average of 1.5 full-time P-2 or P-3 analysts to work on each situation, assuming an average of nine preliminary examinations at any given point of time. These 1.5 staff members, with support from P-1 analysts and under the supervision of the P-5 head of section, are responsible for a wide range of activities in their assigned situations – from analysis necessary to support determinations regarding investigations, to public information, to efforts to deter crimes or encourage na-

---

[34] These reports are available from the Court's web site, *ibid.*

[35] Assembly of States Parties, ICC, "Report of the Court on the Basic Size of the Office of the Prosecutor", ICC-ASP/14/21, 17 September 2015, para. 19. The "basic size" of the Office of the Prosecutor, presented to ICC member countries in 2015, is the size it considers necessary "not only [to] ensure that the Office attains a staffing size which is stable for the foreseeable future, but also one with sufficient depth to absorb new demands without having to continue the present unsustainable practice of repeatedly postponing new investigations which must be pursued in accordance with the Office's mandate, or constantly stripping ongoing activities of critical resources so as to staff the highest prioritised activities". *Ibid.*, para. 3.

tional proceedings, along with the associated field missions, consultations, and other activities necessary to support these functions.[36]

Particularly in preliminary examinations with widespread allegations of crimes, extending over a long temporal period, or where significant national proceedings are under way, the OTP's resources are highly limited as compared to the quantity of needed analysis, let alone the steps that may be necessary to engage national authorities in a way that can effectively catalyse national prosecutions. These resources are also limited as compared to the diplomatic or resources that some governments are likely to allocate to engage with the OTP.

These limited resources give reason to pause in considering what strategies the OTP can reasonably be expected to pursue on positive complementarity. It is worth bearing in mind that these strategies are, appropriately, only secondary to the Situation Analysis Section's primary role of analysis to support decisions regarding whether or not to open ICC investigations.

---

[36] *Ibid.*, paras. 14–21.

INDEX

A

accessory liability, 182, 183, 196

admissibility, 46, 49, 50, 55, 74, 87, 88, 92, 101, 102, 116, 117, 120, 133, 156, 167, 196, 198, 215, 217–219, 224, 238, 242, 259, 263, 264, 276, 279, 302, 324, 332, 373, 375, 376, 379, 403, 414, 419, 423, 442, 459, 470, 471, 473, 489, 490, 492–496, 501–503, 509, 538, 556, 558, 577, 585, 602, 603, 606, 608, 610, 614, 618, 620, 623, 626, 661, 683, 684, 695, 696, 701, 705, 706, 708, 715, 717, 725, 726, 728, 729

Afghanistan, 88, 89, 103, 106, 115, 154, 182, 205–211, 235, 275, 276, 283–287, 330, 332, 333, 342, 353, 355, 356, 367, 383, 384, 396, 457, 486, 494, 499, 529, 531, 533, 560, 622, 658, 660, 661, 668, 670, 673–675, 678, 679

African Union, 60, 81, 283, 359, 363, 365, 673

aggression, 181–183, 195, 201, 210, 262, 605, 705

aiding and abetting, 181–183, 195-201, 203, 204

amicus curiae, 33, 146, 545, 554, 555, 559, 564, 566–568, 574–586

Article 15 communication, 45, 46, 87, 88, 95, 96, 98, 138, 141, 148, 171, 173, 174, 177, 196, 222, 239, 258, 260, 268, 269, 272, 273, 275, 277–279, 288, 297, 303, 307, 309, 310, 315, 323, 327–329, 335, 339, 340, 342, 344, 345, 348, 350, 352, 361, 368, 377, 384–387, 389, 467, 513, 518, 534, 535, 537, 540–543, 546, 547, 549, 554–570, 574–586, 603, 623, 625, 639–642, 650, 653, 670, 679, 698, 699, 701, 702, 714

Assembly of States Parties, 33, 37, 39, 40, 46, 47, 66, 87, 93, 100, 109, 122, 132, 144, 235, 236, 262, 304, 321, 335, 340–342, 345, 351, 354, 368, 374, 379, 380, 397, 451, 460, 463, 602, 664, 697, 718, 719, 726, 729

B

Bensouda, Fatou, 48, 81, 89, 99, 101, 103, 105, 107, 109, 110, 120, 122, 123, 128, 135, 136, 272, 273, 284, 286, 287, 331, 340, 343–345, 350, 354, 360, 361, 365, 368, 369, 418, 447, 458, 460, 561, 562, 570, 602, 628, 656, 673, 704

Burundi, 81, 110, 214, 221, 224, 225, 235, 245, 249, 330, 331, 360, 373, 377–380, 486, 487, 496, 559, 560, 579, 622, 623, 702

United Nations Independent Investigation on Burundi, 378–380

C

case selection and prioritization, 36, 48, 49, 67, 100, 105, 152, 155, 197, 241, 249, 282, 491, 492, 523–526, 532

Central African Republic, 43, 113–115, 133, 184, 204, 216, 235, 242, 280, 302, 330, 341, 343, 344, 350, 351, 360, 397, 411, 414, 415, 418–420, 433–435, 440, 455, 458, 467, 538, 548, 549, 573, 590, 603, 614, 616, 622, 624, 672, 729

children, 29, 36, 48, 157, 158, 190, 241, 405, 582, 593, 601, 613, 632–653

civil law, 30, 290, 291, 299, 327, 607

civil society, 37, 106, 107, 138, 148, 172–174, 252, 259, 265, 278, 298, 408, 409, 475, 482, 516, 517, 521–523, 525–537, 540–551, 553–555, 557, 558, 560–565, 568, 569, 574, 576, 578–581, 583, 584, 586, 670, 677, 683, 690, 700, 711, 719, 724, 727

Coalition for the ICC, 275, 280, 409, 410, 528, 553, 581

Colombia, 88, 89, 103, 134–136, 210, 211, 235, 273–275, 283, 284, 289, 306, 330,

342, 348, 349, 351, 352, 355, 370,
373–375, 457, 503, 536, 537, 549–551,
560, 590, 608–610, 616, 622, 623, 656,
659, 660, 666, 677, 697, 712, 729
FARC, 135, 273, 274
Special Jurisdiction for Peace, 135
common law, 30, 69, 83, 98, 327, 607
Comoros, 49, 88, 113, 115–120, 133, 139,
145, 214, 215, 218, 223, 224, 228, 237,
244–246, 248, 251, 281, 289, 313, 330,
333–336, 345, 346, 351, 356, 449, 455,
456, 458, 472, 486, 488, 491, 493, 500,
502, 539, 540, 544, 545, 570, 571, 580,
622, 661, 725, 729
complementarity, 46, 51, 70, 80, 87, 88,
101, 102, 104, 132, 149, 153, 156, 185,
196, 217, 219, 224, 237, 255–257, 263,
267, 268, 274, 290, 303, 306, 310–312,
321, 325, 336, 374, 375, 379, 396, 403,
404, 414, 415, 457, 478, 489, 492, 494,
495, 503, 522, 536, 538, 556, 557, 591,
592, 602, 603, 606, 607, 609, 620–623,
629, 633, 640, 647, 655, 657, 660, 664,
666, 684, 705–707, 711–713, 715,
718–727, 730
positive, 132, 303, 374, 375, 640, 718–
720, 722
shared, 629
Congo, 7, 28, 31, 43, 55, 62, 110, 113, 114,
118, 157, 178, 184, 200–203, 205, 220,
221, 228, 231, 235, 241, 280, 282, 283,
287, 288, 302, 330, 396, 397, 402, 406,
432, 438, 448, 452, 455, 458, 487, 498,
538, 542, 545, 547, 567, 577, 582, 589,
590, 593, 595, 596, 603, 619, 622, 624,
672
consequentialism, 2, 3, 8, 9, 11, 12, 19, 29,
34, 36, 38, 39, 49, 50, 52, 56–61, 63,
64, 66, 69, 71, 75, 103, 104, 119, 121,
132, 145
Convention on the Rights of the Child,
634–636, 638, 643–646, 648–650, 653
Côte d'Ivoire, 31, 47, 91, 178, 184, 185,
214, 217, 219–222, 225, 234, 235, 242,
244, 248, 249, 271, 272, 288, 325, 330,
334, 342, 360, 389, 396, 397, 401, 403,
425, 429–432, 440, 444, 445, 448, 458,
467, 484, 486, 488, 492–495, 499,

507–509, 512–515, 538, 559, 579, 603,
624, 642, 666
Crimea, 285, 286, 378, 381

D

Darfur, 31, 117, 225, 231, 235, 280, 330,
359, 363, 381, 389, 411, 414–416, 420,
422, 436, 437, 440, 578, 603, 622
deontology, 2, 3, 8–12, 19, 29–32, 34–36,
38, 39, 54, 57, 59–61, 64–66, 72, 75
deterrence, 12, 59, 64, 67, 105, 161, 162,
175, 185, 256, 257, 268, 289, 290, 306,
311, 321, 358, 362, 371, 372, 383, 392,
524, 612, 663, 665, 732

E

European Centre for Law and Justice, 580
European Court of Human Rights, 227,
408, 531, 575
expressivism, 20, 48, 69, 612, 613, 732
Extraordinary Chambers in the Courts of
Cambodia, 28, 291, 293–296, 299, 305,
308, 326
Co-Investigating Judge, 294–296, 305

F

fair trial, 6
fairness
distributive, 8
procedural, 8, 10, 11, 60, 293, 295
substantive, 7
feminism, 590–593, 596, 599, 601, 605,
609, 613, 617, 620–622, 626–629

G

Gabon, 88, 235, 330, 448, 483, 512, 514,
516, 517, 622
Gbagbo, Laurent, 31, 39, 271, 272, 399,
432, 445, 451, 452, 469, 484, 492,
507–509, 512–516, 667
gender, 29, 36, 48, 157, 160, 241, 265,
288, 298, 426, 581, 589–593, 597–601,
605, 610–613, 619–623, 626–628, 635,
642, 644, 645, 655, 699

Q

R

434, 441–443, 446, 454–455, 461,
464, 472–473, 476, 478, 522, 537–
540, 543–544, 546, 554, 556–557,
559, 569, 578, 580, 583, 603, 605,
615, 639, 664–665, 669, 671–672,
680, 696, 698, 702–703, 713–714,
716, 724
UN Independent Investigation on
Burundi. See Burundi
United States, 3, 19, 32, 35, 62, 78, 79, 90,
136, 149, 172, 183, 185, 187, 189,
191–193, 195, 201, 206–211, 221, 272,
275, 285, 290, 291, 316, 367, 381, 443,
444, 496, 511, 529–531, 566, 598, 644,
657, 658, 668–676, 679, 686–689
Central Intelligence Agency, 106, 285,
384, 529, 530, 674, 687, 688
Defense Security Cooperation Agency,
209
universal jurisdiction. See jurisdiction:
universal

V

Venezuela, 91, 106, 107, 235, 273, 283,
330, 344, 350, 352, 560, 570, 598, 622,
661
victim, 11, 20, 29, 33, 36, 40, 43, 54, 55,
57, 67–71, 75, 92, 99, 104, 106, 111,

116, 117, 129, 131–135, 138, 141, 146,
151, 156, 157, 161, 170, 171, 173, 176,
177, 198, 211, 230, 236, 241, 247, 256,
264–266, 269, 274, 277, 278, 289, 290,
292, 294, 296, 298, 299, 308, 309, 312,
315, 357, 365, 367, 383, 390, 401, 402,
409, 410, 424, 425, 428, 437, 469, 470,
475, 477, 478, 481, 482, 497, 505,
511–513, 516–518, 521–529, 531–535,
537, 540–549, 553, 558, 565, 567, 569,
574, 577, 578, 581–584, 586, 593–595,
601, 609, 610, 614, 615, 617, 619, 621,
622, 624, 626–628, 632, 633, 635, 639,
641, 642, 645, 646, 648, 650–653, 675,
707, 712, 724
victims
interests, 85, 133, 198, 261, 264, 276,
296, 308, 315, 316, 524, 614, 628,
638, 646, 652, 708, 715
Vienna Convention on the Law of Treaties,
220, 462, 463, 465, 466

W

Women's Initiatives for Gender Justice,
567, 581, 582
World Bank, 181, 183, 184, 186, 188,
193–195

TOAEP TEAM

Editors

Antonio Angotti, Editor
Olympia Bekou, Editor
Mats Benestad, Editor
Morten Bergsmo, Editor-in-Chief
Alf Butenschøn Skre, Senior Executive Editor
Eleni Chaitidou, Editor
CHAN Ho Shing Icarus, Editor
CHEAH Wui Ling, Editor
FAN Yuwen, Editor
Manek Minhas, Editor
Gareth Richards, Senior Editor
Nikolaus Scheffel, Editor
SIN Ngok Shek, Editor
SONG Tianying, Editor
Moritz Thörner, Editor
ZHANG Yueyao, Editor

Editorial Assistants

Pauline Brosch
Marquise Lee Houle
Genevieve Zingg

Law of the Future Series Co-Editors

Dr. Alexander (Sam) Muller
Professor Larry Cata Backer
Professor Stavros Zouridis

Nuremberg Academy Series Editor

Dr. Viviane Dittrich, Deputy Director, International Nuremberg Principles Academy

Scientific Advisers

Professor Danesh Sarooshi, Principal Scientific Adviser for International Law
Professor Andreas Zimmermann, Principal Scientific Adviser for Public International Law
Professor Kai Ambos, Principal Scientific Adviser for International Criminal Law
Dr.h.c. Asbjørn Eide, Principal Scientific Adviser for International Human Rights Law

Editorial Board

Dr. Xabier Agirre, International Criminal Court
Dr. Claudia Angermaier, Austrian judiciary
Ms. Neela Badami, Narasappa, Doraswamy and Raja

OTHER VOLUMES IN THE PUBLICATION SERIES

Morten Bergsmo, Mads Harlem and Nobuo Hayashi (editors):
Importing Core International Crimes into National Law
Torkel Opsahl Academic EPublisher
Oslo, 2010
FICHL Publication Series No. 1 (Second Edition, 2010)
ISBN: 978-82-93081-00-5

Nobuo Hayashi (editor):
National Military Manuals on the Law of Armed Conflict
Torkel Opsahl Academic EPublisher
Oslo, 2010
FICHL Publication Series No. 2 (Second Edition, 2010)
ISBN: 978-82-93081-02-9

Morten Bergsmo, Kjetil Helvig, Ilia Utmelidze and Gorana Žagovec:
The Backlog of Core International Crimes Case Files in Bosnia and Herzegovina
Torkel Opsahl Academic EPublisher
Oslo, 2010
FICHL Publication Series No. 3 (Second Edition, 2010)
ISBN: 978-82-93081-04-3

Morten Bergsmo (editor):
Criteria for Prioritizing and Selecting Core International Crimes Cases
Torkel Opsahl Academic EPublisher
Oslo, 2010
FICHL Publication Series No. 4 (Second Edition, 2010)
ISBN: 978-82-93081-06-7

Morten Bergsmo and Pablo Kalmanovitz (editors):
Law in Peace Negotiations
Torkel Opsahl Academic EPublisher
Oslo, 2010
FICHL Publication Series No. 5 (Second Edition, 2010)
ISBN: 978-82-93081-08-1

Morten Bergsmo, César Rodríguez Garavito, Pablo Kalmanovitz and Maria Paula Saffon (editors):
Distributive Justice in Transitions
Torkel Opsahl Academic EPublisher
Oslo, 2010
FICHL Publication Series No. 6 (2010)
ISBN: 978-82-93081-12-8

Morten Bergsmo, César Rodriguez-Garavito, Pablo Kalmanovitz and Maria Paula Saffon (editors):
Justicia Distributiva en Sociedades en Transición
Torkel Opsahl Academic EPublisher
Oslo, 2012
FICHL Publication Series No. 6 (2012)
ISBN: 978-82-93081-10-4

Morten Bergsmo (editor):
Complementarity and the Exercise of Universal Jurisdiction for Core International Crimes
Torkel Opsahl Academic EPublisher
Oslo, 2010
FICHL Publication Series No. 7 (2010)
ISBN: 978-82-93081-14-2

Morten Bergsmo (editor):
Active Complementarity: Legal Information Transfer
Torkel Opsahl Academic EPublisher
Oslo, 2011
FICHL Publication Series No. 8 (2011)
ISBN print: 978-82-93081-56-2
ISBN e-book: 978-82-93081-55-5

Morten Bergsmo (editor):
Abbreviated Criminal Procedures for Core International Crimes
Torkel Opsahl Academic EPublisher
Brussels, 2017
FICHL Publication Series No. 9 (2018)
ISBN print: 978-82-93081-20-3
ISBN e-book: 978-82-8348-104-4

Sam Muller, Stavros Zouridis, Morly Frishman and Laura Kistemaker (editors):
The Law of the Future and the Future of Law
Torkel Opsahl Academic EPublisher
Oslo, 2010
FICHL Publication Series No. 11 (2011)
ISBN: 978-82-93081-27-2

Morten Bergsmo, Alf Butenschøn Skre and Elisabeth J. Wood (editors):
Understanding and Proving International Sex Crimes
Torkel Opsahl Academic EPublisher
Beijing, 2012
FICHL Publication Series No. 12 (2012)
ISBN: 978-82-93081-29-6

Morten Bergsmo (editor):
Thematic Prosecution of International Sex Crimes
Torkel Opsahl Academic EPublisher
Beijing, 2012
FICHL Publication Series No. 13 (2012)
ISBN: 978-82-93081-31-9

Terje Einarsen:
The Concept of Universal Crimes in International Law
Torkel Opsahl Academic EPublisher
Oslo, 2012
FICHL Publication Series No. 14 (2012)
ISBN: 978-82-93081-33-3

莫滕·伯格斯默 凌岩(主编):
国家主权与国际刑法
Torkel Opsahl Academic EPublisher
Beijing, 2012
FICHL Publication Series No. 15 (2012)
ISBN: 978-82-93081-58-6

Morten Bergsmo and LING Yan (editors):
State Sovereignty and International Criminal Law
Torkel Opsahl Academic EPublisher
Beijing, 2012
FICHL Publication Series No. 15 (2012)
ISBN: 978-82-93081-35-7

Morten Bergsmo and CHEAH Wui Ling (editors):
Old Evidence and Core International Crimes
Torkel Opsahl Academic EPublisher
Beijing, 2012
FICHL Publication Series No. 16 (2012)
ISBN: 978-82-93081-60-9

YI Ping:
戦争と平和の間——発足期日本国際法学における「正しい戦争」の観念とその帰結
Torkel Opsahl Academic EPublisher
Beijing, 2013
FICHL Publication Series No. 17 (2013)
ISBN: 978-82-93081-66-1

Morten Bergsmo and SONG Tianying (editors):
On the Proposed Crimes Against Humanity Convention
Torkel Opsahl Academic EPublisher
Brussels, 2014
FICHL Publication Series No. 18 (2014)
ISBN: 978-82-93081-96-8

Morten Bergsmo (editor):
Quality Control in Fact-Finding
Torkel Opsahl Academic EPublisher
Florence, 2013
FICHL Publication Series No. 19 (2013)
ISBN: 978-82-93081-78-4

Morten Bergsmo, CHEAH Wui Ling and YI Ping (editors):
Historical Origins of International Criminal Law: Volume 1
Torkel Opsahl Academic EPublisher
Brussels, 2014
FICHL Publication Series No. 20 (2014)
ISBN: 978-82-93081-11-1

Morten Bergsmo, CHEAH Wui Ling and YI Ping (editors):
Historical Origins of International Criminal Law: Volume 2
Torkel Opsahl Academic EPublisher
Brussels, 2014
FICHL Publication Series No. 21 (2014)
ISBN: 978-82-93081-13-5

Morten Bergsmo, CHEAH Wui Ling, SONG Tianying and YI Ping (editors):
Historical Origins of International Criminal Law: Volume 3
Torkel Opsahl Academic EPublisher
Brussels, 2015
FICHL Publication Series No. 22 (2015)
ISBN print: 978-82-8348-015-3
ISBN e-book: 978-82-8348-014-6

Morten Bergsmo, CHEAH Wui Ling, SONG Tianying and YI Ping (editors):
Historical Origins of International Criminal Law: Volume 4
Torkel Opsahl Academic EPublisher
Brussels, 2015
FICHL Publication Series No. 23 (2015)
ISBN print: 978-82-8348-017-7
ISBN e-book: 978-82-8348-016-0

Morten Bergsmo, Klaus Rackwitz and SONG Tianying (editors):
Historical Origins of International Criminal Law: Volume 5
Torkel Opsahl Academic EPublisher
Brussels, 2017
FICHL Publication Series No. 24 (2017)
ISBN print: 978-82-8348-106-8
ISBN e-book: 978-82-8348-107-5

Morten Bergsmo and SONG Tianying (editors):
Military Self-Interest in Accountability for Core International Crimes
Torkel Opsahl Academic EPublisher
Brussels, 2015
FICHL Publication Series No. 25 (2015)
ISBN print: 978-82-93081-61-6
ISBN e-book: 978-82-93081-81-4

Wolfgang Kaleck:
Double Standards: International Criminal Law and the West
Torkel Opsahl Academic EPublisher
Brussels, 2015
FICHL Publication Series No. 26 (2015)
ISBN print: 978-82-93081-67-8
ISBN e-book: 978-82-93081-83-8

LIU Daqun and ZHANG Binxin (editors):
Historical War Crimes Trials in Asia
Torkel Opsahl Academic EPublisher
Brussels, 2016
FICHL Publication Series No. 27 (2015)
ISBN print: 978-82-8348-055-9
ISBN e-book: 978-82-8348-056-6

Mark Klamberg (editor):
Commentary on the Law of the International Criminal Court
Torkel Opsahl Academic EPublisher
Brussels, 2017
FICHL Publication Series No. 29 (2017)
ISBN print: 978-82-8348-100-6
ISBN e-book: 978-82-8348-101-3

Stian Nordengen Christensen:
Counterfactual History and Bosnia-Herzegovina
Torkel Opsahl Academic EPublisher
Brussels, 2018
Publication Series No. 30 (2018)
ISBN print: 978-82-8348-102-0
ISBN e-book: 978-82-8348-103-7

Stian Nordengen Christensen:
Possibilities and Impossibilities in a Contradictory Global Order
Torkel Opsahl Academic EPublisher
Brussels, 2018
Publication Series No. 31 (2018)
ISBN print: 978-82-8348-104-4
ISBN e-book: 978-82-8348-105-1

Morten Bergsmo and Carsten Stahn (editors):
Quality Control in Preliminary Examination: Volume 1
Torkel Opsahl Academic EPublisher
Brussels, 2018
Publication Series No. 32 (2018)
ISBN print: 978-82-8348-123-5
ISBN e-book: 978-82-8348-124-2

All volumes are freely available online at http://www.toaep.org/ps/. For printed copies, see http://www.toaep.org/about/distribution/. For reviews of earlier books in this Series in academic journals and yearbooks, see http://www.toaep.org/reviews/.

CPSIA information can be obtained
at www.ICGtesting.com
Printed in the USA
BVHW08*1516100918
527049BV00007BA/75/P